AMERICA
The Glorious Republic

VOLUME 2 ● 1877 TO THE PRESENT ● WITH READINGS

How little do my countrymen know what precious blessings they are in possession of, and which no other people on earth enjoy!

THOMAS JEFFERSON, *writing to James Monroe from Paris, June 17, 1785*

AMERICA
The Glorious Republic

VOLUME 2 • 1877 TO THE PRESENT • WITH READINGS

Henry F. Graff

Professor of History
Columbia University

Houghton Mifflin Company   BOSTON

Atlanta   Dallas   Geneva, Ill.   Lawrenceville, N.J.   Palo Alto   Toronto

Cover: Watercolor rendering by Elizabeth Moutal of wood carving by John Haley Bellamy.
Half-title: Watercolor rendering by Alfred H. Smith of wood carving by William Beal.
Frontispiece: "Flags, Fourth of July, 1916," by Childe Hassam. **Page 7:** Plains fort. **Page 9:** Roosevelt and Churchill. **Page 10:** Nixon in China. **Page 12:** Automobile assembly line. **Page 13:** NRA poster. **Page 14:** GI's in Korea. **Page 15:** Space shuttle. **Page 17:** Map of world, 1540.

The readings on pages 439–586 of this book also appear in *Voices of America: Readings in American History* by Thomas R. Frazier (Houghton Mifflin Company, 1985).

Printed in the U.S.A.
ISBN: 0-395-38175-4

ABCDEFGHIJ-D-943210/898765

To
Molly Ann Morse
and
Elizabeth Graff Morse,
splendid young women
of the
Glorious Republic

AUTHOR

HENRY F. GRAFF is a noted historian and teacher of history. For many years he has been on the faculty of Columbia University, having risen through the ranks of the Department of History to full professor and serving a term as Chairman. He has also lectured on scores of campuses throughout the country. For six years he was a member of the National Historical Publications Commission, having been appointed by the President. A specialist in the history of the presidency and of United States diplomatic relations, Dr. Graff has published extensively on both subjects. His previous textbooks for high school and junior high school classes have been widely acclaimed. Renowned for the elegance and liveliness of his lectures, he has been honored with Columbia's Great Teacher Award and with the coveted Mark Van Doren Award, bestowed by the student body of Columbia College for distinguished teaching and scholarship.

SUSAN A. ROBERTS, who prepared the study material for *America: The Glorious Republic*, is a teacher at Del Norte High School, Albuquerque, New Mexico.

READERS

TOM ALLEN, Liberty Junior High School, Richardson, Texas.

ARLENE DAWSON, George High School, Atlanta, Georgia.

LINDA FRANCIS, Fort Bend Independent School District, Stafford, Texas.

BALTAZAR GARCIA, Nogales High School, Nogales, Arizona.

NORMAN McRAE, Detroit Public Schools, Detroit, Michigan.

VIRGINIA DRIVING HAWK SNEVE, Flandreau, South Dakota.

GEORGE TURNER, Northeast High School, Philadelphia, Pennsylvania.

Contents

Readings

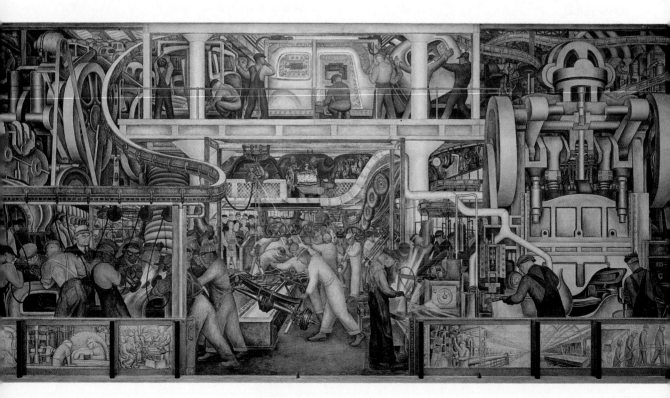

NRA MEMBER
U.S.
WE DO OUR PART

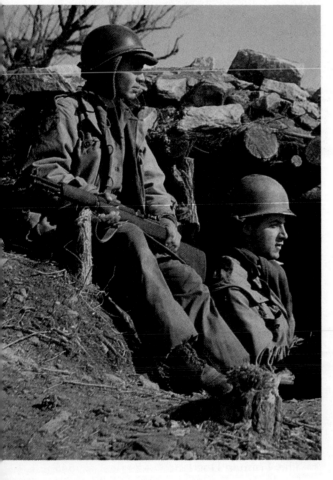

Maps

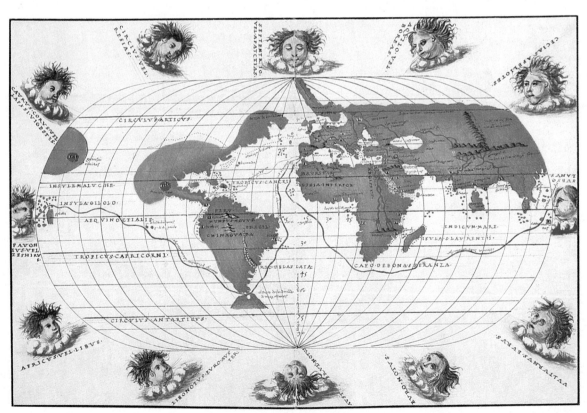

Dear student:

The American past is full of fascinating people, events, and deeds — even a master novelist could not have invented them. A true account of American history, then, has all the surprises, twists and turns of plot, and variety of characters that people expect to find in a good story. In *America: The Glorious Republic* I have sought to tell the history of the United States as it deserves to be told. To my account I have brought knowledge accumulated through years of experience in reading and teaching about America (I made up my mind when I was in grade school that I would one day be an historian).

As you read and study this book, I trust you will enjoy its style and content, addressed especially to Americans like you who are now young and who will live most of their lives in the twenty-first century. In that not-so-far-off time you will need to know and value the formative landmarks of the country's past. From this book you can acquire historical background to help you face public issues that Americans today may not have even guessed will then be before the nation.

To enrich your understanding, I have enhanced my own words with original documents, first-hand accounts, direct quotations, song lyrics, and revealing anecdotes. These materials permit you to see close up some of the footprints that earlier Americans have left on the paths they took in meeting the problems of *their* day. To help make the successive eras of America's history vivid and memorable, my publisher has brought to these pages a matchless array of illustrations drawn from hundreds of collections. Good pictures, as you know, enable the past to remain forever alive.

Each unit of the book will draw your attention to the technological innovations that altered America's course or outlook. Ingenuity has always been an American characteristic, and recognizing its impact is indispensable to understanding the nation's development.

The maps in the book, taken together, constitute a built-in historical atlas. They will enable you to locate precisely — as you should — every American place name mentioned in the text. In addition, the many graphs, charts, and time lines will assist you in fixing firmly in your mind important facts and significant points. Summaries at the end of each chapter will allow you to review conveniently what you have read.

Finally, because the book offers a modern view of America, its history is presented in the context of events taking place in the world at large. A "World Scene" feature in every chapter will help you view American history in the tumultuous international setting in which it has unfolded.

When you have come to the end of the book, you may want to ponder the immense journey the nation has been on since Columbus' men first shouted "Land! Land!" in 1492. You will, I hope, be pleased that through your knowledge of American history you have grown in your ability to make judgments about the dilemmas and concerns of your own time. If this proves to be the case, I will feel well rewarded for my efforts to make the book accurate and interesting. No less important than your personal pleasure and satisfaction, however, will be your ability to take your place in a new generation of voters and officeholders more fully appreciative of what it means to be an American.

Henry B. Graff

A New Nation Takes Shape

In 1877 the United States began its second century of independence. Four centuries had not yet passed since Europeans reached North America. Americans could feel, however, that they and their forebears had dared greatly and accomplished much in such a brief period of history. Brought together in an incredibly beautiful land, they had formed a country that became an inspiration for millions of people everywhere. Because most Americans were able from the start to enjoy steadily widening opportunity in a setting of personal freedom, the very name *America* had become a synonym for hope and self-improvement.

EXPLORATION AND COLONIZATION

The Portuguese sail around Africa to India. The modern story of America began in western Europe in the fifteenth century. Seafarers, sponsored by monarchs aiming to extend their power, were beginning to venture farther and farther from their home ports. Voyagers from Portugal sailed southward along the African coast, eventually rounding the continent and making their way to India in order to trade by sea. Goods from Asia, which formerly had passed through the eastern Mediterranean region, now began to be shipped to western Europe direct.

Columbus reaches America. In 1492 Christopher Columbus, an Italian mariner sailing for the Spanish Crown, set out with a tiny fleet to find Asia by heading westward into the Atlantic. He landed on a Caribbean island and to the end of his life believed that he had reached the outlying islands of Asia. Amerigo Vespucci, sailing under the flag of Portugal, made a new finding. He recognized that a vast continent lay between Europe and Asia. An important

map maker, acknowledging the work of Vespucci, named this "new" half of the earth *America* in his honor.

Europeans encounter native Americans. The Spanish and Portuguese knew practically nothing about the new land they had come upon. Hoping to find gold and silver there, they regarded the Indians, as they called the inhabitants, either as obstacles or as people who could be forced to help in the quest for precious metals.

The native Americans had developed a rich variety of cultures. In the desert of what is now the American Southwest were peoples who had a flourishing agriculture and who built villages out of adobe. On the Plains lived Indians who depended entirely upon the buffalo for their food, clothing, and shelter. In the northeastern part of what is now the United States lived woodlands Indians, some of whom had joined together in powerful confederations. In Mexico dwelt people who had created an elaborate civilization marked by notable engineering feats and astronomical discoveries. In Peru thrived a vigorous empire, organized under an all-powerful ruler.

The coming of the Europeans doomed these native cultures. As first the Spanish and the Portuguese, and soon afterward the French and the English, spread their power over North and South America, tribal society was disrupted and then virtually destroyed.

Spain and Portugal establish colonies. In settling the Americas, Spain established the Spanish language, the Roman Catholic religion, and the authority of the Spanish Crown over a vast region. The immense quantities of American gold and silver that the Spaniards shipped home made Spain the richest country in the world. The Portu-

The *Mayflower* brought the Pilgrims to America in 1620. Seeking a land where they could worship as they pleased, these determined people started the settlement of Plymouth.

guese established themselves in Brazil and introduced the Portuguese language there.

France starts American colonies. Soon France joined in colonizing the Americas. France's leading explorers, Jacques Cartier and Samuel de Champlain, established French influence from the Gulf of St. Lawrence to the Great Lakes, laying the basis for New France. Another explorer, La Salle, journeyed down the Mississippi River and claimed for France both the entire waterway and the lands it washed.

England is a latecomer in starting North American settlements. The English entered the competition through private enterprise. A group of London investors in 1607 landed a hundred men at a place they called Jamestown, in Virginia. The colony, which shortly received women settlers too, took root only after much suffering. The growing of tobacco eventually assured Jamestown's success.

In New England, white settlement began in 1620 at Plymouth, Massachusetts. The tiny band of people who settled there were Pilgrims, seeking sanctuary for their religious views. Soon afterward began a large-scale migration of Puritans to the shores of Massachusetts Bay. Setting stern standards, the Puritan leaders expelled from Massachusetts such people of strong opinion and iron determination as Roger Williams and Anne Hutchinson. These and other opponents of the Puritans attracted followers who were also seeking better economic opportunity. So it was that more New England colonies came into being: Rhode Island and Connecticut as well as New Hampshire and Maine.

Farther south, Roman Catholic settlers established Maryland under a charter from King Charles I. In 1663 Charles II granted to eight friends the region between Virginia and what was then Spanish Florida. They named the region *Carolina* in his honor. Later it was divided into North and South Carolina. In 1733 Georgia, the land immediately south of the Carolinas, was settled by a reformer named James Oglethorpe.

Even as the English were arriving on the Atlantic shore, Dutch people were establishing New Netherland. The colony became New York in 1664 when the English took it over — the name honoring Charles II's brother, the Duke of York. The Duke,

Freedom of religion became a basic American principle. Here, worshipers in colonial Williamsburg, Virginia, gather at a parish church for a Sunday service.

having control over the region known as New Jersey (which by then included a settlement of Swedes at what is now Wilmington, Delaware), granted it to two friends. New Jersey began to attract settlers from other colonies as well as from abroad.

The settlement of Pennsylvania was the work of William Penn, who had received the territory in payment of a debt owed his father by Charles II. Penn created a haven for a religious group called Quakers. He planned his colony as a "Holy Experiment" in which people would live in freedom under the rule of law.

The English colonies develop distinctive ways of life. The English colonies adapted themselves to the particular environment in which each was set. Those to the north depended on family farming. Those to the south focused on plantation agriculture, growing such crops as tobacco and rice.

In addition to agricultural products, the colonies developed a lively commerce in fish, whale oil, forest products, iron, and furs. As a result, there was work for almost everybody who wanted it. Further effects were a steadily rising standard of living and the absence of large-scale poverty.

Throughout the colonies, both north and south, the supply of labor was always short. Some of it was provided by indentured servants, who were bound to a master for a fixed number of years in return for transatlantic passage, and by slaves, brought from Africa by slave-traders.

Trade regulations are designed to favor England. Communication from one colony to another was limited. Each colony, through its governor, was in touch on its own with Parliament. Still, Parliament increasingly saw the colonies as a single entity, convinced that they must serve the interests of England. Beginning in the mid-1600's, England passed Navigation Acts in order to gain the maximum economic benefits from its overseas colonies. Under these laws, colonial exports had to be shipped to England before they could be sold elsewhere. In similar fashion, European goods destined for the colonies had to be shipped through England.

Many colonists objected to the Navigation Acts as an interference with their economic freedom. On the other hand, England supplied the colonies with protection that they could not provide for themselves.

France and England clash for empire. The need for protection was brought home to the colonists by a series of wars between France and England in America. The outcome of the first three conflicts — King William's War (1689–1697), Queen Anne's War (1702–1713), and King George's War (1744–1748) — brought neither side a decisive victory. A final showdown, however, was in the making. Increasingly, Virginians were determined to promote the settlement of the Ohio Valley; the French were no less ready to make the region theirs.

In 1754 the French and Indian War began. It started when a small force of Virginia militiamen, under the command of young George Washington, was defeated by the French at Fort Necessity in southwestern Pennsylvania. Fighting between Britain and France went on for years, in Europe and Asia as well as in America. When the Treaty of Paris (1763) ended the hostilities, New France had ceased to exist. Canada and all of France's holdings east of the Mississippi River, except for two tiny fishing islands off the Newfoundland coast, became English possessions. New Orleans and the vast Louisiana territory went to Spain.

THE AMERICAN REVOLUTION

Relations between Britain and the colonies grow tense. The British now set about reorganizing their American possessions in order to make them pay a larger share of the cost of government. To this end, Parliament decided to enforce the Navigation Acts strictly, putting an end to the smuggling that had long irritated English merchants. Then, in order to halt the fighting between colonists and Indians on the western frontier, Britain issued a proclamation prohibiting settlement beyond the Appalachian Mountains. Finally, to raise revenues in the colonies, Parliament passed a Stamp Act requiring that stamps be affixed to newspapers, pamphlets, legal documents, and other items.

Various segments of the American population felt threatened: merchants, land speculators, lawyers, and editors. Organizations calling themselves Sons of Liberty and

The French and Indian War began when George Washington, a young militia officer, tried to drive the French away from the forks of the Ohio River.

Daughters of Liberty protested the tax. They boycotted imported goods, hoping that English merchants would persuade Parliament to pay attention to the colonists' complaints.

Parliament yielded to the clamor, repealed the Stamp Act, and passed in its place the Townshend Acts, which placed taxes on imported goods. The colonists protested that the Townshend Acts were further examples of "taxation without representation."

Violence breaks out in Boston. Few colonists had yet given serious thought to the idea of independence. As the opposition to London's policies grew, however, committees in the various colonies began to coordinate their activities with one another. When Parliament decided in 1773 to give a British company a monopoly on the sale of tea in the colonies, American merchants became alarmed. Patriots in Boston — where the strongest opposition to Parliament was centered — took up the fight. A group of them dumped into the sea many cases of the arriving tea.

On July 4, 1776, the members of the Second Continental Congress, meeting in Philadelphia, approved the Declaration of Independence.

Parliament angrily passed a series of laws, known as the Intolerable Acts, to punish the people of Boston for the Boston Tea Party. Now a call went out for a Continental Congress, to meet in Philadelphia in September, 1774. The delegates declared that Parliament had no right to tax the colonies without their consent.

The American Revolution begins. When Britain made no concessions, the colonists began to arm themselves. On April 19, 1775, fighting broke out at Lexington, near Boston. There a group of colonial minutemen was dispersed by British troops. Not long afterward the British took heavy losses in the Battle of Bunker Hill.

When the Second Continental Congress gathered at Philadelphia the next month, many colonists could see that a break with Britain was inevitable. Thomas Paine's pamphlet, *Common Sense,* had made a powerful case for independence, and its argument was being widely circulated. The Congress formed an army and appointed George Washington to be its commander. The American force was quickly placed in action against the British in Boston. In March, 1776, the redcoats evacuated the city and withdrew to Nova Scotia.

The Declaration of Independence is written. General Washington moved to New York, awaiting what he expected would be a large-scale invasion. Meanwhile, sentiment in favor of independence was growing. In response, the Congress appointed a committee to draft a declaration of independence, and Thomas Jefferson of Virginia was chosen to write it.

The Declaration of Independence was a lofty and powerful proclamation of liberty as well as of independence. "All men," Jefferson wrote, "are created equal." Among their "unalienable rights" are "Life, Liberty, and the pursuit of Happiness." On July 4, 1776, the Congress approved the Declaration.

American independence is won. In the months that followed, Americans learned the high price of achieving their goal. Nevertheless, when General Burgoyne surrendered an entire British army at Saratoga in October, 1777, Americans began to believe that they would win their independence. The victory at Saratoga, a turning point in the war, persuaded France to sign a treaty of alliance with the United States.

In 1781 American and French troops, aided by a French fleet, trapped a British force under Lord Cornwallis at Yorktown, Virginia. Cornwallis's surrender to Washington convinced the British that further fighting was useless. In the Treaty of Paris of 1783, Great Britain recognized American independence. The boundaries of the United States were set at Canada on the north, at the Mississippi River on the west, and at Florida on the south.

A NEW FORM OF GOVERNMENT

A confederation of states is established. Immediately after the signing of the Declaration of Independence, the former colonies had begun to create new governments. The state constitutions they wrote included bills of rights protecting individual liberty. The stirring ideals of the Declaration, moreover, led to democratic reforms. Even slavery came under attack, with practically all of the states banning the further importation of slaves.

As a result of their colonial experience with Great Britain, Americans had come to distrust any kind of strong central government they could not themselves control. They created, therefore, a loose union under the Articles of Confederation which, following ratification by the states in 1781, provided a central government for the new nation until 1789.

The government under the Articles of Confederation was weak. The states strictly limited the power of the Congress to levy taxes, control trade, and issue money. Under the Articles, moreover, there was no national judicial system. Although the Congress was able to pass laws establishing a system for dividing and governing the public lands, it could not deal responsibly with a variety of international questions that arose in the 1780's. Neither could it deal with the effects of the widespread economic distress and discontent of the day.

Under the guidance of George Washington, steps were taken to remedy the weaknesses of the Articles. After a meeting at Annapolis, Maryland, in 1786, the representatives of the five states who had attended agreed to gather the following year in Philadelphia to amend the Articles.

The Philadelphia Convention meets. In May, 1787, a group of distinguished Americans representing every state except Rhode Island gathered in Philadelphia at what became known as the Constitutional Convention. Because of substantial agreement that a stronger government was required, the delegates began to shape a new frame of government.

The outcome of the deliberations was the Constitution of the United States, a blueprint for a new federal system in which all powers not specifically delegated to the central government would remain with the states. For the first time, a government would derive its power not from a monarch or from the states but from the people.

The Constitution is ratified. The approval of nine of the thirteen states was required to ratify the Constitution. The document's supporters, quickly called Federalists, argued that the new frame of government

In New York, where the Constitution was ratified by a margin of just three votes, Federalists held a parade to celebrate the event.

25

would safeguard liberty. The opponents, called Antifederalists, expressed fear that a strong government would destroy liberty. They insisted that the rights of individuals be protected by law. Shortly after ratification of the Constitution in 1788, such guarantees were offered in appropriate amendments. In 1791, the first ten amendments, called the Bill of Rights, won state approval and became part of the Constitution.

THE FIRST PRESIDENTS

George Washington is the first Chief Executive. Early in 1789, national elections were held. George Washington was unanimously chosen President — the first President in the history of the world. After he assumed leadership, he chose as his advisers the heads of the executive departments created by Congress. These advisers eventually became known as the Cabinet.

Although Washington was opposed to political parties, by 1792 two such organizations had arisen. One, the Federalist Party, centered around Secretary of the Treasury Alexander Hamilton. Favoring a strong national government which would encourage the growth of industry, it drew upon the loyalty of merchants, manufacturers, and the owners of large plantations. The Democratic-Republican (or Republican) Party rallied around Secretary of State Thomas Jefferson. It had as its goal a nation of independent farmers and favored the ideal that "that government is best which governs least."

To encourage manufacturing at home, Congress and the new administration supported passage of the first tariff. By creating the Bank of the United States, moreover, the administration accepted a loose construction of the Constitution. This interpretation allowed for the expansion of governmental powers beyond those expressly provided for in the Constitution itself.

Foreign affairs, meanwhile, troubled the country. Some people feared that the radicalism and violence which had accompanied the outbreak of revolution in France in 1789 would encourage a similar development in the United States. Others believed that the end of tyrannical governments everywhere ought to be an active goal of American policy. When war broke out between France and England, however, Washington decided that the country must remain aloof from foreign struggles. He issued a Proclamation of Neutrality, thus setting a policy of avoiding direct involvement in Europe's squabbles.

John Adams succeeds Washington as President. Washington's successor in 1797 was the man who had been his Vice President, John Adams. In the four years of Adams's term, the struggle between the Federalists and the Republicans grew more intense. When the Federalist Congress passed a series of anti-Republican laws called the Alien and Sedition Acts, opponents argued that the states should have the right to decide if laws are constitutional. For the first time, the issue of nullification had been raised.

THE AGE OF THE JEFFERSONIANS

Jefferson becomes President. In 1800 Thomas Jefferson was elected President and the era of the Republicans began. Although some Federalist policies were reversed, the power of the federal government continued to grow. Furthermore, by a series of bold decisions Chief Justice John Marshall established the principle of judicial review — the power of the courts to decide upon the constitutionality of acts of Congress and of state legislatures.

The most notable action of the Jefferson administration was the purchase of the vast region called Louisiana. Despite his support of a strict construction of the Constitution, Jefferson believed that he could not pass up the opportunity to double the size of the country.

The United States seeks to defend its neutral rights. Jefferson, who had once opposed the building of a bigger navy, discovered the nation had a need for military strength. To protect American citizens and uphold national honor, the United States fought a war against the Barbary pirates of North Africa. The struggle foreshadowed a larger one that grew out of the continued fighting between Britain and France. As they made the high seas a battleground, the two great powers disregarded the interests of neutral nations, including the United States. The British especially did not hesitate to seize American ships on the oceans, impressing the crews into their navy and scoffing at protests from the United States. Jefferson, seeking to avoid war, tried through an embargo to hurt the British economy, but the method did not have the desired effect.

Britain and America fight again. By the time that James Madison followed Jefferson into the White house in 1809, American policy had turned into a fruitless effort to please first Britain, then France. In 1812, having run out of possible solutions to the steady assault on American rights, the United States went to war against Britain. In the first year of the struggle, often called the "second War of Independence," American privateers and naval vessels won a number of dramatic single-ship engagements. The vast power of the British navy was thereafter deployed against America, and the result was near-disaster for the young republic. The burning of the city of Washington by an invading British force remains a low point in American history. When Andrew Jackson destroyed a British army at New Orleans in 1815, the United States redeemed its honor, even though the Treaty of Ghent ending the war had already been signed. In this unusual treaty, neither side won or lost anything. Americans, however, resolved that they must never again be so vulnerable to foreign attack.

UNION AND DISUNION

Sectional differences check the growth of nationalism. Sharing a rich feeling of national pride, Americans often referred to the years of James Monroe's presidency (1817–1825) as the "Era of Good Feelings." In addressing the world at large the nation spoke with a single voice, as, for instance, in 1823 when it issued what came to be called the Monroe Doctrine. This statement

The British attack on the American frigate *Chesapeake* in 1807 raised a cry for war in the United States.

warned that the American continent was no longer open to European colonization.

Despite the show of unity on the surface, the nation was beginning to display marked divisions internally. Each of the sections — North, South, and West — was developing an outlook and political views aimed at serving its own economic interests. Much of the difficulty turned on the issue of slavery. The states in which the "peculiar institution" existed felt threatened by the growing strength and prosperity of the free states. Time and again, compromises arranged by leading members of Congress averted disaster. The Missouri Compromise, for instance, brought Missouri and Maine into the Union and kept a balance between the number of free and slave states.

Despite growing disagreements among the sections, Andrew Jackson, President from 1829 to 1837, was a hero throughout the country. His strong stand against South Carolina's threat to nullify a tariff act helped show how powerful the office of President can be. Many people, observing

Abraham Lincoln's strength of leadership helped the United States survive as a nation.

Jackson's zeal in fighting the Bank of the United States, regarded him as the leader of an emerging democratic era. Indeed, in the 1830's and 1840's a new era of reform, accompanied by the rapid growth of factories and the spread of canals and railroads, seemed to open fresh vistas for all Americans. The admission of Texas, the arrival of Mormons in Utah, the establishment of the Oregon boundary, and a gold rush to California — all taking place in the 1840's — fulfilled the promise of a country extending "from sea to shining sea."

The issue of slavery stirs up an angry debate. The tormenting question of whether slavery ought to be allowed to spread into the newly opened territories became all-consuming. Notable speeches by Daniel Webster, John C. Calhoun, and Henry Clay made the arguments familiar to everybody. In 1850 a compromise once again saved the Union, as the nation made arrangements concerning lands acquired in the war with Mexico (1846–1848). When the Compromise of 1850 came apart in the next few years, however, the Union became more and more divided over the issue of slavery.

By the middle of the 1850's a new Republican Party had come into existence, largely as a result of the fierce struggle to organize the Kansas Territory. The Republicans ultimately found their leader in Abraham Lincoln of Illinois, regarded by many Southerners as an abolitionist. Immediately after he was elected President in 1860, southern states seceded from the Union and formed the Confederate States of America.

The North and South take up arms. Lincoln was determined that, at whatever cost, the Union must be saved. The outcome was the Civil War, a struggle that raged from 1861 to 1865 at a fearful cost in lives and treasure. The Battle of Gettysburg in 1863 marked the turning point. Two years later, at Appomattox in Virginia, General Robert E. Lee surrendered to General Ulysses S. Grant. In the course of the hostilities, the slaves were emancipated and the troubling moral issue that had beset America almost since its founding was laid to rest.

The nation faces the future. When the war was over, the Union had to be reassembled. How to accomplish reconstruction caused conflict between President Andrew Johnson and Congress. When the work was formally completed in 1877, black Americans, under new amendments to the Constitution, had acquired citizenship and the right to vote. Decades would pass, however, before they gained their full civil rights.

Looking ahead, the nation would throw its energies into new challenges and undertakings: the building of a network of railroads, the transformation of the country into an industrial giant, the conquest of the Great Plains, the readjustment of the relationship between employers and employees and between business and government, the absorption of millions of new immigrants into national life, and the assumption of international responsibilities. Yet, even as America shook under the vibration of these mighty movements, the nation would continue to advance steadily toward the unchanging ideal of "government of the people, by the people, for the people."

THE NATION TRANSFORMED

POST-CIVIL WAR – 1900

*Give me your tired, your poor, your huddled
masses yearning to breathe free, . . .
Send these, the homeless, the tempest-tossed, to me:
I lift my lamp beside the golden door.*

EMMA LAZARUS, "THE NEW COLOSSUS," 1886

UNIT OUTLINE

The Last Great West

POST-CIVIL WAR – 1900

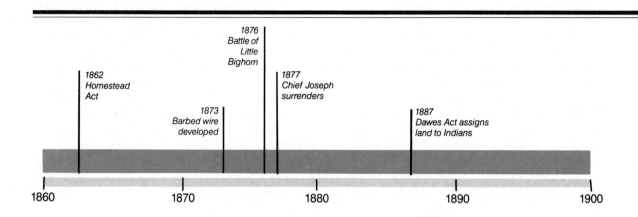

CHAPTER OUTLINE

1. The Plains Indians lose their homelands.

2. Ranchers and miners penetrate the West.

3. Farmers settle the Great Plains.

Americans of the 1840's, venturing westward to Oregon and California from territories along the Mississippi, encountered a vast and varied region. The eastern part of the trans-Mississippi West, extending roughly from the present state of Minnesota south to Texas and west to the foothills of the Rockies, was characterized by a level surface or by low, rolling hills. This region — often called the Great Plains — received less rainfall than the eastern part of the country and became more arid the farther west pioneers traveled.

The second part of the trans-Mississippi West consisted of the Rocky Mountains, explored by Lewis and Clark, Pike, Frémont, and others. This imposing mountain system had long been a barrier to easy passage across the continent.

The third part of the region was the plateau lying west of the Rockies and extending to the Cascades and the Sierra Nevada. Much of this section, particularly its southern part, was a forbidding desert area.

For centuries, the trans-Mississippi West had been the home of Indian tribes. In the years following the Civil War, the arrival of ranchers, miners, and farmers brought far-reaching changes to the Indians' ways of living. This chapter tells the story of the conquest of the Indians and the settlement of the land west of the Mississippi.

1 The Plains Indians Lose Their Homelands

Throughout America's history, white settlers pushed the Indians out of their homes and hunting grounds. In the many battles between whites and Indians, the Indians were occasionally victorious. Never, however, were they able to stop the white settlers for long.

The Indian Territory is organized. In 1834 a region that included most of the present state of Oklahoma was set aside by Congress for the Indians of the Five Civilized Tribes (the Cherokee, Chickasaw, Choctaw, Creek, and Seminole). Known as the Indian Territory, this area became home to those tribes after they were forced to leave their homelands east of the Mississippi River.

Eventually, more than 75,000 Indians were living in the territory.

The Civil War, in part, changed the relationship between the United States and the resettled Indians. The tribespeople believed that under the treaties they had accepted, they had exchanged their historic independence for the protection of the United States. When war broke out between the North and South, however, the Union withdrew United States troops from Texas and Arkansas, convincing the Indians that they had been abandoned. Quickly the Confederacy annexed the Indian Territory and wooed the tribes to the rebel side. The Indians were guaranteed representation in the Confederate Congress and were also promised a state of their own if the South won. The alliance seemed logical, since many Indians were slaveholders and therefore sympathized with the South in the struggle.

After the introduction of the horse, the Plains Indians adopted new methods of pursuing buffalo, their source of food and clothing. Later, buffalo hunting became a sport for white settlers, whose coming greatly altered life on the Plains.

During the Civil War about 5,500 Indians fought on the Confederate side.[1] In fact, the last Confederate leader to surrender was General Stand Watie, a Cherokee chief who did not lay down his arms until a month after Appomattox.

The Indian wars begin. In the period before the Civil War, white settlers had by-passed the Indian Territory, making their way into the traditional hunting grounds of the Plains Indians. Soon, so many white settlers were living on the Plains that territories were organized. After the Kansas and Nebraska territories were created in 1854, other territories were formed one after another: Dakota, Montana, Wyoming, Idaho, and Colorado.

The Indians who had long made their home at the eastern edge of the Rockies soon felt the force of change. In 1858 gold was discovered in the vicinity of Pikes Peak. Almost immediately 100,000 miners entered the region. The local Indians — the Cheyenne and the Arapaho — having no place to go, chose to stand and fight. The ensuing struggle between whites and Indians gradually spread eastward onto the Plains. It was destined to last for thirty years.

The Indian warriors of this period, on horseback with feathered headdresses streaming in the wind, quickly became familiar figures to other Americans. They were celebrated in magazines and books and later in motion pictures. Even today the image of the Plains Indians is burned into people's minds as typical of *all* Indians.

Actually, when Coronado first came into contact with the Plains Indians in 1540, he found that they were generally peaceful people. Three centuries later, however, they had been radically changed by their contact with Europeans. The Indians of the South and West had acquired horses from the Spanish, and the Indian horse-frontier gradually spread up the Rio Grande Valley onto the Great Plains. In the meantime, Indians in the East had acquired guns from the British and later from the Americans. The gun-frontier reached the Plains about the time the Indian Territory was created and merged with the horse-frontier. As a result, mounted Indians armed with guns appeared for the first time, just when white settlers were beginning to settle the trans-Mississippi West.

For a considerable time, the Plains Indians had a decided advantage over their enemies. Then the Colt six-shooter was introduced into the United States Army in the 1850's. Invented by Samuel Colt and patented in 1836, it was the first firearm to have a revolving loading device. The six-shooter enabled soldiers to pursue their enemy without having to stop and reload their rifles after every shot.

The destruction of the buffalo signals an end to the Indians' ways of living. The superior weapons of the United States Army were not the only disadvantage the Indians faced. Their will to resist was also weakened by the destruction of the American buffalo herds. The huge beasts had once provided the nomadic tribes with food and materials for tools and shelter.

Perhaps fifteen million of the buffalo roamed the Plains when Coronado passed through the region. It was possible, Coronado reported, to see as many as 300,000 animals at one time. One of Coronado's men described in amazement what he had learned:

> The Indians live or sustain themselves entirely from the buffalo, for they neither grow nor harvest corn. With the skins they build their houses; with the skins they clothe and shoe themselves; from the skins they make rope and also obtain wool. With the sinews they make thread, with which they sew their clothes and also their tents. From the bones they shape awls [pointed tools for making holes].

The wiping out of the buffalo herds was begun by the Indians themselves. Since the time when Lewis and Clark crossed the Plains, the tribes had been killing off the animals at a rate that reduced their number each year. By the mid-1800's the Indians were selling about 100,000 buffalo hides annually to the American Fur Company.

---

[1] The North recruited Indians as well, and by the war's end some 4,000 Indians had fought for the Union.

"Born Upon the Prairie"

In October, 1867, the chiefs of many Indian tribes met with government commissioners in southern Kansas. Ten Bears, a Comanche chief from Texas, spoke to the gathering about the feelings of his people for their way of life on the open prairie and about their conflicts with white soldiers.

Chief Ten Bears

My people have never first drawn a bow or fired a gun against the whites. There has been trouble on the boundary between us, and my young men have danced a war dance. But fighting was not begun by us. It was you who sent out the first soldiers and we who sent out the second. Two years ago I came upon this road, following the buffalo. But the soldiers fired on us, and since that time there has been a noise like that of a thunderstorm, and we have not known which way to go.

The blue-dressed soldiers came out of the night when it was dark still, and for campfires they lit our lodges. So it was in Texas. They made sorrow come into our camps, and we went out like buffalo bulls when their cows are attacked. When we found white soldiers, we killed them. The Comanche are not weak and blind. They are strong and farsighted like horses.

But there are things which you have said to me which I do not like. You said that you wanted to put us upon a reservation. I do not want that. I was born upon the prairie, where the wind blew free and there was nothing to break the light of the sun. I was born where there were no enclosures and where everything drew a free breath. I want to die there and not within walls. I have hunted and lived like my fathers before me, and, like them, I lived happily. So, why do you ask us to leave the rivers, and the sun, and the wind, and live in houses?

The slaying of the buffalo became more highly organized after 1867. In that year the railroad penetrated the Plains. Hunters, like the experienced scout and Indian fighter William F. Cody, were hired to supply the construction crews with buffalo meat. Buffalo Bill, as Cody became known, slaughtered thousands of the animals.

Between 1871 and 1874 hunters killed about three million buffalo each year. Most of the skins were sold in the East, where owning a buffalo hide became a mark of elegance. The carcasses would be left to rot in the sun. When only the bones were left, they would be picked up and shipped to fertilizer factories in the East. In 1874 about 3,500 tons of bones were shipped out of Kansas and Colorado alone. By 1883 the animals had virtually disappeared. It is said that when the United States Mint in 1913 created a five-cent coin showing a buffalo, the artist had to go to the Bronx Zoo in New York to find a live specimen for a model!

The Indians fight a losing battle. Serious trouble between white settlers and Indians broke out in the Minnesota Territory in 1862. In the summer of that year the Sioux, led by Little Crow, went on the warpath, killing hundreds of settlers. Panic quickly spread and the governor sought aid from Washington. To restore order, President Lincoln put General John Pope in charge of a new Department of the Northwest, which included Minnesota and several other states

Fur traders who moved into Sioux country built outposts such as Fort Laramie in Wyoming.

and territories.[2] Pope's orders regarding the Sioux were clear: "They are to be treated as maniacs or wild beasts, and by no means as people with whom treaties or compromises can be made."

In the Minnesota campaign, the American soldiers showed no mercy. When many of the Sioux surrendered, there was an immediate cry for revenge from local whites. Pope favored condemning to death more than 300 of the 1,800 Sioux prisoners. President Lincoln intervened, however, and prevented the slaughter — although he authorized the hanging of 38 Indians. Pope continued his drive against the Sioux, finally succeeding in pushing them onto new lands in the Dakota Territory. Many of these Indians were reduced to starvation.

In the Colorado Territory the Cheyenne and Arapaho had been forced by the federal government in 1861 to give up their claims to land that had once been guaranteed to them. They were then resettled in eastern Colorado near Sand Creek. Some of the warriors, led by Chief Black Kettle, resisted

---

[2]The Union defeat at the Second Battle of Bull Run had led Lincoln to remove Pope from command of the Army of the Potomac, making necessary a new assignment for the defeated commander.

the removal by raiding mining camps and other settlements. In response, a force of local militia, commanded by Colonel J. M. Chivington, surprised 500 Cheyenne at Sand Creek. Attacking at daybreak, the militiamen killed 270 Indians — 200 women and children and 70 men.

Hardly had the struggle broken off in Colorado when warfare erupted again, this time on the northern Plains. There the Sioux tribes, who had been promised a permanent homeland, had become inflamed by the news of Sand Creek. They were also aroused when a wagon trail was built through their land and when the army sent troops to ensure the safety of white travelers. The Sioux, led by Crazy Horse and Red Cloud, proved a determined foe. Every wagon train came under attack.

The Indians are placed on reservations. Before the fighting ended in 1867, both sides had suffered heavy losses. By then it was clear that new steps would have to be taken to end Indian resistance.

Congress decided that only one solution was possible: all Indians must be settled on *reservations.* These were tracts of land set aside for the different tribes. The government expected the Indians to give up their hunting way of life and get food through government agents on the reservation or through farming.

In 1867, the government established two large reservations. One, located in the western part of the Dakota Territory, was to contain some 54,000 Indians. The other, forced on the Five Civilized Tribes as punishment for having supported the Confederacy, was carved out of the western part of the Indian Territory. It would be the home of 86,000 tribespeople. Both reservations were far from the new transcontinental railroads that were being built, and far, too, from any land that white settlers might want. Other small reservations were scattered throughout the West.

Some Indian chiefs were bribed and flattered into accepting the government's terms. Red Cloud, for one, had the fight taken out of him by the royal treatment he received in Washington when he visited

President Grant. Younger warriors, however, refused to accept retreat to reservations. Beginning in 1868, they waged relentless warfare against the advancing white settlers, ranging far and wide over the Plains from Texas to the Canadian border.

Indian resistance is crushed. The effort to suppress the Indian unrest resulted in many bloody encounters. The most severe was the Red River War of 1874–1875, during which 3,000 United States troops under Generals William T. Sherman and Philip H. Sheridan engaged the Comanche, Kiowa, Arapaho, and other tribes in battle. When that struggle was finally over, Indian resistance on the southern Plains had been broken.

Resistance on the northern Plains was another matter. In the early 1870's surveying parties of the Northern Pacific Railroad were working through the Yellowstone country under the protection of the Seventh United States Cavalry, a group of veteran Indian-fighters. The commanding officer was a handsome, long-haired lieutenant colonel named George Armstrong Custer. The great-grandson of a Hessian officer who had remained in America after surrendering with Burgoyne, Custer had graduated from West Point just in time to take part in the First Battle of Bull Run. His gallantry and dashing manner drew favorable attention and assignments. After Appomattox, General Sheridan presented him with the Confederate flag of truce and the table on which Grant wrote the terms of surrender. Sheridan commented at that time, "I know of no one whose efforts have contributed more to this happy result than those of Custer."

Seeking even more glory, Custer was pleased to be assigned to Indian fighting. Soon the Indians recognized him as a formidable opponent. In 1868 he defeated the Cheyenne, led by Black Kettle, in a battle at the Washita River in the Indian Territory. In addition to killing more than 100 warriors (including Black Kettle), Custer's forces also killed 38 unarmed women and children.

In June, 1876, Custer prepared to surprise a large force of Sioux and Cheyenne who had gathered near the Little Bighorn River in Montana. When the Indians discovered his presence, however, Custer decided to make a frontal attack. To this day no one knows why Custer acted so recklessly. Possibly he thought the Indians were afraid to stand and fight; possibly he hoped

The Indians in the West were resettled on lands set aside as reservations, such as the Pine Ridge reservation in southwestern South Dakota.

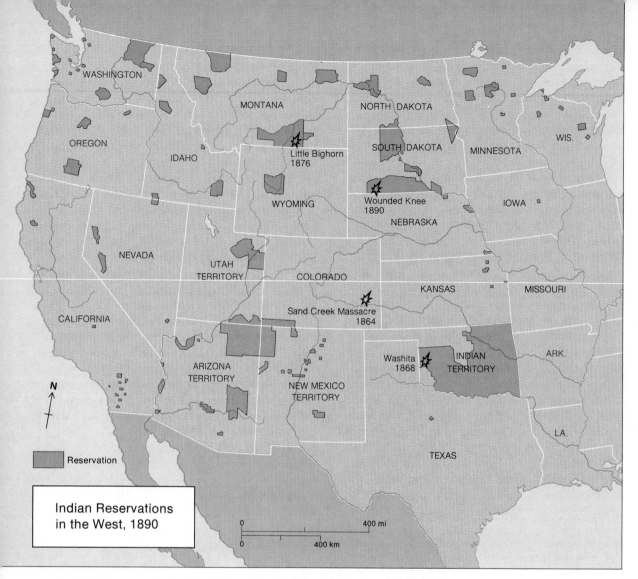

Indian Reservations in the West, 1890

Reservation

Little Bighorn 1876

Wounded Knee 1890

Sand Creek Massacre 1864

Washita 1868

INDIAN TERRITORY

N

0   400 mi
0   400 km

By 1890 the many efforts of the Indians to resist the encroachment of white settlers had ended, and most Indians had been confined to reservations.

to win everlasting fame. At any rate, he died along with his detachment of 264 troops. A Blackfoot chief later said that the rush of Indians toward Custer's column was "like a hurricane . . . like bees swarming out of a hive." The Battle of the Little Bighorn is remembered as "Custer's Last Stand."

The news of Custer's death raised to new heights the fury against the Indians. The nation, celebrating the centennial of its independence, demanded a swift end to further Indian resistance. Troops now relentlessly waged war against the outgunned Indians. By late 1876 fighting in the Dakota Territory had ended.

The Indian wars come to an end. Some Indians continued to resist in the next years, but without real hope. In the Pacific Northwest, Chief Joseph led the Nez Perce in a brilliant campaign against well-equipped army forces who were trying to force his people onto a reservation. His small band traveled more than 1,300 miles across Oregon and Idaho in 1877 before being forced to surrender in Montana. The last major resistance was offered by the Apache Indians in New Mexico. Indian warfare came to an end there in 1886 when the Apache leader, Geronimo, was captured.

The final tragic chapter in the long history of Indian warfare was written on the northern Plains in 1890. A religious revival had spread through the Sioux tribes, based on the belief that a Messiah was about to appear who would defeat the whites and restore the Indians' land. A practice of the religion was to hold long, exhausting dances, which put many of the participants into trances. Settlers, fearing the "Ghost Dance" religion, called in troops to disarm a group of Indians they thought posed a threat. At Wounded Knee Creek, in southwestern South Dakota, the tribespeople — 120 men and 230 women and children — were encamped, prepared to surrender their weapons. In a moment of confusion, someone fired a shot. The troops opened fire with rifles and with their new Gatling guns, the earliest type of machine gun. About 300 of the unprotected Sioux perished.

The government changes its Indian policy. Americans as a whole had long been blind to the question of Indian rights. By the early 1880's, however, after the cruel struggles were over, the public attitude started to change. Reformers began to take a different view of Indian affairs. One reformer was Helen Hunt Jackson. Her book *A Century of Dishonor*, published in 1881, drew national attention to the shameful treatment of the tribespeople. The book has been called "the Indians' *Uncle Tom's Cabin*."

Supporters of Indian rights were soon speaking out in Congress. Under the guiding hand of Henry L. Dawes, senator from Massachusetts, the Dawes Act was passed in 1887. It abolished most tribal organizations and authorized the President to divide up the reservations. Each head of an Indian family would be allotted 160 acres, while smaller tracts would be granted to unmarried men, women, and children. After 25 years, each landholder would receive title to his or her homestead and would be made a citizen of the United States. Any reservation land left over after the distribution would be sold by the government, the proceeds to be set aside for Indian education.

The Dawes Act is a failure. The speedy "Americanization" of the Indian was now the goal of the United States. The Dawes Act, as a government official said, would make the American Indian into an Indian American. However, the Dawes Act did not work as well as its author had hoped. Many Indians had no desire to give up their tribal organizations or to become farmers. The land they received, moreover, was rarely good for farming. Many Indians fell so heavily in debt that they had to sell their land as soon as they obtained title to it. Of the 150 million acres owned by Indians in 1880, about 60 percent was taken from them in one way or another.

The economic condition of the Indians declined steadily, and as their poverty deepened, their health and general well-being declined. By 1900 the situation was so critical that people began talking about the "vanishing" Indians. They noted that in 1900 the entire Native American population had fallen to a mere 237,000. The Indians, however, did not vanish. The twentieth century would see a resurgence of Indian population and culture.

SECTION REVIEW

1. Vocabulary: *reservation.*
2. (a) What was the Indian Territory? (b) Which side did the Indians in that territory choose during the Civil War?
3. What advantages did army troops have in their struggle with the western Indians?
4. Of what significance was the destruction of the buffalo herds?
5. (a) Why did the Indians resist white settlement? (b) Who were some of the Indians' leaders in that struggle? (c) What was the result of the Indian wars?
6. (a) How did the Dawes Act mark a change in the government's Indian policy? (b) How successful was it?

2 Ranchers and Miners Penetrate the West

The Great Plains, which had once been an obstacle to pioneers heading for Oregon or California, became a region of opportunity in the years after the Civil War. Beginning in the 1860's, a colorful new era opened: the day of the cattle rancher and the miner.

THE SPREAD OF RANCHING

Ranching begins in Texas. Soon after the Spanish had arrived in Mexico, they began to raise cattle. By the 1700's they had brought livestock into Texas. When Americans first moved there under Stephen Austin's leadership, they earned their living almost entirely from cattle raising. The San Antonio Valley — a diamond-shaped tract formed by the Gulf of Mexico and the Rio Grande on the south and the town of San Antonio at the north — proved ideal for the purpose. Animals known as Texas longhorns were developed there by crossbreeding English and Spanish cattle. By the 1830's about a million head of cattle roamed the Texas landscape, most of them untended. These animals were valued mainly for their hides.

Cowboys become part of the western scene. Already the cowboy as a distinctive type had appeared. The first cowboys were Mexican *vaqueros* (vah-KAIR-ohz).[3] The *vaqueros* taught the Americans how to handle the animals, how to rope them, trail them, and brand them. The Americans later anglicized the word *vaquero* to "buckaroo." In time other familiar words of the cowboy's trade were adapted from their Spanish forms: *lasso, lariat, chaps, stampede, rodeo,* and others. Some words were taken over unchanged: *corral, bronco, sombrero.*

Cowboys began tending large herds of cattle in the years after Texas won its independence in 1836. The cattle industry expanded, as beef-eating in the United States increased. The cowboys were already guiding small numbers of cattle northward along the Shawnee Trail into Missouri. Then the cattle were shipped to other parts of the country. In 1852 the first longhorns arrived in New York and were quickly acclaimed for the quality of their beef.

Cowboys became American heroes through popular fiction — at first through the dime novels dealing with "the West," then through Wild West shows that toured the country, and later through movies and television. The cowboy was made out to be larger than life, dealing bravely with cattle rustlers, stubborn Indians, evil sheriffs, and brutal outlaws. In reality cowboys were, as one of them said, "merely folks, just plain, every-day bowlegged humans." It is estimated that 5,000 of the cowboys were black. One of them, the rodeo star Bill Pickett, was the greatest of all bulldoggers.

A cowboy's work was hard, usually wearisome, and at times dangerous. The cowboy was almost constantly on horseback. Like the cattle themselves, the mustangs that cowboys rode came originally from Spain — no doubt brought there long before from North Africa. The mustang had what everybody agreed was "cow sense" and an instinctive ability to help the cowboy make the right move in difficult situations — a sudden stampede, a blinding blizzard, an unexpected downpour. Traveling incessantly in the saddle took its toll on the rider, and cowboys tended to wear out physically after a few years. When at the end of a drive cowboys had the relief of seeing a town and other human beings, they were not inclined to search for excitement. Mostly they wanted to rest from the tension and responsibility of their work.

Cow towns help develop a market for cattle. After the firing on Fort Sumter, many cowboys quickly found themselves in Confederate uniforms. The cattle were left untended once more, and most Americans soon forgot the taste of western beef.

When veterans from Texas returned home after Appomattox, however, they again took up cattle raising. Two important conditions had developed in the years the cowboys were away. One was the prosperity in the North, which had created a livelier market than ever for beef. The other was a discovery farmers in Missouri and Kansas had made. They had noticed that their own cattle fell ill from a disease called "Texas fever" shortly after coming into contact with the longhorns. Aiming to prevent the Texas animals from being driven into their region, farmers armed themselves. They began firing on animals and often stampeded herds.

---

[3] *Vaquero* is a Spanish word meaning "one who works with cows."

Cattle that bred and roamed on the open range were gathered in the spring roundup and branded with the distinctive mark of the owner.

The question of how to satisfy the public's hunger for beef without risking conflict — and heavy loss — was solved by Joseph McCoy, an Illinois businessman. McCoy picked out a small village in Kansas named Abilene, on the Kansas Pacific Railroad. The community had only a few log huts but was surrounded by luxuriant grassland. Within sixty days, beginning in July, 1867, McCoy had turned the little place into a beehive of activity — constructing stockyards, pens, and chutes for cattle, and a rooming house for cowhands. In selecting Abilene, McCoy ignored a Kansas law restricting the entry of Texas cattle, but the region was so thinly settled that nobody objected.

McCoy sent his associate, W. W. Sugg, to make contact with cattle ranchers, urging them to bring their herds into Abilene in order to get them to market. Sugg could assure the Texans that the trail to Abilene was far enough west to avoid protests and clashes. By the beginning of August, 7,000 cattle had been driven to Abilene. Early in September the first cattle train, consisting of twenty cars, chugged off for Chicago and its waiting stockyards. Before 1867 was over, at least 36,000 cattle — and possibly twice that number — had passed through Abilene.

The long drive is hard work. Reaching Abilene was the culmination of what came to be called the *long drive.* Herd after herd beat its dusty way north along such well-known routes as the Chisholm Trail. Each herd was led by two cowboys known as "pointers." These were experienced hands, some of them still in their teens, whose task was to guide the cattle and keep them from becoming mixed up with other herds. Behind the pointers rode the "swing riders," (or "flank riders"), who kept the herd from spreading out. Bringing up the rear were the "drag riders," who coaxed straggling cattle. The entire operation was directed by the trail boss, or foreman. He planned the daily

39

Chicago, the rail crossroads of America, became a center for livestock trade, as indicated by these stockyards, and for the meat-packing industry.

drive, found out ahead of time where water was available, and arranged for food and shelter along the way. As the railroads pushed westward, other cow towns developed in the same way as Abilene. After 1875, Dodge City, Kansas — on the Western Trail — became the busiest of them all.

Cattle are wintered on the open range. Hard times in 1873 caused a sharp drop in the price of beef. Cattle dealers decided not to ship the animals to slaughter but to have them spend the winter on the open range of the northern grasslands. Astonishingly, the cattle thrived despite the cold. Soon cattle were kept on the plains as a matter of course. By 1880, four million head of cattle had been driven north, many of them on the Pecos Trail that ran from Texas to Cheyenne, Wyoming, a distance of more than a thousand miles. Where the drive to Abilene took two or three months, the journey to Wyoming took somewhat longer. When the cattle industry spread even farther north, the drives to Montana or the Dakotas often took half a year.

The cattle business on the open range grew rapidly. Gradually better cattle were raised there, with scrawny longhorns being crossbred with stock like the Aberdeen Angus and Hereford.[4] The improved animals combined the stamina of the longhorn with the greater weight of the two more recently imported breeds.

Open-range cattle raising comes to an end. Many of the cattle barons of the 1880's found the open-range cattle industry profitable because their animals were allowed to graze on government-owned land and needed only limited attention from cowboys. For several reasons, however, the days of the long drive and the open range were numbered. First, the open range was rapidly becoming overstocked and the grass overgrazed. Second, destructive diseases were being passed from one animal to another on the open range, and regular inspection of the herds was impossible. Third, the purity of selectively bred animals could not be protected under the conditions of the long drive and the open range.

---

[4]Herefords had first been brought into the United States in 1817 by Henry Clay.

The year 1885 brought hard times to the open-range cattle industry. First, prices fell because of the enormous supply of animals. Then, the weather conspired against the industry. The winter of 1885–1886 was extremely severe. Snows covered the grass early in the season and froze, making it impossible for the animals to graze. By spring, 85 percent of the range cattle were dead.

The following summer a fearful drought was accompanied by withering heat. The temperature often reached 120 degrees in the shade — where there was any. Fighting prairie fires kept the cowboys as busy as tending the animals did.

Weather in the following winter (1886–1887) again proved devastating. From December to mid-February the temperature hovered between 34 degrees and 60 degrees below zero. In late January came a brief *chinook*, or warm southern wind, that partly melted the snow, followed by a cold spell that seemed to turn everything to ice.

The cowboys struggled valiantly to save the animals. Their efforts, however, were mostly in vain, for the day of the open range was ending. By the end of the 1880's farmers began using fencing to enclose pastures on the range. They also began to raise hay on their property and to feed it to the animals during the winter. As one cowboy put it, "I tell you times have changed. You didn't hear the sound of a mowing machine in this country ten years ago." Before long, the sound of the threshing machine was also heard on the Great Plains, in fields where buffalo and cattle had once roamed.

MINING IN THE ROCKIES

Gold is discovered in Colorado and Nevada. Even as the cattle frontier was reaching the edge of the Rockies, the mountains themselves were the scene of another dramatic development: the miner's frontier. In 1859 gold was discovered in Colorado and Nevada almost simultaneously. Practically overnight, thousands of people rushed to the mountains, determined to make a lucky strike. Stories circulated that there were good "pickings" in the vicinity of Pikes Peak. Covered wagons known as "prairie schooners" were soon on their way west, emblazoned with the words "Pikes Peak or bust!" Most of them eventually returned, bearing the sad news "Pikes Peak and busted!"

Only a few prospectors — as in any gold strike — hit pay dirt. Among the luckiest were the shopkeeper H. A. W. Tabor and his wife, Augusta, who was the first white woman in the region. The Tabors had looked for treasure themselves without success. Two prospectors persuaded Tabor in 1878 to lend them money and supplies to go digging, in return for a third of whatever ore they might find. On an investment of just $50, Tabor earned $1 million for his portion of the successful strike made by the two prospectors. Enriched by this and other strikes, he built the Tabor Grand Opera House in Denver in 1879.[5]

The gold rush resulted in the growth of towns in Colorado. By 1860 Leadville — nicknamed Cloud City because it was situated more than 10,000 feet above sea level — had become the main center of activity for gold-seekers. Most of them were young men who knew nothing about mining. A new town, Ore City, flourished for only two years, then became a ghost town as the diggings were exhausted. Still, prospectors continued to sing:

> The gold is there, 'most anywhere,
> You can take it out rich, with an iron
>   crowbar,
> And where it is thick, with a shovel and
>   pick,
> You can pick it out in lumps as big as a
>   brick.

The people who settled in the larger towns that sprang up — towns such as Denver, Boulder, and Canon City — made a living by supplying the miners. The first Colorado farmer to irrigate his land, David K. Wall, soon made money by supplying fresh vegetables to the miners.

Coloradans learned to persevere after the surface gold had been extracted. Crops

---

[5]Not until four years later did the Metropolitan Opera House open its doors in New York.

failed, a grasshopper plague took its toll, and the first transcontinental railroad was built through Wyoming, not Colorado. Still, the region grew. In 1876 Colorado came into the Union as the Centennial State.

The Comstock Lode attracts miners to Nevada. New mining "booms" continued for many years. Soon after the Colorado rush was over, the magnet for prospectors became Nevada, in that day a part of the Utah Territory. At first prospectors were drawn by their pursuit of gold. Soon it was silver that became the lure.

In western Nevada a band of miners in 1859 found the richest deposit of precious ores in history. It was named the Comstock Lode for Henry T. P. Comstock, the miner who claimed to have made the discovery. The nearby town of Virginia City was named, it is said, for Comstock's partner whose nickname was "Old Virginia."

The rush to the region defies description. By the end of 1860 — just before Lincoln took office — 154 businesses had been established in Virginia City to serve the miners. The drinking water, however, contained such harmful minerals that practi-

Mining boom towns were situated along major railroads. Cattle trails ended at points on those same rail lines, which carried ore and beef to eastern markets.

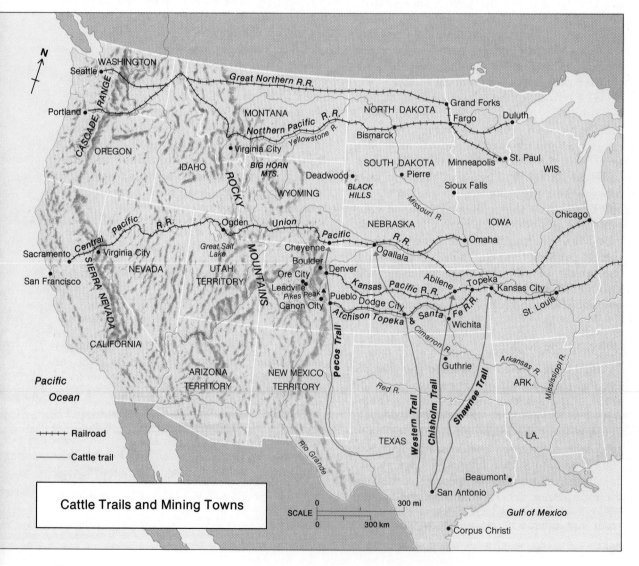

Cattle Trails and Mining Towns

cally everybody fell ill at some time during the next two years. Although Virginia City had six doctors, many hundreds of people died.

The Comstock mines yielded more than $500 million in silver and gold by the time they were worked out around 1880. One mine, the "Big Bonanza," netted about $200 million to four prospectors of Irish immigrant background. John W. Mackay, one of them, gave away half of his money to charities, always anonymously. Most new millionaires, however, showed off their riches. One mine owner shod his horses with silver. Another filled his water tank with champagne in order to serve his wedding guests.

When the silver was exhausted, Nevada suffered economic depression. It was brought into the Union as a state in 1864, however, even though the territory did not meet the population requirement. President Lincoln, believing that one more free state might be needed to ratify an emancipation amendment, signed the proclamation of admission.

The mining rush speeds up the development of the mountain states. The mining frontier also left its mark on the Washington and Montana territories. Idaho on the eve of the Civil War was part of the Washington Territory (which in turn had been carved out of the Oregon Territory in 1853). Congress, yielding to Idaho miners, in 1863 organized the Idaho Territory, which included Montana and practically all of Wyoming.

Montana became the scene of a gold rush beginning in 1862. People here, like others on the mining frontier, were isolated from the rest of the world. Wrote one Montanan, "All the great battles of the season of 1862 — Antietam, Fredericksburg, Second Bull Run — all the exciting debates of Congress and the more exciting battles at sea, first became known to us on the arrival of the newspapers in the spring of 1863."

With the Montana gold rush, so many people filled the region that in 1864 Congress organized the Montana Territory, with another Virginia City as its territorial capital. For almost twenty years gold was found in the maze of gulches in the Rockies. When the surface outcroppings of gold were gone, however, mining became big business. Deep shafts were sunk and ore refineries built. These operations required large sums of money, usually provided by investors in the East.

The last of the mining rushes took place in the Black Hills of the Dakotas. The area, over two hundred miles from the nearest railroad, repeated the pattern of the early mining operations elsewhere. The colorful figures of the region — including Deadwood Dick (the nickname of an English-born frontiersman) and his friend Calamity Jane — were celebrated in the popular dime novels. Probably the most famous hero was Wild Bill Hickok, a soldier, Indian scout, Union spy, and United States marshal, who was slain by a shot in the back in a tavern brawl in the mining town of Deadwood.

The mining communities never had the glamor of the cow towns. They were filled with too much greed and too much squabbling over claims. Criminals were kept under control by *vigilantes.* Secret and outside the law, these citizen committees set out to provide law and order. Using intimidation and threats, the vigilantes insisted that they were the servants of justice, seeking only to put down lawlessness. At times, however, they were the instruments of vengeance and mob violence.

Constituted governments, in any event, quickly began to take control. North Dakota, South Dakota, Montana, and Washington received statehood in 1889, as the country marked the hundredth anniversary of George Washington's inauguration. The following year Idaho and Wyoming entered the Union as the forty-third and forty-fourth states.

SECTION REVIEW

1. Vocabulary: *long drive, vigilante.*
2. (a) Describe the origins of cattle ranching in Texas. (b) What role did cow towns play in the development of ranching?
3. Why did open-range cattle raising come to an end?
4. What part did prospectors play in opening up the Rocky Mountain area?

The Great Plains

When European settlers arrived in North America, they found vast forests covering nearly the entire eastern part of the continent. Near the Mississippi River, the forests gradually gave way to the broad, rolling expanses of the Midwest's tall-grass prairie. Farther west, the climate was drier, and the land became high plateaus. Many kinds of short prairie grasses grew on these high grasslands — the Great Plains — which extend west to the edge of the Rocky Mountains and south to even drier desert areas. From south to north, this short-grass prairie stretches about 1,500 miles, from Texas to western Canada.

A "Breadbasket" of the World

The Great Plains of North America are temperate grasslands. Lying in the middle latitudes (about 30° to 60° north), they are the result of continental patterns of rainfall and temperature. Because they lie inland, far from the oceans, the grasslands have a dry continental climate — warm summers, cold winters, and a low average yearly rainfall. Water is often scarce, particularly in late summer. Because the growing season in some parts is too short for many crops, the land is used for grazing animals. Where there are both enough rainfall and a longer summer, however, the grasslands are ideally suited for growing grains. These conditions have made the Great Plains one of the "breadbaskets" of the world — a major producer of wheat and other grains.

Prairie Soils

It is not only climate and rainfall that make the Great Plains an important grain-growing region. Where prairie grasses had grown for many years, a special type of rich, soft, blackish-brown soil developed. Because the rainfall was generally low, important minerals stayed in the soil rather than being washed away.

The prairie grasses also helped make the soil rich. The long root systems of these grasses reached deep into the top layers of soil, often to a depth of six feet or more. The plants helped recycle essential elements in the soil. Near the surface, the roots and stems of some prairie grasses twined together to make a tough, protective mat of sod. Besides grasses, the original prairies were thick with berries, mosses, and colorful wildflowers, especially daisies, asters, sunflowers, and clover.

Rain and Wind

As the map shows, rainfall decreases steadily from the Mississippi River westward. A sharp break occurs at about the 98th meridian of longitude. This change accounts for the shorter grasses and lack of trees on the Great Plains, where the average precipitation (rain and snow) is about half that of the central Midwest. Because most of this precipitation falls as spring and summer rains, it is well timed for planting and harvesting wheat. Nonetheless, the low average rainfall makes farming on the Great Plains risky in several ways.

Although crops flourish in years of normal or heavy rainfall, these periods commonly are followed by years of drought, in which rainfall may be only half what was expected and needed. Such periods are disastrous for the crops, for farm families, and for the land itself (page 40).

Prairie winds blow strongly and steadily, for there are few trees to act as windbreaks. Wind erosion has always been a problem on the Great Plains. The land was particularly fragile in spots where the tough sod cover was broken — whether by animals' hooves, farmers' plows, or settlers'

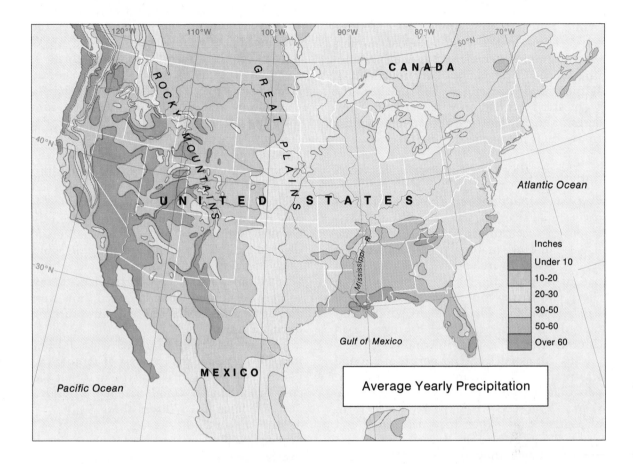

Inches
Under 10
10-20
20-30
30-50
50-60
Over 60

Average Yearly Precipitation

roads. The dark, crumbly prairie soil blew away easily once it had dried out and been exposed to the air.

In periods of abundant rainfall, Great Plains farmers increased the amount of land they planted and moved into areas that normally were too dry for farming. More prairie grasses were plowed under for wheat fields. This made the erosion problem even worse when the drought began. Without the tough roots of prairie grasses to hold the soil in place, tons of rich topsoil might be blown away by dust storms.

As more and more of the Great Plains was turned into farms, the risk increased, and conserving the soil became very important. Periods of drought could not be prevented, but some steps could be taken to reduce the damage. These included planting trees as windbreaks, using different farming methods, and letting wild grasses grow back in some fields.

1. (a) Where are the Great Plains? (b) How are they different from the tall-grass prairies of the Midwest? (c) Why are the Great Plains called a "breadbasket"?

2. (a) What factors have contributed to making prairie soils good for farming? (b) What is sod?

3. (a) What problems does lack of rainfall cause in the Great Plains? (b) What are some ways of protecting the soil of the Great Plains?

3 Farmers Settle the Great Plains

While ranchers and miners were staking their claims in the West, pioneer farmers were beginning to create an agricultural empire on the Great Plains. The movement of farmers had started in 1862, when the Homestead Act had provided a grant of 160 acres of free federal land to anyone willing to live on it for five years.

The settlers endure hardships. The Great Plains forced Americans to use all the ingenuity they could muster. The region had far less rainfall than farmers east of the Mississippi were accustomed to. It also lacked the usual building materials for houses and fences. Fences were essential because crops had to be protected from grazing herds of sheep and cattle. Moreover, nature seemed harsher on the Plains: high winds that fanned raging prairie fires; baking sun in summer; fierce blizzards in winter.

Insects plagued the farmers too. No one was prepared for the invasion of grasshoppers that began in 1874 and lasted for three years. The insects first appeared in the form of a giant cloud; then they descended and chewed up everything green. When no crops were left, they went to work on farm tools, broom handles, the walls of houses, and even harnesses. Falling into the wells, the 'hoppers ruined water supplies.

One of the greatest problems that Plains farmers faced was loneliness. Farm families lived many miles apart and felt their isolation keenly. Few pleasures relieved the hard work and drabness of farm life in the late 1800's.

Hamlin Garland, who wrote about rural life of that period, grew up on midwestern farms. Once, after a few years in the East, Garland returned for a visit and was struck by what he had never noticed before: "The lack of color, of charm in the lives of the people, anguished me. I wondered why I had never before perceived the futility of woman's life on a farm." He remembered the plight of his mother, worn out by years of unending toil: "I recalled her as she passed from the churn to the stove, from the stove to the bedchamber, and from the bedchamber back to the kitchen, day after day, year after year, rising at daylight or before, and going to her bed only after the evening dishes were washed and the stockings and clothing mended for the night."

Many a bride arrived at the new homestead to discover that "home" would be a dug-out or a sod house. A dug-out was a dwelling cut into the side of a hill or into a rise in the ground. A sod house was constructed of strips of sod sliced from the ground. Cut into blocks and fashioned into walls and roofing, the sod thus provided shelter until other materials became available. Some sod houses were carefully chinked with a kind of "native lime" made of sand and clay, which kept the chill wind out. Occasionally the interiors were whitewashed and attractively furnished. Many sod houses leaked when it rained, however, and sometimes collapsed without warning during a storm.

Many settlers who moved west did not take into account the expense of taming the Plains. First of all, it was estimated that the cost of putting a wooden fence around a 160-acre farm in 1870 was about $1,000 — a sum beyond the reach of almost all farmers. Second, getting water on the vast, nearly treeless Plains involved digging wells deeper than farmers had ever gone before — sometimes many hundreds of feet. The cost of digging such wells ran as high as $2 a foot — again a sum very few farmers could raise. Third, to bring water to the surface from such depths required power. The "old oaken bucket" would not answer the need. Windmills were needed to pump water that was deep in the ground, but like the wells themselves, most farmers could not afford them.

Inventions and new techniques help the Plains farmers. A number of inventions enabled the pioneers to cope with their new surroundings. In 1873 Joseph F. Glidden, a native of New Hampshire living in Illinois, developed a way of twisting wire so that it had a sharp barb every few inches, like a thorny hedge. By 1883 Glidden had built a

A settler used the soil from about a half acre to build a typical sod house, a construction that was an adaptation of Indian winter dwellings.

factory that produced enough of the barbed wire each day to make 600 miles of fence. Within a few years mass production methods had lowered the price of 100 pounds of barbed wire to less than $4 — a price that brought decent fencing within the reach of all. This invention ranks with the cotton gin in its revolutionary impact on American agriculture.

If cheap fencing became available to most farmers fairly early, wells and windmills were not generally affordable until about 1890. Meanwhile, farmers turned to a technique called *dry farming.* Actually dry farming is an ancient agricultural practice. In the American Southwest, the Anasazi people had mastered the technique — as had the Arabs and Jews of the ancient Near East. White Americans, however, had never had need of the method before moving onto the Great Plains.

Dry farming requires rainfall of at least ten inches annually. The soil must be plowed to a depth of about ten inches before the arrival of winter rains and snow. The topsoil is cultivated after each rain to keep it loose. In that way the moisture that has soaked in is kept from evaporating.

The thick sod covering the Plains was a problem which had to be overcome even before new farming methods could be introduced. What was required was a plow strong enough to break the tough prairie grassland. John Deere, a native of Vermont, had made an effective steel plow in his Illinois blacksmith shop in the 1840's. Then, in 1868 James Oliver introduced a plow that could cut a smooth furrow in practically any kind of soil. Soon Oliver was turning out 200,000 plows a year in a plant he built in Indiana.

Many other machines also made their appearance, enabling relatively few people to work large farms. The innovations included grain drills for planting seeds in rows; plows that farmers could ride on; and threshing machines that separated the chaff from the wheat.

Railroads encourage settlement. Some of the early settlers broke under the strain of life on the Plains, never becoming accustomed to the loneliness and the relentless howl of the wind. No frontierspeople since the first settlers in Virginia and Massachusetts were so far removed from the daily conveniences they had earlier known. Nevertheless, the pioneers arrived in a ceaseless stream. Some at first were Civil War veterans adjusting to civilian life. Others were immigrants from western Europe seeking wider opportunity. Still others were the footloose adventurers who have been found on every frontier in American history.

The railroad was the means by which most people reached the Great Plains. After the Indian wars the influx of newcomers to Kansas followed the line of the Atchison, Topeka, and Santa Fe Railroad. The people who settled Nebraska set up farms along the route of the Union Pacific. (Nebraska joined the Union as the thirty-seventh state in 1867.) Ranchers trying to preserve the open range opposed the steady increase of homesteads in both Kansas and Nebraska. In the end, though, the farmers won. By 1880, for instance, the population of Kansas was 850,000 and that of Nebraska about 450,000.

Western population grows. The development of the Dakotas was hastened by the construction of the Northern Pacific Railroad as well as by the gold rush to the Black Hills. The area was the home of immense "bonanza" farms. The best-known bonanza farm was run by Oliver Dalrymple, a successful wheat farmer. Dalrymple was hired by the Northern Pacific to prove the fertility of the Red River valley. On 18 sections of land — each one mile square — he produced 600,000 bushels of wheat in 1861. By 1880 over 300 farms flourished in this rich river valley, averaging over 1,000 acres in size; a few were as large as 100,000 acres. While bonanza farms were not typical of the grain-growing region, they gave a hint of the scale on which crops would be raised in the future.

The Dakotas were boosted further by the Great Northern Railroad. Rails laid northwestward from St. Paul, Minnesota, reached Fargo and Grand Forks before heading west to Seattle, Washington. Thousands of European immigrants were drawn to the Dakotas, principally Scandinavians, Germans, and Czechs. Some of the newcomers worked on the bonanza farms, but most of them quickly acquired family holdings of their own. By 1885 all Dakota had been settled east of the Missouri River. The population of over 500,000 people was four times what it had been only five years earlier.

When the Dakotas were divided into two states in 1889, North Dakota's capital was named Bismarck in honor of Ger-many's chancellor — in hopes of attracting German investment. Once, Lewis and Clark had camped near its site; now it was a booming river port and supply center. South Dakota's capital was Pierre, but its largest city was Sioux Falls. Settled in 1856, Sioux Falls had been abandoned during the Indian troubles. Now its name remains as a reminder of the Indians who once dominated the area.

Wyoming and Montana were not reached by farmers until the 1880's. In both of these territories life for farmers was hard. Wyoming's settlers mainly engaged in ranching and its population grew only slowly, being less than 65,000 in 1890. Montana had 132,000 people in 1890, most of them miners.

A land rush takes place in Oklahoma. As white settlement grew larger on the Great Plains, the Indian Territory (page 31) also began to attract the attention of frontierspeople. In 1883, at Wichita, Kansas, an "Oklahoma Colony" of settlers called "boomers" began to call for the opening of Indian lands. The railroads also applied pressure. The particular areas the "boomers" had in mind were the as yet unsettled portions of central Oklahoma. Congress finally agreed to negotiate with the Indians, and land soon was purchased for white settlement.

At noon on April 22, 1889, central Oklahoma was opened for settlement. Some 50,000 people had gathered at the border, waiting for the pistol shot announcing that the "run" was on. (Already, many "sooners" had jumped the gun.) Upon hearing the signal, they surged forward by bicycle, wagon, carriage, on horseback, and on foot to stake out claims. How Guthrie, Oklahoma, was settled is described in this account:

Unlike Rome, the city of Guthrie was built in a day. To be strictly accurate in the matter, it might be said that it was built in an afternoon. At twelve o'clock on Monday, April 22nd, the resident population of Guthrie was nothing; before sundown it was at least ten thousand. In that time streets had been laid out, town lots staked off, and steps taken toward the formation of a municipal government. At twilight the camp-fires of ten thousand people gleamed on the grassy slopes of the Cimarron Valley, where, the night before, the coyote, the gray wolf, and the deer roamed undisturbed.

The population of the Oklahoma Territory grew rapidly, and in 1907 Oklahoma entered the Union as the forty-sixth state — 300 years after the founding of Jamestown.

Arizona and New Mexico join the Union. Other territories which became states as a result of the settling of the last great West were New Mexico and Arizona. In 1905 and 1906 Congress failed in its efforts to admit the two territories as a single state. The effort was unpopular because many New Mexicans feared the extinction of their proud Spanish heritage. Arizonians, for their part, sought to avoid domination by the far more numerous New Mexicans. In 1912 New Mexico and Arizona were admitted as separate states, giving the flag its forty-seventh and forty-eighth stars.

The settlement of the last frontier is completed. Stretching from ocean to ocean, the United States now contained 48 separate states, most of them concerned with problems that would hardly have been recognized by the people who started the original thirteen colonies. An era had ended. The land of America was still sparsely settled in many places, but maps no longer could show a line separating populated areas from unsettled land.

By 1900, a total of 500 million acres of public land had been distributed by the federal government in less than forty years — an achievement unmatched anywhere in the world. Of this total, eighty million acres had been taken by homesteaders. Much of the rest had been acquired by railroads, lumbering interests, and mining concerns. In addition, states had handed out under one arrangement or another millions of acres of their public land.

America was now a country of small farmers to a greater extent than ever before. In the years from 1860 to 1910 the number of American farms increased from 2 million

Many Scandinavian immigrants who arrived in the 1800's became farmers in the Plains states.

to 6.4 million. The number of acres under cultivation more than doubled — from about 400 million acres to more than 875 million acres. The production of wheat — not to mention other crops — rose from about 200 million bushels in 1860 to over 625 million bushels in 1910. Out of the mills and packing houses of Kansas City, Minneapolis, and Chicago flowed an abundance of relatively inexpensive food. Moreover, surplus food now entered the international market, where it could help feed people in other parts of the world.

The new farmers of America were, however, not the free spirits Thomas Jefferson had envisioned. Making the trans-Mississippi region suitable for farming had been the work not only of intrepid individuals but also of railroads, new technology, and complex machinery. The farmer had gradually become dependent on American industry and eastern businesspeople. The adjustment of farming people to this condition would raise concerns that those who had "tamed" the last West never imagined.

SECTION REVIEW

1. Vocabulary: *dry farming*.
2. (a) What hardships did settlers on the Great Plains encounter? (b) What innovations helped relieve the hardships?
3. What western states were admitted to the Union as a result of the influx of new settlers?

Locating Information

In the study of history it is important to be able to locate information about a specific topic. Information may be located either in your textbook itself or in reference books.

Parts of a Book

Good textbooks are designed and organized in such a way that students can easily locate information and understand its significance. Here are the parts of a textbook that you should examine with care and use as aids in locating information.

Contents. Always located at the beginning of a book, the table of contents provides an outline of a book's organization as well as page references for the material being presented. Turn to the front of this textbook and review the table of contents. You will see that the narrative is organized into four units and sixteen chapters. Each chapter, in turn, is made up of a number of sections. The contents pages also inform you that there is an atlas and reference section. A listing of primary sources, special features, maps, and graphs is part of the table of contents too.

Chapter organization. To give you a preview of the information being presented, a chapter outline is included on the first page of each chapter in this book. The chapter outline lists the titles of the sections of the chapter. Within each section, column and paragraph headings in bold type provide an outline of the topics being covered.

Vocabulary. During your reading of any textbook, you will come across unfamiliar words. In this textbook many new words appear in bold type and then are defined in context. The glossary on pages 648–651 provides a means for reviewing the definitions of the important words that appear in the text. What is the meaning of the term *long drive*?

Dates. Since history is a record of the past, it is important to know when events took place. This textbook has a time line at the beginning of each chapter to give you a preview of the period to be covered and the important events that will be introduced. Turn to page 30 and study the time line for Chapter 1. What period of time does it cover? What is the first event that is included on the time line? What is the last event on the time line?

A list of dates in American history is included in the atlas and reference section at the back of the textbook. Turn to pages 633–635 and skim through the dates presented there. What events are listed in bold type? In what year did Benjamin Harrison become President?

Index. A valuable tool for locating specific information is provided at the very end of the textbook. This is the index. The index lists names, places, and subjects in alphabetical order and provides the page numbers on which they can be found. It also includes references to pictures, charts, graphs, and maps, as well as to primary source readings. Look at the following index entry:

Great Plains, 30, 113; settlement of, 32, 33, 35, 37–49; ranching on, 37–41; farming on, 43–49; tree replanting on, 241.

On what pages of the book can information be found about ranching on the Great Plains?

Illustrations. Throughout the textbook there are numerous illustrations. These illustrations, along with the captions, provide additional information about topics discussed in the text. Turn to page 47 and study the picture of a Plains farm. What does the picture tell you about the way settlers on the Great Plains lived? What does it tell you about the material used to build the house?

Reference Books

In your study of American history you will often need to locate information in reference books. Your school or community library has such books. The most commonly used reference books are dictionaries, encyclopedias, almanacs, and atlases.

Dictionary. A dictionary is a book that lists words alphabetically and gives their definitions and pronunciations (and often their origins).

Encyclopedia. An encyclopedia is a book or set of books containing articles on a great many subjects, arranged in alphabetical order. Encyclopedias can cover areas of general interest or they can be specialized, such as an encyclopedia of American history. Use an encyclopedia when you are looking for a clear and concise summary of a specific topic.

Almanac. An almanac is a one-volume book of facts, published once a year. Almanacs are useful sources where you can find up-to-date information on many subjects, especially people, places, events, and statistics.

Atlas. An atlas is a book of maps. Some atlases may contain information about products, population, and climate. Historical atlases show how different areas of the world appeared in the past.

Check Your Skill

Use the information presented on these pages to answer the following questions.

1. When you begin to read a book, where should you first look to find out about its organization and the information being presented?
2. In this textbook, why are column and paragraph headings of special importance?
3. If you come across an unfamiliar word while reading this textbook, how would you go about finding its definition?
4. What is the purpose of the time lines that appear at the beginning of each chapter?
5. Study the picture on page 35 and then describe what the picture reveals about the way of life of the Indians in the West.
6. How would you go about locating a specific subject in this textbook?
7. What type of reference book would you use to find (a) a concise summary of a specific topic, (b) up-to-date statistics, (c) the location of the Rocky Mountains?

Apply Your Skill

1. Write an essay describing how you would locate information about the Plains Indians.
2. Do research using the appropriate reference books to find out the names of your state's senators and representatives in Congress today.

Chapter 1 Review

Summary

In the period from 1820 to 1842, eastern Indian tribes were forced to move to territories set aside for them west of the Mississippi River. Soon, white settlers began to move west too. They bypassed the Indian Territory, but settled on lands that had long been the hunting grounds of the Plains Indians. Faced with being pushed off their lands and having their traditional way of life destroyed, these powerful tribes attacked white settlers, miners, and soldiers.

From the 1850's to the 1880's many tribes, including the Sioux, Cheyenne, Arapaho, and Apache, fought fierce battles with the United States Army. The Indians, who faced overwhelming odds, suffered heavy losses before being subdued and forced onto reservations. Government policies attempted to integrate the remaining Indians into white society, but those policies were not successful and the tribes continued to suffer.

Beginning in the 1860's, meanwhile, cattle ranching became an important occupation in the West. Cattle had first been introduced into Texas by the early Spanish settlers. By the 1830's, about a million head of cattle roamed the Texas landscape. Having learned how to handle the animals from Mexican *vaqueros*, American cowboys rounded up the cattle and drove the herds hundreds of miles north to shipping points on railways in Missouri. As the railroads moved westward, cow towns such as Abilene, Dodge City, and Cheyenne grew up almost overnight. Cattle were later raised on the open range, but by the end of the 1800's the ranchers had begun to fence in their herds and grow hay to feed the animals.

Another attraction for thousands of newcomers at this time was mining. The discovery of precious metals in the mountains of Colorado, Nevada, Idaho, Montana, Wyoming, and the Dakotas produced great wealth for some people and led to the rapid development of these regions.

In the last decades of the nineteenth century, large numbers of pioneer farmers moved onto the Great Plains. Enduring a difficult environment, these hardy farmers learned to use new types of machinery and new techniques to make the fertile soil produce bountiful crops.

Vocabulary and Important Terms

1. Great Plains
2. Indian Territory
3. Sand Creek
4. reservation
5. Little Bighorn
6. Wounded Knee Creek
7. *A Century of Dishonor*
8. Dawes Act
9. *vaquero*
10. cow town
11. long drive
12. open range
13. Comstock Lode
14. vigilante
15. barbed wire
16. dry farming
17. bonanza farm

Discussion Questions

1. (a) How did the introduction of horses and guns affect the Plains Indians? (b) What part did the buffalo play in the lives of the Plains Indians?

2. (a) For what reasons did the Indian wars break out in the late 1850's? (b) What was the result of the Indian wars?

3. (a) Why did Congress decide to settle all Indians on reservations? (b) What was the reaction of many Indians?

4. (a) Why did the public attitude toward the problem of Indian rights begin to change in the early 1880's? (b) What was the goal of the Dawes Act? (c) Why did it not work as well as its author had hoped? (d) What was the situation of the Indians by 1900?

5. (a) Who were the first cowboys? (b) In what ways did the cowboy of legend differ from the real cowboy?

6. (a) What new conditions did the cattle industry face after the Civil War? (b) How did the cattle industry change in response to these conditions?

7. (a) What pattern of mining operations was repeated with each of the mining rushes in the trans-Mississippi West? (b) What was life like in a mining town?

8. (a) How did agricultural conditions on the Great Plains differ from conditions east of the Mississippi? (b) What inventions and new farming techniques helped farmers tame the Great Plains?

9. What role did railroads play in encouraging western settlement?

10. (a) To what extent was America by the early 1900's a land of small farmers? (b) How were American farmers different from the farmers Thomas Jefferson had once envisioned?

Relating Past to Present

1. How do farmers live on the Great Plains today? How have some of the hardships faced by pioneer farmers been eased? What difficulties still exist for today's farmers?

2. Where do Indians live in the United States today? In what ways has life changed for American Indians since 1900?

Studying Local History

1. In what way, if any, was your state affected by the settlement of the trans-Mississippi West? If your state is located in this region, what communities grew up as parts of the ranching, mining, and farming frontiers?
2. How important, if at all, is mining to the economy of your state or region?

Using History Skills

1. *Reading maps.* Study the map on page 42 showing cattle trails. (a) From which state did the cattle trails start? (b) Which trail ended in Abilene, Kansas? (c) Why did the trails run north-south?

2. *Reading source material.* Study Ten Bears' speech on page 33. (a) Why, according to Ten Bears, did fighting start between the Comanche and government soldiers? (b) What solution did the government commissioners offer? (c) What was Ten Bears' response? (d) Based on what you have read in this chapter, what might have been the outcome of this meeting?
3. *Locating information.* Which reference book would be the *best* source of information for each of the following questions? (a) Who was Samuel Colt, and why is he famous? (b) In what part of Texas is the San Antonio Valley located? (c) How is the word *vaquero* pronounced?
4. *Writing a report.* Use an encyclopedia or a history of the trans-Mississippi West to find out about the removal of the Navajo Indians from their homeland to Fort Sumner, New Mexico, in 1864. It is an event the Navajo remember in their history as the "Long Walk."

WORLD SCENE

The New Breadbaskets

After 1865 many foreign families began settling the Great Plains of the United States and the grasslands of Argentina. The knowledge of farming brought by the immigrants helped develop these regions.

Mennonites and Russian wheat. Among the settlers of the Russian steppes were Mennonites, a religious group originally from Holland and Germany. Known to be good farmers, the Mennonites had been invited by Catherine the Great to develop farms in the part of southern Russia called the Ukraine. Before long, the Mennonites had turned the Ukraine into a prosperous wheat-producing area.

In 1871 the Russian czar ordered all men to report for military duty. The Mennonites, being pacifists, refused to serve. As a result, they had to leave Russia or face imprisonment. Enticed by an offer of land and a promise of exemption from military service, nearly 20,000 Mennonites immigrated to the United States, bringing with them seed for a variety of winter wheat known as Turkey Red. They settled on the Great Plains and planted the Turkey Red. It began to replace spring wheat as the nation's most widely raised crop, and in

time made Kansas's reputation as the Wheat State.

The pampas of Argentina. Like the Great Plains, the Argentine pampas were transformed in the late nineteenth century from a sparsely populated grassland into a rich agricultural center. In the 1870's this region — between the Atlantic and the Andes — became accessible through the construction of railroads. At the same time, government-sponsored programs were encouraging Europeans to come and settle on it.

Between 1880 and 1890, more than a million men, women, and children — primarily from Spain and Italy — entered Argentina and started farming the pampas. New types of grains brought by the immigrant farmers grew well on this fertile land. As on the Great Plains, the new settlers also raised sheep and cattle.

In the 1880's the development of ships with refrigerated compartments stimulated the beef-cattle industry, since fresh meat could now be exported safely all the way to Europe. By the early 1900's Argentina had become the leading agricultural nation in South America.

CHAPTER 2

The Making of Big Business

POST-CIVIL WAR – 1900

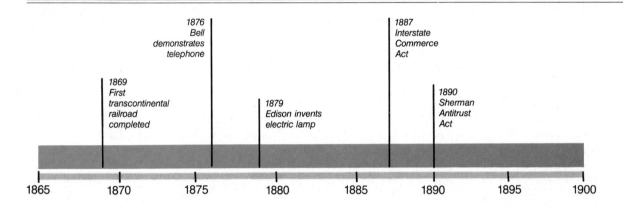

1876
Bell
demonstrates
telephone

1887
Interstate
Commerce
Act

1869
First
transcontinental
railroad
completed

1879
Edison invents
electric lamp

1890
Sherman
Antitrust
Act

1865   1870   1875   1880   1885   1890   1895   1900

CHAPTER OUTLINE

1. Many factors stimulate industrial growth.

2. Railroads tie the nation together.

3. Business leaders contribute to the growth of industry.

Even as ranchers, miners, and farmers were moving into the West, other Americans were making giant strides in business and manufacturing. Factory-made goods had already become commonplace by the 1840's, thanks to the pioneering work of such individuals as Samuel Slater and Eli Whitney. Now, the ability to produce unlimited quantities of consumer goods was looked upon as opening a new time of prosperity and opportunity for all Americans.

The creation of industries mobilized the entire country in a seeming frenzy of activity. Within one generation after Appomattox, Americans had opened up the continent's forest and mineral resources, assembled immense armies of workers, built a variety of manufacturing establishments, and laced the land with a mighty railroad system.

By the end of the century the United States had emerged as the world's leading industrial power. Between 1850 and 1900 the number of American factories soared from 123,000 to 205,000. In those same years the number of factory workers increased almost tenfold. By 1900 more than 60 percent of the American work force had nonagricultural jobs. The value of manufactured goods, furthermore, had long since exceeded the value of agricultural products. More truly than ever, Americans had become a nation. They were bound together by the sinews wrought in their factories and the common belief that a stream of undreamed-of products would help make tomorrow better than today.

1 Many Factors Stimulate Industrial Growth

Several factors help to explain the remarkable increase in America's industrial production in the years after the Civil War.

Inventors help the United States develop industry. Americans had long been said to have a special talent for invention. "Yankee ingenuity," as it was called, may have been stimulated by the constant need of isolated settlers to solve technical problems on the frontier. Widespread experimenting may have also flowed from the curiosity that could sometimes be aroused in people by the free schooling and literacy that most Americans enjoyed. Certainly, Americans were also spurred by the knowledge that industrial development in England was based on imaginative inventions. In the North, the need to save labor — almost always in short supply — also brought out creative ideas. Finally, the Constitution itself provided inventors with a powerful inducement when it gave Congress the power to enact patent laws. A *patent* enabled an inventor to have for a certain period of years the exclusive right to make, use, and sell his or her inventions. In 1836 Congress established the United States Patent Office to administer the patent laws.

A growing work force is available. In the years between 1860 and 1900 the population of the United States more than doubled, growing from 31 million to 76 million. The arrival of fourteen million immigrants during those years provided part of the increase. Although many immigrants took up farming, the bulk of them found jobs in the big cities of the North. There they applied their brawn and brains to the development of American industry. They were joined by thousands of native-born Americans who had left the land and also were flocking to the cities.

Resources are plentiful. In the richness and diversity of its resources, the United States was especially favored. All of the most important minerals required for heavy industry were abundant. These included coal, iron ore, oil, copper, zinc, and bauxite (from which aluminum is manufactured). Almost all of these resources had been discovered by the 1850's, and the means of extracting them were well developed. Moreover, magnificent forests provided lumber for the construction of buildings of every description.

Coal. Coal was the most important resource in the industrial development of the country. It was essential to the iron and steel industries and in powering factory machines of all kinds. Coal was at first mined

An improved steel-making process was recognized by the United States Patent Office in 1857. This and other inventions encouraged industrial growth in the late 1800's.

Gusher in the Oil Fields

As a reporter for the *Derrick*, a newspaper published in western Pennsylvania, Frank Taylor attended a demonstration of a new method for blasting through bedrock to reach trapped oil. He watched as a "torpedo" of explosives was dropped into a deep shaft and detonated. Taylor then wrote about the excitement of seeing a huge geyser shoot into the air, showering oil over the surrounding area.

A Pennsylvania oil well

On October 27, 1884, those who stood at the brick school house and telegraph office and saw the Semple, Boyd, and Armstrong No. 2 well torpedoed, gazed upon the grandest scene ever witnessed in oildom. When the shot took effect and the barren rock poured forth its torrent of oil, it was such a magnificent spectacle that no painter's brush or poet's pen could do it justice. Men familiar with the wonderful sights of the oil-country were struck dumb with astonishment, as they beheld that mighty display of nature's forces.

For over an hour that grand column of oil, rushing swifter than any torrent and straight as a mountain pine, united derrick floor and top. In a few moments the ground around the derrick was covered inches deep with petroleum. The branches of the oak trees were coated and a stream as large as a man's body ran down the hill to the road. Heavy clouds of gas, almost obscuring the derrick, hung low in the woods, and still that mighty rush continued. People packed up their household goods and fled to the hillsides. It was literally a flood of oil.

Several men volunteered to undertake the job of capping the largest well ever struck in the oil region. Three thousand pounds of weight were added before a cap was successfully fitted and the well put in operation. It was estimated that the production of that well later reached ten thousand barrels of oil a day.

---

chiefly in northeastern Pennsylvania, where the largest deposits in the world of the anthracite variety are located. By 1870 the bituminous fields lying in the Appalachian Mountains from Alabama to Pennsylvania were also being developed.[1]

---

[1]Anthracite coal, which burns with very little smoke, was used for home heating; bituminous coal, which produces heavy smoke, was used in smelters and other industrial operations.

Iron ore. A second indispensable mineral resource, iron ore, was the most widely found metal in the United States. It was first mined in quantity in the Lake Superior region, following its discovery in northern Michigan in 1844. The Soo Canal, joining Lake Superior and Lake Huron, was completed in 1855, enabling steamships to move ore to points on Lake Michigan and Lake Erie where it was refined. Farther west, a vast ore belt in the Mesabi (muh-

SAH-bee) Range of northeastern Minnesota was discovered by Leonidas Merritt, a Civil War veteran, and his brothers. The belt, more than 100 miles long and from one to three miles wide, proved to be one of the most extensive iron ore deposits in the world. Ore from the Mesabi Range was sent by rail to Duluth, Minnesota, which became the nation's chief ore-shipping port.

Oil. A third essential resource was oil. Unlike iron, which was important even in colonial times, oil was unfamiliar to most Americans until the 1860's. Indians had long skimmed it from the surface of streams and used it in medicine and for making paints. Some white Americans had also used it for medicinal purposes, believing it to be a cure for various ailments.

A New Yorker, George H. Bissell, long interested in oil chemistry, came up with the idea of drilling into the earth near a creek in western Pennsylvania on which oil had always floated. Bissell arranged with E. L. Drake, a conductor on the New Haven Railroad, to do the work. At a place later called Titusville, Drake began his task. Most people laughed at the project, and it quickly became known as Drake's Folly. Success rewarded Drake's efforts, however, and by August, 1859, he had a well that was producing 25 barrels of oil a day.

Within a short time an oil rush got under way in the region. The chief commercial product made from the petroleum was kerosene, refined at nearby plants. Kerosene lamps became the rage throughout the country, giving much better light than the candles and whale-oil lamps in common use. Oil as a source of mechanical energy awaited the invention of the internal-combustion engine and its application in automobiles, trucks, tractors, and airplanes. When that happened, a seemingly unlimited market opened for gasoline, another petroleum product obtained by refining.

Government interest encourages industrial expansion. The interest of the national government in promoting the growth of industry had been evident ever since the days when Alexander Hamilton had proposed tariff and bank legislation. Subsequent fed-

eral assistance had taken many forms. Land grants had been offered to builders of canals and railroads. Scientific expeditions had been sent out not only to add to general knowledge but also to locate raw materials and find new markets. Rivers and harbors had been improved by the Army Corps of Engineers, and rights of way had been surveyed for railroads. The first telegraph line, between Baltimore and Washington, D.C., had been constructed in 1844 with a direct grant from Congress.

Capital helps the United States develop its industries. The stability of the American government and economy had long attracted Europeans eager to invest their *capital* for a profit. (Capital is wealth, in the form of money or property, that is owned by an individual or business organization.) In addition, these *capitalists* — that is, people with capital available for investment — noticed with much interest that the population

Oil was once used in small amounts chiefly for medicines. After the strike at Titusville, it was produced in abundance as fuel for lamps.

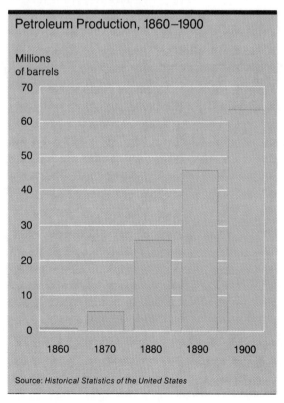

Petroleum Production, 1860–1900

Millions of barrels

Source: *Historical Statistics of the United States*

of the United States was growing rapidly, a strong indication of an expanding market for goods and services. Many Europeans, especially investors from Great Britain, put their money into American factories, mines, and railroads.

American capitalists, for their part, also invested money in the expansion of industry. Factory owners tended to put the capital they accumulated back into the companies they knew best — their own.

The Civil War stimulates business activity. The Civil War played a large role in speeding up the growth of industry. Nevertheless, the outbreak of hostilities, which disrupted the supplies of some raw materials, at first slowed production in many factories. Moreover, the rupture of normal economic ties between the North and South contributed to the failure of almost 7,000 northern businesses. For a time, people became reluctant to invest more money in industry.

By late 1862, however, business was reviving. The fighting had created an enormous government market for factory products, including iron goods, munitions, and clothing. Philadelphia, then the country's center of manufacturing, saw 58 new factories open in 1862, 57 the following year, and 65 in 1864. The large profits that industrialists earned enabled them to accumulate capital for further investment.

The absence of southern representatives in Congress during the war allowed the North to pass laws that the South had long opposed. These laws made it easier for people to accumulate capital. Tariffs were increased, for instance, helping the manufacturers of basic goods to make substantial profits and to use some of them to expand further. The Homestead Act, by encouraging the settlement of the western plains (page 43), created a powerful demand for railroad facilities and for other industrial products such as farm machines.

The Civil War significantly stimulated invention, as industry sought short-cuts in manufacturing. By 1865 Americans were even turning out many new devices unre-lated to war, among them passenger elevators and fountain pens. The war, moreover, gave many leaders in industry and government their first experience in organizing production on a large scale and distributing goods nationally.

Business leaders form corporations. As American industry grew bigger, more and more *corporations* were formed. Already, in the years before the Civil War, the corporate form of business organization had come into use. A corporation is created when three or more people are granted a charter, or license, by a state government. Such a charter permits the corporation to sell shares of stock (certificates of ownership) as a means of raising capital. The shareholders who buy the stock are the actual owners of the corporation and receive a portion of the corporation's profits, or *dividends.*

After 1860, corporations began replacing individual proprietorships (small businesses run by individuals or families) as the leading form of business organization. The corporation offered many advantages over the proprietorship. It provided businesses with an efficient way to raise the large amounts of money needed for expansion. The corporation gave investors the freedom to sell their stock whenever they wished. In the event that the corporation went bankrupt, the shareholders would only lose the money they had paid for the stock; they could not be held liable for any of the corporation's debts. Finally, because stock could be transferred from person to person and from one generation to the next, a corporation had permanent life. It could not be disrupted by the death or resignation of an owner.

SECTION REVIEW

1. Vocabulary: *patent, capital, capitalist, corporation, dividend.*
2. (a) Name five factors that played a part in the growth of American industry. (b) Explain why each was important.
3. What were the advantages of corporations as compared with individual proprietorships?

2 Railroads Tie the Nation Together

Conditions in post-Civil War America were ripe for the rapid expansion of large-scale production. Because railroads had kept pace with the growth of industry, the means were already at hand for carrying raw materials to manufacturing plants and for distributing finished products. Industry and the railroads each depended on the other, and the nation came to depend on both.

The railroads enjoy rapid growth. During the Civil War the importance of railroads had been well established. When the war ended, the demand for new railroad lines was heard throughout America. In 1865 the nation had slightly more than 35,000 miles of railroad track, most of it in the North and East. The railroads of the South, virtually destroyed in the war, had to be rebuilt. The lines between the Atlantic coast and the Mississippi Valley were too few to carry the goods of the country. Meatpackers in Chicago, oil prospectors in Pennsylvania, and grain growers in Iowa all complained about the shortage of rail facilities. In response, a new era of railroad construction swiftly got under way. By 1872 the nation's total railroad mileage had nearly doubled, and in the 1880's and 1890's almost 7,000 miles of track were laid every year. In 1900 the nation had nearly 200,000 miles of roadbed in use.

Along with this remarkable growth came improvements in the quality of train travel, as railroads became safer and more reliable. Brittle iron rails were replaced by steel ones able to sustain the weight of heavier trains. Huge iron bridges capable of bearing great loads were constructed, making possible the use of more powerful locomotives. Freight cars, each large enough to contain twenty tons of goods, were also put into operation. The use of a standard gauge allowed for the easy transfer of cars from one line to another. The chief effect was to speed up long-distance service.

As railroads crossed the nation, the depot became a familiar site at minor junctions and in larger cities, where it was often named "Union Station."

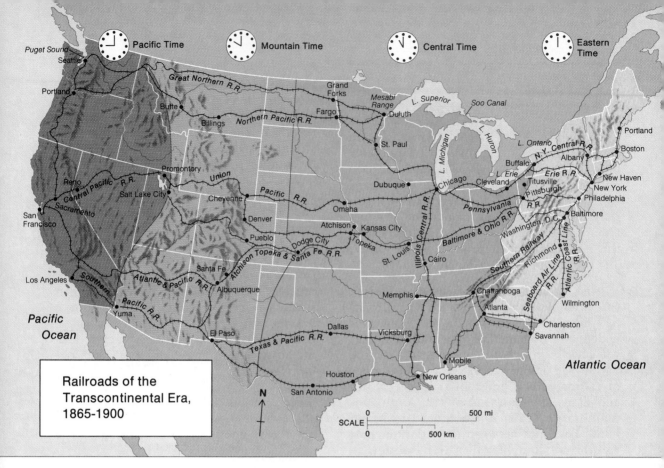

Railroads of the Transcontinental Era, 1865-1900

By 1900, the United States had nearly 200,000 miles of railroad track, almost one third of the world's total railroad mileage.

Passenger service also improved. The accidents that for years had discouraged travel were significantly reduced after George Westinghouse's automatic air brakes came into use in 1869. All the cars of a train could now be stopped in an emergency. Passengers were also attracted by the introduction of the dining car. Travel was made more comfortable, too, when heating systems, drawing on steam from the locomotives, replaced the smoky wood-burning stoves of earlier days.

Great railroad systems are formed. At the same time that railroad construction was going on everywhere, an effort was under way to join together many small railroad lines into major routes, or *trunk lines.* A leader in this movement was Cornelius Vanderbilt, whose New York Central Railroad reached Chicago in 1869. It was now possible to travel from New York to Chicago without transferring from one

railroad to another — eliminating the old need to change trains eight or ten times.

Other trunk lines quickly followed the lead of the New York Central in connecting Chicago with eastern cities. One was the Erie Railroad. Known for the unsavory financial dealings of its owner, Daniel Drew, it was the Central's chief rival. By 1869 it boasted: "1,400 miles under one management; 860 miles without change of cars."

Another trunk line was the Pennsylvania Railroad, a system linking Philadelphia to Chicago. The Pennsylvania also obtained a route to St. Louis, while shrewd deals gave it access to leading cities on the eastern seaboard as well. Not until 1910, however, when the line completed a tunnel under the Hudson River, did the Pennsylvania Railroad have access to a terminal in New York City.

A fourth major trunk line was the Baltimore and Ohio. Following the path of the old National Road, the line reached northward to Philadelphia and as far west as Chicago and St. Louis.

All of these trunk lines had their own depots in Chicago, and the constant arrival and departure of trains created a lively transportation business within the city. The first-class hotels of Chicago had towers from which local coach operators watched with telescopes for incoming trains. Once a train was sighted, carriages rushed out to meet it. Frank Parmelee started a service for transferring passengers between the various railroad stations. It became respected for the quality of its vehicles and the courtesy of the drivers. Later Parmelee organized the first commercial fleet of taxicabs.

Trunk lines are built in the South. In the years following the Civil War, railroad construction took place in the South at a pace faster than the national average. Between 1870 and 1873 alone, over 2,500 miles of new roads were built in the South. The Southern Railway was formed in 1894 by the financier J. P. Morgan, who joined several bankrupt lines. It eventually linked cities of the Mississippi Valley with Washington, D.C., and points south.

A competitor of the Southern was the Atlantic Coast Line Railroad, with connections linking important towns and cities between Richmond and Wilmington, North Carolina. The Illinois Central was yet another major line of the South, its tracks linking cities and towns from Chicago to Mobile. When the Illinois Central developed a connection with Savannah, it became a funnel through which the beef and grain of the Middle West found its way onto southern tables. Another line, the Seaboard Air Line Railroad, consisted of 4,000 miles of track, serving the same region as the Atlantic Coast Line.

A transcontinental railroad is proposed. West of the Mississippi the building of a transcontinental railroad became "the great work of the age." Some Americans predicted that a rail line connecting the east and west coasts would at last provide a "Northwest Passage," threaded through the heart of the United States itself. The lead-

ing advocate of such an iron highway had been a New Yorker named Asa Whitney. Beginning in the 1840's, he relentlessly pressed Congress to finance the construction of a transcontinental railroad. Whitney was convinced that trade with China would enrich America, and that a rail line to the Pacific was essential for that trade.

Congress had been unable to carry out Whitney's plan. The intense rivalry between the sections of the country was the main stumbling block, since it prevented agreement on the location of a route. Then a financial panic struck the nation in 1857, ending the immediate likelihood of constructing a transcontinental line.

Work begins on the first cross-country railroad. By 1862 the importance of railroads had become so obvious that Congress approved funds for a transcontinental line. The Union Pacific Company was established to build a road westward from Omaha, Nebraska, while the Central Pacific was formed to build eastward from Sacramento, California.

The federal government's contribution to the two companies was generous. In addition to the rights of way, the companies received large tracts of public land for each mile of track that was laid. The government also supplied some of the enormous amounts of timber and stone required in the immense task. For every mile of track, furthermore, the government paid a subsidy in the form of a thirty-year loan in United States bonds. The sum varied with the terrain: $16,000 per mile for the relatively level land across the plains east of the Rockies, $32,000 per mile in the plateau region, and $48,000 per mile across the mountains.

The building of the Union Pacific and Central Pacific railroads is one of the triumphant dramas of American history. The heroes were the laborers, numbering 20,000 at the height of the operation. Many of the workers, like the chief engineer of the Union Pacific, Grenville Dodge, were Civil War veterans. The railroads also hired thousands of young men recently arrived in the United States from Ireland and China.

Although the technique of track-laying varied according to local conditions, the procedure was always basically the same. Two gangs of workers, one on each side of the new tracks, walked ahead of a railroad car piled high with rails. The men would throw a pair of rails to the ground — one on each side of the roadbed, on which the wooden "sleepers" or ties were already in place. The rails would then be bolted to the ties, and the railroad car pulled forward. Over and over the process would be repeated. An observer described the action:

> The chief of the squad calls out "Down" in a tone that equals the "Forward" to any army. Every 30 seconds there came that brave "Down," "Down," on either side of the track. They were the pendulum beats of a mighty era; they marked the time of the march and its regulation beat.

The nation followed the progress of the first transcontinental with intense interest. People read accounts of workers facing the blistering heat of the plains in summer or the blizzards and freezing cold of the mountains in winter. At first, laying a mile of

These workers posed proudly at one of the mountain passes they helped to construct for the Northern Pacific Railroad, which was completed in 1887.

track a day was regarded as a good rate of progress. Then, even in the winter months with considerably less daylight, the crews were laying two miles a day. As the competition grew keener between the eastern and western companies, a record was set one day when nearly eight miles of track were put in place between sunrise and sunset. Soon the record was raised to ten miles.

The transcontinental railroad is completed. By the summer of 1868 the Central Pacific had laid tracks across California and was crossing Nevada. The Union Pacific, meanwhile, was pressing westward from Cheyenne, Wyoming.

The two competing companies had agreed that their lines would join at the tiny town of Promontory, Utah. By then the Union Pacific would have laid 1,086 miles of track, and the Central Pacific 689 miles. In an impressive ceremony on May 10, 1869, the junction was made. Two locomotives, as the author Bret Harte put it, were at last "facing on the single track, half a world behind each back." A golden spike was driven into place, completing the road, and Western Union flashed the news from Promontory all over the country. Every city in the Union heard the telegraph clicking the pre-arranged signal: "One, two, three — done!" Chimes rang in New York City, a huge parade got under way in Chicago, and in Philadelphia the Liberty Bell pealed once again. President Grant received a telegram sent from the scene announcing the festive "mountain wedding."

In a short time the high hopes of the original promoters of the transcontinental railroad seemed fulfilled. Along the route of the transcontinental, towns mushroomed, becoming centers of local business. Within a short time, scores of small communities were linked to the transcontinental "lifeline" by feeder tracks.

Other transcontinental lines are built. Even before the ceremony at Promontory, railroad companies were getting ready to build other transcontinental lines. One was the Northern Pacific, chartered by Congress to run from a point on Lake Superior to Portland, Oregon. Building it involved crossing some of the continent's most difficult terrain. Much of the money to accomplish the forbidding task was supplied by Jay Cooke, a Philadelphia banker. When Cooke's bank failed in 1873, the Northern Pacific found itself in financial trouble. The line was not completed until the 1880's, finally reaching Portland through the use of a local railroad's tracks.

Another transcontinental was the Southern Pacific. Started in 1864, it was developed out of a branch of the Central Pacific. In time the Southern Pacific extended as far north as Oregon, and to the south it connected New Orleans and Los Angeles.

The Atchison, Topeka, and Santa Fe, which followed the old Santa Fe Trail, was yet another transcontinental. A promoter of the Santa Fe — as the railroad was known — was a native of Pennsylvania named Cyrus Holliday. He had moved to Kansas in the 1850's and had helped make the state free soil. The construction of his road was begun in 1869 at Atchison, Kansas, and by 1872 the tracks had reached the cow town of Dodge City. Crossing the major cattle trails, the line soon made quick profits from the booming cattle business.

The railroads attract settlers. The managers of the transcontinental lines, recognizing that their profits would be increased if farm communities were built along their rights of way, successfully advertised in Europe for settlers. The Great Northern Railroad, running between Lake Superior and Puget Sound, was one line that actively encouraged settlers to move west. The Great Northern was the work of a railroad builder from Canada named James J. Hill. Hill settled in St. Paul, Minnesota, and began to build what turned out to be a railroad empire. He started by purchasing a small bankrupt line in 1873. Over the years, he built up his rolling stock — cars and locomotives — and began buying other railroad companies. Hill earnestly believed in the future of the region he was serving. He predicted that the northern Great Plains — and the region west, including the northern Rockies and Pacific Northwest — would one day be remarkably prosperous.

To attract settlers to the area, the Great Northern sent agents to Europe to publicize the virtues of what Americans were calling "Hill country." Hill held out the lure of free land under the Homestead Act. He also offered newcomers special arrangements that helped them get a start. He charged emigrants low fares from Chicago to any point on his line, and offered inexpensive freighting of household goods, farm animals, and equipment. He also supplied lumber, fence posts, and even trees and shrubs for the building and landscaping of new homes. Thousands of Europeans found his offer irresistible.

Railroads influence American life. The rapidly expanding railroad lines changed the face of America. Manufacturers were able to send their products into almost every part of the country, creating for the first time a truly national marketplace. Raw materials, moreover, could swiftly and conveniently be shipped to factories, even those located far away. Railroads, for instance, were able to bring iron ore from the Lake Superior region to the site of the coal supply in Pennsylvania for the production of iron and steel. Speeding up traffic from one part of the country to another, the railroads also strengthened contacts between people from different places.

Railroads at first had mostly a local impact. They tied a particular town to the "outside world." Soon, however, the effect of having railroads reaching *everywhere* changed the nation's behavior profoundly. Through railroads, both magazines and newspapers circulated nationally. Moreover, railroads helped to discipline the population in a new way. By establishing regular schedules, they made people be "on time." In addition to making people more punctual, railroads notably increased the tempo of American life. Henry David Thoreau, the poet and essayist, once asked: "Do [people] not talk and think faster in the depot than they did in the stage-office?"

Time zones are introduced. To make schedules easier to follow, the railroads put a system of standard time zones into effect on November 18, 1883. The country was divided into four time zones, known today as Eastern, Central, Mountain, and Pacific. The system replaced a crazy-quilt arrangement that had been based on local times. The terminal at Buffalo, New York, for example, had had three clocks, all showing slightly different times because they served railroad lines coming from different places. In Illinois there had been 27 local times and in Wisconsin 38! Congress formally adopted the time-zone system in 1918.

SECTION REVIEW

1. Vocabulary: *trunk line.*
2. What improvements were made in the quality of railroad travel in the years after the Civil War?
3. (a) Why did small railroads merge to form trunk lines? (b) What were some of the major trunk lines?
4. (a) What role did the federal government play in the building of the first transcontinental railroad? (b) What two companies built that railroad, and when was it completed?
5. Why did railroads encourage western settlement?
6. In what ways did railroads affect American life?

3 Business Leaders Contribute to the Growth of Industry

The forward march of American industry in the years after the Civil War opened new opportunities for people with boldness and energy. Among the business leaders were notable individuals who enlarged American production beyond imagination.

Andrew Carnegie organizes the steel industry. For centuries, people had made steel in small amounts by laboriously removing impurities from melted iron. Prized for its strength and toughness, steel was, nevertheless, too expensive to be manufactured in large quantities. Then, in the 1840's and 1850's, William Kelly in America and Henry Bessemer in England discovered independently that a blast of air directed at melted iron could remove the impurities.

The Bessemer process, as it was called, set the stage for the Age of Steel. In a short time steel rails became standard on all railroads. Before long, moreover, skyscrapers built with steel frames were transforming the look of American cities.

The steel industry came to be identified with the name of Andrew Carnegie. At the age of thirteen, Carnegie had been brought by his parents to America from Scotland. The impoverished Carnegies settled in Pennsylvania, where, after working briefly as a bobbin-boy in a cotton factory, Andrew got a job as a telegraph clerk in Pittsburgh. The young fellow had a keen instinct for opportunity, like successful business people of every era. Moreover, he was not afraid of hard work.

In the telegraph office Carnegie met the head of the Pittsburgh division of the Pennsylvania Railroad, Colonel Thomas A. Scott. Scott took a liking to the young man and decided to hire him as his private secretary. Through Scott, Carnegie met other business leaders, and from then on he advanced rapidly in the business community. He acquired interests in the iron business and in bridge building, and it was only a matter of time before he turned his attention to steel. After traveling in Europe and meeting Henry Bessemer, Carnegie decided to invest all his money in producing steel by the new air-blast method.

In 1873 Carnegie, already a multimillionaire, began building an immense steel plant just outside Pittsburgh. Shrewdly he named it the J. Edgar Thomson Works, after the president of the Pennsylvania Railroad. Carnegie hoped to get orders for rails from "the Pennsy," as people called it. He was not disappointed. Thomson helped make Carnegie the world's largest manufacturer of steel. By 1889 the United States passed Great Britain in the quantity of steel produced annually.

Carnegie was an astute investor. He also had a gift for finding the right people to be his associates. He once said, in jest, that he hoped his grave would be marked "Here lies the man who was able to surround himself with men far cleverer than himself."

The Carnegie organization gained a tight grip on companies that provided the services and supplies it required, including deposits of iron ore, limestone, and coal. Carnegie also established steamer lines on the Great Lakes to control the transportation of iron ore to Pittsburgh, and operated his own railways that carried raw materials to smelters and mills. By 1900, Carnegie controlled most of the steel production in America. When Carnegie finally sold his company to J. P. Morgan's newly created United States Steel Corporation in 1901, he received bonds with a face value of $250 million in payment.

In retirement Carnegie devoted his time to giving away much of his enormous wealth. His gifts included the establishment of public libraries in many American towns and cities. He also devoted himself to advancing the causes of world peace, education, and medical research. In all, Carnegie gave away more than $350 million.

John D. Rockefeller organizes the oil industry. Another master builder of industrial America was John D. Rockefeller. Born in New York State to a family of modest circumstances, Rockefeller eventually made a fortune in the nation's oil business. From his father, who earned a living by selling patent medicines, young John acquired an interest in business. From his mother, who was a stern woman deeply devoted to religion, he acquired self-discipline and a dedication to church affairs.

Born in 1839, Rockefeller was to live for 98 years, from the day of horsepower to the eve of the atomic age. Like Carnegie, Rockefeller kept his eyes open for opportunity — and like Carnegie, he came to maturity just when industry was beginning to revolutionize American life.

Rockefeller was fascinated by the rush to the Pennsylvania oil fields (page 57) and the growing market for petroleum products. He decided, however, that while the drilling for oil could be a wild gamble, the refining of it was practically a sure investment. At the age of 23, Rockefeller put his money into a small Cleveland refinery.

Andrew Carnegie built up the steel industry in America. By 1900, his corporation was providing nearly 75 percent of all United States output, and the nation had become the world's leading steel producer.

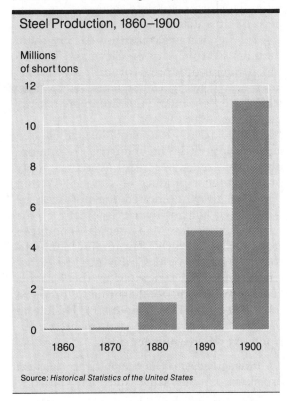

Steel Production, 1860–1900

Millions of short tons

Source: *Historical Statistics of the United States*

A stickler for detail, Rockefeller hated waste. In a short time, he was conducting a more efficient business than his rivals, steadily bringing down the cost of producing and selling kerosene. Success did not change Rockefeller's ways; he continued to reinvest his earnings. He advised his partners, "Take out what you [need] to live on, but leave the rest in. Don't buy new clothes and fast horses; let your wife wear her last year's bonnet. You can't find any place where money will earn what it does here."

Rockefeller developed a business that owned all the sources of most of its supplies. He saw to it that he and his partners controlled the pipelines and tank cars they required and the ships that carried their products. They even had their own plants for manufacturing barrels. Within a few years Rockefeller was pioneering in research. Such products as paraffin and insecticides were developed in his laboratories.

As early as 1867 Rockefeller reached an agreement with the railroads under which his companies were granted special freight rates. The lower shipping costs put his competitors at a disadvantage, and before long Rockefeller was in a position to buy them out. In 1870 the city of Cleveland had 25 independent producers of oil. Two years later only five independents were left: Rockefeller's Standard Oil Company had acquired the other twenty!

By the age of 38 Rockefeller had created a *monopoly* in the oil industry. (A monopoly is the exclusive control over the supply of a particular product or service.) Within 15 years after he entered the business, he had gained control over 95 percent of the nation's refineries. Many people denounced Rockefeller for ruthlessly forcing competitors to join him or face ruin. He, nevertheless, contributed strikingly to the nation's economic growth, for he brought order to what had been a chaotic industry. He left an oil industry well equipped to meet the nation's ever-increasing demands.

Inventor-industrialists contribute to industrial expansion. At the same time that Carnegie and Rockefeller were making their marks

through the processing of natural resources, inventions were helping make possible entirely new industries. Among them was an industry built around an important new source of power — electricity.

For many years inventors had experimented with electricity. In an experiment with a kite, Benjamin Franklin had won international fame as "the man who captured lightning" by demonstrating that lightning and electricity are the same. In 1821 an English scientist, Michael Faraday, had shown that people could generate electricity by spinning a magnet around a wire. In making this discovery, he found a force that eventually would free America from its dependence on steam power.

Electricity was first put to work in a practical way in communication when Samuel F. B. Morse built a telegraph line running between Baltimore and Washington, D.C., in 1844. The first message tapped out by Morse's telegraph was a quotation from the Bible: "What hath God wrought!" Out of this modest beginning later developed the Western Union Company, whose lines helped bind the entire nation together.

Thomas Edison develops the light bulb. The man who dramatized the potential of electricity was Thomas Alva Edison. Edison, like Carnegie, had been trained to be a telegraph operator. His natural inclination, however, was inventing. Edison had a remarkable gift — and infinite patience — for applying to practical purposes ideas that others had put forward. Before he was 23, he had built an improved stock ticker. A few years later — in 1878 — he patented a phonograph able to "store" voices on tinfoil. This invention was Edison's most original work, although he would wait ten years before improving it.

Meanwhile, Edison devoted himself to his most spectacular creation: the electric light bulb. Early advances had taken place in England where Sir Joseph Wilson Swan had constructed a bulb with a carbon filament (the thread within the glass bulb). Edison tackled the problem of introducing a filament that would burn for more than a few hours. In October, 1879, he announced

The Telegraph

In 1836 Samuel F. B. Morse developed a telegraph that was capable of sending electrical impulses over copper wire. Later, Morse perfected two devices that made speedy communication practical: one clicked out a dot-dash code while the other relayed long-distance messages by means of switching mechanisms. The telegraph enabled newspapers to receive timely news by wire from all over the country. The telegraph was also valuable in scheduling the many trains that were crisscrossing the nation. In 1866 another achievement, after repeated failures, was the successful laying of a transatlantic cable. This engineering feat made communication by telegraph possible between Europe and the United States.

his success in getting a cotton thread covered with carbon to glow for forty hours. On the last day of 1879 he ran a special train to bring 3,000 people to his laboratory in New Jersey where he had hundreds of small lamps — all lighted by electricity.

Even before Edison perfected the light bulb, he had made plans for a central power plant from which underground cables would carry electrical current to homes and shops. He had to consider details no one had ever thought about previously: transmission cables, fittings of all kinds, electrical conductors, and switches. Most technicians did not believe that the turning on and off of lights — which would produce a constantly changing energy load — could be handled successfully. Edison solved the problem, however, and by 1882 had his system working in New York City. His company, the Edison Illuminating Company, eventually became Consolidated Edison and served as a model for power companies throughout the United States. Three separate manufacturing companies were established to produce electric light bulbs, generators, and cables. In a few years these companies were combined to form the Edison General Electric Company.

A significant improvement in Edison's system for distributing electric current was made by George Westinghouse, whose transformer enabled electricity to be transmitted as alternating current to far-away points. In 1885 the Westinghouse Electric Company came into existence as a manufacturer of transformers and alternating-current equipment.

The electrical industry — embracing companies selling electrical current and those selling appliances and equipment — had not existed before the Civil War. Now, as the twentieth century was dawning, the number of electric light bulbs in use was approaching 20,000,000. Power stations were also being built as fast as possible. In 1882 there were only 38 of them; by 1900 there were more than 3,000.

Alexander Graham Bell introduces the telephone. Another invention that gave rise to an important new industry was the tele-

phone. It was the work of Alexander Graham Bell, a speech teacher who had come to America from Scotland in 1871 to teach in a Boston school for the deaf. Besides teaching young people, Bell began work on a device he hoped to sell to Western Union. He was making an instrument for transmitting sound over a telegraph wire.

Bell's knowledge of acoustics — the science of sound — enabled him to build a telephone. Where the telegraph transmitted pulses of current translated into dots and dashes, the telephone required a continuous current. The current would vary in intensity exactly as the density of air varies when a given sound is made. As a result, the sound of a voice could be duplicated at the end of the wire.

The telephone was shown for the first time in Philadelphia at the Centennial Exposition of 1876, shortly after it was patented as an "improvement in telegraphy." Bell, then 29 years old, had the opportunity to demonstrate the telephone to the emperor of Brazil, Dom Pedro, who was visiting the exposition. "It talks!" shouted the emperor as he placed the instrument to his ear. Dom Pedro's interest brought the telephone to the attention of other visitors to the exposition. From that moment on, Bell's invention was a sensation.

Soon after the demonstration at Philadelphia, Bell and an assistant talked over a wire strung a distance of two miles between Boston and Cambridge, Massachusetts. In the years that followed, the number of telephone lines increased, and Bell continued to improve his invention. In 1877 a telephone was used for the first time to report a story to a newspaper. That same year the first switchboard was put into use. The first regularly employed operator was a man, in New Haven, Connecticut, who answered the phone "ahoy-ahoy" rather than "hello." Male operators soon were replaced by women, nicknamed "hello girls."

The Bell Telephone Company was formed in 1877 by Gardiner G. Hubbard, a public-spirited man who in the 1850's had introduced gas for lighting purposes in Cambridge, Massachusetts. Hubbard had become interested in Bell's work because the Hubbards' daughter, Mabel, had been left completely deaf by an attack of scarlet fever. Two days before the Bell Company was formed, Mabel Hubbard, then eighteen years old, married Alexander Graham Bell.

The Bell Company eventually became the giant American Telephone and Telegraph Company. Made up of various local companies, it enabled customers to make telephone calls from one end of the country to the other.

New forms of business organization are developed. Throughout the late 1800's, corporations in the same business tended to join together to form large combinations. In so doing, they eliminated competition and reduced waste and the risk of losses.

Pools. One way many corporations acted in combination was by forming *pools.* The pool was an arrangement by which corporations in the same line of business agreed to control their output and divide up the available market. Sometimes business pools went so far as to place the profits of an industry in a joint treasury and later share them according to proportions agreed upon. More commonly, as for example among the railroads in a particular region, the managers would meet and decide what percentage of local business each would control. Such arrangements were finally outlawed in 1887 when the Interstate Commerce Act prohibited railroad pools. Pools might have died out anyway, since their agreements had no legal standing, were not enforceable, and were often violated by the participants.

Mergers. An answer to the shortcomings of the pool was the outright *merger* of rivals in the same industry. Usually the strongest in a group of competitors would buy out the others. The powerful New York Central Railroad came into existence in this way. Similarly, the Edison Electric Light Company merged with other companies to form the General Electric Company.

Trusts. A more common form of business combination was the *trust.* Under this arrangement stockholders deposited their stock certificates with a board of trustees and received trust certificates in exchange.

Through the trust a number of companies actually united into one system.

The first trust was formed in 1882 when John D. Rockefeller organized the Standard Oil Company. This trust established a virtual monopoly of the nation's oil-refining facilities. Soon, other business leaders saw advantages in forming trusts. Competition in a particular industry could be practically eliminated and prices could be controlled. Unlike the pools, trusts were chartered by state legislatures.

By the 1890's, the nation had giant trusts in sugar, tobacco, lead, and whiskey. A large number of smaller trusts had also been organized. Soon the word *trust* was being used to describe any monopoly or near-monopoly.

Many Americans objected to the vast power that trusts could exercise. They pointed out that since its earliest days the United States had prospered under a *free enterprise system.* Free enterprise permits businesses to compete in the selling of goods and services to the largest possible number of people. It is a system, furthermore, in which private individuals have the responsibility for making economic decisions. The creation of trusts, critics charged, was an abuse of the free enterprise system. They pointed out that though business operators liked to say that "competition is the life of trade," in actuality they worked to reduce it as much as possible.

To try and restore some competition and prevent harmful monopolies, Congress passed the Sherman Antitrust Act in 1890. The new law made it illegal for businesses to set up monopolies. However, the Sherman Antitrust Act was vaguely worded and difficult to enforce.

Holding companies. After 1890 still newer forms of business consolidation were being organized. One was the *holding company.* In a holding company, a new corporation is formed and stock is issued. The money raised from the sale of the stock is then used to purchase the stock of other corporations. Without producing any goods or services, therefore, a holding company could control the corporations whose stocks it held.

The Sherman Antitrust Act (1890)

An act to protect trade and commerce against unlawful restraints and monopolies. . . .

Section 1. Every contract, combination in the form of trust or otherwise, or conspiracy, in restraint of trade or commerce among the several states, or with foreign nations, is hereby declared to be illegal. Every person who shall make any such contract or engage in any such combination or conspiracy, shall be deemed guilty of a misdemeanor, and on conviction thereof, shall be punished by fine not exceeding five thousand dollars [now $50,000], or by imprisonment not exceeding one year, or by both said punishments. . . .

Section 2. Every person who shall monopolize, or attempt to monopolize, or combine or conspire with any other person or persons to monopolize any part of the trade or commerce among the several states or with foreign nations, shall be deemed guilty of a misdemeanor. . . .

Interlocking directorates. Another form of business consolidation was the *interlocking directorate.* Under this method, a group of directors of one company served as directors for several other companies. Consequently, they could develop a uniform policy for an entire industry or, for that matter, for several industries.

Finance capitalists provide funds for further investment. As American business continued to expand, a new kind of leader emerged — the *finance capitalist.* Finance capitalists were not usually qualified to provide technical know-how or to show how an industry could be made more productive. They did not deal in the products of an industry as such. Rather, they were bankers who exerted their influence through control of the bonds and stocks that corporations issued to raise money. A finance capitalist's center of activity was not the grimy atmosphere of the factory town but splendid offices in the financial district of a major city.

The most powerful of all finance capitalists was J. Pierpont Morgan. Born to wealth and college-educated — unlike practically all the other industrialists of his time — Morgan opened a branch office of the family banking firm in New York City in 1860. Turning to railroads, he took an important hand in ending stock speculation and in creating consolidated lines out of rival ones. By the end of the century he had helped finance the Hill system (page 63), as well as the New York Central and Pennsylvania systems.

Morgan's influence gradually extended throughout the nation's economy and included control over commercial banks, insurance companies, and a wide range of stock-market operations. The sums of money Morgan dealt in stagger the imagination. When Andrew Carnegie sold out his company to Morgan (page 65), Morgan's payment made Carnegie the richest man in the world. A year or two later the men met again, on shipboard. In the course of conversation, Carnegie said, "I made one mistake, Pierpont, when I sold out to you." "What was that?" asked Morgan. "I should have asked you for a hundred million more than I did," said Carnegie. "Well," replied Morgan, "you would have got it if you had."

In 1912 it was reported that Morgan and his banking associates held positions as directors in 112 corporations with assets of over $22 billion. This sum was said at the time to be three times greater than the assessed value of all the real estate in New York City.

Business leaders dominate American society. Successful business leaders like Morgan, Carnegie, and Rockefeller became well-known public figures. Where politicians had been popular idols in the early days of the republic, many industrialists and finance capitalists were now national heroes. Their dealings created jobs for thousands; they lived like wealthy monarchs; and they were actively changing the very look of America by the railroads they built, by the products they manufactured, and by the standard of living they helped raise. They acted decisively and boldly, and they had an air of authority that Americans found lacking in many of their elected leaders at that time.

Underlying the public's admiration of successful business leaders was a widespread conviction that it was possible for practically anybody to go from rags to riches. The son of an Irish immigrant who rose to prominence as a lawyer pointed out, "In worn-out king-ridden Europe, men must stay where they are born. But in America a man is accounted a failure, and certainly ought to be, who has not risen above his father's station in life."

The most influential children's books of the era, those of Horatio Alger, helped popularize the "rags-to-riches" theme. Alger's books, which poured from his pen in a steady stream, inspired youths who were eager to rise from poverty. Some of the titles tell of their contents: *Strive and Succeed, Brave and Bold, Strong and Steady, Slow and Sure, Try and Trust.* These books reinforced the belief in old sayings like "Genius thrives on adversity," and "There's always room at the top."

The new millionaires, for their part, believed in the theory of the "survival of the fittest," having concluded that they themselves were best suited to run American business. As to swallowing up their weaker competitors, was it not, they said, a law of nature that in the ocean big fish eat little fish, and that on land weak animals become prey to the strong? Rockefeller once summed up the industrialists' point of view about destroying their competitors by comparing the process to the cultivation of a rose. "The American Beauty rose," he said, "can be produced in the splendor and fragrance which bring cheer to its beholder only by sacrificing the early buds which grow up around it. This is not an evil tendency in business. It is merely the working-out of a law of nature and of God."

These thoughts were accompanied by another and kindlier point of view that many of the new millionaires advanced, one that Carnegie called "the gospel of wealth." Monied people, Carnegie said, must not gloat over their wealth. They should, rather, view themselves as guardians of it for the whole community. A rich person, he said, is simply "the agent and trustee for his poorer brethren, bringing to their service his superior wisdom, experience, and ability to administer, doing for them better than they would or could do for themselves." The gifts that Carnegie made (page 65) showed that he tried to live by what he preached.

In 1889, one hundred years after George Washington was sworn in as the nation's first Chief Executive, Benjamin Harrison of Indiana became President. The America he knew was worlds removed from the one in which Washington had made his mark. The new President observed proudly in his inaugural address that America now possessed "power and wealth beyond definition." But what would be their effect on the nation? The lofty principles of the United States faced a new time of testing.

SECTION REVIEW

1. Vocabulary: *monopoly, pool, merger, trust, free enterprise system, holding company, interlocking directorate, finance capitalist.*
2. What parts did Andrew Carnegie and John D. Rockefeller play in the expansion of American industry?
3. (a) Who were some of the leading American inventor-industrialists? (b) What new industries grew up as a result of their inventions?
4. (a) For what reasons did Americans look up to successful business leaders? (b) How did industrialists justify their business methods?

Chapter 2 Review

Summary

In the decades after the Civil War the United States experienced extraordinary economic growth, making it in time the world's leading industrial power. A number of factors contributed to this development. One was "Yankee ingenuity," which produced many of the inventions that spurred the growth of American industry. Another was the availability of an energetic and growing labor force required by large manufacturing concerns. Yet another was access at home to huge amounts of indispensable natural resources — including coal, iron ore, and oil. These factors were enhanced by the encouragement and assistance the federal government gave to industry and by the substantial investments made in America by wealthy European and American capitalists. The creation of the corporation facilitated the raising of money to finance industrial activity.

Hand in hand with industry went the development of an extensive railroad system. The railroads expanded rapidly after the Civil War, reaching a total of nearly 200,000 miles of track by 1900. Small railroads were merged to form trunk systems that linked the large cities of the East and the West. A transcontinental line was completed in 1869.

Railroads were essential to the settlement of the West. They brought thousands of European and American homesteaders to areas once remote. At the same time, they shipped east the products of the new western farms and ranches.

The expansion of industry created opportunities for enterprising individuals. Andrew Carnegie and John D. Rockefeller were two such people, rising from modest backgrounds to become millionaires and leaders of enormous industrial organizations. Carnegie made his reputation and fortune in the steel industry, while Rockefeller took advantage of the wealth to be made in the refining of oil.

Another group that acquired fame and fortune at this time were the inventor-industrialists. Among them were Thomas Edison, who contributed the phonograph and the electric light, and Alexander Graham Bell, who invented the telephone.

To control large manufacturing concerns and growing markets, business leaders devised various forms of business organizations. The pool, merger, trust, holding company, and interlocking directorate were all outgrowths of large industry. As the American economy continued to expand, banks became active in financing industrial growth. Finance capitalists such as J. Pierpont Morgan were powerful participants in all fields of business and industry.

Vocabulary and Important Terms

1. patent
2. capital
3. capitalist
4. corporation
5. stock
6. dividend
7. trunk line
8. "the gospel of wealth"
9. time zone
10. pool
11. monopoly
12. Bessemer process
13. merger
14. trust
15. free enterprise system
16. holding company
17. interlocking directorate
18. finance capitalist
19. Standard Oil Company
20. transcontinental railroad

Discussion Questions

1. (a) What role did inventors play in helping the United States develop industry? (b) For what reasons was a large work force available? (c) What resources were available? (d) How did the government promote the growth of industry?

2. (a) Why were both Europeans and Americans eager to invest their money in the expansion of industry? (b) How did the Civil War help to stimulate economic growth?

3. As American business continued to grow, what role did finance capitalists play in further industrial development?

4. (a) Why did the corporation become the leading form of American business organization after 1860? (b) Why did business corporations later join together to form large combinations?

5. (a) To what extent did railroads grow in the period after the Civil War? (b) Why was the development of railroads important to industrial growth?

6. (a) Why had a transcontinental railroad been proposed as early as the 1840's, and why had Congress been unable to carry out this proposal prior to the Civil War? (b) When did Congress agree to a transcontinental railroad? (c) To what extent were the hopes of the railroad's original promoters fulfilled?

7. (a) Who was James J. Hill? (b) What did he believe would be the future of the northern Great Plains? (c) How was he able to attract settlers to that area?

8. (a) How did Andrew Carnegie become the world's greatest manufacturer of steel? (b) Why in retirement did Carnegie give away much of his enormous wealth?

9. (a) What business practices enabled John D. Rockefeller to organize the Standard Oil Company?

(b) How did Rockefeller contribute to the nation's economic growth?

10. (a) What were some of Thomas Edison's creations? (b) What effects did the electrical industry have on American life?

11. (a) How did Horatio Alger's books popularize the "rags-to-riches" theme? (b) How did that theme contribute to the public's admiration of successful business leaders?

Relating Past to Present

1. One of the reasons for America's rapid industrial growth was the nation's abundance of minerals and other resources required for heavy industry. Which resources are still plentiful in the United States today? Which resources are not plentiful today?

2. New inventions during the period of great industrial growth improved transportation and communication. Among other things, these inventions helped bring people throughout the nation closer together. What are some modern-day inventions involving transportation and communication? How have they affected American life?

3. The "rags-to-riches" theme gained popularity in the late 1800's. Do the American people still believe that anyone can rise from "rags to riches"? Explain your answer.

Studying Local History

The rapidly expanding railroad lines in the period after the Civil War changed the face of America. What railroad building took place in your state between 1865 and 1900? How did this railroad expansion affect the growth of towns and cities in your state or region? In what other ways, if any, did the railroads affect life in your community?

Using History Skills

1. *Comparing graphs.* Study the graph on page 60 showing petroleum production and the graph on page 65 showing steel production. (a) Describe the gains made by the petroleum industry between 1860 and 1900. (b) Describe the gains made by the steel industry in those same years. (c) How does the upswing in production in these two industries correspond to the growth of heavy industry in the late 1800's?

2. *Placing events in time.* Make a time line that shows some events during the period that marked the rise of big business. On that time line include the following: (a) the completion of the first transcontinental railroad; (b) the invention of the telephone; (c) the organization of the Standard Oil Company; (d) the passage of the Sherman Antitrust Act.

WORLD SCENE

Capital for Railroads

Without capital from British, French, and German investors, the remarkable world-wide expansion of railroads during the 1800's could not have taken place so rapidly.

British investment in the Americas. During the 1700's the Industrial Revolution in Britain had led to the accumulation of large amounts of capital. The British, therefore, were in an especially good position to invest money required for railroad construction in other countries.

Helped by British investments, the expansion of railroads in North America was dramatic. In 1840 Canada and the United States had a total of 3,000 miles of track; by 1900 that total had increased to nearly 500,000 miles. In South America, where practically no railroads had existed in 1850, over 27,000 miles of track had been built by the end of the century.

Russian railroad expansion. In 1850 Russia was a sprawling land with only about 850 miles of railroad track. When the Russians lost the Crimean War in 1856, in part because they could not transport their army easily, they saw the importance of having a satisfactory railroad system.

Since Russia had neither the necessary funds nor the industrial strength for railway construction, the czars turned to Europe for help. The French, recognizing the diplomatic advantages in having Russia as a debtor, made substantial loans to finance Russian railroads. The emerging German nation, meanwhile, had an economy that was largely dependent on its iron and steel industries. Supplying Russia with thousands of miles of rails and hundreds of locomotives and railroad cars boosted German industry.

By the early 1900's Russia had been able to add 40,000 miles to its railroads, including the important Trans-Siberian line. This route, stretching across Asia for 4,000 miles, connected Moscow with the Pacific coast port of Vladivostok.

CHAPTER 3

An Urban Industrial Society

POST-CIVIL WAR – 1900

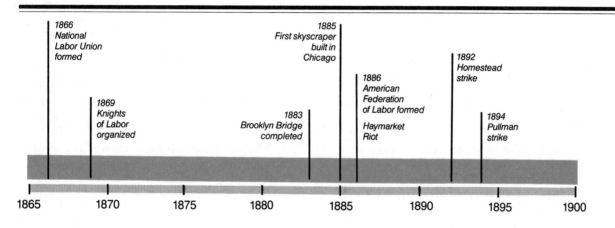

1866
National
Labor Union
formed

1869
Knights
of Labor
organized

1883
Brooklyn Bridge
completed

1885
First skyscraper
built in
Chicago

1886
American
Federation
of Labor formed

Haymarket
Riot

1892
Homestead
strike

1894
Pullman
strike

1865   1870   1875   1880   1885   1890   1895   1900

CHAPTER OUTLINE

1. Immigrants continue to move to the United States.

2. Cities grow rapidly after the Civil War.

3. Laborers organize to improve working conditions.

4. Organized labor faces strong opposition.

The opportunities offered by the expansion of American industry drew millions of immigrants to the United States. Most of them were young people unable or unlikely to make a go of it at home. They felt the force embodied in a song that the labor leader Samuel Gompers had learned as a child in Europe, and that Andrew Carnegie's father also once sang with hope. The tune begins:

To the west, to the west, to the land of the free
Where mighty Missouri rolls down to the sea,
Where a man is a man if he's willing to toil,
And the humblest may gather the fruits of the soil.

The immigrants helped make the wheels of American industry turn faster. Mostly from agricultural regions in their native lands, they went to work in the urban centers of the North and the Middle West, alongside native-born Americans also from the countryside.

As a result of the post-Civil War immigration, the ballooning cities became jumbles of ethnic neighborhoods. The city dwellers were forced to endure overcrowding, poor sanitation, and the threat of raging fires. Still, the combined labors of the millions of workers contributed to a higher standard of living year after year for everybody — including the workers themselves.

1 Immigrants Continue to Move to the United States

Between 1870 and 1900, more than eleven million immigrants entered the United States. Until the 1880's most immigrants came from western and northern Europe — from Great Britain, Ireland, Germany, and Scandinavia. On the eve of the Civil War, natives of Ireland, Germany, and Great Britain had made up 80 percent of America's foreign-born population. By 1890, however, the pattern of immigration had changed. Increasingly large numbers of people began arriving from southern and eastern Europe — from Italy, Greece, Russia (including Poland), and Austria-Hungary.

Most immigrants settle in cities. Unlike earlier immigrants, relatively few of those who came to America in the generation after the Civil War took up farming. Most of them settled in the large urban centers of the North. New York City was the principal point of entry for immigrants from Europe. Vast numbers of the newcomers remained there, finding shelter in neighborhoods filled with relatives or friends. In New York City, they could find familiar foods and also advice in their own language on how to get started in America. Many of the immigrants flowed into Connecticut and New Jersey, finding work in the factories there, or into Pennsylvania's mining and manufacturing towns. The city of Buffalo on Lake Erie became a center of Polish and Italian immigrant life. Many Slavs — people from central, southern, and eastern Europe speaking closely related languages — found work in the Pennsylvania coal fields. Thousands of Slavs also found work in Cleveland's iron

Immigrants gaze at the Statue of Liberty after arriving in New York. For these people, like millions of others, America seemed to be a land of golden opportunity.

and steel plants. Chicago, the hub of the nation's railroad network and the site of a variety of industries, rapidly acquired the largest number of Poles and Czechs in the country.

In New York as well as Philadelphia, Boston, and Cincinnati, German Jews established garment businesses and gave work to many fellow-newcomers. The growth of specialized labor had ended dressmaking at home for most Americans, and the market for mass-produced clothing seemed a likely place in which to make a living. The Irish also tended to settle in cities, and like other newcomers they were often recruited to work at building the railroads, bridges, and tunnels that the emerging industries required.

Reasons for immigration are unchanged. The basic reason for the flood tide of immigration — no matter from what part of the world — remained the same as in earlier decades. People regarded the United States

This graph shows immigration between 1820 and 1900. During that period, more than 19 million immigrants came to American shores.

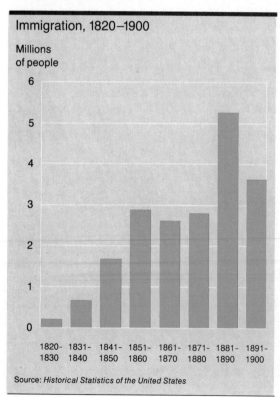

Immigration, 1820–1900

Millions of people

1820-1830	1831-1840	1841-1850	1851-1860	1861-1870	1871-1880	1881-1890	1891-1900

Source: *Historical Statistics of the United States*

as a "promised land" with bright opportunities for themselves and their children. The factors that motivated specific immigrant groups to move to America varied widely, however. The experiences of southern Italian farmers and eastern European Jews offer two illustrations.

Italian immigration. Agriculture in Italy was disastrously affected by events of the 1880's. The rising production of lemons and oranges in California and Florida was wiping out the American market for Italian citrus fruit. Moreover, the market in France for Italian wines was being cut severely by high French tariffs. On top of everything, severe epidemics of cholera had killed tens of thousands of Italians.

America beckoned to the survivors of these bad times. Up to 1879 there had never been a year in which as many as 5,000 Italians immigrated to the United States. Then, in 1880 it seemed as if the floodgates had opened. By the middle 1880's tens of thousands of Italians were arriving each year, with the figure reaching 100,000 in 1900, soaring to more than 230,000 in 1903, and peaking in 1914 at 284,000.

In their flight from poverty at home, the Italian immigrants were often at the mercy of employers who took advantage of their unfamiliarity with the English language. Hundreds of thousands of young Italian men were already in the hands of labor bosses by the time they set foot in the United States. At first the system worked this way: a *padrone* — an Italian American who could speak English and knew American ways — would recruit young men in the villages of southern Italy. He could promise them jobs because he already had made arrangements with American factory owners or construction contractors. The *padrone* paid for the ocean passage of the young immigrants and put them to work as soon as they landed. He made a good living by supplying gangs of workers to American industrialists. In fact, the workers' salaries were usually paid directly to the *padrone*, who deducted a commission for himself.

After 1890 so many Italians came to America on their own that it was no longer necessary to search the Italian countryside

for workers. The *padrone* served simply as an employment agent whose ability to obtain housing for the newcomers made them dependent on him.

The Italians, like all immigrants, took jobs wherever they could find them. When they were able to escape backbreaking labor with the shovel, they opened barber shops, vegetable and fruit stores, ice and coal dealerships, bakeries, and restaurants. Many Italians spent their first years in America working and scrimping in order to send money to enable relatives to join them in the land of opportunity. As time went on, the Italian immigrants could take satisfaction that they were adding to the country's supply of goods and services.

Jewish immigration. Among the newer immigrants from eastern Europe were significant numbers of Jews. Jews, of course, had been present in the United States since colonial times. As late as 1877, however, they totaled only about 250,000 people. Then, by the 1880's, Jews started to arrive in large numbers. Of the more than two million Jewish immigrants who came to the United States between 1870 and 1900, most were from Russia. Relaxed emigration laws enabled them to flee from political and religious persecution in their homeland.

The uprooted Jews streamed into the poorest parts of New York, Philadelphia, and Chicago. Thousands of them found work with Jewish employers in the garment

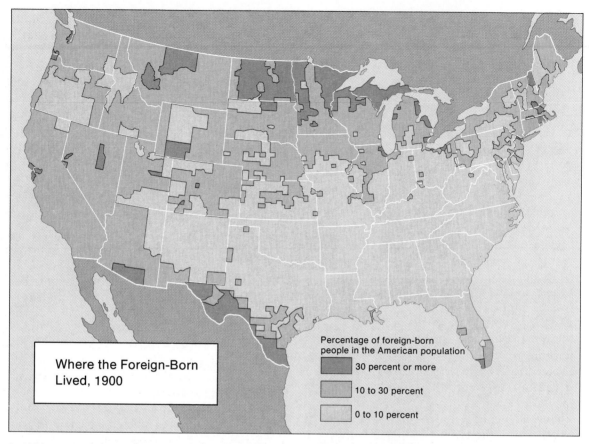

Where the Foreign-Born Lived, 1900

Percentage of foreign-born people in the American population

- 30 percent or more
- 10 to 30 percent
- 0 to 10 percent

In 1900 a number of states had areas where more than 30 percent of the people had been born in other countries.

industry. Others threw themselves into the variety of opportunities that urban living offered to all Americans. Like other immigrant groups, the Jews looked to their children to lift the whole family through economic and social success. Aided by habits of study and learning that had been deeply ingrained through the centuries, the young people quickly took advantage of educational facilities. Their study of science, medicine, and the law often led to brilliant achievement in the expanding society, which had large need for people with such training.

Calls for restriction of immigration are heard.
Some native-born Americans, alarmed by the size of the post-Civil War immigration, began demanding restrictions on the number of newcomers. They pointed out

that during the period of the "old immigration" before the war, the largest number of people who had ever arrived in one year totaled only 400,000. Now, with the "new immigration," as many as 750,000 people were arriving every year. How could so many newcomers be absorbed into American life, they asked?

Critics of the traditional policy of unrestricted immigration offered a variety of arguments. Some of the newcomers, they said, were simply "birds of passage" — people who came to the United States planing to remain a short time and then go back to Europe, without becoming Americans. Indeed, many eastern Europeans immigrated simply to make enough money in order to live comfortably in the old country. It is said, for instance, that most Greek immigrants, deeply devoted to their native land, came to the United States without any intention of staying permanently. They were chiefly peasants forced by crop failures to seek opportunity overseas — temporarily, they assumed. The 500,000 Greeks who came to America in the years 1900 to 1925 represented about 10 percent of the entire Greek population.

Foreigners also aroused criticism because they appeared to be clannish — sticking together in their own well-defined neighborhoods in the cities and factory towns. Most big cities had a "little Italy" or a "little Rumania" or a "little Armenia," as the case might be. Actually, in these neighborhoods the newcomers found the friendship and security they needed to survive in a new country.

Immigrants came under criticism, too, for working in low-paying jobs. Many unions opposed further immigration, maintaining that newcomers were undercutting American labor. In truth, people newly arrived in the United States took jobs at low pay not because they wanted to but because they had no choice. Furthermore, the jobs they took often were the least desirable ones, jobs they would shun in a few years.

Religious prejudice also often lay behind sentiment to restrict immigration. It was more polite to be anti-immigrant than to be anti-Semitic or anti-Catholic, and the effect could be the same. Jews had long felt the barbs of discrimination. In one well-remembered incident in 1877, Joseph Seligman, a financier and long-time friend of President Grant, was turned away from the Grand Union Hotel at Saratoga, New York. The owner had decided to exclude "Israelites as a class" from his establishment. Now, as Jews became more numerous, the ancient shameful prejudice against them often became evident. At many places of employment the sign "No Jews" was familiar by the beginning of the 1900's.

The sign "No Catholics need apply" was also seen — a tragic, bigoted response to the fact that the majority of new immigrants were Roman Catholics. The American Protective Association, an anti-Catholic organization founded in Iowa in 1887,

spread from its rural stronghold to the big cities in the 1890's. This and other similar groups beat the drums for limiting the suffrage to native-born Americans. In this way, they insisted, America could protect itself from the Roman Catholic Church which, they alleged, instructed its members on how to vote. A professor at Columbia College in New York, supporting the restriction of immigration, said that newcomers should not have the suffrage until the "power of American life has had time to loosen the bonds of priestly authority."

Immigration from China is restricted. The first significant steps to restrict immigration were taken against the Chinese. Many Americans had once heartily welcomed the Chinese, who began to arrive in California in the 1850's. A journalist there, watching Chinese people parade in celebration of Washington's Birthday, once called them "our most orderly and industrious citizens." Then, when the Panic of 1873 struck and bad times followed, the competition for jobs became intense. The cry, "The Chinese must go!" was suddenly heard, and anti-Chinese riots broke out in California.

Under a treaty with China in 1868, Chinese immigrants had been formally granted the right to enter the United States in unlimited numbers. Before long, however, a new treaty was negotiated, giving the United States the right to "regulate, limit or suspend" but not "absolutely prohibit" the immigration of Chinese workers. Finally, in 1882 Congress suspended all immigration from China for a period of ten years. This Chinese Exclusion Act was extended several times and remained in effect until World War II. The passage of the law was the first change in the traditional American policy of "come one, come all."

SECTION REVIEW

1. (a) What changes took place in patterns of immigration after the Civil War? (b) Why did most immigrants settle in cities?
2. (a) Why did some Americans call for restrictions on immigration? (b) What restrictive measure was enacted?

Immigrants in a New Land

Although most of the people who migrated to the United States in the nineteenth century were drawn to the great industrial cities, there were still millions who spread out across the nation. They looked for opportunities in farming, fishing, and other fields, and played a large part in the settlement of the Midwest, the mountain states, and the Pacific coast.

Resources and Opportunities

Jobs in industrial cities were not the only opportunities that awaited immigrants to the United States in the 1800's. The growth of railroads not only made traveling easier but also encouraged settlers in other ways. In hopes of building new communities in the Midwest and West, some railroad companies offered special help to settlers from Europe (page 63). In addition, many of the railroad workers who came from Ireland, China, and other countries settled down along the new railroad lines.

Gold and silver mining also drew both Americans and Europeans westward—first to California, then to the Rockies (page 41). Many settled in California and in the mountain states. The discovery of other mineral resources brought experienced miners from England and Wales, Finland, and eastern Europe. Some moved to the lead and tin mines along the Mississippi River in southwestern Wisconsin and northern Illinois. Others worked the copper and iron ore deposits of Michigan's Upper Peninsula.

The rich fisheries of the Atlantic and Pacific coasts drew settlers from seafaring European nations. The Portuguese settled mainly in New England and California; the Scandinavians in the Pacific Northwest.

The Beckoning Land

Even though the United States was becoming less rural, its rich farmlands and prairies were still the goal of many immigrants who had worked the land in their home countries. Often they had not owned their land but had been tenants on the estates of large landowners. In a number of European countries, political upheavals in the 1800's brought changes in society and in agriculture that made life harder for small farmers. In the United States, settlers could farm free land under the Homestead Act or buy inexpensive land from promoters.

The desire for land was a major factor in the settlement of the Midwest in the late 1800's. As the top two maps show, great numbers of people from Germany and Scandinavia were living in this area by 1910. These two groups, in fact, made up more than half the populations of states such as Wisconsin, Minnesota, and North Dakota.

Germans were the largest nationality group over all in the immigration of the nineteenth century. As the map shows, they moved into nearly every northern and western state. A sizable German colony began in Texas in the 1830's. Most, however, settled in the cities and farmlands of the upper Midwest, especially near Milwaukee, St. Louis, and Cincinnati.

Settlers from Norway, Sweden, and Denmark followed a similar pattern of settlement. They played an important role in the growth of wheat farming in Minnesota and the Dakotas.

Immigrants from the Russian Empire (map, lower left) followed a different pattern. The Germans and the Scandinavians each were a single nationality group, but those who emigrated from czarist Russia included many different peoples — mostly non-Russian minority groups such as Poles, Ukrainians, Lithuanians, and Jews. While Jewish immigrants stayed mainly in New York and other eastern cities, others spread

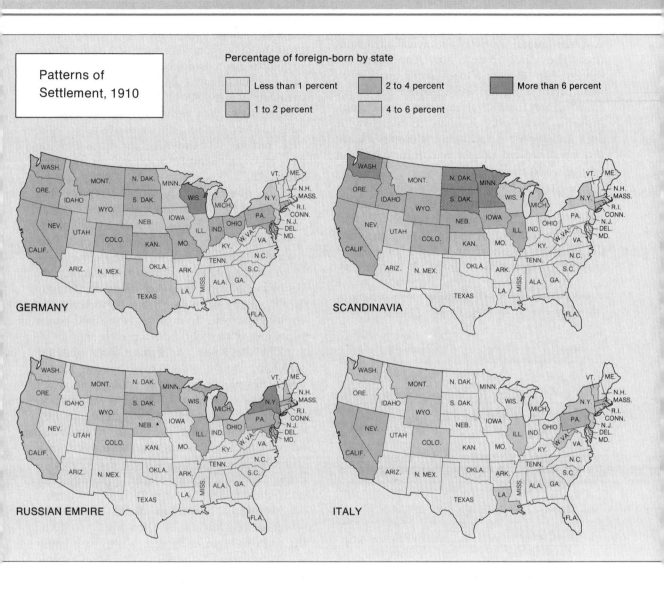

Patterns of Settlement, 1910

Percentage of foreign-born by state

Less than 1 percent   1 to 2 percent   2 to 4 percent   4 to 6 percent   More than 6 percent

GERMANY

SCANDINAVIA

RUSSIAN EMPIRE

ITALY

out to the mining areas of Pennsylvania and the farms of the upper Midwest.

The lower righthand map shows the heavy concentration of Italian immigrants in the northeastern industrial cities (described on page 76). Many other Italians, however, had traveled to California during the gold rush, starting a large settlement in San Francisco. More Italians later moved to the rich California valleys and established farms, orchards, and vineyards.

1. In what ways did the building of railroads encourage settlers from Europe?
2. (a) What natural resources attracted immigrants? (b) Why were European farmers especially drawn to the Midwest?
3. (a) What nationality groups were predominant in the upper Midwest about 1900? (b) What different peoples emigrated from Russia? (c) What attracted Italians to California?

2 Cities Grow Rapidly After the Civil War

A phenomenal growth of cities accompanied the development of American industry. Factories and mills were built in or near urban communities in order to attract immigrants and native-born Americans looking for work. Houses, consisting at first mostly of ramshackle shanties, were quickly thrown up to accommodate the workers and their families.

As street after street filled up, America was on its way to becoming "a nation of cities." In the years between 1870 and 1900, the number of people living in cities of 100,000 or more increased from four million to fourteen million. Only one city — New York — had a million people in 1870. By 1900 Chicago and Philadelphia had also passed the million mark.

Cities face new problems. The rapid growth of urban America brought about problems not quickly solved. The most pressing need was the supplying of safe drinking water. As late as 1878, only 600 communities had reliable sources of water and modern systems to distribute it. The high rate of typhoid fever in cities lacking proper water-supply systems dramatized the need.

The quest for safe water supplies was stimulated by the growing acceptance of the germ theory of disease, which grew out of the work of the French biologist Louis Pasteur. Still, urban public health, closely related to the purity of drinking water, lagged behind that of rural America. As late as 1890, a baby born in a large American city could expect to live only 44 years — ten years less than a child born on a farm.

The disposal of wastes was another problem. While New York, Boston, and a few other places had some sewer lines, they were inadequate for the needs of the expanding population. Most cities simply drained their sewage into nearby rivers and lakes. Chicago's sewage was dumped into Lake Michigan, from which the city also drew its drinking water. Philadelphia poured its wastes into the Delaware River.

Memphis began to build a modern sewer system in 1880 (following a frightening yellow-fever epidemic wrongly blamed on improper waste disposal). Soon, other cities followed suit and built plants to dispose of sewage satisfactorily.

Cities expand in area. Until the 1850's cities and towns were compactly arranged, built in many instances on a waterfront. Commercial activities were carried on along the docks. Close by were warehouses, various manufacturing establishments, and shipping offices. Not far away were banks, churches, shops, and the city or town hall. Scattered among these structures were the dwellings. In the best locations — as, for instance, on the top of a hill — lived the wealthier people. Nearby, however, would

Ten Largest Cities in the United States		
1860	1880	1900
1. New York 813,669	New York 1,206,299	New York 3,437,202
2. Philadelphia 565,529	Philadelphia 847,170	Chicago 1,698,575
3. Baltimore 212,418	Chicago 503,185	Philadelphia 1,293,697
4. Boston 177,840	Boston 362,839	St. Louis 575,238
5. New Orleans 168,675	St. Louis 350,518	Boston 560,892
6. Cincinnati 161,044	Baltimore 332,313	Baltimore 508,957
7. St. Louis 160,773	Cincinnati 255,139	Cleveland 381,768
8. Chicago 109,260	San Francisco 233,959	Buffalo 352,387
9. Buffalo 81,129	New Orleans 216,090	San Francisco 342,782
10. Newark 71,941	Washington 177,624	Cincinnati 325,902

Source: *Twelfth Census of the U.S., 1900*

Advances in transportation and communication contributed to the rapid growth of cities after the Civil War. This 1892 painting shows a busy street in Indianapolis.

be people of lesser means. Rich and poor, immigrant and native-born, lived in close proximity to one another.

The need for everything to be within walking distance of everything else controlled the physical size of these cities. One effect, however, was that they became crowded. Even before big factories, the density of urban population was startling. By 1850 an acre in New York City contained on average 135 people; in Boston and Philadelphia, around 80.

These "walking cities" began to disappear by the time of the Civil War. Bridges and ferries enabled some people to move to nearby towns and villages while still holding jobs in the cities. What broke the limited size of cities and allowed them to sprawl, however, was the development of new systems of urban transportation.

Advances are made in urban transportation. Some experimenting in transportation had already been carried on by enterprising individuals. Omnibuses — long, horse-drawn vehicles with two decks — had operated on the streets of major cities since the 1830's. The first omnibus (copied from a French version) was actually a stagecoach that ran on Broadway in New York City in the time of Andrew Jackson. The omnibus driver rode up and down the thoroughfare, picking up passengers and taking them where they wanted to go. Before long, the system became regular, and the idea behind it spread to other cities.

An improvement on the horse-drawn omnibus was the horse-drawn streetcar which ran on rails. The first one, built by John Stevenson of Philadelphia, was put into service by the New York and Harlem Railway in 1832. Running the vehicle on tracks helped provide a smoother, faster ride. Streetcars, which could hold thirty passengers, were divided into three compartments with ten seats each. Within a few years much bigger vehicles were being constructed, capable of transporting substantially more people.

Despite much experimentation, not until the 1880's did electrically operated streetcars come upon the scene. The first electric streetcar was put into use in 1886 in Montgomery, Alabama. This vehicle, looking much like the horse-drawn streetcar, had a motor at the front powered by a cable attached to a wire strung overhead along the right of way.

The electric streetcar was perfected by Frank Sprague, a young graduate of the Naval Academy who had worked with Thomas Edison. Sprague became an expert builder of motors, and his genius lay in adapting his "constant speed" motor to street-railway service. He completed the first street railway system in Richmond, Virginia, in 1888. This triumph was remarkable because of the many steep grades and sharp curves the cars had to negotiate in Richmond. For the transmission of electric current to his vehicles, Sprague relied on a troller — a wheeled device that moved along on an overhead wire. Soon the word *troller* became "trolley," and trolley-car lines were being built in every city of substantial size.

Some of the largest cities dealt with local transportion by constructing elevated railways. The first of them appeared in New York in the 1870's. These "els" allowed more street room than even the trolley cars. Still, they were unsightly and noisy, and created barriers to air and light for people who lived along their path. As an alternative to "els," major cities such as Boston (1897) and New York (1904) began to build subways or "undergrounds."

Improved transportation helps make suburbs possible. The development of transportation systems had an almost immediate effect on the larger cities and their surrounding communities. Take, for example, the city of Boston. In 1850 Boston was still a walking city with a diameter of four miles. By 1873 the city's limits had been extended half a mile, and another mile and a half was added by the end of the 1880's. The edge of settlement by then was about four miles from City Hall. In the 1890's, the distance to the city line from City Hall had become six miles. Trolleys — accompanied shortly by electric commuter trains — then made their appearance. Now people could travel many miles to the city from out of town, and return at night. When that happened, the first true suburbs came into existence.

Advances in architecture help cities adapt to the growth of population. Devising ways of moving people through and under city streets was made possible by engineering know-how that only an industrial nation develops. Another by-product of advanced technology was the ability to construct taller buildings than ever before.

From the 1850's to the early 1880's cast iron was widely used to erect tall buildings — as high as five stories. The man who first used cast iron in the construction of urban commercial buildings was a New Yorker, James Bogardus. Cast iron — hard, brittle, and heavy — can be inexpensively produced and can support great weight. In the major cities cast iron was first used in constructing department stores. These popular institutions for displaying and selling large amounts of consumer goods were yet another result of industrial growth and response to urban life.

Bogardus's achievement produced a need to be able to transport people safely between floors in a tall building. Elisha G. Otis, a native of New England, answered the need. Otis invented the first elevator with an automatic safety device. If the cables broke, the device kept the elevator from falling. Otis's first elevator was installed in a New York City department store in 1857. Frank Sprague, the trolley-car pioneer, made improvements in elevator motors, and the first electric elevator began operation in 1889. Sprague's elevator business was later taken over by the Otis Company.

Soon, architects and engineers found ways to erect taller and taller buildings. They assembled gigantic steel frames to support structures of many stories. The first skyscraper, completed in 1885, was the Home Insurance Building in Chicago, ten stories high. In the next few years, even taller buildings went up, primarily in New York and Chicago.

The pace of activity in major cities was constantly stimulated by the traffic that new bridges helped deliver. These bridges linked the parts of urban communities separated by rivers. The completion in 1883 of the Brooklyn Bridge, connecting Brooklyn

Until the completion of the Manhattan Bridge, shown here under construction, ferries in New York City connected the boroughs of Manhattan and Brooklyn.

and the island of Manhattan, gave New York a structure of rare beauty. Designed by John A. Roebling, it was also an engineering marvel, the longest suspension bridge in the world.

Only a few years earlier the Eads Bridge, a steel and masonry structure, had been built over the Mississippi River at St. Louis, Missouri. During the late 1800's Boston bridged the Charles River; Pittsburgh, the Allegheny; and St. Paul and Minneapolis, the Mississippi.

The need for city housing is great. As urban transportation systems permitted cities to expand physically, "downtown" in large cities became a distinct place. It was the scene of bustle, crowded roadways, and more and more tall buildings making canyons of the narrow streets and allowing little sunlight to fall upon them. People who could not afford better accommodations were forced to live in run-down dwellings in the shadow of these buildings. Working people who were somewhat better off lived a distance away in buildings known as *tenements.* The word *tenement* originally referred to any dwelling containing room for more than three families. New York's first

tenements, built in 1850, were designed as an improvement for poor people who had been living in cellars and even flimsy shacks. The tenements contained "railroad flats," that is, apartments laid out with rooms leading one to another in a straight line.

New York's Tenement House Law of 1879 was regarded as providing a major improvement in tenement construction. The law required the construction of the so-called "dumbbell" tenement — named after the shape of its floor plan. The buildings, five or six stories high, contained on each floor fourteen rooms in two three-room and two four-room apartments. The arrangement satisfied the legal requirement that every room in the new tenements have a window. In the hall were two toilets to serve the needs of four families.

Ideal for New York's standard lot size of 25 by 100 feet, a dumbbell tenement also provided an air shaft on each side because of the indention in the middle of the building. These shafts gave some light and ventilation to the interior rooms. The airshafts were a curse, however, if fire broke out, because they insured the rapid spread of the flames.

Following the opening of the Metropolitan Museum of Art in 1880, New Yorkers could enjoy looking at paintings once held in private collections.

Cities provide cultural and educational opportunities. If the nation's rapidly growing cities suffered from problems, they also presented advantages. City people had more cultural facilities than did people in rural areas. The larger the population, the easier it was for men and women eager to pursue particular interests to find like-minded people. The Metropolitan Museum of Art in New York, as an example, was opened in 1880. It placed on view some of the artistic treasures of the world. In time, almost every major city had museums.

Music, too, became available for more than a mere few. In 1873 Cincinnati established the May Music Festival, which became an annual civic highlight. A number of large cities also had symphony orchestras which came to be compared favorably with some of the best in the world. Practically every city supported a public library system out of tax revenues.

People were able to find in the cities many other ways to fill their leisure time. They could attend sport events or theaters or simply visit relatives and friends elsewhere in town. They could also have the pleasure of shopping in the multitude of retail stores that lined the principal avenues and side streets.

The department store became an important place for browsing as well as for shopping. R. H. Macy and Company, which had opened in New York in 1858, was one of the first. Later, some of the many types of goods that department stores could provide were made available to isolated farm communities by mail-order houses. The firm of Montgomery Ward, which began operation in Chicago in 1872, pioneered in distributing a catalog of goods for sale by mail. Such catalogs helped to spread city styles to rural areas and thus make those styles national.

Cities also provided educational opportunities not available elsewhere. Large schools, characteristic of the cities, could have a more varied course of study than the small ones found in villages and towns. Moreover, city schools could be more readily supervised. Standards were, therefore, more easily set and maintained than in

Ten tenements to a city block meant that as many as 4,000 people were jammed together under conditions constantly exposing them to disease and vermin as well as fire. So many people died of tuberculosis on one block of New York's Lower East Side that it was known as "lung block." These slum areas were home to thousands of poor people, most of them immigrants, in the nation's teeming cities.

Significant tenement-house reform came only slowly. In 1901 New York passed a law requiring a more open courtyard for each building and a separate toilet for each apartment. Many slum dwellers, however, could not afford to rent a flat, or apartment, in the new buildings. Attempts to limit the number of people who could live in a flat, moreover, were resisted by the very people reformers hoped to help. One of the few ways most slum dwellers could eke out a living was by taking in boarders.

country schoolhouses. The bigger communities, furthermore, had the means for enforcing laws making attendance in school compulsory.

SECTION REVIEW

1. Vocabulary: *tenement*.
2. (a) What problems arose from the rapid growth of cities after the Civil War? (b) What efforts were made to find solutions to those problems?
3. How did advances in urban transportation and architecture contribute to the growth of cities?
4. What cultural and educational opportunities did cities provide?

3 Laborers Organize to Improve Working Conditions

Although the expansion of manufacturing provided jobs for millions of people, industrialization also had unwelcome effects. Working people looked for ways to deal with problems that concerned them.

Factory work is monotonous. The most noticeable fact about factory work was that working people using machines were doing the same task over and over again, making the workday boring and monotonous. The massing of large numbers of people in factories, moreover, made many workers feel that they were mere cogs in a giant system, that they were individuals no longer.

Workers also came to recognize that, like machine parts, they themselves were replaceable parts in industrial America. With so many people competing for jobs, some factory operators felt little concern over the wages and working conditions of their help. An employee who complained could be replaced overnight.

Workers fear loss of jobs. Among the most troubling effects of industrial growth was periodic unemployment. One kind of unemployment was seasonal, resulting from the regular closing down of factories (usually to conform with the ups and downs of the market or the availability of raw materials). The other kind of unemployment was called structural unemployment. It occurred — and still occurs — during hard times, when plants shut down for an indefinite period because of a lack of demand for their products.

Workers in the garment industry were in the forefront of the movement to organize American laborers into unions.

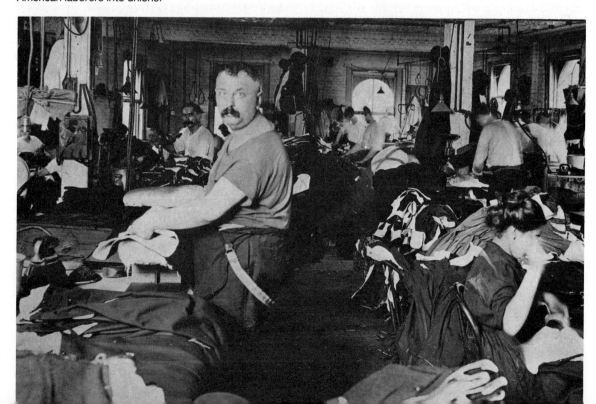

The industrial world also produced periodic panics and depressions, resulting in widespread general joblessness. Before the Civil War, unemployment had not been as devastating to most workers as it would be later on. In the earlier days many of the laid-off people could return to the family farm and wait until things improved. After the Civil War, however, millions of people had permanently moved to the big cities. Now a lay-off could be a calamity. For immigrants especially there was no way to "return to the farm." At best the unemployed could rely on the good will of more fortunate neighbors, or possibly on handouts from local charities. No government agency existed to offer assistance.

Factory work is dangerous. Yet another distressing fact was that many workers were laboring at machines that could maim or kill. The hazards grew worse as new, faster equipment was introduced. Workers' safety was often neglected when employers went forward with plans to speed up production.

New relations exist between worker and employer. Many working people who read about the new millionaires no doubt envied them. Working Americans still remembered that wealthy men had been able to buy their way out of the Civil War draft. Workers never forgot, either, that the increase in prices of consumer goods during the war had not been accompanied by a comparable rise in wages. Added to the old resentments was a particular new one: factory workers rarely experienced the close contact with their employers that had once been common in small workshops. Unable to have ready contact with their employers, working people found it practically impossible to complain about their conditions of work — except among themselves.

William Sylvis organizes the National Labor Union. By the time the Civil War ended, there was fertile ground for organizing factory workers into unions. Labor unions were not new in the United States. Circumstances now presented fresh opportunity, however, for imaginative labor leaders to do their work.

One of the first able organizers was William Sylvis of Pennsylvania. A leader in the iron-molders union in Philadelphia, Sylvis had been instrumental in 1859 in bringing together representatives from eighteen locals to form the Iron Molders International Union. By 1865 Sylvis's union was the strongest labor organization in the country, boasting 53 locals and a total membership of 7,000.

A persuasive speaker, Sylvis was hostile to the new capitalist leaders, denouncing them as "a monied aristocracy — proud and dishonest, blasting and withering everything it comes in contact with." In 1866 Sylvis organized the National Labor Union in Baltimore. Two years later he became its president, bringing to the role his inexhaustible energy. He would say of the union, "I hold it more dear than I do my family or my life."

Sylvis and the other founders of the National Labor Union hoped to combine in "one big family" farmers and workers — skilled and unskilled — all across the United States. The union would seek, too, to improve the conditions of "the sewing-women and daughters of toil in this land." In 1868 the union accepted delegates from women's suffrage groups, and in 1869 it seated black delegates. In an era when most employees worked ten or twelve hours a day, the National Labor Union was calling for an eight-hour working day. It also advocated tenement-house reform, the establishment of reading rooms and educational facilities for working people, and the transfer of public land to genuine settlers only and not to speculators.

The National Labor Union collapses. At the height of its power, the National Labor Union had 600,000 members. However, Sylvis's death after just a year in office was a blow from which the National Labor Union could not recover. The union later tried to turn itself into a political organization — the National Labor Reform Party — but in the presidential election of 1872 it made a very poor showing and collapsed shortly afterward.

The movement for an eight-hour day continues. Union leaders did not give up the fight for an eight-hour work day. A leading spokesman for this reform was Ira Steward, a Bostonian. At the age of nineteen he had served an apprenticeship as a machinist and was forced to work twelve hours a day. His insistence on shorter hours cost him his job. He was dismissed for holding "peculiar views." Steward persisted in his crusade so earnestly that he became known as "the eight-hour monomaniac." He formed the Grand Eight-Hour League of Massachusetts, which soon was copied in many states.

Steward believed that workers should be paid no less for an eight-hour day than for a longer one. A popular jingle that Steward's wife wrote helped make the idea clear:

Whether you work by the piece or work by
the day
Decreasing the hours increases the pay.

Steward contended that if working people had a shorter workday, they would have time to enjoy the use of more goods, including possibly those they themselves were making. In that way, as Steward saw it, employers no less than employees would benefit from a shortening of the hours of work, because the factory products would find a larger market. By 1867 six states had passed eight-hour-day laws, but they contained too many loopholes to have the desired effect.

The labor movement endures hard times. The depression of 1873 set back further efforts to organize laboring people. The mere hint that a worker wanted to join a union could mean instant unemployment. Between 1873 and 1878 total union membership dropped from 300,000 to about 50,000. Where there had once been thirty national craft unions, only seven remained. Labor's prospects seemed grim.

One union that flourished even in the hard times of the mid-1870's was the Knights of St. Crispin, an organization of shoemakers. The leader of the union was Charles Litchman of Massachusetts. The

Union leaders urged the labeling of union-made goods, believing it would assure the American people of high-quality products.

Knights of St. Crispin felt the competition of non-union labor so keenly that Litchman opened a campaign to have a label placed on union-made products to identify them as such. The union label came to stand for quality workmanship performed under satisfactory conditions.

Violence breaks out in Pennsylvania labor disputes. The depression of 1873 produced for the first time large numbers of homeless, jobless, hungry people. The unemployed held mass meetings in the leading industrial cities, considerably alarming the general public. The police did not hesitate to break up these gatherings of protest. In the coal mines of Pennsylvania the struggle was tragic. The work was hard and dangerous, and the wages low. The miner who was fully employed was fortunate; most miners averaged only 130 days of work in a year.

To go on strike would be fatal, however, because management could readily find strike-breakers — men just as desperate for work as those they replaced. As Jay Gould had once cynically observed, "I can hire one half of the working class to kill the other half."

Nevertheless, the miners did strike. Late in 1874, the coal operators cut wages below the minimum that they had earlier agreed to in conversations with miners' organizations. In anguish and outrage, workers walked off the job. The operators promptly hired replacements and brought in armed guards to protect them. There were pitiful scenes as sheriffs' posses evicted the striking miners and their families from homes owned by the coal companies. Women — alongside the men — vainly tried to stand off the sheriffs' deputies with sticks and rocks. In the end the strike was broken.

A number of Pennsylvania miners belonged to a secret society known as the "Molly Maguires," which aimed to spread terror among mineowners. The name of the society was taken from an organization of anti-landlord agitators in Ireland in the 1840's led by one Molly Maguire. Since most of the miners came from Ireland, they were likening their troubles in America to their former situation in the old country. The Mollies intimidated and even murdered uncooperative mine bosses and supervisors.

In 1874 the president of the Philadelphia Coal and Iron Company decided to take steps to destroy the Mollies. He hired a private detective, James McParlan, who worked his way into the inner circle of the terrorist organization, posing as a counterfeiter and killer. As a result of McParlan's testimony, 24 Mollies were convicted of crimes, and 10 of them were hanged for murder. Union-organizing in the coalfields suffered a very serious setback, as a result, from which it did not recover for 25 years.

Federal troops break a railroad strike. Labor unrest also reached the railroads. In July, 1877, following an announcement of a wage cut, employees of the Baltimore and Ohio went out on strike. As the strike spread to other lines, riots broke out in a number of cities, including Baltimore, Pittsburgh, Chicago, and St. Louis. The outburst of violence in Baltimore lasted four days and cost fifty lives. This uprising led many people to believe that as in Paris a few years earlier, a workers' revolution was at hand. The *New York Tribune*, nonetheless, stated that public opinion was "almost everywhere in sympathy with the insurrection."

Later that month, striking railroad workers seized control of trains in Pittsburgh. Because of long-standing resentment over the power of the Pennsylvania Railroad in the state, local authorities tended to sympathize with the strikers. To quell the violence, state militiamen had to be dispatched from Philadelphia. When the soldiers arrived, they fired at the strikers, killing 25 men and wounding many others. Enraged, the strikers rushed to neighborhood gun shops, armed themselves, and drove the soldiers out of town. Joined by others who were unemployed, the strikers took over railroad property. Vandals among them set fire to the freight yards, creating a wall of flame three miles long. Order was not restored until President Hayes sent in federal troops — the first time since Andrew Jackson had called up troops to quell a strike of canal laborers. The trouble subsided and by August, 1877, the men had gone back to work.

Labor violence provokes strong opposition. The leaders of industry were dismayed by the bloody strife. They denounced unions, whatever the kind, and became determined to crush them. Many leading people endorsed the hostile sentiment regarding workers that had been expressed by the preacher Henry Ward Beecher: "God intended the great to be great and the little to be little." Many states revived conspiracy laws that permitted the prosecution of labor unions. Some communities built new armories to prepare for future uprisings.

The Knights of Labor is organized. Laboring people had also learned from their disappointments. They were beginning to see that they must organize more effectively. But how? The leaders who had formed the

Sweatshop Work

At the turn of the century, a young Polish girl named Sadie Frowne arrived in New York with her mother. As immigrants they were fortunate to have relatives who helped them find employment. Sadie Frowne later described her first few years in America.

A factory worker

Mother and I came on a steamship. Aunt Fanny and her husband met us at the gate of this country and were very good to us. Soon I had a position as a servant, while my mother got work in a factory making white goods.

I was only a little over thirteen and a greenhorn, so I received nine dollars a month and room and board, which I thought was doing well. Mother made nine dollars a week.

Mother caught a bad cold and coughed and coughed. She tried to keep on working, but it was no use. She had not the strength. At last she died and I was left alone.

After mother died, I thought I would try to learn a trade. Then I could go to school at night and learn to speak the English language well. So I went to work in what is called a sweatshop, making shirts by machine. I was new at the work, and the foreman scolded me a great deal. I did not know at first that you must not look around and talk, and I made many mistakes with the sewing. But I made four dollars by working six days a week.

After a while I got another job in a factory making skirts. I am earning five dollars and fifty cents a week now. The factory is on the third floor of a brick building. It is a room twenty feet long and fifteen wide.

Often I get to the factory soon after six o'clock and do not leave until six at night. At seven o'clock we all sit down at our machines and the boss brings to each one the pile of work that he or she is to finish during the day. The machines go like mad all day, because the faster you work the more money you get. The machines are all run by foot power, and at the end of the day one feels so weak that there is the temptation to lie right down and sleep.

We have just finished a strike in our business. It spread all over and the United Brotherhood of Garment Workers was in it. We struck for shorter hours, and after being out four weeks won the fight. We only have to work nine and a half hours a day and we get the same pay.

Noble Order of the Knights of Labor in 1869 believed that they had found the formula. At their head was a garment cutter from Philadelphia named Uriah S. Stephens. Having once studied to be a preacher, Stephens was an accomplished public speaker.

Stephens and the six men with whom he founded the Knights decided to permit the admission of all workers — skilled and unskilled, immigrant and native-born, men and women, blacks and whites. The only people barred from joining were doctors, liquor dealers, lawyers, bankers, professional gamblers, and stockbrokers. Stephens created elaborate titles and rituals for the Knights. Officials had names like "Inside Esquire" and "Venerable Sage." As head of the Knights, Stephens enjoyed being called

The nation's leading union in the 1880's, the Knights of Labor provided a way for black and white workers to join together for labor reform.

the "Grand Master Workman." He invented a secret initiation ceremony, a secret password, and a secret handshake.

The secrecy of the Knights of Labor seems excessive today — even foolish. In that day, however, workers were usually safer if their employers did not know that they belonged to a union. The Knights did not begin to drop their secret practices until 1881. By then a strong sense of unity among the members had been established.

The Knights become the nation's leading union. The Knights bluntly attacked the "unjust accumulation" of wealth, arguing that it would lead to poverty for all working people. Many of the demands of the Knights of Labor were familiar to labor movements of the era: an eight-hour day, the distribution of public lands to actual settlers only, "equal pay for equal work" for men and women, and an end to convict and child labor. Later the Knights called for government ownership of the railroads and telegraph lines, and a graduated income tax — that is, one providing for higher rates on larger incomes than on smaller incomes. Because Stephens preached a message of mu-

tual respect between employer and worker, the Knights opposed strikes as a means of achieving their goals.

Like many other labor groups of the time, the Knights believed strongly in *cooperatives.* These were businesses owned and operated by the workers themselves. Among a variety of ventures, the Knights had a coal mine and a shoe-manufacturing plant.

The Knights of Labor grew slowly in the early 1880's. Then, after the organization ceased being secret in 1881, its rolls expanded rapidly. In that year its membership was 19,000; three years later the number had passed 100,000. Ironically a victory in a notable railroad strike in the West — notwithstanding the stated opposition to strikes — raised the Knights' prestige and helped swell their ranks. Within a few months after the 1885 strike, membership had reached 700,000. This figure included some 60,000 black members.

The Knights owed much of their success to the work of Terence V. Powderly, a machinist by trade who had succeeded Stephens as Grand Master Workman in 1879. Powderly, then only thirty years old, had strong ideas. Handsome, impeccably dressed, and displaying formal manners, he did not appear at first glance — as a writer who knew him said — to be "the leader of a million of the sons of toil." Like Stephens, he disapproved of strikes and insisted that working men and women should establish cooperatives.

The popularity of the Knights declines. The Knights were badly hurt by unauthorized strikes, which the organization felt forced to support despite its official anti-strike position. The failure of some of the cooperative ventures also damaged the Knights. In addition, many union people were beginning to dispute the Knights' idea that skilled and unskilled workers belonged in the same organization. Common sense seemed to show that the two segments of the working population had divergent needs and goals. The lofty legislative goals of the Knights, moreover, seemed extravagant to working people primarily interested in a shorter day and higher wages. Many workers had come to the conclusion that employers would respond only to the pressure of strikes, and that unions must sponsor them.

The Haymarket Riot destroys the Knights. The year 1886 proved bad for the Knights. There were strikes in almost every industrial region. Although only a few of them involved the Knights, the public tended to blame all of them on the Order. Worst of all, the Knights received a terrible blow from an event in Chicago that was not of their making.

A number of unions in Chicago had gone on strike for an eight-hour day — against the wishes of the Knights' leaders. The strikers quickly had the support of a group of *anarchists*, people advocating the abolition of all forms of government. The anarchists found an opportunity to spread their views when four strikers were killed in an encounter between strikers and police at the McCormick harvester works.

To protest the slayings, the anarchists held a rally in Chicago's Haymarket Square, in May, 1886. Near the end of the meeting, which was breaking up because of threatening skies, the police arrived. Suddenly a bomb was hurled, killing seven police officers and injuring many other people.

A wave of hysteria swept the city. Although the identity of the culprit was never established, eight anarchists were arrested and tried for the crime. They were all found guilty. Four of them were hanged, one committed suicide, and the rest were sentenced to life in prison. A few years later, the surviving three were pardoned by Illinois governor John P. Altgeld, a friend of labor who declared that the trial had been a miscarriage of justice.

One of those executed was Albert Parsons, who had been a member of the Knights. Powderly repudiated him, saying, "Honest labor is not to be found in the ranks of those who march under the red flag of anarchy, which is the emblem of blood and destruction." Nevertheless, many people linked the Knights to the Haymarket affair. Said the *New York Sun*, "Five men in

this country control the chief interests of five hundred thousand workingmen, and can at any moment [by calling a strike] take the means of livelihood from two and a half million souls. These men compose the executive board of the noble order of the Knights of Labor." The membership in the Knights melted away, from 700,000 in mid-1886 to 200,000 only two years later.

Powderly himself, far from being the dictator some people said he was, was exhausted by the problems associated with his organization. Dejectedly he said, "The position I hold is too big for any ten men. It is certainly too big for me." Lacking forceful leadership, the Knights soon became only a memory. By 1893, another year of depression, the number of members had fallen to 75,000. Soon thereafter the organization died out.

SECTION REVIEW

1. Vocabulary: *cooperative, anarchist*.
2. For what reasons did working people seek to organize unions in the years after the Civil War?
3. (a) What was the National Labor Union? (b) The Knights of Labor? (c) Why did each fail?

4 Organized Labor Faces Strong Opposition

At the time that the Knights of Labor were declining, some labor leaders began organizing separate unions for skilled workers in different trades or crafts. They believed, for example, that carpenters or hatmakers or steamfitters would be better served if they each had a union of their own. In 1881 a number of these trade unions joined to form a federation. Five years later the organization became known as the American Federation of Labor (AFL). It did not enroll individual members. A worker could join only through being a member of an affiliated craft union.

Samuel Gompers leads the American Federation of Labor. One of the guiding spirits in establishing the AFL was Samuel Gompers, president of the International Cigarmakers Union. Gompers had long enjoyed success as head of the cigarmakers. He had put his union on what he called a "business basis." He meant by the phrase that the union collected dues, restricted membership, and made only such demands on employers as seemed reasonable. The union established sickness and death benefits and arranged its finances so that the stronger locals sometimes supplied funds to weaker ones.

Of Dutch-Jewish background, Samuel Gompers had been born in England in 1850 and immigrated to New York at the age of thirteen. As a young man sitting at a worktable rolling cigars, Gompers listened attentively to the older hands discussing politics. Sometimes the workers paid one of their number to read to them. Gompers often had this assignment. Frequently the reading material contained radical ideas for solving some of labor's problems. Gompers did not believe such revolutionary proposals were desirable. He was convinced that "pure and simple" trade unionism was the answer to

Under the direction of Samuel Gompers, shown here at the time of a union drive in West Virginia, the AFL became the nation's leading labor organization.

labor's needs. Later, as president of the AFL he never sought to change the capitalist system. He merely hoped to obtain a fair share of its benefits for working people. Once, at a Senate committee hearing, a senator asked Gompers about the aims of the AFL. Gompers replied straightforwardly, "We have no ultimate ends. We are going on from day to day. We fight only for immediate objects — objects that can be realized in a few years."

The AFL gains popularity. The AFL did not hesitate to support strikes but tried as much as possible to avoid them. It insisted that employers sign binding agreements, or contracts, with their unions. These contracts fixed for a stated period the conditions of work, including wages and hours. Through the efforts of the AFL, the slogan "No contract, no work" became a familiar saying of working people. Contracts had existed as early as 1866 in the iron-and-steel industry, but in the 1890's the AFL made them a symbol of the labor movement.

For a brief time there was rivalry between the Knights of Labor and the AFL. Most skilled workers agreed, however, that the strike and the contract were sensible instruments for advancing labor's interests. By 1904 the AFL, with 1,750,000 members, had become the nation's leading union. The AFL continued to restrict its membership, barring unskilled workers. In addition, reflecting some of the prejudice of the time, the AFL excluded women and blacks.

The AFL faced difficulties and frustrations, for business leaders were as hostile to it as they had been to the Knights. Nevertheless, the dignified Gompers, who with the exception of one year remained president of the AFL until 1924, earned the respect of his opponents. He became a familiar figure before state and congressional legislative committees, pleading the cause of labor. Gompers never forgot the people for whom he spoke, even when he was present at social gatherings with business and banking leaders.

Some labor leaders advocate violence. Scorn for the accommodating methods of the AFL led to the establishment in 1905 of the Industrial Workers of the World (IWW). Its founders hoped to organize unions that would gain control of industry and overthrow capitalism. Under the leadership of Vincent St. John and William ("Wild Bill") Haywood, the Wobblies, as the IWW came to be nicknamed, had about 70,000 members at its peak in 1913. Open to everybody regardless of race, sex, or nationality, the IWW was most active among western miners, lumbermen, and migrant farm workers. When the United States went to war in 1917, many IWW leaders were arrested, indicted, and convicted on charges of sedition and espionage.

Business opposes unions. Business, meanwhile, developed new methods for opposing the efforts of working people to organize unions. A method already familiar was to plant a spy among employees to eavesdrop on their plans. A man who specialized in spying on industrial workers was Allan Pinkerton, a detective who had gained fame for uncovering a plot to assassinate Abraham Lincoln in 1861. Pinkerton's services were advertised in this way: "Corporations or individuals desirous of ascertaining the feelings of their employees, and whether they are likely to engage in strikes or are joining any secret labor organizations . . . , can obtain a detective suitable to associate with their employees and obtain this information." Pinkerton also was in the business of providing employers with forces of strikebreakers.

A second method of intimidating employees was the *blacklist.* Workers who joined unions or went out on strike found they could not get another job in the same town. Their names would be circulated among all local employers. These blacklists closed the door to "troublemakers."

As unions became more powerful, employers devised a third method of controlling union activity: the *yellow dog contract.* This was an agreement that new workers were forced to sign. In it they swore that they were not members of a union, and they pledged not to join one.

Business people also sometimes resorted to seeking an *injunction,* or court order. By

obtaining an injunction from a judge, an employer facing labor problems was able to enlist the power of the government in forbidding a strike or a boycott or picketing.

Labor suffers defeat in the Homestead strike. Well-organized and growing bigger, business held the advantage in its struggle with labor. The balance became more uneven after the failure of two major strikes in the 1890's.

The first of these strikes began in 1892 when workers at the Carnegie Steel Company at Homestead, Pennsylvania, refused to accept new wage cuts. Henry Clay Frick, Andrew Carnegie's right-hand man, thereupon shut down the plant and surrounded it with special guards to protect the property. The guards, however, were soon run out of town by infuriated workers who realized that Frick intended to reopen the plant with strikebreakers.

Frick was glad to take up the challenge to the company's authority because he believed he now had a chance to destroy the union once and for all. On July 6, two river barges filled with 300 hired Pinkerton detectives were towed up the Monongahela River toward Homestead. As the detectives came ashore, armed workers fired on them from behind barricades, and the battle was on. After a thirteen-hour struggle, the Pinkertons finally raised a white flag of truce, laid down their arms, and surrendered. In the fighting, ten men had been killed and dozens wounded.

The Carnegie Company then persuaded the governor of Pennsylvania to provide help, and in short order the state militia was summoned to restore peace. Meanwhile, the company began bringing in strikebreakers to replace workers who had walked off the job. Of the original 4,000 employees at the plant, only 800 were rehired. Many of the leaders of the strike were prosecuted in court for rioting and murder. The steel workers' union was destroyed. Forty years would pass before union organizers once again operated in the steel industry.

While some members of Congress were sympathetic to the Homestead strikers, the public in general was not. The working per-

WORKMEN CANNONADING THE BARGES.

SOLDIERS IN CAMP.

WORKMEN ATTACKING THE BARGES.

GREAT BATTLE OF HOMESTEAD.
Defeat and Capture of the
PINKERTON INVADERS
July 6th 1892.

The artist who drew these pictures of the Homestead strike sympathized with the steel workers. The public, however, disapproved of the strikers' actions.

son, it was widely asserted, must remain free to sell his or her services as an individual and not through a union. Furthermore, many people held that the right to work was sacred. They insisted that union organizers had no business interfering with employees willing to accept whatever terms the company offered. The readiness of the federal government to enter disputes on the side of business, therefore, was firmly supported by people throughout the United States.

Government action breaks the Pullman strike. No event showed better the role of government in labor disputes than did the Pullman strike of 1894. George Pullman, whose sleeping car had revolutionized overnight rail travel, had built for his employees what was widely hailed as a model company town, near Chicago. All the houses, schools, stores, and churches in the town of Pullman were owned by the Pullman Company. Rents in Pullman ran about 25 percent

higher than in neighboring towns. George Pullman bought water from Chicago at four cents a thousand gallons and sold it at ten cents a thousand to the consumers in his town. Employees were not obliged to live in Pullman, but those who did not were likely to lose their jobs.

In 1893 the nation was faced with another financial depression. During the hard times, Pullman cut wages an average of 25 percent without making a comparable cut in rent or in the cost of services. The pastor of a church in Pullman declared that "after deducting rent the men invariably had only from one to six dollars or so on which to live for two weeks."

Into the picture stepped the American Railway Union, a nation-wide organization of all railway workers — skilled or unskilled. By 1894 the union had a membership of 150,000, including some Pullman workers. At its head was Eugene V. Debs, who had made the well-being of working people the passion of his life.

A gentle man, Debs instructed union members at Pullman to avoid violence. On May 11, 1894, however, about 4,000 Pullman employees went on strike, and events were soon out of control.

The strike, up to now local, became national when the American Railway Union instructed its members not to handle trains with Pullman cars attached. By the end of June, 1894, railroad traffic throughout the western United States had come to a standstill. Before much longer every part of the country was affected.

The railroad owners now decided to attach Pullman cars to trains carrying mail. Any attempt to interfere with such trains would be an interference with the mails — a federal crime. The strikers, however, refused to handle these trains. At this point the railroads persuaded the Attorney General, Richard Olney, to hire an army of special deputies — actually in the pay of the railroads — to help keep the trains moving.

Violence broke out as the deputies came under attack from striking workers. President Cleveland ordered federal troops to Chicago to restore order. Governor Altgeld insisted that troops were not needed, but Cleveland sent them anyhow. He is supposed to have said, "If it takes every dollar in the Treasury and every soldier in the United States to deliver a postal card in Chicago, that postal card should be delivered."

When the strike continued to paralyze transportation, the railroads obtained an injunction against the American Railway Union, forbidding it to interfere in any way with their operations. Debs, quickly judged to be in violation of the injunction, was sent to prison for six months. The strike was virtually over; the union had been smashed. By the middle of July, train service was returning to normal. Almost forty years would pass before legislation was enacted preventing strikes from being so readily broken by an injunction.

The America that was being forged in the factories and cities was as dependent as ever on the variety and ingenuity of the people. Once again, finding common goals

Eugene Debs gained national attention for his role in the Pullman strike. Some Americans, like this cartoonist, criticized Debs for bringing the nation's railroad traffic to a halt.

for everybody — worker or industrialist, urban dweller or farmer, native or immigrant — became a national requirement. Would the American "melting pot" — a phrase coined by an English journalist, Israel Zangwill — fuse the people into one great whole? Would the physical landscape, changing into a scene of cities and factories, continue to allow Americans to pursue happiness as well as economic progress? Would America continue to offer opportunity for all? "I lift my lamp beside the golden door," were words inscribed on the base of the Statue of Liberty, which was unveiled in New York harbor in 1886. Fulfilling the promise was the duty all Americans assumed, as the nineteenth century completed its course.

SECTION REVIEW

1. Vocabulary: *blacklist, yellow dog contract, injunction.*
2. (a) What were Samuel Gompers's goals for the American Federation of Labor? (b) How successful was the AFL?
3. What methods did business use to try to prevent the forming of unions?
4. What effects did the Homestead and Pullman strikes have on the labor movement?

Improving Reading Skills

The ability to understand and remember what you have read is important in studying American history. There are a number of ways in which you can improve your reading skills.

SQRRR

A five-step method called SQRRR can help you become a better reader. SQRRR stands for *Survey, Question, Read, Recite, Review.* The SQRRR method is easy to learn and apply.

Survey. Begin any new assignment by making a survey of the material to be read. This can be done in *America: The Glorious Republic* by reading the section titles and the boldfaced headings.

Question. Set a purpose for your reading by turning each section title and heading into a question. Form your questions by using the words *who, what, when, where, why,* and *how.* Here is one example. The heading "Most immigrants settle in cities" could become "Why did most immigrants settle in cities?" Write down your questions and use them as a guide when reading your assignment.

Read. Read the assignment thoroughly. While you are reading, be thinking of answers to the questions you have just formed.

Recite. Using your own words, recite the answers to your questions. Forming these answers will help you to organize the information you have read and will fix it in your memory.

Review. Finally, review the headings you have surveyed and once again answer the questions you created from the headings. If you are unsure about the answer to any question, reread the passages that pertain to that subject. Writing out your answers is the best way to remember them.

Skimming and Scanning

Skimming and scanning are two skills that will help you better utilize your time in reading an assignment. Each method is applied for a specific purpose.

Skimming a reading selection is useful when you want to get a general idea of the information being presented. To skim a reading effectively, you should take the following steps:

(1) Read the chapter and section titles and any boldfaced headings of the selection.

(2) Look at pictures, maps, charts, and graphs to see what information they contain.

(3) Read the first two or three paragraphs of a selection. Introductory paragraphs usually preview the contents of a selection.

(4) Read the first and last sentences of all other paragraphs.

(5) Read any summary that might be included at the end of the selection.

Scanning is a technique used when you want to locate specific information in a reading assignment — an answer to a review question, for example. To scan effectively you should have a definite idea of what you are looking for. You should read, therefore, only those passages that refer to that subject. Use section titles, headings, boldfaced words, first and last sentences of paragraphs, and illustrations as clues to help you locate the information you need.

Taking Notes

Note-taking is one of the most important skills you can master. Taking notes requires you to concentrate on the information you are reading and identify the main ideas and supporting details. Here are several guidelines to follow when you take notes on a reading assignment:

(1) Finish reading each passage before making any notes. It is usually necessary to read a complete paragraph, for instance, before you can determine its main idea.

(2) Write down only the main ideas and the most important supporting details. Your notes should focus on the main topics and include only enough detail to help you understand your notes when you reread them.

(3) Use abbreviations and symbols. Abbreviations and symbols can help you take notes quickly. Examples of abbreviations include *GB* for Great Britain, *Fr* for France, *pol* for politics, and *gov't* for government. Examples of note-taking symbols are *w/* (with) and *w/o* (without). You can, of course, create your own abbreviations and symbols. Keep your own abbreviations and symbols simple so that they make sense when you review your notes.

Summarizing

Summarizing is a way to organize the important information in a reading assignment. Written in paragraph form, a summary is a brief and concise statement of the main topics covered in a passage. The following guidelines will help you write a good summary:

(1) Locate key words and use them in your summary.

(2) Be as brief as possible but be careful not to leave out anything that might alter the meaning of the selection you are summarizing.

(3) Write full sentences, using your own words. Do not copy, word for word, sentences from the reading.

Check Your Skill

Use the information presented on these pages to answer the following questions.

1. What is the meaning of SQRRR?
2. How would you go about surveying a reading assignment?
3. In the SQRRR method, how do you form questions from a reading?
4. How do the last two steps of SQRRR help you remember what you have read?
5. What is the advantage of using skimming and scanning?
6. What are good clues to look for when you are scanning a passage?
7. Why is note-taking a valuable skill to develop?
8. When taking notes, what details from a passage should you include?

Apply Your Skill

1. Using the SQRRR method, read Section 2 (pages 82–87) of Chapter 3. Write out your questions and answers.
2. Skim Section 3 (pages 87–93) of Chapter 3 and then write a short paragraph telling what the section is about.
3. Scan Section 4 (pages 93–97) of Chapter 3 to help you answer the following question: "What methods did business leaders use to prevent unions from organizing working people?"
4. Take notes on Chapter 3 and then use them to help you write a summary of the main topics and themes covered in the chapter.

Chapter 3 Review

Summary

The population of the United States changed dramatically by the end of the nineteenth century. In the generation after the Civil War millions upon millions of immigrants arrived in the United States — many of them from southern and eastern Europe — and settled, for the most part, in northern cities.

Like most previous immigrants, the new ones came to America to improve their lives and make a future for themselves and their families. They faced, however, ethnic and religious prejudices. Demands were heard among some native-born Americans for laws to restrict the number of newcomers.

The expansion of industry stimulated urban America in the decades after the Civil War. The unprecedented growth of cities put severe strains on their basic facilities. Water service, sewer lines, and housing were everywhere inadequate, making living conditions difficult and unhealthful for many city dwellers.

Working people, in addition to finding fresh opportunities, suffered some disadvantages. Factory work often was monotonous and dangerous. Moreover, lay-offs could be unexpected and long. Usually having no direct contact with their employer, workers in big plants organized unions with the aim of making their voices heard. In 1866 the National Labor Union was founded. It advocated improved working conditions and an eight-hour work day, but lasted only a short time. Following the economic depression of 1873, union membership in general fell off. Moreover, violent confrontations during mining and railroad strikes damaged the reputation of unions and set back their cause.

Another attempt to create a national labor union was made by the Knights of Labor. This union admitted practically all workers — regardless of race, color, sex, national origin, or degree of skill — and by the mid-1880's had a membership of over 700,000. The Knights disapproved of strikes, advocating instead negotiations with employers for improved conditions. Once again violent labor strife, this time in Chicago in 1886, led to public fear of unions and to a decline in union strength. The depression of 1893 dealt the final blow to the Knights of Labor.

Just as the Knights of Labor disappeared, a federation of craft unions was created under a dynamic labor leader named Samuel Gompers. The organization, known as the American Federation of Labor, accepted the idea of the strike but only as a last resort. In its place, the AFL encouraged the signing of contracts that specified wages, hours, and working conditions. By the early 1900's, the AFL had become the nation's leading union.

Vocabulary and Important Terms

1. *padrone*
2. American Protective Association
3. Chinese Exclusion Act
4. "walking city"
5. omnibus
6. streetcar
7. suburb
8. tenement
9. National Labor Union
10. eight-hour day
11. "Molly Maguires"
12. Knights of Labor
13. cooperative
14. anarchist
15. Haymarket Riot
16. American Federation of Labor
17. Industrial Workers of the World
18. blacklist
19. yellow dog contract
20. injunction
21. Homestead strike
22. Pullman strike

Discussion Questions

1. (a) What was the basic reason for immigration after the Civil War? (b) How did the post-Civil War "new immigration" differ from the "old immigration," both in terms of national origin and numbers of immigrants? (c) What specific factors motivated Italian immigrants and Jews from eastern Europe to move to America?

2. (a) How were Chinese immigrants originally received when they began to arrive in California? (b) Why did the attitude toward Chinese immigrants change? (c) What was the result of this change in attitude?

3. Describe the relationship between the rapid expansion of American industry and the growth of American cities.

4. (a) How did tenements provide an answer to the problem of urban housing? (b) What kinds of problems were created by tenements? (c) What attempts at housing reform were undertaken? (d) How successful were those attempts?

5. (a) What kinds of periodic unemployment were created by the development of the factory system? (b) Why did unemployment become a more serious problem after the Civil War than it once had been?

6. How did the factory system affect relations between worker and employer?

7. (a) What were some of the demands of labor unions in the years after the Civil War? (b) How did working people try to win their demands? (c) How successful was the labor movement in this period?

8. (a) In what ways were the Knights of Labor and the American Federation of Labor similar? (b) In what ways were they different? (c) Why was the American Federation of Labor the more successful organization?

Relating Past to Present

1. As American cities grew, they underwent many changes, in part as a result of advances in transportation. How do the transportation systems of today's cities compare with those that were developed in post-Civil War America? Explain the similarities and differences.
2. By 1900 three American cities had population of over one million. How many American cities today have more than a million people?

Studying Local History

1. What cities in your state or region grew larger as a result of the rise of industry? What kinds of factories were developed in those cities? What groups of immigrants, if any, were drawn to them?
2. Study the map on page 78. Did your state have a large or small percentage of foreign-born people in 1900? What percentage of your state's population today is foreign-born?

Using History Skills

1. *Improving reading skills.* Examine Sadie Frowne's description of sweatshop work on page 91. (a) Why did Sadie Frowne go to work in a sweatshop? (b) What hardships did she encounter on the job? (c) Do you think she felt optimistic or pessimistic about the future? Give reasons for your answer.
2. *Using the index.* In the index find the entry for unions. On what pages in your book are labor unions mentioned or discussed? Look up each of those references. Based on the information you find, write a brief account of the history of the American labor movement.

WORLD SCENE

The Spread of Industry

During the last decades of the nineteenth century, manufacturing developed rapidly in a number of countries. In addition to the United States, Germany and Japan were emerging as industrial powers.

German industry. From 1870 to 1900 Germany experienced extraordinary industrial expansion. The political unification of Germany sparked this extraordinary expansion. At last, Germany's abundant resources of coal and iron ore and highly motivated labor could be brought together efficiently.

Government policies did much to encourage new German industries. High tariffs were instituted, offering protection from foreign competition. Monopolies, furthermore, were allowed in heavy industry, giving large companies tight control over production and distribution.

The most dramatic example of German industrial growth was in the manufacture of steel. Dominated by companies such as Krupp and Thyssen, the German output of steel rose from 1.5 million tons in 1880 to 7.4 million in 1900. The talent of its scientists and inventors also gave Germany a running start in the development of new industries. The nation became a leader in the manufacture of chemical and electrical products.

Manufacturing in Japan. At the same time, on the other side of the world, Japan was laying the foundation for becoming a major industrial power. In 1868 a new Japanese government embarked on a program of modernization that would transform the country.

Opening up Japan for the first time to the influence of western technology, the government raised taxes to pay for the construction of railroads, telegraph lines, shipyards, mines, and factories. A banking system was organized along western lines. Japanese students were sent abroad to schools, and foreign advisers were invited to Japan. A national education system emphasizing technical training was created within a few years.

A result of these changes in Japanese society was the growth of large companies, especially for the manufacture of textiles, glass, and weapons. By 1900 production of industrial goods had increased twenty times over that of 1868. In three decades the Japanese had established the industrial base of what would become one of the most impressive economies in the world.

CHAPTER 4

Politicians and Protest

POST-CIVIL WAR – 1900

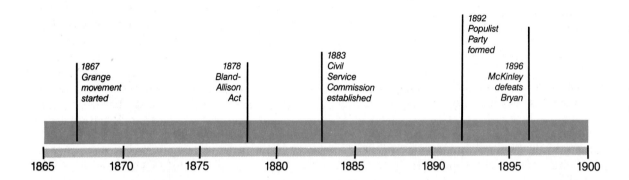

1867
Grange
movement
started

1878
Bland-
Allison
Act

1883
Civil
Service
Commission
established

1892
Populist
Party
formed

1896
McKinley
defeats
Bryan

1865   1870   1875   1880   1885   1890   1895   1900

CHAPTER OUTLINE

1. Corruption marks party politics.

2. Efforts at reform continue.

3. Farmers begin to join together.

4. The Populists propose far-reaching reforms.

The rapid economic and social changes that the United States underwent in the years after the Civil War put severe strains on the nation's political institutions. Politicians had had no experience — nor had anyone else — in dealing with industrial problems. No national officeholders, for instance, had ever before had to think about railroad strikes, or industrial unemployment, or the pollution of the environment. The Presidents continued to come from farms or small-town America. They were unfamiliar with slums and the world of the immigrant, because all of them had grown to adulthood far from such concerns. The vast majority of congressmen had similar backgrounds. Since most seats in Congress were filled by representatives from rural districts, urban matters were seldom discussed.

The Presidents of the post-Civil War period, moreover, did not think that Chief Executives should produce new ideas and programs in government. The public, as a whole, agreed. Some of the worst suffering in the history of the United States took place during the depression of 1873. The hard times were seen as inevitable, for the most part, and the federal government was not inclined to adopt measures that might assist the victims of economic disaster. Some voices, however, called for reform, most notably among labor organizations, associations of farmers, and the new political parties that were appearing.

1 Corruption Marks Party Politics

What posed a threat to the American political system was not the transformation that big business and big cities were bringing about, but unprecedented graft and corruption in government. Nationally it made no difference which party controlled Congress. Members of both parties were guilty of wrongdoing. A change of party after an election brought new faces before the public but had little effect on how politics was conducted.

Corrupt lobbyists wield influence. During the post-Civil War period, Congress had fallen into the habit of passing out special favors to powerful groups that had the means to hire lobbyists. The best-known lobbyist was Sam Ward. Ward was called "King of the Lobby" in tribute to his efforts on behalf of wealthy financiers. There were hundreds of individuals like Ward, operating not only in Washington, D.C., but also in state capitals throughout the United States.

The method of lobbyists was to offer public officials bribes in the form of expensive gifts. In return, the lobbyists obtained for their clients some desired governmental action. State legislatures were often honeycombed with members who had been "bought" by big-business magnates. A magazine sadly complained in 1876, "Legislative bribery and its satellite, lobbying, have become the most grievous political evil of the country."

Many business leaders had concluded that bribery was an appropriate way to deal with government officials. Collis Huntington, one of the owners of the Southern Pacific Railroad, candidly told an aide, "If you have to pay money to have the right thing done, it is only just and fair to do it." The Crédit Mobilier affair, a massive stock swindle that came to public attention during Grant's presidency, was a perfect example of corruption at work in the national government.

By the mid-1870's, some people had recognized that the sale of political favors was

In his painting "Electioneering," artist E. L. Henry portrays townspeople gathering around to hear a candidate discuss the issues of the day.

a danger to the well-being of the republic. Representative government could not exist if the men conducting it were dishonorable and unscrupulous. Reform became a lively topic for discussion in a few circles, but the public at large continued to be indifferent to the subject. People were distracted by the intense campaigns waged for office, seeing them as a form of entertainment.

The parties avoid major issues. Neither of the major parties took much interest in reform. Each party represented a wide variety of interests, and each sought to avoid taking clear positions on most issues.

The two parties were fairly evenly matched. The Republican Party — which called itself the "Grand Old Party" (GOP) — almost always saw its candidate elected President in the postwar years. Its supporters included the industrialists of the East and the grain-growing farmers of the Middle West. In addition, most laborers in the industrial cities followed the lead of their employers and voted Republican. The Republicans also had the backing of the war veterans and of their organization, the Grand Army of the Republic (GAR), because the veterans credited the party with having saved the Union.

Thousands of Americans in every part of the country voted Republican out of respect for the memory of Lincoln. Still others, never forgetting the idealism with which the Republican organization had begun in 1854, supported it as the humanitarian party. Black people, understandably, revered it as the party of emancipation.

The Democratic Party relied heavily on the support of voters in the South. After 1876, the former Confederate states always voted Democratic, producing the expression "the solid South." In cities throughout the country the Democrats were strong and in political control. Immigrants — particularly the Irish — tended to vote Democratic. They were attracted by the Democrats' traditional support for easy naturalization of newcomers. Business leaders and their employees who opposed the tariff also voted for the Democrats, who since Jackson's time had advocated a low tariff.

For many years after 1865, the Democrats insisted on keeping the Civil War issues alive. They opposed suffrage for blacks; they continued to argue for states' rights; and they identified themselves generally with the lost cause of the Confederacy. Thoughtful Democrats, however, realized that the party could not continue to live in the past. Ironically, Clement Vallandigham, a former Ohio congressman who had been banished to the South during the Civil War for his pro-Confederate views, urged the Democrats in 1871 to shift to new issues. In 1872, when they nominated the reformer Horace Greeley for President, however, the Democrats were soundly defeated by General Grant.

Hayes breaks with the party bosses. After the disclosures of corruption in the Grant administration, the Republicans knew that to hold the White House they must elect a man of undoubted integrity and good sense. Moreover, they knew the country required such a President, for the Democrats too had established a sad reputation for being corrupt. A leading Republican, striking hard at them, bellowed extravagantly: "That party never had but two objects — grand and petty larceny."

The Republicans believed that in Rutherford B. Hayes of Ohio they had found a figure the people could admire. When Hayes came to the White House in 1877, he was known as someone interested in reform. His motto was, "He serves his party best who serves his country best."

The new President's choice of Cabinet officers made the party bosses indignant. Hayes named William M. Evarts to be Secretary of State. Evarts was well-remembered for his role as chief counsel to Andrew Johnson during the impeachment trial. Another of Hayes's appointments also angered party regulars. David M. Key, a former Confederate from Tennessee, was named to be Postmaster General. This apparent gesture of reconciliation with the South was part of the Compromise of 1877 (page 28).

To be Secretary of the Interior, Hayes selected Carl Schurz (pronounced SHIRTS). Schurz had come to the United States from

"Who stole the people's money?" was the caption of this cartoon, one of many drawn by Thomas Nast to expose the activities of the Tweed ring. The Hayes administration sought reforms to stop such political corruption.

Germany in 1852. Briefly the United States minister to Spain and then a general in the Civil War, he had helped organize the Liberal Republican Party in 1872. Schurz had a fervor for honesty in government. In the Hayes Cabinet, he came to be noted also for his fair dealings with the Indians and for his support of reform.

Hayes begins the fight for civil service reform. A decent man of high intelligence, Hayes made Congress recognize again the dignity of the presidency — badly damaged by Johnson and Grant. Early in his administration, the new President decided to make changes in the way public officeholders were appointed.

Hayes detested the spoils system, which had been widely used ever since the days of Andrew Jackson's presidency. He believed that appointments to government positions should be made on the basis of ability and experience, not as a reward for political support. He favored use of a **merit system** as a basis for government appointments. Under the proposed system, jobs would go to those applicants scoring highest on competitive examinations. The movement to establish the merit system was called civil service reform.

Hayes faces a difficult situation. Few people in Congress shared Hayes's enthusiasm for civil service reform and little was done about it during his administration. Meanwhile, Hayes had four difficult years in the White House. His role in calling on federal troops to bring order in the Baltimore and Ohio Railroad dispute angered working people (page 90). In addition, many farmers had come to the conclusion that the high-tariff policy of the Republican Party was placing too heavy a burden on them. Farmers deeply resented the fact that they had to buy household goods and farm equipment that were protected from foreign competition, while having to sell their crops in a market totally unprotected. Why, they asked, should they not receive prices for their produce comparable to prices they were forced to pay for manufactured items?

The parties select candidates for the 1880 election. When he was nominated in 1876, Hayes had stated that he would not run a second time. The Republican Party did not try to make him change his mind. The Republican convention in 1880, which met in Chicago, was one of the stormiest ever held. The party had become split between two factions. The Stalwarts, led by Senator Roscoe Conkling of New York, were enemies of reform and of the President. The Half-Breeds, on the other hand, were followers of the President. Their leader was James G. Blaine of Maine, one of the most influential members of the Senate.

Hayes had been an enemy of Conkling's ever since 1877, when he had directly challenged the senator's power in New York. In that year, the President sought the resignation of Chester Arthur, a Conkling appointee who was Collector of the New York Custom House and who had been accused of cheating the government. Conkling, who strutted like a peacock in the Senate, often wearing white flannel trousers and brightly colored vests, raged at the President. "Parties are not built up by deportment," he shouted, "or by ladies' magazines, or gush!" Parties, he said, would die if "the faithful" could not be rewarded with jobs. Conkling was able to block the confirmation of Arthur's successor for three years. The fight, however, was far from settled.

Conkling and the Stalwarts were intent upon bringing General Grant back for a third presidential term, but Blaine, who could not obtain the nomination for himself, was able to prevent Grant from receiving it. The convention turned instead to a dark-horse candidate, James A. Garfield of Ohio. To appease the Stalwarts, Chester Arthur was nominated to be Vice President.

Garfield, who had served in the House and in the Senate, had been a Civil War general too. Earlier he had been head of Hiram College in Ohio. A pious man, he was an outstanding debater and preacher. To make him seem a "man of the people," the Republicans publicized him as a former canal boy, since he had once worked on a barge. "From the tow path to the White House" was the theme of the Republican campaign.

The Democrats, meeting at Cincinnati, also selected a Civil War veteran, General Winfield Scott Hancock of Pennsylvania. Hancock was remembered as a hero of the Battle of Gettysburg. His nomination, it was hoped, would quiet those people who continued to view the Democrats as the party of former Confederates and their sympathizers. Although inexperienced in politics, Hancock was once described as "a good man, weighing 250 pounds with a record as stainless as his sword."

Garfield is elected President. The Democrats waged a lackluster campaign in 1880, mainly denouncing Garfield for having received a dividend check of $329 on Crédit Mobilier stock. Again and again audiences jeered, "Three twenty-nine!" Although the campaign was without issues, Hancock was long remembered for a remark he made to a newspaper reporter: "The tariff question is a local question." Manufacturers who regarded the tariff as an important national issue thought the statement foolish.

In the election, out of nine million ballots cast, Garfield led by fewer than 10,000 votes. He carried the key states, however, and scored an impressive victory in the electoral college.

Garfield and the Stalwarts clash. As soon as Garfield was inaugurated, the battle between the Stalwarts and the Half-Breeds was resumed. Blaine, who had been appointed Secretary of State, tried to use his influence to limit Senator Conkling's power. He had Garfield nominate one of Conkling's foes in New York to be Collector of the New York Custom House. Conkling was furious. Once more he had been challenged.

In a dramatic gesture, Conkling and the other senator from New York, Thomas

Platt, resigned their Senate seats. At that time (before the Seventeenth Amendment to the Constitution went into effect) senators were elected not by popular vote but by their state legislatures. Conkling, therefore, expected the legislature at Albany, the state capital, to restore him and Platt to their places in the Senate — thus rebuking the President. To their astonishment, the legislature refused to reseat them, despite a humiliating trip Vice President Arthur made to Albany on their behalf. They had violated an unwritten rule of politics: politicians must never level an attack on a President from their own party. Those who do suffer the consequences.

Garfield is assassinated. During Garfield's brief administration, he was hounded day and night by people trying to obtain political appointments in the civil service. Garfield had written in his diary, "My day is frittered away with the personal seeking of people when it ought to be given to the great problems which concern the whole country."

Then tragedy struck. On July 2, 1881, Garfield left the White House for a trip to New England, intending to show his two sons Williams College, where he had been educated. As the President stood in the Washington, D.C., railway station, he was shot in the back by one Charles Guiteau, a disappointed office-seeker. Garfield lingered through the summer while the nation prayed for his recovery. When James Garfield died on September 19, Chester Arthur became President.

SECTION REVIEW

1. Vocabulary: *merit system.*
2. (a) What dangers confronted America's political institutions during the 1870's? (b) What was the response of the public? (c) Of the two major parties?
3. (a) What were the views of President Hayes on civil service reform? (b) What problems did Hayes face during his administration?
4. (a) Who were the Stalwarts? (b) Who were the Half-Breeds? (c) Why did James Garfield clash with the Stalwarts during his very short time as President?

2 Efforts at Reform Continue

The assassination of President Garfield opened the door wider on the burning issue of civil service reform. The shocked nation was now more aware than ever of the abuses of the old spoils system.

The movement for political reform gains strength. In the years after the Civil War, government at every level had become more complex, requiring officials in the various bureaus to have specialized knowledge. People recognized that it was no longer acceptable for appointees to have as their main qualification the fact that they knew the "right" politician.

The leading voices in the movement for civil service reform were two magazine editors — George W. Curtis of *Harper's Weekly* and E. L. Godkin of *The Nation.* Many of the people who joined them in the movement came from old New England families. The reformers were also often men and women who had been working to secure civil rights for the freed slaves.

The reformers' opponents, the bosses who defended the old system of providing jobs for political supporters, were not evil people. The spoils system, after all, had grown out of democracy itself. In order to win voters and "get out the vote" on Election Day, politicians had built local "machines." These machines consisted of local, state, and federal employees whose jobs depended on victory for "the boss." In large cities, bosses often enlarged their base of support by the favors they could dispense through friends in government. A political boss could arrange for an ailing father to be put into a hospital; he could rescue a wayward boy from the clutches of the court; he could find a job for the daughter of a poor family. All that the boss demanded for running this private social security system were votes. Although the boss system worked unevenly and unfairly, it filled a need not being met in any other way.

The city machines continued to function in many parts of the country, but the idea of appointing people to civil service positions on the basis of merit took hold following Garfield's assassination. Declared *The Nation*, "We do not think we have taken up a newspaper during the last ten days which has not in some manner made the [assassination] the product of 'the spoils system.'"

The Pendleton Act is passed. Ironically, it was Chester Arthur, the Stalwart, who presided over the beginning of reform. In his first annual message to Congress, Arthur strongly endorsed civil service reform. In January, 1883, he signed into law a bill introduced by Senator George H. Pendleton, a Democrat from Ohio. The law created a Civil Service Commission empowered to hold examinations and make appointments on a merit basis. Broadened from time to time, the Pendleton Act eventually ended the spoils system in the federal government.

President Arthur supports reforms. Chester Arthur was a widower when he came to the White House. He looked impressive, for he was such a stylish dresser that some people called him "the Dude President." Mrs. Blaine, who kept close tabs on the White House, said in 1882 that Arthur had bought 25 new coats that year. Arthur's interests were not limited to clothes, however. An honors graduate of Union College in New York, he had become a lawyer. In one of his first cases, he won $500 in damages for a black woman who had been forced off a street car because of her race. Black people in New York thereafter had received better treatment on public transportation.

Arthur proved to be a better President than most people expected, conducting the affairs of the country honestly and effectively. For instance, he vigorously prosecuted criminals when irregularities were discovered in the operation of the Post Office. Some of the culprits included high-ranking figures in his own party.

Arthur was fortunate that there was a surplus in the United States Treasury, owing to substantial tariff and tax yields. Determined that the money should not be wasted on the rash schemes of congressmen, Arthur proposed restoring the United States Navy to strength. Of late it had fallen into a deplorable condition. Under Arthur's direction, the navy began to construct modern ships. Within a short time America's naval vessels could be favorably compared with those of Great Britain and France.

The Democrats win the presidency in 1884. Although an effective President, Arthur's endorsement of civil service reform had cost him the support of Republican bosses. In 1884 they denied him the nomination for a presidential term in his own right. Arthur thus joined John Tyler, Millard Fillmore, and Andrew Johnson — the previous "accidental Presidents" who also had failed to receive their party's highest honor.

In 1884 the Republicans finally turned to James G. Blaine — "the Plumed Knight," as admirers called him. The Stalwarts, however, refused to support Blaine. Asked to deliver a speech on behalf of the candidate, Roscoe Conkling replied, "I am not engaged in criminal practice." Reform Republicans who were called Mugwumps (from an Indian word meaning "big shot") also withheld their support from Blaine because of political favors he had once done for a railroad in Arkansas. They hoped that, in the expression of the day, they could "go in for" the Democratic choice. It turned out that they could.

The Democrats' nominee was the big, burly governor of New York, Grover Cleveland. Earlier elected mayor of Buffalo, New York, Cleveland had aroused admiration for his political courage and honesty. As governor, he had battled Tammany Hall (the Democratic machine in New York City) and endeared himself to reformers.

The campaign of 1884 raised no social or economic question on which the candidates had to express opinions. Both parties resorted to mudslinging. The Republicans spread gossip about Cleveland's personal life. The Democrats harped on Blaine's political past. One of their taunts went:

Blaine, Blaine, James G. Blaine
Continental liar from the state of Maine!

The campaign was also enlivened by the candidacy of Belva Lockwood. A lawyer,

The Pendleton Civil Service Act (1883)

. . . It shall be the duty of (the Civil Service) commissioners . . . to aid the President . . . in preparing suitable rules for carrying this act into effect. . . . And . . . said rules shall provide . . . as follows:

First, for open, competitive examinations for testing the fitness of applicants for the public service. . . . Such examinations shall be practical in their character, and so far as may be shall relate to those matters which will fairly test the relative capacity and fitness of the persons examined to discharge the duties of the service into which they seek to be appointed.

Second, that all the offices, places, and employments so arranged . . . in classes shall be filled by selections according to grade from among those graded highest as the results of such competitive examinations. . . .

Fifth, that no person in the public service is for that reason under any obligations to contribute to any political fund. . . .

Sixth, that no person in said service has any right to use his official authority or influence to coerce the political action of any person or body. . . .

Belva Lockwood was the first woman to plead a case before the United States Supreme Court. Nominated by the National Equal Rights Party as a candidate for President, she ran on a ticket urging voting rights for women.

The outcome of the 1884 election may have been determined a few days before Election Day. A minister in New York City made a speech at a meeting of Protestant clergymen referring to the Democrats as the party of "rum, Romanism, and rebellion." Blaine, who was present, allowed this insult to Catholics to go unanswered. His failure to respond may have cost him votes.

Cleveland won the popular vote in a close race, receiving only 29,000 more votes than Blaine. In the electoral college, however, Cleveland's margin was more substantial: 219 to 182. Minor parties, including the National Equal Rights Party, failed to make a significant showing.

Grover Cleveland occupies the White House.
The election of Cleveland brought the first Democratic President to the White House since Buchanan left it in 1861. Cleveland's inaugural ball was one of the most lavish in history — and the first ever lighted by electricity. Two years later, Cleveland celebrated another important event. At the age of 49, he became the first President to be married in the White House. His bride was Frances Folsom, then 21 years old. The young First Lady adopted a policy of holding receptions in the White House on Saturday afternoons. Her aim was to greet young women who worked during the week. Sometimes she welcomed as many as 8,000 visitors on one day — a tribute not only to public curiosity but to the increasing number of working women.

Cleveland hoped to live by his motto: "A public office is a public trust." Still, he had little imagination or sensitivity to social injustice. He said he was in favor of civil service reform. Nevertheless, he yielded to the pressure of his party, so long out of power, in dismissing thousands of jobholders simply in order to put Democrats in their place. The Mugwumps were dismayed.

Cleveland vetoes pension bills. Cleveland, though, could also show backbone. He vetoed a bill, for example, that would have given a pension to any Union army veteran who had served at least ninety days. Cleveland also unhesitatingly vetoed the pension bills that members of Congress introduced on behalf of favored veterans in their home districts. One family, for instance, sought a pension for the service of a son who had drowned in a canal — after deserting from the army! No previous President had vetoed pension bills. In the northern states, former soldiers were exasperated, especially because Cleveland had not himself served in the armed forces.

Cleveland further angered Union veterans by ordering the return of captured Civil War flags — Union and Confederate alike — to the various states. The commanding officer of the GAR, Lucius Fairchild, turned a wrathful tongue on the President: "May God palsy the hand that wrote that order. May God palsy the brain that conceived it, and may God palsy the tongue that dictated it." Despite Fairchild's outburst, Cleveland had helped to put the Civil War in the past.

Cleveland takes other firm stands. Cleveland's vetoes of the pension bills were in keeping with his view of the presidency. He believed it was the President's job to be an impartial "umpire," making sure that no individual or group was either granted special favors or deprived of their rights.

Cleveland also vetoed a bill which would have provided federal assistance to Texas farmers who had suffered losses in a drought. The President expressed the dominant view of the time in his message: "I do not believe that the power and duty of the general government ought to be extended to the relief of individual suffering which is in no manner properly related to the public service or benefit." The President stated a principle: "Though the people support the government, the government should not support the people."

Cleveland, however, did not oppose other kinds of intervention by government. In 1887 he signed into law the Interstate Commerce Act to regulate railroad rates. This act provided for the creation of an Interstate Commerce Commission (ICC), the first of a long series of regulatory agencies that involved the federal government directly in the lives of individuals.

In addition to accepting regulation of the railroads, many Americans had concluded that the tariff on manufactured goods was too high. Cleveland agreed with this view. The tariff, he had come to believe, was bringing unnecessarily large returns to business at the expense of consumers. Most Democrats supported him when, in an unheard-of step, he devoted one entire annual message to Congress to his call for a reduction in tariff rates.

Cleveland knew he might be hurting his chances for re-election by his strong stand, but he was determined to do what he thought right. He told one of his advisers, "What is the use of being elected or re-elected, unless you stand for something?" To his intense disappointment, a bill providing for lower tariff rates failed to pass Congress.

The Republicans win the election of 1888. Cleveland was enthusiastically renominated by the Democratic Party in 1888. His opponent was Benjamin Harrison of Indiana. Harrison's great-grandfather, also named Benjamin Harrison, had signed the Declaration of Independence. His grandfather was "Old Tippecanoe," President William Henry Harrison. A forbidding person, Benjamin Harrison earned the nickname "Old Ice Water."

Although Cleveland won about 100,000 more popular votes than Harrison, the Republican candidate carried the electoral college. It seems clear that fraudulent returns in New York, Rhode Island, Ohio, and Indiana gave those states to Harrison. Harrison was a devout man who regularly studied the Bible and held a prayer service in his library daily. When told of his victory by Matt Quay, chairman of the Republican Party, Harrison said, "Providence has given us the victory." Quay, who knew how the votes had been counted in the doubtful states, repeated Harrison's words to a friend in private and commented, "Think of the man. He ought to know that Providence hadn't a thing to do with it."

Cleveland's policies are reversed. Harrison was content to follow the advice of party leaders during his years in office. James Blaine, who had played a key role in getting Harrison the nomination, was again named Secretary of State. John Wanamaker, a wealthy dry-goods merchant from Philadelphia, was appointed Postmaster General. So many prominent businessmen were in the new official family that people called it "The Millionaire's Cabinet." The Cabinet members quickly followed traditional practices. Wanamaker, for instance, fired some 30,000 Democrats in his department and replaced them with Republicans.

From its start, the Harrison administration came under heavy pressure from interest groups seeking favorable treatment. Aided by the Speaker of the House, Thomas B. Reed, appropriation bills — most of them "pork-barrel" proposals[1] — were sent in a steady stream to the White House for signature. Among the bills was one entitling all Union veterans to pensions.

The highest tariff ever passed to date also went through Congress. The man who worked hardest for it — and who gave his name to the bill — was Representative William McKinley of Ohio. To aid American sugar refiners, the McKinley Tariff removed the levy on raw sugar. It protected American sugar growers, however, by paying them a bounty of two cents a pound for their crop. On imported manufactured goods, it set duties so high that western farmers, traditional supporters of Republican Presidents, were infuriated. They could see the cost of the factory products they would buy going higher than ever.

The farmers' criticism of the Republicans was quieted temporarily by the passage in 1890 of two laws named for Senator John Sherman of Ohio. The Sherman Silver Pur-

Grover Cleveland's re-election in 1892 is celebrated in the painting with great triumph and fanfare. In actuality, the campaign had been a lackluster one.

chase Act increased the amount of silver the government purchased annually and allowed for the printing of paper money backed by silver. Farmers believed that these steps would increase the amount of money in circulation and make it easier for them to repay their financial obligations. The Sherman Antitrust Act (page 69) made illegal the creation of any "combination . . . or conspiracy" that produced a monopoly "in restraint of trade."

The Democrats regain the White House in 1892. By the time of the 1892 election, the clamor for reform was rising again. A new political organization, the Populist Party, had been formed by distressed farmers. Attracting strength from other discontented people, it nominated a candidate for President and expected to make a good showing in the election.

The Republicans renominated Harrison, while the Democrats once again chose Grover Cleveland to be their standard-bearer. The campaign was dull. There were few torchlight parades or huge rallies. Possibly the ordeal of the Homestead strike (page 95) and other unrest contributed to the

---

[1]*Pork-barrel* is a slang term applied to legislation that chiefly benefits the locale of the legislator obtaining it. The expression originated in the pre-Civil War practice of distributing pork to plantation slaves from huge barrels.

lack of spirit. At any rate, the Democrats won, with Cleveland achieving the most overwhelming presidential victory at the polls since Lincoln's in 1864. The strength of the Populist candidate, James Weaver, surprised the country. He polled over a million popular votes and took 22 electoral votes. The Populists were the first *third party* to win electoral votes since 1860. (A third party is any party organized in opposition to the two major parties.)

The depression of 1893 hits the country. Cleveland's new term in the White House opened just as hard times — the depression of 1893 — struck the country. Economic conditions remained bad for the four years Cleveland was in office. Thousands of businesses failed, and farm prices gradually fell to new lows. One fifth of all the country's factory workers lost their jobs. Some Democrats blamed the depression on the McKinley Tariff which, they said, had reduced the demand for foreign goods and consequently produced a decline in customs revenue.

Cleveland was not prepared to give aid to the victims of the depression. In the four years between his two terms, Cleveland had practiced law in New York City. The experience had made him even more sympathetic to the concerns and interests of eastern bankers and businessmen. In truth, the leading politicians of *both* parties seemed blind and deaf to the needs of farmers and working people.

A sign of the hard times was a march on Washington of protesting citizen groups from many parts of the country. The most publicized of these "armies" was one led by Jacob S. Coxey, a successful Ohio businessman. A reformer by instinct, Coxey favored a massive road-building program financed by the federal government. He also supported a public-works program for unemployed people in the cities.

The orderly little ragtag army that Coxey led from Ohio to Washington numbered about 500. The men traveled about fifteen miles a day, slept under a circus tent, and relied for food on handouts from local authorities and union people. The marchers' goal was to dramatize the plight of the jobless. When Coxey reached Washington, he was arrested and sent to jail for twenty days for walking on the grass at the Capitol. Coxey's army soon broke up, and nothing came of his proposals.

The Sherman Silver Purchase Act is repealed. Cleveland believed that prosperity would return only if Americans had confidence in the backing of their paper currency. Ever since the passage of the Sherman Silver Purchase Act (page 111) in 1890, Cleveland believed that the people's faith in the nation's currency had been destroyed. He argued that basing paper money on both silver and gold as provided in the law was a mistake. People were using silver to obtain paper money, turning it in for gold and then hoarding it. By 1893 the hoarding of gold — both by banks and individuals — was threatening the nation's gold reserves. Cleveland maintained that for a healthy economic climate, *a gold standard,* or currency based solely on gold, was necessary. He succeeded in persuading Congress to repeal the Sherman Silver Purchase Act in 1893, much to the dismay of the silver-producing states and of farmers.

In the face of the dwindling supply of gold in the Treasury, Cleveland also concluded what people came to call the "Morgan bond deal." A group of bankers, headed by J. P. Morgan, agreed to pay $62 million in gold for government bonds. Because Morgan profited handsomely from the transaction, many people believed that Cleveland was himself in league with the "money trust." By showing that leading bankers were supporting the government, however, Cleveland stopped the flow of gold and re-established confidence in United States currency.

Congress approves the Wilson-Gorman Tariff. Cleveland continued to put his faith in tariff reduction. Through his efforts, Congress in 1894 passed the Wilson-Gorman Tariff. In its orginal form, the bill provided for overall lower tariff rates. During the Senate debate on the bill, however, hundreds of amendments were added to protect special interests. In the version passed by Congress, the Wilson-Gorman Act was nearly as protectionist as the McKinley Tariff.

The Wilson-Gorman Tariff finally became law without the President's signature. Among the many amendments to the bill was an income-tax provision. The Supreme Court, however, declared the income tax unconstitutional in 1895. The Court ruled that the income tax, being a direct tax, was contrary to the Constitution since it was not apportioned according to population.[2]

SECTION REVIEW

1. Vocabulary: *third party, gold standard.*
2. (a) What was the Pendleton Act? (b) Why was it enacted?
3. (a) Why did Chester Arthur fail to gain the Republican nomination for President in 1884? (b) What factors led to Grover Cleveland's victory in that election?
4. What stand did President Cleveland take on each of the following? (a) Pension bills (b) Federal assistance to farmers (c) Railroad regulation (d) Tariff rates
5. What tariff policy did Benjamin Harrison follow after he won the presidency in 1888?
6. (a) What was the Sherman Silver Purchase Act? (b) Why did Grover Cleveland support the effort to repeal it after he was re-elected President?

3 Farmers Begin to Join Together

Although the United States had become, as Speaker Reed said, "a billion-dollar country," signs of unrest showed that many people felt left out of the benefits. Southern and western farmers, particularly, had long been struggling to organize and to seek answers to the problems they confronted.

Farmers join the Grange. The first significant organization of farmers was founded in 1867. Called the National Grange of the Patrons of Husbandry, it was the brain child

Women as well as men were admitted to the Grange. At meetings like this one in Illinois, Grangers met to exchange ideas and solve common problems.

of Oliver H. Kelley, a clerk in the Department of Agriculture. A man of boundless energy, Kelley planned to bring farmers together in intellectual and social activities. He recognized that one of the results of settling the Great Plains was the loneliness imposed on people by the immense distances between settled places. He understood, too, that farmers needed a place where they could discuss ways of improving farming. Kelley planned that each local unit, or Grange, would have among its officers a "lecturer" who would at each meeting present a report on some topic of general interest.

Kelley talked over his plans with his niece, Carrie Hall, who convinced him that if his organization were to attain its goals, it would have to include women. Kelley soon began conducting a drive for members, and by the early 1870's was having incredible success. Said Kelley of the Grange, "It must be advertised as vigorously as if it were a patent medicine." By 1873, 20,000 local Granges had sprung up, located in all but four states (though concentrated mainly in the South and West). These locals contained about 800,000 members.

Like the Knights of Labor, the Grangers started cooperative enterprises, the aim being to eliminate middle agents and

---

[2]The Sixteenth Amendment to the Constitution, which went into effect in 1913, removed the constitutional barrier to this kind of tax.

Farmers and the Grange

The writer Hamlin Garland (page 46) grew up on midwestern farms in the 1860's and 1870's. He moved from Wisconsin to Iowa, and then to the Dakotas, and later wrote about life in rural America.

Many of our social affairs were now connected with "the Grange." During these years on the new farm, while we were busy with fencing and raising wheat, there had been growing up among the farmers of the west a social organization officially known as The Patrons of Husbandry.

My father was an early and enthusiastic member of the order, and during the seventies its meetings became very important dates on our calendar. In winter "oyster suppers" with debates, songs, and essays drew us all to Burr Oak Grove schoolhouse, and each spring the Grange picnic was a grand "turn out." It was almost as well attended as the circus.

The central place of meetings was usually in some grove along the river to the west and south of us. Early on the appointed day the various lodges of our region came together one by one at convenient places, each one moving in procession and led by great banners on which the women had blazoned the motto of their home lodge. Some of the columns had bands and came preceded by far faint strains of music, with marshals in red sashes galloping to and fro in fine assumption of military command.

It was grand, it was inspiring to us, to see those long lines of carriages winding down the lanes, joining one another at the

A poster depicting agricultural life

crossroads till at last all the Granges from the northern end of the county were united in one mighty column advancing on the picnic ground, where orators awaited our approach with calm dignity and high resolve. Nothing more picturesque, more delightful, has ever risen out of American rural life. Each of these assemblies was a most grateful relief from the loneliness of the farm.

thereby make prices lower. The most successful cooperatives were grain elevators — buildings equipped to load, unload, clean, and store grain. Many farmers had become convinced that elevators owned by the railroads were overcharging for their use.

The Supreme Court upholds Granger laws.
The Grange also turned to politics, urging that railroad and warehouse rates be regulated. Between 1869 and 1874, so-called Granger laws were passed by legislatures in

Illinois, Iowa, Wisconsin, and Minnesota. These laws were designed to fix maximum freight and storage charges. In a number of states, official commissions were appointed to help enforce the legislation.

The railroads strongly opposed the Granger laws and in some instances appealed to the courts. In 1877 the United States Supreme Court acted on a number of cases, which came to be called the "Granger cases." The main question the Court had to deal with can be summarized: Has a state the right to regulate a private corporation on grounds that the business involved affects the public welfare?

In the best known of the cases, *Munn v. Illinois,* the Supreme Court held that states have the power to regulate private property when it is "clothed with a public interest." In other words, a state did indeed have grounds for regulating private property devoted to public use. The Court modified the decision somewhat in 1886, however, when it held in a case called *Wabash, St. Louis and Pacific Railroad Company v. Illinois* that a state could regulate a railroad only within the state's own borders.

Since most railroads ran between states, clearly only the federal government was in a position to regulate them. The Interstate Commerce Act, passed in Cleveland's first term (page 490), had provided the beginning of an answer to the problem of railroad abuse. This momentous law forbade pools, rebates, and the setting of high rates for short hauls. Railroads were required to post their rates and to make them "reasonable and just." The Interstate Commerce Act was a monument to the work begun by the Grangers.

Grange membership declines. For all its success in bringing farmers together, the Grange was, like the Knights of Labor, ultimately the wrong *kind* of organization. By concentrating on cooperatives — which often failed — the Grangers proved incapable of solving the farmers' specific problems. During the 1880's, membership fell off. Still, the Grange had proved to farmers the advantages of political action.

The Greenback Party is formed. Many farmers were heavily burdened by debts contracted during the Civil War. At that time the market for grain had been good, and money for buying more land had been easy to borrow. When the price of grain declined, these debts were more difficult to pay off. The harder the farmers worked, the larger the crops they produced. This abundance forced prices lower.

Some farmers began to be attracted by the program of the Greenback Party. This group had organized for the purpose of convincing the federal government to keep in circulation the large amounts of greenbacks, paper money issued during the Civil War which had to be accepted in payment of debts. The members also believed that if additional paper money without backing were added to the money supply, farm prices would rise. Farmers would then be better able to pay off their debts. After a financial panic struck the nation in 1873, Greenback parties arose in a number of states. A national organization was formed in 1876, and Peter Cooper of New York, then 85 years old, was nominated for President. In 1880 the Greenback candidate for President was James Weaver. In those elections, however, neither Cooper nor Weaver received a significant number of votes.

The Greenbackers ran the eccentric Ben Butler for President in 1884, but they had long since gone into decline. The party never recovered from a decision by Congress in 1875 to redeem all greenbacks in gold and retire them. This Resumption Act deeply disappointed farmers and other "cheap money" advocates who had hoped that the issuing of *more* greenbacks would solve their problems.

The Farmers' Alliances appear. By the beginning of the 1880's, farmers were once again seeking reform through politics. They began establishing pressure groups called Farmers' Alliances. The goals of the Alliances included more paper money in circulation, the unlimited coinage of silver, government ownership of the railroads, and the return to the federal government of the public land the railroads had received.

Step by step the alliances came into existence. Farmers first banded together locally, then the locals became state-wide; afterward, state units came together in regional organizations. Eventually there were two major sectional voices of farming people: the Southern Alliance and the Northwestern Alliance. The Southern Alliance became highly influential, with three million white members and one million black members in an affiliated Colored Farmers' Alliance.

Although idealized in this painting of harvest time, the lives of farmers in the late 1800's were strained by devastating weather, high costs, and fluctuating prices.

In 1889 an effort was made to link the Southern and Northwestern Alliances. Representatives of labor were also invited to participate in order to join together "the organized tillers and the organized toilers." There were, however, serious obstacles to such unity. The Southern Alliance, for one thing, insisted upon separate white and black lodges, a proposal the Northwestern Alliance rejected.

In the election of 1890, the Southern Alliance, tying itself to the Democratic Party, captured four governorships, forty-four seats in the House of Representatives, three seats in the Senate, and control of eight state legislatures. On the Plains, the Northwestern Alliance was able to send six representatives to Congress from Kansas and Nebraska.

The considerable time it took farmers to begin running their own candidates for political office can be accounted for by the relative slowness with which people communicated in this period. The telephone had not yet entered the lives of most farmers. Furthermore, the ferocity of the Civil War had tied farmers — like all people — to the traditional political parties. The ties were based on sentiment as well as interest. To northern farmers, forsaking the Republicans seemed a betrayal of the party that had saved the Union. To white farmers of the South, forsaking the Democratic Party was unthinkable.

Farmers face complex new problems. By the end of the 1880's, however, hard times had loosened old political loyalties. Farmers confronted a combination of falling prices, unusually bad weather, and above all, heavy *mortgages.* (A mortgage is a pledge of property to a creditor — often a bank — usually against the repayment of a money loan.)

The increase in the population of the western states had been so sudden and substantial that the region had become a powerful magnet for eastern investors with money to lend. The number of people in Kansas and Nebraska between 1880 and 1890, for instance, went from 1,448,000 to almost 2,500,000. In those same years, the population of North and South Dakota jumped from 135,000 to 511,000. Most of these people could not have survived without borrowing money. They required it to put up houses and farm buildings and to purchase equipment, fencing, and seed grain. To obtain the money they needed, many farmers mortgaged their property, often beyond what they could readily afford. Meeting the payment on the mortgages was a heavy burden. It became a severe problem when things turned sour at the end of the 1880's. By 1887 the number of mortgages in Kansas was three times greater than in 1880. Half the farmers of Kansas and North Dakota had taken mortgages, most of them heavy.

Nature played a cruel hand in the calamity that followed. The terrible weather from 1885 to 1887 that had devastated the cattle industry (page 40) also ravaged the grain growers. Within a short time, thousands of farmers were unable to pay the installments due on their mortgages. Soon they lost their farms as creditors took them over. It was said that if the farms covered by the failed mortgages were laid end to end, they would form a tract of land thirty miles wide and ninety miles long.

The farmers who survived knew they must pay back the money they owed. But how? They had always noticed that when railroads went bankrupt, they were reorganized under court orders. This meant that the debts of the railroads were cut down, but that the trains continued to run. As a result of such practices, many farmers considered railroad managers, judges, and eastern bankers to be "the enemy." The editor of a farm journal expressed it this way:

There are three great crops raised in Nebraska. One is a crop of corn, one a crop of freight rates, and one a crop of interest. One is produced by farmers who by sweat and toil farm the land. The other two are produced by men who sit in their offices and behind their bank counters and farm the farmers.

Farmers began to leave the Plains states in droves. Many a covered wagon departed bearing a sign that read: "In God We Trusted, In Kansas We Busted." Some farmers held on for a while by borrowing from "loan sharks" at exorbitant interest rates. In the end they were defeated too.

As farmers tried to understand what had gone wrong, they began to accept the simple idea that not enough money was available to do what they called "the money work." The reasoning appeared logical enough. At the time of the Civil War the country had about $1 billion in circulation. Twenty-five years later the population had almost doubled, but the money in circulation had increased only slightly. No wonder that farm prices were so low, said the farmers. There were too few dollars on hand to buy the increased amount of farm products. It took $1.20, for example, to buy a bushel of wheat in 1871; in 1892 the same amount of money could buy two bushels. Farmers thought the solution was to inflate the currency, that is, to somehow get more money into circulation. Few of them gave thought to the rise in the price of manufactured goods that would surely follow putting the idea into practice.

The coinage of silver becomes a political issue. The failure of the Greenback Party, which had advocated expanding the currency, had keenly disappointed many farmers. In the same years, however, rich veins of silver were being discovered in the mountains of the West. These silver strikes suggested another solution. Why not freely issue silver coins?

The struggle to put more silver into circulation had grown out of earlier developments. During most of the nation's history, both gold and silver coins had circulated. Both were legal tender, which meant that a person who was owed money *had* to accept either gold or silver in repayment of the debt. Silver and gold had been valued for coinage purposes in 1834 at a ratio of 16 to 1. In other words, 16 ounces of silver were equal in value to 1 ounce of gold. To put it another way, there was sixteen times as much silver in a silver dollar as there was gold in a gold dollar.

After the discovery of gold in California in 1849, the metal became more plentiful and its value in relation to silver fell. Still, the old ratio of 16 to 1 remained the official relationship between the two precious metals. People soon were aware that the silver in a silver dollar was worth more than the gold in a gold dollar. A silversmith making silver jewelry, umbrella handles, snuffboxes, silver comb-and-brush sets, and hundreds of other items would pay more for the metal than would the United States Mint. Consequently, so little silver was brought to the Mint for coinage that in

1873 Congress removed the silver dollar from the list of standard coins. At the time, the decision attracted almost no attention.

By the end of the 1870's, however, the increased silver production in the West was having a noticeable effect. The value of silver in relation to gold was declining sharply. By 1875, as the price of silver at the silversmiths' shops fell lower and lower, silver producers were denouncing Congress for having committed the "Crime of '73!" They called for the coinage of silver once again. "Give us back the dollar of our daddies," they pleaded.

The silver controversy continues. The mine owners raised this cry, of course, hoping to induce the government to buy the total output of the silver mines. The interests of the silver producer and the farmer — the one in disposing profitably of the ore, the other in enlarging the currency — came together. Congress responded to the clamor in 1878 with the Bland-Allison Act. It provided for the Secretary of the Treasury to purchase not less than $2 million and not more than $4 million worth of silver each month.

The law satisfied neither the silver producers nor the farmers, and both groups pressed hard for even larger purchases of silver by the government. The admission to the Union in 1889 and 1890 of several silver-producing states increased the pressure on Congress. Finally yielding, Congress in 1890 passed the Sherman Silver Purchase Act (page 111). In spite of expectations, however, the operation of the law did not dramatically increase the amount of money in circulation.

New farm leaders attract national attention. The farmers were interested in more than currency reform. Meeting in St. Louis in 1889, representatives of the Alliances adopted a wide-ranging political platform. It called for a graduated income tax, government ownership of railroads, and an end to national banks.

Leaders of the Alliances had, by this time, become nationally recognized names. Among them was "Pitchfork Ben" Tillman of South Carolina. Once, when Tillman was running for the Senate, he told an audience,

"send me to Washington and I'll stick my pitchfork into [President Cleveland's] old ribs." Another notable was Tom Watson of Georgia. Like Tillman, Watson had special affection for the nation's poor farmers, and he became a dogged spokesman for them in the House of Representatives.

From Kansas came the fiery Mary Elizabeth Lease. Those who admired Mrs. Lease called her a "Patrick Henry in petticoats." Another impressive advocate of immediate action was Annie Diggs of Kansas, an editor and political organizer. Yet another influential figure from Kansas was "Sockless Jerry" Simpson. He had earned the nickname after claiming that a political rival — a banker — wore silk socks. A newspaper reporter twisted the statement to mean that Simpson wore none!

Possibly the most persuasive orator among all the farm politicians was Ignatius Donnelly of Minnesota. He cultivated many interests. He believed, for instance, that he had proved Francis Bacon was actually the author of the plays of Shakespeare. The figure known to the public the longest was James Weaver. As the Greenback candidate for President in 1880 (page 115), Weaver, a Civil War general from Iowa, had spoken to crowds in towns and villages from one end of the country to another. With his white hair and earnest manner, he seemed a fatherly figure to his admirers and had earned respect.

Through the work of these people, the farmers' concerns were brought to the attention of all Americans. In the next few years, those concerns would have an extraordinary impact on national politics.

SECTION REVIEW

1. Vocabulary: *mortgage.*
2. (a) What was the Grange? (b) What kinds of laws did it support? (c) What was the significance of *Munn v. Illinois*?
3. (a) What program did the Greenback Party offer? (b) Why did it attract the support of farmers?
4. (a) What were some of the serious problems faced by farmers in the late 1800's? (b) What solutions to those problems did the Alliances propose?

4 The Populists Propose Far-Reaching Reforms

By 1890 many farmers were talking about forming a new political party. Alliance members, Grangers, Greenbackers, Knights of Labor, and many other reformers met in St. Louis in February, 1892, for that purpose. The convention adopted the name "People's Party," though in time the new organization became known as the Populist Party. The excitement created by the Populists swiftly gained momentum.

The Populists call for a new direction. Meeting at Omaha in July, 1892, the Populists adopted a platform that embraced proposals farmers and union members had advocated for years. The planks included a call for legislation to tighten control over the railroads, the free and unlimited coinage of silver at a ratio of 16 to 1, and a graduated income tax. The extensive platform also contained pleas for the secret ballot in elections and liberal pensions for Union veterans. It also proposed the direct election of senators and a one-term limit for the President and the Vice President. Reaching out for labor's support, the platform advocated the eight-hour day and condemned the use of Pinkerton detectives in labor disputes.

The Populists get off to an encouraging start. The enthusiasm that greeted the adoption of the platform had the air of a religious revival meeting. The Populists nominated James Weaver to be their presidential candidate. When the 1892 election returns came in (page 112), the Populists had a right to be encouraged. Immediately, they began making plans for 1896. Weaver predicted, "The Republican Party is as dead as the Whig Party was after the Scott campaign of 1852, and from this time forward will diminish in every state of the Union and cannot make another campaign."

The Populists were overestimating their strength. In the congressional elections of 1894, only 12 states gave more than 30 percent of their votes to Populist candidates. Still, the Populists were confident that they would carry the day in 1896. They assumed

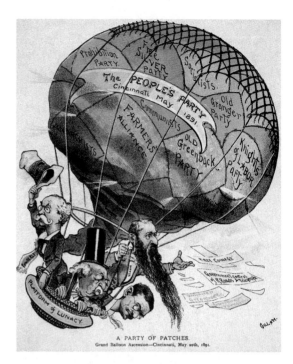

A PARTY OF PATCHES.
Grand Balloon Ascension—Cincinnati, May 20th, 1891.

Satirized as a patchwork of interests, the Populists had their own presidential candidate by 1892.

that the Democrats and the Republicans would reject the free-silver issue. Then *they* would use it to win the support of the silverites in both major parties. The result, they hoped, would be a widened base of support for their own program of reform.

The Republicans prepare for the election of 1896. In June, the Republicans gathered in St. Louis for their convention. The dominant figure was Mark Hanna, a wealthy industrialist from Ohio and the very symbol of the "enemy" the Populists had in mind. Hanna began lining up delegates to make William McKinley — a Civil War veteran who had twice been elected governor of Ohio — the party's nominee. The naming of McKinley on the first ballot was assured even before the delegates arrived.

The Republican platform, denouncing the idea of free silver, stated firmly that "the existing gold standard must be maintained." McKinley's own views on the matter were less solid. Some people tagged him "Wobbly Willie." He would often speak out for "sound money" (meaning the gold standard) and sometimes in favor of bi-metallism (meaning money based on gold *and* silver). He understood, however, that the Republican platform could win him votes in the East from big businessmen and from people afraid that a shift to silver might endanger business and eventually their jobs. Moreover, being an advocate of a high tariff (page 111), he counted on the backing of working people who saw tariffs as necessary to keeping wages up. McKinley knew, too, that many workers would support him because he had once defended in court a group of strikers arrested in a riot.

The Democrats nominate Bryan. The Democrats gathered in Chicago for their convention early in July. Already they had been weakened by six years of the Populist onslaught that drew supporters away from their ranks. Party leaders saw that the silver issue could be theirs now that the Republicans had passed it by. Silver Democrats were calling for a rejection of the "gold Democrats" and sought to make the issue a weapon for victory.

The Democrats' platform showed who was in charge. The most important plank was a clear call for "the free and unlimited coinage of both gold and silver at the . . . ratio of sixteen to one." The huge audience cheered when Ben Tillman denounced Grover Cleveland — the party's own sitting President — as a "tool of Wall Street."

One of the delegates who had spoken in favor of the party platform was William Jennings Bryan, a handsome, broad-shouldered, 36-year-old Nebraskan. A brilliant orator with a melodious voice that carried to the farthest corners of the hall, he hypnotized the crowd with his speech. When he reached his final words, the people were on their feet, cheering wildly. He concluded: "You shall not press down upon the brow of labor this crown of thorns; you shall not crucify mankind upon a cross of gold."

The Democrats had found their new leader. On the fifth ballot they made Bryan the party's choice for President. He was destined to be the dominant figure of the Democratic Party for the next sixteen years.

The Populists support Bryan. The Populists were in deep gloom when they came together in St. Louis two weeks later. Should they too make Bryan their candidate? He was not in sympathy with many of the Populist proposals. Yet a separate candidate would only assure a victory for the Republicans. Many Populists resisted the idea of being joined with the Democrats. Tom Watson, deeply distressed, said that the Democrats wanted the Populists to "play Jonah while they play the whale."

In the end the Populists decided they had no choice but to nominate Bryan. Still, they balked at taking Bryan's running mate, Arthur Sewall of Maine. A shipyard owner, Sewall was also a bank president and a railroad director. The Populists nominated their favorite, Tom Watson, for the vice presidency.

McKinley wins the 1896 election. Bryan waged a fiery and strenuous crusade for the White House. In so doing he introduced the modern presidential campaign, one in which candidates themselves play the chief part. Sometimes making as many as six speeches a day, Bryan was greeted everywhere by brass bands and hoopla. He tried to persuade the faithful that he represented "the people" in their mighty struggle with "Wall Street."

The Republicans campaigned along traditional lines. McKinley, a devoted husband, refused to be away from his ailing wife for any length of time. He conducted his campaign from the front porch of his house in Ohio. Week after week he greeted thousands of people, who came from all parts of the country to hear him speak. McKinley kept in touch by telephone with politicians throughout the country, thus becoming the first presidential nominee to use the phone extensively for campaigning.

On Election Day, McKinley won convincingly. He carried not only the nation's industrial areas — where employers had threatened mass dismissals if Bryan won — but also the important farming states of Iowa, Minnesota, and North Dakota. Many farmers, possibly influenced by a slight rise in wheat prices at the end of the summer, had decided to vote Republican, as they always had. Many working people also

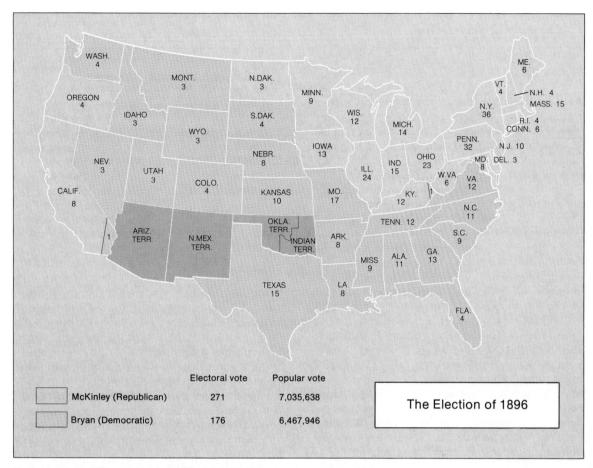

	Electoral vote	Popular vote
McKinley (Republican)	271	7,035,638
Bryan (Democratic)	176	6,467,946

The Election of 1896

Bryan's nationwide speeches in 1896 and the well-financed campaign of McKinley resulted in the largest popular vote in any presidential election to date.

voted for McKinley, not so much out of fear for their jobs but out of fear that Bryan's proposals could lead to cheap dollars and inflation that would hurt wage earners. To the silverites, Bryan's defeat was a deep disappointment; to the Populists, it was an unrelieved disaster.

The gold standard is formally established. The silver issue soon disappeared. When gold was discovered in western Canada and in Alaska shortly after the election, the supply of money began to increase rapidly. The United States went on the gold standard in 1900, and the silver question faded from public interest.

The Populist legacy was mixed. Some of the party's suggestions were eventually enacted into law, including the graduated income tax and the direct election of senators.

After a generation of protest, however, the batteries of reform had run down. Meanwhile, the country was looking abroad for new opportunities. Suddenly, domestic affairs were pushed into the background as foreign issues took center stage. Within two years, William Jennings Bryan was in a colonel's uniform training troops in the state of Nebraska. Tom Watson would write, "The blare of the bugle drowned the voice of the reformer."

SECTION REVIEW

1. (a) Who were the Populists? (b) What did the Populists call for in their platform of 1892?
2. (a) Who won the Republican and Democratic nominations for President in 1896? (b) Which candidate did the Populists support? (c) What was the outcome of the election?

Chapter 4 Review

Summary

After the Civil War, the American political system was marked by graft and corruption. Lobbyists, representing special interest groups, interfered with the effective functioning of government by seeking special favors through the use of bribes. The Crédit Mobilier affair was characteristic of the era.

In 1876 the Republicans were aware that they needed to select a candidate of unquestionable integrity to run for President. The man they chose was Rutherford B. Hayes of Ohio. When Hayes was elected President, he tried to change the method by which public officeholders were appointed. Opposed to the spoils system, Hayes favored a merit system as a basis for government appointment. Civil service reform, however, met with little enthusiasm in Congress.

James A. Garfield was elected President in 1880, with Chester Arthur as his Vice President. As soon as Garfield took office, the battle over reform began again. The issue came to a tragic climax when Garfield was assassinated by a frustrated office-seeker. Shocked by this event, the public now demanded immediate action. In January, 1883, the Pendleton Act established a Civil Service Commission to make appointments on the basis of merit.

In 1884 Grover Cleveland won the presidency, becoming the first Democrat to occupy the White House since 1861. Cleveland tackled two particularly sensitive issues: the pension bills and tariff rates. Possibly because of Cleveland's forthrightness, Republicans once again were able to take over the presidency in 1889 with the inauguration of Benjamin Harrison.

Cleveland returned to the White House in 1893, just as a devastating depression was about to begin. Lasting for four years, the hard economic times caused the failure of numerous businesses, and thousands of Americans suffered keenly.

One group that felt victimized by economic fluctuations were the farmers. To deal more effectively with their situation, farmers began to join together. In 1867 the National Grange was formed. Then, in the 1880's farmers formed organizations called Farmers' Alliances. By 1892, Alliance members, Grangers, and other farmers and workers joined together to form the Populist Party. In the 1896 election, the Populists backed William Jennings Bryan, the Democratic candidate for President, who was running on a free-silver platform. Republican candidate William McKinley won, however, and his election was a victory for the gold standard.

Vocabulary and Important Terms

1. "solid South"
2. merit system
3. Stalwarts
4. Half-Breeds
5. Pendleton Act
6. Mugwumps
7. Interstate Commerce Act
8. McKinley Tariff
9. third party
10. Coxey's army
11. gold standard
12. Wilson-Gorman Tariff
13. National Grange
14. *Munn v. Illinois*
15. Greenback Party
16. Farmers' Alliances
17. mortgage
18. Bland-Allison Act
19. Populist Party

Discussion Questions

1. (a) What groups gave their support to the Republican Party during the post-Civil War period? (b) Which voters tended to back the Democratic Party? (c) To what extent was the Republican Party dominant during this period?

2. (a) In the debate over civil service reform, what arguments were offered in support of the spoils system and the merit system? (b) What effect did President Garfield's assassination have on the reform movement? (c) What setbacks did civil service reform suffer during the Cleveland and Harrison administrations?

3. (a) Why did many farmers oppose high tariffs? (b) What stand did President Cleveland take on the tariff question? (c) Why did he not sign the Wilson-Gorman Tariff?

4. (a) What effect did the depression of 1893 have on the country? (b) What did President Cleveland believe to be the cause of the depression? (c) What step did he take as a result?

5. In what sense was the Interstate Commerce Act a monument to the efforts of the Grangers?

6. (a) Why were farmers slow to organize their own political parties and run candidates for office? (b) Why, by the end of the 1880's, had old political loyalties begun to loosen?

7. (a) Why, in the 1870's, did mine owners and farmers call for government coinage of silver? (b) How did Congress respond to these demands? (c) Why were neither silver producers nor farmers satisfied with the laws passed? (d) What part did the silver issue play in the election of 1896? (e) What happened to the silver issue after that election?

8. (a) What groups joined together in 1892 to form the organization known as the Populist Party? (b) What proposals were made in the Populist platform of 1892? (c) What electoral successes did the Populists enjoy? (d) What was the Populist legacy?

Relating Past and Present

The late 1800's saw the rise of a number of third parties. What third parties have been formed in recent years? What platforms have they adopted? What successes have they had? In what ways, if any, have these third parties affected the major parties and the outcome of recent elections?

Studying Local History

Find out about the history of the Granger movement in your state or region. How popular was the Grange? What Granger laws, if any, were passed in your state? What social and educational activities did the Grange sponsor? What activities does the Grange carry on in your state or region today?

Using History Skills

1. *Reading maps.* Study the map on page 121 showing the election results of 1896. (a) What sections of the country supported McKinley? (b) What sections supported Bryan? (c) What divisions in national politics are revealed in the map?
2. *Reading source material.* Study Hamlin Garland's description of the Grange on page 114. (a) What social activities did the Grange sponsor in Hamlin Garland's county? (B) Where were regional Grange meetings held? (c) How does Garland's account convey the importance of the Grange to rural Americans?
3. *Making connections.* List the planks of the Populist Party (page 119). Then do research to find out which planks were later enacted into law.

WORLD SCENE

Citizen Participation

The period from 1865 to 1900 saw efforts in many countries to bring about some degree of citizen representation in government.

The Third French Republic. The collapse of the French army and the capture of Emperor Napoleon III at the end of the Franco-Prussian War (1870) gave groups in Paris favoring the establishment of a republic an opportunity to take over the government of France. The new government was named the Third Republic (previous republics had been created in 1792 and 1848), and national elections were held to choose an assembly.

The election returns of 1870 showed that rural areas had chosen representatives who wished to restore the monarchy in France. Radical groups, adamantly opposed to the return to any form of monarchy, quickly set up their own independent government in the city of Paris. Known as the Paris Commune, this revolutionary government was crushed within two months by the French army.

A coalition of monarchist groups governed France until 1875. In that year republicans gained control of the National Assembly and wrote a new constitution which provided for a more representative government. The Third Republic lasted well into the twentieth century, but it was unstable because competing interests in France, all of them represented in the assembly, were unable to work together effectively.

Self-government in Canada. By the end of the American Revolution, thousands of Loyalists had moved to Canada, most of them settling around the Great Lakes. This influx of English-speaking people led in 1791 to the division of the old province of Quebec into two parts. The region occupied by the Loyalists became Upper Canada (present-day Ontario), while the French-speaking area became Lower Canada (present-day Quebec).

In the late 1830's rebellions against British rule erupted in both parts of Canada. These uprisings were quickly subdued, but the British government, deeply concerned, sent Lord Durham to investigate the troubles. The Durham Report, submitted in 1839, was a document of considerable insight. It recommended that to keep Canada loyal to the British Crown, Parliament should grant the Canadian people self-government. Soon after Lord Durham made his suggestions, Upper and Lower Canada were united in a single province under one governor. It was several years before Britain granted Canada self-government.

In 1864 Canadian representatives, meeting in Quebec, produced the basis for a constitution and outlined a plan for the political union of the various provinces. The plan was accepted by the British, and in 1867 Parliament passed the British North America Act. The new union, calling itself the Dominion of Canada, became the first self-governing nation within the British Empire.

UNIT 1 REVIEW

Important Dates

1862 Homestead Act.

1866 National Labor Union formed.

1867 Grange movement started.

1869 First transcontinental railroad completed.
Knights of Labor organized.

1876 Battle of Little Bighorn.
Bell invents telephone.

1877 *Munn v. Illinois.*

1879 Edison invents electric lamp.

1882 John D. Rockefeller organizes Standard Oil Company.

1883 Pendleton Act signed into law.

1886 Haymarket Riot.
American Federation of Labor formed.

1887 Interstate Commerce Act.
Dawes Act assigns land to Indians.

1890 Sherman Antitrust Act.
Sherman Silver Purchase Act.

1892 Homestead strike.
Populist Party formed.

1893 Sherman Silver Purchase Act repealed.

1894 Pullman strike.

1900 United States goes on gold standard.

Review Questions

1. (a) Why was the trans-Mississippi West the last region of the continental United States to be opened to white settlement? (b) What different groups moved into that region during the 1800's? (c) What conditions attracted each group?

2. (a) Why were the Indians who lived in the Great Plains unable to stem the tide of white settlers? (b) What Indian policies did the federal government enact in the years after the Civil War? (c) What was the effect of those policies on the Indians?

3. (a) What factors contributed to the rapid industrial growth experienced by the United States after the Civil War? (b) How did the business activities of Andrew Carnegie and John D. Rockefeller reflect some of the changes in the ways Americans conducted business during this period? (c) What effect did industrial growth have on America's cities?

4. (a) What factors contributed to the building of America's railroads? (b) Why were railroads important to industrialists? (c) To average citizens?

5. How did inventions in the post-Civil War period play a part in the growth of American industry?

6. (a) Why did an increasing number of immigrants come to the United States after the Civil War? (b) Why and how did some native-born Americans oppose this "new" immigration? (c) To what extent was immigration restricted during this period?

7. (a) With the rise of big business, what new relationship grew up between workers and their employers? (b) In what ways did working people seek to change their working conditions, and what changes did they demand? (c) What obstacles did labor unions encounter?

8. (a) Why did civil service reform, tariff reduction, and free silver become important national issues in the period after the Civil War? (b) What was the fate of each of those issues by 1900?

9. (a) What problems did farmers face in the late 1800's? (b) What actions did farmers take to solve those problems? (c) How successful were they?

Projects

1. On an outline map of the United States write in the date of admission for those states that joined the Union as a result of the settlement of the trans-Mississippi West. Also, illustrate what brought settlers into each new state after the Civil War.

2. Find out more about life on the Great Plains in general and about the role of pioneer women in particular by reading the writings of one or more of the following authors: (a) Hamlin Garland, (b) O. E. Rölvaag, (c) Willa Cather, (d) Laura Ingalls Wilder. Select one or more descriptive passages to read to the class. Tell how this and other passages have contributed to your understanding of ways of living on the Plains.

3. Submit an imaginary application to the United States Patent Office for a patent on one of the inventions described in this unit. On the application form name the invention and how it works. Also briefly describe the usefulness of the invention and its anticipated effect on American life. Read your patent application to the class.

4. Write an essay on the topic "The post-Civil War period was a time of political corruption, ignored issues, and hard times for most Americans." You may either agree or disagree with this statement, but be sure to support your position with evidence.

5. Create a set of five handbills in which you illustrate some of the demands of farmers in the late 1800's. On these handbills include pictures, slogans, and other information that shows the determination of farmers to solve their problems.

6. Make a bulletin-board display that depicts American society in the year 1900. Your display should illustrate significant changes in American ways of living and working in the period after the Civil War.

CRUSADING AT HOME AND ABROAD

1880 – 1920

We must make up our minds that, whether we like it or not, we are a great people and must play a great part in the world.

THEODORE ROOSEVELT, 1910

A Force in the World

1880 – 1900

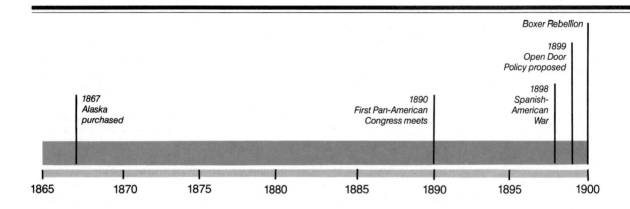

Boxer Rebellion

1899
Open Door
Policy proposed

1867
Alaska
purchased

1890
First Pan-American
Congress meets

1898
Spanish-
American
War

1865   1870   1875   1880   1885   1890   1895   1900

CHAPTER OUTLINE

1. Americans begin to look beyond their borders.

2. Interest in expansion grows.

3. The United States fights a war with Spain.

During the 1870's and 1880's, most Americans had little interest in foreign affairs. They were absorbed with such domestic matters as reconstruction, the dazzling changes in the look and behavior of the nation, and the boundless physical exertion required in developing the West. The Presidents, furthermore, reflected the habit Americans had acquired of knowing little about other countries. From Lincoln until the end of the century, no Chief Executive had ever traveled abroad before taking office.

America, nevertheless, was being drawn slowly into world politics. The Atlantic cable, made permanent in 1866, enabled news from Europe to be transmitted instantaneously. To follow the course of diplomatic and military events no longer required waiting for the next ship to arrive. Moreover, there was no escaping the fact that the world was growing smaller. Steamships, which had begun crossing the Atlantic in the unheard-of time of ten days in 1850, were coming across the water in the 1880's in seven days. By 1900, they made the trip in five and a half days.

The United States finally began to recognize its interest in helping maintain peace among nations. Not only did foreign trade depend upon world peace, but shortened distances were putting Europe's international troubles — and shortly those of other continents — close to America's backyard. By the 1890's, Americans would look "outward" and the United States would become active in foreign affairs.

1 Americans Begin to Look Beyond Their Borders

Even though Americans as a whole gave little thought to the world outside, the United States was involved continually in diplomacy abroad. Immediately following the Civil War, it carried on delicate negotiations that resulted in overseas expansion.

THE BEGINNINGS OF EXPANSION

The United States seeks to buy islands in the Caribbean. The acts of marauding Confederate cruisers during the Civil War had convinced many officials that the United States should have naval bases in the Caribbean. As a result, Secretary of State William H. Seward in 1865 asked Denmark to sell the United States the Danish West Indies. Following a favorable vote by the inhabitants of the islands, Denmark agreed to terms.

The treaty had scarcely been signed when the islands were ravaged in rapid succession by an earthquake, a hurricane, and a tidal wave. Seward was roundly assailed for having made such a foolish deal. The navy, furthermore, had by now fallen into disuse, and it had no need for bases outside the country. The House of Representatives humiliated Seward by refusing to vote the money to complete the sale. When General Grant became President, he put the treaty aside. The islands would remain Denmark's until 1917 when a new set of circumstances led to their purchase by the United States.

Seward was also eager to obtain Samaná Bay in the Dominican Republic, offering in 1868 to pay $2 million for it. The Dominican government replied by inviting the United States to buy the entire island! Although President Johnson recommended that Congress accept the offer, it was rejected. Later, President Grant wished to go ahead with the arrangement, but his Secretary of State, Hamilton Fish, opposed it. Still, a treaty of annexation was submitted to the Senate. It ran into unshakeable opposition from the chairman of the Senate Foreign Relations Committee, Charles Sumner. To Sumner, the deal looked like a scheme to

Ships from the United States Navy paraded on the Hudson River in 1899. Naval strength was instrumental in the spread of American influence in the late 1800's.

enrich some of Grant's White House staff and various corrupt Dominican politicians. In Sumner's view, the United States would do better by backing a free confederation of the West Indian islands, where the "black race should predominate" under American protection. After the treaty failed, Grant was so angry — he had once believed he had Sumner's support — that for a long time whenever he passed Sumner's house in Washington, he shook his fist at it.

Seward purchases Alaska. Seward's expansionist ideas were grand in scope. The Secretary envisioned the annexation of Haiti, as well as of various Spanish and French islands in the Caribbean. As his gaze swept further, he could see the United States purchasing Iceland and Greenland and annexing Hawaii.

Seward's ambitious ideas would never be fully realized, but in 1867 he seized an opportunity to extend America's frontiers by purchasing Alaska from Russia. The Russians had feared that if war ever broke out in Europe, Britain might use the opportunity to take over this territory, then known as Russian America. Only a few years earlier, furthermore, the governor of Siberia (the Russian domain in Asia) had warned the czar, "The ultimate rule of the United States over the whole of [North] America is so natural that we will sooner or later have to pull back from there." When the Russians let it be known that they were interested in selling Alaska, Seward was eager to negotiate. He drew up a treaty by which the United States agreed to pay Russia $7,200,000 for the vast territory. Word that Russia had accepted Seward's terms arrived on the newly laid Atlantic cable.

Alaska contained almost 600,000 square miles — twice the size of Texas. Many people ignorantly regarded the territory as worthless. Some members of Congress ridiculed the proposed purchase as "Seward's Folly" and, more playfully, as "Frigidia" and "Walrussia." Charles Sumner, however, came to Seward's side. Sumner argued that Alaska's rich resources were necessary for America's future development. Believing that the purchase of Alaska could be com-

pared with the purchase of Louisiana, Sumner saw the following significance: "One by one they have retired, first France, then Spain, then France again; and now Russia; all giving way to the absorbing unity which is declared in the national motto, *E Pluribus Unum*."[1] The treaty transferring Alaska was ratified by the Senate on April 9, 1867, by a vote of 37 to 2.

The United States watches the situation in Cuba. The Spanish colony of Cuba was high on Seward's list of places to be acquired. Because slavery still existed there, however, the Radical Republicans in control of Congress would not hear of any scheme to take it over. Still, because France and Britain had an active interest in Cuba as the "world's sugar bowl," the United States felt it must keep a watchful eye on the island. Located on an approach to the Gulf of Mexico, Cuba could become a threatening base if it fell into the wrong hands.

In 1868, when a rebellion broke out in Cuba, officials in Washington were tempted to intervene, but held back. A few years later, in 1873, a Spanish naval vessel captured a rebel ship, the *Virginius*, off the Cuban coast. Fifty-three passengers, some of them United States citizens, were taken ashore and shot as "pirates." The American outcry could have led to war, but the United States accepted an apology and a money indemnity. In time, Spain put down the rebellion, and abolished slavery. Cuba, nevertheless, remained a potential trouble spot in the Caribbean, for Spain's presence was a standing invitation to Americans to intervene there.

The United States becomes interested in Asia and the Pacific islands. Americans had long sought a toehold in Asia too. The annexation of Alaska, bordering on the northern Pacific, gave fresh life to the notion of expanded trade with Asian peoples. Japan, for instance, had fascinated American merchants and seafarers ever since 1852, when Commodore Matthew C. Perry had set out

---

[1]This Latin phrase, meaning "out of many, one," appears on the seal of the United States.

with a naval expedition for the "Land of the Rising Sun." For two centuries, the rulers of this ancient empire had forbidden its people to have contact with foreigners. Received hesitantly by Japanese officials, Perry persuaded them in 1854 to sign a treaty highly favorable to the United States. The treaty ended Japan's seclusion by giving American traders access to Japanese ports.

Other Pacific islands also attracted American attention. In 1867, the year of the Alaska purchase, the United States annexed Midway Island (map, page 143), discovered a few years earlier by Americans. In 1878, the United States acquired a coaling station, Pago Pago, on Tutuila, one of the Samoa Islands. Germany and Great Britain were also active in Samoa and their rivalry led to serious squabbling. Finally, in 1899 the two European powers entered into an agreement with the United States. Germany received the islands of Western Samoa and the United States acquired what became known as American Samoa (map, page 143).

Interest in Hawaii develops. Hawaii's strategic importance had long been clear to Americans hoping for influence in the Pacific. As early as 1842, Daniel Webster, then Secretary of State, declared that the United States would not permit any other country to take over those islands, then independent. In 1849, French forces seized Honolulu but quickly pulled out when the United States protested.

Hawaii's place in American thinking loomed larger in the 1880's. The United States was engaged in rebuilding and modernizing its navy and expanding the range of naval operations. In 1887, America acquired from the Hawaiian monarchy the right to establish a coaling and repair station at Pearl Harbor, the magnificent land-locked harbor on the southern coast of the island of Oahu. The agreement was especially satisfying to American sugar planters, traders, and missionaries, already influential on the islands. This new tie with the United States strengthened the hope of

American interests in Hawaii included pineapple and sugar plantations. Owners of these plantations sought annexation in 1893 and finally won it in 1898.

these Americans that Hawaii would soon come under United States protection.

Hawaii is annexed. Matters came to a head in 1891 when Liliuokalani (lee-LEE-oo-oh-kah-LAH-nee) became queen of Hawaii. A forthright person, she was generally unfriendly to the American planters on the islands. Those settlers were already in an angry mood over the McKinley Tariff (page 111), which permitted *all* foreign sugar — not just sugar from Hawaii — to enter the United States duty-free.

Early in 1893, fearing that Queen "Lil" might rid the government of American influence, the planters staged a revolt against her. They toppled the queen from her throne and then quickly formed a provisional government.

Less than a month of Benjamin Harrison's administration was left when the President sent the Senate a treaty providing for the annexation of Hawaii. The treaty was still in the Senate when Grover Cleveland came to the White House. Cleveland was, in general, against the acquisition of colonies, and his sense of justice led him to withdraw the treaty. He declared himself "unalterably opposed to stealing territory, or of annexing a people against their consent." Moreover, he said, "The people of Hawaii do not favor annexation." Still, the only way to put the queen back in power was to use force against the Americans who had helped depose her. Democrats disappointed by Cleveland's position pointed out sarcastically that it was not their party's tradition to restore monarchs to their thrones.

Cleveland, unwilling to send troops, turned the Hawaiian question over to Congress, which did nothing about it for the next few years. Not until the United States went to war with Spain in 1898 did Congress approve a resolution annexing Hawaii.

STRENGTHENING THE MONROE DOCTRINE

The United States promotes Pan-Americanism. Ever since it was proclaimed in 1823, the Monroe Doctrine had been the cornerstone of American foreign policy. The United States had already invoked the Doctrine when France tried to install an Austrian archduke, Maximillian, as emperor of Mexico in 1864. Another kind of challenge to the Doctrine developed during the presidency of Rutherford B. Hayes. At that time a private French company was attempting to build a canal across the Isthmus of Panama. Many Americans were made uneasy by the enterprise, fearing that the French government itself might become involved in the Americas.

By the 1880's the United States was taking an even more active role in the Western Hemisphere. It tried to promote *Pan-Americanism* — that is, the spirit of economic and political cooperation among all American nations. The individual who deserves much credit for furthering this movement was Secretary of State James G. Blaine. Like most Americans of his era, Blaine knew little about international relations. He came to office at a time when the United States was just beginning to recognize the need for a trained corps of diplomats. His achievements, nonetheless, were impressive.

In Blaine's few months as Secretary under President Garfield in 1881, he made arrangements for a conference of representatives from all the American nations. The plans were canceled, however, after Garfield's assassination. When Blaine returned to the Department of State under President Harrison in 1889, the idea of a Pan-American Congress was renewed, and representatives of the American nations met in Washington, D.C., in 1890.

Blaine made a number of proposals at the conference. While he had general concern for the peace of Latin America, he also worried about the growth of European influence in that region. He was particularly troubled that British manufactured goods were widely sold there and that products from the United States often were not given a chance to compete. Blaine hoped to remedy the situation by a program to foster the unity of the Western Hemisphere. He called for an inter-American customs union, better transportation between North and South America, a uniform system of weights and measures, and even a common silver coin to be used in all the Americas.

Uncle Sam reminds European powers of the United States' policy by pointing to the Monroe Doctrine in this cartoon and warning, "That's a live wire, gentlemen."

The Pan-American Union is established. At the 1890 meeting, the delegates agreed to establish the Pan-American Union. The purpose of this organization was to encourage the exchange of information about the customs, laws, and trade of American countries. It also aimed to encourage economic, social, and cultural cooperation. Although few other concrete decisions came from the Pan-American gathering, some observers were optimistic that the Monroe Doctrine had passed "into a stage of higher development." They could foresee that Pan-Americanism would extend the principles of the Monroe Doctrine. Maintaining the peace and security of the hemisphere would become a shared responsibility. Most Latin American nations, however, remained distrustful of the United States.

The United States becomes involved in a boundary dispute. A dramatic example of the defense of the Monroe Doctrine was provided by the Venezuela boundary dispute of 1895. Ever since 1840 there had been disagreement over the dividing line between Venezuela and British Guiana (map, page 165). Whe Britain seemed to be extending its territorial claims in the mid-1880's, the United States, no less than Venezuela, was concerned. Was Britain violating the Monroe Doctrine as well as infringing on a neighbor's territory?

Anti-British feeling in the United States was especially high. Irish-Americans were helping keep it stirred up. Also, many people believed that British trade practices had caused the depression of 1893.

The Monroe Doctrine, it appeared, would have to be defended. Early in 1895, Congress asked President Cleveland to urge the British and Venezuelan governments to submit their boundary dispute to *arbitration,* that is, to have the dispute settled by a board of fair-minded, neutral persons. At the same time, a pamphlet entitled *British Aggression in Venezuela, or the Monroe Doctrine on Trial* was circulating in Washington and having noticeable influence. The title suggests its inflammatory contents.

Not long after the publication appeared, Cleveland appointed Richard Olney to be Secretary of State. A brusque, no-nonsense man, Olney took action. He sent a message to London in which he declared that if Britain seized the disputed territory by force, it would be violating the Monroe Doctrine. Olney assured the British that the United States would not sit idly by and watch the violation of a neighbor in the hemisphere. He recommended that they give up British Guiana altogether. Then Olney added words that infuriated not only Britons but most Latin Americans as well: "Today the United States is practically sovereign [supreme] on this continent." (By "this continent" he meant both of the Americas.) Olney's startling assertion of power was followed by an equally bold explanation. Said the Secretary, the United States' "infinite resources combined with its isolated position render it master of the situation and practically invulnerable as against any or all other powers."

Cleveland threatens war over Venezuela. The British rejected this assertion of American authority. They had never accepted the Monroe Doctrine in the first place. Now they said that even if they had accepted the Doctrine, it did not apply in this case. They could not see, furthermore, why they must entrust their interests in the Venezuela dispute to the United States.

President Cleveland was infuriated by the British response, describing himself as "mad clear through." Politically, he could not afford this type of rebuff, for Irish-Americans were staunch supporters of the Democratic Party. He believed, moreover, that Britain was not only violating the Monroe Doctrine but also bullying Venezuela — something that offended his sense of decency. Unless Britain accepted arbitration in the dispute, Cleveland said, the United States would use "every means in its power" to protect Venezuelan territory. Because the British were having even more serious difficulties in South Africa and because they feared that in a war with the United States they might lose Canada, they finally agreed to cooperate. The dispute was settled by arbitration in 1899.

The episode undoubtedly strengthened the Monroe Doctrine. The peaceful solution also marked the end of sniping between the United States and Great Britain. Never again would the British challenge America's dominant position in the Caribbean region.

SECTION REVIEW

1. Vocabulary: *Pan-Americanism, arbitration.*
2. (a) What efforts did William Seward make to buy islands in the Caribbean? (b) What were the results? (c) How did the United States purchase Alaska?
3. (a) What was the *Virginius* affair? (b) How was it resolved?
4. (a) Why did Americans become interested in Asia and the Pacific islands? (b) What Pacific islands did the United States acquire?
5. (a) What proposals did Blaine make to the first Pan-American Congress? (b) What was the outcome?
6. (a) What was the cause of the dispute between Britain and Venezuela in the 1890's? (b) How was the issue settled?

2 Interest in Expansion Grows

In spite of prodding by Seward and a handful of other expansionists, the United States, as we have seen, did not readily seize opportunities to acquire overseas territories. The celebration of the nation's one-hundredth birthday in 1876 had reminded the nation anew of how much they prized their independence. Most thinking Americans held political liberty to be so sacred that they believed it should not be denied to any people. Nevertheless, a number of factors were leading to an active interest in taking over territories far from home.

European powers set an example. The most important cause for the change in Americans' attitudes was the example Europe was providing. Since the 1870's the major countries there had been engaged in establishing overseas colonies. By the end of the century, European countries had taken control of much of Asia and Africa and most of the islands of the Pacific. Because Britain's colonies were situated on every continent and in time zones all around the world, its people boasted that "The sun never sets on the British Empire." Germans, deeply envious, believed they could explain the success of the British: "The Lord wouldn't trust them in the dark!"

Many Americans wanted to join in the lively competition for colonies in order to have a place among the mighty nations of the earth. Said Henry Cabot Lodge, a senator from Massachusetts and a leader of the American expansionists, "As one of the great nations of the world, the United States must not fall out of the line of march."

The United States reaches for new markets. The nation's industrial and agricultural growth also helped arouse interest in acquiring possessions. American industrialists and farmers were beginning to seek overseas markets for their products. Senator Albert J. Beveridge of Indiana recognized the economic profits that could be gained abroad. In a speech in 1898, he said:

> American factories are making more than the American people can use; American soil is producing more than they can consume. Fate has written our policy for us; the trade of the world must and shall be ours. We will establish trading posts throughout the world as distributing points for American products. We will cover the ocean with our merchant marine. We will build a navy to the measure of our greatness. Great colonies governing themselves, flying our flag and trading with us, will grow about our posts of trade.

New ideas gain popularity. Additional support for expansion came from writers and professors who believed in the racial superiority of white America. One of them was a historian, John Fiske, who taught at Harvard College. Another was a Congregational minister, Josiah Strong. Both of them wrote popular books in which they argued that among all living things there is a ceaseless "struggle for existence." Both believed that the principle of the "survival of the fittest," which biologists claimed to have found in the world of nature, also applied to the world of international politics.

In the competition among nations, Fiske and Strong asserted that the "English

In this cartoon, Uncle Sam is obviously pleased with United States expansion overseas, which many Americans in 1898 viewed as almost an obligation.

race" (by which they meant white, English-speaking peoples) had moral, intellectual, and technological superiority. Wrote Fiske, "The two great branches of the English race have the common mission of establishing throughout the larger part of the earth a higher civilization and more permanent political order than any that has gone before."

In his book *Our Country*, Strong wrote in 1885 of what the United States specifically could contribute to this task of dominating other peoples. The American nation, he was convinced, had inherited from Britain the energy and perseverance required "to spread itself over the earth." Other writers quickly added to this idea the notion that the United States had a divine obligation to hasten the fulfillment of its destiny as a colonizing power.

One of the most influential of the men who accepted this belief was John W. Burgess, a professor at Columbia College in New York. Burgess found it deplorable that "by far the larger part of the surface of the globe is inhabited by populations which have not succeeded in establishing civilized states." America, he believed, had a vital role to play in correcting this situation. He argued that the United States should acquire colonies in order to train people in the art of self-government. Failure to do so, he asserted, would be a "disregard of duty."

Theodore Roosevelt was influenced by Alfred T. Mahan's writings on naval power. In 1897, Roosevelt became Assistant Secretary of the Navy.

A new generation of political leaders urges expansion. A group of striving political leaders also spoke out for colonies. The most powerful of these advocates were Theodore Roosevelt of New York and two friends and associates — Senator Lodge and John Hay. They were men with deep roots in the nation's past, who claimed to speak for the future. Roosevelt belonged to the seventh generation of Roosevelts living in New York City. Lodge could relate how a grandfather of his as a young boy hid under a sideboard at home in order to watch George Washington, a guest of the family, eat breakfast. Hay, at the age of 23, had gone to Washington, D.C., from Indiana in 1861 to be a private secretary to Abraham Lincoln.

These up-and-coming leaders claimed to be irritated by both the industrialists' single-minded concern with making money and the ordinary politicians' careless disregard of public honor. They considered themselves, on the other hand, to be "well-born and intelligent men" who would direct the nation's attention toward noble ends. High on their list of goals were a clash of arms and the acquisition of colonies. Roosevelt wrote in 1895, "This country needs a war." He dismissed people willing to have "peace at any price"; with exasperation he identified them as "bankers, brokers, and Anglo-maniacs [lovers of England]." Hay, also favoring a "large policy" — which meant the conquest of distant peoples and territory — wrote to President McKinley that "the greatest destiny the world ever knew is ours."

Mahan favors a strong navy. Yet another person strongly urging the necessity of colonies was Captain Alfred Thayer Mahan. A magnetic teacher and a writer of rare gift, he preached that Americans needed colonies because the country had reached the limit of expansion. "In our infancy," Mahan wrote, "we bordered upon the Atlantic only; our youth carried our boundary to the Gulf of Mexico; today maturity sees us upon the Pacific." Regarding expansion as something needed by every vigorous country, he insisted that "whether they will it or no, Americans must now begin to look outward." Mahan called for a strong navy, a canal across the Isthmus of Panama, and the establishment of coaling stations and naval bases in the Caribbean and the Pacific.

Politicians took up Mahan's call. Lodge proclaimed in the Senate, "It is sea power which is essential to every splendid people." He added, "We have too great an inheritance to be trifled with. . . . It is ours to guard and extend." Acting on Mahan's advice and with broad support in Congress, administrations during the 1890's brought into being a modern navy. By 1900 the United States had the third largest fleet in the world.

A revolt breaks out in Cuba. The growing interest in foreign affairs and expansion could be seen in 1895 when a rebellion against Spanish rule broke out in Cuba. Steadily worsening economic conditions had made Cuba ripe for trouble. The island suffered badly in the depression of 1893. Then the tariff of 1894 had placed such a high duty on raw sugar that Cuba's ability to sell it in the United States was substantially reduced.

Many of the leaders of the Cuban revolt had lived or traveled in the United States. Because they admired America, they hoped to turn their homeland into a republic too. Their rallying cry was *"Cuba Libre!"* (meaning "A Free Cuba!").

The rebels, lacking sufficient arms to fight openly against the Spanish troops, resorted to guerrilla tactics. They set fire to villages, raided sugar plantations, and disrupted railroad lines. They reserved their harshest treatment for people who supported the Spanish authorities, not hesitating to execute them. Deep down, the Cuban revolutionaries did not believe they could oust the Spanish from the island. They hoped, rather, to win concessions by causing so much damage that the island's plantations and trade would be paralyzed.

To counter the insurgents, the Spanish adopted what they called a reconcentration policy, which meant forcing thousands of people out of their homes and into camps enclosed by barbed wire. Through this program, the rebels in the countryside were cut off from their civilian supporters. The reconcentration camps became places of unimaginable torment, with starvation and disease widespread. As many as 200,000 people had died in these camps by 1898.

Americans watched the events in Cuba with interest — and with increasing dismay. The desperate situation called forth their humanitarian instincts. They also sympathized with the effort to establish an independent republic. Some Americans, furthermore, had never forgotten the *Virginius* incident (page 128).

Newspapers inflame public opinion. The Cuban struggle was made to order for American newspapers. Catering to the tastes of their growing number of readers, the papers had become more and more sensational. In their columns, journalists could blow up the slightest international incident into a life-or-death crisis. The invention of the Linotype machine had made it possible to "break open" the front page of a newspaper and quickly replace a story with a new one fresh off the telegraph wire or cable. Improved methods of reproducing pictures made it possible to illustrate even ordinary stories and make them vivid and intimate.

Interest in the latest news was heightened by the keen competition for circulation among New York newspapers, which were widely copied throughout the country. The chief rivals were Joseph Pulitzer's New York *World* and William Randolph Hearst's New York *Morning Journal.* Both of these newspapers practiced what came to be called "yellow journalism." This meant that they casually took liberties with the truth and felt no need to provide balanced reporting. Yellow newspapers did not hesitate to fake the "news," either. Nevertheless, the theatrical character of yellow journalism — including exaggerated headlines, melodramatic cartoons and sketches, and gruesome crime stories — appealed to millions of readers.

In the Cuban struggle, Hearst early advocated American intervention on the side of the rebels. He also quickly saw the insurrection as useful in his contest with Pulitzer. Pulitzer, too, saw he could put the struggle to profitable use. Soon, the newspapers were vying with each other in presenting accounts of atrocities said to have been carried out by Spanish authorities. A favorite villain was Spain's commander in Cuba, General Weyler (or, as he came to be called in the press, "Butcher" Weyler).

In a short time, the newspapers were acting as if they had government authority. They sent "commissions" to meet with insurgent leaders and sometimes even to carry official messages from rebels in Cuba to those in the United States. They also assigned correspondents to the island to search out stories. Some of the reporters sent dispatches without ever visiting the areas they described. Hearst once sent the artist Frederic Remington to sketch the scenes of a battle. Remington, finding things quiet, wired the home office for instructions. Hearst is reported to have replied, "You furnish the pictures and I'll furnish the war."

McKinley tries to avoid war. President McKinley, who had personally known the horror of the American Civil War, was unwilling to become involved in the Cuban tangle. He expressed his hope that a new government in Spain would make the changes necessary to end the rebellion in Cuba. Throughout 1897 he practiced patience. He was pleased when Spain removed General Weyler and began a policy that was expected to bring peace to the island.

The New York newspapers, nevertheless, kept up their calls for American intervention. Hearst excited the country with the touching story of Evangelina Cisneros, a young Cuban who had voluntarily accompanied her father, a rebel, into imprisonment. Eventually she, too, was charged by the Spanish with antigovernment activities. The *Journal* reported, however, that her sole crime had been to resist the advances of a Spanish officer and that she was about to be shipped to a prison colony in Africa. The word went out from Hearst, "Enlist the women of America!" Well-known women responded swiftly. Mrs. Jefferson Davis appealed to the queen of Spain to release Evangelina Cisneros and turn her over to American women. Julia Ward Howe implored Pope Leo XIII to use his influence to make Spain show mercy. A petition to the Spanish government signed by 20,000 American women included many famous names: Julia Dent Grant, General Grant's widow; Nancy McKinley, the President's mother; and Mrs. Mark Hanna. The Spanish would have liked to release Miss Cisneros and silence the distressed Americans. To do so, however, would have seemed a surrender to pressure.

The *Journal*, displaying its impatience, sent one of its adventurous reporters to Cuba to rescue the young woman. He snatched her out of her cell by reaching down from a next-door rooftop, and rushed her to a waiting ship. She was soon in the United States, a heroine of the insurrection. The *Journal's* headline trumpeted: AN AMERICAN NEWSPAPER ACCOMPLISHES AT A SINGLE STROKE WHAT THE BEST EFFORTS OF DIPLOMACY FAILED UTTERLY TO BRING ABOUT IN MANY MONTHS. As congratulations poured in, the governor of Missouri

suggested to Hearst that he send 500 reporters to Cuba and liberate the island!

The De Lôme letter angers Americans. On February 9, 1898, the *Journal* published another scoop, a letter that the Spanish minister to the United States, Dupuy de Lôme, had sent a friend in Cuba. Intercepted by a rebel spy in the Havana post office, it was delivered to the *Journal* in New York.

The De Lôme letter created a fresh sensation. In it, the minister described McKinley as "a would-be politician who tries to leave a door open behind himself while keeping on good terms with the jingoes [war advocates] of his party." The *Journal's* headline exaggerated wildly the importance of the diplomat's unwise comment: THE WORST INSULT TO THE UNITED STATES IN ITS HISTORY. When De Lôme promptly resigned his post, the *Journal* published a cartoon showing an irate Uncle Sam snarling at the crestfallen Spaniard, "Git!" That the letter had been stolen and that much worse was being said about McKinley in the daily press were points few Americans seemed to recognize.

The "Maine" sinks. Six days after the De Lôme letter was published, a truly momentous event occurred. The battleship *Maine*, which had been sent by the United States to Havana harbor to protect American lives and property, was torn apart there by an explosion. In the inferno, 260 sailors perished, and many others were injured. The destruction of the *Maine* stunned the American people. The actual cause of the disaster will likely never be known. Recent investigations have concluded that in all probability the *Maine* was destroyed by an accident which took place inside the vessel.

From the start, most of the American press and public charged Spain with responsibility for the loss of the vessel. In the tidal wave of national anguish, the *World* screamed in a headline that it was sending its own divers to Havana to find out if the explosion had been caused by a bomb or a torpedo. The *Journal* already had an explanation: THE WARSHIP "MAINE" WAS SPLIT IN TWO BY AN ENEMY'S SECRET INFERNAL

Calls for American intervention in the Cuban revolt became more intense after the mysterious explosion of the United States battleship *Maine* in Havana harbor.

MACHINE. A popular song expressed the common judgment:

Spain, Spain, Spain!
You ought to be ashamed
For doing such a thing
As blowing up the *Maine*.

A new slogan — "Remember the Maine!" — swept the country.

The United States moves closer to war. The expansionists were for going to war against Spain. The most active of them was Theodore Roosevelt, now Assistant Secretary of the Navy. He was more and more irritated by McKinley's apparent reluctance to fight. Roosevelt wrote, "I would give anything if President McKinley would order the fleet to Havana tomorrow."

Roosevelt was using his boundless energy to make preparations for a war he was sure was coming. One day in February,

1898, when Secretary of the Navy John D. Long took the afternoon off, Roosevelt acted as if he were responsible for the Department of the Navy. He put himself in touch with important senior naval officers, redistributed the vessels of the fleet, and placed orders for ammunition. Moreover, Long later wrote, the Assistant Secretary sent "messages to Congress for immediate legislation authorizing the enlistment of an unlimited number of seamen." To Commodore George Dewey, commander of the Pacific fleet (then based in Hong Kong), Roosevelt sent a fateful cable. In the event of war, Roosevelt ordered, Dewey's duty would be to sail to the Philippine Islands, a possession of Spain, and see to it that the Spanish naval squadron did not get away.

President McKinley was in the painful position of having a war forced upon him that he did not want. He called in a group

The Examiner.

Circulation of The Examiner
Easter Sunday
115,510 Gross

THE EXAMINER was delivered
at more than 40,000 homes in
San Francisco yesterday. There
are about 48,000 inhabitants in San Francisco.

VOL. LXVI. SAN FRANCISCO, TUESDAY MORNING, APRIL 12, 1898. NO. 102.

AMERICANS LOOK TO CONGRESS TO SAVE THE NATION'S HONOR.

THE HOUR HAS COME.

Now It Is for Congress to Declare Freedom for Cuba.

MCKINLEY FAILS IN PURPOSE

His Message Does Not Fulfill Promises of Intentions That Were Humane.

BY EX-SENATOR JOHN J. INGALLS.

EX-SENATOR JOHN J. INGALLS.

CONGRESS MAY DECLARE WAR.

Determination to Save the Nation From a Humiliating Position.

Elkins and Other Friends of the Administration Are Scheming to Block Action.

MR. BENNETT'S PAPER.

Fierce Words in the European Edition of the New York "Herald."

ALL DEVOLVES UPON CONGRESS.

The Legislators Must Extricate the Nation From Its Difficulty.

SUBMARINE MINES PLANTED IN HAVANA HARBOR.

On April 12, 1898, the *Examiner*, a San Francisco newspaper, urged Congress to declare war on Spain.

of congressmen and told them, "I must have money to get ready for war. I am doing everything possible to prevent war, but it must come and we are not prepared for war." Early in March, Congress unanimously passed a bill providing $50 million for "national defense."

The news of the congressional action took the Spanish by surprise. It also intimidated them. As the United States minister there reported, "To appropriate fifty millions out of money in the Treasury, without borrowing a cent, demonstrates wealth and power. Even Spain can see this."

The United States declares war on Spain. On April 9, 1898, the Spanish, under extreme pressure from the United States, agreed to an armistice in Cuba. In Washington, the ambassadors of six European powers called upon President McKinley to halt the preparations for war. In spite of the news of the armistice, McKinley finally asked Congress to declare war on Spain. He had spent many a sleepless night in coming to his decision, but the pressure to declare

war was too great. Roosevelt, fretful over what he considered to be foot-dragging, told a friend that McKinley had actually prepared two messages for Congress — "one for war and one for peace, and he doesn't know which one to send in!"

The United States formally declared war on Spain on April 25, 1898. A few days earlier, Congress had recognized Cuba's independence and had given McKinley the authority to use force to drive the Spanish from the island. An amendment to the war resolution was proposed by Senator Henry M. Teller of Colorado. Approved by Congress, the Teller Amendment stated that when the fighting in Cuba was over, the United States would "leave the government and control of the island to its people."

SECTION REVIEW

1. (a) Why did interest in overseas expansion grow in the late 1800's? (b) How did this attitude affect the navy?
2. (a) Why was the Cuban revolt of interest to Americans? (b) What role did newspapers take in the debate over American intervention?
3. (a) What events led to the outbreak of war between the United States and Spain? (b) What was the Teller Amendment?

3 The United States Fights a War with Spain

The long-awaited war with Spain was fought with purpose and bravery — and not a little awkwardness resulting from inexperience. The navy was ready to move swiftly, but the army was unprepared for war.

Dewey defeats the Spanish fleet at Manila. In accordance with instructions, Commodore Dewey had been waiting in Hong Kong for news of the war declaration. On April 27, he received orders to proceed to the Philippines. British officers whom Dewey knew believed that the Americans were headed toward certain defeat. Their view, Dewey later wrote, was that the Americans were "a fine set of fellows, but unhappily we shall never see them again."

Dewey at Manila Bay

The naval battle at Manila Bay in 1898 made Commodore George Dewey a national hero and proved the worth of America's navy. In this passage from his autobiography, Dewey described the victory at Manila Bay, including the issuing of his famous order to Charles Gridley, captain of the flagship *Olympia*.

Commodore Dewey

The misty haze of the tropical dawn had hardly risen when at 5:15, at long range, the Spanish forts and squadron opened fire. Our course was not one leading directly toward the enemy, but a converging one, keeping him on our starboard bow. Our speed was eight knots and our converging course and ever-varying position must have confused the Spanish gunners. My assumption that the Spanish fire would be hasty and inaccurate proved correct.

So far as I could see, none of our ships was suffering any damage, while, in view of my limited ammunition supply, it was my plan not to open fire until we were within effective range, and then to fire as rapidly as possible with all our guns.

At 5:40, when we were within a distance of 5,000 yards (two and one half miles), I turned to Captain Gridley and said: "You may fire when you are ready, Gridley."

. . . Gridley took his station . . . and gave the order to the battery. The very first gun to speak was an 8-inch from the forward turret of the *Olympia*, and this was the signal for all other ships to join the action. . . .

There was no cessation in the rapidity of fire maintained by our whole squadron, and the effect of its concentration, owing to the fact that our ships were kept so close together, was smothering, particularly upon the two largest [Spanish] ships, the *Reina Cristina* and *Castilla*. . . .

Victory was ours, though we did not know it. Owing to the smoke over the Spanish squadron, there was no visible signs of the execution wrought by our guns. . . . It was a most anxious moment for me. So far as I could see, the Spanish squadron was as intact as ours. I had reason to believe that their supply of ammunition was as ample as ours was limited.

Therefore, I decided to withdraw temporarily from action for a redistribution of ammunition if necessary. . . . But even as we were steaming out of range, the distress of the Spanish ships became evident. Some of them were perceived to be on fire and others were seeking protection behind a point. . . . Moreover, the Spanish fire, with the exception of the Manila batteries, to which we had paid little attention, had ceased entirely. It was clear that we did not need a very large supply of ammunition to finish our morning's task.

At midnight on April 30, 1898, Dewey's ships sailed into Manila harbor. For unexplained reasons, the Spanish allowed them to pass unchallenged. As the sun rose, Dewey confronted the Spanish fleet. Less than two hours later, the entire Spanish naval force of ten ships had been sunk or destroyed, and the American squadron was pounding the Spanish shore batteries. By sunset, Dewey's ships were anchored off the city of Manila as safely as if it were peacetime. Their brass bands played "the usual evening concert."

When news of the victory at Manila arrived in Washington, the nation went wild with joy. Dewey became an instant hero. A popular jingle began:

Oh, Dewey was the morning
Upon the first of May,
And Dewey was the admiral
Down in Manila Bay. . . .

To take the city itself, Dewey waited for help from an American army unit. Late in July a force of 11,000 troops under General Lesley Merritt arrived. By the middle of August, after light resistance, Spanish forces had surrendered Manila to the Americans and to Filipino guerrillas led by Emilio Aguinaldo (ah-gwee-NAHL-doh).

The American fleet blockades Santiago. Meanwhile, the war was also being fought in the Caribbean. Before troops could be sent to Cuba, the American navy was given the task of controlling the seas. Its orders were to find and destroy the Spanish fleet of Admiral Cervera (sair-VAY-rah), which had left the Cape Verde Islands for Cuba soon after the declaration of war. Many Americans living along the Atlantic coast were in a panic, fearing that they were about to be hammered by Cervera's guns. Rear Admiral William T. Sampson, commander of the American Atlantic fleet, lay in wait for Cervera in the Caribbean. Off the coast of Virginia, Commodore Winfield Scott Schley patroled with an American squadron, ready to cut off the Spaniards if they came into his path.

The Spanish fleet managed to slip past the Americans and sail safely into the Cuban port of Santiago. Admiral Sampson, however, quickly bottled up Cervera by blockading the harbor.

Land forces are sent to Cuba. Meanwhile, an American expeditionary force of 17,000 regulars and volunteers had been assembled at Tampa, Florida. These troops were under the overall command of General William R. Shafter. Shafter weighed 300 pounds — not perfect condition for fighting a demanding

campaign in tropical heat, but made to order for mischievous cartoonists.

Included among Shafter's officers was General Joseph ("Fighting Joe") Wheeler. Now 61 years old, the former Confederate cavalry commander was wearing once again the Union blue — a symbol of the reconciliation between the North and South. Also among Shafter's troops was a volunteer unit known as the Rough Riders. Although led by Colonel Leonard Wood, the Rough Riders' second-in-command drew far more attention than Wood. He was Lieutenant Colonel Theodore Roosevelt, who had left Washington for the thick of the battle.

The training of the American land forces had been inadequate and their embarkation from Tampa was a model of confusion. The single railroad line to the docks at Tampa was insuffient for handling a modern army. Black troops suffered the additional indignity of being refused service in local restaurants. They would have remained unfed if they had not been able to buy food from street vendors.

On June 14, 1898, the troops, including the Rough Riders, set sail for Cuba. Wearing woolen uniforms, they were ill-clad for a war in the tropics. The broiling heat on the five-and-a-half-day sea journey to Cuba added to their discomfort. Still, they were eager to fight. They sang a favorite tune, "Hot Time in the Old Town Tonight," which Theodore Roosevelt would later turn into a political campaign song.

The United States defeats Spain in the Caribbean. Landing just east of Santiago, the American troops went into action almost immediately. Their goal was to capture that city, install guns on the heights overlooking the harbor, and pound Cervera's fleet below. On the morning of June 24, the land battle began.

Two fortified positions outside of Santiago blocked the Americans' advance. One was at the village of El Caney. Spanish sharpshooters had set themselves up in the church where Cortés was said to have prayed the night he went forth to conquer Mexico. Only after a savage, eight-hour battle did the Americans gain control of El Caney.

The volunteers known as the Rough Riders charge up San Juan Hill in this famous painting by Frederic Remington, who was sent to Cuba by newspaperman Hearst.

After El Caney fell, the Americans pushed on to San Juan Hill. Again, the outnumbered Spanish forces put up stiff resistance. Their sharpshooters pinned down 8,000 Americans for hours. At one point a force of Rough Riders under Colonel Roosevelt found itself under heavy fire. Roosevelt's men, aided by two regiments of black soldiers, worked their way through tall grass to the top of San Juan Hill. Roosevelt fought with a bravado equal to his warlike words before the war. Barely able to see without his glasses, he went into battle with a dozen pairs sewn in the lining of his uniform — in case a few should get shot off!

The victories at El Caney and San Juan Hill were later described by a young lieutenant named John J. Pershing: "White regiments, black regiments, regulars and Rough Riders, representing the young manhood of the North and the South, fought shoulder to shoulder, unmindful of color, . . . and mindful only of their common duty as Americans." Having taken the heights dominating Santiago, the Americans could now bring the city and the Spanish fleet under direct fire from strategic artillery positions.

Two days after San Juan Hill fell to the Americans, Admiral Cervera, under instructions not to surrender his ships, made a desperate attempt to escape into the open sea. July 3 was a Sunday, and the church bells were sounding when Cervera ordered the bugle blown for the beginning of the battle. Cervera guessed the outcome, for he nodded knowingly when an aide whispered "Poor Spain!" as the grave gamble began.

In a battle lasting just four hours, the technical superiority of the American fleet asserted itself. The Spanish ships were destroyed. Admiral Sampson cabled Washington, "The fleet under my command offers the nation as a Fourth of July present the whole of Cervera's fleet." Unable without their ships to reinforce their troops in Cuba, the Spanish realized they had been defeated. Santiago surrendered on July 17, 1898. The Spanish flag — first brought to the city in 1513 — was hauled down for the last time. Spanish resistance in Cuba was now at an end.

After the surrender of Santiago, General Nelson A. Miles led an American force to the Spanish island of Puerto Rico. The

141

RTO RICO, CLOSE OF THE WAR

General Miles and his forces met little resistance as they crossed Puerto Rico. Their march ended when an armistice was signed on August 12, 1898.

troops took Puerto Rico without significant opposition. Meanwhile, as America celebrated its victory over Cervera, a small detachment from the Philippines landed on Wake Island, which the United States formally occupied in 1899.

Peace brings the United States new responsibilities. After its defeats in the Caribbean and the Pacific, Spain sued for peace. On August 12, 1898, the day before Manila fell, an armistice was arranged.

As the Spanish withdrew from their possessions in the Caribbean and the Pacific, the world recognized that the United States had become a great power. A French politician could see that America had been transformed. He explained, "When a people have interests everywhere, they are called upon to involve themselves in everything. The United States intervenes thus in the affairs of the universe. It is seated at the table where the great game is played, and it cannot leave it."

Under the terms of the Treaty of Paris, signed on December 10, 1898, Spain granted Cuba its independence and ceded the Philippine Islands, Guam, and Puerto Rico to the United States. The United States agreed to pay $20 million to Spain for the Philippines.

Annexation of the Philippines presents a problem. Following the peace treaty, the United States faced the question of what to do with the new possessions. President McKinley admitted that when he first heard of the Philippines, he could not have said within 2,000 miles where they were located. Now he had to decide whether to keep the islands or not.

McKinley agonized over the fateful decision on the Philippines. At one point he said, "If old Dewey had just sailed away when he smashed the Spanish fleet, what a lot of trouble he would have saved us." Finally the President decided, as he told a group of clergymen, that the United States must take control of the islands in order "to educate the Filipinos, and uplift and civilize and Christianize them."[2] Most members of Congress supported the decision and, indeed, would have resisted efforts to abandon the islands. Senator Beveridge spoke for the new generation of national leaders: "We cannot fly from our world duties. . . . We cannot retreat from any soil where Providence has unfurled our banner; it is ours to save that soil for liberty and civilization."

---

[2]McKinley apparently did not know that most Filipinos were Roman Catholics.

Filipinos resist American rule. In spite of the high motives of McKinley and Beveridge, many Filipinos were not satisfied to exchange Spanish domination for American rule. A revolutionary group had arisen earlier in the Philippines under the leadership of Emilio Aguinaldo. At the time that he had joined his forces with the Americans to defeat Spain (page 140), Aguinaldo believed he had assurances that the United States would not claim the Philippines at the end of the struggle. When the United States decided to keep the islands, a second war broke out — in February, 1899. Called the Philippine Insurrection, it did not formally end until July 4, 1902. United States soldiers suffered over 7,000 casualties, while Aguinaldo's forces lost between 16,000 and 20,000 men. Possibly a quarter of a million civilians also died in the struggle. Many were victims of disease and starvation as well as of violence.

By 1900, American expansionists had succeeded in extending United States influence beyond the boundaries of the continent. American possessions included Puerto Rico and many islands in the Pacific Ocean.

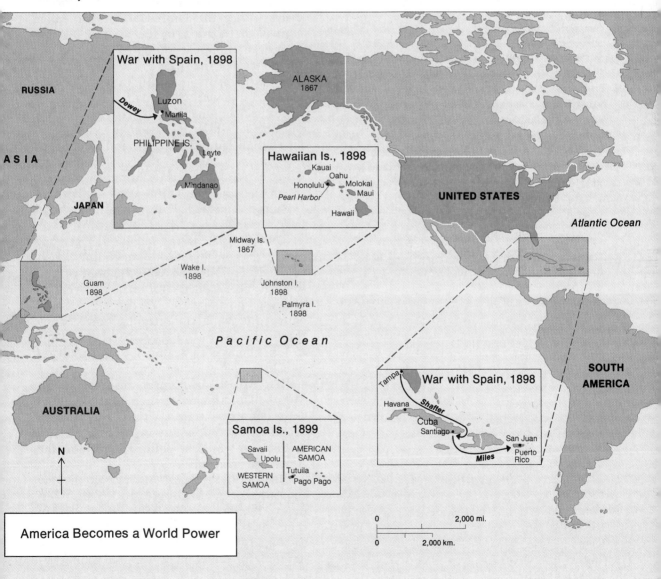

America Becomes a World Power

Imperialism becomes a campaign issue in 1900. Americans who had opposed annexing the Philippines pointed to the insurrection on the islands as one of the dangers of following a policy of *imperialism* — the establishment of political or economic control over other peoples. William Jennings Bryan told an audience in Omaha, "Our guns destroyed a Spanish fleet but can they destroy that self-evident truth, that governments derive their just powers, not from superior force, but from the consent of the governed?" Many Americans agreed with these thoughts, contending that the highest ideals of the nation had been violated when it decided to have an empire.

A group opposing the possession of colonies formed the Anti-Imperialist League in Boston in 1898. By 1900 the League claimed to have 30,000 members and over 500,000 contributors. Its chief financial supporter was Andrew Carnegie. Members of the League also included Carl Schurz, Samuel Gompers, and Jane Addams. "We regret," the League declared, "that it has become necessary in the land of Washington and Lincoln to reaffirm that all men, of whatever race or color, are entitled to life, liberty, and the pursuit of happiness."

Troops bearing the colors of the United States helped to end the Boxer Rebellion that raged in China.

In 1900, Bryan, again nominated for the presidency by the Democrats, made an issue of anti-imperialism. The party platform, in words echoing Lincoln's, stated, "No nation can long endure half republic and half empire." The Republicans renominated McKinley, now a victorious war President. His running mate was Theodore Roosevelt, recently elected governor of New York. The Republican ticket won overwhelmingly, mostly because McKinley was a symbol of the triumph over Spain, but also because he promised to maintain "the full dinner pail" for every worker.

The United States urges equal treatment in China. Once the United States had taken control of territory in the western Pacific, American diplomats became embroiled in the politics of that part of the world. China was the focus of much diplomatic activity. Crushed in a war with Japan in 1894–1895, China seemed unable to defend itself. After the defeat, China had been forced to give Japan the island of Formosa and to agree to the independence of Korea. Recognizing China's weakness, the European powers began to force the Chinese to grant them "spheres of influence" in which they would have special trade privileges.

The British were deeply alarmed by what they considered the impending break-up of China. They disliked the policy of allowing special rights for major powers in Chinese port cities, advocating instead equal commercial opportunity for all. When the British asked the United States in 1898 to join them in opposing special privileges in China, Americans were reminded of a similar British offer made just before the Monroe Doctrine was issued. Once again — as in Monroe's time — the United States decided to act alone, knowing that eventually Britain would be obliged to support the American position.

In 1899, Secretary of State John Hay sent almost identical notes to Britain, Germany, Russia, France, Italy, and Japan. In them he set forth what became known as the Open Door Policy. Hay asked the other nations for assurances that all countries would "enjoy perfect equality of treatment for their commerce and navigation" in China. Although most of the answers were noncommittal, Hay went ahead and announced that the major powers had approved the Open Door Policy.

The Chinese rebel against foreign interference. The Chinese people understandably resented the efforts of foreign powers to carve up their country. A patriotic organization called the "Society of the Righteous and Harmonious Fists" (shortened, by Westerners, to "Boxers") began a movement to drive all foreigners from China. In a campaign of violence in 1900, the Boxers attacked western missionaries and then seized parts of Peking, the capital city. Foreigners took refuge in the British legation there.

Widespread fear existed in the West that all foreigners in Peking would be killed. At the same time, the United States was afraid that if the European countries sent troops to crush the rebellion, they might also take over more Chinese territory. Concerned, Hay in July, 1900, sent a new note to the powers of Europe. In it, he declared that America supported a policy of seeking to preserve China's territorial unity. The nations replied that they accepted this position of the United States as desirable.

In the end, the siege of Peking was lifted by a joint expedition of western troops — 2,500 of whom were American. The expedition freed the foreigners and forced the Chinese government to pay large sums of money for damages caused by the uprising.

———

As the nineteenth century passed into history, Americans were sure they stood on the threshold of such progress and prosperity as no people had ever enjoyed. The *New York Times* was pleased to point out that the United States was helping to bring "the regenerating forces of popular government to the uttermost parts of the earth." Few people could have guessed, however, that

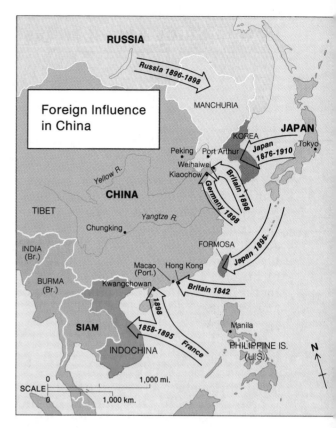

China's government in the late 1800's was too weak to resist foreign powers. The Open Door Policy was the American diplomatic response to this situation.

the energies unleashed by the Spanish-American War could also be harnessed for a peaceful remaking of life at home.

SECTION REVIEW

1. Vocabulary: *imperialism.*
2. (a) Where did fighting take place during the Spanish-American War? (b) What were the results of the fighting?
3. What territory did the United States gain in 1898 as a result of the Treaty of Paris?
4. (a) What arguments were put forward by Americans who supported annexation of the Philippines? (b) What arguments were put forward by opponents? (c) What was the reaction on the part of many Filipinos? (d) How did the election of 1900 reveal the thinking of American voters on the subject of expansion?
5. (a) Why did the United States propose the Open Door Policy in China? (b) What was the Boxer Rebellion? (c) How was it suppressed?

Using Historical Sources

All history books depend on a variety of sources for the information they contain. No matter what period or subject is being covered, historians must do research to assemble the details and gain the insights that, when put together, constitute a work of history. The sources available to historians are of two types — primary sources and secondary sources.

Primary Sources

The most common kind of *primary source* is a document that was written at the time of the event it describes. Diaries, letters, newspapers, public records, and official documents are all primary sources. Graphic representations such as paintings, maps, architectural plans, and political cartoons can also be primary sources.

The following cable, sent by Assistant Secretary of the Navy Theodore Roosevelt to Commodore George Dewey, is an example of a primary source. Read the message and then answer the questions that follow.

Washington, February 25, 1898

Dewey, Hong Kong:

Order the squadron . . . to Hong Kong. Keep full of coal. In the event of declaration of war with Spain, your duty will be to see that the Spanish squadron does not leave the Asiatic coast, and then offensive operations in the Philippine Islands. . . .

Roosevelt

What was the purpose of Roosevelt's message to Dewey? In the event of war with Spain, what was Dewey ordered to do? Why can this cable be considered a primary source?

Secondary Sources

All historical sources that are not first-hand accounts are classified as *secondary sources*. Biographies, history books, accounts in reference books, and graphic illustrations done at a later time by someone who was not an eyewitness are all examples of secondary sources.

The following passage, written by historian Richard Hofstadter, in *The Age of Reform* (1955), is an example of a secondary source. Read the passage and then answer the questions that follow.

The Spanish-American War, a triumph of the new journalism, was nowhere fought more brilliantly than in the columns of the newspapers, and it was covered by a battery of reporters numerous enough . . . to be used in an emergency as military reinforcements. As the reporter's job rose in status . . . more and more young men with serious literary aspirations were attracted to it. . . . These men brought to the journalistic life some of the ideals, the larger interests, and the sense of public responsibility of men of culture.

Where, according to Hofstadter, was the Spanish-American War brilliantly fought? What did the new class of reporter bring to journalism? Why can this passage be considered a secondary source?

Using Source Material

When reading primary and secondary sources, you should ask yourself questions that will help you evaluate the information. Are the facts presented accurately? Do the sources depend heavily on fact or on opinion? Is there bias in the source? Is the author using figurative language rather than stating directly the facts of a situation? Let us examine each of these points.

Establishing accuracy of facts. In reading both primary and secondary sources, you should be concerned about the accuracy of factual material. The best way to check facts is to consult a number of established sources and compare how the facts in question are stated. If all the sources present the facts in the same manner, you can be reasonably sure they are correct.

Distinguishing fact from opinion. Statements of fact can be checked for accuracy. Statements of opinion represent the personal views of an individual. The quotation by Henry Cabot Lodge on page 134 that "It is sea power which is essential to every splendid people," is a statement of opinion, not fact. Lodge was expressing his own preference for a strong navy. Many people would disagree with his emphasis on the need for every great nation to have a navy.

Recognizing bias. A source expresses bias when the author has an established preference that prevents impartial judgment. The statement by John Fiske on page 133 in which he describes the worldwide civilizing mission of the English race is an example of bias. Fiske's views were influenced by his belief in the racial superiority of white, English-speaking people. All statements by Fiske, therefore, should be read with this bias in mind.

Understanding figurative language. You will often encounter figurative language in your reading of source material. Rather than describe something directly, an author may use word images to make a point. Figurative language adds color and expression to source material, but you must read it carefully to understand fully the information being presented.

Check Your Skill

Use the information presented on these pages to answer the following questions.

1. What is a primary source?
2. What are some examples of secondary sources?
3. How can you check the accuracy of facts in source material?
4. Why is it important to distinguish between fact and opinion when reading source material?
5. What is the definition of bias?
6. Why do some authors of source material use figurative language?

Apply Your Skill

Use the readings for Chapter 5 on pages 478–483 to answer the following questions.

1. In the first selection, find three instances where Alfred Mahan states an opinion.
2. In the second selection, what bias is evident in the editorial on the Cuban rebellion?
3. Is the picture of Mark Twain on page 482 a primary or secondary source? Explain your answer.
4. Identify instances where Theodore Roosevelt, the author of the fifth selection, uses figurative language to make his point.

Chapter 5 Review

Summary

In the years after the Civil War, the United States gradually took on new international responsibilities. The change began slowly when Congress, in 1867, approved a treaty purchasing the vast territory of Alaska from Russia. Midway Island was annexed in that same year, while a coaling station on Tutuila was acquired in 1878. The influence of American traders, sugar planters, and missionaries on Hawaii, meanwhile, had been growing steadily. In 1893 a group of these Americans staged a revolt against the Hawaiian queen. The islands were annexed by the United States in 1898.

To enhance the role of the United States in the Western Hemisphere, Secretary of State James Blaine sponsored a congress of American nations. At that meeting, held in 1890, the delegates agreed to create the Pan-American Union as a means of promoting inter-American unity. United States commitment to the Monroe Doctrine was tested in 1895, when President Cleveland rose to the defense of Venezuela in a boundary dispute with Britain.

Throughout the late nineteenth century, the nations of Europe were engaged in sharp competition for colonies. Many Americans, recognizing the need for foreign markets, believed the United States also should possess colonies. These expansionists were influenced, furthermore, by popular ideas about American superiority.

In 1895 a rebellion broke out against Spanish rule in Cuba, arousing deep concern in the United States. President McKinley tried to avoid American involvement in the revolt. Nevertheless, the publication of the De Lôme letter and the destruction of the battleship *Maine* aroused Americans, and led to a declaration of war against Spain.

The war was quick and decisive. By the end of July, 1898, the navy had destroyed Spanish fleets in the Caribbean and the Pacific. The United States Army, meanwhile, had captured the Philippines, Cuba, Puerto Rico, and Guam. On December 10, 1898, the Treaty of Paris was signed. Cuba was granted independence, while Spain ceded the Philippines, Puerto Rico, and Guam to the United States.

The annexation of the Philippines was opposed by the Anti-Imperialist League, formed in 1898 to protest the acquisition of overseas possessions. American voters seemed to approve of the nation's new foreign policy, however, when they gave President McKinley a decisive majority over William Jennings Bryan in the election of 1900.

Vocabulary and Important Terms

1. "Seward's Folly"
2. *Virginius* incident
3. Pan-Americanism
4. Pan-American Union
5. arbitration
6. yellow journalism
7. De Lôme letter
8. Teller Amendment
9. Rough Riders
10. Treaty of Paris (1898)
11. Philippine Insurrection
12. imperialism
13. Anti-Imperialist League
14. Open Door Policy
15. Boxer Rebellion

Discussion Questions

1. (a) What plans for expansion did Secretary of State William H. Seward make? (b) Which of Seward's goals were realized?
2. (a) Why did Hawaii begin to interest Americans in the 1880's? (b) Describe the steps by which Hawaii was annexed.
3. (a) On what occasions in the 1860's and 1870's was the Monroe Doctrine invoked? (b) How did the United States expand its role in the Western Hemisphere during the 1880's and 1890's? (c) What was the position of the United States in the dispute over the boundary between Venezuela and British Guiana? (d) What was the significance of the peaceful settlement of the boundary dispute?
4. (a) Why, in the years immediately following the Civil War, did the United States not readily seize the opportunity to own overseas territories? (b) For what reasons did public opinion shift on the question of overseas expansion by the 1880's?
5. (a) Who were the leading American spokesmen for expansion? (b) What were some of the arguments used by the expansionists?
6. (a) Why were American newspapers increasingly influential in shaping public opinion? (b) What role did those newspapers play in helping push the United States toward war with Spain?
7. What was the state of American preparedness at the start of the Spanish-American War?
8. (a) What did the victory of the United States over Spain indicate to the rest of the world? (b) What question did the United States face as a result of its acquisition of new territory? (c) How did imperialism become a political issue in 1900?

Relating Past to Present

1. The sensational measures used by newspapers in the late 1800's often influenced public opinion.

How influential are newspapers in shaping opinion today? What other sources of news are available?

2. Arbitration led to a peaceful settlement of the Venezuelan boundary dispute in the late 1890's. What are some recent examples of international disputes that have been settled by arbitration?

3. Secretary of State Blaine promoted Pan-Americanism at a meeting in 1890. What organization exists today as a result of those first efforts of cooperation among all American nations?

Studying Local History

Find out if the newspapers of your state or region played a part in helping push the United States into the Spanish-American War. What evidence is there that they did or did not follow the lead of the Hearst and Pulitzer newspapers?

Using History Skills

1. *Reading maps.* Study the map on page 143 showing America's rise to world power. (a) What island possessions had the United States gained by 1900? (b) What strategic advantages did each of those possessions offer the United States?

2. *Using historical sources.* Study Senator Beveridge's statement on page 133. What are the chief characteristics of the colonial empire described by Beveridge?

3. *Writing a summary.* Use the information presented in this chapter to write a short summary explaining American expansion in the late 1800's. Explain how the United States became interested in acquiring new territory, what new territories the United States acquired, and what new responsibilities and involvement in world affairs resulted.

WORLD SCENE

European Imperialism

European imperialism reached its height in the last half of the nineteenth century as nations competed with one another to establish overseas empires.

The French in Indochina. In the late 1700's French missionaries and traders began arriving in what is now Vietnam. When rulers hostile to Christianity came to power after 1820, the French decided to intervene. French forces were sent to Southeast Asia in 1858. Eventually they forced the local ruler to hand over territory around the city of Saigon to France and to allow the free exercise of the Catholic faith.

French imperialists soon persuaded their government to expand from this base and claim more and more of Southeast Asia. Cambodia was made a French protectorate in 1863, and all of what is today Vietnam was occupied by French forces by 1885. In 1887 the French joined these provinces into a colonial possession they called Indochina, with a governor-general in charge. Laos became part of the confederation in 1893.

Indochina was a lush and productive region that the French quickly developed. Mining operations were undertaken in the north, while in the south large plantations were established for the production of rubber and rice.

The division of Africa. Africa was the last major land area to be colonized by European nations. Over the centuries footholds had been established along the coasts, but by 1880 only about 10 percent of the African continent had been claimed by European colonial powers. During the next two decades, however, the map of Africa changed drastically. Eager to acquire overseas territories to improve their access to raw materials and dependable markets, Britain, France, Germany, Italy, Portugal, Spain, and Belgium vied for colonies.

The British, in particular, had grandiose ambitions in Africa. By the early 1880's they controlled Capetown in southern Africa and Egypt in the north. They hoped to expand their influence on the continent. British colonies stretching from the Cape to Cairo would give them dominance in Africa — a situation which other nations opposed.

As tensions increased over colonial claims in Africa, Otto von Bismarck, the chancellor of Germany, arranged a meeting of all interested countries. Fourteen nations, including the United States, sent delegates to the Berlin Conference in 1884. In a short time the Europeans divided nearly all of Africa among themselves. By 1900 the only African nations that had escaped becoming part of a colonial empire were Liberia and Ethiopia.

CHAPTER 6

The Progressive Presidents

1900 – 1920

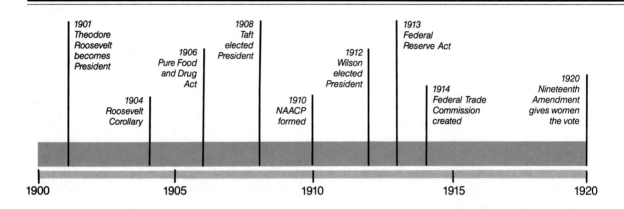

| 1900 | 1905 | 1910 | 1915 | 1920 |

1901 Theodore Roosevelt becomes President

1904 Roosevelt Corollary

1906 Pure Food and Drug Act

1908 Taft elected President

1910 NAACP formed

1912 Wilson elected President

1913 Federal Reserve Act

1914 Federal Trade Commission created

1920 Nineteenth Amendment gives women the vote

On September 5, 1901, President McKinley delivered a speech at the Pan-American Exposition in Buffalo, New York. He spoke optimistically about the nation's future and about peace among nations. He also offered what was at that time a new idea: "Isolation is no longer possible or desirable," he said. "God and man have linked the nations together." The following day, as the President stood in a receiving line to greet the public, a 28-year-old anarchist stepped up to him and fired two bullets. Early in the morning of September 14, McKinley died, and Theodore Roosevelt took the oath of office as President.

Theodore Roosevelt's powerful personality and considerable popularity would soon make a strong impression. A patriot who loved American history, he saw himself as helping to mold the future. He believed it his mission as President "to look ahead and plan out the right kind of civilization."

By the time Roosevelt became President, many deep-seated problems caused by the rapid growth of industry and cities had aroused nationwide concern. In many states and cities attempts were made to solve some of these problems through legislation. Gradually, the interest of Congress was enlisted, as the movement to find solutions attracted support from middle-class Americans. The effort at reform taken as a whole has come to be known as the Progressive Movement.

1 The Progressives Call for Reform

During the late 1800's a number of people had spoken out against political corruption, industrial monopolies, and the inequities faced by farmers and workers. By 1900 a new generation of reformers — the progressives — were getting ready to face these nagging issues.

Progressivism has its roots in earlier political movements. The Progressive Movement resulted from a number of political ideas and movements that came together as the new century opened. The first was that of populism, which had called not only for good government but also for specific reforms in American economic and social life. Most of the people who became progressive reformers, ironically, had been opposed to the rural-based Populists. The progressives, mostly city people, could never accept the Populists' hostility to business or their radical proposals that included government ownership of the railroads. Nevertheless, the new reformers took over the Populist idea that government must work to ensure the public's economic well-being. They also approved of the Populist idea that the average citizen must be allowed to play a more direct role in politics.

Progressives are disturbed by inequalities. Another element nourishing a new era of reform was the growth of a well-educated urban middle class. It included professors and teachers, lawyers, social workers, small business operators, and rising numbers of women who had leisure time. These people were offended that the advantages of America were not being distributed more widely. Possessed of a keen sense of justice, these people had developed a fuller consciousness of the conditions of life borne by so many fellow Americans. They turned a spotlight on many blemishes of society, and sometimes they saw more of them than they could readily remove: hazardous sweatshops and cruelty to children, fire-trap slums and unhealthful food, infant mortality and ineffective schools.

Writers awaken public opinion. Still another element in shaping the Progressive Movement was the so-called "mugwump literature." Appearing in the late 1800's, these books had fostered a desire for laws

Despite prosperous times, reflected in this painting of New York's Central Park, many Americans called for reform in the early 1900's.

that would make government more responsive to the needs of the people. Henry George's *Progress and Poverty*, for example, which appeared in 1879, was widely read. In it, George argued that any increase in national wealth always brings with it a matching increase in poverty. He sought to explain this seemingly impossible connection. He concluded that it resulted from the steady increase in the value of land, which he called "unfair." He maintained that the increase enriched a mere handful of people, even though it was made possible only by the existence of the entire community. He proposed a single tax to replace the existing variety of taxes. The single tax would be based on what he labeled the "unearned" increase in the value of land.

Another popular writer was Edward Bellamy. His fame stemmed from his novel *Looking Backward, 2000–1887*, published in 1888. Describing an imaginary society of the future, Bellamy painted a vivid picture of a world no longer burdened by the shortcomings he found in the America of his day. Read by millions, *Looking Backward* stirred readers to imagine the possibilities of social and economic change.

Still another influential author was Henry Demarest Lloyd, who was greatly distressed over the growth of monopoly. His *Wealth Against Commonwealth*, which came out in 1894, made a fierce attack on the Standard Oil Company. Lloyd was not able to provide a solution to the question of how to regulate trusts. Nevertheless, he piled fact upon fact so convincingly that a reader felt a powerful urge to do *something* about the situation.

One of the first books to deal with a specific urban problem was *How the Other Half Lives*, published in 1890 by Jacob Riis (REES), an immigrant from Denmark. A description of life in the slums of New York, the book shocked its readers and helped launch a crusade for improved housing.

The muckrakers expose social problems. Lloyd and Riis were the first of a group of writers and editors who came to be called *muckrakers*. The name was coined by Theodore Roosevelt in 1906. Highly critical of sensationalism in the press, Roosevelt said that people who wrote such articles reminded him of the man in John Bunyan's *A Pilgrim's Progress* (1678) who "could look no way but downward with a muckrake in his hand." Despite Roosevelt's barb, the name *muckraker* became a badge of distinction. Through magazine articles and novels, the muckrakers drew attention to abuses that had crept into American life.

During the early 1900's, muckraking magazines, having picked up some tricks from yellow journalism, gained large circulations, some of them in the hundreds of thousands. The articles dealt with political graft, street crime, fraudulent advertising of patent medicines, and other topics.

The first notable muckraking magazine began under the inspiration of S. S. McClure. As an immigrant youth from Ireland, he had started his career in the 1880's, publishing a magazine devoted to bicycling, a craze beginning to sweep the country. Among those writing for *McClure's* was Ida M. Tarbell, a trained historian, who in 1903 wrote a series of articles describing the excesses of the Standard Oil Company. Her articles became a model for other muckrakers. Lincoln Steffens, for instance, produced a series on municipal corruption called "The Shame of the Cities." In yet another series, Ray Stannard Baker wrote about railroad abuses.

Magazines all over the country copied *McClure's*. For *Everybody's*, Thomas W. Lawson in 1905 and 1906 attacked the "money kings" in a number of articles. David Graham Phillips's account of bribery in high places, "The Treason of the Senate," ran as a serial in *Cosmopolitan* in 1906.

Other writers criticize American life. A number of muckraking books also became best-sellers. The most important was Upton Sinclair's novel *The Jungle* (1906), which revealed the unsanitary conditions in Chicago's large meat-packing plants. Other influential novels were written by Frank Norris on what he called "the epic of wheat." The first was *The Octopus* (1901), a recounting of the struggle in California between wheat farmers and the railroads. Another, *The Pit* (1903), examined business transactions on the Chicago wheat exchange. Two wealthy sisters-in-law, Marie and Bessie Van Vorst, published in 1903 a startling book called *The Woman Who Toils.* They had gathered their material on women in industry by disguising themselves as workers. A persuasive book on still another problem was *The Bitter Cry of the Children* by John Spargo, an Englishman. Appearing in 1906, it provided a heart-rending account of boys and girls at work in sweatshops.

The progressives seek legislative solutions. Muckrakers provided ammunition for the progressive reformers. But what could be done to rectify specific situations?

The progressives assumed that once the evils of society were revealed, proper laws could be framed to deal with them. The progressives, in fact, were sure that through legislation America could eventually achieve "social justice" for all.

The progressives were not radicals. They opposed the call of *Socialists* for government ownership of the means of production. The progressives, it is true, were willing to enlarge the power of the federal government. They saw the things that were wrong simply as flaws, however, capable of being remedied without significantly altering institutions or upsetting society.

Most progressives believed that the federal government should be a referee in what they saw as the contest between big business and "the people." They believed, too, that people in small businesses needed help against larger competitors. The progressives regarded the accumulation of wealth in fewer and fewer hands as a particularly serious danger to the republic. They concluded, therefore, that monopoly — of all kinds — must be their prime target.

Individuals recognize the need for reform. As the spirit of progressivism spread, people from many walks of life became crusaders in the work of improving social

Ida Tarbell contributed to *McClure's*, one of the mass-circulation magazines that was responsible for uncovering abuses in government and in business.

conditions. An outstanding figure was Jane Addams, the daughter of a well-to-do miller in rural Illinois. She gave up the idea she had once had of becoming a doctor, and instead became a "doctor" to the troubled cities. She created Hull House in the heart of Chicago's tenement district in 1889 to help the underprivileged of the neighborhood. Hull House was a settlement house, a community center offering a wide range of services to people of all ages, many of them immigrants recently arrived in America.

Jane Addams's example inspired reformers elsewhere. A wealthy young woman named Lillian Wald organized the Henry Street Settlement on the Lower East Side of New York. Lillian Wald, who had once started training to be a nurse, also established a pioneering visiting nurse service for the needy.

SECTION REVIEW

1. Vocabulary: *muckraker, Socialist.*
2. (a) What ideas did the Progressive Movement draw from the Populists? (b) How were the progressives influenced by "mugwump literature"?
3. What were some of the problems exposed by the muckrakers?
4. How did the progressives seek to remedy social evils?

2 Reform Begins at the City and State Levels

The progressive crusade took to heart the observation of James Bryce, a noted English observer of the United States, that city government was the nation's greatest single failure. People in many cities went to work on the problem.

Reformers attack municipal problems. Municipal reform soon had a number of heroes. Toledo, Ohio, for example, benefited from the election to city hall of a businessman named Samuel "Golden Rule" Jones.[1] First elected in 1897, Jones spent the next seven years as mayor fighting dishonesty and political corruption. His most important action was the establishment of the merit system for civil servants in city departments. He also set up the city's first kindergarten and public playgrounds. Jones's successor, Brand Whitlock, became a national figure in the work of reforming city government.

In Cleveland, Mayor Tom L. Johnson was a leader of reform. Johnson had achieved success in business through his control of street-railway systems in Indiana and Ohio. Henry George's writings had greatly influenced him. As mayor of Cleveland, he gathered together a group of bright young advisers who helped him make their city the best-governed in the United States. Johnson worked hard to establish public ownership of electric power plants and the street railway system.

New forms of city government are introduced. In attempting to adapt to modern needs, some cities began experimenting with new types of government. One arrangement, known as the "Des Moines idea," provided for a commission to run the city. Under this system, five commissioners were selected in a nonpartisan election. Another arrangement was the city-manager form of government. The city manager, hired under contract, was responsible to a commission or to a city council. By 1923, some 300 cities had city managers.

Reforms are instituted on the state level. State government also came under the influence of progressive ideas. A memorable figure at the state level was Robert La Follette of Wisconsin, known as "Fighting Bob." As governor of his state from 1901 to 1906 and United States senator for the next nineteen years, La Follette gained a national reputation as a reformer. In 1903, Wisconsin adopted the *direct primary.* This allowed for candidates for state office to be chosen by the people in preliminary, or primary, elections rather than by party bosses. Within the next ten years, almost every state had a similar law. The ambitious program that La Follette pushed through was known as the "Wisconsin idea." In addition to primary elections, it introduced the merit system in the state civil service and regulation and taxation of the railroads.

Other states also enacted reforms intended to give the people tighter control of government. The *referendum* was widely adopted. Under this plan, the people were allowed to vote directly on proposed bills. The *initiative* — a process by which citizens propose legislation or constitutional amendments — also gained popularity. First adopted in South Dakota in 1898, it spread from there to other parts of the country. The *recall* — a process enabling voters to dismiss public officials before the end of their terms — was adopted by the city of Los Angeles in 1903. Oregon put a provision for recall into its constitution in 1908, and a number of other states quickly followed suit.

Progressives also supported the adoption of the *secret ballot* (sometimes called the Australian ballot). Until the early 1890's, political parties had printed their ballots in distinctive colors. How a person voted, therefore, was easy for all to see. Placing the names of all candidates on a single ballot and allowing voters to make their choices in secret put an end to open voting and to the abuses it brought.

---

[1]Jones had acquired his nickname after posting a card bearing the golden rule as a guide for the treatment of employees in his machinery-manufacturing plant.

The Seventeenth Amendment is ratified.
The progressives took up, in addition, the old Populist call for the direct election of United States senators. The pressure became so great that by 1912 Congress passed the Seventeenth Amendment. Ratified the following year, it took from the state legislatures, and gave to the people, the right to elect United States senators.

Women gain the right to vote. The progressives' desire to widen the people's role in politics helped advance the cause of women's suffrage. Ever since 1848, when the first women's rights convention was held at Seneca Falls, New York, the question of voting rights for women had been debated. For many years, Susan B. Anthony and Elizabeth Cady Stanton, leaders of the National Woman Suffrage Association, carried on the campaign, often in the face of unbending opposition. The dam began to break in 1869 when Wyoming Territory gave women the vote. When Wyoming came into the Union in 1890, it retained suffrage for women.

In the next few years, the movement for women's voting rights grew stronger. By 1900, Colorado, Utah, and Idaho had joined Wyoming in granting women the ballot. Then, as the impulse to reform generally took hold, the movement gained victories in other states. By 1919, women had acquired equal suffrage in fifteen states, and a number of other states were allowing partial suffrage.

The work of Carrie Chapman Catt, Alice Paul, and Lucy Burns — and many other dedicated women's rights advocates — led finally to the ratification in 1920 of

Around 1900, women's groups, chiefly in the Midwest, were working to secure female suffrage in individual states and localities. In 1914, Alice Paul formed a national organization to champion women's right to vote.

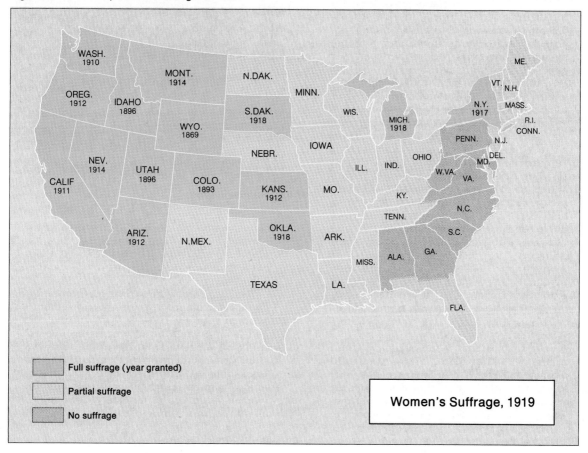

Women's Suffrage, 1919

Full suffrage (year granted)

Partial suffrage

No suffrage

the Nineteenth Amendment to the Constitution. It prohibited the denial of the vote to anyone "on account of sex." Women continued to face discrimination in seeking entry into many jobs and professions. Still, the new amendment was a springboard to fuller rights that women would win in the years ahead.

Reform affects other aspects of American life. The work of the progressives cannot be measured only by the reforms they undertook. Part of what they accomplished was to help reshape important American attitudes. To a greater degree than ever before, people focused attention on individual hygiene and public health. Moreover, they

---

EYEWITNESS TO HISTORY

Suffragist Tactics

Gertrude Foster Brown left a career in music to devote herself to the suffragist cause. As president of the New York State Suffrage Association from 1913 to 1915, she helped plan strategies to convince the public of the injustice done to women by denying them the right to vote. In this passage Gertrude Foster Brown described how attention was drawn to the suffrage issue.

There were no radios and no effective talking pictures at that time. The only way of reaching voters was through a personal appeal. It was useless to invite men to come to suffrage meetings. Where they were not opposed, they were indifferent or considered the whole business a joke. Since they would not come to women, suffragists had to go to them wherever they were.

In the days of trailing skirts and picture hats, to see a woman mount a soap box on a street corner, or stand on the back seat of an automobile and begin to orate, was so startling that men could not help but stop and listen. The street meetings were so effective that soon, all over the state, women held their meetings on street corners or public squares, wherever the traffic was heaviest, with [colorful] banners and much literature. They haunted every place where men gathered. His clubs, his conventions, his amusement places, were never safe from the danger of a speech demanding votes for women. Vaudeville performances were staged by suffragists. They spoke between the acts in theaters.

The first parades were small and timid affairs. In May, 1911, three thousand women and eighty-nine men were in line. A year later, ten thousand women marched, and, in 1915, forty thousand. Always in New York, women were re-

A suffragist rally

ceived with respect. Not so the men sympathizers. Jeers and scurrilous remarks showered on them. The mildest was "Go home and wash the dishes" or "Rock the baby."

The parades were striking evidence of the sweeping progress of the movement. Women from every class and walk of life, and from every kind of employment were in line. Women from luxurious homes, from the tenement districts, girls from the workshops of the lower East Side, trade union women, teachers and professional women, young girls and elderly women — all united for a common cause.

began to make a virtue of looking and "staying" young. The boyish President Roosevelt and his family were the very symbols of this new attitude.

The concern over cleanliness accompanied a growing awareness that germs can cause disease. Major cities established departments of public health. Some of them set up child-care "stations," offering free milk and medical examinations to needy children. In many parts of the country, laws were passed requiring the vaccination of school children against smallpox and diphtheria.

The worth of outdoor living in promoting health took hold too. Leading cities had started in 1885 to build public playgrounds. Still, young people seemed to require more organized activities. As one answer, the Boy Scouts of America were established in 1910, followed two years later by the Girl Scouts and the Camp Fire Girls. Progressives believed that scouting would help make citizens stronger — mentally and physically. President Roosevelt was especially interested in the scout movement.

Reform does not touch the lives of all Americans. Most progressives were white, middle-class city dwellers whose reforming instincts went only so far. Immigrants during the Progressive Era found themselves scorned as "the foreign element" or talked-down to as "our foreigners." Even Irish-American Catholics, who controlled many a city hall and sometimes a state house, frequently were excluded from business and professional opportunities. Although Oscar S. Straus, who served under Theodore Roosevelt as Secretary of Commerce and Labor, was the first Jew appointed to a Cabinet office, prejudice against Jews in general was widespread.

Black Americans fight discrimination. Blacks benefited very little from progressive reforms. In the decades after the Civil War, black Americans had advanced economically. Many black people owned their own homes or farms and ran their own businesses. However, after the last federal troops were removed from the South in

People imitated the fashions and lifestyles made popular by the magazines of the day. In this formal portrait, Alice Roosevelt presents a good example of what was known as the "Gibson Girl" — upswept hairdo, large hat, elegant clothes, and an air of sophistication.

1877, state laws had been passed restricting the rights of black citizens. These *Jim Crow laws,* as they were known, forced black Southerners by 1890 to use separate restaurants, hospitals, railroads, and streetcars. Through the introduction of literacy tests and poll taxes, furthermore, many southern states prevented blacks from voting.

Although some black people went to court to challenge the Jim Crow laws, the courts usually upheld the state laws. The worst defeat for blacks came in 1896, when the Supreme Court ruled in *Plessy v. Ferguson* that "separate but equal" transportation facilities were legal. The Court offered the following explanation: "If one race be inferior to the other socially, the Constitution of the United States cannot put them upon the same plane." For more than fifty years, "separate-but-equal" laws were in effect in the South. Despite the Fourteenth

Amendment (page 626), blacks were second-class citizens.

Discrimination, unofficial and only a little more subtle, was practiced in the North. Ray Stannard Baker wrote a revealing account of discrimination in his muckraking book *Following the Color Line* (1908). In it, he spared neither the North nor the South.

Blacks responded in various ways to the obstacles they faced. The educator Booker T. Washington was the best-known black leader of the late 1800's and early 1900's. He preached that blacks must accommodate themselves to their circumstances and make the best of the situation. In a speech in Atlanta in 1895 he made public his acceptance of the separation of the races, declaring, as he held up his hand with the fingers spread wide, "In all things that are purely social we can be separate as the fingers, yet one as the hand in all things essential to mutual progress." Washington pressed upon his people the value of vocational education. Tuskegee Institute in Alabama, which he established, became famous as a training place for young black people. Privately, Washington hoped for equality of the races. He emphasized in his speeches, however, that this could only be a long-term objective.

Many black critics of Washington insisted that Jim Crow laws must be overturned immediately. One of these voices was W. E. B. Du Bois (doo-BOYS), for many years a professor at Atlanta University. Du Bois delivered a blistering attack on Washington, accusing him of urging black people to do only menial work. In his book *The Souls of Black Folk* (1903), Du Bois argued that only through political agitation could blacks put an end to segregation. In 1905 he brought together a group of black leaders at Niagara Falls to protest the steady curtailment of the civil and political rights of black people. Five years later, along with sixty other prominent Americans, Du Bois helped organize the National Association for the Advancement of Colored People (NAACP). Lawyers for the NAACP took the fight against discrimination to the courts.

SECTION REVIEW

1. Vocabulary: *direct primary, referendum, initiative, recall, secret ballot, Jim Crow laws.*
2. (a) What new forms of city government were introduced during the Progressive Era? (b) What political reforms were introduced at the state level?
3. (a) How did the Seventeenth Amendment change the way United States senators were selected? (b) What steps led to passage of the Nineteenth Amendment?
4. (a) How were the rights of black Americans restricted in the late 1800's? (b) What was the Supreme Court's decision in *Plessy v. Ferguson*? (c) How did the NAACP fight discrimination?

3 Theodore Roosevelt Offers Americans a "Square Deal"

Theodore Roosevelt's exuberance and energy made many progressives regard him as their leader. His feeling that people deserved a "Square Deal" from their government made him one of the nation's most popular Presidents.

Theodore Roosevelt is an inspiring leader. Theodore Roosevelt was born to wealthy parents in 1858 in New York City. Frail and weak, he suffered from asthma, and only his father, Theodore Roosevelt, Sr., could comfort him when he battled for breath. Then, as his health began to improve, "Teedy," as his brothers and sisters called him, took up boxing and began to lead the "strenuous life."

A man of great vigor, Roosevelt turned his energy to the field of government soon after his graduation from Harvard College in 1880. He served for three years as a member of the New York state legislature. Then for two years he took up ranching in what is now North Dakota, spending time shooting big game in the Rockies. He wrote about his experiences and also penned several volumes of history and biography. When he returned to New York in 1886, he made an unsuccessful run for mayor. President Harrison shortly made him a member of the United States Civil Service Commission, on which Roosevelt served until he became head of New York City's board of police commissioners. In 1897 President McKinley appointed him Assistant Secretary of the Navy. From there on, his career was a stirring adventure — first as a Rough Rider in the Spanish-American War and then as a hero elected to the governorship of New York. In 1900 he was elected Vice President. By September, 1901, Roosevelt was President and people were calling him Teddy[2] or TR, with affection.

The Roosevelt family filled the White House with a joyfulness it had not recently known. There were six children. The eldest was Alice, who was seventeen years old in 1901; the youngest was Quentin, not yet turned four. Theodore Roosevelt imparted to his children his own burning love of action. As they grew up, they tried to live by his standard of public duty.

Roosevelt could inspire unmatchable admiration in other people too. William Allen White, a famous Kansas newspaper editor, wrote of his first meeting with the President: "He overcame me. And in the hour or two we spent that day . . . he poured into my heart such visions, such ideals, such hopes, such a new attitude toward life and patriotism and the meaning of things, as I never dreamt men had."

Roosevelt made the office of the President the center of news and public attention. He understood that his personal popularity readily made him spokesman for the poor as well as the rich, factory owners as well as working people. The White House, he believed, must be a "bully pulpit" for defining national obligations and pointing to possible ways of meeting them.

Roosevelt settles a coal strike. Roosevelt's sympathy for working people was tested during a strike in the anthracite coal mines in 1902. Over 150,000 men had walked off

Theodore Roosevelt's family was energetic and much in the public eye while they lived in the White House. Alice Roosevelt (middle) was married there in 1906.

their jobs in May. Led by John Mitchell of the United Mine Workers, they demanded a pay increase, a shorter work day, and recognition of their union. The mine owners refused to meet any of these demands.

After the dispute had dragged into autumn, the President called union and company leaders to a conference in Washington. At the meeting, the mine owners refused to budge, calling the strikers "a set of outlaws." In an unprecedented action, Roosevelt threatened to send 10,000 troops into the mines to get production started again. The operators finally yielded and agreed to submit the issues to arbitration.

In the settlement, the miners received a wage increase — about half of what they had sought. More important in the long run, Roosevelt earned national esteem for taking steps to get coal for the public. Laboring people were delighted that he had appeared to side with the workers — an extraordinary departure from the government's usual support of management.

Roosevelt tackles the trusts. Theodore Roosevelt had a knack for assuming leadership of a cause as if he had discovered the cause himself. One such issue of growing

---

[2]In a joking reference to Roosevelt's love of big-game hunting, the cartoonist of the *Washington Evening Star*, Clifford K. Berryman, drew the first teddy bear in 1902. Within a few years, teddy bears were helping to enrich childhood everywhere.

concern to the public was the spread of trusts. During the late 1890's, new combinations had been formed, greatly alarming the public. Roosevelt was not opposed to big business in general. Instead, he applied his own yardstick to decide which businesses were good and which were bad. He believed that certain trusts ought to be brought under the regulation of the government. Roosevelt was determined that trusts be responsive to the public interest.

In an important trust-busting action, Roosevelt took on the Northern Securities Company, a corporation that had created a railroad monopoly in the Pacific Northwest. The organization included some of the leading names of railroading and finance: James J. Hill, J. P. Morgan, Edward H. Harriman, and, indirectly, John D. Rockefeller. The government brought suit against this company for violation of the Sherman Antitrust Act (page 69).

In 1904 the Supreme Court ruled that the Northern Securities Company should be broken up. Roosevelt was overjoyed at the news. "The most powerful men in this country were held to accountability before the law," he declared. The public cheered him on.

Through the creation of the Bureau of Corporations in 1903, the government was able to gather facts that enabled it to keep watch on big businesses. Using evidence collected by the bureau, Roosevelt brought cases against Standard Oil, the American Tobacco Company, and some forty other trusts. Roosevelt used these cases and the Northern Securities case to enhance his reputation as a "trust-buster."

Roosevelt wins the election of 1904. As the 1904 presidential race neared, business interests in the Republican Party talked about replacing Roosevelt with Senator Mark Hanna, William McKinley's old friend. Hanna, however, died early in 1904. In any event, Theodore Roosevelt had gained control of the Republican Party machinery through shrewd appointments. When he sought the Republican nomination, therefore, he had virtually no opposition. He became the first "accidental" Chief Executive

to be nominated for the presidency in his own right.

Roosevelt's Democratic opponent in 1904 was a colorless New York judge, Alton B. Parker. Remaining on the bench but fearing he would no longer seem impartial, Parker did not campaign purposefully. A third candidate was Eugene Debs (page 96), who ran on the Socialist ticket.

Roosevelt easily defeated his opponents. On the eve of his inauguration, he blustered, "Tomorrow I shall come into my office in my own right. Then watch out for me!"

New railroad regulations are imposed. Roosevelt believed that a call for reform was now sweeping the country, and he was determined to be at its head. He made railroad rate abuse an object of his attention.

Roosevelt had already persuaded Congress in 1903 to begin to deal with the railroad question by passing the Elkins Act. This law, which expanded the powers of the Interstate Commerce Commission, made it illegal for railroad officials and shippers to give rebates (discounts) to favored customers. Three years later, Roosevelt oversaw the passage of a stronger law, the Hepburn Act. This law broadened the authority of the Commission over railroad rates, even allowing it to reduce objectionable rates — subject to court approval. Moreover, the Hepburn Act gave the Commission power to regulate sleeping car companies, oil pipelines, ferries, bridges, and railroad terminals.

Regulations curb the sale of harmful products. Other federal legislation was aimed at protecting the public from the sale of harmful products. In 1906, the very year that Upton Sinclair published *The Jungle* (page 152), Congress passed the Pure Food and Drug Act. It provided for the elimination of abuses in the processing of food and the manufacturing of patent medicines. Enforcement of this law was up to Dr. Harvey W. Wiley, chief chemist in the Department of Agriculture. Wiley sent inspectors throughout the country to check on methods of preparing foods and medicines.

Another law passed in 1906 was the Meat Inspection Act. This law made com-

Theodore Roosevelt's Message to Congress on Conservation (1907)

... The conservation of our natural resources and their proper use constitute the fundamental problem which underlies almost every other problem of our national life. ... As a nation we not only enjoy a wonderful measure of present prosperity, but if this prosperity is used aright it is an earnest of future success such as no other nation will have. ... But there must be the look ahead, there must be a realization of the fact that to waste, to destroy, our natural resources, to skin and exhaust the land instead of using it so as to increase its usefulness, will result in undermining in the days of our children the very prosperity which we ought by right to hand down to them amplified and developed. For the last few years ... the government has been endeavoring to get our people to look ahead and to substitute a planned and orderly development of our resources in place of a haphazard striving for immediate profit.

pulsory the federal inspection of all meat sold in interstate commerce to see that it came from healthy animals and was packed under sanitary conditions.

Serious efforts at conservation are begun. In the conservation of natural resources, Roosevelt also made an original and lasting contribution. He believed that America's natural resources belonged to *all* of the people. His passion for conservation grew out of a deep love of America's West and the incomparable beauty he had first encountered there as a youth. The President's affection for the great outdoors was matched by his intimate knowledge of nature.

The need to protect the nation's timber resources had been a growing concern for many years. The first step in preserving them had been taken in 1828 when President John Quincy Adams set aside 30,000 acres of oak forest in Florida for the use of the navy. Yellowstone National Park was created in 1872, and Yosemite in 1891. Nevertheless, because of the indiscriminate cutting of trees without replanting, the nation's forests were rapidly disappearing.

Beginning in 1891, Congress authorized the Presidents to withdraw timber land from public sale. Benjamin Harrison set aside seventeen million acres as national forest reserves, and succeeding Presidents followed his example. By the time Theodore Roosevelt left office in 1909, over 230 million acres of forest land had been set aside for future use — almost five times the acreage in 1900.

Roosevelt also helped bring about passage of the Newlands Act in 1902. Under this law, money received from the sale of public lands in sixteen western states was set aside to pay for the irrigation of wasteland. Through the Newlands Act, millions of acres of arid land were brought under cultivation.

In 1903 the first wildlife refuge was established. By 1909 there were 51 such refuges. The Antiquities Act of 1906 put under federal protection land of historic or scientific interest. This law helped protect such locations as New York's Niagara Falls, Arizona's Grand Canyon and Petrified Forest, Oregon's Crater Lake, Colorado's Mesa Verde, California's Muir Woods, and Wyoming's Devils Tower.

The Inland Waterways Commission was established in 1907 to create a comprehensive plan for improving and controlling the nation's rivers. Plans were also made for protecting lowlands from floods, improving navigation on rivers and streams, and increasing water supplies.

Leisure and Recreation

The game of tennis was sweeping the country in 1900, and by 1908 there were 115 tennis clubs. The bicycle remained a favorite means of recreation. Vacationing Americans flocked to the national parks, four of which were created during Theodore Roosevelt's presidency.

The administration deals with the Panic of 1907. Near the end of his presidency, Roosevelt suffered a disappointment. Following a slump on Wall Street in the summer of 1907, a number of banks and businesses failed. Roosevelt said he believed that the "malefactors of great wealth" were to blame for the economic downturn. Nevertheless, in dealing with the Panic of 1907, the trust-busting President was put into the embarrassing position of approving an increase in the power of United States Steel — organized by J. P. Morgan in 1901. The President had been told that he could prevent a stock-market collapse by allowing the giant steel company to purchase its largest competitor, the Tennessee Coal and Iron Company. Roosevelt gave Morgan advance assurance that United States Steel would not be prosecuted under antitrust laws if the deal went through.

The Panic of 1907, fortunately, was not followed by a prolonged depression. As a result, Roosevelt's popularity remained high.

SECTION REVIEW

1. (a) Describe Theodore Roosevelt's concept of the presidency. (b) What was his attitude toward the coal strike? (c) Toward the trusts?
2. (a) What reforms were advanced by the Elkins Act? (b) The Hepburn Act? (c) The Pure Food and Drug Act? (d) The Meat Inspection Act? (e) The Newlands Act? (f) The Inland Waterways Commission?

4 The United States Strengthens Its Interests in the Caribbean and Asia

Theodore Roosevelt's reputation as a man of energy and action was strengthened by his handling of foreign affairs. In dealing with other countries he claimed to be guided by an old West African proverb: "Speak softly and carry a big stick, and you will go far." He did not always speak softly, but he sometimes used "a big stick" to get what he wanted.

Plans for a canal across Central America are revived. The United States had long been interested in building a canal across the Isthmus of Panama (map, page 165). An episode during the Spanish-American War had dramatized the need for a waterway between the Caribbean and the Pacific. After the *Maine* blew up in Havana harbor (page 136), orders were sent to the battleship *Oregon*, then in San Francisco, to sail to the Caribbean. The nation waited anxiously while the ship took nearly 70 days to make the 14,000-mile journey. For weeks, its location and progress were unknown. The "matchless race of the *Oregon*" — as a popular poem called it — made Americans deter-

mined never again to endure such a nerve-tingling time.

When Roosevelt became President, he announced that he intended to get busy on a canal project. Immediately, he faced the diplomatic obstacle of the Clayton-Bulwer Treaty, which had been agreed to in 1850. Under that treaty, the United States and Great Britain had agreed that neither country would exercise exclusive control over a Central American canal. By the beginning of the new century, however, the British had become alarmed over Germany's growing power and were beginning to appreciate the value of a friendly America. Britain was willing to reduce its fleet in the Caribbean and recognize the United States as the primary power in the region. Britain was also willing to permit the United States to construct, own, and defend a canal alone.

A route across Panama is chosen. Roosevelt now had to answer a difficult question: should the canal be constructed through Nicaragua or through Panama? The Panama route would be shorter but more difficult to build. A Nicaraguan canal would be longer but, being entirely at sea level, it would be easier to construct and operate.

In 1879 a French company had started to build a canal across Panama — at that time ruled by Colombia — but had abandoned the project. The French company offered to sell the United States its right of way, equipment, and agreement with Colombia. The United States decided that the asking price was too high and turned its attention to building across Nicaragua.

The chief agent of the French company, a crafty lobbyist named Philippe Bunau-Varilla (boo-NOH vah-ree-YAH), grew concerned. He dropped the company's price for its Panama interests from $109 million to $40 million. He also warned Americans about recent volcanic activity in Nicaragua. Luck was on the side of the French company. In May, 1902, Mount Pelée, a volcano on the Caribbean island of Martinique, erupted with devastating effect, killing more than 30,000 people. A few days later a volcano in Nicaragua began to rumble. Astutely, Bunau-Varilla sent to every United

The Panama Canal, shown here under construction in 1907, uses a system of locks to enable ocean vessels to pass between the Pacific Ocean and the Atlantic.

States senator a copy of a Nicaraguan postage stamp depicting a smoking volcano. Accompanying the picture was the Frenchman's note: "An official witness of the volcanic activity in Nicaragua." The senators were persuaded. In June, Congress enacted a bill providing for the construction of a *Panama* canal.

The consent of Colombia was now required. In 1903 Secretary of State John Hay reached an agreement with Tomás Herrán, the Colombian representative in Washington. The Hay-Herrán Treaty provided that the United States would lease a six-mile-wide strip of land across Panama for a lump sum of $10 million in gold and a yearly rental of $250,000. However, when the treaty was sent for ratification to Bogotá, the Colombian capital, the government responded that the sums agreed to were unacceptable. The Colombians, hoping to win better terms, were blocking the project.

Panama revolts against Colombia. A small group of Panamanians, fearing that the United States might build its waterway across Nicaragua and deprive them of this important artery, took steps to break away from Colombia. They soon had the active cooperation and assistance of the United States. In fact, details of the revolt were worked out in Room 1162 of the Hotel Waldorf-Astoria in New York City. The principal planner was Philippe Bunau-Varilla! Roosevelt and Secretary of State Hay were aware of the scheme, although they did not encourage it. Still, Roosevelt let it be known that the warship U.S.S. *Nashville* would be sent to Panama. Its mission would be to maintain "free and uninterrupted transit" across the isthmus in accordance with an 1846 treaty between the United States and Colombia.

On November 3, 1903, the day after the *Nashville* arrived in Panama, the revolt broke out. Panama City quickly fell under rebel control. Some 400 Colombian troops had already been landed at Colón, but marines from the *Nashville* prevented them from marching across the isthmus to Panama City (map, page 165). The success of the revolution was thus guaranteed.

The United States gains a right of way through Panama. Within three days the United States recognized the independent Republic of Panama. Revolutionary leader Manuel Guerrero became the nation's first president. Philippe Bunau-Varilla, although a French citizen, was named as the first Panamanian minister to the United States. Already Panama's first flag had been designed and fashioned by Madame Bunau-Varilla! On November 18, 1903, Bunau-Varilla and Secretary Hay agreed to a treaty satisfactory to both sides. The Hay-Bunau-Varilla Treaty was the same as the Hay-Herrán Treaty, except that the zone of land across the isthmus was widened to ten miles and granted "in perpetuity" (meaning forever).

Early in 1904 the Senate ratified the treaty. Roosevelt had assured Congress that the acquisition of the Canal Zone had been conducted in the most ethical way, but later he boasted, "I took Panama." Many Americans felt guilty and angry about the methods used to acquire the Canal Zone.

Latin Americans were outraged by Roosevelt's "big stick" method. In 1921, two years after Roosevelt's death, the United States gave $25 million to Colombia. Observers regarded the gift as a diplomatic way of apologizing to that country.

The Panama Canal is constructed. The building of the Panama Canal, begun in 1904, was the stiffest challenge to the nation's engineers since the construction of the first transcontinental railroad a generation earlier. The workers who labored on the "big ditch" risked disease and injury. They were directed by Colonel George W. Goethals (GOH-thalz), who gave the undertaking a quality of leadership that the French company had never known. Goethals was assisted by Colonel William C. Gorgas, surgeon-general of the army, who worked valiantly to wipe out the threat

of yellow fever. The Panama Canal, fifty miles long, was opened on August 15, 1914. The feat of building it had involved removing about 240 million cubic yards of rock and earth and setting in place a complicated system of canal locks.

Within a short time the canal was playing a major part in world commerce. Travel between New York and San Francisco was now 7,000 miles shorter. The canal also enhanced the nation's naval strength by making possible a quick move of ships from one ocean to another.

The Panama Canal affects American foreign policy. The construction of the Panama Canal gave the United States important new interests in the Caribbean. The need to protect the canal also provided the President with new opportunities to wield the big stick in the region.

United States interest in the entire Caribbean region was heightened after the completion of the Panama Canal, whose strategic importance is shown on this map.

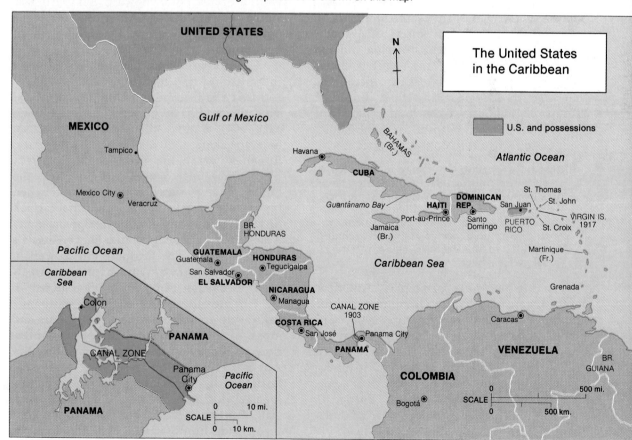

Political instability had long been characteristic of many of the Latin American republics. The persistent gulf separating rich and poor people had created arrogance on one side and envy on the other. Moreover, the lack of easy contact between people living along the coasts and those in the interior prevented the rise of strong national feeling in many of these countries. Government in practically all the Latin American lands remained under the control of a handful of people and was often passed around from one faction to another.

The United States had already felt forced to intervene in Latin American countries to prevent interference from abroad. In 1902 Germany, Britain, and Italy sent warships to blockade Venezuelan ports in order to force the payment of debts. The United States objected strenuously to the naval blockade. The Department of State persuaded Venezuela to accept arbitration in order to end the episode peacefully.

Theodore Roosevelt issues the Roosevelt Corollary. To avoid any such incidents in the future, the United States took a new stand. If a Latin American nation did not repay its debts, then the United States claimed a right to intervene. In his annual message to Congress in 1904, President Roosevelt announced the bold policy. His words, now famous, are known as the Roosevelt Corollary to the Monroe Doctrine:

> Chronic wrongdoing . . . may in America, as elsewhere, ultimately require intervention by some civilized nation, and in the Western Hemisphere the adherence of the United States to the Monroe Doctrine may force the United States, however reluctantly, . . . to the exercise of an international police power.

Acting on these principles, American troops were sent to the Dominican Republic in 1905 and to Cuba in 1906. The United States, in short, had taken on the role of "policing" the Caribbean. Because the United States had appointed itself for this task, many Latin Americans were gravely offended. Still, unlike Europeans who were continuing to seek new colonies, the United States showed no desire to annex more territory. On the subject of the Dominican Republic, Roosevelt once said, "As for annexing the island, I have about the same desire to annex it as a gorged boa constrictor might have to swallow a porcupine the wrong end to."

"Dollar diplomacy" extends American influence. After Roosevelt left the White House in 1909, his foreign policies were maintained by other Presidents. His immediate successor, William Howard Taft, adopted a stance known as "dollar diplomacy." Under this policy, American banks and businesses were encouraged to invest in Latin America. If the investments were endangered by defaults or by failure to make interest payments, the United States would intervene.

Taft applied dollar diplomacy to several Latin American countries. In 1912, for example, he sent troops to Nicaragua to put down an insurrection and restore order.

American influence in Asia grows stronger. United States policy toward Asia also was aimed at protecting American interests, now expected to grow. One goal was to maintain the stability of China.

China's problems had not ended with the crushing of the Boxer Rebellion (page 145). At the beginning of the century Russia had begun to take over Manchuria (map, page 144), a move that alarmed American policy makers. China's territorial integrity, it seemed, was being threatened by Russia.

Because of concern over China, the United States watched approvingly when Japan struck at Russia in a surprise attack in 1904. A modest victory for Japan, many Americans believed, would blunt Russia's aggressiveness. The Japanese did so well in the Russo-Japanese War that they threatened the balance of power in the region.

Hoping to avoid such an outcome, Roosevelt invited delegates from Russia and Japan to meet with him in a peace conference at Portsmouth, New Hampshire, in August, 1905. The resulting Treaty of Portsmouth considerably strengthened Japan's position on the Asian continent. Still, Roosevelt had been able to prevent Japan from humiliating Russia. As a result, he may have saved China from being dominated by either power. For his work at Portsmouth, Roosevelt was awarded the Nobel Peace Prize in 1906 — the first American to be so honored.

Relations between Japan and America are strained. Many Japanese, who expected a better settlement at Portsmouth, felt that Roosevelt had let them down. American-Japanese relations were further strained when San Francisco school authorities insisted that Japanese-American children attend a separate school. The President succeeded in getting the school order reversed. In return, however, he promised Californians that he would seek to halt further Japanese immigration.

In 1907 Roosevelt concluded what came to be known as the Gentlemen's Agreement with Japan. The agreement, which remained in force until 1924, effectively ended Japanese immigration to the United States.

The Great White Fleet circles the globe. Roosevelt expected the anti-American sentiment in Japan to pass. Tensions on both sides of the Pacific reached a point, however, where there was even talk of war. Suddenly Roosevelt decided upon the dramatic step of sending the entire United States fleet around the world. Behind the decision lay several motives. Most important, the President wanted to impress the Japanese with America's naval power. He also wanted to demonstrate to Germany — then expanding its navy — that the United States had the means to enforce its will in the Western Hemisphere. Finally, he was eager to persuade what he regarded as a penny-pinching Congress to support a new ship-building program.

The ships departed from a Virginia port just before Christmas, 1907, as the bands played "The Girl I Left Behind Me." Many young men had left school in order to sign on with the Great White Fleet — so-called because the vessels were painted white.

The journey was enormously successful and the war fever abated. In Japan thousands of school children turned out to sing "The Star-Spangled Banner." The ships returned to American waters on Washington's Birthday, 1909. It became Theodore Roosevelt's firm belief that the sending of the fleet around the world was "the most important service I rendered to peace."

In a demonstration of national strength, the sixteen ships of the Great White Fleet visited all the inhabited continents and paused twice for military maneuvers.

The United States supports plans for world peace. Part of the reforming spirit of the progressives was seen in their support of efforts to promote world peace. The fledgling peace movement was encouraged by two conferences that met at The Hague in the Netherlands in 1899 and 1907. At the first Hague Conference, 26 nations agreed to outlaw poison gas, the dropping of bombs, and the use of explosive bullets. The delegates also created a Permanent Court of International Arbitration. Countries involved in a dispute could bring their quarrels to this Court for settlement. The second Hague Conference was unable to do anything beyond extending the agreements made eight years earlier.

The United States gave arbitration a boost by helping to call the Algeciras (al-jeh-SEER-us) Conference in Spain in 1906. The purpose of the gathering was to settle differences between France and Germany that had arisen over the North African state of Morocco. The Senate condemned the President's support of the conference, arguing that it represented a departure from the pledge in the Monroe Doctrine to stay out of European affairs. Nevertheless, many people were proud that an American President had taken a hand in protecting the peace of the world.

SECTION REVIEW

1. (a) Why was American interest in building a canal across Central America revived following the Spanish-American War? (b) Why was a route across Panama chosen?
2. (a) How were the Panamanians helped in their revolt against Colombia by the United States? (b) What was the Hay-Bunau-Varilla Treaty? (c) How did the Panama Canal affect American foreign policy?
3. (a) What was the Roosevelt Corollary? (b) How was it applied? (c) What was "dollar diplomacy"?
4. (a) Why did the United States mediate an end to the Russo-Japanese War? (b) What were the causes of tension between Japan and the United States? (c) Why was the Great White Fleet sent around the globe?
5. (a) What was the purpose of the two conferences held at The Hague in 1899 and 1907? (b) What was achieved at those conferences?

5 Taft Tries to Follow in Roosevelt's Footsteps

Theodore Roosevelt's popularity was so commanding that he was able to dictate to the Republicans his successor in 1908. The man he chose was William Howard Taft of Ohio — experienced, affable, and weighing over 300 pounds.

Taft is elected President. In 1904 Taft had joined Roosevelt's Cabinet as Secretary of War. Earlier, he had been a federal judge and had served as the first governor of the Philippines. Roosevelt enjoyed Taft's company and admired his achievements. One night early in 1908, the Roosevelts had invited the Tafts to the White House for dinner. After the meal the two families went to the library to talk. There, in the sing-song fashion of a fortune-teller, the President made believe he could foretell the future: "I see a man standing before me weighing about 350 pounds. There is something hanging over his head. I cannot make out what it is; it is hanging by a slender thread. At one time it looks like the presidency — then again it looks like the chief justiceship."

With great enthusiasm, Mrs. Taft shouted, "Make it the presidency!"

"Make it the chief justiceship," said Taft in a quiet voice.

Taft was sincere about what he wanted, and so was Mrs. Taft. She soon had her wish. In the election that year she became First Lady as her husband decisively defeated William Jennings Bryan, the Democrats' candidate for the third time. Years later, Taft was appointed Chief Justice — becoming the only person who has ever held the two highest offices in the land.

Mounting troubles mark Taft's presidency. On his own, Taft was much like Martin Van Buren: a brilliant lieutenant unable to fill a famous predecessor's shoes. Taft once said that whenever he heard the words "Mr. President," he turned around expecting Roosevelt to be there. Roosevelt, for his part, was certain that "Taft will carry on the work substantially as I have. He will do all in his power to further the great causes for which I have fought." Taft, however, could see problems ahead. "There's no use trying to be William Howard Taft with Roosevelt's ways," he said. "Our ways are different."

As Taft's term began, Roosevelt retired from the scene and sailed for Africa to hunt big game. "Health to the lions!" was said to be the toast offered by political enemies as he departed. However, Roosevelt was not off the scene for long.

In his years in office, Taft pleased many progressives with his record of accomplishments. He continued Roosevelt's trust-busting program and strengthened the Interstate Commerce Commission. He tried to lower the tariff substantially and extended federal control over public lands. He saw to it, finally, that New Mexico and Arizona were admitted to the Union in 1912, completing the continental base of 48 states.

In spite of these accomplishments, Taft's years in office were marked by conflict with fellow Republicans. One faction, which included Senator La Follette, considered themselves insurgents — that is, politicians opposed to the policies of their own party. The insurgents believed that Taft had not worked hard enough for tariff reduction, which western farmers supported in order to bring down the cost of manufactured goods.

During Roosevelt's absence, Taft wrote him, "I have been conscientiously trying to carry out your policies, but my method of doing so has not worked smoothly." Roosevelt was soon home again and could see for himself the trouble Taft was in. For one thing, Taft was involved in a bruising fight with Gifford Pinchot, a well-known conservationist whom Roosevelt had appointed Chief Forester. Taft finally fired Pinchot, an action that made the President seem opposed to conservation. Then, in 1910 when insurgents in Congress succeeded in stripping Speaker of the House Joseph Cannon of some of his powers, Taft failed to take a clear-cut stand on the issue. He thus gave the impression that he was opposed to what was termed the "Revolution of 1910," and many progressives were infuriated.

President Taft posed with his family in 1911. His son Robert (right) became a senator, daughter Helen a history professor.

Roosevelt re-enters politics. Roosevelt believed that he had been let down by Taft. Still ambitious and vigorous, Roosevelt decided to enter political life again — as if he had ever left it. Late in the summer of 1910, he delivered a speech in Kansas, asserting that "property shall be the servant and not the master" of the people. The speech showed the influence of a new book, *The Promise of American Life*, written by Herbert Croly. Croly, a superb writer, was the son of Jane Cunningham Croly, the first widely read female newspaper correspondent. Croly's book called for social planning by the federal government as a way to promote prosperity. Roosevelt adopted this viewpoint as his own, calling his program the "New Nationalism." Said he, "The New Nationalism regards the executive power as the steward of the public welfare."

By late 1911 Roosevelt was openly supporting the insurgent Republicans. The insurgents had hoped to nominate La Follette for President, but Roosevelt had his eye on the White House again. Taft said privately, "If you were to remove Roosevelt's skull now, you would find written on his brain '1912.'" After La Follette collapsed while making a speech early in 1912, Roosevelt announced, "My hat is in the ring."

President Taft decided to resist his old friend's campaign for the nomination.

Taft told his military aide, Archibald Butt, "It is hard, very hard, Archie, to see a devoted friendship going to pieces like a rope of sand." It would be some time before Taft and Roosevelt spoke to each other again.

The Republicans are split in 1912. Taft's friends controlled the Republican convention of 1912, and only allowed the seating of nineteen progressive delegates. Angered, Roosevelt's backers refused to have anything to do with the convention. The remaining delegates then nominated Taft on the first ballot.

The Roosevelt people quickly held their own convention, choosing the old Rough Rider in a tumultuous gathering. With religious fervor, Roosevelt told his followers,

"We stand at Armageddon, and we battle for the Lord." Thus, the Progressive Party was launched, sometimes nicknamed the Bull Moose Party.[3] The Progressive platform called for the adoption in all states of the initiative, referendum, and recall, and backed a corrupt-practices act to guard against election fraud. It also contained a call for women's suffrage, federal aid to agriculture, laws to protect women in industry, an end to child labor, and minimum-wage and maximum-hour legislation.

In spite of the enthusiasm of his Progressive backers, Roosevelt must have

---

[3]The name grew out of a Roosevelt remark, "I am as strong as a bull moose."

The Democrats and Woodrow Wilson won an easy presidential victory in 1912 because the Progressive faction, with Theodore Roosevelt as its candidate, split the Republican ranks. The Democrats also won majorities in both the Senate and the House.

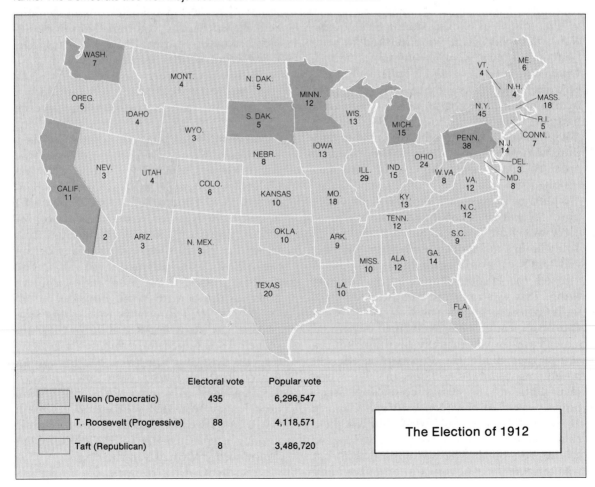

	Electoral vote	Popular vote
Wilson (Democratic)	435	6,296,547
T. Roosevelt (Progressive)	88	4,118,571
Taft (Republican)	8	3,486,720

The Election of 1912

known that he and Taft would split the Republican vote and open the way to victory for the Democrats. In the words of a prominent New Yorker, "The only question now is which corpse gets the most flowers."

Woodrow Wilson leads the Democrats to victory. In the Democratic Party, William Jennings Bryan worked hard for the nomination once again. When the convention became deadlocked, however, he threw his support to Woodrow Wilson, the reform governor of New Jersey. Finally, on the forty-sixth ballot, Wilson won the party's nomination.

Wilson's campaign for President had one leading idea — that the country needed new laws to protect people in small businesses. Wilson was eager to restore free economic competition and put an end to trusts. He knew that no one could turn back the clock to the days before the trusts. He hoped, however, that some of the spirit of that time could be revived — that the "curse of bigness" in business could be eliminated. Wilson called his program the "New Freedom."

Taft ran a listless campaign, acting long before Election Day as if he had already been defeated. Roosevelt directed his campaign to his old admirers, who saw him as a fighter-hero re-entering the battlefield. On one occasion Roosevelt refused to cancel a scheduled speaking date even though he had just been shot by a would-be assassin. He told his audience, "I am going to ask you to be very quiet and please excuse me from making a long speech. I'll do the best I can but there is a bullet in my body. I have a message to deliver and will deliver it as long as there is life in my body."

Wilson was a brilliant speaker, but it was the split in Republican ranks that assured his election. He won only 42 percent of the vote. In the three-way race it was sufficient, however, to give him 435 electoral votes and carry him to victory. Roosevelt was second in the popular and electoral votes, and Taft was third (map, page 170). The Progressive Era was entering a new stage — one that would be its final stage.

(map, page 170)

1. (a) What progressive legislation was passed during Taft's years as President? (b) What political problems did Taft encounter?
2. (a) Why did Theodore Roosevelt re-enter politics? (b) What was the "New Nationalism"?
3. (a) What caused a split in Republican ranks in the election of 1912? (b) What was the result of that election?

6 The Progressive Era Draws to a Close

The 1912 election had been a clear-cut victory for progressives. When he came to the White House, Woodrow Wilson could count on widespread public support for his "New Freedom" program.

Wilson brings strong leadership to the presidency. Woodrow Wilson was the most scholarly man to occupy the White House since John Quincy Adams. Born in Virginia in 1856, Wilson had begun his career as a lawyer, but very early he decided to make his mark in politics. Receiving a Ph.D. in political science, he became one of the most stimulating college professors of his time. He wrote influential books and articles on government and in 1902 became president of Princeton University. As an academic man, however, he felt he could not fulfill his keen "longing to do immortal work." In 1910 he ran for the governorship of New Jersey, convinced that all his reading and training had prepared him for high public office. He had the support of the state Democratic Party bosses, who thought he would only be a figurehead governor. Once in office, however, he proved to be beyond their control. He quickly transformed the state into a model of reform as he drove out corrupt officials. Two years later, he was elected President.

Wilson had come to admire Theodore Roosevelt's aggressive use of the power of the presidency, and he intended to be a strong Chief Executive too. He even revived the practice, broken by Jefferson, of presenting his messages personally to Congress. The purpose, Wilson said, was to show that the President "is a human being trying to cooperate with other human beings in a common service." With confidence he presented his programs, and his energetic leadership brought practical results.

Tariffs are reduced. One of President Wilson's first steps was to seek a reduction in tariff rates. After publicly denouncing lobbyists who opposed tariff reform, Wilson encouraged Congress to pass the Underwood Tariff Act of 1913. Rates were lowered on almost 1,000 items. To make up for the anticipated loss of revenue, the Underwood Tariff included a provision for an income tax. Wilson proudly said, "I have had the accomplishment of something like this at heart ever since I was a boy."

The Federal Reserve System is set up. Wilson also sought reforms in the nation's banking system. Along with other progressives, he argued that a handful of private

Legislation passed during Wilson's administration sought to curb the increasing concentration of money and credit in the hands of the "money trust."

investment firms in the East controlled the existing banks. Wilson's views were reminiscent of Andrew Jackson's. Whereas Jackson had wanted to get the government out of banking, however, Wilson supported a government-controlled system that would be able to provide an elastic currency. In other words, the volume of currency could be increased or decreased according to the changing needs of the economy, thus providing greater stability for the banking structure of the country.

After intricate negotiations with Congress, Wilson agreed to sign the Federal Reserve Act into law in 1913. The act divided the United States into twelve banking districts, each with a Federal Reserve Bank. All national banks had to become members of the Federal Reserve System, while all state banks were invited to join. The Federal Reserve Banks were strictly "banker's banks," with considerable power over the money and credit policies of member banks. A central Federal Reserve Board directed the whole system.

Wilson deals with the trusts. Another goal of Wilson's "New Freedom" program was stricter control of the trusts. The Clayton Antitrust Act, passed in 1914, strengthened the Sherman Act (page 69) by defining unfair business practices. It prohibited a company from acquiring the stock of another company for the purpose of forming a monopoly. It made interlocking directorships illegal. The new law also seemed, for the first time, to exempt labor and farm organizations from being prosecuted as conspiracies in restraint of trade. The Clayton Act brought union people to the side of the Democrats. In 1917 Wilson became the first President to address a convention of the American Federation of Labor.

At the President's request, Congress also created the Federal Trade Commission in 1914 to deal with the trust problem. The purpose of the Commission was to keep an eye on big corporations and to issue "cease and desist" orders — subject to court review — whenever antitrust laws were violated. The act creating the Commission also outlawed certain unfair methods of competition in interstate commerce.

Other progressive laws are passed. During his years in office, Wilson could claim credit for several other laws. The La Follette Seamen's Act of 1915 gave merchant seamen improved working conditions. The Federal Farm Loan Act of 1916 provided farmers with long-term credit. The Adamson Act, also passed in 1916, established an eight-hour workday for railroad employees.

Still, the work of the progressives, many leaders believed, remained incomplete. The laws that Wilson and his associates advocated were not as far-reaching as those that some progressives supported. Wilson, furthermore, remained blind to the situation of black people. Many people, in fact, blamed him for the increase in Jim Crow regulations in the city of Washington during his presidency. W. E. B. Du Bois had supported Wilson in 1912 and had urged other black leaders to do likewise. Once in office, however, Wilson would not budge from his belief that segregation was the best policy for both races. Even Booker T. Washington was saying, as Wilson's term went on, that he had never seen black people "so discouraged and bitter as they are at the present time."

The Progressive Movement brings important changes in American life. By the time Woodrow Wilson won election to a second term of office (Chapter 7), the Progressive Movement had run its course. Its accomplishments, nevertheless, were noteworthy. It had enlisted the leaders of the urban communities in attacking problems that had earlier been ignored. It had made an effort to root out privilege and monopoly. It had established the principle that big business must exercise public responsibility. Much remained to do, but even Wilson believed that to remake America would require "a generation or two."

Meanwhile, the constant revelations of what was wrong with American life had brought a reaction: people gradually became inattentive to them. Moreover, fresh pride

President Wilson was deeply saddened when his first wife, Ellen, died in 1914. The next year he met Edith Bolling Galt, shown with him here, and they were married in December, 1915.

in the nation, generated by the completion of the Panama Canal, was drowning out the chorus of complaints.

The next era of history was being glimpsed too. Already the automobile was on the scene: the Ford Motor Company had been organized in 1903. Already airplanes were flying: the first powered flight had taken place in that same year as the Wright Brothers kept their four-cylinder machine aloft for twelve seconds. Theodore Roosevelt in 1902 had become the first President to ride in an automobile and in 1910 the first to ride in an airplane.

The engines of Europe's military machines were beginning to whir too. Few Americans could hear them. Still, those sounds from abroad were not lost on Wilson. He had written just before taking the train to his inauguration in 1913, "It would be the irony of fate if my administration had to deal chiefly with foreign affairs."

SECTION REVIEW

1. How did Woodrow Wilson view the role of the President?
2. (a) Why did Wilson support passage of the Underwood Tariff Act? (b) The Federal Reserve Act? (c) The Clayton Act?
3. (a) What were some of the progressives' chief accomplishments? (b) For what reasons did the Progressive Movement slow down?

Chapter 6 Review

Summary

At the beginning of the twentieth century a spirit of reform, known as the Progressive Movement, swept the nation. The movement was stimulated by the growth of a well-educated middle class which objected to corruption in government and to unfair practices in the world of business. Many of the shortcomings of government and of monopolistic businesses were brought to light by a crusading group of writers and journalists.

One goal of the progressives was to reform municipal government. Programs carried out by such mayors as Samuel Jones in Toledo and Tom Johnson in Cleveland were copied by other cities. On the state level, Robert La Follette of Wisconsin led the way with a sweeping program of reform. The direct primary, the secret ballot, the direct election of senators, women's suffrage, and the referendum, initiative, and recall were adopted during the Progressive Era. The progressives made little progress, however, in alleviating resentment toward foreign immigrants or in ending discrimination against blacks.

When Theodore Roosevelt became President in 1901, he brought to the White House a spirit of enthusiasm. He was sympathetic to the Progressive Movement and undertook a program of antitrust suits. He also persuaded Congress to pass laws to regulate railroad rates, limit the sale of harmful products, and conserve national resources.

Theodore Roosevelt took an active role in strengthening America's interests in the Caribbean and Asia. One of the most dramatic projects during his presidency was the construction of the Panama Canal. Roosevelt acquired for the United States a right of way across the Isthmus of Panama and immediately organized the building of a canal to connect the Pacific with the Atlantic Ocean. To reaffirm the Monroe Doctrine, Roosevelt issued a statement of policy — known as the Roosevelt Corollary — under which the United States claimed the right to intervene in Latin American countries to prevent intervention by European powers. In Asian affairs, Roosevelt negotiated a peace between Russia and Japan and won a Nobel Peace Prize for his efforts. To impress the world with America's military strength, Roosevelt sent the United States fleet around the world in 1907–1909.

William Howard Taft, hand-picked by Roosevelt as his successor, was elected President in 1908 but ran into trouble trying to fill his predecessor's shoes. Disillusioned with Taft's policies, Roosevelt re-entered politics in 1912 and split the Republican Party when he ran as a candidate of the newly formed Progressive Party. This division assured the election of the Democratic candidate, Woodrow Wilson. A scholarly, accomplished man, Wilson brought strong leadership to the White House and continued the reforms begun by Roosevelt.

Vocabulary and Important Terms

1. Progressive Movement
2. "mugwump literature"
3. muckraker
4. Socialist
5. direct primary
6. "Wisconsin idea"
7. referendum
8. initiative
9. recall
10. secret ballot
11. Seventeenth Amendment
12. Nineteenth Amendment
13. Jim Crow laws
14. *Plessy v. Ferguson*
15. Northern Securities Company case
16. Hepburn Act
17. Pure Food and Drug Act
18. Meat Inspection Act
19. Hay-Bunau-Varilla Treaty
20. Roosevelt Corollary
21. "dollar diplomacy"
22. Treaty of Portsmouth
23. Great White Fleet
24. Underwood Tariff Act
25. Federal Reserve Act
26. Clayton Act
27. Federal Trade Commission

Discussion Questions

1. (a) When did the Progressive Movement get its start, and what were its roots? (b) What kinds of problems were the progressive reformers seeking to correct?

2. (a) What, according to the progressives, was the proper role of the federal government in the world of business? (b) What progressive measures at the local, state, and national levels gave people increased participation in government?

3. (a) Why did many progressives regard Theodore Roosevelt as their leader? (b) How did Roosevelt display his conviction about right and wrong in handling the coal strike? (c) In dealing with big business? (d) In acquiring the Panama Canal? (e) In settling the Russo-Japanese War?

4. (a) How did Roosevelt interpret his election victory in 1904? (b) What steps did he take as a result? (c) What contributions did Roosevelt make to the conservation of natural resources?

5. (a) Why did the United States take an active interest in building a canal across the Isthmus of Pan-

ama? (b) How did the Panama Canal affect American foreign policy? (c) What role did the United States assume for itself in Latin America? (d) In what countries did the United States intervene during the Roosevelt and Taft administrations?

6. (a) Who were the three major candidates for President in 1912? (c) Why did Wilson win?

7. What progressive legislation was passed during Woodrow Wilson's years in office?

Relating Past and Present

In the eyes of today's reformers, what aspects of American society need attention? Are today's reformers more likely to be active at the local, state, or national levels? What do they see as the most effective methods of achieving reform?

Studying Local History

1. The Progressive Movement began at the local and state levels. Which progressive reforms, if any, affected your state? For example, does your state have a direct primary? Initiative? Referendum? Recall? If so, to what extent have they been used?

2. Study the map on page 155 showing women's suffrage. What voting rights had women gained in your state by 1919?

Using History Skills

1. *Reading source material.* Study Gertrude Foster Brown's description of suffragist tactics on page 156. (a) Why did the suffragists find it necessary to take their appeals directly to men? (b) How did they go about doing so? (c) How were the suffragist parades ''striking evidence of the sweeping progress of the movement''?

2. *Writing a report.* Choose one of the following American authors, all of whom are classified as muckrakers, and report on him or her to the class. Tell what abuses the author uncovered and what reforms, if any, resulted from the author's writings: (a) Ida M. Tarbell, (b) Lincoln Steffens, (c) Ray Stannard Baker, (d) Upton Sinclair, (e) Frank Norris.

3. *Comparing.* What personal characteristics and accomplishments made Theodore Roosevelt and Woodrow Wilson outstanding Presidents?

WORLD SCENE

Political Reform

In the early 1900's the spirit of reform prompted people in many parts of the world to demand more responsive governments.

The Russian Revolution of 1905. For many years there had been dissatisfaction with the inept rule of Czar Nicholas II and criticism of the corruption of the Russian government. The humiliating Russian defeat in the Russo-Japanese War of 1904–1905 contributed to unrest among the Russian people.

On a Sunday in January, 1905, thousands of workers assembled peacefully in front of the imperial palace in St. Petersburg. They intended to present a petition seeking improved working conditions and a representative assembly. Without warning, the palace guards fired on the protesters, killing and wounding hundreds. ''Bloody Sunday,'' as the incident came to be called, triggered upheaval throughout Russia.

To head off full-scale revolution, Nicholas agreed to certain reforms. He authorized the establishment of an elected assembly and permitted freedom of speech and other basic liberties for the Russian people. Once order had been restored, however, Nicholas took away many of the concessions he had been forced to make.

Revolution in China. By 1900 the Chinese government was on the verge of collapse. Pressure was mounting from Britain, France, and Russia for increased trading rights. There was pressure, too, from many young people filled with a desire to ''Westernize'' their country.

In a desperate effort to modernize the government, the young Manchu emperor, Kuang Hsü, began extensive reforms in 1898. These measures were seen as a threat by many traditional Chinese, and after only a few months Kuang Hsü was dethroned. He was succeeded by his aunt, Tz'u Hsi, then 62 years old. Although she gradually made important reforms, the Manchus were unable to control the revolutionary groups active throughout China.

In 1911 a spontaneous uprising led to a revolution that finally toppled the dynasty. An exiled Chinese revolutionary, Sun Yat-sen, was in America when he heard news that the Manchus had fallen. Quickly returning to China, he helped establish a Chinese republic and was chosen its first president.

Defending Democracy

1910 – 1920

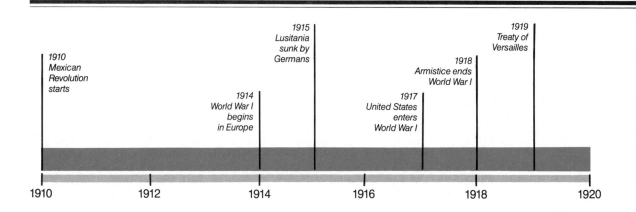

Although Woodrow Wilson had had no experience in foreign relations, fate thrust him into the role of international leader. The perplexing issues of the day caught him, as they did the nation, by surprise. In dealing with them he could not even turn to trained people in the Department of State, for there were none. His Secretary of State, William Jennings Bryan, knew practically nothing about the world outside America, and he was an amateur in diplomacy.

Wilson, for his part, took as a guide in facing his duties the moral instruction that he had received as a boy. His father, a Presbyterian minister, had instilled in the youth the idea that knowing right from wrong meant fighting for the right at whatever the cost. From his adoring mother, Wilson acquired a belief that he was superior in mind and morality to his associates. As President, living up to his parents' teaching made him feel keenly that wrong in the world could be made right through the will of the United States.

If, then, the path of international politics was for Wilson unknown territory, he was confident he could make his way on it successfully. He believed, furthermore, that he understood the place of the United States in the world. He once said, "My dream is that as the years go on and the world knows more and more of America . . . that America will come into the full light of day when all shall know that she puts human rights above all other rights, and that the flag is the flag not only of America, but of humanity."

1 Latin American Policy Remains Unchanged

President Wilson had hoped to complete his program of domestic reform. Foreign affairs, nonetheless, became his consuming concern. Eager to help remodel American life at home, he was quickly caught up in helping shape international politics.

Wilson continues the policy of intervening in Latin America. Shortly after he became President, Wilson declared himself to be firmly set against imperialism. In an unprecedented pledge in October, 1913, he said, "the United States will never again seek one additional foot of territory by conquest. She will devote herself to showing that she knows how to make honorable and fruitful use of the territory she has."

Wilson's words were reassuring, especially to Latin Americans who had grown deeply distrustful of their powerful neighbor to the north. Still, Wilson carried out more armed intervention in Latin America than any of his predecessors. He sent marines to Haiti in 1915 to insure the payment of debts, and in 1916 installed an American government that remained for eight years in the Dominican Republic. America extended its influence in the Caribbean, furthermore, with the purchase in 1917 of the Danish West Indies (now called the Virgin Islands) for $25 million (page 127).

Fighting breaks out in Mexico. Relations with Mexico proved most serious during Wilson's presidency. In 1911 the dictator of Mexico, Porfirio Díaz, who had ruled with an iron hand for almost all of the preceding 34 years, fell from power in a sudden upheaval. Mexico under Díaz had been a country controlled by a small privileged class. The vast majority of Mexicans were peons, or peasants, who did not own the land they worked. Díaz had sold about 75 percent of Mexico's mineral resources to foreign interests and had disposed of millions of acres of land to his friends.

Textile workers draped their factory with a huge flag. President Wilson hoped that the flag of the United States would symbolize freedom and human rights for all people.

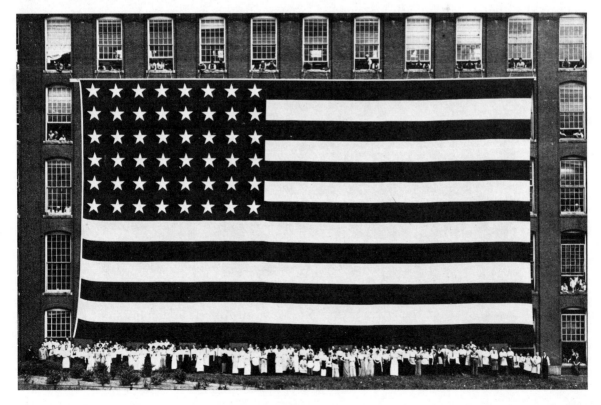

Díaz's successor was Francisco Madero, a democratic idealist who had led the revolution. Madero was too inexperienced, however, to put into effect the reforms he had planned. His followers, moreover, were badly divided. One group was led by General Victoriano Huerta (WEHR-tah), a former supporter of Díaz, who secretly plotted against the new president and finally drove him out of office. The counter-revolution reached its climax when Madero was assassinated — a deed most people blamed on Huerta himself.

Wilson follows a policy of "watchful waiting." When Wilson moved into the White House, he inherited the knotty problem of whether or not to recognize "the unspeakable Huerta," as he called the general. Wilson decided he would have nothing to do with Huerta. His hope was for a "tranquil and righteous government in Mexico." He desired it also to be democratic.

Many Americans were made uncomfortable by Wilson's refusal to extend diplomatic recognition to Huerta. A prominent editor asked, "What legal or moral right has a President of the United States to say who shall or shall not be President of Mexico?" Actually, Wilson was expressing a novel point of view: that the United States would only establish diplomatic relations with governments chosen in free elections. The policy of the United States had long been to recognize governments regardless of how they had come into existence.

Wilson decided to follow a policy of "watchful waiting," that is, of sitting by until the Huerta regime was toppled. The President was dismayed, however, when the Huerta government hung on. He had already cut off the shipment of arms to Mexico. In 1914 he lifted the embargo so that weapons and ammunition would flow to Huerta's chief opponents, Venustiano Carranza and Francisco ("Pancho") Villa (VEE-yah). Still, Wilson would go no further. He did not wish to endanger the investments — totaling nearly a billion dollars — that Americans had made in Mexican enterprises. These included ranches, oilfields, railroads, mines, and public utilities. Wil-

son feared, furthermore, for the safety of the 50,000 Americans living in Mexico.

American troops occupy Veracruz. Eventually, though, the President decided he had to try stronger methods. Following an incident involving American sailors in Tampico, Mexico, the President asked Congress for the authority to use force against Huerta's government. American naval units pounded the Mexican port of Veracruz, and marines and sailors went ashore to occupy the city. Wilson had expected the operation to be carried out without loss of life. Cadets of the Mexican Naval Academy resisted the attackers, however, taking heavy losses.

Wilson felt frustrated and quickly accepted an offer of the ABC countries (Argentina, Brazil, and Chile) to mediate the dispute. Under intense pressure, Huerta finally resigned in July and fled the country. Carranza became Mexico's new president.

American forces pursue Pancho Villa. Wilson, who believed that the Mexican Revolution could now go forward, was appalled when civil war broke out. Carranza was beset by troops under Pancho Villa. Villa, who had been angered by American aid given Carranza, crossed the United States border in March, 1916, and raided a town in New Mexico, killing nineteen inhabitants. The American public was outraged. Wilson felt he must act decisively.

The President sent Brigadier General John J. Pershing into Mexico on an expedition to find Villa and punish him. Villa cleverly eluded Pershing, however, and the Americans eventually clashed with Carranza's forces, who resented American soldiers on Mexican soil. When Carranza demanded their withdrawal, Wilson sent more troops to the border.

Tension mounted alarmingly. Still, Wilson shunned the idea of waging war against people struggling for freedom. In the end, he accepted Carranza's proposal that a joint Mexican-American commission try to settle the difficulties. The commission produced no solution, but Carranza soon destroyed Villa's forces, enabling Wilson to withdraw Pershing and his troops.

Brigadier General John J. Pershing and his troops crossed into Mexico in pursuit of Pancho Villa.

In spite of the frustrating events, the President remained friendly to the lofty goals of the Mexican Revolution. His actions had not led to the democratic Mexican government he had hoped for. He was satisfied, nevertheless, that Carranza had wide popular backing.

———

Wilson's diplomacy seemed sufficiently successful in Mexico to try it on a larger scale. Indeed, the opportunity came to him to preach democracy to the entire world. The occasion was war in Europe — long-threatened and long-anticipated.

SECTION REVIEW

1. Why may it be said that President Woodrow Wilson carried on the Latin American policy of his predecessors?
2. (a) Why did the Mexican people overthrow Díaz? (b) What was the policy of "watchful waiting"? (c) What circumstances led Wilson to follow that policy?
3. (a) What actions did Wilson take against the Huerta regime? (b) Why did he send General Pershing into Mexico? (c) What was the outcome of the dispute with Mexico?

2 World War I Begins

On June 28, 1914, Archduke Francis Ferdinand, heir to the throne of Austria-Hungary, and his wife Sophie were shot and killed in the city of Sarajevo, capital of the province of Bosnia (map, page 194). The assassinations were the work of conspirators from Serbia,[1] a neighboring country angered by Austria-Hungary's recent annexation of Bosnia, which it claimed as its own. Austria-Hungary, backed by Germany, its main ally, decided to use the incident as an excuse for crushing Serbia. On July 28, 1914, Austria-Hungary declared war on Serbia.

Within a week the war had spread with astonishing speed, as Europe's two mighty alliance systems found themselves locked in combat. In one camp were the *Central Powers*, led by Germany and including Austria-Hungary and the Ottoman Empire (Turkey). In the other camp were the *Allies*, consisting of Great Britain, France, Russia, Serbia, and, from 1915 on, Italy.

What were the causes of World War I? The rivalries of the powers of Europe were deeply rooted. The rise of the German Empire in the years following Germany's victory over France in the Franco-Prussian War in 1871 had greatly alarmed Britain and France. The Germans quickly made a virtue of military life and developed an aggressive foreign policy. With their formidable army and navy, they entered into competition with Britain and France to set up colonies in Africa and in the Pacific.

Situated in central Europe, Germany had fear of having one day to fight a "two-front" war, that is, a war on its eastern and western borders at the same time. To assure itself of some security, Germany signed a secret treaty of friendship with Austria-Hungary in 1879. The Ottoman Empire, fearing Russian designs on its port city of Constantinople (now Istanbul), had moved steadily closer to Germany by 1914.

Britain, France, and Russia were afraid that Germany and its allies might be able to

———

[1] Serbia is today part of Yugoslavia.

Citizens of Paris welcomed France's mobilization against Germany in 1914. As the "great war" broke out in Europe, the United States maintained neutrality.

control the continent of Europe. France and Russia put aside their old feuds and became allies in 1894. Britain and France, long-time enemies, resolved their differences by signing a treaty in 1904. When Russia joined England in an agreement in 1907, the three countries were linked together in a pledge to assist one another in the event of war. They hoped their combined strength would counterbalance that of the Central Powers.

Throughout Europe the international rivalry was fueled by an uncontrolled arms race that reinforced overheated national feelings. The huge armies of the European nations consisted of millions of men, expensively equipped and distinctively attired. The senior officers' dress uniforms were adorned with yards of gold braid. Their hats, trimmed with feathers or fur, seemed worthy headgear for gods. When these armies marched on parade, the civil-

ian populations swelled with pride at the show of *their* troops, *their* flag, *their* national strength.

The United States follows a policy of neutrality. Despite these ominous developments in Europe, Americans felt removed from any possible danger. Few people regarded European affairs as the business of the United States. On the whole, Americans continued to think that the Atlantic and Pacific oceans protected the United States from dangers outside — in much the way that moats once protected medieval castles.

Americans were astounded when the war broke out in 1914. They followed the news from Europe with fascination. Most people assumed that the hostilities would be over quickly. No one imagined the prophetic truth uttered by Edward Grey, Britain's foreign secretary: "The lamps are going out all over Europe; we shall not see them lit again in our lifetime." A new world was in the making.

Wilson was personally stunned by the news of war. He was especially dismayed when Germany marched against France through Belgium, a neutral country. He regarded the assault on the Belgians as lawless and uncivilized. Still, he issued a statement proclaiming America's neutrality. He urged all Americans to be "neutral in fact as well as in name . . . impartial in thought as well as in action."

Most Americans favor the Allies. To be neutral "in thought as well as in action" was not easy. Americans regarded the British and French as friends. The United States, it is true, had fought two wars against the British, and the millions of Irish immigrants who had come to America helped keep alive the feeling of hostility and distrust. By the late 1800's, however, relations between America and Great Britain had at last become friendly. The two nations were drawn closer by their common concern over Germany's commercial and military strength.

The revived feeling of kinship with the English came easily to Americans. The two nations shared the same language, the same faith in representative government, and the same view of personal freedom. American laws and customs were based on English traditions. Practically every American was familiar with the novels of Charles Dickens, the adventures of Sherlock Holmes, and the works of William Shakespeare. Millions of Americans who had never visited England knew its famous place names: Trafalgar Square, Windsor Castle, the Tower of London, and countless others.

United States relations with France were also cordial. Any American who had studied history could recall with gratitude the aid France had given during the War for Independence. Americans applauded the thought expressed in a poem penned soon after the outbreak of hostilities:

Forget us, God, if we forget
The sacred sword of Lafayette.

At first, few Americans felt hostility or even irritation toward Germany or Austria-Hungary. Germany was a comparatively new nation with which America had had little experience. Austria-Hungary also was only a name. A mention of Vienna, its capital, might bring to mind the lilting music of Johann Strauss, the "waltz king," who had lived there.

Trade with the Allies is important. The fighting in Europe gradually changed American feelings. One observer said that public opinion became, "Sure I'm neutral. I don't care who licks the Hun." ("Hun" was hostile slang for "the Germans.")

The people's sympathy with the Allied cause grew as American prosperity seemed more and more dependent on trade with the Allies. Being a neutral nation the United States could sell supplies, including munitions, to either or both sides in the struggle. At first, Americans sold only a little more than usual to Britain and France. As the war heated up, however, the trickle of goods to those countries became a mighty Niagara. Because the British navy controlled the seas and had clamped a blockade on Germany's coastlines, the Central Powers could not readily obtain products from America.[2]

Americans also lent money to the Allies to help them purchase food and war equipment. By the end of 1916, the Allies had borrowed about $2.3 billion in the United States, compared with Germany's modest $20 million. Plainly the eventual recovery of their money gave Americans a heavy stake in an Allied victory. The outcome was by no means certain, however, for the war had already taken unpredicted turns.

Germany devises a strategy for attacking France. The war planning of the major European powers had been under way since the beginning of the century. The French and the Germans both viewed Belgium as

---

[2]Despite the much-publicized build-up of naval forces before the war, the only important naval engagement was the Battle of Jutland, fought off the west coast of Denmark in 1916. Although the British took heavy losses, the German fleet was forced to return to its home base and remain there during the rest of the war.

the highway each would have to use in order to strike at the other. In 1905 the Germans had adopted as their strategy the plan of Count Alfred von Schlieffen (SHLEEF-un), the chief of the German general staff. Schlieffen's strategy called for sending his best troops in a wide, wheeling movement through Belgium into northeastern France. In a gigantic hammer blow the troops would sweep down upon Paris, entrapping the French armies and destroying them. Meanwhile, a defensive war would contain the slow-moving Russians in the east. Then, after Paris had fallen, German troops would be dispatched to the Eastern Front to deal with the enemy there.

Schlieffen had said that everything depended on keeping strong the right wing of the attacking German army. Moreover, he wanted that right wing to travel in an arc that would take it as far west as possible. "When you march into France," he had said, "let the last man on the right brush the [English] Channel with his sleeve."

These Allied soldiers were entrenched in northeastern France. By one estimate, the trenches of the Allied and the Central Powers totaled 25,000 miles.

The surprises that war inevitably produces defeated the plan. Schlieffen's successor as chief of staff, Helmuth von Moltke (MOLT-kuh), grew alarmed when three things went wrong: (1) the Belgians, led by Albert, their king, resisted the Germans fiercely; (2) the supposedly inefficient Russians were able to get their troops to the front much earlier than expected; and (3) Britain sprang swiftly to the defense of Belgium. Moltke, in panic, weakened the right wing of the German army by detaching units of his army and sending them east to help stem the Russian advance.

The German advance is stopped. Germany's plan for a quick victory, therefore, was shattered. French forces stopped the Germans just north of Paris early in September, 1914, at the First Battle of the Marne. The French were aided by troops hurriedly brought to the front from Paris in 1,200 taxicabs — the first time troops had ever been moved into battle by motor vehicle. The Germans now tried to reach the English Channel, extending their lines as far west as they could. Determined to win this "race to the sea," the Allied armies — British, French, and Belgian — slugged it out with the Germans at Ypres (EE-pruh) during October and November. In the carnage, the British Expeditionary Force of 100,000 men was reduced by more than half.

Both sides use trench warfare and new types of weapons. A tragic stalemate soon developed. The armies, constantly reinforced with new conscripts, burrowed into trenches running from Belgium across northern France and southward to the border of Switzerland. The troops held fixed positions that for the next three years never shifted more than a few miles forward or backward.

The machine gun became the war's supreme firearm. It was ideal for trench warfare. When troops went "over the top," seeking to advance across "no man's land," they faced the withering fire of these diabolical weapons. A frontal assault on enemy trenches inevitably produced a hideous number of casualties.

In 1915 the war was made even more horrible by the introduction of poison gas by the Germans. Then, in 1916 at the Battle of the Somme, the British unveiled still another new weapon — the tank.

Fighting takes place on other fronts. On the Eastern Front, the Russians, having been rolled back from East Prussia, recovered to prevent the Germans from taking the Polish capital of Warsaw. By the fall of 1915, after a year of invasions and counterinvasions, neither side was making progress.

A British-French fleet, meanwhile, sought to attack Constantinople. The effort failed, and the scheme to isolate Turkey from the other Central Powers was foiled.

Germany uses its submarines. During 1914 and 1915 both sides tried to observe the rights of neutrals, which meant the rights chiefly of the United States. Nevertheless, by 1915 Britain and Germany had become like two huge bloody giants blindly battling each other to the death. The mounting casualties and the search for a means to bring the war to a victorious conclusion made both sides bolder. The British declared that food was essential to the war effort and, therefore, subject to seizure if found on a neutral vessel bound for Germany. They began to halt American ships on the high seas. Sometimes the British took American vessels into port and held them so long that the cargoes rotted. To fool German submarines, British ships occasionally displayed the American flag — also a violation of international law.

Still, British actions affected only property. Claims for damages could be adjusted after the war. German actions produced loss of life because they employed a relatively new naval weapon: the submarine, also called the U-boat (from the German word *Unterseeboot*).

The submarine changed the nature of warfare at sea. Formerly a neutral ship that had been stopped at sea would have been boarded and searched; passengers and crew would have been removed before sinking the vessel. Submarines, however, had thin metal hulls easily pierced by the guns of enemy ships. Submarines were obliged to fire their torpedoes and flee.

Early in the war, Germany made known its plan to torpedo, without warning, enemy or neutral merchant vessels sailing in the waters around the British Isles. The Wilson administration responded to the German announcement with a stern warning. If Germany's new policy — clearly a violation of international law — led to a loss of American lives or property, Germany would be held "to a strict accountability." Nevertheless, the notice to the Germans neither defined the threat nor dealt with the question of what would happen if American lives were lost aboard an Allied, not an American, vessel.

The "Lusitania" is sunk. The German government instructed its U-boats to avoid attacks on American ships. Still, the conduct of any war has a way of slipping out of control, almost as if it has a life of its own. An American was killed when a British merchant vessel was torpedoed in March, 1915, and an American tanker was sunk on May 1, with the loss of two American lives. The United States had not yet decided how to respond to these German actions when a great turning point occurred on May 7: a U-boat torpedoed the British liner *Lusitania* within sight of the Irish shore. The liner sank within a few minutes. Almost 1,200 people perished, including 128 Americans.

Chance, always a factor in war, had played a part in the disaster. The U-boat commander had been disappointed over his assignment to the vulnerable little vessel. During his time at sea, moreover, he had seen nothing exciting to aim at. Running out of fuel and other supplies, he had decided to head home when suddenly the *Lusitania* loomed in his periscope. He did not know that it was carrying a cargo of munitions. The *Lusitania*, furthermore, would not have been in the U-boat's range of fire if its captain had followed orders to pursue a zig-zag course across the Atlantic from New York, in order to avoid submarines. He had placed such supreme confidence in his luxurious "Lucy" and especially in its speed that he had sailed a straight path.

An undated German recruiting poster bears remarkable resemblance to the British poster of 1914. More and more enlistments were needed to fill the ranks of those killed.

Wilson reacts to the crisis. Americans were outraged by the sinking of the *Lusitania*. Theodore Roosevelt denounced the attack as "piracy on a vaster scale of murder than old-time pirates ever practiced." The Wilson administration sent a series of stern diplomatic notes to Germany, insisting upon an apology, compensation for the losses, and a pledge to stop attacking unarmed merchant ships.

The position of the United States had now been made clear. Americans claimed the right to travel anywhere — even on Allied merchant ships and regardless of what cargoes those ships might be carrying. The United States, in short, would protect its citizens, even when they were sailing under a foreign flag. The United States remained committed, nevertheless, to a policy of neutrality toward the warring nations. In response to those critics who called for war with Germany, Wilson declared, "There is

such a thing as a man being too proud to fight. There is such a thing as a nation being so right that it does not need to convince others by force that it is right."

Germany issues the "Arabic" and "Sussex" pledges. While the American public was still inflamed over the *Lusitania* incident, further distressing news arrived: On August 19, 1915, a U-boat had sunk the British steamer *Arabic*, causing the loss of two American lives. Eager to avoid further trouble with the United States, the German ambassador to Washington issued the so-called *Arabic* pledge. Germany promised not to sink unarmed vessels without warning, unless they tried to escape. The *Arabic* pledge was short-lived. In March, 1916, a U-boat torpedoed the unarmed French passenger ship *Sussex* in the English Channel. The German commander had assumed, he said, that the *Sussex* was laying mines.

When President Wilson learned that several Americans aboard the *Sussex* had been injured, he was furious. He warned the German government that if it did not "immediately declare and effect an abandonment of its present methods of submarine warfare against passenger and freight-carrying vessels, the government of the United States can have no choice but to sever diplomatic relations with the German Empire altogether." When Germany's ruler, Kaiser Wilhelm II, read the note from the United States, he was furious. He scribbled on it what he considered to be his sad choices: "Either starve at England's bidding or face war with America!" In what became known as the *Sussex* pledge, however, Germany renewed its promise not to sink unarmed ships without warning. Germany added the condition, however, that the United States must persuade the British government to give up its blockade.

Wilson wins the election of 1916. Wilson's desire to keep the United States at peace was a barrier to his making preparations for the possibility of going to war. Nevertheless, a program to strengthen the armed forces was begun in 1916. The regular army was doubled in size and the National Guard was vastly increased and strengthened. The navy began a building program aimed at giving the United States the largest fleet in the world by 1920.

Since most Americans still favored neutrality, the President's slowness stood him in good stead in the 1916 presidential campaign. The Democrats' slogan, "He kept us out of war," made a favorable impression upon peace-loving Americans. Wilson was proud to explain, moreover, that he had maintained "peace with honor." In the big industrial cities, laboring people regarded the President as a friend whose policies they valued. Election posters showing a worker's family bore the caption, "He has protected me and mine." The Republicans, making an issue of America's alleged lack of preparedness, issued placards showing the widow of a drowned American and her children with the words, "He has neglected me and mine."

In 1916, President Wilson campaigned on his policy of neutrality, although the aggressive attacks of German U-boats were drawing the United States closer to war.

Many Republicans believed they could win in 1916 if they nominated Theodore Roosevelt once again. He was eager to make the race, but important party leaders could not accept the man who had deserted them four years earlier (page 170). Besides, they wanted a "safer" candidate. They found him in Charles Evans Hughes of New York. Stately and handsome, Hughes had gained fame as a reform governor of New York, a position he resigned when President Taft named him to the Supreme Court in 1910. Now he stepped down from the Court in order to accept the Republican nomination.

Hughes's slogan was "America first and America efficient." Hughes earnestly courted the so-called "hyphenate vote," especially the Irish-Americans and the German-Americans. Many people assumed that Wilson's apparently pro-Britain and anti-Germany stance had already cost him the support of those people.

On election night, Hughes appeared to have won. Many of the Bull Moosers of four years earlier were back in the Republican Party again, and they had given Hughes their support. It was said of the Democrats receiving the returns at the Hotel Biltmore in New York that never was there "such a morgue-like entertainment in the annals of time." Hughes went to sleep believing he would be the next President.

The following day, however, the returns from California came in, making Wilson the victor after all. For the first time since the days of Andrew Jackson, a Democrat had been elected for a second consecutive term in the White House.

SECTION REVIEW

1. (a) What incident touched off the First World War? (b) What were the underlying causes of that conflict?
2. (a) What policy did the United States follow at the beginning of World War I? (b) Which side did most Americans favor? Why?
3. (a) How successful were Germany's plans for scoring a quick victory? (b) Why did both Britain and Germany try to restrict American shipping? (c) What methods did each use?
4. (a) What was the effect on American public opinion of the sinking of the *Lusitania*? (b) Why did Germany issue the *Arabic* and *Sussex* pledges?
5. (a) What steps did President Wilson take to prepare the United States for war? (b) What slogan did he use in his successful bid for re-election in 1916?

3 The United States Enters the War

As 1916 drew to a close, things were looking up for Germany. German forces had been victorious on the Eastern Front and were on the verge of forcing Russia out of the war. Germany had also won an impressive victory over Rumania, which had recently entered the war on the Allied side. Perhaps the Germans could defeat *all* their enemies.

Wilson urges negotiations. Meanwhile, Wilson had been working to end the war. In 1915 he had sent abroad his close friend and adviser, Colonel Edward M. House, to discuss possible peace terms. Both sides were still convinced they could win, however, so the efforts of House came to nothing. In early 1916, Wilson again sent House to Europe for a round of talks. German leaders were eager for Wilson to call a peace conference. They hoped a settlement would reflect the military situation, which favored the Central Powers. The Allies, of course, were afraid to negotiate until their military position had improved. Again the peace effort failed.

In December, 1916, Wilson asked each side to state privately its terms for peace, aiming to mediate an end to the fighting. The answers were so extravagant that they offered no possibility for successful negotiation. Wilson knew that Germany would now try to end the war by resuming unrestricted submarine warfare. In that event, he might not be able to keep the United States from being drawn into the struggle.

Germany gambles on a quick victory. On January 31, 1917, the German ambassador in Washington informed the American government that all ships found in the war zone would be subject to submarine attack. Germany, in other words, had gone back on its *Sussex* pledge and was about to resume unrestricted submarine warfare. Three days later the United States broke off diplomatic relations with Germany. Despite the opposition of a handful of senators, whom Wilson called "a little group of willful men," the President announced that American merchant vessels would now be armed with naval guns. The country had moved from "strict neutrality" to armed neutrality.

The "Zimmermann telegram" pushes the United States closer to war. The German government further shocked Americans by proposing an alliance between Germany and Mexico if Germany and the United States went to war. In return, Germany would help Mexico recover Texas, New Mexico, and Arizona. The message containing this secret proposal was sent by Foreign Minister Arthur Zimmermann to the German minister in Mexico City. Transmitted in code, it was intercepted and decoded by British intelligence officers. The British government passed on the message to authorities in Washington, knowing the effect it would have.

Made public, the Zimmermann telegram created a sensation. In the Southwest, where the issues of the war had not aroused much excitement, people were aghast. Wilson had more support than ever for the strong stand he was taking against Germany's decision to return to unrestricted submarine warfare.

Wilson still hoped that somehow there could be "a peace without victory," as he told Congress early in 1917. "Only a peace between equals can last," he declared. Fundamentally, he hated the idea of war, believing that it might weaken democracy in America and turn the country into an armed camp. Still, he spoke of Germany privately as "a madman that should be curbed." He was becoming convinced that a victory for Germany would mean the triumph of militarism in the world, and that America's free way of life could be a casualty of such an outcome.

The United States goes to war. From March 12 to March 19, 1917, Wilson was confined to the White House by illness. During that time he seems to have pondered deeply the choice he felt he must make: war with Germany or a continuing effort to defend neutral rights through diplomacy and armed neutrality. During that week, submarines sank three American merchant vessels as the Germans pressed relentless attacks against shipping in the waters around the British Isles, France, and Italy.

During those days also, the czar of Russia, Nicholas II, was forced to give up his throne. Military reverses and incompetent leadership had brought to the surface a long-smouldering hostility to the Russian royal family. Russian revolutionaries quickly set up a provisional government that aimed to carry on the war. Headed by Alexander Kerensky, the new government offered hope that Russia might create a parliamentary regime. A democratic Russia fighting on the Allied side would make Germany stand out even more as a repressive country dominated by its "military masters."

When the week was over, Wilson was sure of what he must do — absolutely sure, it appeared. He issued a call for Congress to assemble on April 2, 1917. Standing before its members, he asked them to recognize the state of war that Germany had forced upon the United States. "The present German submarine warfare against commerce is a warfare against mankind," he declared. "[We] will not choose the path of submission and suffer the most sacred rights of our nation and our people to be ignored or violated," he went on. Then the President abruptly shifted gears — from defending American rights to asserting that as long as the existing German government was in power "there can be no assured security for the democratic governments of the world." He added a sentence that became America's rallying cry: "The world must be made safe for democracy." Suddenly Wilson was transformed from being a man "too proud to fight" into a man willing to wage war for a lofty end.

Wilson may still have had doubts that he had done right in asking for war. That night, when he was alone with his secretary in the White House, he recalled the cheering of the crowd that had greeted him as he rode to Capitol Hill. "My message today," the President said softly, "was a message of death for our young men. How strange it seems to applaud that." He then put his head on the table and wept.

The public approved overwhelmingly of the war resolution that Congress voted on April 6, 1917. Being joined with England and France — now underdogs in the fighting — satisfied millions of Americans who believed that the Allies embodied the same democratic ideals as the United States. Americans were also reassured by the idea that winning the war would ensure permanent world peace. Many people itched for the troops to be sent to Europe in order to get on with the task. A popular song was

Many artists contributed their talents in support of the war. Norman Rockwell illustrated this sheet-music cover.

the rousing "Over There," written by a stage star, George M. Cohan:

> Over there — over there —
> Send the word, send the word over there —
> That the Yanks are coming, the Yanks are coming,
> The drums rum-tumming ev'rywhere. . . .

The armed forces are strengthened. With America's entry into the struggle, Allied representatives began to arrive in the United States, pleading for quick assistance to save their nations from defeat. The United States, however, was not yet prepared for heavy military participation. It did not have a single complete army division. The navy was ill-equipped. The air force, simply a section of the army, consisted of 35 pilots and 50 aging planes.

Still, a crusading spirit developed. The nation mobilized with lightning speed, astonishing the world and especially Germany. The Germans had concluded that American troops would not arrive in Europe in time to affect the fighting.

Because the Defense Act of 1916 had provided for a regular army of only 175,000 men, Wilson turned to a military draft to provide a force large enough for the nation's needs. The Selective Service Act, which went into effect in May, 1917, aroused opposition among people who feared that it would cause the nation to glorify military life. The Speaker of the House, "Champ" Clark, said he could see "precious little difference between a conscript and a convict." In general, however, the public accepted the draft. The Selective Service Act eventually made all men between the ages of 18 and 45 subject to induction. By the end of the war, almost five million men had served in the armed forces.

Among the troops who served in the armed forces were some 370,000 black Americans. Blacks served in every branch of the army. They were not allowed to enlist in the Marine Corps, however, and the navy took them solely for noncombat duties. Only through much agitating, moreover, was a school established for the training of black army officers. Blacks, nevertheless, distinguished themselves. The first Allied unit to break through to the Rhine River was the 369th, an all-black regiment.

Convoys protect American shipping. United States naval forces in the Atlantic were under the command of Rear Admiral William S. Sims, who helped devise a way of outfoxing the U-boats: the convoy system. The vulnerable merchant ships would travel the Atlantic surrounded by a convoy (an escort of destroyers and cruisers). As a result, despite the presence of German submarines, the United States Navy did not lose a single troopship sent abroad. Moreover, the navy shipped about five million tons of essential supplies to Europe.

Government agencies expand their operations. President Wilson understood from the beginning that the fighting front depended on the well-organized support of people at home. Through sweeping powers granted him by Congress, he set about making this possible. The daily life of Americans was soon regulated by dozens of government committees, boards, and councils. These bureaus greatly expanded the role of the federal government. Many Americans for the first time began to complain that Wilson had instituted a *bureaucracy,* that is, a government run by rules and regulations made by unelected officials.

The War Industries Board placed centralized controls on the nation's economy. The Board's chief work was to obtain supplies for the United States military forces and for the Allies. It also managed the distribution of raw materials at home and abroad. The chairman was Bernard M. Baruch, a successful financier. Baruch persuaded many business executives to give up well-paid positions in private business and become "dollar-a-year men," donating their talent to the war effort.

In 1917 the President chose Herbert C. Hoover, a California mining engineer and businessman, to head the Food Administration. Hoover had earlier demonstrated rare ability in distributing food in war-torn Belgium. Hoover and the volunteers who worked with him toured the United States urging the public to conserve food. The government proclaimed wheatless and meatless days and preached "the gospel of the clean plate." "To Hooverize" became a popular verb meaning "to save food."

The President also appointed a fuel administrator to see that the public conserved coal for the war effort. "Gasless Sundays" and "heatless Mondays" were introduced to dramatize the need.

The government took over the management and operation of the nation's railroads. To supervise the Railroad Administration, Wilson named his son-in-law, Secretary of the Treasury William Gibbs McAdoo. Meanwhile, the United States Shipping Board was placed in charge of an accelerated program of shipbuilding. In one day — July 4, 1918 — 95 vessels were launched. A sign in many shipyards read, "Three ships a week or bust."

Support for the war effort by laboring people was important to the nation's military success. The National War Labor Board was created in April, 1918. It sat as the final judge in labor disputes. One of its chairmen was former President Taft.

Money is raised to help finance the war. About a third of the war's cost was met through increased taxation. The remainder was raised through the sale to the public of Liberty Bonds, long-term bonds with face values as low as $50. The series of five issues — including a final "Victory" Loan — brought in more than $21 billion. Actors and actresses, sports figures, and government officials helped to sell the bonds at meetings, in theaters, hotel lobbies, and in restaurants. In all, over twenty million Americans purchased Liberty Bonds.

The war provides new opportunities for women. As men answered the call of the draft and left their jobs, women found they were welcome in many fields previously closed to them. Soon they were making ammunition, running elevators, collecting fares on streetcars, and doing many other indispensable tasks. When the navy found it was short of clerks, the Secretary of the Navy, Josephus Daniels, asked, "Is there

This college student earned credit for her work on an American farm during the war.

any law that says a yeoman must be a man?" He quickly answered his own question by putting more than 10,000 women into uniform. Some women eventually served with the troops as nurses, Red Cross and Salvation Army workers, ambulance drivers, and canteen hostesses.

Black migration from the South gathers force. Black Americans also found fresh opportunities. For the first time in the nation's history, blacks were invited to participate in a great national undertaking. The beckoning jobs in war factories lured many black people northward and westward. Blacks could find jobs in all the war industries, mainly doing heavy work such as riveting the hulls of ships, cutting coal in the mines, and butchering cattle in the slaughterhouses. Still, the *Christian Recorder*, a black church paper, said in 1917 that the job openings the war created were the best thing that had happened to blacks "since the Emancipation Proclamation."

In the cities of the North, where blacks had traditionally lived in white neighborhoods, large, exclusively black "ghettos" quickly developed. In New York there was Harlem; in Chicago, the South Side; in Cleveland, the Hough section; and so forth. The National Urban League, organized in New York in 1911 with the help of concerned whites, played a significant role in helping southern blacks shift from rural to big-city life. The League shortly had branches throughout the country.

Public opinion is mobilized. Despite strong support for the war effort, some Americans had been against Wilson's declaration of war. Opposition came from some Americans of German and Irish extraction. It also came from pacifists opposed to war, whatever the purpose, as well as from radical groups who regarded the struggle solely as a means of defending capitalism.

To counter the voices of opposition, the government took positive steps. It established the Committe on Public Information to "sell" the war to the people. George Creel, a successful journalist, was named to head the Committee. He so dominated it that it became known as the Creel Committee. To whip up public enthusiasm, the Creel Committee enlisted poster artists, college professors, and novelists. An army of 75,000 lecturers delivered "Four-Minute Speeches" — in theaters, at church gatherings, at union meetings — on such topics as "Why We Are Fighting" and "The Meaning of America."

Critics charged that the Creel Committee was attempting for the first time in American history to manipulate public opinion. Creel stirred up much hatred of Germans, suggesting that German spies were everywhere. Still, those Americans who agreed with Wilson that a better world would come from the struggle, admired Creel's work in publicizing at home and abroad the President's stirring speeches.

A climate of intolerance is fostered. Just before the United States entered the conflict, President Wilson expressed his concern to an editor. "Lead this people into war," he said, "and they'll forget there ever was such a thing as tolerance." The dire prophecy was partly fulfilled when Congress made stern arrangements for dealing with disloyal individuals. The Espionage Act (1917) provided severe punishment for people engaging in spying, sabotage, or obstruction of the war effort. The Sedition Act (1918) extended these penalties to individuals who made disloyal remarks. In time, over 1,500 people were arrested for sedition. Eugene Debs (page 96), who expressed pacifist sentiments, was sent to prison for violation of the Espionage Act. (He received a presidential pardon in 1921.)

Local vigilante committees sometimes took things into their own hands. In one midwestern town, a minister who had been forbidden to use German was caught speaking it as he comforted a dying woman who spoke only German. Local anti-German feeling was so great that he was tarred, feathered, and run out of town. In many places throughout the country, schools dropped the teaching of German. The playing of music by German composers was commonly banned. On menus everywhere sauerkraut became "liberty cabbage" and hamburgers became "Salisbury steak."

The Fourteen Points (1917)

Open covenants of peace, openly arrived at, after which there shall be no private international understandings of any kind, but diplomacy shall proceed always frankly and in public view.

Absolute freedom of navigation upon the seas . . . in peace and in war. . . .

The removal, so far as possible, of all economic barriers and the establishment of an equality of trade conditions among all the nations. . . .

Adequate guarantees given and taken that national armaments will be reduced. . . .

A free, open-minded, and absolutely impartial adjustment of all colonial claims, based upon . . . the principle that . . . the interests of the populations concerned must have equal weight with the . . . claims of the government whose title is to be determined.

A general association of nations must be formed under specific covenants for the purpose of affording mutual guarantees of political independence and territorial integrity to great and small states alike.

Wilson issues the Fourteen Points. Still, the war aroused high-mindedness in Americans too. Millions found inspiration in Wilson's public addresses. In them he put on display his idealism, his vision, and his gift of language. None of them was more influential than the statement of war aims that became known as the "Fourteen Points." He delivered it before Congress on January 8, 1918.

In the speech — the main parts of which are summarized above — the President tried to appeal to thinking people everywhere. He set forth fourteen "points" or proposals for helping to reduce the risk of war in the future. The first five were general in scope. They called for an end to secret diplomacy; the establishment of freedom of the seas; the removal of economic barriers to international trade; the reduction of arms; and a readjustment of "all colonial claims, based upon . . . the interests of the populations concerned. . . ." The eight points that followed called for specific territorial changes to relieve the distress of various peoples living under foreign domination. In recommending, for example, independence for Poland, Wilson was advancing the principle of "national self-

determination," an end being pursued by a number of nationalities in Europe.

The fourteenth point expressed Wilson's chief goal for the postwar world: the creation of a League of Nations. Wilson, a year earlier, in the "peace without victory" speech, had stated his belief that the United States would willingly join a "League for Peace." Such an organization, Wilson was convinced, would help guarantee the political independence and territorial security of all countries, small as well as great.

SECTION REVIEW

1. Vocabulary: *bureaucracy.*
2. Why were Wilson's efforts to end the war in Europe unsuccessful?
3. What events led the United States to declare war against Germany?
4. (a) How did the United States strengthen its armed forces? (b) What agencies administered the war effort on the home front? (c) What steps were taken to finance the war?
5. (a) What opportunities did the war create for women? (b) For black Americans?
6. (a) How was public opinion mobilized? (b) What were the Espionage and Sedition acts?
7. What were the Fourteen Points?

4 The United States Helps Win the War

By early 1918 the war had reached a decisive stage. The Germans, in control of most of Belgium and northern France, were attempting once again to take Paris. The Allies' situation seemed desperate. To make matters worse, at the end of 1917 Italy had been decisively defeated by Austrian troops at the Battle of Caporetto, losing 300,000 men and 30,000 pieces of artillery.

A new government comes to power in Russia. Adding to the Allies' woes, Russia was about to leave the war. The Kerensky government (page 187) had been driven from power in November, 1917, by a small party called the Bolsheviks. The Russian people, tired and exhausted, had lost their heart for fighting. They responded to the slogan of the Bolsheviks: "Peace, Land, Bread." They were enticed, too, by the Bolsheviks' announced plan to create a government of workers, soldiers, and peasants.

The new regime signed a humiliating peace treaty with Germany at the city of Brest-Litovsk. The Germans were now free to transfer to the Western Front the huge armies on duty in the east. The Bolsheviks, meanwhile, established a Communist dictatorship in Russia, doing away with private ownership of property and allowing no opposition parties, no free elections, and no freedom of the press, speech, or religion.[3]

American forces arrive in Europe. Upon entering the war, the United States had speedily organized an American Expeditionary Force, called the AEF for short. Its commander was John J. Pershing, now 57 years old and a major general. Pershing had made the headlines in 1906 when President Roosevelt "jumped" him in rank from captain to brigadier general. He became a national name in 1916 by his pursuit of Pancho Villa (page 178). Because he had commanded black troops early in his career, he had acquired the nickname "Black Jack."

The American soldiers, "Yanks" as they were known,[4] were untried but enthusiastic. Their arrival on French soil, beginning in June, 1917, heartened the Allies and shook the morale of the Germans. France's Marshal Ferdinand Foch (FOHSH), the supreme commander of the Allied forces, was impressed by the quality of the Americans. He hoped to use them to fill in the badly mauled ranks of the Allies. Reluctantly, he honored Pershing's instructions from Washington that the United States forces must fight as a separate unit.

The Germans quickly discovered the fighting ability of the Yanks. In the first offensive in which Americans were engaged, they captured from the Germans the key town of Cantigny (kahn-tee-NYEE) on the road to Paris.

Germany launches an offensive. At the beginning of June, 1918, the Germans had fought to within about fifty miles of the French capital. They now knew they must deliver a knockout blow before more Amer-

United States Army pilots first downed German aircraft in April, 1918. The excitement of air combat contrasted greatly with the grimness of trench warfare.

---

[3]In 1922 the Bolsheviks changed the official name of Russia to the Union of Soviet Socialist Republics. It is often referred to as the Soviet Union or the USSR.
[4]They also were called "doughboys." The word probably originated from the white dust of the adobe soil in the Southwest that covered mounted troops. From early days, the Spanish had applied the word *adobe* to all military people. The step from there to "dobie" and then to "doughboy" was short.

Americans to the Front

An American war correspondent and writer, Frederick Palmer, was with the United States forces when they landed in France in 1917. In his book *America in France*, he described the scene as the first American troops took their place alongside the French in the front-line trenches.

We were moved into the trenches with all the care of father teaching son to swim. The French are thorough people. They believe in no short cuts to learning, but in gradual process.

Our battalions, three at a time, were to be placed between French battalions in the line in what was to be distinctly considered as another step in our course of training. Every American battery was to be paired off with a French battery. The French regulated the amount of our artillery fire and their observers named our targets.

The artillery moved up on the night of October 22nd. Battery C, of the Sixth Field Artillery, wanted the honor of firing the first shot of the war. Without waiting to go into position at the time set, the men dragged a gun forward in the early morning and sent a shell at the enemy. There was no particular target. The aim was in the general direction of Berlin.

The night of October 23rd, when our infantry left their barracks for the trenches, was chill and rainy. Down the street you heard a sturdy rhythmic tread; and then a moving shadow, taking form in the darkness, developed into a column of soldiers with their faces much alike in the gloom. For all they knew they might be going into violent action. They had been drilled and drilled and schooled and lectured, warned

An American doughboy

by their veteran instructors what a tremendous, formidable enemy, with all his preparation and experience, the German was in the complicated techniques of trench warfare, with its sudden surprises of raid and artillery concentration.

There was nothing downhearted about their mood. They were worried lest they should make a mistake and not remember all their training in case of a crisis. It did not matter so much to them that they might be killed as they might be killed in a manner that was contrary to instruction. If they had been told to charge machine guns then and there, I think that they would have let out the cry of hounds off the leash.

ican divisions were put into action. In this crucial moment for the Allies, doughboys were pressed into action in the Battle of Chateau-Thierry (shah-TOH tyeh-REE), where they helped the French halt the enemy advance.

Substantial numbers of Americans also took part in recapturing Belleau Wood from the Germans — west of Chateau-Thierry and on the path to Paris too. In the struggle,

United States marines obeyed their orders: "We dig no trenches to fall back on. The marines will hold where they stand."

An Allied counteroffensive helps win the war. By the end of July, the German offensive had finally been slowed. Then, in the Second Battle of the Marne, the Allies, reinforced by 85,000 Americans, halted the Germans. The tide of the war was turning.

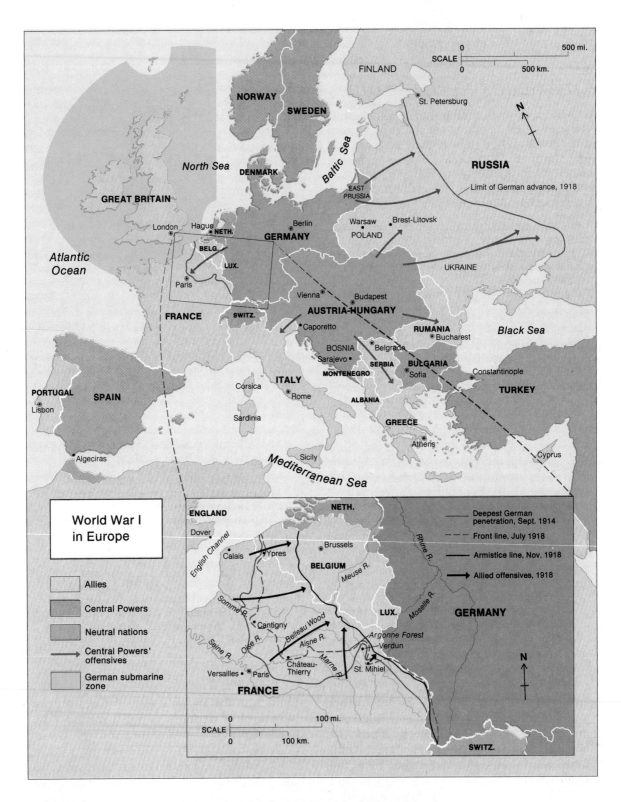

World War I in Europe

Legend:
- Allies
- Central Powers
- Neutral nations
- Central Powers' offensives
- German submarine zone

Inset map legend:
- Deepest German penetration, Sept. 1914
- Front line, July 1918
- Armistice line, Nov. 1918
- Allied offensives, 1918

In the east, Germany achieved relatively easy victories over Russia's disorganized and ill-equipped forces. In the west, the Allied powers defended their positions in northern France. The inset map shows that the line of deepest German penetration in 1914 was barely a hundred miles from the line of armistice four years later.

The Allies began to force the Germans into retreat on a line from the Aisne (AYN) River to the Marne (map, page 194). About 270,000 United States troops participated in this mighty effort.

The first major United States offensive took place in September, 1918, as part of the final stages of the war. The Americans were assigned the task of driving the Germans out of the St. Mihiel (SAN mee-YEL) area, which had been held by the enemy since 1914. After four days of bloody fighting that cost 7,000 American lives, St. Mihiel came under American control.

The troops in the St. Mihiel offensive were aided by airplanes that strafed the enemy and helped spot artillery positions. This was the first significant use of air support in the history of warfare. The planes were English or French, but many of the fliers were American. Most of them were members of the Lafayette Escadrille, under the command of Colonel "Billy" Mitchell. The Escadrille was a group of devil-may-care young men who had originally entered the French air service and had only recently transferred to the United States forces. Because they expected their lives to be short, they flew without parachutes. Some of the pilots became public heroes — like Eddie Rickenbacker, who was eventually credited with shooting down 26 German planes.

American forces were now sent to the area between the Meuse River and the Argonne Forest. The attack, launched on September 26, 1918, was part of a general Allied offensive.

Over a million Americans were engaged in the Meuse-Argonne operation. In the densely wooded Argonne Forest, the troops often could not see more than a few yards ahead. The Yanks crawled inch by inch over barbed wire covered by heavy undergrowth. The setting was made to order for the German defenders, who had regarded the terrain, heavily fortified with concrete entrenchments, barbed-wire entanglements, and sheltered machine-gun pits, as impenetrable. Before the battle was over, the Americans had sustained 120,000 casualties. They had, nevertheless, severely weakened the German military position. In this cam-

These American troops waited at St. Mihiel. Under General Pershing, they would soon begin their rigorous drive against the German lines of defense.

paign, Alvin C. York of Tennessee became a household name for his exploit of single-handedly taking on an enemy platoon. He captured more than 100 prisoners before the shooting was over.

An artillery captain who earned a reputation for effective leadership in the Argonne campaign was a peppery Missourian named Harry Truman. For brave generalship, Douglas MacArthur won a promotion and a decoration. For his craft in maneuvering troops, Colonel George C. Marshall won the admiration of the Germans as well as of his own superiors. A generation later, these men's lives would again be intertwined in common purpose.

SECTION REVIEW

1. (a) Describe the military situation facing the Allies by the end of 1917. (b) Why did Russia sign a peace treaty with Germany?
2. What part did American troops play in the Allied drive that finally ended the war?

5 The United States Rejects World Leadership

On November 11, 1918, an armistice finally silenced the guns. In the sudden stillness the nations could take stock. The total casualties staggered the imagination: 8.5 million soldiers had been killed on both sides, while an equal number of civilians had lost their lives. The United States had suffered a small number of casualties by comparison with other nations. Still, America had had a preview of what the rest of the twentieth century might be like.

Wilson decides to go to Europe. With the signing of the armistice, Wilson was in excellent spirits. Said one of his Cabinet officers, "He is certainly in splendid humor. And why shouldn't he be, for the world is at his feet, eating out of his hand! No Caesar ever had such a triumph!"

Wilson saw his role as that of peacemaker and shaper of a new order for people everywhere. Domestic politics, however, had set the stage for disappointment. The first blow was delivered by the congressional elections of 1918. Wilson asked for a "vote of confidence" from the voters, that is, for a new Democratic Congress. The American people, for a variety of reasons mostly unconnected with the war, turned him down, as they elected a Republican House and Senate. Many Europeans, and some Americans, wondered how Wilson could speak for the world's people now that he had been rejected at home.

A second blow was the growing anger of Republicans. Wilson had decided to attend the peace conference in Europe personally. Some Americans believed it was wrong for him to leave the country, because no President had ever done so. Others were dismayed because no Republicans were being included in the official American peace delegation. Americans of both parties had backed the war effort, Wilson's critics pointed out. Was the fashioning of the peace to be an honor for *Democrats* only? Former President Taft charged that Wilson simply wanted "to hog the whole show."

The weakened support at home did not seem to concern Wilson as he set forth for Paris early in December, 1918. He was certain that he could bring back a peace treaty that the Senate would not dare reject. His reception in Europe would show his critics at home that the world expected him to have his way.

He was right about the fervor with which Europeans greeted him. In Paris his motorcade proceeded under banners reading "Honour to Wilson the Just." Hundreds of thousands of French people cheered him deliriously. The cry "Vive Wilson! Vive Wilson! [Long live Wilson!]" rolled across Paris like a tidal wave. In other countries he was welcomed with similar frenzy. Wounded soldiers in Italy even reached to touch him in hope of being miraculously healed.

The Allies disagree over terms of peace. Wilson's colleagues among the Allied leaders did not share the popular enthusiasm for the American President; nor did they share Wilson's idealism. French premier Georges Clemenceau (kleh-mahn-SOH), "the tiger of France," was 77 years old. Clemenceau had seen his country overrun by German troops in 1870 and again in 1914. Now he wanted no visionary peace, but a harsh one that would keep Germany from invading his country a third time. David Lloyd George, prime minister of Great Britain, also had little patience for Wilson's high-flown goals. He and Clemenceau privately made sarcastic comments about the Fourteen Points, with Clemenceau calling them "the Fourteen Commandments" and adding that "even the Almighty had only Ten." The Italian premier, also at Paris, was Vittorio Orlando. His chief aim was to acquire the territories that the other Allies had secretly promised Italy in return for entering the war in 1915. Of the Big Four leaders, then, President Wilson often stood alone against Clemenceau, Lloyd George, and Orlando.

Peace treaties are written. Representatives from 27 nations attended the peace conference held in Paris, but matters were

The Treaty of Versailles officially ended the First World War. The treaty was signed on June 28, 1919, in the elegant Hall of Mirrors at the Palace of Versailles, near Paris. In this painting Woodrow Wilson, Georges Clemenceau, and David Lloyd George (seated center, left to right) look on as the German representatives sign.

decided by the Big Four. For instance, in treaties signed with the Central Powers, they redrew the boundary lines of eastern Europe to create new, independent countries. These countries were formed out of the defeated German, Austro-Hungarian, Russian, and Turkish empires. The new countries were Poland, Czechoslovakia, Finland, Yugoslavia, Estonia, Latvia, and Lithuania. In addition, Austria and Hungary became separate states (map, page 199).

Despite Wilson's earlier call for a "peace without victory," the Versailles Treaty (vehr-SIGH),[5] in the end, forced harsh peace terms on Germany. The treaty made Germany accept responsibility for having started the war. Germany had to agree to remain disarmed. It was deprived of its colonies. The new German government was saddled with staggering *repara-*

<hr />

[5]The treaty was signed at the Palace of Versailles, just outside the city of Paris.

tions — the bill for war damages. Germany ultimately was assessed $33 billion.

The Covenant of the League of Nations establishes a world organization. Although the Versailles Treaty was harsher than Wilson had wished, he was able to have some of his ideas incorporated in it. To him the most important of these was the Covenant (terms of agreement) of the League of Nations. The Covenant provided for a League of Nations which had the task of keeping peace in the world. The "heart" of the Covenant was Article X, which made the members of the League promise to defend one another's territory against aggression. The League would have a permanent Secretariat (that is, an administrative and secretarial staff), an Assembly, and a Council. The Assembly would consist of representatives from the member nations of the League, each having one vote. The Council, composed of delegates from the United States, Great Britain,

France, Italy, Japan, and four non-permanent members chosen by the Assembly, would be given the duty of mediating disputes between members and devising plans for bringing about disarmament.

The League was Wilson's proudest effort in behalf of world peace. Still, he gave his attention to other matters, for he aimed to be remembered as the architect of a world without war. Believing that imperialism had been a powerful cause of the struggle just ended, he succeeded in preventing the former colonies of Germany and Turkey from being handed over to the Allies. Instead, on his suggestion, they were made part of a *mandate system.* Under this system, specially named countries, answerable to the League, were assigned the task of preparing the colonies for self-government.

Opposition to the League arises in the Senate. When Wilson eloquently presented the Versailles Treaty to the Senate in July, 1919, opposition to it had already been organized. (Two senators failed even to rise out of courtesy to the President when he entered the chamber.) A few months earlier, more than a third of the senators had signed a statement asserting that the treaty was not acceptable in the form then proposed.

The critics' chief objection was to the League Covenant, which Wilson insisted was indispensable to the treaty. Opponents of the League concentrated their attack on Article X. They maintained that if the United States joined the League, the Monroe Doctrine and the nation's power to declare war and peace would be destroyed. Some people even argued that the United States would be drawn into wars to save the British Empire. One angry senator denounced the President as "Britain's tool — a dodger and a cheater." Another said the President's words were mere "soap bubbles of oratory." Wilson replied that the nation must "follow the vision" of world leadership. As the battle over ratification proceeded, Wilson said of the hostile senators, "They have poisoned the wells of public sentiment."

The senators who opposed the treaty were divided into two main groups. One, known as the "irreconcilables," or "bitter-enders," included Hiram Johnson of California, William E. Borah of Idaho, and Robert M. La Follette of Wisconsin. They were determined to battle to the bitter end against acceptance of the treaty with the League under any conditions.

A second group, called "reservationists," was led by Henry Cabot Lodge of Massachusetts. Lodge's followers favored participation in the League, provided certain reservations (limiting conditions) were agreed to that would protect American national interests. Lodge drew up a list of fourteen such reservations. Many people were sure that Lodge, who envied and disliked Wilson, was spitefully mocking the President's Fourteen Points.

Wilson appeals to the American people. In the face of senatorial opposition, Wilson grew stubborn and uncompromising. The series of mild strokes he apparently had suffered beginning in the 1890's may have begun affecting his personality. Gone was the gracious manner he often displayed. Now, when urged to accept the Lodge reservations, he shouted, "Accept the treaty with the *Lodge* reservations? Never! Never!"

In September, against the counsel of his advisers, Wilson set out on a speaking tour of the Middle West and West to win public support. Even a much younger man in excellent health would have been taxed by Wilson's exhausting schedule. With his usual eloquence, Wilson spoke of his glowing dream. He told an audience in Ohio, "When this treaty is accepted, men in khaki will not have to cross the seas again." He seemed to be making progress among his listeners. However, the traveling and speaking were wearing him out — and he seemed near collapse.

After addressing an audience in Colorado on September 25, 1919, Wilson spent a distressful night. His doctor and his wife appealed to him to break off the tour. He was concerned that his opponents would call him a quitter, but he agreed to return to the White House. There, on the night of October 2, he suffered a stroke that paralyzed his left side.

Wilson's advisers tried to keep from the public the severity of the President's illness. Mrs. Wilson carefully screened her husband's visitors and even dealt with official documents. Still, when she urged him to compromise on the League issue, he would not yield. "Little girl, don't you desert me; that I cannot stand," he pleaded.

The treaty is defeated. The original favorable sentiment toward the League began to wane. Other issues seemed more pressing: the world-wide epidemic of "Spanish flu," which cost half a million lives in the United States alone; labor disputes in the coal mines and the steel mills; a fear of radicalism after the Bolshevik Revolution in Russia; and the question of how to dispose of the railroads (which were still in government hands). The public was more interested in reading about the exploits of a young heavyweight boxer named Jack Dempsey and a Boston Red Sox player named Babe Ruth, who was attracting crowds with his home-run hitting.

When the Senate voted on the Versailles Treaty on November 19, 1919, with the Lodge reservations, a combination of Wilson Democrats and "irreconcilables" defeated it. A vote on the treaty *without* the Lodge reservations also failed. Upon hearing the news, Wilson said quietly, "They have shamed us in the eyes of the world." Soon afterward, Congress passed a resolution declaring the war with Germany ended. Wilson, never angrier, vetoed it, calling it a "stain upon the gallantry and honor of the United States." (In 1921, a new President signed a similar resolution and the war with Germany was officially over.)

As his administration drew to a close, Wilson, now only a shadow of his former self, waited hopefully for the election of 1920. He was confident the Democrats would win handsomely and that a Democratic-controlled Senate would ratify the Versailles Treaty. In the meantime, Wilson was satisfied with the fight he had waged — although he had never been a good loser. "I would rather fail in a cause that will ultimately triumph than triumph in a cause that will ultimately fail," he said.

Europe After World War I

The map of eastern Europe, altered by treaties in 1919, looked vastly different than it did before the war.

When Wilson returned from Paris after the peace conference, a newspaper had commented sarcastically: "Just think, we are going to have a President all by ourselves from now on." Many Americans must have shared this sentiment by 1920. They wanted to go back to "the good old days." The zeal to crusade abroad had vanished.

SECTION REVIEW

1. Vocabulary: *reparations, mandate system.*
2. (a) What evidence was there of weakened support at home for Wilson's peace plans? (b) What were the positions of France, Great Britain, and Italy concerning a peace treaty? (c) What were the terms of the Versailles Treaty?
3. (a) Describe the organization of the League of Nations. (b) For what reasons did opposition to the League arise in Congress? (c) What was the fate of the Versailles Treaty in the Senate?

Understanding Maps and Graphs

When you read history, most information is presented in the form of written text. In many instances, however, this information is easier to comprehend when it is illustrated. A review of the elements of a map and the characteristics of different types of graphs will help you make use of these sources of information.

Maps

Title. The first thing you should look for on a map is the title. The title will tell you the purpose of the map.

Symbols. Every map uses symbols to show information. The map on this page uses a number of symbols. Arrows depict the direction of French and American troop advances. Dots represent the location of cities and towns. Shaded areas show *relief*, or physical characteristics of the land. Different types of lines show national boundaries, battle lines, and roads.

Key. A key is often included to explain the important symbols that are used on a map. As you can see, the key on the map below shows the American and French forces, roads, and the change in the battle line.

Scale. The scale on a map helps you determine distance. Using the scale on the map below, you can calculate approximately how far Allied troops advanced in the St. Mihiel campaign. What is the greatest distance the Allied forces advanced during the St. Mihiel battle?

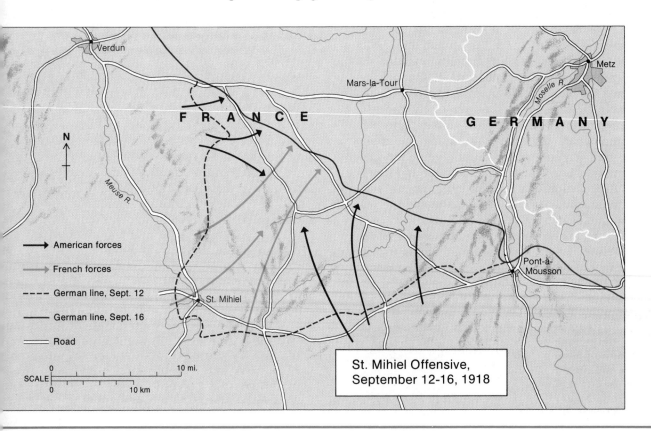

St. Mihiel Offensive,
September 12–16, 1918

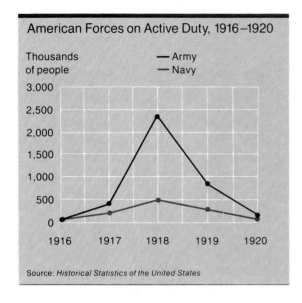

American Forces on Active Duty, 1916–1920

Thousands of people
— Army
— Navy

Source: *Historical Statistics of the United States*

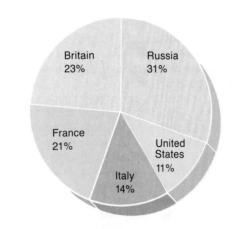

Total Allied Forces, 1914–1918

Britain 23%
Russia 31%
France 21%
United States 11%
Italy 14%

Source: *The Encyclopedia of Military History*

Graphs

Bar graphs. A bar graph consists of a horizontal axis and a vertical axis on which the amounts to be measured are marked off in equal intervals. Bars are drawn on the graph to represent data at a specific time. Bar graphs appear on pages 29, 37, and 48 of this textbook. Notice that these bar graphs are an effective way of comparing data for different years.

Line graphs. A line graph is constructed in the same manner as a bar graph. Instead of using bars, however, the data are presented by placing dots on the grid and then connecting them with a line. Line graphs, like the one above, are the best type of graph to use when showing change over time, or trends.

Circle graphs. A circle graph is used to show how a whole is divided into parts. The circle represents the whole of what is being measured and is given the value of 100 percent. The parts are shown as sections of the circle and labeled with the percentage they signify. The circle graph on this page repre-

sents the total military force mobilized by the Allies during World War I.

Check Your Skill

Use the information presented on these pages to answer the following questions.

1. On the map, how are American forces distinguished from French troops?
2. On the line graph, what do the different lines indicate?
3. What trend does the line graph show?
4. According to the circle graph, which Allied nation mobilized the greatest number of troops in World War I?

Apply Your Skill

1. Use the map on page 194 to determine which European countries remained neutral during World War I.
2. Make a circle graph from this table.
   Military Casualties, 1914–1918

France, 33%	Italy, 8%
Britain, 17.5%	United States, 1.5%
Russia, 40%	

Chapter 7 Review

Summary

When Woodrow Wilson entered the White House in 1913, the nation's attention was focused on American responsibilities in the Caribbean. Wilson followed the interventionist policies established by earlier Presidents. During his years in office, American troops were sent to Haiti, the Dominican Republic, and then to Mexico.

In 1914 the outbreak of fighting in Europe took Americans by surprise. Rivalries among the great powers of Europe had finally led to war between the Central Powers (Germany, Austria-Hungary, and Turkey) and the Allies (France, Britain, Russia, and Italy). Although President Wilson declared that the United States would remain neutral, most Americans strongly favored the Allies. During the conflict, Germany ordered its submarines to prevent American supplies from reaching Britain and France. When American lives were lost with the sinking of the *Lusitania* and other ships, Wilson's protests brought a temporary halt to the submarine attacks. The resumption of unrestricted submarine warfare in 1917 finally brought the United States into the conflict on the side of the Allies.

Following the declaration of war, the nation's armed forces were strengthened by a draft, and industry was placed under central control. Support for the war was mobilized by the Creel Committee, while the Espionage and Sedition acts were passed to control dissent. Wilson made clear his administration's war aims when he issued the Fourteen Points.

Although the first American fighting units arrived in France in June, 1917, they did not become engaged in heavy combat until the following spring. At that time they helped turn back the last offensive staged by Germany. An Allied counteroffensive in the summer of 1918, in which over one million American troops took part, led to Germany's call for an armistice on November 11, 1918.

President Wilson went to Europe for the peace conference and was hailed as a hero by the European people. Disagreement over the terms of the peace treaty arose, however, with Wilson trying to impose his Fourteen Points on the other Allied leaders. He did succeed in getting the Covenant of the League of Nations accepted as part of the peace settlement, and returned home to present the Versailles Treaty to the Senate for ratification. There he was greeted by intense opposition from senators who objected to American involvement in an international organization. The President toured the country to encourage support for the League but suffered a stroke during his journey. The treaty was defeated, and Wilson left office a disappointed man.

Vocabulary and Important Terms

1. "watchful waiting"
2. Central Powers
3. Allies
4. Schlieffen plan
5. U-boat
6. *Sussex* pledge
7. *Arabic* pledge
8. Zimmermann telegram
9. Selective Service Act
10. convoy
11. bureaucracy
12. Liberty Bonds
13. National Urban League
14. Creel Committee
15. Espionage Act
16. Sedition Act
17. Fourteen Points
18. Bolsheviks
19. Treaty of Versailles
20. reparations
21. League of Nations
22. mandate system

Discussion Questions

1. (a) Why did President Wilson try to influence events in Mexico? (b) What steps did he take?
2. (a) What was the reaction of most Americans to the news of war in Europe? (b) Why did the American people's sympathy with the Allied cause grow as the war progressed?
3. (a) According to international law, to what rights was the United States entitled as a neutral nation? (b) How did the United States respond to Germany's announcement early in the war that it would sink all vessels in waters around the British Isles? (c) On what occasions prior to entering the war did the United States restate its position on German submarine warfare? (d) Why did Germany decide in early 1917 to resume unrestricted submarine warfare, and what was the result of this decision?
4. (a) In his war message to Congress, what did President Wilson say were the main reasons for going to war against Germany? (b) What phrase became America's rallying cry? (c) What was the attitude of the public regarding United States entry into the war? (d) What did Americans believe the war would accomplish?
5. (a) What was the state of American preparedness when the United States entered the war? (b) Why did the military situation in Europe make it essential that the United States mobilize its armed forces quickly? (c) In what areas of American life was the role of the federal government expanded during the war years?

6. (a) What contributions did the United States make to the Allied war effort? (b) In what battles did American troops play a key role?

7. (a) Why did Woodrow Wilson decide to go to Europe when the war was over? (b) What feelings at home and among Allied leaders frustrated Wilson's goal of becoming a peacemaker? (c) In what ways did the Versailles Treaty favor the Allies?

8. (a) What two groups of senators opposed the Versailles Treaty? (b) How did Wilson respond to senatorial opposition? (c) What action did the Senate finally take concerning the Versailles Treaty?

9. (a) What did Woodrow Wilson believe were his main accomplishments? (b) How had the outlook of the American people changed by 1920?

Relating Past to Present

1. What opportunities are there for American Presidents to play the role of peacemaker in the world today? What recent Presidents have tried to serve as peacemaker? What successes have they had?

2. What is the present-day status of each of the countries created at the end of World War I (page 199)?

Studying Local History

What contributions did people in your community make to the American war effort during World War I? What memorials of the First World War are in or near your community?

Using History Skills

1. *Comparing maps.* Compare the map of Europe during World War I (page 194) with the map of Europe as it was redrawn after the war (page 199). (a) Which countries gained territory at the end of the war? (b) Which countries lost territory? (c) What new nations were established? (d) Which country was divided in two?

2. *Reading source material.* Study Frederick Palmer's description of action in World War I on page 193. (a) What was the relationship between the French troops and the Americans? (b) What was the mood of the American troops as they took their positions in the trenches? (c) What was their main worry? (d) How extensive was the cooperation between the French and American forces? Explain your answer.

WORLD SCENE

The World at War

Hostilities during the First World War were not confined to Europe. The war also spread to the colonial empires.

Fighting in the Middle East. A leading concern of the British throughout the First World War was the protection of their interests in Egypt. In particular, Britain was determined to keep the Suez Canal out of German hands. When the Ottoman Turks, who controlled much of the Middle East, allied themselves with Germany, they presented a formidable threat to Egypt. To prepare for a campaign to drive the Turkish and German forces out of the Middle East, the British constructed roads and a railroad leading from the Nile to the Sinai Peninsula.

The British launched their attack in November, 1916, but were stalled by a Turkish-German force at Gaza in April, 1917. A magnetic young British colonel named T. E. Lawrence, now remembered as Lawrence of Arabia, succeeded, however, in persuading Arab chieftains to help the British defeat the Turks. With Arab help, Britain was able to drive the Turks out of Palestine and Syria, and then force Turkey to withdraw from the war. The defeat of the Turks ended their four-centuries-old grip on the Middle East.

Fighting in East Africa. At the outbreak of the First World War, the German colony of East Africa had for its defense the warship *Königsburg* and an army consisting of 260 German soldiers and 4,600 African troops. This force was led by Colonel Paul von Lettow-Vorbeck. The British moved quickly to seize Germany's African possessions, but Lettow-Vorbeck and his men put up a spirited defense.

The little German army led the British on a never-ending chase through swamps and forests and across mountains. Lettow-Vorbeck used hit-and-run tactics to disrupt British supply lines and communications.

Lettow-Vorbeck's men eluded the British for four years. Only when the general received news of the armistice in November, 1918, did he surrender. In Germany, he was recognized as a national hero.

UNIT 2 REVIEW

Important Dates

1867 Alaska purchased.
1889 Jane Addams founds Hull House.
1890 First Pan-American Congress meets.
1895 Venezuelan boundary dispute.
1896 *Plessy v. Ferguson.*
1898 Spanish-American War.
Hawaii annexed.
1899 Open Door Policy in China announced.
1900 Boxer Rebellion.
1901 Theodore Roosevelt becomes President.
1903 Right of way through Panama acquired.
1904 Roosevelt Corollary.
1905 Treaty of Portsmouth ends
Russo-Japanese War.
1906 Pure Food and Drug Act.
1910 NAACP formed.
1911 National Urban League organized.
1912 Wilson elected President.
1913 Federal Reserve Act.
1914 Panama Canal opened.
World War I begins in Europe.
1915 The *Lusitania* sunk.
1916 Border campaign against Villa.
1917 United States enters World War I.
1918 Armistice ends World War I.
1919 Treaty of Versailles.

Review Questions

1. (a) Why did the views of some Americans regarding overseas territories change between the end of the Civil War and the beginning of the twentieth century? (b) What territories did the United States acquire during those years?
2. (a) Why did the United States begin to take an interest in the Far East in the late 1800's? (b) In what ways did the United States become involved with China and Japan in the late nineteenth and early twentieth centuries?
3. (a) In what ways did the United States seek to expand its role in Latin America during the post-Civil War period? (b) During the administrations of Roosevelt, Taft, and Wilson?
4. (a) What political reforms did the progressives bring about at the local, state, and national levels? (b) How did those reforms enable citizens to participate more directly in the affairs of government?
5. (a) What obstacles did black Americans face during the late nineteenth and early twentieth centuries? (b) How did black leaders differ in their response to the situation? (c) What progress did blacks make within American society, especially during the First World War?
6. (a) What activities helped to bring about national suffrage for women? (b) When the United States entered World War I, what contributions did women make to the effort?
7. (a) Before 1917, to what extent were the American people "neutral in fact as well as in name" when it came to favoring sides in World War I? (b) Why did the United States finally enter the war? (c) What contributions did America make to the Allied victory?
8. (a) What were Wilson's goals at the time the United States entered World War I? (b) At the end of the war, what opposition to his plans did he encounter both at home and abroad? (c) Which of his goals were accomplished, and which were not?

Projects

1. On an outline map of the world, indicate the territories that were gained by the United States between 1867 and 1917. Give the date each became an American possession, and tell how each territory was acquired.
2. Create a set of three handbills, one each for the candidacies of William Howard Taft, Woodrow Wilson, and Theodore Roosevelt in the election of 1912. On these handbills include pictures, slogans, and other information that illustrate the political positions of each of the three presidential candidates and his respective party.
3. Make a model of one of the new weapons introduced during World War I. Your model might be of a submarine, an airplane, a tank, or of some other World War I innovation. Show your model to the class and explain how it affected warfare.
4. Find out more about the shaping of public opinion at home during World War I by reading the words to songs that encouraged the Allied war effort and by locating posters that encouraged Americans to buy Liberty Bonds, to conserve food and fuel, to enlist in the armed forces, to aid wartime agencies, and to support in all other ways the American war effort. Share this information with the class.
5. Participate in a classroom debate on the question of whether the United States should have ratified the Versailles Treaty and entered the League of Nations. One group should argue for American participation in the League of Nations, while the other group should argue against membership in the League.

GOOD TIMES, HARD TIMES, AND WAR

1919 – 1945

This generation of Americans has a rendezvous with destiny.

FRANKLIN D. ROOSEVELT, 1936

CHAPTER 8

A Roaring Decade

1919 – 1929

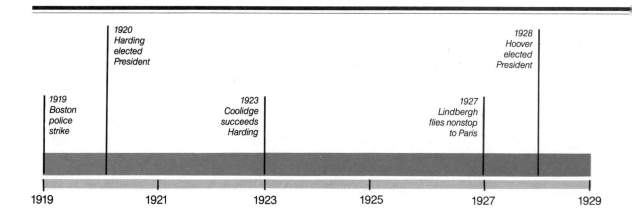

| 1919 Boston police strike | 1920 Harding elected President | 1923 Coolidge succeeds Harding | 1927 Lindbergh flies nonstop to Paris | 1928 Hoover elected President |

1919   1921   1923   1925   1927   1929

CHAPTER OUTLINE

1. The postwar years are marked by political and economic unrest.

2. The Republicans provide presidential leadership during the 1920's.

3. American society undergoes rapid change.

When the "doughboys" returned from Europe in 1919, Americans felt satisfaction and relief. The United States had been tested in battle overseas and had triumphed. Millions of citizens were convinced that the war had truly been the "war to end war." Now they looked forward to better and calmer days. They also hoped for a return to more familiar times. They were tired of Wilson's idealistic struggle for peace in the world and reform at home.

Nevertheless, in the postwar era the nation underwent rapid change. Some of it resulted from the economic downturn of the early 1920's, marked by distress among farmers and by labor unrest. Some of it came from the continued growth of cities at the expense of rural America. As the decade wore on, change produced conflict and confusion. Many older people were shocked by what they saw: the boldness of young people; open disrespect for the law; and the many new ways of working, living, and thinking.

Although times were hard for farmers and some other groups, most Americans were prosperous during the 1920's. The majority of Americans were now living in cities. The air was filled with the sounds of factories, radios, telephones, phonographs, automobiles, "talking" pictures, crowds of cheering sports fans, airplanes, electrical appliances — and occasionally a raucous mob or a gangster's machine gun. This noisy, fast-paced decade has been called the "Roaring Twenties."

1 The Postwar Years Are Marked by Political and Economic Unrest

Within a few months after the armistice ended the First World War, over three million Americans were discharged from the armed forces. In the same period, hundreds of thousands of wartime workers were cut from the payrolls of government and industry. Unemployment suddenly became a serious problem. Farmers, meanwhile, were confronted with sharply falling crop prices. Wheat, which sold for over $2 a bushel in 1919, was selling for 52 cents in 1921. The nation was entering a period of economic and political unrest.

Labor troubles break out. Workers had taken a no-strike pledge when the United States went to war. Since the nation was in a state of emergency, laboring people had agreed not to force their demands until the conflict had ended. Now, with the return of peace, working people had become increasingly discontented. The cost of living had almost doubled since 1916, while in many industries wages lagged behind. Also, factory workers were no longer willing to endure wartime working conditions — which, in the steel industry, consisted of a 69-hour, 7-day work week. They were ready to fight for improvements in their standard of living and in their working conditions. In 1919 there were almost 4,000 strikes, many of them violent.

One of the most dramatic incidents took place when the Boston police went on strike for higher wages and improved working conditions. With the police off the scene, looters had a field day, smashing shop windows and stealing merchandise. The mayor of Boston finally called for troops, and Governor Calvin Coolidge responded by sending the National Guard. Meanwhile, a volunteer corps, largely made up of Harvard students and recently returned veterans, patrolled the streets of the city. Coolidge had moved slowly in the

Many developments in the 1920's had lasting impact. Assembly-line production, particularly in the automobile industry, created new jobs and spurred demand for additional mass-produced items.

crisis but nevertheless gained a national reputation as a strong leader. He condemned the strike in blunt words: "There is no right to strike against the public safety by anybody, any time, anywhere." President Wilson congratulated the governor on a "victory for law and order."

The trouble in Boston had scarcely ended when two disruptive industrial strikes broke out. The first was called at a plant of the United States Steel Corporation in Indiana. The second, under the shrewd leadership of John L. Lewis, head of the United Mine Workers, was directed against the operators of soft-coal mines.

The steel strike, aimed at organizing the workers in a union, ended in failure. Before it was broken, the strike had involved more than 350,000 workers. The coal strike was halted by a federal court injunction ordering the workers back to their jobs.[1]

The "Red scare" begins. Many Americans had been deeply disturbed by the Bolshevik victory in the Russian Revolution of 1917 (page 192) and the subsequent spread of communism. German Communists were able to hold the city of Berlin for a few days in 1919. For five months Communists ruled Hungary, which had regained its independence from Austria following the First World War. Communist sympathizers in the United States and western Europe seemed to many people to have great power. The labor turmoil alarmed people who feared that America, too, was turning radical.

During the First World War, moreover, people had been made suspicious of anything "un-American." Those old suspicions were now revived, this time with Communists in mind. For instance, the chief speaker for the coal operators declared, without any evidence, that the coal strike was financed by Bolshevik gold on direct orders of the Russian leaders. This feverish suspicion of Communist revolutionaries became known as the "Red scare."

---

[1]Although the strikes were failures, the mine workers received a wage increase through arbitration, and a few years later the steel companies agreed to establish an eight-hour workday.

Americans were further distressed by a number of acts of terrorism. One involved Mayor Ole Hanson of Seattle. Hanson had gained nationwide publicity when he had called in troops to break up a strike of shipyard workers in February, 1919. Soon afterward he received a bomb in the mail. Fortunately, the bomb was found before anyone was hurt.

Other terrorist incidents followed. Senator Thomas Hartwick of Georgia, a well-known anti-Communist, received in the mail a bomb that did explode, injuring the maid who opened the package. Another bomb destroyed the home of Attorney General A. Mitchell Palmer. During the spring and summer of 1919, postal authorities discovered more than thirty bombs addressed to citizens known to be opposed to organized labor or unrestricted immigration.

The high point of tension came on September 16, 1920, when a bomb exploded on Wall Street at noon, killing more than thirty people and injuring hundreds of others. Palmer's opinion that Communists were preparing "to rise up and destroy the government at one fell swoop" was widely accepted as true.

Beginning in the fall of 1919, Palmer, a zealous man, led law-enforcement agencies in a series of raids against suspected Communists. Over 6,000 people were arrested, and about 550 of them were deported. During the "Red scare," even governmental officials were not immune from attacks on their civil liberties. In New York in 1920, five Socialists who had been legally elected were denied their seats in the state legislature.

The effects of the "Red scare" linger. Many Americans became concerned about violations of constitutional rights. They said that claims about the dangers of radicalism had proved to be wildly exaggerated. The strong emotions sparked by the national debate over radicalism, nevertheless, lingered throughout the decade. Nowhere was this seen more clearly than in the case of Sacco and Vanzetti.

Nicola Sacco and Bartolomeo Vanzetti, two anarchists, were arrested in 1921. They

The bombing of Wall Street in 1920 took place near the offices of the financier J. P. Morgan. The terrorist who threw the bomb was never identified.

were charged with the slaying of two uniformed guards in a payroll robbery at a shoe factory near Boston. In a widely publicized trial, the two men were found guilty and condemned to death. After mass demonstrations at home and abroad in protest of the death sentence, they were executed in 1927.

Americans were deeply aroused by the Sacco-Vanzetti case. Many legal experts insisted that there was no solid evidence against the convicted men and that they had been convicted because of their political beliefs. Others were convinced that justice had been done.

New demands are heard for the restriction of immigration. At the same time that Americans debated the dangers of radicalism, the movement to restrict immigration into the United States gained new force. Old values had been rudely shaken by the great wave of immigrants from southern and eastern Europe who poured into American cities from the 1890's until the First World War. As the war industries shut down, scores of factory workers found themselves unem-

ployed. Many were convinced that foreigners, who were so numerous, were occupying jobs that otherwise would be filled by native-born Americans. When disappointment with the outcome of the war set in — for the world had not been made "safe for democracy" — they found it easy to blame foreigners. After all, they asserted, foreigners had caused the war in the first place.

The "Red scare," moreover, had planted the belief that radical ideas were being brought into the country by aliens. Further, because many of the new immigrants were Catholic or Jewish, it was convenient to turn anti-Catholicism and anti-Semitism into "antiforeignism," which was less embarrassing to express. Also, rural people, fearing the spread of urban influence, could show their concern by opposing immigration. They could sense that the newcomers were an important source of strength to the cities. Finally, economic conditions were so discouraging in so many countries that, it was said, "the whole world is preparing to move to the United States."

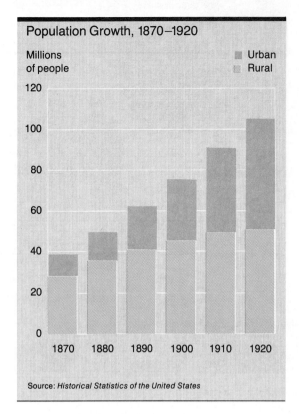

Population Growth, 1870–1920

Millions of people

- ■ Urban
- ■ Rural

120

100

80

60

40

20

0

1870　1880　1890　1900　1910　1920

Source: *Historical Statistics of the United States*

By 1920, an increasing proportion of the American population was living in urban areas.

The first attempt to limit immigration had already been taken. This was the passage of a bill requiring that people seeking to enter the country pass a literacy test. The bill had been vetoed by President Taft in 1913 and by President Wilson in 1915 and again in 1917. Congress, however, enacted it over Wilson's second veto.

Congress establishes immigration quotas. In response to public pressure, Congress passed the Emergency Quota Act of 1921, which restricted the admission of foreigners to 3 percent of the number of each nationality living in the United States in 1910. It also limited the total number of immigrants to about 350,000 a year.

Many considered this law unsatisfactory. The year 1910 was the wrong one to choose, they argued, because by then millions of eastern and southern Europeans had entered the country. The critics insisted that northern and western Europeans made more desirable Americans. Therefore, they

said, the year 1890 was a better year to use because the country had relatively few eastern or southern Europeans at that time. As a result, the National Origins Act was passed in 1924, with the base year set at 1890. The quota was reduced from 3 percent to 2 percent. The law forbade all immigration from Asia — which caused Japan to hold a day of national mourning and anger. The act did not, however, restrict immigration from Canada or Latin America. In 1927 the number of immigrants allowed to enter the country each year was reduced to 150,000.

Black Americans face hostility. During the war years, hundreds of thousands of southern black workers had moved north to find jobs in war industries. Many thousands more served with the American army in Europe. Black veterans, many of them treated as heroes in France, returned home with a sense of pride and with hope for the future. Nevertheless, the demands of blacks for better jobs, housing, and fair treatment were resisted by many whites, who feared the competition of black workers for jobs. Racial tension rose.

The summer of 1919 witnessed more than 25 race riots. In Washington, D.C., Omaha, Chicago, and other cities hundreds of people were injured and dozens were killed. The worst riot was touched off by an incident at a public beach in Chicago. For three days violence raged. By the time it ended, 38 people had been killed and more than 100 injured. Moreover, a vast amount of property had been destroyed.

Black music, art, and literature are recognized. In spite of the obstacles they faced, many black Americans made brilliant contributions to music, poetry, drama, and painting during the 1920's. For the first time in American history, large numbers of black literary and artistic people were recognized for their work by the nation as a whole. Because so many creative blacks lived in the Harlem section of New York City, their outpouring of work was called the "Harlem Renaissance."

The literature of the Harlem Renaissance brought new pride to black people. In 1925, Alain Locke, a professor of philosophy at Howard University, published a collection of poems, stories, and essays entitled *The New Negro.* The "New Negroes" represented in Locke's book were young writers — penetrating, assertive, and imaginative. Locke, through his work, helped bring the literary output of black writers to the attention of the nation at large. The poets Langston Hughes, Claude McKay, and Countee Cullen also contributed significantly to American literature as a whole with works about the treatment of blacks. Along with the historians Carter G. Woodson and W. E. B. Du Bois, these writers and poets explored the story of blacks in America, as well as reminding readers of the African heritage of black people.

A leading spokesman of the new feeling of black pride was Marcus Garvey, a Jamaican who captured the imagination of large numbers of black Americans. He preached in his weekly paper, *Negro World*, that

blacks should leave America and build a country of their own in Africa. A splendid organizer, he created the Universal Black Cross Nurses and the Black Star Steamship Line to advance the cause of black nationalism. He also declared himself president of the Empire of Africa and gave impressive titles to the most faithful of his 500,000 followers. Garvey, however, never realized his dream of founding a black homeland. He had, nevertheless, helped awaken among many black people a sense of cultural pride.

The Ku Klux Klan is revived. The race consciousness of the day also produced intolerance. The most flagrant example was the organization of a new Ku Klux Klan. It had no formal connection with the infamous organization that had flourished during reconstruction, but it adopted many of the methods of its predecessor. It revived the

Many black musicians moved from New Orleans to cities like Chicago and New York City in the 1920's. Their new and spontaneous music was a blend of blues, spirituals, and West African rhythms and was called jazz. Louis Armstrong and his band, shown here, recorded some of the finest music of the period.

secret rituals, the white-hooded robes, and the burning of crosses.

A goal of the Ku Klux Klan was to preserve America for white Protestants. Although it resumed the antiblack campaign of the old Klan, the new organization also carried out campaigns of violence against Catholics, Jews, and immigrants.

By the mid-1920's, the Klan claimed a membership of between four and five million Americans. Especially active in the small towns of the South and Midwest, the Klan also had branches in such far-flung states as New York and Oregon. Its power was so extensive that at one point five United States senators and four governors were members. Klan influence, however, faded rapidly after 1925. A scandal involving a powerful Indiana Klan leader, as well as publicity about corruption within the organization, dealt the Klan heavy blows.

The Eighteenth Amendment is added to the Constitution. Nothing better illustrates the clash of values in American society during the 1920's than the national debate over *prohibition* — the effort to eliminate the sale and consumption of alcoholic beverages. The prohibition movement had begun in earnest during the middle of the nineteenth century when the first prohibition legislation was passed in Maine. The early prohibitionists had believed that persuasion through individual contact alone would end the drinking of alcoholic beverages. The work became more systematic in 1874 when the Woman's Christian Temperance Union (WCTU) was organized in an attempt to bring the Protestant churches into the effort. Before long, some of the energy that Protestant ministers had only a few years earlier put into the antislavery crusade was being marshaled against "Demon Rum." The new crusade did not become truly effective, however, until the Anti-Saloon League was established in 1893. The League's lobbying effort was so successful that by 1917, 24 states had passed local-option laws, which allowed individual counties to adopt prohibition. In addition, Michigan, Montana, Nebraska, South Da-

kota, and Utah established prohibition on a state-wide basis.

By the time the United States entered the First World War in 1917, the Anti-Saloon League was lobbying Congress for a constitutional amendment that would forbid the sale of liquor anywhere in the country. The sense of high moral purpose created by entering the war was an advantage for the movement.

On December 18, 1917, Congress approved the Eighteenth Amendment, which prohibited the manufacture, transportation, and sale of beverages containing more than one half of one percent alcohol. By January 16, 1919, two thirds of the states had ratified the amendment, and it went into effect a year later. The Volstead Act was passed in October, 1919, to provide the government with the power to carry out the intent of the amendment.

Prohibition proves hard to enforce. Enforcing prohibition became an enormous and expensive battle. Many otherwise law-abiding Americans violated the Volstead Act. Others who respected the new law themselves refused to help enforce it by reporting people who broke it. In the face of the public's attitude, the enforcement of prohibition became impossible.

By the middle of the 1920's "bootlegging" — the illegal manufacture and sale of liquor — had become big business. Liquor was smuggled into the country from Canada and Mexico or from rum-running vessels lying off the coasts. In place of saloons, "speakeasies" sprang up. In speakeasies, drinks were served to those who were known to the proprietor or who had been sent by other customers.

Criminal gangs are organized. The disregard of prohibition weakened respect for laws in general. Meanwhile, violating the liquor laws was immensely profitable. Gangs of criminals, busily engaged in transporting liquor across state lines, came to be linked together.

The gangs that controlled the liquor traffic were as well-organized as the law-enforcement agencies. The gangsters, moreover, were ruthless in their operations. Violence, including murder, was their method of maintaining discipline in the ranks. Between 1920 and 1929, more than 500 gang-style killings took place in the city of Chicago alone.

The best-known criminal in the prohibition era was Al Capone. He controlled the flow of "bootleg" whiskey into Chicago's 10,000 speakeasies. By 1925 Capone had even gained control of the town government of the Chicago suburb of Cicero.

The task of combating organized crime fell to the Federal Bureau of Investigation, a division of the United States Department of Justice. In 1924 the FBI was placed under the leadership of J. Edgar Hoover, a young lawyer. Eventually, FBI agents worked their way into Capone's gang and collected enough evidence to send him to prison — for income tax evasion.

Despite widespread dissatisfaction with prohibition, few people believed that a movement that had been eighty years in the making would ever be called off. Besides, prohibition had been written into the Constitution. No amendment had ever been removed. A senator said in 1930, "There is as much chance of repealing the Eighteenth Amendment as there is for a hummingbird to fly to the planet Mars with the Washington Monument tied to its tail." The issue, nevertheless, was by no means settled.

SECTION REVIEW

1. Vocabulary: *prohibition*.
2. (a) Why were there labor troubles in the years immediately following the First World War? (b) What major strikes were called in 1919? (c) What was the outcome of each?
3. (a) What was the "Red scare"? (b) What actions were taken against suspected Communists?
4. What steps were taken to restrict immigration during the 1920's?
5. (a) What obstacles did black Americans face after the First World War? (b) What was the Harlem Renaissance?
6. (a) How did the Eighteenth Amendment come to be passed? (b) Why did it prove to be difficult to enforce?

2 The Republicans Provide Presidential Leadership During the 1920's

Throughout the 1920's Republican Presidents occupied the White House. In 1920 the party's candidate was Warren G. Harding, an Ohio senator and newspaper publisher. Many people doubted that Harding would be equal to the job. By comparison with his predecessors — Wilson, Taft, and Roosevelt — Harding appeared to be an uninspired choice for the White House.

Harding is elected President in 1920. Harding selected as his running mate Calvin Coolidge, the governor of Massachusetts who had become a national hero through his handling of the Boston police strike. The Democrats' candidate for President was another Ohio newspaper publisher, James M. Cox. For Vice President the Democrats chose the former Assistant Secretary of the Navy, Franklin D. Roosevelt of New York.

President Harding, shown throwing the first pitch at a baseball game, won the election in 1920 with more than 60 percent of the vote.

Personally a genial man, Harding was eager to get along with people. He loved to be among people in a "folksy" way, to shake their hands, and to make long speeches — "bloviating" he called it. He conducted his campaign from the front porch of his home in Ohio. There he met visitors who flocked to catch a glimpse of him. "Keep Warren at home," said a leading Republican politician. "Don't let him make any speeches. If he goes out on tour, somebody's sure to ask him questions, and Warren's just the sort of fool that'll try to answer them."

Handsome and distinguished in appearance, Harding looked every inch a President. He was, furthermore, made-to-order for the nation's new mood. The public seemed tired of the Democrats and all that Wilson represented: internationalism, idealism, and do-goodism. Where Cox and Roosevelt supported United States entry into the League of Nations, Harding called the organization a fraud. He called for a "return to normalcy," meaning, it was assumed, a return to what were considered the calmer days of before the war. When it came to the regulation of big business, Harding promised he would "put less government in business and more business in government."

The election results suggested that Harding had correctly interpreted the public's mood. He received sixteen million votes compared to just nine million for Cox. The Republicans also increased their margins in the House and Senate.

Harding chooses a Cabinet. Harding was not prepared by training or temperament for the tasks he would face in the presidency. Indeed, early in his administration he told a visitor to the White House, "I knew that this job would be too much for me." There was still the peace treaty to be taken care of; unemployment was growing; agriculture demanded help; relations with Latin America, Asia, and Russia had to be restudied; and the problem of war debts needed attention.

Harding knew his limitations and said he would choose some of the "best minds" to help him govern the nation. He appointed to his Cabinet some of the ablest men in his party. Charles Evans Hughes, the Republican presidential candidate in 1916, was appointed Secretary of State. Andrew Mellon, a millionaire and reputed financial wizard, became Secretary of the Treasury, while Henry C. Wallace, a distinguished Iowan, was named Secretary of Agriculture. Herbert Hoover, famous for his relief work **during World War I (page 189), was made** Secretary of Commerce. Mellon and Hoover set in motion a program to balance the federal budget. They also promoted economy in government and trade opportunities abroad for American manufacturers.

Some of Harding's other appointees were totally wrong for the job. They eventually made his administration the most corrupt since Grant's. Harding had been unable to resist placing many unqualified friends — who became known as the "Ohio gang" — in important government positions. He soon was confessing to a reporter, "I can take care of my enemies. But my friends. . . . They're the ones that keep me walking the floors nights!"

President Harding dies in office. Although troubled and worried by the dishonesty of many of those around him, the exhausted Harding went on a fact-finding trip to the Pacific Northwest and Alaska in 1923. He was visibly ill upon his return from Alaska. Then, on August 2, 1923, he died suddenly in San Francisco of a heart attack.

At the time of Harding's death, Calvin Coolidge was vacationing at his father's home in Vermont. His father, a justice of the peace, administered the oath of office by the light of a kerosene lamp.

Coolidge's coming to the White House may well have saved the Republicans from political disaster. The new President was a man of integrity and character. He was a symbol of the old-fashioned, thrifty, small-town American. Coolidge helped to restore people's faith in the high office.

The nation learns of the Harding scandals. Immediately after his death, Warren Harding was praised by a friend as "one of the knightliest, gentlest, truest men who ever lived in the White House." Disclosures soon showed how wrong that judgment was. The Harding administration had been riddled with the misconduct of important officials. Harding, who was weak but honest himself, had permitted dishonest, self-seeking politicians to occupy positions of trust in the national government.

The most shocking case concerned the leasing of two oil fields. When oil replaced coal as fuel for most of the navy's warships around 1912, oil deposits became vital to national defense. By 1919, the navy was using seven million barrels a year. Still, Secretary of the Interior Albert B. Fall persuaded Harding to transfer from the Department of the Navy to the Department of the Interior certain reserve oil fields in California and Wyoming. Fall then secretly leased the Elk Hills Reserve in California to an oil company controlled by Edward L. Doheny. He also leased the Teapot Dome Reserve in Wyoming to Harry F. Sinclair, another wealthy oilman. For his cooperation, Fall received $100,000 from Doheny for Elk Hills and $300,000 from Sinclair for Teapot Dome. He was also given expensive gifts, including a herd of cattle. After a long trial, Fall was convicted in 1929 of accepting a bribe. He was fined $100,000 and sentenced to a year in prison — the first Cabinet member ever so punished.

Other revelations about the "Ohio gang" now followed. The head of the Office of Alien Property, Jess Smith, and the director of the Veterans' Bureau, Colonel Charles Forbes, had both accepted bribes. Smith busily sold pardons and paroles to criminals as well as performing other "favors." He at times was heard to mutter, "My, how the money rolls in!" In return for payoffs, Forbes systematically sold off government supplies badly needed by former soldiers. His swindling is said to have cost the taxpayers $200 million. Attorney General Daugherty, personally involved in these scandals, was tried twice for accepting bribes. Each time, however, the jury failed to reach a decision, and he went free.

Coolidge is elected President. In 1924 the Republicans nominated "Silent Cal" as

After being informed that President Harding had died, Calvin Coolidge was sworn in by his father, a justice of the peace.

their candidate for President. He ran on the simple slogan "Keep cool with Coolidge."

The Democrats, on the other hand, had a hard time settling on a candidate. They battled fiercely for seventeen days in the sweltering heat of summer at their convention in New York. The struggle centered on William Gibbs McAdoo of California, a former Secretary of the Treasury (page 189), and on Alfred E. Smith, the popular governor of New York.

The conflict reflected the national debate over the changes America was undergoing. Smith, a Roman Catholic, represented the nation's emerging urban centers. He had been born in a slum on New York City's Lower East Side. He was a "wet" — that is, he was opposed to prohibition — and he denounced the Ku Klux Klan without hesitation. McAdoo, on the other hand, was a Protestant. He was a "dry," supported mainly by southern and western delegates who favored prohibition.

After three weeks of deliberation, the exhausted delegates chose John W. Davis of West Virginia on the 103rd ballot. A former member of Congress and ambassador to Great Britain, Davis was a capable man. However, he had no popular following.

Both major parties had turned their backs firmly on the progressivism that had marked their recent past. The voters who

The Farm Tractor

The development of the internal-combustion farm tractor was of great significance for American farmers in the early 1900's. By replacing a team of horses with a tractor, a farmer had the capacity to do many times more work in a fraction of the time once required. With the invention in 1918 of a device called a power takeoff, the tractor could be used to drive many kinds of attachments. This improved, multi-purpose tractor could not only pull a plow and cultivator but also run planters, harvesters, loaders, winches, and even post-hole diggers. The need for draft animals on a farm was greatly reduced. By 1920, there were nearly a quarter million tractors in operation in the United States, and farm families were relieved of the worst drudgery of farming. These gasoline-powered vehicles revolutionized American agriculture and farm life.

continued to seek reform found a champion in Robert M. La Follette who ran on the ticket of the Progressive Party, a new third party. Still, the Progressives, who favored union activity and government ownership of railroads, seemed out of touch with the views of most Americans.

Coolidge was easily elected, carrying 35 of the 48 states. The Republicans also retained control of Congress. The Progressive Party polled nearly five million votes, more than any third party in American history, but carried only La Follette's home state of Wisconsin.

Farmers suffer hard times. Much of the success of Republican candidates during the 1920's can be explained by the booming economy and the rise in the standard of living. The market for industrial and consumer products seemed unlimited, especially as Europe recovered from the war and sought American goods. Business profits were high, and the future of American industry seemed rosy. Millions of Americans felt prosperous.

This prosperity, though, rested on a shaky foundation. Many working people did not have the means to buy the consumer goods that were well advertised and much desired. Nor could most blacks, Mexican Americans, or Indians afford them. Excluded, too, from the general prosperity were the nation's farmers.

In 1920 agriculture slipped into a depression from which it did not emerge for many years. During World War I, the high price of wheat had led farmers to overextend their operations. Then, as European nations resumed production, the price of wheat and other farm crops fell dramatically. Total net income from farming dropped from $9 billion in 1919 to $3.4 billion in 1921. This collapse came just when young men were returning to the farms from the army. Many of the veterans returned to find that the mortgage on the family homestead had been foreclosed.

In 1921, members of Congress from the farm states organized themselves into what was called the farm bloc. The farm bloc had enough votes to hold a commanding posi-

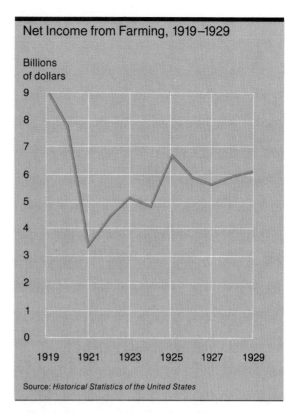

Net Income from Farming, 1919–1929

Billions of dollars

Source: *Historical Statistics of the United States*

The income of farmers plummeted in the 1920's, and they sought legislation to alleviate their difficulties.

tion in Congress and proposed a number of solutions to the farmers' problems. Farmers complained, for instance, that the importation of Canadian foodstuffs had forced down the price of the crops they sold. Attempting to satisfy them, Congress passed an "emergency" tariff on May 27, 1921, that placed duties on wool, sugar, meat, wheat, and corn. This act was replaced the following year by the Fordney-McCumber Act, which raised tariffs generally to the level where they had been during the Taft administration.

The farm bloc succeeded in enacting other important laws. One was the Grain Futures Trading Act, which gave the Secretary of Agriculture broad control over the farm commodity markets, or grain exchanges. A second was a law exempting farm cooperatives from the operation of the antitrust laws. A third was the Agricultural Credits Act of 1923, which made it easier for farmers to obtain loans.

217

The huge annual crop surpluses, however, remained the biggest problem for farmers. The McNary-Haugen Farm Relief Bill of 1924 sought to raise the domestic price of farm products by setting up a federal farm board that would buy surpluses and then sell them on the world market. Twice President Coolidge vetoed the proposal, objecting to it as government price-fixing. He expressed a general feeling when he said, "Farmers have never made much money. I don't believe we can do much about it."

Signs of economic trouble appear. The farmers were not alone in their difficulties. By 1927 the coal and textile industries were depressed. In 1928 the oil industry, owing to a glut of its products, faced a sharp slump in prices. By late 1929 the construction industry was 25 percent below the performance of the previous year.

The nation as a whole, however, accepted the view of President Coolidge: "The business of America is business." People believed that business would expand and all would be well. In any event, the stock market was regarded as the *real* index of business activity, and it was going up, up, up.

In many fields, corporations made substantial profits, so the price of their stock was high. Some companies, instead of borrowing the money they needed, simply sold new shares of stock. With the additional funds, they enlarged their plants and produced more goods. Again, profits went up and so did stock prices. The cycle then repeated itself. But what would happen if the goods could not be sold because the market for them suddenly collapsed? Also, what would happen if the stock market suddenly fell sharply and stayed down?

A couple of times in 1928 stock prices broke sharply, but each time they rebounded quickly. Nobody seemed to regard these events as indications of things to come. Indeed, twice in 1928 President Coolidge reassuringly declared that stocks were "cheap at current prices."

Herbert Hoover is elected President. Calvin Coolidge's name had become a synonym for the prosperity that many Americans were enjoying. Most people believed he would run for re-election, but in the summer of 1927 he calmly announced, "I do not choose to run for President in 1928." He may have had a feeling that serious economic troubles were about to occur. Indeed, Grace Coolidge, the First Lady, referring to the President, said casually to a friend, "Papa thinks a depression is coming."

Republican eyes turned to Herbert Hoover. Although he lacked a sparkling personality, Hoover was well-regarded for his work as Secretary of Commerce under Harding and Coolidge. He represented big business, rural America, Protestantism, and prohibition.

Born in Iowa in 1874, Hoover had been orphaned at eight and went to live with an uncle in Oregon. In time he became independently wealthy as a mining engineer and business promoter. At the Republican convention in 1928, Hoover was nominated on the first ballot.

Having lost his bid for the Democratic nomination in 1924, Al Smith again drew support from those who championed the interests of the cities. His big-city manner, combined with his religion and his opposition to prohibition, made him popular in many urban areas. An accomplished reformer in New York, Smith seemed the ideal choice for the Democrats. His name was placed in nomination by Franklin Roosevelt, who labeled him the "happy warrior." Smith easily won the nomination on the first ballot.

It was a fierce campaign, with prohibition and Smith's Catholicism as the main issues. Only rarely, however, has the party controlling the White House been defeated when economic conditions have appeared to be good. Herbert Hoover won an overwhelming victory in 1928, receiving 444 electoral votes to Smith's 87.

For the first time since reconstruction days, the Republicans had carried five states in the formerly solid South. Still, the twelve largest cities in the country, carried by the Republicans in 1924, were now in the Democratic column. The Democrats, in other words, had made major gains in the Republican North. If the trend continued, the

Democrats next time might become the nation's majority party.

But why should such a trend continue? During the campaign, Hoover had stated, "We in America today are nearer to the final triumph over poverty than ever before in the history of any land. The poorhouse is vanishing from among us." As Hoover took the oath of office on March 4, 1929, the outlook for the nation seemed bright.

SECTION REVIEW

1. (a) Why was Harding elected President in 1920? (b) What scandals marred his presidency? (c) Who succeeded him in office?
2. (a) Who were the leading candidates for President in 1924? (b) Who won the election?
3. (a) Why did farmers suffer hard times after World War I? (b) What was the farm bloc? (c) How did it try to help farmers?
4. (a) Who was elected President in 1928? (b) Why did most people look to the future with optimism? (c) What signs of coming trouble were appearing?

3 American Society Undergoes Rapid Change

During the 1920's a number of new technological developments transformed American society. None was more important than the automobile. The automobile had already seized the imagination of the American people. Early in his term, President Taft had converted the White House stables into a garage and startled many people by riding around Washington in a "horseless carriage." His chauffeur was under strict orders never to run the machine faster than 20 miles per hour. Warren Harding in 1921 was the first President to ride to his inauguration in an automobile. The day of the elegant horse-drawn carriage for state occasions was over.

Henry Ford puts America on wheels. America, with its wide-open spaces and great distances, was made to order for the automobile. The potential market for car sales was almost unlimited. Any manufacturer who could produce an efficient, easily maintained, and inexpensive car could count on success.

Such a man was Henry Ford. His Model T, eventually the most famous car ever built, was the most revolutionary invention of the young century. The impact of Ford's automobile was comparable in American history to that of the cotton gin.

Ford was a mechanical genius who believed he could make a car that practically everybody could afford. After long experimentation with various designs, he produced the first Model T in 1908. The high-sitting, ungraceful vehicle was practical if not elegant. It soon found a huge market. By 1913 Ford was producing over 500 cars a day, and two years later his one-millionth car was on the road.

Car production grows rapidly. The amazing increase in car production was made possible by the use of the *assembly line.* The assembly line was Henry Ford's most important contribution to American industry. Under this system, the hundreds of parts used in an automobile were manufactured by specialized machines. The parts were then placed on a conveyor belt which passed from worker to worker. As the belt moved along, each worker performed a single operation: fastening mudguard brackets

Henry Ford's Model T was produced in mass volume at low cost, enabling many Americans to buy one.

or installing the engine or simply putting in place a bolt on which the next worker would place a nut. The production of an automobile at Ford's plant was accomplished in 45 such operations. On operation 44 the radiator was filled, and on operation 45 the car was driven off the line. By 1925 Ford had so perfected the process that a car came off the assembly line every ten seconds.

Tourists came to the Ford plant and watched in awe as these cars "for the great multitude" — to use Ford's phrase — rolled in a steady stream from the assembly line. Because Ford cut his price almost every year (the lowest price was $290 in 1924), sales kept rising. He became the most successful manufacturer in history.

Henry Ford had established a minimum wage for his factory employees in 1914: $5 a day, at a time when the national average for unskilled workers was $1 a day and for skilled workers $2.50. This rate of pay seemed excessively high to many of Ford's critics. Ford argued, however, that unless his employees were paid well, they would never be able to buy Ford cars. If some people thought Ford had made a mistake, they were soon surprised. Ford's profits raced even higher. By 1926 he was paying his workers $10 a day.

Powerful competitors of Ford, including Chrysler, Packard, and Studebaker, also achieved remarkable success. General Motors' Chevrolet was making friends too. In addition to being an inexpensive car, the Chevy — as it was popularly called — had a "refined" look copied from high-priced cars like the Cadillac.

Ford himself saw the change in taste and in 1927 ended production of the Model T. The following year he put the Model A on the market to compete with the Chevy.

By 1920 there were about 8 million cars on the road. Ten years later, Americans owned over 23 million cars, and the automotive industry had become the nation's biggest business. General Motors developed the system of introducing a new model each year. Owning an automobile became a mark of personal success. By the late 1920's, having "two cars in every garage" seemed a worthy goal for every American family.

The automobile brings many changes. The automobile made it possible for Americans to travel more widely. Families with automobiles could enjoy picnics and vacations in distant places. This new mobility also meant that people could commute greater distances to their jobs. It meant, too, that young people were beginning to spend less time at home. Many of them, driving their own "tin lizzies," enjoyed more personal freedom than any previous generation of youth. Their new-found freedom led to social changes. The idea, for instance, that a young woman needed a chaperone on a date vanished.

The wide use of the automobile resulted in a doubling of the number of miles of paved roads during the 1920's. At the same time, traffic jams and accidents became common. By 1930 more than half the accidental deaths in the country were caused by auto crashes.

Americans were on wheels to stay. Whereas most people a few years earlier lived and died only a few miles from where they had been born, now they had new choices as to where they would make their home. The automobile produced a boom in the development of suburbs, which created thousands of jobs in the construction industry as homes, schools, libraries, churches, stores, motels, service stations, garages, and post offices were built. By 1930 one out of nine workers had jobs in glass, steel, rubber, or other industries related to automobile production.

Accompanying the rise of the automobile was the development of the trucking industry, which more and more competed with the railroads in the shipment of goods. There were only a million trucks in 1920, but more than three times that number in 1930. Furthermore, in the same decade, the number of buses went from about 18,000 to almost 41,000.

The automobile brought increased demands for petroleum products, and people constantly searched for new oil fields. The modern oil industry had its beginnings at the turn of the century when a huge oil field was found in eastern Texas, just south of Beaumont. For most of his life a Texan named Pattillo Higgins had been convinced that the land in that area contained oil. Sometimes he would take his Sunday school classes to a place named Spindletop, near Beaumont. With a cane he would poke holes in the ground there and light the natural gas as it escaped. Fascinated by the underground gas, he finally bought the land at Spindletop and, along with an Austrian-born mining engineer named Anthony Lucas, began drilling on it.

The determination of the men paid off. On January 10, 1901, a deafening roar shook the earth as oil gushed to the surface. Spindletop was the biggest oil strike that had ever been made. Soon the field was producing between 85,000 and 100,000 barrels of oil daily, and an oil boom was on. Prospectors crowded into Texas, searching for more Spindletops. New fields were found, and soon Texas was the nation's leading oil-producing state.

Mass media creates mass markets. To sell automobiles and all the other products pouring out of America's factories, advertising itself became big business. Advertising created new tastes and persuaded people that they had new needs. More and more Americans measured their status in society by their ability to buy new and more intriguing goods.

The use of advertising slogans and alluring models had started at the turn of the century. As ads whetted the nation's appetites for consumer goods, new customers were also created by the introduction of the installment plan. By selling "on time," merchants expanded the ready market for expensive products such as automobiles, radios, refrigerators, and typewriters.

Movies set the style. The motion-picture industry, also new, played a large part in fastening the mass-production economy on the country. Movie audiences saw their heroes driving up-to-date models of cars, wearing the latest style of clothing, dancing the newest step, and singing the newest tune. Thousands of people imitated what they saw on the motion-picture screen.

In this way the film industry contributed to raising the expectations of average

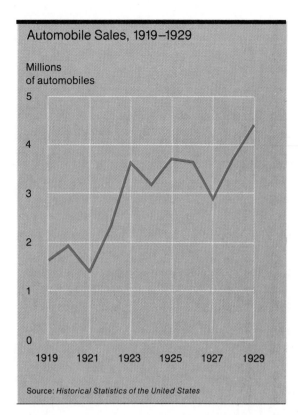

During the 1920's, sales of automobiles more than doubled.

people — and increasing their dissatisfactions. How shabby one's own house seemed in comparison to those in the movies! How carefree the characters appeared, living in mansions without visible means of support and enjoying boundless luxury! Millions of people began to follow the lead of the "stars" in their demands for pleasure, leisure, and material goods. Where people once saved their money for a rainy day — a time of need — they now saved for a sunny day — a time of vacation.

The motion-picture industry had produced its first screen story, *The Great Train Robbery*, in 1903. Soon afterward, a promoter in Pittsburgh set up facilities in a warehouse for projecting one-reel shows, charging five cents admission. These "nickelodeons" spread quickly to other cities. By 1907 nearly every city had a movie theater, and more were being built every year.

The actors and actresses of the screen were constantly in the public eye: the Gish sisters, Charlie Chaplin, Mary Pickford,

Douglas Fairbanks, and many others. Some of their names and even the stories about their lives were made up by promoters — all a part of the make-believe that movies were fostering. Clara Bow, known as the "It" girl, dramatized her glamour daily. She liked to draw attention by driving on the streets of Hollywood in an open convertible, accompanied by seven chow dogs whose color matched her flaming-red hair.

In 1922, forty million movie tickets were being sold each week; by the end of the decade the figure had doubled. The production of motion pictures had quickly become big business.

The radio serves America. The beginning of commercial radio broadcasting went hand-in-hand with the movies in changing American tastes and use of leisure time. In millions of homes, families gathered around the radio to hear Paul Whiteman's orchestra or long-running serials like the Goldbergs with Molly Berg. Others enjoyed hearing songs by the A&P Gypsies or the Connecticut Yankees.

The first commercial radio station was KDKA in Pittsburgh which, on November 2, 1920, broadcast the presidential election returns. In 1922 the White House acquired its first radio. Within a few years the radio was a familiar item in American life.

Radio seemed to speed up American life. The regular broadcasting of news reports gave listeners immediate access to what was going on. People not only knew what their leaders looked like — an element added to political life in the 1880's with the invention of quick methods of reproducing pictures. Now they knew what their leaders sounded like too.

Women have new opportunities. The 1920's also saw the rise of the "new woman." As the decade progressed, women began to experience new freedom and opportunity. Many women who had taken jobs outside the home during the First World War continued to be gainfully employed. Furthermore, the number of fields open to women gradually increased, however slowly.

A giant step toward a new era for women was the ratification in 1920 of the Nineteenth Amendment (page 155). After almost a century of effort, women had at last gained the right to vote. Soon, organizations such as the League of Women Voters were formed to help women participate more fully in political life.

Equally important for many women was the introduction of new labor-saving devices, freeing them from age-old drudgery. Much of this new freedom came from the

New movie theaters opened in every American city. Broadway in New York City was so brightly lighted by movie marquees that it became known as the Great White Way.

A Working Woman

In 1924 a team of sociologists began a pioneering study of life in a typical Midwestern city. In 1929 Robert and Helen Lynd published their work in a book entitled *Middletown: A Study in American Culture.* The following statement was made by a married woman who had two sons and worked six days a week outside her home.

I began to work during the war when everyone else did; we had to meet payments on our house and everything else was getting so high. The mister objected at first, but now he [does not] mind. I'd rather keep on working so my boys can play football and basketball and have spending money their father can't give them. We've built our own home, a nice brown and white bungalow, by a building and loan like every one else does. We have it almost all paid off and it's worth about $6,000.

No, I don't lose out with my neighbors because I work; some of them have jobs and those who don't [have jobs] envy us who do. I have felt better since I worked than ever before in my life. I get up at five-thirty. My husband takes a dinner and the boys buy theirs uptown and I cook supper. We have an electric washing machine, electric iron, and vacuum sweeper. I don't even have to ask my husband any more because I buy these things with my own money. I bought an icebox last year — a big one that holds 125 pounds; most of the time I don't fill it, but we have our folks visit us from back East, and then I do.

We own a $1,200 Studebaker with a nice California top, semi-enclosed. Last

An office worker

summer we all spent our vacation going back to Pennsylvania — taking in Niagara Falls on the way. The two boys want to go to college, and I want them to. I graduated from high school myself, but I feel if I can't give my boys a little more, all my work will have been useless.

---

widespread use of electrical appliances. Nowhere were the effects clearer than in homes equipped with electric irons, refrigerators, vacuum cleaners, and washing machines.

Many women showed how free they were by shortening their skirts and even rolling their stockings to below their knees. In so doing they earned the admiring nickname "flappers." A fashion editor wrote in 1920 that "the American woman . . . has lifted her skirt far beyond any modest limi-

tations." The hem was then nine inches from the ground. It soon reached the knee. Lipstick and rouge, once seen only on actresses, were now used by millions. Many women also decided that hair worn in braids or in a bun was a thing of the past. When a popular dancer named Irene Castle "bobbed" her hair — that is, cut it short — millions of women imitated her.

Fads and sports capture the public imagination. As life speeded up, the nation became

Fads and Spectacles

Americans danced the Charleston in the 1920's, solved crossword puzzles, and cheered when Helen Wills won tennis championships. Pole-sitting drew much attention but was not widely practiced!

more than ever addicted to fads — popular crazes that lasted for a season or two and then faded out. For a time, millions of Americans were caught up in the crossword-puzzle fad and then in the game of *mah jongg*. The opening in 1922 of the tomb of the Pharaoh Tutankhamen in Egypt led to the popularity of clothing with a "King Tut" motif.

The search for leisure-time activities had much to do with the popularity of organized sports. A reflection of the growing size of cities was the increasing interest in spectator sports. Professional baseball, which had started in 1869, grew in popularity in the 1920's. Yankee Stadium, opened in 1922, became a showcase for Babe Ruth's dramatic home-run hitting. Ruth revolutionized a game that had previously concentrated on base-running and crafty pitching. Professional football and hockey were also introduced in the 1920's, but baseball remained "the national sport."

Other sports also produced popular idols: Bobby Jones in golf, Bill Tilden and Helen Wills in tennis, and Jack Dempsey and Gene Tunney in boxing. In 1926 Gertrude Ederle, the daughter of a New York butcher, became the first American and the first woman to swim the English Channel. New York City lauded her with a homecoming parade upon her return.

The airplane comes of age. The greatest hero of the 1920's, however, was Charles A. Lindbergh, who received the public's acclaim for his solo flight across the Atlantic in 1927. His extraordinary achievement grew out of a series of events that took place early in the twentieth century.

The airplane industry, which was American in origin, had its beginnings in 1903. In that year Orville and Wilbur Wright made a successful flight at Kitty Hawk, North Carolina. During the First World War, airplanes were at first assigned to the signal corps for use in observing enemy movements. By the end of the fighting, however, they were being used in combat.

The first regular airmail route was opened in 1918 between Washington, D.C., and New York. The service was extended within a few years to routes between New York, Chicago, and San Francisco. The planes were owned by the Post Office Department. Beginning in 1925, Congress started the practice, already common in Europe, of subsidizing private airlines to carry the mail.

Commercial air travel began in 1926. In that year 18 lines carried more than 5,000 passengers. Innovators soon dotted the scene. One was 26-year-old Juan Trippe, who combined his love of flying with skill in obtaining the financial backing necessary to make commercial flying a success. In 1927 he and his friends launched Pan American Airways. Another innovator was William Boeing, an airplane designer and manufacturer who helped start United Airlines. Still another was Eddie Rickenbacker, an air ace of World War I (page 195), who later became head of Eastern Airlines. Auxiliary industries were also established. Frederick B. Rentschler, the son of a German immigrant iron maker, helped establish Pratt and Whitney Aircraft, an engine manufacturer. Within a few years Rentschler had turned his original cash investment of $253 into over $35 million.

Lindbergh crosses the Atlantic. The drama and the risk of flying created constant news. The United States Navy seaplane NC–4 in 1919 had become the first to fly across the Atlantic. The most sensational flight, however, would be a nonstop journey from New York to Paris.

In 1919 a New York hotel owner offered a prize of $25,000 to the first pilot who succeeded in such an undertaking. On May 20, 1927, from a muddy field on Long Island, Charles A. Lindbergh took off in his plane, *The Spirit of St. Louis,* on one of the most memorable flights in history. He had planned the flight with infinite care. Half the weight of the plane was fuel. Some of the fuel was carried in tanks in front of Lindbergh's seat, blocking his forward view. His few personal supplies included a canteen of water and a brown bag containing five sandwiches.

On the way, Lindbergh battled sleet, snow, and sleep. Thirty-three and a half hours after takeoff, he put his plane down at Le Bourget airfield near Paris. "Well, I made it," he said modestly.

"Lucky Lindy," as he was quickly dubbed, became an instant international hero. He was an unassuming young man who had dared to reach for an "impossible" goal. When he refused to cash in on his sensational journey by signing testimonials and accepting movie contracts, Americans were both astonished and pleased. One newspaper called him "the fair-haired boy that every man would like to have been." In Lindbergh, who had now opened the era of intercontinental flight, Americans saw a reminder of days now gone forever. He was an American frontiersman in an increasingly urban time.

SECTION REVIEW

1. Vocabulary: *assembly line.*
2. (a) What economic and social changes were brought about by the introduction of the automobile? (b) By movies? (c) By the radio?
3. How did the role of American women change during the 1920's?
4. What fads and sports held the attention of the American public during the 1920's?
5. (a) Who were some of the individuals responsible for the development of commercial air travel? (b) How did Charles Lindbergh capture the imagination of the American people?

Chapter 8 Review

Summary

The years immediately following World War I were unsettled ones for the United States. The adjustment from a wartime economy to normal operations was not entirely smooth. Prices during the war had increased dramatically, and workers in every sector now demanded higher wages. Police officers in Boston, steel workers in Indiana, and miners in the soft-coal fields were just three groups who went out on strike over salary demands.

News from Europe about Communist uprisings combined with the labor unrest to frighten many Americans. People became suspicious that outsiders were threatening American society. Increased demands for restrictions on immigration were one consequence of these fears of foreign influence.

Black Americans who had served in the armed forces or worked in war industries looked forward to greater opportunities after the war. Competition with white workers for jobs, however, resulted in tension, and in the summer of 1919 race riots took place in many cities. Still, black creativity flourished during the 1920's, producing a wealth of music, art, and literature.

The movement to prohibit the sale and consumption of alcohol gathered strength during the war, resulting in the ratification of the Eighteenth Amendment in 1919. Measures to enforce prohibition, however, were ineffective.

In the presidential contest of 1920, the Republican candidate, Warren G. Harding, emerged victorious. After Harding died in 1923, numerous scandals involving members of his Cabinet came to light. Calvin Coolidge finished Harding's term and was elected President himself in 1924. During Coolidge's administration much of the American economy boomed. Foreign imports and huge farm surpluses caused agricultural prices to fall sharply, however, and slumps in the coal, textile, and construction industries by the end of the decade foretold economic problems ahead. When Coolidge decided not to run again, his Secretary of Commerce, Herbert Hoover, received the Republican nomination for the presidency and then won the election of 1928.

The decade after the First World War brought profound changes to American life. The automobile, thanks in large part to Henry Ford, became available to millions of Americans. Motion pictures, the radio, and professional sports provided new entertainment. Commercial air travel began and Charles A. Lindbergh became a national hero by flying nonstop from New York to Paris.

Vocabulary and Important Terms

1. "Red scare"
2. quota
3. National Origins Act
4. Harlem Renaissance
5. prohibition
6. Volstead Act
7. Federal Bureau of Investigation
8. "Ohio gang"
9. farm bloc
10. McNary-Haugen Bill
11. Model T
12. assembly line

Discussion Questions

1. (a) Immediately after World War I, what difficulties did the nation's economy face? (b) Why were many workers discontented?

2. (a) Why did Congress establish immigration quotas in the 1920's? (b) Why did those who supported immigration restriction insist that 1890 was the best year on which to base quotas?

3. (a) What effects did the general disregard for prohibition have on American society? (b) Why did few people believe prohibition would be repealed?

4. (a) How did the presidential election of 1920 reflect the national debate over America's involvement in international affairs? (b) What was the outcome of that election? (c) Why was Coolidge's succession to the presidency important both for the Republican Party and for the American people?

5. (a) Why are the 1920's remembered as a time of prosperity? (b) What groups did not share in that prosperity? (c) What evidence was there that the prosperity rested on a shaky foundation?

6. (a) What were the main issues in the presidential campaign of 1928? (b) Why did Herbert Hoover win the election? (c) What new voting trends were revealed by the 1928 election?

7. (a) Why was Henry Ford's Model T a revolutionary invention? (b) Why might Ford's treatment of factory workers also be considered "revolutionary"?

8. How did advertising, movies, radio, and consumer credit help create mass markets for the vast outpouring of products from America's factories?

9. What were some of the ways in which Americans spent their newly created leisure time during the 1920's?

Relating Past and Present

1. Al Smith's religion was a major issue in his race for the presidency in 1928. What Catholics have run for President in recent years? Was their religion an issue?

2. What fads and sports have captured the imagination of the American public in recent years? Besides participating in organized sports, in what other ways do Americans fill their leisure time?

Studying Local History

1. Find out which candidate received your state's electoral votes in the presidential elections of 1920, 1924, and 1928. Then try to explain *why* your state voted as it did.
2. The radio station KDKA began operation in 1920. Find out when the first commercial radio station began in your local area. What kinds of programs were popular?

Using History Skills

1. *Reading source material.* Study the account of the working woman on page 223. (a) When did this woman first find a job? (b) What was the reaction of her husband? (c) For what reasons did she enjoy working outside the home?

2. *Reading graphs.* Study the graph showing farm income on page 217. How does the graph help explain the difficulties that American farmers faced during the 1920's?

3. *Using the dictionary.* Find the word *normalcy* in the dictionary. (a) What part of speech is *normalcy*? (b) From what word is it derived? (c) What did President Harding have in mind when he called for a "return to normalcy"?

4. *Writing a report.* Choose one of the following American authors and write a report based on his or her life: (a) F. Scott Fitzgerald, (b) Ernest Hemingway, (c) Willa Cather, (d) Sinclair Lewis, (e) Eugene O'Neill. In your report describe the impact the author had on literature during the 1920's. What were some of the settings of the author's works?

WORLD SCENE

The Collapse of Empires

The impact of the First World War was far-reaching. Centuries-old empires had collapsed, and new nations arose in their place.

The breakup of the Ottoman Empire. The decision of the Ottoman Turks to side with Germany in World War I proved costly. The Ottoman Empire, badly defeated, was stripped of much of its territory. The new nations of Palestine, Trans-Jordan, Syria, Lebanon, and Iraq, all of which were created out of former Ottoman territory, were placed under the supervision of either Britain or France.

A nationalist group known as the Young Turks had forced reforms on the Ottomans before the war. They now organized an army to challenge the Ottoman sultan. By the end of 1922 the Young Turks had abolished the office of sultan and had even persuaded the Allies to negotiate a new, less harsh peace treaty for their country.

In October, 1923, a democratic republic was proclaimed in Turkey, and the leader of the nationalist movement, Mustafa Kemal, was elected president. A resourceful and resolute man, Kemal believed his nation could not prosper without rapid modernization. He initiated sweeping changes — Western dress, the Roman alphabet, and the Christian calendar were adopted, as was a law requiring all Turks to choose a surname, in the European style. Kemal himself became Kemal Atatürk, meaning "father of the Turks."

The new state of Czechoslovakia. Czechoslovakia was one of the nations created following the breakup of Austria-Hungary in 1918. The new state was fortunate in inheriting the most valuable industrial areas of the old empire. Czechoslovakia was also fortunate in the leadership that guided its new constitutional government. The first president was Tomáš Masaryk, a widely respected statesman and scholar. Married to an American, Masaryk was well known in the United States, where he had many friends.

Masaryk had the difficult task of mediating the often-conflicting interests of the country's ethnic groups. Czechoslovakia was largely made up of two Slavic elements — the Czechs, constituting 60 percent of the people, and the Slovaks, constituting 30 percent. The remaining 10 percent of the population consisted of Germans, Poles, and Hungarians. Tomáš Masaryk, who greatly admired Thomas Jefferson's achievements, helped mold Czechoslovakia into a democracy by the end of the 1920's.

CHAPTER 9

Fashioning the New Deal

1929 – 1940

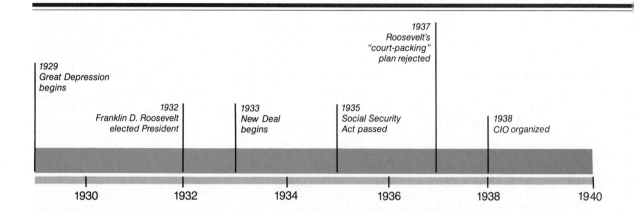

1929
Great Depression
begins

1932
Franklin D. Roosevelt
elected President

1933
New Deal
begins

1935
Social Security
Act passed

1937
Roosevelt's
"court-packing"
plan rejected

1938
CIO organized

1930   1932   1934   1936   1938   1940

CHAPTER OUTLINE

1. The Great Depression begins.

2. The New Deal takes shape.

3. The second New Deal introduces reforms.

4. The New Deal comes to an end.

Herbert Hoover was sworn in as President in an atmosphere of high optimism. Although March 4, 1929, was a rainy day, Hoover's words were sunny: "Ours is a land rich in resources . . . blessed with comfort and opportunity. In no nation are the fruits of accomplishment more secure. . . . I have no fear for the future of the country."

If Hoover had misgivings, they included one that he confided to a newspaper editor. The public, Hoover had observed, considered him "a sort of superman, that no problem is beyond my capacity. . . . If some unprecedented calamity should come upon the nation, I would be sacrificed to the unreasoning disappointment of a people who expected too much." The calamity came soon enough — the deepest economic depression the nation had ever experienced. It put Hoover on the defensive throughout his presidency and paved the way for the election of Franklin Delano Roosevelt in 1932.

Franklin Roosevelt had grown up in the time of Theodore Roosevelt and Woodrow Wilson. From them he acquired his admiration for strong and active leadership. He showed clearly that he enjoyed the exercise of power and responsibility. He also demonstrated a willingness to use his office to propose a seemingly endless series of measures to restore the nation's economic health. Deeply rooted in American history, he considered himself a conservative man guided by the motto "Reform, if you would preserve."

1 The Great Depression Begins

In 1929 Americans everywhere were buying shares of stock and creating a record boom on Wall Street. The average price of common stock in 1926 had been below $100 a share; by late summer in 1929, the average price had climbed to over $216. The Secretary of the Treasury, Andrew W. Mellon, answered those who urged caution: "There is no cause to worry. The high tide of prosperity will continue."

Warning signs appear. Words, however, could not alter facts. By the middle of 1929 consumer spending had slackened noticeably, a slowdown in new construction was setting in, and the boom in automobile sales had come to an end. A potential source of trouble was the large amount of money — running into billions of dollars — that people had borrowed to buy stocks on margin. (Buying on margin is a method by which investors put up only a fraction of the purchase price for stock shares and borrow the remainder from their brokers.) Despite warnings that stock prices were too high, more and more Americans invested in stocks.

The Federal Reserve Board (page 172), which had inflated the money supply during the 1920's, may have helped set the stage for disaster. The easy-money policy probably stimulated the public's urge to speculate. Recognizing the danger of over-speculation, the "Fed" finally warned its member banks not to lend money for speculative purposes.

By 1930 the nation was faced with the worst depression it had ever known. Factories stood idle, farms were abandoned, and millions of people were out of work.

The stock market crashes. Disaster struck on October 23, 1929, when stock prices dropped sharply. The trend continued the following day — which has ever since been remembered as Black Thursday. Stock shares began to be sold in huge quantities and the bottom fell out of the market. Orders from thousands of people desperate to sell their stock jammed the wires from every part of the country.

A group of bankers gathered on Black Thursday, amid much publicity, at the office of J. P. Morgan and Company. After a short meeting they announced they were going to support the market by buying stocks — with millions of dollars supplied by their banks. Prices rallied somewhat, and for a few days a measure of confidence returned. The words of President Hoover were reassuring too: "The fundamental business of the country — that is, the production and distribution of goods and services — is on a sound and prosperous basis."

Actually, the business of the country was *not* soundly based. Some economists pointed out that the prosperity of the previous years had been unevenly spread. Factories, as a result, were producing more goods than workers and other consumers could afford to buy.

The pattern of American international trade also contributed to economic weakness. The United States had emerged from the First World War as a creditor nation, with other countries owing Americans billions of dollars. The debtor nations could repay their obligations — and continue to buy American products — only by selling goods in the United States. High tariffs, however, prevented this. Consequently, foreigners borrowed more and more money from the United States. When the foreigners could not repay what they had borrowed, American investors were hurt. After the stock market began to slide, the flow of dollars abroad was reduced to a mere trickle. Foreign markets for American goods dried up, causing American factories to shut down.

On Tuesday, October 29, the stock market began to sink again with another big sell-off. More than sixteen million shares were sold that day. In the weeks that followed, stock prices moved steadily downward. By the middle of November it was apparent that stock prices were not going to "bounce back" quickly. In fact, for the next two and a half years the market continued to drift lower and lower.

Prosperity comes to an end. The stock market "crash" was the first stage of the disastrous Great Depression. Stock market losses from mid-October to mid-November, 1929, amounted to $30 billion, wiping out the resources of millions of Americans. People began to cut down on their purchases. As more and more factories closed or went on part-time operation, thousands upon thousands of jobs simply disappeared. Construction of new homes and buildings ground to a halt, throwing more people out of work. By the autumn of 1931, eight million people were unemployed.

The Depression spreads. It is impossible today to imagine the fear and anxiety that came into countless homes. The wages of those fortunate enough to have jobs were slashed again and again as the business collapse deepened. The average yearly income of a working person fell from $703 in 1929 to only $375 in 1933. People with savings, meanwhile, quickly used them up. Credit companies reclaimed furniture, automobiles, radios, refrigerators — even clothing — that had been purchased on the installment plan. Millions of families, unable to make mortgage payments, lost their homes. In the cities, families that could not pay the rent were forced out of their apartments. Sometimes people would sit on the street with all their possessions, hoping that a friend or neighbor would give them a helping hand.

Farm conditions grew worse as the Depression settled in. Farm income, which had been $6 billion in 1929, dropped to $2 billion in 1932. When farmers tried to increase their return by raising more crops, prices slipped even lower. To add to the problem, large parts of the nation were beset by drought beginning in 1930. In a short time, so many dust storms had struck

Drought and wind turned much of the Great Plains into a "Dust Bowl" during the Depression years. Here an Oklahoma family struggles against a raging dust storm.

the entire area from Texas to the Dakotas that it came to be labeled the "Dust Bowl." The scope of the disaster is suggested by the grim joke told by a Nebraska farmer during one such storm: "I'm counting the Kansas farms as they go by."

Industrial workers and farmers were not the only Americans affected by the Depression. Middle-class people were also badly hurt by hard times. Few jobs were available to a laid-off school teacher, or a clergyman whose salary was not being paid, or a lawyer unable to collect fees. The effect on morale was devastating, as people like these went door to door shining shoes or selling newspapers.

People tried to keep up their courage. They struggled to assure themselves that "prosperity was just around the corner." In Cincinnati someone distributed thousands of buttons that read "I'm sold on America. I won't talk depression." There was a kind of cheerfulness in a popular song of 1931, "Life is Just a Bowl of Cherries." As things grew worse, however, optimism faded, and in 1932 people began singing a gloomier tune, "Brother, Can You Spare a Dime?"

Hoover urges voluntary action. Because the Republicans had claimed credit for the pros-

perity of the 1920's, they could not escape blame for the nation's predicament. In the White House, Herbert Hoover was filled with anguish. Many people, mistaking his unsmiling face for hard-heartedness, jeered him in public. Soon, the homeless unemployed had given the name "Hoover blankets" to the newspapers they covered themselves with at night. The shanties in which these unfortunates huddled became known as "Hoovervilles." An empty pocket turned inside out was called a "Hoover flag."

Hoover did not believe that extraordinary measures were required. He firmly insisted that voluntary activities would bring the nation out of its doldrums. He urged people, for instance, to be more generous than usual in donating money to charity. He opened a Give-A-Job campaign in which job-holding Americans were encouraged to provide a day's work to their unemployed neighbors, allowing them, for instance, to clean out a cellar or whitewash a fence. Most people were embarrassed to offer such work to someone they knew. Many people who needed help were too proud to ask the family next door for assistance. Hoover, meanwhile, turned a deaf ear on an idea being discussed in many quarters — that

"Broken Hopes and Dreams"

Mahalia Jackson, who later became a world-famous singer, was a young woman in 1928 when she moved from the South to live with her aunt in Chicago. In the hard times that began soon afterwards, she observed what happened to people around her. She wrote about the period in her autobiography *Movin' On Up.*

Mahalia Jackson

When the Depression hit Chicago, the life the Negroes had built up for themselves in Chicago fell apart. On the South Side it was as if somebody had pulled a switch and everything had stopped running. Every day another big mill or factory would lay off all its colored help. Suddenly the streets were full of men and women who'd been put out of their jobs. . . . Banks all over the South Side locked their doors, and I'll never forget seeing the long lines of people outside them crying in the streets over their lost savings and falling on their knees and praying.

The Depression was much harder on the city Negroes up North than it was on the Negroes down South because it cost them all the gains they had struggled for. Many of the Negroes in the South didn't feel the Depression too much. Some of them could hardly tell the difference from prosperity. They never had had much for themselves and still had their little vegetable gardens and their chickens and maybe a pig or two, so they could still get enough to eat.

But in Chicago the Depression made the South Side a place of broken hopes and dreams. It was so sad that it would break your heart to think about it.

The big fine cars disappeared from the streets. People's clothes began to look more and more shabby, and families began to pile in together to save rent money. . . .

The city parks were full of people living in shanties made out of tin and wood scraps. All over the city, people were lining up to eat at bread lines and soup kitchens. If you earned a dollar, you felt guilty about spending it on yourself. I remember one day I earned $1.75 washing clothes, and on the way home I had to pass the people standing in one of those bread lines. I fished the money out of my pocket and told those people to follow me. We bought a sack of potatoes and a mess of smoked ribs . . . with that money and took it all back to my place and had one big supper.

the federal government assist the unemployed by giving them relief through direct payments. To Hoover the idea of a government "hand-out" was not permissible under a system of free enterprise.

City governments tried as best they could to relieve the suffering, but by 1932 many of them could not provide any more help. When city governments ran out of money, the states lent a hand. New York

State, under Governor Franklin D. Roosevelt, took the lead in giving direct assistance to the unemployed. Before long, other states were doing likewise.

Even as they agonized over their condition, most Americans retained confidence in capitalism as a system of production and distribution of goods. Moreover, although there was widespread discontent, it produced little violence. The public, accustomed to self-discipline, did not destroy property — even to get food or obtain shelter. Some hunger marches took place, and on occasion people prevented bank agents from foreclosing farms. In general, however, the orderly processes of public life went on as usual.

Hoover tries to stop the downward trend. In spite of his desire to keep the government out of the economy, Hoover early accepted the idea that the government would have to take on certain responsibilities. In 1929, for instance, the Hoover administration supported passage of the Agricultural Marketing Act. The measure set up a Federal Farm Board, which had a special fund of $500 million to stabilize farm prices and discourage the growing of surplus crops. Farm cooperatives could borrow money from the fund to pay for the costs of storing produce until prices were higher. The Agricultural Marketing Act was the first instance where federal funds were used in an attempt to regulate farm prices. It failed, however, to stop the fall in farm prices or to prevent the continued growth of surpluses.

Hoover strongly believed that if business could somehow be revived, the rest of the country would share in the benefits. Following the failure of a number of banks in 1931, therefore, he called for the establishment of the Reconstruction Finance Corporation (RFC). Set up by Congress in 1932, the RFC was granted the authority to lend money to banks, railroads, and other institutions in financial trouble. Some critics denounced the RFC as "a federal breadline for business." At any rate, despite advancing nearly $2 billion in loans during Hoover's years in office, the RFC proved unable to restore prosperity.

When President and Mrs. Hoover moved into the White House in 1929, there were few indications of the trouble that lay ahead.

Hoover also recommended a cut in income taxes. The effect, he hoped, would be to put additional money in circulation so that people could purchase more consumer goods. The results were modest, however, because millions of Americans had no income at all.

The "Bonus Army" marches on Washington. Nothing dramatized the agony of the times better than the march of the "Bonus Army" on Washington, D.C., in 1932. Made up of 15,000 veterans of World War I, the "Army" consisted of marchers from many parts of the country. Their purpose was to petition Congress for immediate payment of a bonus for wartime service. The bonus was not scheduled to be distributed until 1945.

Congress rejected the petition of the Bonus Army but offered to pay their fare home. All of them departed except about 2,000 die-hards, who had set up a camp of shacks and tents on the banks of the Poto-mac. Following a scuffle between a band of veterans and the police, the government of the District of Columbia declared itself unable to maintain order. On July 28, 1932, Hoover finally called in the army to disperse the holdouts. Soldiers led by the Chief of Staff, General Douglas MacArthur, set fire to the camp and scattered the occupants with bayonets and tear gas.

SECTION REVIEW

1. What were some of the advance signs of economic trouble in 1929?
2. Describe the effects of the stock market crash.
3. (a) What was President Hoover's attitude toward government relief projects? (b) What programs did he institute in an effort to halt the Depression?
4. (a) Why did the "Bonus Army" march on Washington? (b) What happened to the "Bonus Army"?

2 The New Deal Takes Shape

In 1932 the Republicans nominated Herbert Hoover for a second term as President. Only the most optimistic members of the party believed, however, that he could be re-elected. Most voters felt certain that *anybody* the Democratic Party named would win the election. Interest, therefore, centered on the struggle among the Democratic hopefuls.

The Democrats nominate Franklin Roosevelt. Al Smith longed for a second nomination, but most Democratic leaders, remembering the religious issue in 1928 (page 218), did not want to see it raised again. An eager contender with a magical last name was Franklin Delano Roosevelt, who had been re-elected governor of New York in 1930. Roosevelt had a winning smile and a warm public manner. Still, he had no clearly thought-out program for dealing with the problems the Depression had brought. As a practiced politician, he, of course, found it an advantage not to be in favor of any specific plan of action.

In a victory mood, the Democrats gathered in Chicago in late June, 1932, and on the fourth ballot nominated Roosevelt for President. John Nance Garner of Texas, Speaker of the House of Representatives, was named as their candidate for Vice President. The Democratic platform called for reduced government spending, a sound currency, aid to agriculture, and repeal of the prohibition amendment.

Roosevelt had been born in 1882 at Hyde Park, New York, in a mansion overlooking the Hudson River. Young Roosevelt grew up in a protected world of wealth and leisure. His father, James, who was 52 years old at the time of the boy's birth, was a gentleman farmer, who had known Sam Houston. The mother, Sara Delano, half her husband's age, came from a family that had made its money in the trade with China.

Educated by private tutors until he was fourteen years old, Roosevelt received a good background in French and German. As a youth, he traveled abroad more widely than any President since John Quincy Adams. After graduating from Harvard College in 1904, he entered the Columbia University Law School. The following year he married his distant cousin, the gifted and energetic Anna Eleanor Roosevelt. Her "Uncle Ted," then President of the United States, traveled to New York for the ceremony.

After serving in the New York State legislature, Roosevelt was named by Woodrow Wilson to be Assistant Secretary of the Navy. In 1920 Roosevelt became well-known nationally when he ran unsuccessfully for Vice President. Then, in 1921, a personal tragedy struck. While vacationing with his family in Canada, he was stricken with polio and his legs became paralyzed. With the encouragement of his wife and family, he gradually regained his strength. Still, he would never again be able to stand or walk without assistance.

Roosevelt, spurred by his wife and many friends, remained active in politics. His rousing nominating speech for Al Smith at the Democratic convention in 1924 brought him public acclaim. In 1928, he was elected governor of New York. To silence opponents during the campaign who whispered about Roosevelt's paralysis, Smith had had an answer: "We do not elect [a governor] for his ability to do a double back flip or a handspring." By the time the Depression struck, FDR, as people referred to him, was becoming a symbol of an afflicted nation determined to stir and be itself again. In millions of people, he inspired fresh confidence that determination and hard work could bring triumph over adversity.

Roosevelt promises a New Deal. Ignoring the custom that a candidate must wait for formal notification of his nomination, Roosevelt flew to Chicago in June, 1932, to address the Democratic convention. In his speech, he pledged that he would provide a "new deal for the American people." Roosevelt did not — because he could not — say in detail what he meant. Still, people could hear in the phrase "New Deal" an echo of the earlier Roosevelt's "Square Deal." The ring of familiarity hinted that whatever changes took place would be in keeping with tradition.

The Democrats win the election. The Democrats' theme song, "Happy Days Are Here Again," held promise for millions of people laid low by the Depression. They ignored Hoover's assertion that if Roosevelt became President, "grass will grow in the streets of a hundred cities."

On Election Day, Roosevelt carried 42 of the 48 states, receiving 23 million votes in contrast to Hoover's 16 million. The electoral vote was 472 for Roosevelt and 59 for Hoover. The landslide signaled the beginning of the longest hold on power of any politician in American history.

Prohibition is repealed. Responding to the election results, Congress in February, 1933,[1] approved an amendment that would bring an end to prohibition. Later that year, the Twenty-First Amendment became effec-

Franklin Roosevelt refused to let a severe disability destroy his political career. In 1932 the voters elected him President, believing he could bring the Depression to an end.

tive, repealing the Eighteenth Amendment. The controversial experiment of national prohibition was over.

The crisis deepens. In the months between November, 1932, and March, 1933, economic conditions had greatly deteriorated. Banks closed at a faster rate than ever before, wiping out the savings and deposits of millions of people. As panic spread, so many people withdrew their money that

---

[1]Until it was abolished in 1933 by the Twentieth Amendment, a "lame duck" session of Congress was held from the December following a presidential election to March 4, when the new President was inaugurated.

Franklin D. Roosevelt's First Inaugural Address (1933)

This is pre-eminently the time to speak the truth, the whole truth, frankly and boldly. Nor need we shrink from honestly facing conditions in our country today. This great nation will endure as it has endured, will revive and will prosper.

So first of all let me assert my firm belief that the only thing we have to fear is fear itself — nameless, unreasoning, unjustified terror which paralyzes needed efforts to convert retreat into advance. . . .

Our greatest primary task is to put people to work. This is no unsolvable problem if we face it wisely and courageously.

It can be accomplished in part by direct recruiting by the government itself, treating the task as we would treat the emergency of a war, but at the same time, through this employment, accomplishing greatly needed projects to stimulate and reorganize the use of our national resources. . . .

I am prepared under my constitutional duty to recommend the measures that a stricken nation in the midst of a stricken world may require.

These measures, or such other measures as the Congress may build out of its experience and wisdom, I shall seek, within my constitutional authority, to bring to speedy adoption. . . .

even banks with sound management faced disaster.

Some angry farmers began taking the law into their own hands. In the Midwest, the National Farmers' Holiday Association refused to permit any crops to reach market until prices were boosted. Farmers even dumped milk on highways in order to reduce supplies and, presumably, lift prices. Charles M. Schwab, chairman of the board of Bethlehem Steel, confessed, "I'm afraid; every man is afraid." As Hoover prepared to attend the swearing-in of his successor, he said grimly, "We are at the end of our string."

Roosevelt seeks to restore the nation's confidence. On Inauguration Day, Roosevelt addressed the stricken country with words of reassurance. The speech, portions of which appear on this page, electrified the country. Hundreds of thousands of people wrote to the President, applauding his words and offering support. Their backing encouraged him as he began his administration.

A Cabinet is named. Roosevelt's Cabinet consisted of strong personalities also ready to try new ways. In the Department of State was Cordell Hull, a long-time senator from Tennessee, eager to batter down the tariff walls between nations. In charge of the Department of Agriculture, Roosevelt put Henry A. Wallace of Iowa, an agricultural economist who was well-known for developing a hybrid corn. The Secretary of the Interior was Harold L. Ickes of Illinois, a former Progressive, an outspoken foe of business interests, and a devoted conservationist. As Secretary of Labor, the President appointed Frances Perkins, who had been Industrial Commissioner in New York in the late 1920's. Once a worker at Hull House (page 153), she was the first woman ever to serve in a President's Cabinet.

The "brain trust" advises Roosevelt. Roosevelt also depended on the suggestions of a group of advisers affectionately labeled the "brain trust." In the group were several Columbia University professors. They included Raymond Moley, a political scientist; Rexford G. Tugwell, a specialist in agricultural affairs; and Adolf A. Berle, an expert in corporate finance. Other consultants included William Green, president of the AFL, and Bernard Baruch, a well-known financier.

The First Lady, Eleanor Roosevelt, provided her husband with an extra set of eyes and ears. Restless and untiring, Eleanor Roosevelt traveled incessantly and, upon returning to the White House, reported to the President on a variety of subjects. Her interests included areas of American life that had been long ignored — poverty in coal-mining communities, the plight of black people and other minorities, and the violation of civil liberties. She later wrote that she became a better observer as the years went by and as she came to anticipate her husband's wide-ranging questions.

A "bank holiday" is declared. Upon taking office, Roosevelt immediately declared a "bank holiday," a four-day period during which all the nation's banks were closed. The banks were allowed to reopen only after government inspectors had examined their records and confirmed their soundness. Roosevelt then told the nation over the radio, "I can assure you that it is safer to keep your money in a reopened bank than under the mattress." Roosevelt's move brought an end to bank failures resulting from the withdrawal of savings by frightened depositors.

The New Deal is inaugurated. From March 9 through June 16, 1933, Congress met in

When Roosevelt took office, many of the nation's banks were on the verge of collapse. Scenes like the one below were commonplace, as rumors of bank failures created panic and sent depositors rushing to withdraw their savings.

special session. Its members were eager to follow the leadership of the White House. The legislation they passed during the "Hundred Days" profoundly changed American life. The new laws fell into three categories: *relief* measures for emergency assistance; *recovery* measures to try to bring an end to the Depression; and *reform* measures to provide a means of solving or preventing the recurrence of long-standing problems.

Relief is provided for the unemployed. The most urgent problem facing the President after the banking crisis was the situation of millions of unemployed Americans. To provide them with immediate help, the administration moved quickly. Congress, through a much-publicized measure, established the Civilian Conservation Corps — generally called the CCC. It dealt on a massive scale

The Civilian Conservation Corps combined work relief for unemployed men between the ages of 18 and 25 with badly needed conservation projects. This corpsman is learning how to survey land.

with the problem of unemployment. The law eventually put some 2,500,000 young men to work constructing dams, clearing beaches and camp sites, and planting trees. Most CCC members were allowed to keep only a small part of the meager wages they were paid. The balance was sent home to their needy families. The law was generally popular because the work done under its terms aided in protecting the natural environment — and because so many young people now could escape the need to stand in breadlines.

A second relief measure authorized the setting up of the Federal Emergency Relief Administration (FERA). Congress provided the agency with funds — $500 million at first and, later, $3 billion more. These funds were to be distributed to the states for direct relief to the unemployed.

The FERA was a departure in American history, and it was not a success. Direct relief seemed like an undeserved gift to many recipients, who were embarrassed to receive it. Harry Hopkins, administrator of the FERA, persuaded Roosevelt that the country needed a program to provide people with work. As a result, the Civil Works Administration was established before 1933 ended, with Hopkins at its head. The CWA swiftly provided four million jobs, most of them "make-work" projects with little permanent value, like raking leaves. (Cynics were soon calling these jobs "boondoggles" — a word once applied to the trivial chores cowboys performed when they were not managing their herds.)

The sale of stocks and bonds is regulated. A step to restore trust in financial institutions was embodied in the Federal Securities Act, passed in May, 1933. This law required corporations offering new stock or bonds to register them with the Federal Trade Commission and to disclose accurate information on them. The aim was to prevent fraud and misrepresentation. This new measure appealed especially to investors who believed, rightly or wrongly, that they had been cheated by brokers during the stock market boom of the late 1920's.

In 1934 Congress went further by establishing the Securities and Exchange Commission. The SEC — an independent commission appointed by the President — was given broad powers to regulate the stock exchanges in order to weed out unscrupulous operators.

Legislation is passed to promote recovery. To launch the nation's recovery, Roosevelt moved to assist various segments of the population. The names of the agencies he established told of their functions. The Home Owners Loan Corporation (HOLC) was created in 1933 to help people avoid the loss of their homes through the foreclosure of mortgages. The law eventually lent a total of $3 billion to more than a million homeowners, enabling them to save their dwellings.

Suitable housing, a vital factor in restoring public morale, was often on the President's mind. In 1934 the Federal Housing Administration (FHA) began to offer federally guaranteed loans to middle-income families who wanted to repair an old house or build a new one. In the six years after its passage, the law made possible 554,000 loans totaling $2.3 billion for the construction of new housing.

In an effort to help farmers recover economic health, Congress passed the Agricultural Adjustment Act (AAA). This law provided for direct payments to farmers who reduced the production of such crops as wheat, corn, rice, and tobacco. The subsidies were made possible through a processing tax placed on industries — flour mills and slaughterhouses, for instance — that prepared products for market. The tax, of course, was passed on to consumers through higher prices.

For a time the most widely discussed recovery law was the National Industrial Recovery Act (NIRA), the crowning law of the "Hundred Days." It provided that each industry — with the aid of the National Recovery Administration (NRA) — would cooperate in preparing "codes of fair competition" to establish standard prices, wages, and hours in their businesses. Sec-

Following passage of the National Industrial Recovery Act in 1933, manufacturers and retailers proudly displayed the NRA poster in store windows, on factory doors, and on delivery trucks.

tion 7a of the law also guaranteed labor's right to organize unions and to bargain collectively with employers through agents of their own choosing.

The NRA was inaugurated with high hopes and much publicity. A likeness of an eagle with the slogan "We Do Our Part" was made the symbol of the NRA and exhibited in store windows and on factory walls throughout the country. The presence of an eagle poster was evidence that the company displaying it had promised to abide by the code of fair competition established in that industry.

The NRA act also created the Public Works Administration (PWA) with an appropriation of $3.3 million to stimulate the construction industry. In addition to providing jobs on public works, PWA projects were intended to help revive the economy through the sale of building materials such as steel, cement, and lumber.

The United States goes off the gold standard. Roosevelt did not believe that world-wide remedies for the Depression would be effective, so he felt free to take independent steps. For example, he decided that inflation was needed to raise prices. He therefore took the country off the gold standard. This meant that the nation's currency would no longer be redeemable in gold. The President expected that the cheaper dollars would lead to a rise in prices. Business profits would also rise, he believed, followed soon by higher wages and substantial re-employment.

Critics predicted that going off the gold standard would lead to catastrophe. Bernard Baruch bluntly commented, "Maybe the country doesn't know it yet, but I think we may find that we've been in a revolution more drastic than the French Revolution." For a brief period in 1933, prices and production did indeed rise. Wages, however, lagged behind, and ordinary people were unable to buy the consumer goods that had begun to pour from the factories. By late summer, business activity was in the doldrums again.

Congress increases banking security. No one could say how long the recovery measures would be required, nor when the tinkering with the economy would end. The New Deal's reform measures, however, were meant to be a permanent part of American life.

A step to reform the banking business was the Glass-Steagall Act that Congress

Heeding President Roosevelt's proposal that the government undertake the development of the Tennessee River valley, Congress established the Tennessee Valley Authority in 1933.

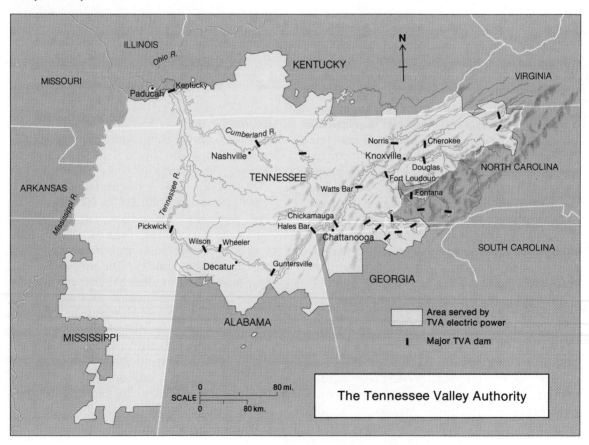

The Tennessee Valley Authority

passed in 1933. It provided for the separation of commercial banking and investment banking. In short, it prohibited banks from speculating in stocks and bonds with the money of depositors. The act also established the Federal Deposit Insurance Corporation — the FDIC. Its function was to insure customers' deposits, up to a certain amount. Americans as a whole quickly regained confidence in the banking system.

The TVA is a new kind of experiment. One reform measure of the early New Deal that raised controversy was the development of the Tennessee Valley, a region that had been plagued for years by floods and erosion. In 1933, Congress established the Tennessee Valley Authority (TVA). This vast project had a number of purposes — flood control, improved river navigation, irrigation, and the generation of hydroelectric power. All in all, the TVA was an enormous effort to develop and rehabilitate the entire region drained by the Tennessee River. The undertaking affected parts of Tennessee, Kentucky, North Carolina, Virginia, Mississippi, Alabama, and Georgia — a 41,000-square-mile region containing three million people.

By 1944, scores of dams had been constructed on the Tennessee River and its major tributaries. The dams made possible the construction of an inland waterway system with a nine-foot channel extending 650 miles from Knoxville, Tennessee, to Paducah, Kentucky. In time, the TVA acquired facilities that gave it control over the production and sale of electricity throughout the Tennessee Valley.

Run as an independent public corporation by a board of three directors, the TVA had as its goal the economic and social well-being of the entire region. The agency and its work became a model for similar river projects throughout the world. In addition to the improvements brought about by better management of the land, the region benefited from the electrification of millions of homes.

Nonetheless, the TVA had many critics, some of whom argued that the program seemed like government interference with private enterprise. Utility companies pointed out, moreover, that the TVA could charge low rates for electricity because, as a government agency, it was exempt from paying taxes. Opponents of the TVA were able to prevent similar projects — such as a proposal for an "MVA" in the Missouri River valley — from being started.

Other conservation measures are proposed. The TVA was just one of the New Deal's conservation programs. Boulder Dam on the Colorado River (begun in the Hoover Administration and later called Hoover Dam) was completed in 1936. The Bonneville and Grand Coulee dams, started under Roosevelt, were constructed on the Columbia River. Like the TVA dams, these immense triumphs of American engineering aided flood control, improved the navigation of the affected rivers, made irrigation of the land more efficient, and produced enormous amounts of electric power.

Land conservation was another area in which the Roosevelt administration had a deep interest. To deal with the "Dust Bowl" (page 231), the President ordered the planting of a vast belt of trees on the Great Plains. The aim was to break the stiff winds there, anchor the soil, and hold moisture. Today the millions of trees planted during the 1930's are mighty reminders of a far-sighted policy.

SECTION REVIEW

1. (a) Who were the candidates in the 1932 presidential election? (b) What were the main issues? (c) What was the outcome of the election?
2. For what reason was the Twenty-First Amendment adopted?
3. (a) What was the nation's mood when Franklin Roosevelt was sworn in as President? (b) What steps did Roosevelt take to restore confidence in the nation's banks?
4. (a) What steps were taken to help unemployed Americans? (b) Homeowners? (c) Farmers? (d) Business? (e) Labor?
5. (a) What was the TVA? (b) What did it achieve? (c) On what grounds was it criticized? (d) What other conservation measures did the New Deal take?

Water for Dry Lands

The "Dust Bowl" conditions that followed a severe drought on the Great Plains increased the hardships of the Depression of the 1930's and brought a new awareness of the need to conserve water and land resources. This concern inspired a number of conservation programs that have grown and expanded since the 1930's.

Where Our Water Supply Comes From

Almost all of the world's water — more than 97 percent — is stored in the salty oceans. A little more than 2 percent is locked up in glaciers and ice sheets. Less than 1 percent, therefore, is left to supply the fresh water that people depend on — water stored in the ground, in lakes and rivers, and in the atmosphere as water vapor (the source of rain and snow).

Varying amounts of water can be stored in the ground, depending on the type of rock and soil and on the available rainfall. The top level of the water-saturated underground layer is the *water table.* Wells for water must be dug or drilled to the level of the water table. Water stored below that level is called *ground water.* Lakes and ponds are actually visible parts of the water table; ground water may also feed rivers and streams. Large areas in which ground water is stored naturally in beds of gravel or porous rock are called *aquifers.* Aquifers lie beneath most parts of the United States and are an important source of the water supply for cities, towns, and farms.

Rapidly increasing demands for water — for irrigation, industry, and fast-growing populations — mean that people draw water from the aquifers more quickly than it is replaced by rain or snowfall. This problem is particularly serious in drier parts of the western United States where rainfall is low. To supply water for thirsty cities and farmlands, people have sought ways to use the surface water of distant lakes and rivers rather than the water in the aquifers.

Huge systems of dams, artificial lakes, and reservoirs for water have been built on a number of great rivers in the United States since the water conservation programs of the 1930's (page 241). These projects usually have several purposes — water storage, flood control, hydroelectric power, new areas for recreation. Sometimes they are controversial, for people at different places along the river may have conflicting needs and demands for water. People may also object to the changes that a dam makes in the landscape and the natural environment.

The Colorado River

One of the most extensive western water-development projects has been along the Colorado River. Named for its reddish color, the Colorado is a swift-flowing river fed by the ice and snow of the Rockies. It runs for more than a thousand miles through the Southwest, crossing through Mexico to flow into the Gulf of California. In northern Arizona the river has cut sharply down through many layers of rock to form the spectacular Grand Canyon.

Much of the Colorado Basin — the area drained by the river — receives little rainfall and has few aquifers to provide ground water. The waters of the river have therefore become essential for the cities and farmlands of a seven-state region. The region is often divided into the Lower Basin (California, Nevada, and Arizona) and the Upper Basin (Colorado, New Mexico, Utah, and Wyoming). All the states, as well as Mexico, claim the right to use the water of the Colorado River.

Beginning in the 1920's, the federal government encouraged and approved plans made by the states to share the river water and the power generated by hydroelectric dams. Hoover Dam, completed in 1936, was the first of several major dams (shown on the map) built along the Colorado River and its branches between the 1930's and the 1960's. These dams control floods, divert water for storage, produce electric power, provide irrigation, and supply much of the water used by Los Angeles and neighboring cities in southern California. Huge aqueducts carry millions of gallons of water to reservoirs that supply water to the coastal cities.

As the map shows, the dams also created large artificial lakes in the "drowned" valleys behind them. These lakes have become popular spots for fishing, boating, swimming, and other kinds of recreation.

A very large percentage of the water saved and stored from the Colorado goes for irrigation. In Mexico and southern California, near the mouth of the river, a rich delta was built up over thousands of years from the silt and soil carried from upstream. Without irrigation, however, this land was too dry for farming. Since 1940, the All-American Canal has carried water from the Colorado to California's Imperial Valley and other valleys that are now rich, productive agricultural regions.

In Mexico, the Morelos Dam diverts water from the Colorado River to a similar canal that irrigates farmlands near the border. One continuing problem in this lower part of the river, however, is the build-up of minerals in the water, which sometimes makes it too salty to use.

While the Colorado is vitally important to the Southwest, water from the upper part of the river is also diverted eastward over the Rockies. The Colorado-Big Thompson project carries water over the Continental Divide (the crest of the Rockies) by a system of dams, tunnels, and reservoirs to supply irrigation for land in eastern Colorado.

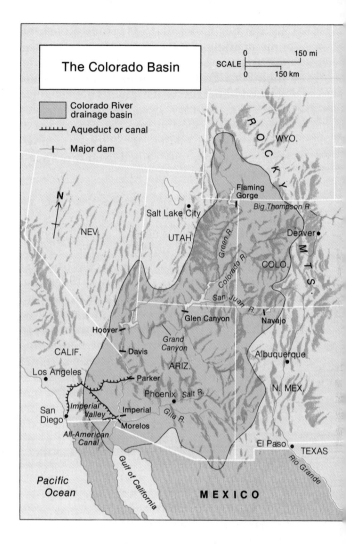

The Colorado Basin

SCALE
0 — 150 mi
0 — 150 km

Colorado River drainage basin
Aqueduct or canal
Major dam

1. (a) About what percentage of the world's water is available for people's use? (b) Where is this water located?
2. What effect do growing populations have on aquifers?
3. (a) What is the route of the Colorado River? (b) What is the source of the water in the river?
4. (a) Name four of the purposes of the dams on the Colorado River. (b) What is most of the water used for?

3 The Second New Deal Introduces Reforms

By the beginning of 1934, some Roosevelt opponents — mostly Republicans but also dissatisfied Democrats like Al Smith and John W. Davis — joined together and formed the Liberty League. They charged that the country was being destroyed through overspending and the pampering of jobless people. In the 1934 elections, however, the Democrats gained even more seats in both houses of Congress.

Hard times continue despite New Deal efforts. Most of Roosevelt's opponents accused him of conducting a "give-away" government. A number of other critics, though, attracted attention by charging that the government was too tight-fisted. Senator Huey P. Long of Louisiana, making himself a spokesman for poor people, advocated a "share-our-wealth" program that would have entitled every family in the nation to a yearly income of $2,500. Another figure who drew crowds was Dr. Francis E. Townsend of California, who organized a national movement calling for a monthly pension of $200 for every person over sixty years of age. Yet another man with a ready solution was Father Charles E. Coughlin, a Roman Catholic priest who advocated government ownership of banks, public utilities, and natural resources.

Roosevelt was well aware of the strong appeal of these seemingly easy solutions to hard times. Moreover, the Depression was by no means over. The jobless still numbered more than eleven million at the end of 1934, about 22 percent of the labor force. (To be sure, the figures were an improvement over early 1933, when more than thirteen million people had been out of work.) In the view of many Democratic leaders it was time to seek further reforms, for recovery had not taken place as anticipated.

The second New Deal begins. The President's annual message to Congress on January 4, 1935, marked the beginning of what is now known as the second New Deal.[2] The major theme of the address was that the federal government had to take greater responsibility for the economic well-being of the American people. The administration had broad new goals: better housing, and protection from the effects of old age, unemployment, and disability. Roosevelt proposed to treat the economy as a tree that had to be watered at the roots. He would help the victims of the Depression increase their ability to buy consumer goods and lift their standard of living, thereby stimulating production and bringing about economic recovery.

The Social Security Act is passed. The most far-reaching law adopted by the new Congress was the Social Security Act, passed in August, 1935. It established benefits for retired workers, unemployment insurance, and a health and child-welfare program. The old-age benefits would be paid out of an insurance fund to which both employers and employees would contribute. The unemployment insurance would be paid for by a compulsory payroll tax on employers. Federal grants matched by state grants would aid widows, dependent children, blind people, and certain other handicapped persons. A number of classes of employees were not eligible for social security coverage: agricultural workers, domestic servants, civil servants, and most professional people, including doctors and lawyers.

Herbert Hoover denounced the measure. He maintained that "social security, [must be built] upon a cult of work, not a cult of leisure." Many other Americans agreed. Some critics insisted that the Social Security bill would destroy the freedom of the American people by substituting government control for free enterprise.

Work relief programs are continued. The driving force of the second New Deal was

---

[2]The idea that there were "two New Deals" is merely a convenience for studying the period. Roosevelt himself did not differentiate between a first and a second New Deal.

Newspaper cartoonists often poked fun at the multitude of federal agencies, designated by initials, created by the New Deal.

the Emergency Relief Administration Act, passed by Congress in April, 1935. It enabled Roosevelt to take strong measures to cope with unemployment. Under the act, the President established by executive order the Works Progress Administration (WPA) and appointed Harry Hopkins to be its head. The CWA, which Hopkins had administered (page 238), had been terminated in 1934, when Roosevelt had become concerned over its cost and over rumors of corruption in its management. As a result, the United States had once more returned to direct relief for the unemployed. By the end of 1935 approximately twenty million Americans were receiving some form of public assistance.

The WPA had an initial appropriation of $5 billion — the largest that had ever been made in peacetime in America. The aim of the WPA was to give people work as soon as possible. People in WPA jobs, administration officials hoped, would feel once again the dignity that comes from working purposefully.

Projects had to be found that had public usefulness and local sponsors. Moreover, the projects had to be planned so that they did not call for excessive amounts of equipment and supplies. As much as possible, the available funds were to be spent on wages. Also, projects had to be completed in one year since Congress made only annual appropriations.

By 1941 the WPA had an average of over two million people on its payroll each month. WPA workers constructed more than a hundred airports throughout the country, built or rebuilt over a hundred thousand public buildings, laid half a million sewer lines and 650,000 miles of roads, and improved thousands of parks and school grounds. A WPA project was built in almost every town and city in the nation: a new swimming pool, or hospital, or post office, or bridge.

The WPA also broke fresh ground in the realm of the arts. The Federal Theater, organized under its auspices, presented plays in parts of the country that had never previously seen live stage performances. For the first time the lobbies of public buildings were adorned with colorful murals. They were the work of artists who would not otherwise have had a showplace for their talent.

Still, many WPA undertakings were a waste of time and money, for the ways of putting people to work were often farfetched. John Steinbeck, the author, was once assigned as a WPA worker to take a census of dogs in a California community. Furthermore, on construction projects many WPA workers loafed shamefully, knowing they would not be fired. Another problem was that the WPA was sometimes used for partisan purposes. Some politicians found it easy to corral the votes of people so dependent on the Democratic Party's remaining in office.

Congress created a "junior" WPA for young people — the National Youth Administration (NYA) — in June, 1935. During the eight years the NYA was in existence, it created jobs for over 1,500,000 high school students and 600,000 college students. The work consisted of helping in laboratories, libraries, and school and college offices. The small salaries that went with the jobs enabled many young people to stay in school. The NYA funds were distributed through the states. One of the most energetic state administrators was a future President, Lyndon B. Johnson of Texas.

The Works Progress Administration was the first federal agency to give jobs to artists. This WPA-financed mural glorifies American workers.

The second New Deal passes more reform measures. The administration's experiments made the White House a constant source of news and excitement. One such undertaking was the establishment of the Rural Electrification Administration (REA) in 1935. Its goal was to bring electricity to the rural areas of the country. Whereas power lines had reached only 4 percent of America's farms in 1925, they reached 25 percent by 1940.

A less successful experiment was the Resettlement Administration, created in 1935. This agency was given funds to buy up poor and infertile land occupied by destitute farmers, tenants, sharecroppers, or migrant workers, and to resettle the people in more promising places. The RA eventually purchased about nine million undesirable acres and removed them from cultivation. The RA also created so-called "greenbelt towns" — planned suburban communities outside Milwaukee, Cincinnati, and Washington, D.C. The degree of federal involvement that this type of activity required, however, received little public support.

Another controversial measure was a tax bill passed by Congress in August, 1935. It was directed at eliminating what Roosevelt considered "an unjust concentration of wealth and economic power" in the hands of a small fraction of the population. The bill provided for a significant increase in individual and corporate income taxes. The proposal boosted the inheritance tax. To prevent evasion of that levy, the gift tax, too, was increased. Opponents labeled the measure a "soak-the-rich" scheme.

Organized labor makes gains under the Wagner Act. In July, 1935, Congress passed the National Labor Relations Act. The guiding spirit behind it was Senator Robert F. Wagner of New York. The law — often called the Wagner Act — made stronger the provisions of Section 7a of the NRA (page 239). It guaranteed the right of workers to organize and to bargain with employers for better wages and working conditions. The act was to be enforced by a National Labor Relations Board. The NLRB was authorized to hear testimony about unfair labor practices by employers. Such practices included forcing workers to join company unions and preventing them from joining unions of their choice. The NLRB could issue binding orders compelling companies to stop these practices.

Perhaps no piece of legislation aroused so much controversy as the Wagner Act. Employers insisted that it unfairly tied their hands while giving unions a free rein.

The CIO is formed. As the second New Deal proceeded, the strengthened labor movement became more forceful. The AFL had remained true to its traditional reliance on organization by craft unions (page 93). Some AFL members, however, regarded this outlook as stodgy and old-fashioned. The AFL's policy, moreover, irritated the hundreds of thousands of noncraft workers — mostly unskilled — who remained unorganized. Now, encouraged by the pro-labor legislation of the New Deal, these workers began seeking ways to organize unions.

Some labor leaders set about organizing unions for workers in the mass-production industries (automobile, rubber, steel, cement, radio). An important figure in this movement was John L. Lewis, head of the United Mine Workers. Lewis knew the labor movement from the inside out. His father had been a member of the Knights of Labor, and he himself had gone into the coal pits to work at the age of twelve. Joined by Sidney Hillman and David Dubinsky of the garment workers' unions, Lewis in November, 1935, formed the Committee for Industrial Organization — the CIO — and began trying to organize entire industries into one union. Lewis became the Committee's chairman. When the AFL suspended the members of the Committee in 1938, the CIO turned itself into a separate organization. It kept its initials and adopted the name Congress of Industrial Organizations. At once the CIO began to organize industrial unions that included unskilled as well as skilled members.

Labor violence breaks out. The attempt to organize the steel industry in 1936 and the

In 1937 industrial workers began making use of a new weapon in their drive to organize unions—the sit-down strike. Here, workers in a Flint, Michigan, auto plant refuse to leave their posts.

automobile industry in the following year resulted in some of the angriest labor strife in American history. In the steel industry, ten men were killed in 1937 during a labor disturbance at a Chicago plant of the Republic Steel Company. In that same year, however, the giant United States Steel Corporation recognized the CIO steelworkers' union. Four years later, the National Labor Relations Board forced several smaller steel companies to recognize the CIO union as the employees' representative.

In the automobile industry, workers made use of the "sit-down strike," simply refusing to leave their posts until their unions had won recognition from management. Even when plant managers turned off the heat in the dead of winter, the strikers remained in the factories.

The AFL disclaimed responsibility for the sit-down strikes, and the CIO never gave them official approval. Opinion polls showed overwhelming public opposition to labor's new-found weapon. In any event, as the NLRB continued its work, elections were held to name collective bargaining units, and the sit-downs no longer served a purpose.

By the end of 1937 the CIO had done a remarkable job of organizing unskilled workers. Unions in the mining, automobile, steel, textile, and garment industries all had hundreds of thousands of members. In addition, the CIO brought into the ranks of organized labor more women, blacks, and immigrants than ever before. For the first time in the heavy industries, working people were union members, able to bargain effectively with management. Because the New Deal had hastened this development, Roosevelt was widely regarded as labor's best friend. Labor became a powerful source of New Deal support.

The Supreme Court declares New Deal legislation unconstitutional. Critics in Congress, frustrated by their inability to prevent passage of New Deal legislation, sometimes called Roosevelt's program the "Raw Deal." Nonetheless, the only effective roadblock to Roosevelt's programs, as it turned out, was the Supreme Court. In 1935, decisions in two important cases struck hard at important New Deal measures.

The first of the cases was *Schechter v. United States*. These were the facts: A Brooklyn, New York, poultry company had violated its industry's "code of fair competition" by paying wages below the minimum and by selling unhealthful chicken. The company argued that it was not engaged in interstate commerce and that, therefore, the code did not apply to it.[3]

The Court, in a unanimous decision handed down on May 27, 1935, held that the NRA was unconstitutional. The Court ruled that if the federal government could regulate *everything* affecting interstate commerce, then "there would be virtually no limit to federal power." The Court declared also that in giving the NRA control over wages and hours, Congress had improperly delegated legislative authority to the executive branch.

---

[3]Congress, which had created the NRA, had taken the position that anything affecting interstate commerce — even commerce conducted entirely within a state's borders — was subject to national legislative control.

Franklin Roosevelt frequently took to the radio airwaves during his years in office to speak directly to the American people.

Roosevelt, angered by the decision, denounced the Supreme Court for using a "horse-and-buggy definition of interstate commerce." He knew, nevertheless, that the NRA had probably outlived its usefulness. It was badly run, and many small businesses had been hurt by its operation, because the "codes of fair competition" usually favored bigger companies. Some labor leaders, furthermore, were calling the NRA a failure and were even referring to it as the "National Run-Around."

On January 6, 1936, the Supreme Court wiped out another recovery law. In the case of *United States v. Butler*, the Court declared the Agricultural Adjustment Act unconstitutional. The justices held that the processing tax established by that act (page 239) was invalid because it took "money from one group" of citizens for the "benefit of another."

The administration quickly obtained passage of laws allowing it to salvage useful parts of the legislation the Court had knocked down. For example, to get around the decision on NRA, Congress in August, 1935, passed the Bituminous Coal Conser-

vation Act. It established standards for regulating wages and working conditions in the soft-coal industry. The provisions of the AAA that paid farmers to reduce the size of their crops, moreover, were revived in a new way. Under the Soil Conservation and Domestic Allotment Act, passed in February, 1936, farmers were compensated for planting grasses and other soil-holding plants instead of cash crops like tobacco, corn, and wheat. Farmers, therefore, were being paid for aiding in soil conservation, not for reducing production.

Further Court decisions weaken the New Deal. In the late spring of 1936, the Supreme Court delivered two decisions that shook the Roosevelt administration to its foundations. In the first ruling, the Court struck down the Coal Conservation Act as unconstitutional. Roosevelt and his advisers were stunned by the Court's view that the federal government could not regulate hours and wages. They concluded that the people would have to rely on the state governments to do this work. That idea, too, was shattered when on June 1, 1936, the

Supreme Court declared unconstitutional New York State's minimum wage law. The law, passed in 1933, had been designed to protect working women and children. The Court maintained that by establishing a minimum wage for women, New York was denying people the freedom, guaranteed by the Fourteenth Amendment, to make contracts. Roosevelt — and reformers in both parties — were appalled by the decision. At a press conference, the President asserted that there was now a no-man's land where neither the state *nor* the federal government could act.

Some groups denounced the decision and made proposals that would have altered the Court's power of judicial review. Because a number of the important recent decisions had been by a 5 to 4 vote, some people suggested that a vote on the Court of at least six to three ought to be required to overturn a law. Other people proposed giving Congress the power through a constitutional amendment to override decisions of the Court by a two-thirds vote. Still other commentators maintained that Congress should forbid judicial review altogether. Whatever the answer, the New Deal seemed at an impasse.

Roosevelt runs for re-election. The presidential campaign of 1936, meanwhile, was about to begin. Roosevelt felt he needed a new mandate from the people to go forward with the New Deal.

The President's renomination was certain. Meeting at Philadelphia, the Democrats in wild enthusiasm named him and Vice President Garner without a formal ballot. The party platform contained a bold promise to seek a constitutional amendment if the Supreme Court should continue to declare New Deal legislation unconstitutional.

The Republicans gathered in Cleveland to nominate a candidate. Herbert Hoover was hoping for a new nomination — and personal vindication. The party turned, however, to Governor Alfred M. Landon of Kansas, who had been a Bull Moose Republican in 1912. Landon had gained national attention for balancing his state's budget at a time when state and federal deficits had become commonplace. Landon's running mate was Colonel Frank Knox, a Chicago newspaper publisher who had fought as a Rough Rider in the Spanish-American War. The convention sang a parody of "O Susanna." It began:

> If Roos-e-velt would have his way
> We'd all be in his grip,
> And soon he'd change the ship of state
> To his dictatorship.

In spite of their scorn for Roosevelt, the Republicans adopted a platform endorsing

Auto license tags like this one urged Roosevelt's re-election in 1936. The Democrats won the contest in a landslide.

many New Deal measures, including unemployment insurance, old-age pensions, and benefit payments for farmers. The Republicans maintained that they could run these programs better than the Democrats.

The Democrats are returned to office. Roosevelt understood the issue of the campaign: "It's myself, and people must be either for me or against me." On Election Day, 1936, Roosevelt swamped the hapless Landon. Roosevelt, who won the electoral votes of every state except Maine and Vermont, was now at the height of his popularity. He had received 61 percent of the popular vote. No President since Monroe in 1820 had won such a sweeping victory.

SECTION REVIEW

1. What were some of the criticisms of the New Deal offered by Roosevelt's opponents?
2. What programs were provided in the Social Security Act?
3. (a) Why was the WPA established? (b) The National Youth Administration?
4. (a) How did the Wagner Act help organized labor? (b) Why was the CIO formed?
5. What New Deal programs did the Supreme Court declare unconstitutional?
6. (a) Who were the candidates in the 1936 election? (b) What was the outcome?

4 The New Deal Comes to an End

Seeing his re-election as a ringing endorsement of the second New Deal, President Roosevelt set about extending his programs. He could proceed without delay, for he became the first President to be inaugurated in the month of January, in accordance with the Twentieth Amendment, ratified in 1933 (page 235).

The President attacks the Supreme Court. Roosevelt had declared in his campaign that the nation was on the road to recovery. But how far did it still have to go? In his second inaugural address he spoke of the work ahead: "I see one third of a nation ill-housed, ill-clad, ill-nourished. It is not in despair that I paint you that picture. I paint it for you in hope — because the nation, seeing and understanding the injustice in it, proposes to paint it out. . . ."

At the same time that Roosevelt considered new programs, he felt concern that the Supreme Court might now invalidate some of the administration's reform measures as well. He was particularly fearful about the fate of the Wagner Act and the Social Security Act. In 1937 he proposed that a new justice be appointed for each one who did not retire upon reaching his seventieth birthday. (The total membership of the Court, however, was not to exceed fifteen.) At the time, six of the nine justices were seventy or older. Under Roosevelt's scheme, therefore, six new justices would be appointed. This would be more than enough to establish a pro-New Deal majority on the Supreme Court.

The Court issue weakens the New Deal. The response to Roosevelt's "court-packing" plan, as it was soon called, was generally unfavorable. Many members of the President's own party were dismayed at his attack on the "Nine Old Men," as the Court was sometimes called. After a long battle and seemingly endless discussion of the proposal in the newspapers, Congress would not go along with it.

While Congress was debating the Court plan, decisions handed down in the spring of 1937 upheld the Wagner Act and the unemployment-insurance tax provision of the Social Security Act. Soon afterward the Court upheld a minimum-wage law passed by the state of Washington, reversing the decision in the New York case of two years earlier (page 250). Some people had a clever explanation for the Court's new opinions: "A switch in time saves nine." In any case, a number of retirements from the Court soon enabled Roosevelt to appoint justices who supported New Deal legislation. Roosevelt could claim that he had lost a battle but won the war.

By now, however, the President's political support was noticeably weaker. Many

THAT COMPASS
DOESN'T POINT THE WAY
I WANT TO GO.
CHANGE IT.
NOW!

Roosevelt's "court-packing" plan cost him support. One cartoonist compared the President to an admiral trying to change a basic law of nature.

Americans felt less comfortable with his policies. They complained that the federal government had grown too large in size and power, and that labor unions had acquired too much influence in the Democratic Party. The attack on the Court, furthermore, had cost Roosevelt much popular support.

Another cause of popular dissatisfaction with the New Deal was its unconventional attitude toward government finances. Some of Roosevelt's advisers had been influenced by the English economist John Maynard Keynes (pronounced CANES). Keynes had argued that it is acceptable for the government to use monetary and fiscal policies to stimulate the economy. Millions of people were aghast, however, as the administration began to spend more than it took in through taxes. The national debt rose every year during Roosevelt's term of office. Standing at $22.5 billion in 1933, it had almost doubled by 1940.

Business slumps in 1937. Roosevelt was concerned about the unbalanced budget and in 1937 insisted on a sharp cut in government spending, including the outlays for relief. His aim was to assure Americans that he was working to keep expenditures from exceeding income. Unfortunately, private business was not yet strong enough to offer jobs to people dropped from the relief rolls. At the same time, industrial output was slowing down because the Federal Reserve Board had raised interest rates. Higher Social Security taxes, in addition, were taking a bigger bite of business profits. As a result, by the fall of 1937 Democrats had to admit that the country was in a *recession* (a moderate slump in business). Republicans, on the other hand, spoke of "Roosevelt's depression."

Roosevelt soon asked for a large "lend-spend" program for public works and other projects. Meanwhile, he searched for other ways to reduce unemployment, which in 1938 still stood at ten million. Critics charged that the immense number of people who still had no jobs after five years of the New Deal demonstrated the failure of Roosevelt's policies.

More New Deal legislation is passed. By 1938 the New Deal had lost its momentum. Only a few more important New Deal measures were put on the books. The Farm Security Administration, set up in 1937, was designed to enable tenant farmers to borrow money at low interest rates so that they could buy the land they worked. The United States Housing Authority was also formed in 1937. Its function was to lend money to state and local agencies for the purpose of clearing slums and building housing for the poor.

In 1938 Congress passed a second Agricultural Adjustment Act. The measure was aimed, as the first one had been (page 239), at reducing crop production. This time, however, subsidies would be provided by the Treasury itself, rather than through a tax. Farmers would be paid to store surplus quantities of wheat, corn, cotton, rice, and tobacco in warehouses. The deposited surpluses would help establish an "ever-normal granary" for use in years of scarcity.

Congress in 1938 also passed a Fair Labor Standards Act which affected all companies engaged in interstate commerce. The law provided eventually for a maximum workweek of forty hours and a minimum wage of forty cents an hour. The act also prohibited the employment of children under sixteen years of age.

Minority groups receive little attention. Despite his wide range of concerns, Roosevelt gave little attention to the subject of minority rights. He regarded those issues as politically unimportant. The plight of minorities, consequently, never became a significant concern for officials in the Roosevelt administration.

The Depression was a dreadful time for most black Americans. In the South, black tenant farmers and sharecroppers suffered terribly from the sharp drop in agricultural prices and from the persistent drought that blighted the region in the early thirties. In the North, many blacks who had started their own businesses during the 1920's saw their enterprises go bankrupt. Black industrial workers became victims of the "last hired, first fired" practice. At the depth of the Depression, over two thirds of all black Americans working in industry had lost their jobs.

Assistance and employment from such New Deal programs as the WPA helped thousands of black Americans survive the bad times. By 1939, only agriculture and domestic service provided more jobs for

Mary McLeod Bethune, shown here with Eleanor Roosevelt, supervised the administration's job-training program for minority youth.

black Americans than did the WPA. In all the New Deal programs, however, blacks usually had to accept lower wages than white workers.

Roosevelt slowly began to place blacks in significant federal positions. Practically every New Deal agency appointed an adviser on black affairs. By 1936 these people were being called the President's "black cabinet." Noteworthy members of the black cabinet included Mary McLeod Bethune, a college president who was named director of the Division of Negro Affairs of the National Youth Administration; Robert L. Vann, who was appointed Special Assistant to the United States Attorney General; and Robert C. Weaver, who served as a lawyer in the Interior Department. In addition, some black architects, engineers, and other professionals found work in government positions that had never before been open to black people. In 1937, Roosevelt appointed William Hastie, the dean of Howard University's law school, to be a judge in the Virgin Islands — the first black to sit on the federal bench.

Out of gratitude for what was provided by the Roosevelt programs, black voters began to leave the party of Lincoln and shift to the Democratic Party. This trend was apparent in the 1936 election, and by the end of the decade black Americans were giving Democratic candidates solid support at the polls.

Mexican Americans felt the force of the Depression as keenly as any other disadvantaged group. During the years of the Mexican Revolution (page 177), thousands of people had crossed the border from Mexico into the United States searching for work. The barrier of language and lack of education forced most newly arrived Mexicans to take low-paying jobs in agriculture, mining, or railroad construction. By the 1930's, over a million Mexicans had come to the United States — seeking a chance to improve their lives.

At the time the Depression took hold, most Mexican Americans were employed as migrant laborers, going from farm to farm harvesting crops. As a result, they were rarely affected by New Deal programs. To make matters worse, established labor groups often resented the migrant workers for accepting substandard wages — not recognizing that the newcomers were doing so out of necessity. Ill will reached such a level during the Depression that the United States and Mexico agreed on a program that would encourage migrants to return to Mexico. Some American officials went further, urging a policy of deportation. The resettlement program never accomplished its goals. Many people who went back to Mexico vowed they would one day live in the United States again.

American Indians were already in a state of economic and social disorder by the time the Depression set in. The Dawes Act of 1887 (page 37) had caused great confusion and distress among the tribes. The few non-Indians who bothered to inform themselves about the plight of the tribespeople regarded the Dawes Act as a failure. New programs and policies were considered, but the only positive result came in 1924 when Indians were granted citizenship.

In 1933, Roosevelt appointed John Collier to be Commissioner of Indian Affairs. Under Collier's guidance, the Indian Reorganization Act was passed by Congress in 1934. The act halted the allotment of land to individuals and re-established tribal ownership. It also provided for local tribal government, made loans available for businesses owned by Indians, and recognized the need for programs to teach new methods of farming, irrigation, and land development. Of no less significance to American Indians was a provision encouraging efforts to reintroduce traditional customs, beliefs, and crafts to the communal life of the tribes.

Efforts at reform come to an end. The President continued to believe that new measures of reform were required to restore prosperity to America. As international events took more and more of his time, however, the steam went out of domestic efforts. In 1939 Roosevelt proposed to Congress no new major legislation. The need, he said, was "to preserve our reforms." The New Deal was coming to an end.[4]

How effective was the New Deal? Roosevelt's domestic policies aroused in people either blind devotion or burning distrust. Few could be neutral about FDR. Even today Americans disagree in assessing his role in the nation's history. Still, the legacy of the New Deal shows itself most prominently in the idea that people in the United States are a national resource. The belief that no individual should ever want for the necessities of life became firmly rooted in the American mind. A companion of this view is that government, far from being the master of the people, must be its servant — and a reliable friend in time of need.

New Deal programs, furthermore, transformed the physical condition of the country. The thousands of WPA projects, the TVA complex, and many other enterprises remain visible reminders of the remarkable era in which they burst upon the scene.

Nevertheless, the New Deal failed to end large-scale unemployment and thus cure the Depression. Nor did Roosevelt make even a dent in the hard-core poverty afflicting many people, both urban and rural. Moreover, during his time in office the federal bureaucracy swelled from 600,000 employees to 3,800,000, turning government into big business. The new federal agencies in which these civil servants worked often created rules and regulations that business people found a discouraging obstruction to private enterprise.

Roosevelt sometimes seemed to foster governmental activity for its own sake. He counted on the unshakable loyalty of his followers to make whatever he tried seem necessary and right. He saw himself, though, as working in a noble purpose with fellow-citizens, whom he often spoke to informally on the radio in what he called "fire-

---

[4]Roosevelt never lost his exuberance for breaking fresh ground. He enjoyed being the first President ever to appear on television — at an experimental telecast at the 1939 New York World's Fair.

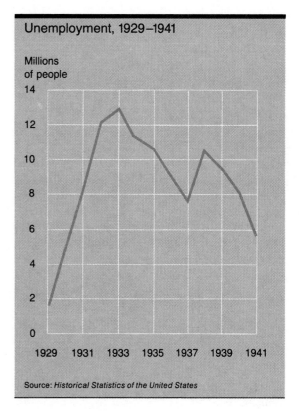

Unemployment, 1929–1941

Millions of people

Source: *Historical Statistics of the United States*

The unemployment rate, at a record level when Roosevelt was inaugurated in 1933, remained high throughout the decade.

side chats." The aim was to renew and restore the nation's flagging spirit. Will Rogers, a beloved humorist of the day, once visited the White House and asked Mrs. Roosevelt, "Where is the President?" She replied, "Wherever you hear the laugh." Even though Roosevelt was so disabled that he had to lock his legs into heavy steel braces before he could be helped to stand, he taught Americans to laugh again. It was the laugh of a people whose confidence was reviving and who could believe that once more the nation was on the way.

SECTION REVIEW

1. Vocabulary: *recession.*
2. (a) What was Roosevelt's "court-packing" plan? (b) What was the outcome?
3. (a) What New Deal measures were passed in 1937 and 1938? (b) Why did the reform program come to an end after 1938?

255

Analyzing Information

History is much more than a collection of facts. It is also a record of such things as opinions, attitudes, and decisions. It is important, therefore, not only to know the facts but to understand what is behind them. There are several methods that can help you analyze information.

Understanding Frame of Reference

When you read history you will come upon statements by many individuals. To evaluate these statements correctly, you must first understand that what people say is always influenced by their *frame of reference.*

Frame of reference is a term used to describe all the factors that go into shaping a person's point of view. These factors may include an individual's upbringing, experiences, values, and feelings. The statement by Herbert Hoover on page 230, for example, describing the fundamental soundness of business in America, was made from the frame of reference of someone who had great confidence in the country's business community. The account on page 232 by Mahalia Jackson was written from the frame of reference of someone who had actually experienced the impact of the Depression on Chicago's black population. It is important to understand these frames of reference in order to evaluate fully the statements these individuals are making.

Defining Problems and Choosing Options

By defining a particular historical problem and then identifying the possible options that could provide a solution, you will be better able to understand events. For example, President Roosevelt faced a problem when the Supreme Court declared several New Deal programs unconstitutional. As you study this period, think about the various options Roosevelt could have chosen — from reforming the objectionable programs to influencing the Court to be more favorable to his legislation. The option Roosevelt chose was to propose that new justices favorable to his policies be added to the Court. Knowing what other choices were possible, however, can help you understand why this plan was received so unfavorably.

Determining Cause and Effect

History is fundamentally the story of cause and effect. A particular development or action will produce a certain consequence or effect. This effect may itself become the cause of yet further effects. Your understanding of historical events will be enhanced when you read history with the concept of cause and effect in mind.

Perhaps the simplest way of finding cause and effect is to ask two questions as you read. *What happened?* The answer will give you the effect. *Why did it happen?* The answer will give you the cause.

An instance of cause and effect in this chapter can be seen in the developments that led to the Great Depression. Why did the American economy become so unstable at the end of the 1920's? Possible answers (or causes) include the buying of stocks on margin, the easy-money policy of the Federal Reserve Board, and a surplus of consumer goods.

Making Inferences and Drawing Conclusions

Since there are so many facts and details in history, no historical account can include them all. Historians must depend on their readers to make inferences — that is, to draw their own conclusions from the evidence at hand — about certain trends or movements.

On page 241, in the account of the development of the TVA, the author describes the accomplishments of this federal project. What is not directly stated, but can be inferred, is the fact that the Roosevelt administration believed that only a program initiated and controlled by the government could undertake so large a project.

When you draw conclusions, you must think beyond the facts given in a reading. You should consider all aspects of the information presented and then decide for yourself what meaning it has. On pages 234–235 you read about the presidential election of 1932. In that election Franklin D. Roosevelt won a landslide over the incumbent Republican President Herbert Hoover. You could conclude from this result that during the campaign Roosevelt was successful in his effort to attract support. He convinced the great majority of voters that he was capable of providing the kind of leadership the country needed to end the Depression and restore economic prosperity.

Forming Generalizations

A generalization is a broad statement that describes a situation or trend in terms of what is *generally* or *mostly* true — not in terms of specific cases. Historians find generalizations useful in giving an overall picture of events. As you read, however, you should notice generalizations and be sure they present a situation accurately. For example, on page 254, the following statement is made: "At the time the Depression took hold, most Mexican Americans were employed as migrant laborers. . . ." This generalization is true because of the large number of Mexican Americans who held

such jobs in the 1930's. It would be misleading, however, if the sentence said "*All* Mexican Americans. . . ."

Learn to look for generalizations when you read, and practice making accurate general statements in your own notes or summaries. Key words to notice are *most, a few, some, sometimes, often, many, almost,* and *usually.* Try to be aware of the exact meaning of each of these words.

Check Your Skill

Use the information presented on these pages to answer the following questions.

1. Why is it helpful to understand frame of reference?
2. Explain why the concept of cause and effect is important in the study of history.
3. Why is it necessary for historians to depend on their readers to make inferences when studying history?
4. What should you consider when drawing a conclusion?
5. Why do historians use generalizations when writing history?

Apply Your Skill

Use the readings for Chapter 9 on pages 516–523 to answer the following questions.

1. In the first selection, identify an example of cause and effect.
2. In the second selection, what is the frame of reference of the newspaper reporter who wrote the article on the "Dust Bowl"?
3. Identify at least three examples of generalizations in the third selection.
4. What are two inferences you can make after reading the fourth selection?
5. What conclusion can you draw after reading the seventh selection?

Chapter 9 Review

Summary

When Herbert Hoover became President in March, 1929, Americans looked forward to a prosperous future. Before the year was out, however, the United States was entering the worst economic depression in its history. As the Great Depression deepened, it affected every sector of society. Unemployment soared to record levels, and thousands of families lost their homes and possessions. Farmers suffered not only from falling crop prices but also from a severe drought that turned part of the country into a "dust bowl."

President Hoover believed that the road to recovery lay chiefly in voluntary actions. By 1932, however, voters responded to Franklin Delano Roosevelt's promise of a "new deal." Immediately upon taking office as President, Roosevelt recommended new laws to provide emergency relief. He also backed recovery measures intended to end the Depression, and reform measures that he hoped would solve long-standing economic problems.

The key pieces of New Deal legislation extended the power of the federal government and created a series of agencies to administer relief and recovery programs. Direct relief was distributed to the unemployed, while millions of young men were put to work in special relief projects. Farmers were given payments to reduce production of certain crops in order to raise prices. Industry was asked to cooperate in setting fair prices and wages. The Tennessee Valley Authority built dams, irrigation systems, and hydroelectric plants on a scale never before attempted by the government. Laws were also passed to protect bank depositors and to regulate the sale of stocks and bonds.

Early in 1935, Roosevelt proposed legislation that called for government to assume far-reaching responsibility for the well-being of its citizens. The Social Security Act and the Wagner Labor Relations Act were the principal pieces of new legislation.

After his re-election in 1936, Roosevelt attacked the Supreme Court, which had declared important New Deal measures unconstitutional. His plan to "pack" the Court was criticized by many Americans, however, and was defeated in Congress. By 1939 all the major New Deal laws had been passed.

New Deal legislation never brought an end to large-scale unemployment. Still, Franklin Roosevelt's place in American history is secure. His influence restored the faith of Americans in the power of representative government to deal with its problems, boldly and imaginatively.

Vocabulary and Important Terms

1. margin
2. Dust Bowl
3. Agricultural Marketing Act
4. Reconstruction Finance Corporation
5. Bonus Army
6. brain trust
7. Civilian Conservation Corps
8. Agricultural Adjustment Act
9. National Industrial Recovery Act
10. Tennessee Valley Authority
11. Liberty League
12. Social Security Act
13. Works Progress Administration
14. Wagner Act
15. recession
16. Indian Reorganization Act

Discussion Questions

1. (a) What was the first stage of the Great Depression? (b) As the Depression got under way, what did Hoover believe to be the cure for the nation's economic problems?
2. (a) How well-defined was Franklin Roosevelt's pledge to provide a "new deal for the American people"? (b) What did the words "new deal" suggest?
3. (a) Describe the banking crisis that Roosevelt faced when he took office. (b) What steps did he take to meet the crisis?
4. (a) What was the "Hundred Days"? (b) Into what three categories did the laws of the New Deal fall?
5. (a) What was the second New Deal? (b) How was the responsibility of government expanded under the second New Deal?
6. How did each of the following criticize the New Deal? (a) Liberty League (b) Huey Long (c) Francis Townsend (d) Father Coughlin (e) Herbert Hoover
7. (a) Why was the Roosevelt administration regarded as being friendly to labor unions? (b) How did labor repay Roosevelt?
8. (a) Why did Roosevelt see the Supreme Court as a major barrier to the success of the second New Deal? (b) How did his "court-packing" plan actually play into the hands of New Deal opponents?
9. (a) Describe the problems faced by blacks, Mexican Americans, and American Indians during the Depression. (b) How was each group affected by New Deal programs and measures?

Relating Past and Present

1. The passage of the Social Security Act marked an important change in America's economic and so-

cial life. What is the status of the Social Security System today? What concerns do the American people have about it? What changes have been proposed to ensure that the system is on a sound footing?

2. Which of the programs initiated by the Roosevelt administration has had lasting significance? Explain why in each case.

3. Union membership grew steadily during Roosevelt's years in office, reaching almost 36 percent of the work force in 1945. Find out what percentage of the American work force belongs to labor unions today. What factors help explain the change in percentage?

Studying Local History

Find out if any buildings, parks, or roads were built in your community as part of a New Deal program. If so, find out what kind of project it was and if it is still in use today.

Using History Skills

1. *Reading source material.* Study Mahalia Jackson's recollections of the Depression on page 232. (a) What, according to Mahalia Jackson, was the effect of the Depression on black people in Chicago? (b) Was that effect sudden or gradual? (c) Why did she believe that the Depression hit northern blacks harder than southern blacks?

2. *Reading graphs.* Study the graph on page 255 showing unemployment figures. (a) Approximately how many million people were out of work in 1931? (b) In 1939? (c) How would a critic of the New Deal interpret the information contained in this graph?

3. *Analyzing information.* Turn to the list of Presidents at the back of the book. Which Presidents were defeated when they ran for re-election? Then, using the index to locate the appropriate pages in your book, find out the reason for the defeat of each of those Presidents. Explain these reasons in a sentence or two.

WORLD SCENE

International Transportation

In the 1920's and 1930's developments in ocean and air transportation significantly reduced the time of travel from one part of the world to another. Journeys that once took weeks could now be made in days or even hours.

Commercial aviation. After the First World War hundreds of American military aircraft were fitted out for civilian use. By the mid-1920's these planes were flying everywhere, seemingly shrinking the distances between the continents. The popularity of air travel grew rapidly: a total of only 18,000 people flew in 1927; that number had reached 3,500,000 by 1938.

In 1928 Germany inaugurated transatlantic flights to North and South America. The Germans used huge, lighter-than-air craft called Zeppelins — in honor of Count Zeppelin, who had designed them. These airships carried up to fifty passengers in plush accommodations. Zeppelins were slow and expensive, however, and flights were often delayed by bad weather. When the *Hindenburg* exploded while landing in New Jersey in 1937, the day of the airship was suddenly over.

Ocean liners. The vast majority of travelers in the 1920's and 1930's crossed the Atlantic in fast, luxurious, passenger liners. Many of these giant ships could make the voyage to North America in just over four days.

The French liner *Ile de France* was launched in 1926 and was the first modern ocean liner built for speed as well as comfort. France stayed in the forefront of transatlantic passenger service with the launching of the *Normandie* in 1932.

The British Cunard Line, whose *Lusitania* had been one of the fastest liners before the First World War, decided to challenge French dominance of the North Atlantic passenger trade. Cunard built the *Queen Mary* and the *Queen Elizabeth*, both of which rivaled the French liners in speed and luxury.

The ocean liners were floating palaces. Passengers could feast in elegant dining rooms, dance in ballrooms to the music of famous orchestras, lounge around huge swimming pools, or enjoy the latest movies in the ships' theaters. By the late 1940's, however, airplanes were flying daily to Europe in a fraction of the time and at about half the cost of traveling by ship. As more and more people chose to fly, the age of the luxurious liners came to a close.

CHAPTER 10

From Isolation to Involvement

1920 – 1941

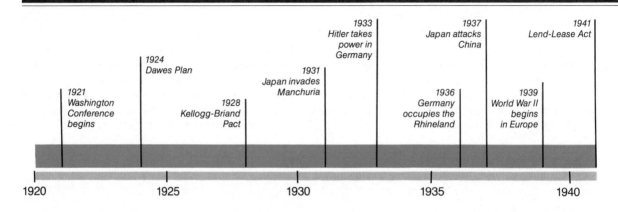

1920	1925	1930	1935	1940

1921
Washington Conference begins

1924
Dawes Plan

1928
Kellogg-Briand Pact

1931
Japan invades Manchuria

1933
Hitler takes power in Germany

1936
Germany occupies the Rhineland

1937
Japan attacks China

1939
World War II begins in Europe

1941
Lend-Lease Act

CHAPTER OUTLINE

1. The United States plays a limited role in world affairs during the 1920's.

2. The United States governs its possessions.

3. Dictators menace world peace.

4. World War II begins.

With the end of the First World War, Americans could see that the United States had the most powerful economy in the world. Woodrow Wilson spoke exuberantly of the future: "The financial leadership will be ours. The industrial primacy will be ours. The commercial advantage will be ours. The other countries of the world are looking to us for leadership and direction."

By 1920 the picture of American economic power was awesome. The United States was pumping nearly 70 percent of the world's petroleum and digging 40 percent of the world's coal. The nation lacked supplies of some raw materials, but in general it was more nearly economically independent of the rest of the world than any other country.

Americans were making serious inroads, furthermore, in markets formerly dominated by Europeans. American automobiles, especially, were on the shopping list of many wealthy foreigners. The center of world banking and finance, moreover, had shifted from London to New York.

A comparable shift in world political authority was also taking place. Though the United States had not joined the League of Nations, its voice was a weighty factor in foreign affairs. That voice was, nevertheless, uncertain. Masters of industrial production, Americans were still only apprentices in conducting international relations. Their education, which could no longer be postponed, would come during decades that were fateful for all humanity.

1 The United States Plays a Limited Role in World Affairs During the 1920's

The First World War had a far-reaching effect on the world's economic situation: it changed the United States from a debtor to a creditor nation. By 1919, European governments owed the United States more than $10 billion.

WAR DEBTS AND TARIFFS

The question of war debts divides the Allies. By the end of the war, the bankrupt nations of Europe had no idea how they could pay off their debts to the United States. The British and French, who owed the most money, assumed that they could use reparations payments collected from Germany (page 197) to repay their war debts to the United States. Germany, however, was in the midst of a severe economic crisis and soon fell behind in its payments.

A number of Europeans suggested solutions to the problem. The proposal heard most often was that both the German reparations and the war debts be scaled down. There were also suggestions that the debtors be permitted to pay their obligations in industrial goods — an idea that no American manufacturer wished to hear. Some Europeans went so far as to advocate the outright cancellation of all war debts. It was only fair, went the argument, that the

The United States was the world's leading industrial power by the time the artist Charles Sheeler painted *American Landscape* in 1930.

United States bear this burden because the European allies had fought much longer than the Americans and had also suffered heavier losses in life and property. Spokesmen from France, moreover, did not hesitate to point out that the French had never been reimbursed for their military assistance during the War for Independence. The United States, they maintained, should absorb the war debts, just as France had once borne the cost of its aid to America.

Woodrow Wilson and his successors in the White House refused to accept the arguments against full repayment. Calvin Coolidge expressed a view shared by most Americans: "They hired the money, didn't they?" There were other sound reasons for saying no. One was that the arguments of the debtors surely did not apply to the substantial loans that had been made in the years following the war. (During the 1920's, American bankers lent Europe nearly $5 billion.) Futhermore, American military sacrifices in the war had been substantial too. Finally, it was not the United States that had insisted on reparations from the defeated Central Powers, but the Allies themselves. In addition, the United States had neither sought nor received territory from the defeated countries, as the other victors had.

The war debts are never repaid. Despite its unwillingness to connect the payment of reparations to war debts, the United States government lent its support to various plans devised to help Germany meet its payments — originally set at $33 billion. Charles G. Dawes, a Chicago banker, came up with a plan in 1924 that was readily adopted. It called for American and Allied bankers to lend Germany millions of dollars for the purpose of boosting industrial recovery and making the German currency stable. In 1928 the Young Plan — the work of Owen D. Young, an American industrialist — cut down Germany's annual payments and limited them to 59 years. In return, the Allies agreed to end their occupation of German territory and to end their controls on the German economy.

These plans strengthened the confidence of American investors who were buying German government and corporation bonds. When the worldwide economic collapse began in 1929, however, the American investments ended, and the reparations could no longer be paid. The European nations agreed in 1932 to accept cancellation of Germany's reparations payments. Then, in the following year, all the governments that owed war debts (except Finland) defaulted on their payments. In all, Germany paid about $4.5 billion in reparations. The Allies, in turn, paid off about $2.5 billion in war debts to the United States.

The United States raises tariff rates. America's mostly unsuccessful attempts to collect war debts caused resentment in Europe. So, too, did America's tariff policy. Many European countries had looked forward after the war to being able to sell their products in the United States. The sale of such products, these countries assumed, would enable them to pay off their obligations. Soon after the war, however, the leading industrial nations were battling one another with a new weapon: tariffs. In the United States the Fordney-McCumber Tariff Act of 1922, for example, increased import duties on hundreds of items.

During the 1920's, many Americans believed the protective tariff to be the basis of prosperity. Indeed, the idea was so well accepted that in response to the onset of the Great Depression, Congress in 1930 passed the Hawley-Smoot Tariff, raising rates yet again. After first protesting the enactment of this tariff, one foreign nation after another put into effect self-protecting tariffs aimed at the United States. Many American businesses and farms were thus deprived of needed markets.

NEW ROADS TO SECURITY

Debate over the League of Nations continues. In the years after the First World War, many people remained gravely concerned over the failure of the United States to join the League of Nations. To be formally linked with other nations, these people said, could provide *collective security* — the mutual protection that becomes possible when countries stand together against peace-breakers. John H. Clarke, a Democrat who had recently retired from the Supreme Court, was in favor of the United States entering the League. He insisted, "If we remain out of it, the next war will come as the last one did, without our having any opportunity to prevent it and with only the privilege of fighting our way out of it."

Arguments on the other side were no less passionate. Proponents of remaining out of the League maintained that the United States must not be burdened with permanent obligations. These people were not shunning the rest of the world. They were simply arguing that the United States must keep itself free to work on behalf of justice wherever help might be required.

The United States cooperates with the League. Although the United States had no formal association with the League of Nations, it cooperated with the League's nonpolitical agencies. It participated in world health programs, in the control of international drug traffic, and in efforts to improve the conditions of labor. It may be said that United States policy, which began as "nonrecognition," gave way to "unofficial cooperation." By 1931 there were five permanent American representatives at Geneva, Switzerland — the headquarters of the League — to monitor issues that concerned the United States.

It is pointless to guess whether international problems would have been more satisfactorily handled if the United States had joined the League of Nations. Americans came quickly to see that the United States would have to cooperate with other nations for its own well-being. The Harding administration, soon after taking power, was seeking ways to accomplish this goal. It focused attention on *disarmament* (a reduction in the size of military forces).

A disarmament conference is held in Washington. Even before the First World War ended, an intense naval race had developed involving the United States, Great Britain, and Japan. After the peace, Japan began building naval bases on Pacific islands that had come under its control. Many people, remembering how the arms race in Europe before 1914 had led finally to war, feared that a naval armaments contest might lead to a similar outcome.

Since most Americans wished to avoid such a competition, not to mention a war with Japan, the time seemed ripe to take steps. The task of finding a solution to the problem was undertaken by Senator William E. Borah. Borah had taken a leading part in keeping the United States out of the League of Nations. Now he felt forced to find a substitute arrangement for the nation's security.

In the spring of 1921, Borah proposed that the United States invite Great Britain and Japan to a conference in Washington, D.C., for the purpose of discussing naval disarmament. Both houses of Congress approved the proposal. President Harding then sent invitations to the nine major powers having interests in Asian affairs.

The conference, held in Washington's Memorial Continental Hall, pleased many Americans, who continued to think that Wilson should never have traveled to Europe in 1918. A well-known journalist wrote of his feelings as he entered the simple meeting chamber, whose chief adornments were portraits of George and Martha Washington: "How infinitely more beautiful is this room than the glaring red and gold of the room at Paris where the Peace Conference was held."

The sessions began on November 12, 1921. The delegates had been deeply moved the day before — the third anniversary of the armistice — when the Unknown Soldier was buried with the highest military honors at Arlington National Cemetery in nearby Virginia. The representatives had had an opportunity to reflect on the terrible cost of war. Only a few people knew about the startling proposal Secretary of State Charles Evans Hughes was about to present.

Hughes entered the hall with an air of confidence. Newspaper reporters liked to say they could tell the state of American foreign relations by the condition of Hughes' beard. This day, an observer wrote, "every hair was at a satisfactory upward angle." Within minutes of beginning his speech, Hughes surprised his audience. He suggested that the major powers set limits on the number of battleships in their navies. This meant the scrapping of ships already built or under construction. Hughes also called for a ten-year "holiday" in the construction of all capital ships (that is, battleships and heavy cruisers).

The British and the Japanese were stunned by Hughes's proposal. An English military commentator said that the Secretary was proposing to sink "in 35 minutes more ships than all the admirals of the world have sunk in a cycle of centuries." When the conference reassembled after a weekend to think over the American proposal, however, world opinion seemed to be firmly behind it.

Subsequent negotiations produced a number of agreements. The first and most dramatic of these was the Five-Power Treaty, so called because the signers were the five great sea powers. Signed in February, 1922, it provided for a ten-year "holiday" in naval shipbuilding that would bring the capital-ship strength of the United States, Britain, and Japan into a ratio of 5:5:3. France and Italy were each to have a ratio of 1.67 to the other powers. Some Japanese diplomats were displeased with the treaty. Still, the arrangement was advantageous to Japan, because the United States and Britain also agreed not to fortify further their possessions in the western Pacific — including the Philippines and Hong Kong.

The Washington Conference seeks international cooperation in Asia. A second agreement reached that year at Washington was the Four-Power Pact, entered into by the United States, Great Britain, Japan, and France. The nations signing the pact agreed to respect one another's possessions in the Pacific. What made the treaty remarkable was that it rested upon the word and pledge of the signing nations — not on a specific military commitment or international organization. A third agreement signed by all the delegates at the conference, and known as the Nine-Power Treaty, guaranteed the independence and territorial unity of China. For the first time, an international gathering had recognized the doctrine of the Open Door (page 145).

Later disarmament conferences are held. Most Americans applauded the results of the Washington Conference (1921–1922), and the Senate gave its approval to the three treaties. In the years that followed, however, concern grew over a new naval competition in the construction of smaller vessels (submarines and destroyers). In 1927 President Coolidge invited all the nations that had signed the Five-Power Treaty to meet at Geneva. Only Britain and Japan accepted the invitation, and the conference was a failure. Seemingly more successful was another meeting held in London in 1930. It produced an agreement among Great Britain, the United States, and Japan to extend the naval holiday for five more years. It also set limitations on the building of smaller vessels. In 1935, however, a year before that treaty was set to expire, Japan demanded naval equality with the United States and Great Britain. When this demand was refused, Japan withdrew from the treaty.

An attempt is made to outlaw war. While the United States was participating in the naval disarmament movement, it also took the lead in an effort to outlaw war. The intriguing proposal to declare war illegal was first made by a Chicago lawyer named Salmon O. Levinson. Levinson captivated Senator Borah with the idea. Another group that eventually supported the proposal were backers of American entry into the League of Nations. They believed that if all nations renounced war, the League would become the agency of enforcement.

The movement was getting nowhere when a Columbia University professor named James T. Shotwell persuaded the French foreign minister, Aristide Briand (bree-AHN), that the United States and France ought to conclude a "pact of perpetual friendship." On April 6, 1927, the tenth anniversary of America's entry into World

War I, Briand made such a proposal. He called, in addition, for an agreement between the United States and France to outlaw war between the two countries. The French saw such a treaty as possible protection against any revival of German military power.

Not enthusiastic about Briand's proposal, Secretary of State Frank B. Kellogg was slow in responding. The public, however, still imagining a world without war, supported the French suggestion. On August 27, 1928, the United States and France, joined by thirteen other nations (all of the major countries except the Soviet Union) signed the Pact of Paris — sometimes called the Kellogg-Briand Pact. They solemnly renounced war "as an instrument of national policy" in their relations with one another. In time the treaty was signed by more than sixty nations.

There were critics of the Pact. One of them called it "an international kiss." Senator Carter Glass of Virginia hoped, he said, that the people of his state did not think he considered the treaty "worth a postage stamp." Many Americans, along with people everywhere, could see that the treaty said nothing about enforcement. Nor did it exclude wars fought in self-defense — a label that even aggressors could apply to their adventuring.

RELATIONS WITH LATIN AMERICA

Diplomacy repairs relations with Latin America. In the days of Roosevelt, Taft, and Wilson, the United States had periodically intervened in Latin American countries, in part to keep out meddling European powers. After the armistice ending the world war, no European nation dared challenge United States military and naval authority in the Western Hemisphere. As a result, there were signs that the United States was modifying the Roosevelt Corollary (page 166). Secretary Hughes, for instance, allowed marines stationed in the Dominican Republic in 1916 to leave in 1924 after a constitutional regime was established there.

Under the terms of the Kellogg-Briand Pact, signed in Paris in 1928, more than sixty countries agreed to ban war as an instrument of national policy.

Efforts to pull American troops out of Nicaragua were more halting. Marines had been sent to that country in 1912 to monitor a government deeply in debt. They were withdrawn in 1925 after the financial situation improved. Civil war soon broke out, however, as rebels sought to oust the government, and in 1927 President Coolidge sent troops to Nicaragua once more.

In the United States there was so much opposition to Coolidge's action that he sent Colonel Henry L. Stimson (who had been Secretary of War under Taft) to Nicaragua to seek a settlement between the competing groups. Stimson succeeded in bringing to power the Nicaraguan rebels, and they quickly received United States support. As relations between the Americans and the Nicaraguans improved, the United States gradually pulled out its troops — the last of them in 1933. Almost immediately Anastasio Somoza began to rise to power. He and his family would rule Nicaragua for the next 45 years.

Relations with Mexico improve. Tension between the United States and Mexico had been high ever since the withdrawal of American troops from Mexican soil in 1917 (page 178). The key to the dispute was a provision in the Mexican constitution of 1917 giving the Mexican people control over all oil and mineral resources. An unanswered question was whether or not the provision applied to mineral and oil properties acquired by Americans before 1917. In 1923 Mexico agreed not to interfere with those rights. Then, in 1924 an ardent nationalist, Plutarco Calles (KAH-yays), became president of Mexico. He made clear that he intended to abandon the arrangement of 1923 in favor of a new one.

A desire on both sides for a peaceful resolution of the dispute led President Coolidge in the summer of 1927 to send his Amherst College classmate, Dwight W. Morrow, to Mexico City as United States ambassador. Morrow was uncommonly successful. His warm personality attracted the good will of the rough and ready Calles. The two men worked out a compromise on American rights to Mexican oil and minerals. Companies that had begun to work their subsoil holdings before 1917 would be permitted to keep them. Meanwhile, the Mexican public's view of America was greatly helped by a good-will flight late in 1927 from Washington to Mexico City by Charles A. Lindbergh, fresh from his conquest of the Atlantic (page 225) and soon to become Morrow's son-in-law.

Hoover travels to Latin America. Stimson and Morrow had contributed notably to the idea that the Roosevelt Corollary was now out of date. Shortly after Herbert Hoover was inaugurated President, he went on a tour of the Latin American republics. In his speeches he emphasized America's desire "to maintain not only the cordial relations of governments with each other but the relations of good neighbors."

Nothing helped to demonstrate America's change in policy better than a memorandum written by Undersecretary of State J. Reuben Clark in 1928 and made public in 1930. "The Monroe Doctrine," said the Clark Memorandum, "states a case of the United States vs. Europe, not of the United States vs. Latin America." The Doctrine could not be used, therefore, as justification for American intervention in the internal affairs of its neighbors. Clark's statement was unofficial — and was even treated as unimportant by President Hoover — but it helped somewhat to clear the air in United States-Latin American relations.

SECTION REVIEW

1. Vocabulary: *collective security, disarmament.*
2. (a) What problem arose when Germany failed to make its reparations payments? (b) Why did the United States reject the suggestion that the Allies' war debts be reduced or canceled?
3. In what ways did the United States cooperate with the League of Nations?
4. (a) What conditions led to the Washington Conference of 1921–1922? (b) What agreements were reached concerning disarmament? (c) Concerning cooperation in Asia? (d) Why did Japan later withdraw from the treaty?
5. (a) What was the Kellogg-Briand Pact? (b) Why was it hailed by some and criticized by others?
6. (a) Why did relations with Latin America improve in the years after World War I? (b) What was the Clark Memorandum?

2 The United States Governs Its Possessions

Throughout the 1920's and 1930's the United States prepared its major possessions for self-government and eventual independence. The mood of the late nineteenth century, when so many voices had been lifted in favor of having colonies, had passed. Americans were finding that they had no enthusiasm for ruling other peoples. Moreover, they had learned that it is more difficult and expensive to manage possessions than to acquire them.

The constitutional status of the territories is fixed. A difficult question for Americans from the time they first acquired possessions was whether or not the people living in the territories were entitled to the rights

The United States established public schools in the Philippines to help train Filipinos in the ways of self-government.

and privileges of American citizens. The question was often stated this way, "Does the Constitution follow the flag?"

A number of Supreme Court cases, known as the Insular Cases, answered this question and related ones. Beginning in 1901 the Supreme Court ruled that there were two kinds of possessions to be considered — incorporated and unincorporated. The Court went on to say that in the incorporated possessions — those which were destined for statehood — inhabitants could enjoy the fundamental rights guaranteed by the Constitution. In the unincorporated possessions — those which were *not* destined for statehood — the inhabitants would enjoy life, liberty, and the right of property. They would not, however, be entitled to all constitutional guarantees.

The United States sets up territorial governments. Having had no experience in governing colonies, Americans invented their methods as they went along. After 1900, for instance, Hawaii was under the rule of a governor and a territorial legislature — the way American territories had always been governed. The Department of the Interior was responsible for Hawaii (and for Alaska).

Being primarily naval stations, the Virgin Islands, Guam, Tutuila, and Wake Island (map, page 143) were placed under the jurisdiction of the Department of the Navy. The Philippines, and a few years later the Panama Canal Zone, were put under the control of the Department of War. This department also took over responsibility for Puerto Rico after 1901.

In 1931 a Division of Territories and Island Possessions was organized in the Department of the Interior. This body became responsible for all of America's possessions except Guam, American Samoa, Wake Island, the Virgin Islands, and the Canal Zone. The three Pacific islands and the Virgin Islands remained under the Department of the Navy; the Canal Zone remained under the Department of War.

Guam in 1950 and American Samoa in 1951 were transferred from the Department of the Navy to the Department of the Interior. In 1950 Congress granted United States citizenship to the residents of Guam, along with the right to send a nonvoting representative to Congress. Guam has a governor and a legislature, who, since 1970, have been popularly elected. American Samoa, meanwhile, elected its first governor in

267

1977 and also sends a nonvoting representative to Congress. The Virgin Islands have elected their own governor since 1970. The residents of the Virgin Islands have been United States citizens since 1927.

The Panama Canal, beginning in 1951, has been operated by a federal agency, the Panama Canal Company. The governor of the Zone, chosen by the President, also serves as president of the company. A treaty signed by the United States and Panama in 1978 was designed to provide for the future of the Canal Zone. Under the treaty, the United States agreed to give Panama full control over the canal at the end of 1999.

American influence remains strong in Cuba. In accordance with the Teller Amendment (page 138), the United States promised to leave Cuba after the island had won its independence from Spain. The American government expected, however, to exercise some control over the new republic. In 1901, therefore, Congress set forth in the so-called Platt Amendment certain conditions that it insisted be incorporated in the Cuban constitution. Cuba's treaty-making powers and its right to borrow money were restricted. Cuba, furthermore, could not refuse to sell or lease lands to the United States for coaling or naval stations. (Accordingly, in 1903 the United States acquired the land around Guantánamo Bay for the construction of a naval base.) Lastly, the United States retained the right to intervene in Cuba "for the protection of life, property, and individual liberty." During the next decades the United States frequently intervened in Cuban affairs, aiming to protect American interests there. The Platt Amendment remained a bone of contention until it was canceled in 1934.

Puerto Rico gains some self-government. When Puerto Rico was acquired by the United States (page 142), General Miles had assured the people that they would receive "the guarantees and blessings of the liberal institutions of our government." Many Puerto Ricans, however, were disappointed in the civil government set up under the terms of the Foraker Act of 1900. Under that law, Puerto Rico was granted a House of Delegates elected by popular vote. Legislation passed by the House of Delegates had to be approved by the governor, who was appointed by the President of the United States. The President also appointed the members of the upper house, which was known as the Executive Council. The United States Congress, furthermore, had the power to overturn any law passed by the House of Delegates. The Foraker Act declared the island's people to be citizens of Puerto Rico, not of the United States. Puerto Ricans were represented in Washington by a resident commissioner with a seat, but no voice or vote, in the United States House of Representatives. Many Puerto Ricans were offended because under Spanish rule they had been equal in status to citizens residing in Spain. They had also been represented in the Spanish parliament.

Puerto Ricans soon began to seek a larger role in their own political destiny. In 1910 Luis Muñoz Rivera became Puerto Rico's resident commissioner in Washington. Muñoz Rivera had led Puerto Rico's movement for self-government in the last days of Spanish rule. Now he directed his energies toward gaining from the United States more rights for his people.

Muñoz Rivera's efforts began to bear fruit in 1917 when Congress passed the Jones Act. Under this law, citizens of Puerto Rico were granted United States citizenship. (Some Puerto Ricans objected on the ground that the island's people had not been formally consulted about their wishes in the matter.) A senate to be elected by Puerto Ricans was also established. The governor of the island, however, continued to be an appointee of the President. Congress, furthermore, reserved the right to annul or amend any act passed by the island's legislature.

The Jones Act failed to satisfy most Puerto Ricans. The continued campaign of the islanders for more self-government was rewarded in 1947 when Congress passed a law enabling them to elect their own governor. The governor, whose term would be four years, was also empowered to appoint the heads of the executive departments, with the consent of the island's senate. (Judges of Puerto Rico's highest court continued to be appointed by the President of the United States.)

Puerto Rico becomes a commonwealth. In 1948 the leading candidate for governor was Luis Muñoz Marin, son of the revered Muñoz Rivera. Muñoz Marin was the most popular politician on the island and he was easily elected. He then proposed a new status for the island.

In 1952 a new constitution was approved by Congress and by the voters of Puerto Rico. It made the island a self-governing commonwealth under United States protection. As residents of a commonwealth, Puerto Ricans would pay no federal income taxes and would be able to move to the mainland without being subject to immigration restrictions.

For the first time, the islanders had voted on their own relationship to the United States. It was understood, furthermore, that no future alteration in the status of Puerto Rico would be made without the express consent of the Puerto Ricans.

The Filipinos seek independence. The Philippines were the most distant and most populous of American possessions. In 1901 William Howard Taft was named the first governor of the islands. In the following year, Congress passed an act declaring the inhabitants to be citizens of the Philippine Islands "entitled to the protection of the United States." A law enacted in 1907 provided for a two-house legislative assembly, the lower house to be elected every two years. The upper house would consist of members of a commission appointed by the President.

In 1912 the Democratic platform contained a pledge to set the Philippine Islands free as soon as practicable. President Wilson sought to fulfill this promise with passage of the Jones Act of 1916 (not to be confused with the Jones Act of 1917 regarding Puerto Rico). Under this law an elective senate replaced the commission as the upper house of the Philippine legislature. The Jones Act

Luis Muñoz Marin, the first elected governor of Puerto Rico, helped make his island a self-governing commonwealth.

promised independence "as soon as a stable government can be established."

During the 1920's the Filipinos made repeated requests for independence. Finally, in 1934 the Tydings-McDuffie Act provided for complete independence for the Philippines, following a transition period of ten years. The outbreak of World War II interrupted that period, delaying fulfillment of the promise. On July 4, 1946, independence came to the islands, and the Republic of the Philippines was born.

SECTION REVIEW

1. According to the Supreme Court, what was the difference between incorporated and unincorporated possessions?
2. How is each of the following possessions governed? (a) Guam (b) American Samoa (c) Virgin Islands (d) Canal Zone
3. (a) Describe the government set up in Puerto Rico under the Foraker Act. (b) What rights did Puerto Ricans gain in 1917? (c) What rights did they gain in 1947? (d) What step did the voters of Puerto Rico take in 1952?
4. Describe the steps by which the Philippines gained independence.

Alaska and Hawaii

In the early 1900's, there were forty-eight states — all on the North American continent and all contiguous (that is, with boundaries that touched). By the second half of the century, however, two distant American possessions would become new states. One, Alaska, shared many geographical links with what its residents called the "Lower 48." The other, Hawaii, was part of the world of the Pacific Ocean.

Alaska

Purchased from Russia in 1867 (page 128), Alaska is a huge peninsula at the northwest tip of the North American continent. It is the largest state, with an area of nearly 600,000 square miles. Part of the state is only about fifty miles from the Soviet Union, separated from Asia by the Bering Strait. Historically, this is where the first settlers in the Americas — ancestors of the American Indians — crossed from Asia.

Two mountain chains — the Rockies and the Pacific coastal mountains — run the length of the North American continent to end in Alaska. The Coast Ranges hug the Pacific coast in the southern part of the state. Their towering peaks are covered by glaciers and ice fields. Submerged peaks of this mountain range form a group of rugged offshore islands. Between the coastal mountains lie basins and valleys with farms and forests. Though Alaska lies far north, winds from the warm Japan Current give some parts of the state a fairly mild, wet climate.

The coastal mountains continue northward as the Alaska Range, whose summit is the tallest peak in North America — Mt. McKinley, 20,320 feet high. The mountains then curve into the Aleutian Range. The

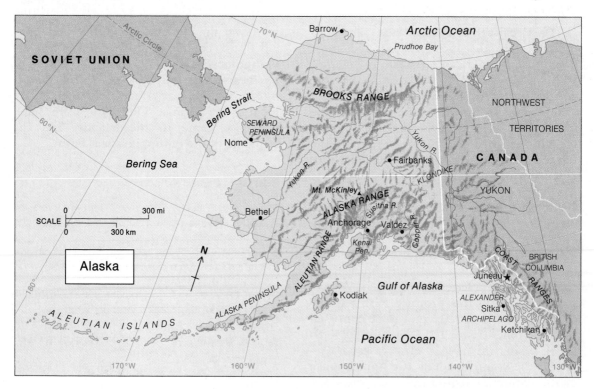

Aleutians, where many volcanoes are still active, stretch out into the ocean as a chain of rugged islands.

In the north of the peninsula is the Brooks Range, the northernmost end of the Rocky Mountains. Between these mountain chains is a hilly region crossed by broad river valleys. The huge Yukon River connects the interior with the sea.

Beyond the Brooks Range, in arctic Alaska, a broad treeless coastal plain slopes down to the Arctic Ocean. This tundra region blooms with wildflowers and grasses in the short summer season but lies over permafrost — ground that is frozen the year round. Also called the North Slope, this is the region where vast oil reserves were found in the 1960's.

Hawaii

Hawaii is unique among the states in that it is made up entirely of islands — eight major islands and over a hundred small islands of rock, sand, or coral. The main islands were formed by lava pouring out of huge shield volcanoes on the ocean floor, building a chain of dome-shaped islands. The broad tops of some of these volcanoes are more than 13,000 feet above sea level, but their undersea bases make them actually more than twice that high.

The landscape of Hawaii is dominated by volcanoes, some still active. Streams have cut deep gorges in the rock; there are steep cliffs and spectacular waterfalls. Where the volcanic rock has been weathered, the soil is rich. As Hawaii also has a mild, tropical climate, there are lush wild forests as well as plantations growing fruit and sugar. Hawaii lies in the path of the trade winds, and rainfall is especially heavy on the windward sides of the mountains. Mt. Waialeale, on the island of Kaui, receives some 480 inches of rain a year and may be the wettest spot on earth.

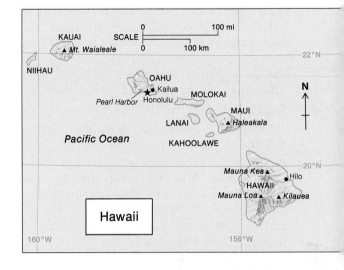

The largest island, Hawaii, has two active volcanoes — Kilauea and Mauna Loa — which give off fiery flows of lava. The volcanoes that formed the island of Maui are both extinct, but the huge crater of Haleakala is one of the largest in the world. (Several Hawaiian volcanoes are now part of the National Park System.) About three fourths of the state's population live on Oahu, the third largest island. Between the mountains that rim each edge of Oahu, there is a wide lowland that slopes to the sea. The southern coast of the island has beautiful beaches and the protected natural harbor of Pearl Harbor. The smaller islands, all volcanic, are Kaui, Lanai, Molokai, Kahoolawe, and Niihau.

---

1. (a) Where is Alaska located? (b) What geographical links does it have with the rest of the United States?
2. (a) What kind of mountains make up the Aleutian Islands? (b) In what part of Alaska was oil found?
3. (a) How were the major islands of Hawaii formed? (b) What kind of climate does the state have?

3 Dictators Menace World Peace

While the United States was making adjustments in the governing of its territorial holdings, the long shadow of a possible new war dominated relations with Europe. By the mid-1930's, changed conditions were upsetting the structure of peace that had been established in Paris in 1919.

Dictators come to power in Europe. In central and eastern Europe, governments seeking democratic reforms had arisen after the First World War, replacing the defeated monarchies. Few democratic governments, however, lasted long. They were too weak and inexperienced to cope with the chaos that war and hard times had left behind. People began to heed the promises offered by demagogues — leaders who appeal to emotion and to prejudice.

In a number of countries *totalitarian* regimes were set up, so named because a single leader and his close supporters exercised absolute control over all spheres of life. Opposition parties were not tolerated. Indeed, all opposition was cruelly suppressed. In ad-

Adolf Hitler, shown reviewing troops, set up a totalitarian regime in Germany.

dition, traditional freedoms were not allowed: every individual had to bow to the will of the state. Meanwhile, arms industries were expanded and the military spirit was glorified.

The first of the totalitarian governments had been established in the Soviet Union after the Bolsheviks seized power in 1917 (page 192). The Bolsheviks' use of a single-party system, of secret police, and of murder as a political tool provided a model for similar brutality in other countries. By the mid-1920's the Soviet Union had come under the control of Joseph Stalin. Through systematic "liquidation" of his political opponents, Stalin made his dictatorship unchallengeable in the Soviet Union. The reign of terror he let loose on his own people was unmatched in history.

By the early 1930's, concern in the West over developments in Russia was overshadowed by events in Germany. There, under the direction of Adolf Hitler and his Nazi Party subordinates, Germany made bold plans for the future.

Shortly after World War I (in which he had served as a corporal in the German army) Hitler began plotting to overthrow the republican government of Germany. While serving a prison term in 1923 for political activities, Hitler wrote *Mein Kampf* ("My Struggle"). The book, ferociously anti-democratic as well as anti-Semitic, gradually became the guide to the future for disillusioned Germans. By 1933 Hitler had attracted millions of followers and was named to the high office of chancellor. Within the next few years he gained control of all branches of the Germany government. Meanwhile, he was making plans to restore Germany's military power.

In Italy, too, plans were being laid to carry out military adventures. Benito Mussolini had made himself Italy's dictator in 1922. In the next few years, with the aid of his Fascist Party, he wiped out the republican institutions of his country. By the 1930's he had made the very word *fascism*, the name of his dictatorial system, a synonym for anti-democracy. Mussolini's announced goal in foreign affairs was to convert the Mediterranean Sea into an Italian lake by taking control of neighboring territory. Mussolini saw himself as belonging in the company of the Roman emperors of old, whose glories he wanted to revive. His enemies regarded his grandiose schemes with contempt, dubbing him the "sawdust Caesar."

Japanese expansion threatens world peace. In Asia, too, aggressive military planners were menacing world peace. Japan had been steadily expanding since the 1870's. It had taken over the Kurile Islands in 1875 and Taiwan (Formosa) in 1895. After the Russo-Japanese War (page 166) Japan had acquired control of the southern half of the island of Sakhalin. As one of the victorious Allies in the First World War, it had been granted control of a number of Germany's Pacific islands.

In 1931 China became a target of Japan's aggressive appetite. In a short time the Japanese swallowed up the rich province of Manchuria and created a puppet government there. In the presence of this serious threat to peace, the League of Nations proved powerless. When the League condemned the Japanese action in Manchuria, Japan responded by withdrawing from membership in the organization. In messages that Secretary of State Henry L. Stimson sent to China and Japan on behalf of the Hoover administration, he set forth America's position. It has come to be known as the Stimson Doctrine. The United States, Stimson said, would refuse to recognize any territorial change brought about as a result of aggression.

Isolationists gain strength in the United States. Words alone, however, could not stop nations from attacking their neighbors. The United States and other peace-loving countries faced the painful truth that no sure force stood in the way of the aggressor nations. In devising foreign policy, however, American statesmen had to take into consideration a number of facts. The most important was that throughout the country many people were determined that the United States should stay out of future wars — at all costs. Known as *isolationists,* they maintained that the United States should avoid foreign entanglements and concentrate on the problems of the Depression. Some isolationists in Congress feared that the New Deal reforms would be endangered if the United States took action against the aggressor nations.

The United States recognizes the Soviet Union. The burden of countering Japan's aggression seemed increasingly to be falling to the United States. A step that some Americans believed could help blunt Japanese military moves was to raise the prestige of the Soviet Union, a natural rival of Japan. This end, they said, could be accomplished by granting diplomatic recognition to the Soviet Union. Other Americans optimistically believed that recognition might open fresh markets for American products and possibly reduce unemployment.

Throughout the 1920's, the United States had refused to recognize the Communist government of the Soviet Union. One reason for withholding recognition was that upon assuming power the Bolshevik revolutionists had refused to pay the debts owed to the United States by the czars. Moreover, the new Communist government had confiscated millions of dollars' worth of American property. A third reason for withholding recognition was the continued effort by the Soviet Union to subvert institutions of the United States in the interest of world communism. The Secretary of State had pointed out that even Soviet diplomatic representatives could be regarded as "agitators of dangerous revolt."

In the negotiations over diplomatic recognition, the Soviet Union agreed to discontinue Communist propaganda in the United States. Any discussion of the debts and other claims, however, was postponed. Late in 1933, President Roosevelt announced that diplomatic recognition of the Soviet Union had been granted.

Many Americans soon regarded recognition of the Soviet Union as a blunder. The anticipated trade never materialized, and Communist propaganda continued. Later, when Soviet leaders were refused a loan by the United States, they broke off discussion of the debts and other claims.

Tensions mount in Europe. In Europe, threats to world peace developed with increasing frequency. In March, 1935, Hitler renounced the clauses of the Versailles Treaty which had stipulated that Germany must be disarmed. Britain and France did not lift a finger to hold Germany to this obligation.

Within a few months, Mussolini made a move. No doubt motivated by the German action and by the display of British and French weakness, he attacked the East African kingdom of Ethiopia in October, 1935. Lacking the weapons to resist, Ethiopia was defeated in eight months. The League of Nations passed a resolution calling Italy an aggressor and imposed economic sanctions on Italy. Oil, however, which was indispensable to Mussolini's armies, was left off the list of products that could not be sold to Italy. Britain and France were afraid to push Italy too hard, fearful of bringing on unwanted hostilities. Moreover, the peace-loving nations were concerned that they might force Mussolini to seek an alliance with Germany.

Roosevelt, ever watchful not to offend isolationists, would not officially associate the United States with the League's action. Some American oil-producers placed a voluntary embargo on shipments of oil to Italy, but it had little effect.

Further breaches of the peace took a variety of forms. In 1936 civil war broke out in Spain. By the time it had ended three years later, General Francisco Franco, a dictator backed with arms and troops sent by Hitler and Mussolini, had come to power.

Meanwhile, the Germans continued to make menacing moves. In 1936, again defying the Treaty of Versailles, Germany sent troops into the Rhineland, an area along the French border that had been demilitarized after the First World War. In that same year Germany and Italy formed the Axis alliance, sometimes known as the Rome-Berlin Axis. (In 1940 Japan joined, making it the Tripartite Pact, sometimes known as the Rome-Berlin-Tokyo Axis.)

The United States adopts a Neutrality Act. Italy's attack on Ethiopia in 1935 prompted the United States to pass neutrality legislation. The supporters of these laws hoped to avoid the kinds of events that many people believed had brought about United States involvement in the First World War.

The first Neutrality Act — signed by Roosevelt in August, 1935 — required the President to prohibit the shipment of arms to belligerents (that is, nations engaged in war). The President, at his discretion, could forbid American citizens to travel on the ships of warring powers, except at their own risk. Clearly, America was hoping to avoid an incident like the *Lusitania* disaster (page 281).

Six months later the Neutrality Act was extended, and restrictions were laid on the granting of loans or credits to nations at war. This law satisfied people who maintained that the war loans to Britain and France made by American bankers had drawn the United States into the struggle in 1917.

The neutrality legislation left the United States almost powerless to restrain Mussolini or Hitler by force. As Roosevelt watched the rising tide of aggression abroad, he was deeply concerned over the ability of isolationists to influence national policy. Still, he did not believe he could defeat them in a showdown. During the presidential campaign of 1936, he made only one reference to foreign affairs. When he did — in a speech in New York State — he unreservedly satisfied the isolationists: "We shun political commitments which might entangle us in foreign wars. . . . I have seen war on land and sea. . . . I have seen the agony of mothers and wives. I hate war."

Congress passes a second Neutrality Act. On May 1, 1937, in response to the Spanish Civil War, Congress passed a second Neutrality Act. By a joint resolution it retained the restrictions against loans and arms sales made in the earlier act and prohibited travel aboard the vessels of warring nations. A new feature was included in this Neutrality Act — a "cash-and-carry" plan. Nonmilitary goods could be sold only to belligerents who sent their own ships for them and paid in cash.

The neutrality legislation was, in truth, unneutral. First, it failed to distinguish between aggressor and victim — a fact that offended many Americans. Second, Germany, Italy, and Japan already had large stockpiles of arms and did not require such supplies from the United States. Third, the cash-and-carry program gave an advantage to nations that had both money and vessels.

Japan wages war on China. Almost as soon as the second neutrality law went into effect, Japan resumed large-scale fighting against China. The Chinese, under the leadership of Chiang Kai-shek (jee-AHNG KYE-SHEK), refused to give in. Yet they lacked sufficient arms to keep Japanese forces from capturing coastal ports and from pushing inland up river valleys. Roosevelt, eager to help China, decided not to recognize that a war existed, since that would have forced him to invoke the neutrality law. The President also relied on the fact that Japan referred to its operations not as hostilities, but as an "incident."

Roosevelt offers his "quarantine speech." Roosevelt was in a predicament. He wanted to support political leaders in Britain, France, and China who were seeking to stand up to aggression. But how? In October, 1937, he tried to alert the country to the dangers that loomed and to suggest a principle for dealing with them. He put his warning and proposal in a speech he delivered in Chicago — a stronghold of isolationist sentiment. In the address, he declared that "the epidemic of world lawlessness" was spreading. Countries that loved peace, he said, would have to organize "a concerted effort to uphold laws and principles on which alone peace can rest secure." They would have to do this, he went on, the way a community faced by an epidemic disease "joins in a quarantine of the patients in order to protect the health of the community. . . . "

The "quarantine speech," an effort to test whether public opinion was changing, was not well received. The people were not yet ready to see the threats to peace abroad as threats to America itself.

Germany becomes an aggressor. Meanwhile, Germany had built up a powerful army and had begun to threaten its neighbors. In early 1938, Hitler's forces occupied Austria. Joining Austria to Germany had always been a Nazi aim. By threats amounting to an ultimatum, Hitler forced his small neighbor to surrender its independence.

After Hitler had annexed Austria, he began to menace the neighboring democratic nation of Czechoslovakia. He demanded that Czechoslovakia give up the Sudetenland, an area with a large German-speaking population. Once that happened, he pledged, there would be "no further territorial problems in Europe."

As the situation grew tense, the leaders of Britain and France agreed to meet with Hitler at Munich, Germany, in September, 1938, to find a solution. There the British prime minister, Neville Chamberlain, and the French premier, Edouard Daladier, consented to the separation of the Sudetenland from Czechoslovakia. Chamberlain claimed that through this surrender to Hitler he had obtained "peace for our time." Many people, however, were shocked by this example of *appeasement* (granting concessions to a potential enemy in order to maintain

The failure of the appeasement policy was made clear when German troops completed their take-over of Czechoslovakia in March, 1939, less than six months after the Munich Conference.

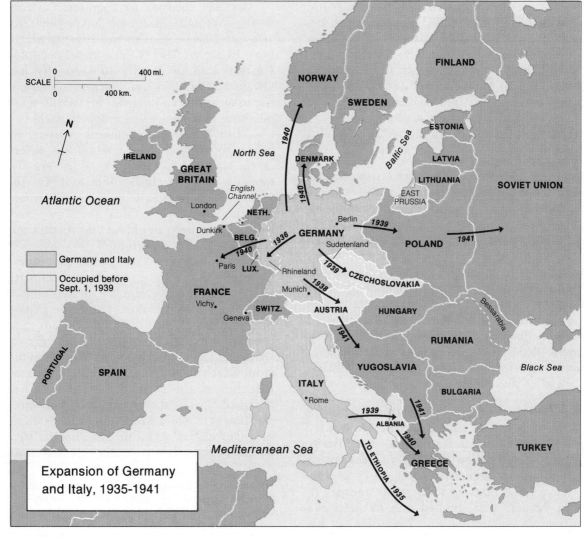

By 1939 Germany and Italy had seized strategic territory in Europe. In the years that followed, Axis attacks spread across the continent.

peace). In any event, Hitler soon ignored his promise to make no more territorial demands, and in March, 1939, seized the rest of Czechoslovakia. Within weeks, Mussolini, made bold by Hitler's success, followed his example and took over Albania (map, above).

Observing these moves with growing anxiety, Britain and France began to see the foolishness of relying on a policy of appeasement, and they hastened to build up their armed forces. They also pledged to defend the independence of Poland, a country which Hitler was now starting to threaten. In addition, Britain and France tried to per-suade the Soviet Union to join with them in resisting further German aggression. While waiting hopefully for a favorable response, they were shocked on August 23, 1939, to learn that the Soviet Union had signed a nonaggression pact with Germany. The Nazis and Communists had long been rivals. The fact that they were now linked together stunned the world. The public did not yet know that Germany and the Soviet Union had agreed secretly to divide Poland. The pact also made clear that Germany would not oppose Soviet moves to take Finland, Estonia, Latvia, Lithuania, and Bessarabia (in Rumania).

The United States formulates the Good Neighbor Policy. Roosevelt, in view of the dismaying events abroad, had long seen the need to cultivate the friendship of countries in the Western Hemisphere. In his inaugural address in 1933, he had declared, "In the field of foreign relations I would dedicate this nation to the policy of the good neighbor." Late in 1933, a Pan-American conference held at Montevideo, Uruguay, adopted a "Convention on the Rights and Duties of States," which was heartily supported by the United States. This agreement proclaimed the equality of all nations in their right to be free of outside interference. Before the year ended, Roosevelt announced that henceforth it would be United States policy to oppose armed intervention in Latin American countries.

The Good Neighbor Policy having been launched, the United States showed it would adhere to it despite provocation. For instance, when the government of Cuba was overthrown in 1933, the United States refrained from sending troops there. Indeed, it was in this period that the United States canceled the Platt Amendment (page 268), which had troubled relations with Cuba for years. As further evidence of the Good Neighbor Policy, the last marines were brought home from Haiti in 1934.

For the purpose of increasing trade with Latin America, Roosevelt backed passage of the Trade Agreements Act of 1934. This law, which passed Congress after much debate, empowered the President to reduce tariff rates by as much as 50 percent, in return for similar concessions from other nations. Soon, tariff rates among the nations of the Western Hemisphere had been lowered, paving the way for the desired increase in trade.

Another milestone was reached in December, 1936, when Roosevelt traveled to Buenos Aires, Argentina, to attend an inter-American conference for the maintenance of peace. The American nations pledged to consult with one another in the event of threats to peace in the Western Hemisphere. Then, at Lima, Peru, in December, 1938, the capstone of the Good Neighbor Policy was set in place. There, at the eighth Pan-American Conference, the American republics pledged to defend themselves from any outside threat. The transformation of the Monroe Doctrine was completed at Mexico City in 1945. By the Act of Chapultepec, the American nations accepted the principle that an attack from abroad on one of them was to be considered an attack upon them all. The Monroe Doctrine was no longer the policy of the United States alone; it had become a shield to be used in time of need by all the American republics.

SECTION REVIEW

1. Vocabulary: *totalitarian, isolationist, appeasement.*
2. (a) Why did dictators come to power in Europe in the years after World War I? (b) What methods did those dictators use?
3. (a) How did Japan threaten world peace in 1931? (b) What was the response of the League of Nations?
4. (a) How did Italy take over Ethiopia? (b) Why did Italy's attack lead to passage in Congress of neutrality legislation?
5. How did Hitler take over Austria and the Sudetenland?
6. (a) What was Roosevelt's Good Neighbor Policy? (b) How was the policy put into effect?

4 World War II Begins

On September 1, 1939, with dive bombers wailing overhead, Hitler's troops stormed into Poland. Having promised to aid the Poles, Britain and France declared war on Germany — slightly more than 25 years after the beginning of World War I.

The outbreak of war affects American neutrality. Immediately upon the eruption of hostilities, President Roosevelt issued a declaration of American neutrality. He called Congress into special session, nevertheless, to bring about a repeal of the embargo on arms. The debate in Congress was furious as isolationists declared that in the end, as Senator Borah put it, the United States "would be sending armies as well as arms." In a radio address, the President responded: "The simple truth is that no person . . . has ever suggested . . . the remotest possibility of sending the boys of American mothers to fight on the battlefields of Europe." In November, 1939, Congress lifted the embargo, and arms and munitions began to flow freely to Britain and France on a cash-and-carry basis.

By then, Poland, invaded in the west by Germany and in the east by the Soviet Union, had been crushed. Winter now closed in, and the war settled into a period of inactivity. Taking advantage of the lull, Roosevelt sent Undersecretary of State Sumner Welles to Europe to see if a peace conference could be organized. The effort failed. The President knew now that the immediate future was dark. He warned the American people that they could not expect to remain untouched if the war destroyed European civilization.

The war spreads over western Europe. In the spring of 1940, Hitler's war machine went into high gear. In April, Nazi forces overran and occupied Norway and Denmark. In May, just as the tulips were blooming, the Netherlands, Belgium, and Luxembourg fell. Before the month was out, France's armies had been sent reeling into retreat. A British expeditionary force of 350,000 troops, which had been rushed to France to help, was pushed back to the French port of Dunkirk on the English Channel. Hundreds upon hundreds of vessels — some simply pleasure craft manned by civilians — slipped across the Channel under the protection of the Royal Air Force to rescue the beleaguered troops. By June 4, the troops had been evacuated in one of the memorable actions of British naval history.

Within a few weeks of the Dunkirk evacuation, France had signed an armistice with Hitler, yielding half the country to German occupation forces. The rest of France would be run from Vichy (VEE-she) by a French government under Marshal Henri Philippe Pétain, who was willing to obey Hitler's orders.

On June 10, just before the French laid down their arms, Italy declared war on France. Roosevelt was infuriated. He said of Italy's action, "The hand that held the dagger has struck it into the back of its neighbor."

The United States aids Great Britain. More and more, Americans were beginning to understand the Fascist threat. A widely re-

After German armies swept into northern France in 1940, the British expeditionary force and other Allied soldiers were evacuated from the port of Dunkirk.

Report from London

In September, 1940, Hitler ordered the German air force to concentrate its attacks on the city of London. Hoping to break the morale of the British people, German bombers unmercifully pounded Britain's capital city. In radio broadcasts to the United States, an American commentator, Edward R. Murrow, reported on the German raids.

Edward R. Murrow

> This is London at 3:30 in the morning. This has been what might be called a "routine night" — air-raid alarm at about nine o'clock and intermittent bombing ever since. I had the impression that more high explosives and less incendiaries [fire bombs] have been used tonight. Only two small fires can be seen on the horizon. Again the Germans have been sending in their bombers singly or in pairs. The anti-aircraft barrage has been fierce, but sometimes there have been periods of twenty minutes when London has been silent. Then the big red buses would start up and move on till the guns started working again.
>
> That silence is almost hard to bear. One becomes accustomed to rattling windows and the distant sound of bombs, then there comes a silence that can be felt. You know the sound will return, you wait, and then it starts again. That waiting is bad. It gives you a chance to imagine things.
>
> I have been walking tonight — there is a full moon, and the dirty-grey buildings appear white. The stars, the empty windows, are hidden. It's a beautiful and lonesome city where men and women and children are trying to snatch a few hours' sleep underground [in bomb shelters].

spected journalist, Walter Lippmann, cautioned that the United States must prepare for the worst: "Before the snow flies again, we may stand alone and isolated, the last great democracy on earth."

Hitler now was menacing Great Britain. In May, 1940, Winston Churchill had become prime minister. Churchill had vehemently opposed his nation's appeasement policies. Now he had finally been called to power. He promised the British people only "blood, tears, toil, and sweat" as they made ready for the expected German onslaught.

As the summer of 1940 drew on, the British Isles were subjected to a daily pounding by Nazi bombers. The Battle of Britain was under way. Opinion polls now showed that more than half of all Americans were willing to aid Britain, even at the risk of war. Roosevelt released planes and arms and ammunition for use by the British. The public was unprepared, however, for the boldness of the President's announcement on September 3, 1940. Roosevelt reported that he had concluded a deal with Great Britain, swapping 50 over-age destroyers for 99-year leases on air and naval bases in Bermuda, Newfoundland, and the Caribbean. The British needed the destroyers — small, speedy vessels — to fight off German submarines and keep open the shipping lanes to the United States. The

United States required the bases to strengthen the defenses of the Western Hemisphere.

Roosevelt called the destroyer deal the most important contribution to the national defense since the Louisiana Purchase. Many Republicans, while applauding the arrangement, were distressed that the President had made it through an executive agreement,[1] rather than by a treaty. Clearly, neutrality was ended.

The United States strengthens its defenses. In September, 1940, Congress passed a Selective Service Act. It created the first peacetime draft of men in American history, calling for the registration of all males between the ages of 21 and 35. The draftees would be subject to one year's military training, but they were not liable for service outside the Western Hemisphere.

As a result of the draft, the military services, which had fewer than 500,000 men in uniform in 1940, had 1,800,000 by the end of 1941. Congress, more and more responsive to the President's view of the dangers to America, increased its appropriations for military defense from $1.7 billion in 1940 to over $6 billion the following year.

The United States was linking its fate to that of other democracies standing against aggression. But how far would the United States go? Roosevelt had an answer for the American people: "I have said this before, but I shall say it again and again and again. Your boys are not going to be sent into any foreign wars." Previously, Roosevelt had always added "except in case of attack." He explained the omission: "If we're attacked, it's no longer a foreign war."

Roosevelt wins a third term. At this juncture the American people were preparing to vote in the 1940 presidential election. Roosevelt had for a time been uncertain whether or not he should seek a third term. Everything, he stated, cried out to him to go back to his home on the Hudson. Then, in May — as France was on the verge of surrender — he announced that he would run again. By so doing, Roosevelt was breaking the tradition established by George Washington that a President serve no more than two terms. Renominated at the Democratic convention in Chicago, Roosevelt dropped Vice President Garner from his ticket and replaced him with Henry A. Wallace, the Secretary of Agriculture and an ardent New Dealer.

The Republicans nominated Wendell L. Willkie, formerly of Indiana and now a Wall Street lawyer. A powerfully built man with tousled hair, he appealed to Americans as a person without pretense. He made his main campaign issue Roosevelt's quest for a third term. A typical Republican campaign button read: "I'm against the third term. Washington wouldn't. Grant couldn't. Roosevelt shouldn't." On international affairs, however, Willkie and the President saw eye to eye. Like Roosevelt, Willkie favored all possible aid to Britain — short of joining in the fighting.

Clearly the outcome of the election would be influenced by the course of the war. A Republican member of the House put it this way: "Franklin Roosevelt is not running against Wendell Willkie. He's running against Adolf Hitler."

The public followed the news from Europe with growing alarm. An invasion of the British Isles seemed next on the Nazis' timetable. As the German air assaults over Britain grew more intense, opinion polls showed the President's popularity rising. Roosevelt, not Willkie, would know what to do if the situation grew even grimmer, people seemed to be saying.

On Election Day, 1940, Roosevelt won easily. He received over 27 million votes compared to somewhat more than 22 million for Willkie. The triumph in the electoral college was overpowering: 449 votes to 82. Willkie had carried only ten states. Nevertheless, the popular vote was the closest in a presidential election since 1916.

The Lend-Lease Act is passed. Soon after the election, the President received a momentous letter from Churchill. The prime minister informed Roosevelt that Britain

---

[1] Executive agreements do not require the approval of the Senate. They do not bind future Chief Executives, who may or may not choose to keep them in force.

had virtually run out of cash. Soon the British would no longer be able to buy munitions in the United States and thus would be unable to conduct offensive operations against the Nazi forces. Roosevelt's response was quick. The United States, he said, would lend or lease to Great Britain the equipment and supplies required to make "our common cause" succeed. "We must be the great arsenal of democracy," the President told the nation.

The Lend-Lease Act, introduced in Congress early in 1941, was passed after extensive debate. Under this law the President was granted the authority to rent, sell, exchange, lease, or even give war materials to any country whose security he regarded as necessary to America's defense. Roosevelt explained that goods lent would be returned or replaced at the end of the war — in the way a neighbor returns a hose borrowed to put out a fire. Congress appropriated $7 billion to carry out the law's intent.

The United States moves closer to war. Shortly after the Lend-Lease bill passed, Roosevelt said, "Ours is not a partial effort. It is a total effort. . . . Our country is going to play its full part." In order to guarantee the safe delivery of aid to Britain, the United States started providing naval convoys to escort merchant ships. Meanwhile, American troops began setting up air and naval bases in Greenland in April, 1941. Then, in May the President proclaimed a state of "unlimited national emergency," putting into operation some 99 laws giving him broad special powers. Included was the power to repel "acts or threats of aggression directed against any part of the Western Hemisphere." In July, American troops landed on Iceland to prevent that island from being occupied by German forces.

Germany's attention, at that time, was riveted elsewhere. In June, 1941, despite the nonaggression pact signed by the two countries less than two years earlier, Germany had suddenly invaded the Soviet Union. Hitler explained to his generals his startling decision to turn on his ally: "We have the chance to smash Russia while our own back is free. That chance will not come

Following passage of the Lend-Lease Act in 1941, the United States began providing the Allies with arms, munitions, and equipment. Here, lend-lease supplies are loaded for shipment to Europe.

again soon." He was confident he would defeat the Russians in two or three months, thus making Germany master of the European continent. Then he would dispose of Britain and be ready to take on the United States.

For many Americans, Hitler had already stated the issue clearly: "Two worlds are in conflict; one of these worlds must break asunder." Roosevelt, profoundly worried over what might lie ahead, called upon Americans in early 1941 to heed the fate of the nations the Nazis had conquered. The lesson to be learned was simple: "It would be suicide to wait until they are in our front yard." Then he added, "Our Bunker Hill of tomorrow may be several thousand miles from Boston."

SECTION REVIEW

1. (a) What effect did Germany's invasion of Poland have on Britain and France? (b) How did the United States react?
2. (a) What European countries did Germany conquer in 1940? (b) How did the United States help Great Britain?
3. (a) What was the main campaign issue in the presidential election of 1940? (b) What was the result of that election?
4. (a) What was the Lend-Lease Act? (b) How did the United States move closer to war?

Chapter 10 Review

Summary

As a consequence of the First World War, the United States was owed large sums of money, especially by Great Britain and France. The British and French counted on reparations from Germany to help pay their war debts, but a severe economic crisis in Germany caused this scheme to fail. During the 1920's, the United States devised plans to help Germany pay its reparations. The economic collapse of 1929, however, frustrated efforts to collect either the reparations or the war debts.

Throughout the 1920's, American Presidents concerned themselves with creating a system of worldwide collective security. Disarmament conferences, held in Washington in 1921 and in London in 1930, limited the number of warships built by the major world powers. In 1928 the United States, France, and twelve other nations signed the Kellogg-Briand Pact, which outlawed war as an instrument of national policy.

After the First World War, efforts were made by the United States to improve relations with Mexico and the nations of Central and South America. The Clark Memorandum, made public in 1930, declared that the Monroe Doctrine did not give the United States the right to interfere in the internal affairs of its neighbors.

Overseas possessions were a new responsibility for the United States and required special attention. Supervision of these territories was divided among the Departments of Navy, War, and the Interior. Various plans were devised to help prepare the territories for statehood, self-government, or independence.

In the 1920's and 1930's totalitarian governments took control of Italy and Germany, creating a dangerous situation in Europe. In Asia, meanwhile, Japan became an aggressive military power. Following Italy's invasion of Ethiopia in 1935, President Roosevelt issued the first Neutrality Act, forbidding the sale of arms or the granting of loans to warring nations. In 1936 world tension increased as civil war broke out in Spain, as Germany occupied the Rhineland, and as Japan resumed its attacks on China.

After 1937, as war in Europe seemed more likely, the United States moved away from a policy of strict neutrality. Once war had broken out in September, 1939, Congress permitted the sale of war supplies to Britain and France.

By the summer of 1940, most of Europe had fallen to Germany. Expecting the worst, the United States increased its aid to Britain, and President Roosevelt ordered the strengthening of American military forces.

Vocabulary and Important Terms

1. Hawley-Smoot Tariff
2. collective security
3. disarmament
4. Washington Conference
5. Kellogg-Briand Pact
6. Clark Memorandum
7. Insular Cases
8. Platt Amendment
9. Stimson Doctrine
10. commonwealth
11. totalitarian
12. isolationist
13. Axis alliance
14. appeasement
15. Good Neighbor Policy
16. Battle of Britain
17. Selective Service Act
18. Lend-Lease Act

Discussion Questions

1. (a) Why did American efforts to collect war debts after World War I cause resentment in Europe? (b) Why was United States tariff policy another source of friction?
2. (a) To what extent was the United States willing to cooperate with the League of Nations? (b) What role did the United States play in the disarmament movement? (c) What role did it play in the quest for world peace?
3. (a) Why did the United States deliberately prepare its major possessions for independence? (b) Which possession became independent, and under what circumstances did it gain its independence? (c) Which possessions remained under United States control?
4. (a) What nations threatened world peace in the 1930's? (b) What expansionist activities did they carry out?
5. (a) Why did many Americans in the 1920's and 1930's want the United States to keep out of foreign entanglements? (b) What effect did isolationist sentiment have on the actions of the Roosevelt administration?
6. (a) What were the provisions of the neutrality acts of 1935 and 1937? (b) What effect did those acts have on the ability of the Roosevelt administration to restrain the aggressor nations? Explain your answer.
7. (a) In what ways did President Roosevelt try to move the United States away from isolationism and neutrality? (b) What effect did the outbreak of war in Europe have on American foreign policy?

8. (a) By 1941 what was the relationship of the United States to its Latin American neighbors? (b) To Great Britain? (c) To Germany and Japan?

Relating Past to Present

1. In the period between the two world wars, the United States sought to improve relations with Latin America through the Good Neighbor policy. What is the state of relations between the United States and Latin America today?
2. Are there Americans today who believe the United States should isolate itself from involvement in world affairs? What arguments for isolationism might be offered today? What might be the arguments against isolationism?
3. After the First World War the United States tried to collect the money it had lent its wartime allies, thereby causing resentment in Europe. Find out what countries owe the United States money today and the circumstances under which they contracted their debts. Should the United States insist on the repayment of those debts? Explain your answer.

Studying Local History

Choose one of the following world events: Mussolini's invasion of Ethiopia; Hitler's takeover of Austria; the Munich conference; the Dunkirk evacuation; or the Battle of Britain. Then do research to find out how newspapers in your state or community covered the event.

Using History Skills

1. *Reading source material.* Study Edward R. Murrow's description of the German attack on London on page 279. (a) What, according to Murrow, was a "routine night"? (b) What defense did the British have against the air attacks? (c) Suppose you were in the United States listening to Murrow's broadcast. What words would you use to describe the people of London? Explain your answer.
2. *Placing events in time.* Look back through the chapter and find five important events that led to the outbreak of World War II. Make a time line showing those events.

WORLD SCENE

New Tools of War

From 1919 to 1939, military theorists analyzed the new weaponry that had been introduced in the First World War. They focused on the airplane and the tank in contemplating future battlefield tactics.

Air power. One of the first to write about the potential of air power in warfare was an Italian army officer named Giulio Douhet. In a book published in 1921, Douhet described how the airplane could be used to break enemy morale. He argued that if a nation took control of the air at the outbreak of war and attacked enemy cities, factories, and military installations, a quick victory would be assured.

Another advocate of air power was an American general named Billy Mitchell. As commander of United States aircraft in the First World War, Mitchell knew how potent a weapon the airplane could be. He pleaded with the War Department and with members of Congress to allocate funds for a large independent air force. When his recommendations fell on deaf ears, he publicly criticized the nation's military leaders. Charged with insubordination, he was court-martialed and suspended from the army.

Tank warfare. The British introduced tanks during the First World War. Difficult to maneuver and extremely slow-moving, these early armored vehicles were the cause of much debate.

In the 1920's two British military experts — J. F. C. Fuller and B. H. Liddell Hart — made startling predictions about the use of tanks on the battlefield. They believed that massed armored units could be used to penetrate enemy lines and then push rapidly forward. The confusion that the tanks would create among the enemy would allow the infantry to move in to do its work.

Despite those arguments, the British government paid little attention to developing tank warfare. The German army, on the other hand, took keen interest in the writings of Fuller and Liddell Hart. General Heinz Guderian, commander of Germany's tank corps, studied the idea of massed armored units. Guderian emphasized that "not a drizzle, but a downpour" of tanks was needed to invade enemy territory and create terror among the populace. Beginning in 1939, Germany combined this tactic with the use of air power to seize control of much of Europe.

Global War

1941 – 1945

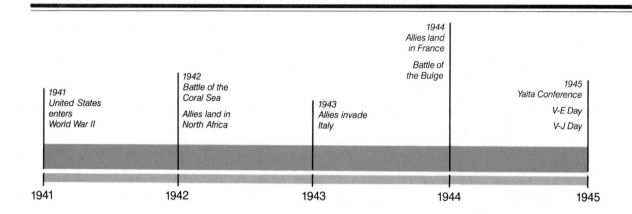

					1944 *Allies land in France* *Battle of the Bulge*	

1941
United States
enters
World War II

1942
Battle of the
Coral Sea

Allies land in
North Africa

1943
Allies invade
Italy

1945
Yalta Conference

V-E Day

V-J Day

1941   1942   1943   1944   1945

CHAPTER OUTLINE

1. The United States enters the war.

2. The United States mobilizes for war.

3. The Allies win the war in Europe.

4. The war in the Pacific is won.

In August, 1941, President Roosevelt and Prime Minister Churchill met aboard the British battleship *Prince of Wales* off the coast of Newfoundland. The two men recognized the symbolic importance of their meeting. Each wanted the world to know that the English-speaking nations would stand shoulder to shoulder against the enemy who meant to destroy them.

Roosevelt was the senior partner in the close friendship that existed between the two leaders. Churchill had admired Roosevelt for many years. He deferred to the President because Roosevelt had been in office longer than he, and because the United States was much more powerful than Great Britain. Roosevelt, for his part, admired Churchill's eloquence and determination. He once wrote his friend, "It is fun to be in the same decade with you." The relationship between the two men led to a degree of military cooperation unparalleled in modern history.

Out of the discussions held on shipboard came a statement of principles, known as the Atlantic Charter, on which the two nations rested their hopes for the future. The principles included the right of all people to self-government; economic cooperation among all nations; free access of all nations to trade and raw materials; freedom of the seas; and an abandonment of the use of force in settling international disputes. A world shaped by the attainment of such goals, however, was only a distant dream in August, 1941.

1 The United States Enters the War

One weighty question hung in the air in August, 1941. Would the United States extend more than moral and financial support to the Allies? Most Americans opposed the commitment of United States troops, although many people feared that the chances of staying out of the fighting were slim.

Relations with Japan deteriorate. Germany, policy-makers assumed, would likely provide the occasion for American entry into the war. Still, Japan's behavior was a constant concern. Japan's decision to join the Axis in 1940 (page 274) had left no doubt that the Land of the Rising Sun was solidly in the camp of the aggressors. Japan continued to fight in China, while the United States stepped up its aid to the forces of Chiang Kai-shek. At the same time, Japan sought to take advantage of the situation in Europe by seizing French, British, and Dutch possessions in Asia.

In July, 1941, Japanese troops occupied French Indochina. Alarmed by this move, and fearing that the Japanese intended further aggression to the south, Roosevelt froze Japanese assets in the United States and placed an embargo on oil, steel, and other essential war supplies that American firms had been selling to Japan. He then issued a stern warning to the Japanese: if they seized any more territory, the United States would take "any and all steps" necessary to protect its national interests.

At a shipboard meeting off the coast of Newfoundland in August, 1941, President Roosevelt and Prime Minister Churchill drew up the historic Atlantic Charter.

Japan began to make plans to attack Pacific possessions of the United States, Great Britain, and the Netherlands, but in the meantime it continued to take part in peace negotiations. In November, 1941, the Japanese government sent a special ambassador, Saburo Kurusu, to Washington, D.C., to assist in talks with the Americans, which had been going on since early in the year. The Japanese were demanding that the United States recognize Japanese conquests in China and Indochina, stop aid to China, unfreeze Japanese assets, and supply Japan with oil. The United States, in turn, was demanding that Japan withdraw from China and Indochina, recognize the Nationalist regime of Chiang Kai-shek as the only government of China, and sign a nonaggression pact with other Pacific nations. Although the Japanese rejected these proposals, they demanded that the negotiations be continued. The chief American negotiator, Secretary of State Cordell Hull, told Secretary of War Henry L. Stimson late in November, "I have washed my hands of [the Japanese situation], and it is now in the hands of . . . the Army and Navy."

Hull was pessimistic because he had special information. American intelligence agents had broken the Japanese code and knew, from the radio messages being exchanged among Japanese diplomats around the world, that the Japanese were planning something. What that plan was, however, the Americans did not know. They knew only that the Japanese negotiators had received word from Tokyo that if no settlement was reached by November 29, "things are automatically going to happen." The United States was not aware that, on November 25, a Japanese fleet had left home waters on a deadly mission to Hawaii.

Pearl Harbor, shown in this photograph before the Japanese attack, was the home base of America's Pacific fleet.

Roosevelt's War Message to Congress (1941)

Yesterday, December 7, 1941 — a date which will live in infamy — the United States was suddenly and deliberately attacked by naval and air forces of the Empire of Japan. . . .

The attack yesterday on the Hawaiian Islands has caused severe damage to American naval and military forces. Very many American lives have been lost. In addition American ships have been reported torpedoed on the high seas between San Francisco and Honolulu.

Yesterday the Japanese Government also launched an attack against Malaya. Last night Japanese forces attacked Hong Kong. Last night Japanese forces attacked Guam. Last night Japanese forces attacked the Philippine Islands. Last night the Japanese attacked Wake Island. This morning the Japanese attacked Midway Island.

Japan has, therefore, undertaken a surprise offensive extending throughout the Pacific area. The facts of yesterday speak for themselves. The people of the United States have already formed their opinion and well understand the implications to the very life and safety of our nation.

As Commander-in-Chief of the Army and Navy, I have directed that all measures be taken for our defense. . . .

No matter how long it may take us to overcome this premeditated invasion, the American people in their righteous might will win through to absolute victory. . . .

I ask that the Congress declare that since the unprovoked and dastardly attack by Japan on Sunday, December seventh, a state of war has existed between the United States and the Japanese Empire.

War comes at Pearl Harbor. Japanese naval officers had long considered the possibility of one day attacking the powerful American naval base at Pearl Harbor in Hawaii. Always the idea had been discarded as impossible. Admiral Isoroku Yamamoto, however, believed that such an attack could deal a fatal blow to American power in the Pacific. In December, 1940, he began to plan in earnest. Yamamoto possessed, said a close colleague, "a gambler's heart."

On December 7, 1941, a clear Sunday morning, a wave of 183 Japanese dive-bombers zoomed in to strike Pearl Harbor. The American fleet was riding at anchor along Battleship Row, the ships lined up like ducks on a pond. The surprise was complete. A bomb pierced the armor of the *Arizona*, setting afire its powder magazine, which exploded with such force that the vessel split in two and settled into the deep. In all, eight battleships were sunk or badly damaged, and eleven other vessels were put out of action. An eyewitness later said, "It was awful, for great ships were dying before my eyes! Strangely enough, at first I didn't realize that men were dying too." More than 2,300 Americans were killed; almost 1,200 others were wounded.

In Washington, D.C., it was 1:50 P.M. when the first news arrived from Hawaii: AIR RAID PEARL HARBOR. THIS IS NO DRILL. Reading it, Secretary of the Navy Knox exclaimed, "This can't be true; they must mean the Philippines!" American leaders could hardly bring themselves to believe that the Japanese had outfoxed them in this way. In any case, the wrangling and uncertainty in the United States were now over. The nation was united as never before.

On December 8, the President asked Congress to recognize that a state of war existed between the United States and Japan. Roosevelt, who had a keen sense of history, had invited Mrs. Woodrow Wilson to be present in the hushed House chamber where he spoke. Calling December 7 "a date which will live in infamy," he calmly promised to avenge Pearl Harbor. "Always," he said, "will we remember the character of the onslaught against us. No matter how long it may take . . . , the American people in their righteous might will win through to absolute victory." The approval of the President's proposal was one vote short of unanimous. The single no vote was cast by Representative Jeannette Rankin of Montana, who had also voted against United States entry into the First World War in 1917. The first woman to serve in Congress, she said that on principle *someone* ought to vote no, and that it ought to be a woman.

Germany and Italy declare war on the United States. Hitler was not obliged under the Tripartite Pact (page 274) to assist Japan now that it had made war. Yet on December 11, he declared war on the United States. Why?

Hitler may have decided he had had great good luck, that the United States would be tied up in the Pacific so thoroughly that it could not be further involved in the war in Europe. Possibly he also had a romantic view of how his country ought to behave in the embarrassing situation Japan had created. At any rate, he declared his country to be at war with the United States. "A great power like Germany declares war itself," he said, "and does not wait for war to be declared on it." That same day Italy, too, declared war on the United States. The United States thus found itself arrayed against the Axis powers on the side of Great Britain, China, and the Soviet Union, who were known as the Allies.[1]

The war in Europe takes priority. The Roosevelt administration had already decided that if war came the United States would concentrate on defeating Germany. Many Americans were upset when the administration went ahead with a "Europe-

---

[1]By the end of the war the Allies numbered 49 nations.

first" strategy. They were more eager to strike back at the Japanese than to defeat the Germans and Italians. Still, most people could see that the more immediate danger was in Europe.

Japanese aggression continues. Despite the decision to give priority to the struggle in Europe, the United States was not idle in the Pacific, and the fighting there was intense. The Japanese boasted of having reduced the United States to the status of a third-rate power. The statement was absurd, but the damage to American naval and air power in the Pacific had been substantial. The Japanese took quick advantage of their success not only in knocking out the battle fleet at Pearl Harbor and most of America's heavy bombers at Manila, the Philippine capital, but also in wrecking the British battle squadron at Singapore. Before the end of December, 1941, Japan had captured Guam, Wake Island, and the British colony of Hong Kong. In February, Japanese forces overran the Malay Peninsula and the British naval base at Singapore. By the end of March the Dutch East Indies were also in Japanese hands. Meanwhile, a battle was being fought for possession of the Philippine Islands.

The Philippines are conquered. In January, 1942, Japanese forces occupied Manila. American and Filipino troops, under the command of General Douglas MacArthur, withdrew to the Bataan Peninsula. There, against overwhelming odds, they continued to fight, hoping to hold out until reinforcements could arrive. Lacking air and sea support, and with no help forthcoming, the defenders surrendered in April. A remnant of the forces escaped to the nearby island of Corregidor. Now under the command of General Jonathan Wainwright, they, too, surrendered — on May 6. General MacArthur, who had been evacuated by submarine to Australia in February, declared solemnly upon his arrival, "I came through and I shall return."

The Japanese forced the defeated garrison of Americans and Filipinos to march 85 miles to board a train for internment in a prisoner-of-war camp. The overland journey proved to be a death march for thousands of the men. They were beaten, starved, and tortured by their captors. As word drifted back to America of this episode, Americans resolved that they would have revenge. MacArthur's words, "I shall return," became a battle cry, a pledge the United States intended to redeem.

American forces achieve victories in the Pacific. In the spring of 1942 — the low point of American fortunes, as it turned out — many people believed that Australia, too, would soon fall to the enemy. Two American victories at sea, however, encouraged the Allies. The surviving American fleet in the Pacific was under the command of Admiral Chester W. Nimitz. On May 7 and 8, 1942, immediately following the surrender of Corregidor, the United States Navy battered a Japanese force heading for New Guinea, thus ending the immediate threat to Australia. This encounter, known as the Battle of the Coral Sea, was the first instance in which the Allies had succeeded in blocking Japan's lightning-like progress.

The following month, American naval forces again won a mighty victory, this time at the Battle of Midway. The encounter was a turning point in the war because it ended the possibility of a Japanese occupation of Hawaii.

These victories, combined with the first American air raid on Tokyo and other Japanese cities in April, 1942, lifted American spirits. The situation, nevertheless, remained grim. By May, 1942, six months after Pearl Harbor, the Japanese had under their flag an area extending eastward to the Aleutian Islands, south almost to Australia, and west to the borders of India (map, page 306). To root the enemy out of their strongpoints would require savage fighting, some of it hand-to-hand. Furthermore, much of the fighting would take place on almost impenetrable jungle terrain, or on bleak coral or volcanic islands that provided no natural shelter or means of concealment.

The Japanese advance is halted at Guadalcanal. The Japanese, bent on controlling the South Pacific, began building an air base on Guadalcanal (one of the Solomon Islands) in

The scene of heavy fighting, Guadalcanal was freed from Japanese occupation early in 1943. Here, Japanese ships burn following an American air strike.

July, 1942. Such an installation could be used for attacks on New Guinea and Australia and could block efforts to retake the Philippines. Consequently, 20,000 American troops were sent to seize the island in early August. At heavy cost, they finally cleared Guadalcanal of the enemy in February, 1943. The hard-earned victory brought a halt at last to the relentless southward advance of the Japanese. Victory over Japan, however, was still far in the future.

Submarine warfare is checked. From the start, the European theater of war was better supplied with both personnel and equipment than the Pacific theater. The first year after Pearl Harbor, however, was a bleak one for the Allies in Europe.

During much of 1942, the center of the American effort was in the North Atlantic, where the Nazis were trying to prevent convoys carrying war supplies from reaching Britain and the Soviet Union. The Germans had discovered that they could increase the effectiveness of their submarines by sending them out in groups, or, as they called them, "wolf packs." The wolf packs, usually consisting of ten U-boats, would circle a convoy and strike it simultaneously — often at night.

Gradually, the Allies found ways to counter the wolf packs. Air patrols and improved detection devices helped the navy find its targets. In addition, army bombers, operating out of Britain, kept the main German submarine base at St. Nazaire, France, under steady attack. In September, 1943, the Allies announced that ninety U-boats had been sunk in as many days. By then the Germans had lost their most experienced submariners, and morale in the service was low. The United States, moreover, was now building merchant ships faster than the U-boats could sink them. The Battle of the Atlantic had been won. Allied troops and supplies could flow to Europe unhindered.

The Russians stop the German advance. Meanwhile, the Germans were finding themselves bogged down in Russia. The invasion of the Soviet Union (page 281) at first went well for the Nazis. So confident was Hitler of a quick victory that his troops had not even been supplied with winter uniforms. Within four months, the German army took a million prisoners and forced the Russians to draw back toward Moscow. Soon, however, Hitler had immense problems. First, his troops were deep inside the Soviet Union when the fierce Russian winter set in, making supply and communication more difficult. Second, the Soviet "scorched-earth" policy — a policy of destroying the resources of the country as the Red Army retreated — made it impossible for the Nazis to live off the land.

At Moscow and Leningrad the Russians made a stand during the winter of 1941–1942. Not only did they prevent the Germans from capturing those cities, but they managed to gain back nearly a quarter of the territory they had lost. When warm weather returned, however, so did the Nazis' determination to conquer Russia. In the summer of 1942, the Germans launched an offensive that won control of the oil fields of the Caucasus and reached the city of Stalingrad on the Volga River.

At Stalingrad the Russians broke the back of the Nazi invasion. For three months the besieged defenders fought the Germans street by street, house by house, and even room by room, for control of the city. Finally, in November, help arrived. Russian reinforcements surrounded the Germans and cut off their supply routes. At the beginning of February, 1943, the battered, frozen, starving, and demoralized German troops surrendered — about 94,000 of them, including 24 generals. Hitler's Russian campaign was in ruins.

The Axis powers threaten Egypt. At the same time that the fighting at Guadalcanal and the Battle of the Atlantic were taking place, the Allies faced another critical struggle — this time in Africa. German and Italian forces, led by General Erwin Rommel, a hero of the Nazi conquest of France, occupied much of northern Africa, from Tunisia to the Egyptian border. The Axis strength there presented a threat to the Suez Canal, Britain's "lifeline" to the oil fields of the Middle East and to India.

After invading the Soviet Union in June, 1941, the Germans at first had great victories. Their advance ground to a halt at Stalingrad, where Russian soldiers and civilians put up a heroic defense of the city.

In May, 1942, the astute Rommel, nicknamed "the Desert Fox," began an offensive to take Egypt. Pushing back British troops, the Axis forces were within seventy miles of the ancient city of Alexandria by July. Mussolini, sure of the outcome, had already shipped his favorite white horse to Africa to be ready for a victory parade through Cairo, the Egyptian capital. Then, at El Alamein, a village on the Mediterranean Sea in northern Egypt, British troops under General Bernard Law Montgomery powerfully rallied and stopped Rommel's advance. To save his forces, Rommel pulled back to Tunisia in one of the longest retreats in history.

The Soviet Union, meanwhile, was pressing the United States and Britain to open a second front against the Germans in France in order to relieve the pressure on Soviet forces in Eastern Europe. Stalin, distressed over the heavy casualties his troops were taking, charged angrily that the United States and Great Britain were delaying an invasion of Europe. Stalin did not seem to recall that in 1940 when the British were fighting the Nazis in France, and also desperately needing help (page 279), he had been an ally of Hitler!

Churchill argued that the Allies did not yet have the strength to retake France. He urged, instead, an invasion of North Africa to secure the Suez Canal and reopen the Mediterranean to Allied shipping. Roosevelt found Churchill's arguments persuasive, and it was decided that American and British forces would join together in driving the Axis out of Africa.

Allied forces triumph in Africa. On November 8, 1942, American and British units under General Dwight D. Eisenhower made landings in the French colonies of Morocco and Algeria. The Vichy French government in North Africa, supposedly obedient to Germany, offered only token resistance and soon surrendered to Eisenhower.

"Ike," as he had been known at West Point, had recently been named commander

Erwin Rommel, shown here during the North African campaign, was one of Germany's most brilliant generals. Later implicated in a plot to kill Hitler, Rommel chose to commit suicide rather than face certain execution.

of all United States forces in Europe. Born in Texas and reared in Kansas, Eisenhower had an open manner and an infectious grin. A descendant of Germans who had settled in Pennsylvania in the 1730's, he was raised to respect pacifism. For some years he had served on the staff of General MacArthur in the Philippines. By the time of the attack on Pearl Harbor, General George C. Marshall, the Chief of Staff, had already identified Eisenhower as deserving of a high command.

The men of Rommel's famed Afrika Korps put up tremendous resistance, but they were doomed to failure. Cut off from their supply lines by Allied sea and air power, they were caught between the advancing armies of Eisenhower from the west and those of Montgomery from the east. On May 12, 1943, after seven months of intense fighting, the last of Rommel's forces laid down their arms. The 55,000 men who surrendered that day in Tunisia were some of the enemy's best fighting men. By their defeat the Axis had lost control of North Africa and the Mediterranean. Now what Winston Churchill termed "the soft underbelly of Europe" lay open to an Allied attack.

SECTION REVIEW

1. (a) What steps taken by Japan in 1940–1941 alarmed the United States? (b) What demands did the United States and Japan make on each other? (c) What action brought the United States into World War II?
2. (a) What attacks did Japan make following United States entry into the war? (b) What was the significance of the Allied victories in the Coral Sea, off Midway, and at Guadalcanal?
3. How did the Allies check German submarine warfare?
4. How were the Russians able to stop the German invasion?
5. (a) What threat did the Axis pose in North Africa? (b) How did the British and Americans defeat the Axis in that region?

2 The United States Mobilizes for War

In the United States people had closed ranks after the attack on Pearl Harbor. Now that war had come, said Charles A. Lindbergh, a former isolationist critic of the President's views on foreign policy, "we must meet it as united Americans regardless of our attitude in the past. . . . "

Fifteen million people serve in the armed forces. American military forces were vastly expanded immediately following the attack on Pearl Harbor. The mustering of troops from civilian ranks, an American tradition, depended on the Selective Service System. The draft was administered by local boards under the supervision of Major General Lewis B. Hershey. Most of the draftees were single men under the age of 30, but all men between the ages of 18 and 45 were eligible for military service, and all men between 18 and 64 were required to register with their draft boards. About ten million men were drafted in the course of the war. Five million other Americans — men and women alike — volunteered to serve.[2]

For the first time the armed forces established women's branches. Women volunteered for military service so that men would be free to go to the front. Over a quarter of a million women served the country in uniform as ambulance drivers, mechanics, pilots, radio operators, clerical workers — as everything but actual combatants. Many other women served in the armed forces as nurses.

United States industry gears up for war. In January, 1942, President Roosevelt created the War Production Board to mobilize the economy. The Board supervised American industry to ensure that the country would meet the needs of the Allied troops. The en-

tire automobile industry, for example, switched to the production of tanks, airplanes, trucks, and other military vehicles. Other industries made similar changeovers. The Board decided on the distribution of government contracts and on the allocation of scarce resources. Certain consumer goods, such as new automobiles, became unavailable. Other goods were in short supply — including sugar, coffee, meat, gasoline, fats and oils, butter, cheese, and shoes — and were rationed by means of stamps distributed through local rationing boards.

The government demands sacrifices from the American people. Taxes were heavy during the war years. By 1945, 42 million citizens were subject to income taxes — ten times the number that had been required to pay them in 1939. In order to ensure that these taxes were collected, the government introduced the practice of withholding income taxes. Employers were required, under this plan, to deduct employees' taxes from their paychecks and turn the money over directly to the government. Still, only 40 percent of the cost of the war was met by taxation. The remainder was raised by heavy borrowing. As a result, between 1941 and 1945 the national debt rose from $50 billion to $250 billion.

One way the government borrowed money was through the sale of war bonds. Millions of workers at home and soldiers in the field purchased bonds through a vigorously promoted payroll-deduction plan. Movies, for instance, invariably closed with "The End — Buy War Bonds." From 1941 to 1946 bond sales totaled over $61 billion.

Americans were also constantly urged to conserve resources. Doing little things helped many civilians to feel the pride of participating in the war effort. To save material, women wore straight skirts, instead of full or pleated ones. Families also planted "victory gardens" to help increase the available food. Communities contributed by collecting scrap metal of all kinds.

Shortages caused increases in the prices of most goods, and the government took

---

[2]The citizen-soldiers were quickly dubbed "GI's" — the initials standing for "government issue," an old phrase applied to equipment distributed by army supply depots.

The Home Front

During the Second World War, Ray Hartman was a student in Chicago. In this account, he remembers how his school helped the American war effort.

A war bond

Everybody was campaigning to sell war bonds. The school set a goal. They were selling stamps. Each kid would buy stamps and try to fill books to get an $18.75 bond. We were using our allowances and paper drives and whatever way we could to get money to purchase the stamps. In those days we were going around selling war stamps similar to the way children now sell chances on raffles. We'd go door-to-door and ask people to contribute dimes and quarters and fill up a book of stamps and buy the bonds.

The goal of the school, I believe, was somewhere in the $79,000 to $80,000 range, and we were told that this would be sufficient money to purchase a P–38 fighter plane. We reached the goal. I was the student chairman of the drive, and after probably eight or nine months of work, we were successful, and there was a P–38 named after the school. Alphonsus was the name of the school, and they named the plane "The Spirit of Saint Al's." We went to the Douglas Aircraft Company where they painted the name on the plane, more or less christened it, and took pictures. I was thrilled, being the chairman of the student drive. I did the ribbon cutting or something like that. We received a letter of commendation from a general for the school.

---

measures to control inflation. The Office of Price Administration — the OPA — was established early in the war to keep a lid on the prices of a large number of commodities. Ceilings were also placed on rents. These controls did not eliminate inflation, but they kept it from reaching disastrous levels. In late 1942 the Wage Stabilization Act empowered the government to control wages.

For the most part, Americans accepted these sacrifices without grumbling, remembering the men at the front and the stakes for which they were fighting. Gradually, people realized that the war was disposing of a long-standing problem. As factories geared up for maximum production — many working around the clock — the unemployment that had plagued the country for a decade disappeared. Farm production rose too, and farmers' incomes almost doubled. The Great Depression had ended at last.

Japanese Americans are interned. A blot on the country's record during the war was its treatment of Americans of Japanese ancestry. After the attack on Pearl Harbor, many people feared that there might be some Japanese Americans — perhaps many — whose loyalty lay with Japan rather than the United States. People on the West Coast, which was regarded as a potential target of Japanese invasion, were especially alarmed at the prospect of sabotage. Although no such activity was ever discovered, the President was convinced that the Japanese Americans were a threat to the nation's security. In February, 1942, he authorized the forcible relocation of 100,000 people of Japanese ancestry, about two thirds of whom were American citizens. With little warning, these people had to leave their houses and businesses, suffering heavy financial losses. They were then moved to isolated camps and held there for the duration of the war.

Despite this harsh treatment, Japanese Americans remained loyal to the Allied cause. Not a single Japanese American was convicted of espionage. When given the opportunity to enlist in the armed forces, more than 1,200 of the interned men volunteered to fight for the United States. The 442nd Regimental Combat Team served valiantly in the campaign against Italy, along with another Japanese American unit from Hawaii.

Black Americans make advances during the war. The effect of the war on black Americans was felt even before Pearl Harbor. Black leaders had long pointed out the contradiction in opposing unjust governments abroad while tolerating racial discrimination and segregation at home. Many Americans were more and more troubled by this argument.

In 1941, before the United States entered the war, A. Philip Randolph, president of the Brotherhood of Sleeping Car Porters, threatened to lead a march on Washington, D.C., unless the President took steps to give black workers access to jobs in defense industries. As a result, Roosevelt issued an executive order forbidding racial discrimination by defense contractors. A Committee on Fair Employment Practices was also established. By the end of the war, the work of the Committee, helped by the general shortage of labor, had opened doors previously closed to black people.

In the armed forces, barriers to black advancement also began to break down. About one million black men and women were in uniform, serving in all branches of the military and in every campaign of the war. At the beginning, they served under white officers, but by the end of the war even the navy, which had traditionally taken blacks only as mess workers and porters, had started to commission black officers.

In the army the walls of discrimination came down somewhat faster. At the height of the war in 1944, black officers were being commissioned at the rate of about 200 a month. Benjamin O. Davis, whose military service had begun in the Spanish-American War, was promoted to Brigadier General in 1940 — the first black ever to hold that rank. His son, Colonel Benjamin O. Davis, Jr., who had graduated from West Point in 1936, commanded a black unit, the 332nd Fighter Group in Italy, which played a key role in the Mediterranean campaign. In the South Pacific an outstanding black unit was the 93rd Combat Division, which

Colonel Benjamin O. Davis, Jr., commanded a unit which destroyed over 200 enemy planes. Davis later became America's first black major general.

SAVE FREEDOM OF SPEECH

BUY WAR BONDS

LIFE IN AMERICA

The Arsenal of Democracy

Following the attack on Pearl Harbor, Americans worked day and night to provide needed war materials. Women filled vital jobs in defense factories, citizens bought bonds to finance the war effort, and drives were held to collect rubber.

saw heavy action beginning with the landings in the Solomon Islands in 1942.

Despite such progress, black soldiers fighting for their country still faced serious discrimination. Most units continued to be racially segregated. Most blacks, furthermore, remained in the lowest ranks, and in many parts of the nation black military personnel confronted strict social segregation in camp as well as in nearby towns.

Mexican Americans experience both opportunities and problems. Mexican Americans also benefited from the shortage of labor the war produced. Many industrial jobs in the American Southwest became available to Mexican Americans for the first time during the war. The need to step up food production to feed the army created new agricultural jobs as well.

Mexican Americans found, however, that these new opportunities created tension with the larger community. As they competed with other groups for housing and jobs, ill will often showed itself. In Los Angeles in 1943 resentment exploded as a brawl between servicemen and Mexican American youths touched off a week of rioting.

Many women enter the labor force. The war opened many new opportunities for American women too. Not only did women serve in the military for the first time, but they became an important part of the civilian labor force. Immediately after the attack on Pearl Harbor, women quickly moved into jobs as truck drivers, lumberjacks, welders, chemists, and mechanics. Without their contribution, the "arsenal of democracy" could not have performed the miracles of production needed to bring victory. By August, 1945, women constituted over a third of the labor force in the United States. About 18,000,000 women who had not previously worked now held jobs.

Roosevelt wins a fourth term. In the summer of 1944, as the fighting raged in Europe, Americans held their presidential nominating conventions as usual. Though ailing and tired, Roosevelt consented to run again — for an unprecedented fourth term. He was virtually unopposed within the Democratic Party. As his running mate, the party named Senator Harry S. Truman of Missouri. The Republicans nominated Thomas E. Dewey, the governor of New York, for President, and Governor John W. Bricker of Ohio for Vice President.

Not surprisingly, the war was the chief issue on the minds of the voters. Some Republicans privately condemned "Roosevelt's war" and whispered about the President's failing health. Dewey, however, confined himself to criticizing the administration's handling of military matters. In the end, people were convinced that this was no time to elect a President inexperienced in the management of foreign affairs. In November, Roosevelt was re-elected, winning 53 percent of the popular vote and 432 of the 531 votes in the electoral college. The drama of a democratic election held during wartime — the first such in the United States since 1864 — was an inspiration to people everywhere who loved freedom.

SECTION REVIEW

1. (a) How did the United States expand its armed forces following its entry into World War II? (b) By what means was industrial production mobilized?
2. (a) Why were Japanese Americans living in the West Coast interned during the war? (b) How did wartime conditions affect black Americans? (c) Mexican Americans? (d) American women?

3 The Allies Win the War in Europe

By the end of 1942, the terrifying successes of Germany and Japan had ceased, and the Allies were ready to go on the offensive.

Churchill and Roosevelt confer at Casablanca. In January, 1943, while the fighting for North Africa was still going on in Tunisia, Churchill and Roosevelt met at Casablanca, Morocco, to discuss their next moves. Stalin had been invited to attend but did not, to the annoyance of FDR and Churchill. No American President had ever before left the country during wartime, but Roosevelt was convinced that it was essential for him to see his commanders and troops. He was also fascinated by the idea of making a trip to places he had never before visited.[3]

---

[3]In traveling by airplane on this occasion, Roosevelt became the first Chief Executive to fly while in office. Nine years earlier Mrs. Roosevelt, visiting lands in the Caribbean, traveled by plane, the first wife of a President to do so.

The two English-speaking leaders reached conclusions on three crucial matters at their Casablanca meeting. First, they decided that as soon as the fighting in Africa had ended, the Allies would invade Italy. Second, the two leaders decided that it was time to send enough men and supplies to the Pacific to allow General MacArthur and Admiral Nimitz to launch an offensive against the Japanese. Third, and most important, they decided to accept nothing less than unconditional surrender from the enemy. The two men were determined that politicians in the Axis countries would never be able to claim that their soldiers had been "stabbed in the back" by a government eager to make peace. (Hitler had used this argument to explain Germany's defeat in 1918.) They also sought to reassure Stalin that they had no intention of making a separate peace with Hitler.

The Allies invade Italy. In July, 1943, two months after the fighting ended in Africa, a combined American and British force of 160,000 men landed on the Italian island of Sicily. By mid-August, they had secured the island. The loss of Sicily led to the overthrow of Mussolini. As the first of the enemy leaders fell from power, American newspapers trumpeted: ONE DOWN AND TWO TO GO! A new Italian government ordered the arrest of the would-be "Caesar." Two months later, a daring German rescue party freed Mussolini and took him to northern Italy where he was put in charge of a puppet Italian government.

On September 3, the Allies set forth from Sicily to conquer the rest of Italy. The Germans, suspecting that the Italians were about to give up, had occupied most of the country. The Allies now faced veteran Nazi troops determined to hold Italy.

President Roosevelt shares a jeep with General Eisenhower in North Africa. Eisenhower had just been given command of the operation to launch an invasion of France.

To take Italy, Allied troops were forced to fight a long and costly campaign, as they slowly drove the Germans northward. By October 1, the G.I.'s under General Mark W. Clark entered Naples. Attempting to outflank the Germans, they landed at Anzio, south of Rome. They ran into a relentless German defense, however, and suffered heavy casualties. It was June, 1944, before Allied forces, led by Clark, entered Rome. Even then, months of hard fighting lay ahead. Not until May, 1945, did the Germans finally surrender their hold on Italy. A few weeks earlier, Mussolini had been captured and executed by anti-Fascist Italians.

Plans are made to invade France. The Italian campaign gave the Russians some relief by pinning down German troops who otherwise could have been transferred to Eastern Europe. Nevertheless, the long-awaited second front in France was about to be opened. Germany would be caught in the middle as Soviet forces pressed westward and the Americans and British pressed eastward.

In the greatest secrecy, Allied strategists laid their plans — the most elaborate in the history of warfare. The Supreme Commander of Operation Overlord — the code name for the invasion of France — was General Eisenhower. Over two million British, American, and other Allied troops were mobilized and given special training in the British Isles. Allied planes, meanwhile, bombarded the French coast, attempting to destroy Nazi lines of communication and transportation. Having held France for four years, the Germans were well-entrenched there. Expecting an invasion, they had tried to make their defenses invincible.

The Allies also took care to mislead the enemy as to the precise place they intended to land. They set up dummy installations in the British Isles and used false radio signals to convince the Nazis that plans were being made to invade France at Calais. Even the strategic bombing of northern France throughout early 1944 was designed to keep secret the planned site of invasion: the Normandy coast.

By the late spring of 1944, the invading forces were ready. As the troops waited anxiously for orders, "Axis Sally," a notorious Nazi propagandist who made English-language broadcasts, played a popular wartime tune called "I Double Dare You." Now she had new words for it, including the jeering lines:

> I double dare you to venture a raid.
> I double dare you to try and invade. . . .
> I double dare you to come over here.
> I double dare you.

France is liberated. Shortly after midnight on June 6, 1944 — D-Day — the mighty invasion began. Three divisions of paratroopers dropped silently behind German lines to sabotage transportation and communication systems. At 3:30 A.M., Eisenhower's Order of the Day was broadcast to the troops of the expeditionary force: "You are about to embark upon a great crusade. . . . " it said. "The hopes and prayers of liberty-loving people everywhere go with you." The Allied ground forces were under the command of General Omar Bradley. Superb at devising tactics, Bradley came to be called with affection "the G.I.'s general."

Although casualties on the Normandy beaches were high, the Allies succeeded in establishing five beachheads where they could land more men and supplies. These footholds were gradually linked together and then widened. Illustrating the surprises that war can produce despite planning, the toughest fighting took place on a landing area called Omaha Beach. There the Allies encountered a German division that they did not know had been moved into position.

By nightfall of D-Day about 155,000 men were ashore. Within a month, a million Allied troops had been landed in Normandy, along with 172,000 vehicles and more than half a million tons of supplies. The invasion was a success. Now the troops began to fan out over French soil, pressing toward Paris. On August 25, 1944, after less than three months of fighting, Allied troops moved into the French capital.

Meanwhile, on August 15 a combined force of American, British, and French

COURTESY TIME-LIFE BOOKS INC.

Having broken through German defenses at the town of Saint Lo in Normandy, American forces were ready to advance toward Paris.

December 16, 1944, taking the Allies off guard, the Nazis attacked along a fifty-mile front in the thinly held area around the Ardennes Forest in Belgium. Hitler hoped to cut the Allied forces in two, leaving the northern half without supplies. The Allies were driven back some 65 miles, creating an enormous bulge in their line of defense. The attack thus became known as the Battle of the Bulge.

After their initial retreat, Allied troops stood their ground at the town of Bastogne in the freezing winter weather. Surrounded by Nazi troops, the place was held by an airborne division commanded by a young brigadier general, Anthony C. McAuliffe. To a demand that he surrender, McAuliffe fired back a one-word answer: "Nuts!" His division dug in bravely until it was rescued.

By the end of January, the Germans had lost every inch of territory they had retaken, and 120,000 men besides. The American price for wiping out the bulge was 77,000 casualties. The Germans had only delayed the outcome of the war. By the beginning of 1945, Allied troops were converging on Germany.

The Allies confer at Yalta. In early February, 1945, President Roosevelt traveled to Yalta, in the Crimea, to meet with Churchill and Stalin. Victory over Germany appearing certain, the leaders had come together to discuss strategy for ending the war and to agree on postwar settlements.

The Big Three, as these leaders were called, concluded plans for the unconditional surrender of Germany. They agreed that Germany would be divided into three zones, to be occupied separately by the victorious Allies. (France would be given a zone out of the territory assigned to the United States and Great Britain.) The city of Berlin, deep inside the Soviet zone, would also be split into three zones. East Prussia would be divided between Poland and the Soviet Union. The Big Three also announced that a meeting would be held at San Francisco to establish a new organization for keeping world peace.

At the Yalta conference, Stalin made several commitments. He restated his

soldiers had landed at Toulon on the southern coast of France and was racing northward along the Rhone Valley. At the same time, General George S. Patton, in command of the United States Third Army, was spearheading with his armored units a spectacular advance from Normandy through Brittany and northern France. By November the Germans had been cleared out of France.

The Germans launch their final offensive. As planned, Stalin's troops had launched an offensive to coincide with the British and American push through Western Europe. The Russians marched west, retaking the Ukraine, the Crimea, White Russia, eastern Poland, and most of Lithuania. By October, 1944, the Red Army had moved into Rumania, Bulgaria, Hungary, and Yugoslavia.

At this point, Hitler personally directed one last, desperate counteroffensive. On

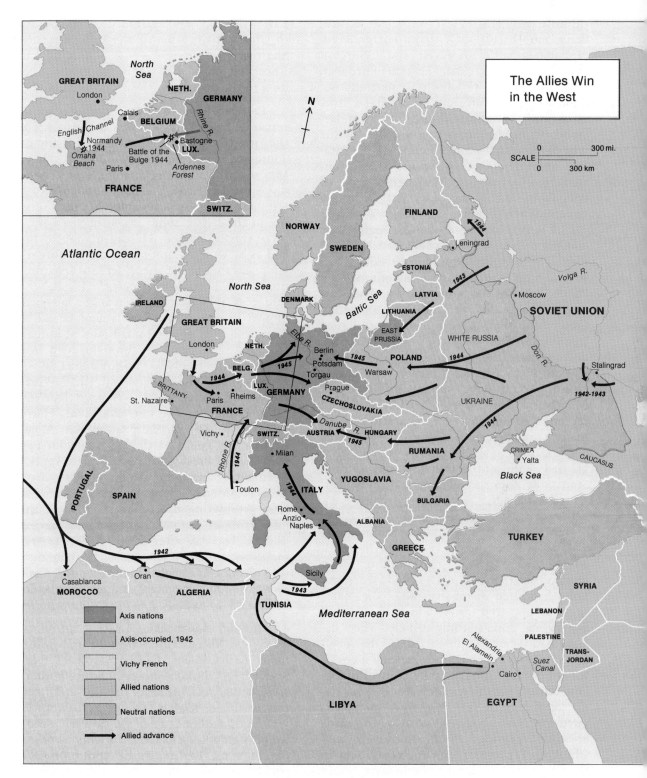

The Allies Win in the West

North Sea

GREAT BRITAIN
London

NETH.

GERMANY

Calais
BELGIUM
Normandy
1944
Omaha
Beach

English Channel

Rhine R.

Bastogne
LUX.

Battle of the
Bulge 1944

Paris

Ardennes
Forest

FRANCE

SWITZ.

N

SCALE

0   300 mi.
0   300 km

Atlantic Ocean

NORWAY

SWEDEN

FINLAND

1944

Leningrad

North Sea

DENMARK

Baltic Sea

ESTONIA

LATVIA

1943

Volga R.

Moscow

SOVIET UNION

IRELAND

GREAT BRITAIN

London

NETH.

Elbe R.

LITHUANIA

EAST
PRUSSIA

WHITE RUSSIA

BELG.

1944

Berlin
Potsdam
Torgau

1945

POLAND

Warsaw

1944

Don R.

Stalingrad

BRITTANY

St. Nazaire

Paris
Rheims

LUX.

GERMANY

Prague
CZECHOSLOVAKIA

UKRAINE

1942-1943

FRANCE

Vichy

SWITZ.

Danube R.

AUSTRIA

1945

HUNGARY

1944

Rhone R.

1944

Milan

RUMANIA

CRIMEA
Yalta

CAUCASUS

Toulon

1944

ITALY

YUGOSLAVIA

Black Sea

Rome
Anzio
Naples

ALBANIA

BULGARIA

TURKEY

PORTUGAL

SPAIN

GREECE

1942

Casablanca

Oran

Sicily

SYRIA

MOROCCO

ALGERIA

1943

Mediterranean Sea

LEBANON

PALESTINE

TUNISIA

Alexandria
El Alamein

TRANS-
JORDAN

Suez
Canal

Cairo

LIBYA

EGYPT

Axis nations

Axis-occupied, 1942

Vichy French

Allied nations

Neutral nations

Allied advance

To defeat the Axis, the western Allies counterattacked in North Africa and then invaded
Italy and France. In the East, meanwhile, Russian armies advanced westward toward
Germany. Following the death of Hitler and the fall of Berlin, Germany surrendered to the
Allies on May 7, 1945.

301

promise to declare war on Japan within three months after Germany surrendered. He agreed with Roosevelt and Churchill that Poland and other Eastern European countries that were wholly or partially occupied by Russian troops would have "free elections." These would lead, it was understood, to governments "responsible to the will of the people" and "broadly representative of all democratic elements." He promised, finally, that he would sign a "pact of friendship and alliance" with the Chinese government of Chiang Kai-shek.

In return for these pledges, Stalin won concessions from Roosevelt and Churchill. First, the Russians would gain control of several important Japanese islands off the Pacific coast of the Soviet Union. The Russians would also be allowed to occupy Outer Mongolia, a portion of Central Asia that bordered on the Soviet Union. Second, despite an earlier promise that Roosevelt had made to Chiang Kai-shek, the Soviet Union would have special privileges in Manchuria. Third, the Soviet Union would receive half of any war reparations Germany would be forced to pay.

The Yalta agreements were at first greeted with enthusiasm in the United States. By the end of the war, however, many Americans were deeply concerned, believing that the West had given away more than it had received from Stalin. Some critics said that Roosevelt and Churchill had been foolish to trust Stalin. They pointed out that in August, 1944, when the Poles had risen in revolt against the Nazis in Warsaw, the Soviet army stationed nearby had done nothing to help. The Russians had seemed willing to allow the rebellious Poles to be wiped out, making it easier for the Soviet Union to take control of Poland once Germany was defeated.

Defenders of the Yalta agreements argued that Stalin had held most of the cards at that meeting. First, Roosevelt and Churchill expected a long and costly war in the Pacific in which they would have found the help of the Soviet Union indispensable. It was reasonable to make concessions in order to spare their own troops. Second, Stalin's forces were already in possession of

Eastern Europe and stationed on the border of China at the time of the Yalta meeting. Short of war, there was little Churchill and Roosevelt could have done to assure freedom to the peoples of these occupied lands.

President Roosevelt dies. When Roosevelt returned from Yalta, he was exhausted. For the first time, he remained seated while he addressed Congress. In April, he traveled to Warm Springs, Georgia, for a rest. There, on April 12, 1945, he died suddenly of a stroke. Mrs. Roosevelt cabled her sons serving in the battle zones: "Darlings: Pa slept away this afternoon. He did his job to the end as he would want you to do." Churchill later said that he sat speechless for five minutes after hearing the news. "I felt," he said, "as if I had been struck a physical blow." In a eulogy to Parliament he called Roosevelt "the greatest champion of human freedom who has ever brought help and comfort from the New World to the Old."

Roosevelt had occupied the White House for twelve years — longer than any other President. The new President, Harry S. Truman, was virtually unknown. A policeman on guard at the Capitol who had seen many Presidents commented sourly, "Truman's only a Coolidge with eyeglasses." Many people shared this view at first, wondering if Truman was up to the job. Truman himself confessed to having doubts. The day after taking office he said modestly to the press corps, "When they told me yesterday what had happened, I felt like the moon, the stars and all the planets had fallen on me."

Germany surrenders. In the spring of 1945, the Allied armies were bringing Germany to its knees. Germany's cities were under heavy bombardment, and its borders were being overrun from the east and from the west. In March, General Eisenhower was faced with a crucial decision. He could lead his troops eastward as quickly as possible to seize Berlin, or he could proceed slowly, wiping out all Nazi resistance in the territory he occupied.

Churchill had urged that the Western Allies take territory as far to the east as possible, especially the capital cities of Berlin

Thousands of mourners lined the streets of Washington, D.C., to honor Franklin Roosevelt. The President died on April 12, 1945, while vacationing at Warm Springs, Georgia. He was buried at his home in Hyde Park, New York.

and Prague. The more Eastern European territory the West held, he believed, the more power it would have to force Stalin to live up to his promise of free elections for the countries in that region. Eisenhower, backed first by Roosevelt and then by Truman, decided not to follow Churchill's advice. On April 27, American forces linked up with the Russian army at the town of Torgau, on the Elbe River — sixty miles south of Berlin.

Germany was in chaos, its leaders holed up in an underground bunker in the capital, its people dazed and dispirited. Hitler, finally recognizing the certainty of defeat, died by his own hand on April 30, 1945. Berlin fell to the Russians two days later. On May 7, at Eisenhower's headquarters in Rheims, France, a German field marshal signed an unconditional surrender. The war in Europe ended the next day (V-E Day).

Nazi atrocities are revealed. During the war, word of unspeakable crimes committed by the Nazis had reached America, but it was not until Allied troops entered German territory that the extent of those horrors came to light. The Nazis had set up enormous concentration camps for the purpose of murdering their political enemies, including the entire Jewish population of Europe. The world, stunned and sickened by this program of extermination, called it the Holocaust. The Nazis had systematically killed millions of men, women, and children in these camps. Among their number were six million Jews.

Throughout his political career Hitler had made the Jewish people his particular scapegoat. Building on the long-standing, unreasoning hostility to Jews, Hitler had come to power partly on the legend that Germany had been defeated in 1918 because of the disloyalty of Jews on the home front. The Nazi leader, maintaining that the Germans were a superior race, succeeded in driving his people into a frenzy against the German Jews as a domestic enemy.

Hitler's campaign against the Jews went through a number of increasingly brutal stages. The first stage came in 1933 when gangs of Nazis, prodded by the government, looted and boycotted shops and other businesses owned by Jews. The second stage was the enactment of laws a few years later that disfranchised all people who had "Jewish blood" — which included anybody with at least one Jewish grandparent. The third stage began in 1939 with mass arrests of Jews, soon followed by the establishment of concentration camps. In these wretched places Jews were kept on the verge of starvation and forced to labor like slaves. The fourth stage began in 1941 after Hitler had sent his armies into the Soviet Union. He ordered that some of the concentration camps be converted into extermination camps. In these camps, the Nazis operated gas chambers and crematoriums to carry on the mass murders "efficiently." Even near the end of the war, German energies were systematically devoted to rounding up Jews and shipping them to their destruction.

Although recognizing that nothing could atone for the atrocities of the Nazi regime, people of the Allied nations demanded that those responsible for committing them be brought to justice. In 1945 and 1946, Allied courts tried Germans accused of these war crimes. Hundreds were executed; many thousands of others received lesser punishments.

SECTION REVIEW

1. (a) What agreements did Roosevelt and Churchill reach at Casablanca in 1943? (b) Why did the Allies invade Italy? (c) What were the results?
2. (a) How did the Allies strike at Germany from the west? (b) How did the Germans try to counter the Allied advance? (c) What were the results?
3. (a) What agreements were reached at Yalta? (b) For what reasons were those agreements controversial?
4. (a) How did the war in Germany come to an end? (b) Why were war-crime trials held?

4 The War in the Pacific Is Won

By 1943 the Allies had taken the offensive in the Pacific. Their task was forbidding, because in the early years of the war Japanese troops had occupied many islands in the Pacific. As defenders of these islands the Japanese were fearsome enemies. They considered surrender a disgrace — even when no possibility of victory remained. Grimly, the Allies prepared to fight the Japanese to the bitter end.

The Allies prepare the way for the invasion of Japan. Allied strategy in the Pacific had three main objectives: to recapture the Philippines; to cut Japanese lines of transportation and communication; and to set up bases from which Japan itself could eventually be attacked. These objectives were to be accomplished through a strategy called "island-hopping." Instead of clearing the enemy out of every island on the route north toward Japan, Allied troops would capture only certain strategic ones. The others, cut off from reinforcements and supplies, would cease to pose a threat.

There were two major lines of Allied advance. The first, assigned to Admiral Nimitz's forces, was to move on Japan from the central Pacific, taking the Gilbert, Marshall, Caroline, and Mariana Islands as they went. From airbases on these islands, the Japanese had been attacking Allied troops under General MacArthur, who was leading the second Allied advance by way of New Guinea.

Allied forces under Admiral Nimitz succeeded in taking key islands in the central Pacific, capturing, in the summer of 1944, Guam and Saipan in the Marianas. These victories placed Allied troops within striking distance of Japan. As soon as the islands were cleared of resistance, enormous airfields were built and B-29 bombers were turned loose in strikes against Japan.

The Philippines are liberated. In October, 1944, General MacArthur fulfilled his long-standing promise to liberate the Philippine Islands. He declared dramatically, "People of the Philippines! I have returned. . . . Rally to me." After two years of slogging their way up from New Guinea and fighting one bloody engagement after another, his men went ashore on Leyte (LAY-tay), in the central Philippines. In the ensuing clash of navies known as the Battle of Leyte Gulf — the greatest naval engagement of all time — the Allies smashed the Japanese fleet once and for all. The way was now clear for Allied troops to move on to the main Philippine island of Luzon, where the capital city of Manila is located. Japanese forces offered stiff resistance. Finally, on March 9, 1945, after three months of struggle, the Japanese troops on Luzon surrendered to the Americans.

American troops advance toward Japan. While MacArthur's troops battled for control of the Philippines, Nimitz's powerful units moved even nearer to the Japanese homeland. A fleet under the command of Admiral William F. ("Bull") Halsey was beginning to roam at will along the coasts of Japan, pounding what remained of enemy shipping. In February, 1945, American marines landed on the tiny island of Iwo Jima. This desolate spot had been selected because it was close enough to Japan to be a base for stepped-up bombing of Japanese cities. Using flamethrowers and dynamite, the marines rooted out the Japanese defenders on the way to the island's high-point, Mt. Suribachi. At its top, the marines succeeded in planting a pole bearing the Stars and Stripes.

From Iwo Jima, American forces pushed on toward the large and strategically important island of Okinawa, less than 400 miles from Japan. On April 1, 1945, 100,000 American soldiers and marines began to go ashore, backed by an armada of 1,300 ships of all kinds. In a last-ditch gesture, Japanese pilots flew suicide missions against American vessels, crashing their planes on the decks of the ships in order to deliver the bomb loads.[4] Nearly 200 American ships were damaged or destroyed by these tactics.

---

[4]The Japanese airmen were known as *kamikazes*, a word meaning "divine wind."

General MacArthur fulfilled his promise to return to the Philippines when he waded ashore at Leyte, 948 days after he had left the islands.

By the time the G.I.'s had gained control of Okinawa, in June, 1945, they had suffered almost 50,000 casualties. The Japanese, too, had suffered fearsome losses, but they showed no sign of weakened resolve.

Scientists develop the atomic bomb. Ever since 1938, scientists had known that it was possible to split the atom, once regarded as the smallest particle of matter. This procedure, they believed, would release the enormous energy at the atom's nucleus or core. In August, 1939, Albert Einstein, acknowledged to be the most brilliant scientist of the century and recently arrived in the United States as a refugee from Nazi Germany, wrote President Roosevelt a fateful letter. In it Einstein stated that the ability to unlock the nucleus of the atom could be used to create "extremely powerful bombs."

Acting on Einstein's suggestion, Roosevelt in 1940 ordered a top-secret project to begin work on an atomic weapon. He knew it was necessary to beat out the Germans and the Japanese, who were working — in separate undertakings — on similar projects. In early 1943 the Manhattan Project, as the American research effort was

305

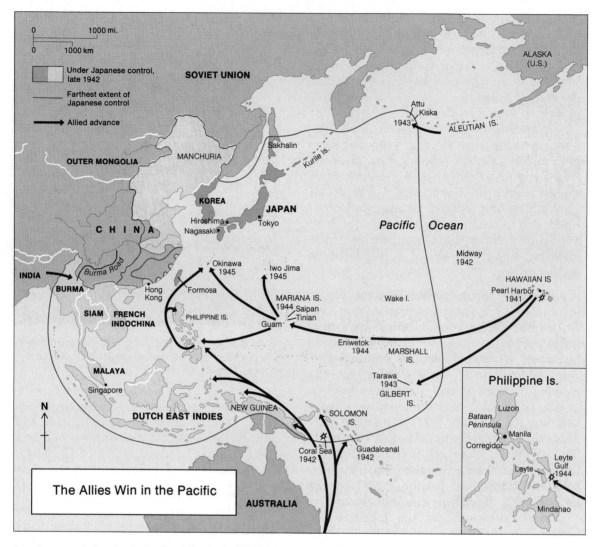

American naval victories in the Coral Sea and off Midway marked turning points in the war in the Pacific. Allied forces then began their advance on Japan.

called, was established at Los Alamos, New Mexico, where its work could be carried on in total secrecy. On June 16, 1945, the first atomic bomb was tested in the New Mexican desert.

President Truman was conferring with other Allied leaders in Potsdam, Germany, when news of the successful explosion reached him. He told Stalin only that the United States had a new weapon capable of vast destruction. (Stalin, through espionage agents, already knew about the Manhattan Project.) Then, on July 26, 1945, the Allied leaders issued this warning to Japan: "The alternative to surrender is prompt and utter destruction." The Japanese decided to ignore the ultimatum.

Truman was thoroughly convinced that the Japanese military forces would never surrender unless American troops actually invaded and conquered their homeland. American military strategists estimated that such an operation could not be accomplished in less than eighteen months and without the loss of a million Allied lives. Truman therefore ordered that the new bomb be dropped on a Japanese city. He used it, he explained, "in order to save the lives of thousands and thousands of young Americans."

As Americans celebrated Japan's formal surrender, held aboard the *Missouri,* President Truman addressed the nation on radio. "It was the spirit of liberty," he said, "which gave us our armed strength and which made our men invincible in victory."

Atomic weapons end the war. On August 6 a B–29 carrying an atomic bomb took off from Tinian Island in the Marianas and headed for Hiroshima, one of the few Japanese cities so far spared by Allied bombers. At 8:00 A.M. the plane dropped its awesome new weapon. The bomb exploded with the force of 20,000 tons of TNT. The city was leveled. Almost 78,000 people were killed and 70,000 were wounded.

In spite of the fearful destruction, the Japanese still did not give up. On August 8 the Soviet Union declared war on Japan and invaded Manchuria. The next day, the Allies dropped another atomic bomb, this time on the city of Nagasaki. Finally, on August 14, the emperor of Japan ordered his military leaders to surrender unconditionally.

The war ended formally on September 2 (V-J Day) in Tokyo Bay. General MacArthur was in charge of the surrender ceremonies, held aboard the American battleship *Missouri.* Among the high-ranking Allied military and naval officers present was General Wainwright (page 288), recently released from a Japanese prison camp. From the foremast of the *Missouri* floated the same American flag that had flown over the Capitol in Washington, D.C., on December 7, 1941. Near it was flying the 31-starred flag that Commodore Perry had brought to Tokyo Bay nearly a century earlier. As the proceedings ended, MacArthur spoke solemnly: "Let us pray for peace . . . and that God will preserve it always." In the moment of joyful relief that the war was over, people could not forget that in this most destructive combat in human history as many as fifty million lives had been lost.

No one knew, that day, whether the terrible memory of the Second World War would prevent future wars. No one knew, either, whether the Allies, who had worked together so magnificently, would be able to sustain their close relationship in peacetime. Of one fact, however, there was no doubt: the United States was now the world's most powerful country, to which free people and those yearning for freedom everywhere looked for leadership.

SECTION REVIEW

1. (a) What were the Allies' main objectives in the Pacific campaign? (b) Why was the "island-hopping" strategy used?
2. What islands did Allied forces capture as they moved closer to Japan in 1944–1945?
3. Why did the Japanese finally agree to an unconditional surrender?

Preparing Reports

In studying American history, you will sometimes have the opportunity to prepare reports. These reports, which may be either written or oral, will be based on research you do.

In preparing a report, you will need to investigate a number of sources, organize the information you collect, and then put together a presentation that is clear, interesting, and informative. The following suggestions will help you divide this task into simple steps.

Choosing a Topic

Select a subject that interests you and that you will enjoy reading about. Once you have chosen a general subject, narrow your topic to fit the assignment. As you begin to do your research and collect information, do not hesitate to keep narrowing your topic to make it suitable for your report. Broad historical subjects can be limited, for instance, by focusing on an important person, event, or development.

Finding Information

An important part of your work will be to locate good sources of information about the topic you have selected. Use the card catalog in the library to look up books covering the topic. Also use the *Reader's Guide to Periodical Literature* to find magazine articles that relate to the topic. Each source you locate may include a bibliography. Be sure to examine the bibliography for additional information about books and articles that might be useful.

As you locate sources, list information about them on note cards. For books, list the author's name, the title, the publisher, and the city and year of publication. For magazine and newspaper articles, include the journalist's name, the title, the name and date of the publication, and the page numbers. In written reports, you may be expected to include a bibliography of your sources. For oral reports, you may be asked to tell where you found the information you are presenting.

Taking Notes

As you read your sources, you should take notes. Use separate note cards for different ideas and subjects, but be sure to include the title of the source and page number on each card. Summarize the main information you need. You should, however, carefully record, word for word, any quotations you think you might use in your report. Take notes on as many sources as will help you become fully informed about your topic.

Organizing Information

The next step in preparing your report is to organize the information you have collected. Read over all your note cards and separate them into stacks that contain similar ideas. For each stack, decide on a phrase that identifies the topic of that group of cards. Determine a logical order for these phrases and make an outline by using the phrases as the outline headings.

Once again reread the note cards in each group and pick out subheadings to fill in the outline. This outline will become the guide for planning your oral presentation or for structuring your written report.

Completing Your Report

Following your outline, use the information in your note cards to create a first draft of your oral presentation or written report. Express your thoughts freely at this stage, getting down on paper all the information you want to include in your report. Check your draft to make sure you have covered all important points in the outline. At this point you should also decide whether charts, graphs, or maps are needed to help you present information more clearly.

Now you are ready to put your report into final form. For a written report, check to see that headings are introduced to help organize the information being presented, that paragraphs are used to present different ideas, and that all your sentences are clear. You may need to write several drafts before you write or type the final paper. On your final copy, be sure to check for correct spelling, punctuation, and grammar. At the end of your report, include a bibliography listing your sources in alphabetical order.

For oral reports, revise the draft to organize your thoughts and smooth out your presentation. Then read it aloud and time yourself to see how long it takes to give the report. If the report is too short, expand the main points; if too long, eliminate some of the supporting details. Create a series of note cards containing key ideas or modify your outline to use as a guide in presenting your report. When your report is in its final form, practice giving it before an audience of your family and friends. Remember to speak clearly, slowly, and to the point.

Check Your Skill

Use the information presented on these pages to answer the following questions.

1. What should you consider when choosing a topic for a report?
2. How would you go about finding information on a topic?
3. Why is it important to record information about the sources you use?

4. As you read different sources for your report, what is the best way to keep track of the information you collect?
5. When you have finished your research, how should you organize the information you have assembled?
6. What steps should you follow when you are ready to write your report or make an oral presentation?
7. What should be included at the end of a written report?
8. What can you use to assist you in presenting an oral report?

Apply Your Skill

1. Suppose you were writing a report on Franklin D. Roosevelt. Rearrange this list to make an outline with the main topics in their proper sequence. Then write at least two subtopics under each one.

   The New Deal
   "Quarantine Speech"
   Roosevelt as President during World War II
   His early life
   Roosevelt as governor of New York

2. Prepare a five-minute oral report on one of the following topics:

   The Attack on Pearl Harbor
   The War in the Pacific
   The North African Campaign
   The Home Front
   D-Day

3. Write a one-page report on one of the following topics:

   Winston Churchill
   The Battle of Stalingrad
   The Battle of the Bulge
   The Yalta Conference
   The Holocaust

Chapter 11 Review

Summary

When Roosevelt and Churchill met in the summer of 1941, they pledged mutual support against totalitarian aggression. At this time, Japan was making clear its intention of dominating Asia. Relations between the United States and Japan deteriorated, and on the morning of December 7, 1941, Japanese planes attacked the American naval base at Pearl Harbor, Hawaii. In the following days the United States recognized the existence of a state of war with Japan; Germany and Italy, in turn, declared war on the United States.

Japan moved quickly to consolidate its position in the Pacific. Guam, Wake Island, Hong Kong, Singapore, and the Philippines fell to the Japanese. American victories in the battles of the Coral Sea, Midway Island, and Guadalcanal finally contained Japanese expansion.

The first priority for the United States was to help control the advance of German armies in Europe and North Africa. In the winter of 1941–1942 the Russians fought the German army to a standstill. After an Allied force defeated the German army in North Africa during the spring of 1943, Roosevelt and Churchill turned their attention to an invasion of Europe.

On the home front, the country quickly mobilized for war. The military was expanded through the Selective Service System, and industry was organized for war production. Increased taxes and the sale of war bonds helped finance the American war effort.

Allied forces landed in Sicily in July, 1943, and for the next year fought their way northward to Rome. Italy surrendered in September, 1943, but the German army continued to hold most of northern Italy. Plans to invade France, meanwhile, were made with great care. On June 6, 1944, an Allied army under the command of General Dwight D. Eisenhower landed on the beaches of Normandy. By August, Allied troops liberated Paris and then began to close in on Germany itself. Hitler ordered one last desperate offensive in December, but Allied soldiers held their ground and repulsed the German advance. The war ended in Europe when Germany surrendered on May 7, 1945.

In 1944 and 1945 the Allies used a strategy of "island-hopping" as they made their way toward Japan. With America now in possession of the atomic bomb, Japan was asked in July, 1945, to surrender or face destruction. When the Japanese ignored this warning, President Truman ordered atomic bombs to be dropped on Japan. On September 2, 1945, Japan formally surrendered — ending the Second World War.

Vocabulary and Important Terms

1. Allies
2. Battle of the Coral Sea
3. Battle of Midway
4. War Production Board
5. war bond
6. D-Day
7. Committee on Fair Employment Practices
8. Battle of the Bulge
9. Yalta agreements
10. V-E Day
11. Holocaust
12. Manhattan Project
13. V-J Day

Discussion Questions

1. (a) Following the entry of the United States into World War II, why did the Roosevelt administration adopt a "Europe-first" strategy? (b) What fighting, nevertheless, took place in the Pacific? (c) How large an area had come under Japanese control by mid-1942?

2. (a) Why was winning the Battle of the Atlantic so critical to the Allies? (b) Why was Hitler unable to defeat the Russians? (c) What effect did Hitler's losses in the Soviet Union have on the outcome of the war?

3. (a) Why were American and British troops sent to Morocco and Algeria in 1942? (b) How did the decision to send troops to North Africa reflect a division in Allied thinking on the question of how best to prosecute the war?

4. (a) What role did the United States government play in the mobilization of resources during the war? (b) What impact did the war have on the American economy?

5. (a) What did the holding of elections in 1944 show about the American system of government? (b) Why were Japanese Americans relocated during the war?

6. (a) Why did Allied leaders decide to demand the unconditional surrender of their enemies? (b) When, and under what conditions, did Italy, Germany, and Japan surrender?

7. (a) Why did the United States develop the atomic bomb? (b) Why did the United States use the bomb against Japan? (c) What effect did the use of the atomic bomb have on the outcome of World War II?

Relating Past to Present

1. Under what circumstances do world leaders meet today and make decisions that potentially have long-lasting effects? Are these decisions as important as those reached by Allied leaders during World War II? Why or why not?

2. Scientists began work in 1940 on the top-secret Manhattan Project. How do the results of their research affect all people today?

Studying Local History

1. Find out how the war effort affected your community. Were there armed forces facilities or military camps in your region? What contributions did high school students make to the war effort? How did your community honor those who died in the war?

2. Study the headlines and editorials of newspapers published in your community in December, 1941. Find out the reaction of people to the news of Japan's attack on Pearl Harbor. What do subsequent newspaper stories tell you about early wartime mobilization efforts in your community?

Using History Skills

1. *Reading source material.* Study Ray Hartman's description of the student war bond drive on page 294. (a) How did the students in Ray Hartman's school raise money for the war effort? (b) What did the school buy with the money the students had collected? (c) Would you infer from this passage that Ray Hartman was an effective leader? Explain your answer.

2. *Preparing reports.* Do research to find out about the role of the federal government during the First World War and the Second World War. How was industry mobilized during each conflict? What efforts were taken to control public opinion? What opportunities were opened to women and to members of minority groups? Write a report on your findings.

3. *Reading maps.* Study the map on page 306 showing the Pacific campaign during World War II. (a) How does the map indicate the farthest extent of Japanese control? (b) From what directions did Allied forces advance on Japan? (c) Explain how the strategy of "island-hopping" enabled Allied forces to advance across the Pacific.

WORLD SCENE

Naval Warfare

Advances in the design and construction of warships brought changes in naval warfare during the Second World War.

German pocket battleships. Germany had created in the early 1930's a new classification of warship, the "pocket battleship." Not a true battleship as measured in size or armament, it was equipped with eleven-inch turret cannon and could travel extremely fast.

At the outbreak of war in 1939, the Germans had three pocket battleships. One, the *Graf Spee,* was at sea when the fighting began. Immediately, it began to sink Allied ships in the South Atlantic. British and French task forces were sent to hunt down the *Graf Spee.* In December a British squadron located it off the coast of Uruguay. After a fierce two-hour battle, in which both sides suffered heavy damage, the *Graf Spee* broke off the action and took refuge in the harbor of Montevideo.

In the days that followed, British diplomats stationed in the port spread rumors that additional Allied ships had arrived and were in position outside the port. Rather than subject his crew to what he thought would be a hopeless battle, the German captain ordered the *Graf Spee* to be blown up. The sinking of the *Graf Spee* was a stirring victory for the Allies.

Japanese and American aircraft carriers. No development since the coming of ironclads had a greater impact on warfare at sea than the introduction of aircraft carriers. With aircraft carriers, naval forces could launch squadrons of torpedo bombers to seek out and destroy enemy ships.

In the months after Pearl Harbor, Japanese and American task forces assembled in the South Pacific and carefully stalked one another. Then, in May, 1942, the Battle of the Coral Sea was fought, marking the first time in naval history that two fleets were engaged in battle without ever coming in sight of each other. The entire battle consisted of a duel between airplanes that took off from the carriers.

This battle, in which the Americans emerged victorious, changed the way nations organized their naval task forces. No battle group could be without at least one aircraft carrier, and all ships were now outfitted with antiaircraft weapons and thicker armor.

UNIT 3 REVIEW

Important Dates

1920 First American radio broadcasting station.
Harding elected President.
1921 Washington Conference begins.
1924 National Origins Act passed.
Coolidge elected President.
1927 Lindbergh flies nonstop to Paris.
1928 Kellogg-Briand Pact.
Hoover elected President.
1929 Great Depression begins.
1931 Japan invades Manchuria.
1932 Franklin Roosevelt elected President.
1933 New Deal begins.
Hitler takes power in Germany.
1934 Indian Reorganization Act passed.
1935 Social Security Act passed.
1936 Supreme Court declares AAA
unconstitutional.
1937 Roosevelt's "court-packing" plan rejected.
1938 CIO separates from AFL.
1939 World War II begins in Europe.
1941 Lend-Lease Act.
United States enters World War II.
1944 Allies land in France.
1945 World War II ends.

Review Questions

1. (a) To what extent were the years after the First World War marked by political and economic unrest? (b) Why was immigration policy a matter of concern to many Americans? (c) What major changes were made in American immigration laws?

2. (a) Why are the 1920's often remembered as a time of prosperity? (b) How was the Great Depression a consequence of some of the economic conditions present in the United States during the 1920's? (c) How was the Great Depression influenced by economic conditions outside the United States?

3. (a) Why was Hoover unwilling to use the powers of the national government to end the depression? (b) To what extent did Roosevelt's attitude differ?

4. (a) How successful was Roosevelt in ending the Depression? (b) What New Deal measures were especially controversial? (c) In each case explain why.

5. (a) Describe the situation minority groups faced during the 1920's and 1930's. (b) How did the role of American women change in the 1920's and 1930's?

6. (a) To what extent did the United States involve itself in world affairs during the 1920's and 1930's?

(b) What changes took place in relations between the United States and its possessions? (c) What changes took place in the nation's Latin American policy?

7. (a) In what ways was world peace threatened during the 1930's? (b) What was the attitude of the United States? (c) Why did this country enter World War II?

8. How did each of the following countries contribute to the defeat of the Axis powers in World War II? (a) The United States (b) The Soviet Union (c) Great Britain

Projects

1. Make a display featuring American society in the 1920's. Your display should illustrate some of the significant changes in ways of living that took place during that decade.

2. Create a set of three handbills on which you indicate either support or criticism of the Agricultural Adjustment Act, the National Industrial Recovery Act, and the Tennessee Valley Authority. On your handbills include pictures, slogans, and other information to back up your point of view.

3. Simulate key aspects of a debate over the effectiveness of the New Deal by re-enacting the roles of supporters and critics. Roles should include (a) supporters of Roosevelt and the New Deal; (b) critics who charged Roosevelt with doing too much; and (c) critics who accused Roosevelt of doing too little (including representatives of the philosophies of Huey Long, Francis Townsend, and Father Coughlin).

4. On an outline map of the world indicate the possessions of the United States. Then list the acts of Congress passed for each territory between 1900 and 1952 and the dates of those acts. Also state the current status of each territory.

5. Write an essay on the topic "The neutrality legislation of the 1930's was a proper response by the United States to the growing threat of another world war." You may either agree or disagree with this statement, but be sure to include evidence to support your point of view.

6. Do research to find out what songs were popular during the Second World War. Present your findings in class.

7. On an outline map of the world indicate the key battles of World War II. Include both sea and land battles. On the back of the map briefly state why each battle was important and what effect, if any, it had on the outcome of the war.

CONFIDENCE AND CONCERN
1945–1968

If we falter in our leadership, we may endanger the peace of the world — and we shall surely endanger the welfare of our own nation.

HARRY S. TRUMAN, 1947

Cold War and Hot

1945 – 1952

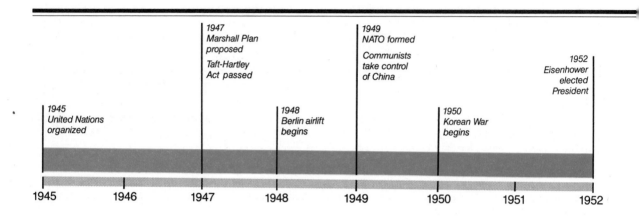

1945
United Nations
organized

1947
Marshall Plan
proposed

Taft-Hartley
Act passed

1948
Berlin airlift
begins

1949
NATO formed

Communists
take control
of China

1950
Korean War
begins

1952
Eisenhower
elected
President

1945   1946   1947   1948   1949   1950   1951   1952

CHAPTER OUTLINE

1. The nation returns to peacetime pursuits.

2. The cold war begins.

3. The cold war leads to a hot war in Korea.

The opening of the postwar era coincided with the beginning of Harry Truman's time in the White House. An able politician and a popular member of the Senate, Truman had been chosen to run with President Roosevelt in 1944. Less than three months after inauguration day in 1945, Roosevelt died and Truman was on his own. Like all "accidental" Presidents, he promised to continue the policies of his predecessor. Problems soon arose, however, for which there were no clear answers.

Truman proved a match for his responsibilities. He was not awed by the people with whom he would have to deal. He wrote his mother after meeting Churchill for the first time, "We had a most pleasant conversation. . . . He gave me a lot of hooey about . . . how he loved Roosevelt and how he intended to love me, etc., etc. . . . I am sure we can get along if he doesn't try to give me too much soft soap." When the new President met the Soviet foreign minister, Vyacheslav Molotov in May, 1945, he severely scolded him for Russia's failure to honor its pledges in Poland. Molotov, livid, responded that no one had ever talked to him that way. Truman retorted, "Carry out your agreements, and you won't get talked to like that!"

The leader of the wartime alliance had been Roosevelt; the cement had been the struggle against Hitler. With both now gone, a new international scene had opened.

1 The Nation Returns to Peacetime Pursuits

Americans in 1945 greeted the end of the war with relief and anticipation. Most people — as after all wars — hoped to return to their old patterns of living. Much, however, would never be the same.

The armed forces return home. Almost immediately President Truman faced demands to "bring the boys home." Although he would have preferred to demobilize the armed forces gradually in order to ease the burden on civilian society, he bowed to the public's wishes to get the troops out of uniform as quickly as possible. By August, 1946, a year after the war ended, the number of troops had been reduced from twelve million to three million.

To ease the transition of discharged military personnel back to civilian life, Congress had passed the Servicemen's Readjustment Act in 1944. Known as the "GI Bill of Rights," this legislation provided veterans with a variety of benefits. In addition to priority for many jobs, veterans were guaranteed wide-ranging educational and financial assistance. The GI Bill's popularity rested in large part on the fact that it enabled millions of young Americans to start over again — if that was what they wanted — with better schooling or in a better job or in better housing than they had known previously. The GI Bill helped wipe out the handicaps resulting from lack of opportunity that the Depression had imposed on so many young people. Nearly eight million veterans were assisted in obtaining education and training — at a cost of about $13.5 billion. The Veterans' Administra-

Servicemen are welcomed home in a victory parade. The GI Bill of Rights helped ease the transition of veterans to peacetime conditions.

The DC-3

The most widely used aircraft in aviation history was the DC-3. When it appeared in 1936, the DC-3 was the first plane to meet the essential requirements of commercial flight—speed, safety, and economy. Operated by a crew of three and able to hold up to 36 passengers, the DC-3 had a pressurized cabin for high-altitude flying. It could maintain a cruising speed of 170 miles per hour. Many DC-3's flew 70,000 hours without major repair.

During World War II the DC-3 was converted to military use and became America's standard medium-range transport and cargo plane. Following the return of peace in 1945, the amazingly dependable and durable DC-3 was put back into commercial use as more and more Americans began to travel by air.

tion, which administered the GI Bill, guaranteed more than $16.5 billion worth of loans to veterans for homes, farms, and businesses. Those generous benefits to the returned veterans aided them enormously in adjusting once again to civilian life.

The economy converts to peacetime. Truman recognized the importance of taking steps to head off the kinds of economic problems that had plagued the country after previous wars. He struggled hard for passage of a full employment bill in 1945, calling for the creation of sixty million jobs — with the understanding that if private business could not provide jobs the government would use all its resources to guarantee full employment. Congress, however, refused to pass the bill.

In general, unemployment did not turn out to be a major problem after the war. Inflation, however, quickly became one of Truman's chief concerns. In 1946, when wartime price controls were removed, prices immediately shot up, increasing nearly 25 percent during 1946–1947. The pent-up demand for goods after four years of austerity was astounding. There was a waiting market for practically every type of consumer product — from automobiles to washing machines, from pots and pans to tables and chairs. A headline in the New York *Daily News* referred to the rising cost of meat:

PRICES SOAR, BUYERS SORE
STEERS JUMP OVER THE MOON

Inflation leads to labor unrest. Working people felt the squeeze of rising prices keenly. The end of the war had put a stop to Sunday, holiday, and overtime work in most branches of industry. For many people, the result was a reduction in take-home pay. In order to catch up with current prices, unions sought substantial wage increases. The problem was that higher wages would increase the cost of manufactured goods, forcing consumer prices higher in an endless upward spiral.

At the end of 1945, automobile workers, electrical workers, and steel-workers took part in crippling strikes.

Many of these walk-outs ended with significant wage increases — soon followed by higher prices for the goods the industries produced. In the spring of 1946 a long coal strike came to an end only when Truman had the government seize the mines.

An even more ominous development came when union members threatened to shut down the nation's railroads. To head off this possibility, Truman called for government operation of the lines. When union leaders went ahead with the strike anyhow, the President sought authority from Congress to draft the strikers. Truman ignored the advice of the Attorney General that such action would be unconstitutional. "We'll draft 'em first," he said, "and think about the law later." Many members of Congress were shocked by the President's stand. The day was saved when, even as the President was speaking, word was handed to him that the labor unions had agreed to settle the strike.

The Taft-Hartley Act is passed. Many Americans blamed the Democratic administration for the strikes and inflation of 1946. Campaigning with a simple but pointed slogan — "Had Enough?" — Republicans swept the congressional elections that year. For the first time since 1928 they won control of both houses of Congress. Among the new members of the House of Representatives were John F. Kennedy from Massachusetts and Richard M. Nixon from California — both destined to be President in the 1960's.

Republican leaders interpreted their victory as a sign of the public's desire for stricter government regulation of organized labor. In June, 1947, Congress passed the Labor-Management Relations Act, also known as the Taft-Hartley Act. The law affirmed labor's right to bargain collectively, and it authorized the continuance of the National Labor Relations Board. Nevertheless, it changed the ground rules for labor-management relations in several respects:

(1) It required a "cooling-off period" of sixty days before a contract could be ended by either an employer or a union. If the Attorney General believed that an impending

As reflected in this cartoon, President Truman vainly hoped for public rejection of the Taft-Hartley Act.

strike or lock-out would threaten the national health or safety, he could obtain an injunction postponing that action for eighty days.

(2) The law forbade the closed shop (in which only workers who were already union members could be hired), allowing instead the union shop (in which workers were required to join a union immediately upon being hired) if the majority of workers voted for it.

(3) State governments were authorized to pass *right-to-work laws.* Such laws allow workers to obtain and keep jobs without joining a labor union at all.

(4) Unions were prohibited from making contributions to political campaigns, establishing secondary boycotts (boycotts against a firm other than the one being struck), putting pressure on nonunion workers to join the union, or charging unusually high initiation or membership fees.

(5) Both employers and unions were permitted to sue for damages resulting from breach of contract.

(6) Union officials were required to sign affidavits saying that they were not Communists and did not advocate the violent overthrow of the United States government.

Supporters of the Taft-Hartley Act argued that it restored the balance of power between labor and management that had been upset (in favor of labor) by the Wagner Act (page 247). To the delight of union members and their leaders, who had only recently been denouncing him as anti-labor, Truman vetoed the bill. Congress, however, overrode the veto. Despite dire predictions, tension between labor and management lessened in the years after the Taft-Hartley Act went into effect.

The Republican Congress passes other measures. Another piece of legislation enacted over Truman's veto was a $5 billion tax cut. Republicans argued that wartime tax increases had been excessive, and especially unfair to wealthy Americans. In 1948 Congress cut taxes across the board, giving special consideration to people in upper-income brackets.

The Republican Congress also expressed disapproval of Franklin Roosevelt's long tenure in office by passing the Twenty-Second Amendment, limiting future Presidents to two terms in office. This Amendment was ratified and became part of the Constitution in 1951. In addition, Congress changed the order of presidential succession. An act adopted in 1947 made the Speaker of the House and the President *pro tempore* of the Senate (instead of Cabinet members) the first and second officials in line after the Vice President.

Truman proposes new social legislation. In the tradition of Franklin Roosevelt, Harry Truman wanted the federal government to take an active role in solving the nation's domestic problems. In addition to guaranteed full employment, his goals included an extension of Social Security benefits, a national health insurance program, federal aid to education, and an enlarged public-housing and slum-clearance effort. Despite his determination, Truman had little success in pushing his program through Congress.

Black Americans find new opportunities.
Along with these proposed reforms, President Truman backed steps to end discrimination against black Americans. Truman seemed to many observers to be the ideal person to bring the issue of civil rights to national attention. Truman had a good sense of the country's mood. He knew that many Americans were troubled by the toleration of racial segregation and discrimination at home while standing as champions of freedom and justice abroad. He believed that people would be receptive to efforts to end racial injustice.

In some areas of American life, racial barriers were already beginning to fall. For the first time, for instance, black athletes began to enter organized baseball. The man who broke the "color bar," as it was called, was Jackie Robinson, who was signed by the Brooklyn Dodgers in the fall of 1945. After a year in the minor leagues, he became the first black man to play major league baseball. Elected as the National League's Rookie of the Year in 1947, he was Most Valuable Player in 1949.

Robinson's success on the baseball diamond helped open the door to black athletes in all professional sports. The color bar in professional football was broken in 1946, tennis in 1949, and basketball in 1950.

Discrimination against black people in other fields was also ending. In 1945 Todd Duncan became the first black man to join a major American opera company. The following year, Camilla Williams became the first black woman to break the color bar in opera when she appeared in the title role of *Madama Butterfly*. Both of these performers were members of the New York City Center Opera Company. In 1955 Marian Anderson became the first black member of the Metropolitan Opera Company.

Parallel with these developments was a movement calling for the end of segregation in the nation's armed forces. In June, 1948, A. Philip Randolph (page 295) organized the League for Nonviolent Civil Disobedience Against Military Segregation. Randolph threatened to urge blacks to resist induction into the armed forces unless segregation and racial discrimination were ended. In

Harry Truman was the first President to address a convention of the NAACP. At this meeting, held in 1947, he endorsed the association's views.

July, Truman issued Executive Order 9981, forbidding segregation in military facilities.

The issuance of Executive Order 9981 was not merely the result of pressure from black leaders like A. Philip Randolph. Truman had been pressing for civil rights legislation since he came into office, though with little success. In February, 1948, he had taken the unprecedented step of sending Congress a special message on civil rights. In it he called for an anti-lynching law, an anti-poll tax law,[1] a permanent Fair Employment Practices Commission, and a permanent Commission on Civil Rights. Truman was seeking, he said, "modern, comprehensive civil rights laws, adequate to the needs of the day and demonstrating our continuing faith in the free way of life."

Truman's re-election chances look slim.
When the Democrats looked ahead to the 1948 presidential election, many members of the party agreed with the assessment of the *New York Times* that "the President's influence is weaker than any President's has been in modern history." The Republicans

---

[1]The payment of a poll tax as a requirement for voting was used by some states as a means of discouraging black people — and poor white people — from going to the polls.

were jubilantly expecting to take over the White House. Clare Boothe Luce, a former Republican congresswoman from Connecticut, said simply, "Mr. Truman's time is short; his situation is hopeless. He is a gone goose." The Republicans again turned to Thomas E. Dewey (page 297) as their candidate for President. Earl Warren of California was nominated for Vice President.

Two splits in the Democratic Party made Republican victory seem certain. The first split came when a group of southern delegates, known as Dixiecrats, formed the States' Rights Democratic Party and named Governor J. Strom Thurmond of South Carolina as their candidate for President. The principal argument of the Dixiecrats was that, in pressing for federal civil rights legislation, the Democrats were violating state sovereignty.

The other dissident group called itself the Progressive Party. The new Progressives advocated sweeping social reforms and cooperation with the Soviet Union. They chose as their candidate former Vice President Henry A. Wallace.

Truman was not discouraged. In a rousing acceptance speech at the Democratic convention in Philadelphia, he issued a challenge to the Republicans. He was going to call the Republican-dominated Congress back in session, he declared, so that it could enact the promises of domestic reform included in the Republican platform. When nothing came of this session, Truman made the 80th Congress a campaign issue. He traveled the length and breadth of the country by train on what he called a "whistle-stop tour." Tens of thousands of people turned out to hear Truman deliver folksy, sometimes rambling, attacks on the Republicans. Dewey, meanwhile, gave lofty addresses, treating the campaign as a formality that would soon be over. The major public-opinion polls predicted that Dewey would win easily.

Truman wins a surprise victory. On election night, the nation awaited a Dewey landslide. By 10 P.M. newsboys in Chicago were hawking an "extra" edition of the *Tribune* bearing the following headline: DEWEY DEFEATS TRUMAN. The President later said, "Of course, he *wished* he had, but he didn't and that's all there was to it." In the astounding upset, Truman polled 24 million votes, two million more than Dewey. Moreover, the Democrats won a majority in both houses of Congress.

Congress rejects Truman's programs. At his inauguration in January, 1949, a confident Truman was accompanied by an honor guard from his old World War I outfit, Battery D. In his inaugural address he dedicated himself and his administration to obtaining a "fair deal" for the American people. He restated the goals he had worked for during his first term.

Despite the election returns, the 81st Congress, like the 80th Congress, showed little interest in passing Truman's Fair Deal legislation. It refused to pass civil rights legislation or a program of national health insurance. It did, however, increase and extend Social Security benefits, raise the minimum wage from 40 to 75 cents an hour, and appropriate money for the construction of low-income housing.

The government investigates internal security. Truman's presidential years from the beginning were marred by a nagging concern over loyalty in government. The issue had come to public attention in 1946, when a Soviet defector revealed that a spy ring in Canada had conspired to steal atomic secrets and hand them over to the Russians. Although he himself did not believe there were any disloyal people in the United States government, President Truman bowed to public pressure and in 1947 created the Loyalty Review Board. The Board's task was to judge whether government workers considered by the FBI to be security risks should be kept on the job. During the rest of Truman's term of office, some 300 government employees were dismissed as the result of the Board's investigations.

Some of these people, like other Americans, had been drawn into the Communist Party in the 1930's during the terrible suf-

Celebrating his stunning victory in the 1948 presidential contest, Harry Truman displays an early edition of the *Chicago Tribune*, which mistakenly announced Dewey's victory.

fering caused by the Great Depression. At that time, Communist promises of universal brotherhood and equality had seemed to some people to offer a possible solution to the harsh realities of the Depression. The terrible repression of Stalin's regime in the Soviet Union was ignored. Some of the men and women who became Communists in the 1930's were well-educated and later gained positions of responsibility in American society and government. By the time of the Second World War, many of these people had become disillusioned with the Soviet Union. Others, however, had not.

Charges of Communist espionage startle the nation. In 1948 the House Un-American Activities Committee (HUAC) revealed that charges of espionage had been brought against a trusted State Department official. Alger Hiss, who had been in the delegation that accompanied Roosevelt to Yalta, was accused by Whittaker Chambers, an editor of *Time* magazine and a former Communist agent, of handing over important secret documents to the Russians during the 1930's. Despite vigorous denials by Hiss and expressions of disbelief by his friends, Chambers could not be shaken in his story. In 1950 Hiss was convicted of perjury (for lying under oath in court about his relationship with Chambers) and sent to prison.

Public anxiety was heightened after the Soviet Union successfully tested its first atomic bomb in September, 1949. This disturbing development was soon followed by the shocking charge that Americans had apparently aided the Soviet Union in developing nuclear weaponry. In 1950 Klaus Fuchs, a British physicist who had worked at Los Alamos (page 306), confessed to being a Soviet agent. As a result of his confession, an

American couple, Julius and Ethel Rosenberg, were arrested and charged with having passed atomic secrets to the Soviet Union. A jury found them guilty, and they were executed in 1953.

These two cases convinced many Americans that there was good reason for concern over internal security and that President Truman had been seriously mistaken in believing that there were no disloyal people in the government. In 1950, Congress passed the McCarran Internal Security Act, which required Communist organizations to register with the Attorney General's office and to furnish membership lists and financial statements. Truman strongly opposed the law, believing it unconstitutional. Congress passed the McCarran Act over his veto.

SECTION REVIEW

1. Vocabulary: *right-to-work laws.*
2. (a) What benefits were provided veterans after the Second World War? (b) What was the chief economic problem facing the nation? (c) Why was there labor trouble?
3. (a) What was the Taft-Hartley Act? (b) What were its main provisions?
4. (a) How did Congress show its disapproval of reforms advocated by Truman? (b) Why did it pass the Twenty-Second Amendment?
5. What gains did black Americans make during the Truman years?
6. (a) What splits developed in the Democratic Party in 1948? (b) What candidates ran for office in 1948? (c) What was the outcome?
7. (a) How did the question of loyalty in government become a concern? (b) Why was the McCarran Internal Security Act passed?

2 The Cold War Begins

Even before the end of the Second World War, tension had begun to appear in relations between the Western powers and the Soviet Union. Already Soviet leaders were insisting on putting into power in Poland and Rumania governments under Russian control. The Red Army was also removing vast amounts of industrial equipment from Germany and was violating the arrangements for reparations agreed to at Yalta. Many Americans were becoming convinced that Roosevelt had been wrong in counting on Russia's cooperation in the postwar world. Senator Robert A. Taft, the son of a former President and himself known as "Mr. Republican," said that Roosevelt had been basing his policy "on the delightful theory that Mr. Stalin in the end will turn out to have an angelic nature."

The United Nations is formed. The drama of establishing the United Nations Organization at San Francisco on the very day, April 25, 1945, that American and Soviet troops were meeting on the Elbe (page 303) covered over the ill will that was developing between Russia and its allies. The UN, founded to promote peace and security for all people in the postwar world, had officially come into being the previous October. Its creation was the result of years of planning by leaders of the Allied nations.

The United Nations Charter, adopted by delegates from 46 nations at the San Francisco Conference, contained a preamble modeled on the preamble to the Constitution of the United States. It expressed the high-minded spirit in which the founding members formed the organization:

> We the peoples of the United Nations, determined to save succeeding generations from the scourge of war . . . to reaffirm faith in fundamental human rights . . . to promote social progress . . . and to ensure that armed force shall not be used, save in the common interest, . . . have resolved to combine our efforts to accomplish these aims.

The Charter included the following provisions:

(1) Each member nation would have one vote in a General Assembly, which was authorized to discuss any matter within the scope of the UN Charter. Although the Assembly had no power to compel action by any government, it could make recommendations that, it was hoped, would carry moral authority.

Delegate to the United Nations

In January, 1946, when the first meeting of the United Nations General Assembly was held in London, President Truman asked Eleanor Roosevelt to serve as a member of the United States delegation. Mrs. Roosevelt recorded her experiences at that historic assembly in this passage from her autobiography, *On My Own.*

Eleanor Roosevelt

I drove to the first session of the General Assembly in London with Mr. Stettinius, who was then Assistant Secretary of State, accompanied by Mr. Sandifer and two younger advisers. We drove slowly through the streets, past the Parliament buildings and the impressive statue of Abraham Lincoln that stands nearby, to the doors of the big auditorium where huge crowds of spectators had gathered to see the delegates of many nations arrive. The people were very hospitable and there was quite a lot of cheering, probably because people who had just survived a terrible war were desperately eager for the world's statesmen to find some better way to solve international problems. . . .

I might point out here that during the entire London session of the Assembly, I walked on eggs. I knew that as the only woman on the delegation I was not very welcome. Moreover, if I failed to be a useful member, it would not be considered merely that I as an individual had failed, but that all women had failed, and there would be little chance for others to serve in the near future.

I tried to think of small ways in which I might be more helpful. There were not too many women on the other delegations, and as soon as I got to know some of them, I invited them to tea in my sitting room at the hotel. . . . The party was so successful that I asked them again on other occasions, either as a group or a few at a time. I discovered that in such informal sessions we sometimes made more progress in reaching an understanding on some question before the United Nations than we had been able to achieve in the formal work of our committees.

(2) A Security Council was to be made up of representatives from the "Big Five" — the United States, Great Britain, France, China, and the Soviet Union — plus six (later ten) nonpermanent members who would be elected to two-year terms by the General Assembly. The Security Council would be authorized to investigate disputes between nations, foster their peaceful settlement, and take military action against peace-breakers. Decisions on substantive issues could be made only with the assent of all five permanent member nations. A veto by any of the permanent members could prevent action by the Council.

(3) An Economic and Social Council, responsible to the General Assembly and not subject to veto by the Security Council,

would be established to seek solutions to social and economic problems.

(4) An International Court of Justice would be established to pass judgment on the legal aspects of international disputes.

(5) A Trusteeship Council would advise the UN on the government of territories held in trust by the organization.

(6) A Secretariat would carry out the day-to-day work of the UN. The organization's chief administrator was to be called the Secretary-General.

The state of Israel is founded. The first major problem facing the United Nations was that of the conflicting claims of Jews and Arabs to the area of the Middle East known as Palestine. Hundreds of thousands of Jewish refugees from Europe were seeking to enter Palestine. The British, who had ruled the area since the First World War, had pledged support to a Jewish national home in Palestine with the understanding that the rights of non-Jewish peoples in the region would be protected.

In early 1947, Britain turned over the Palestine question to the United Nations. In November the United Nations voted to divide Palestine into two states: one for Jews and one for Arabs. Jewish leaders agreed to this solution, but the Arab

For his work in the Middle East, Ralph Bunche was awarded the Nobel Peace Prize in 1950, the first black person thus honored.

spokesmen refused to accept it, insisting that all of Palestine was rightfully theirs.

On May 14, 1948, the independence of the new state of Israel was proclaimed. Within a few minutes of the announcement, President Truman granted Israel formal recognition. The next day, Israel was invaded by Arab armies from Syria, Lebanon, Trans-Jordan, Iraq, Saudi Arabia, Yemen, and Egypt. The Arab League, as these nations called themselves, refused to recognize the legitimacy of the partition of Palestine and were determined to bring about the destruction of Israel. The League's armies were unable to defeat the Israelis, however, and in 1950 an American diplomat, Ralph Bunche, working for the United Nations, was able to arrange an armistice. Despite Bunche's success, the peace was an uneasy one because the basic problem remained: the refusal of the Arab nations to accept Israel's very existence.

Friction develops over the fate of Germany. Meanwhile, the German question was troubling Europe. The trials of Nazi war criminals in 1945 and 1946 (page 304) had been conducted by the former Allies. On other matters concerning the handling of Germany, however, the Western leaders were at odds with Stalin.

As had been planned at Yalta and Potsdam, Germany was divided into four zones that were administered by the United States, Great Britain, France, and the Soviet Union respectively. Problems arose, however, over the way the Soviet Union was handling its zone. In addition to dismantling entire German factories and sending them back to the Soviet Union, the Russians were shipping home food and other goods that they had earlier agreed to deliver to the Western zones. Moreover, the Russians set up a Communist government in their part of the divided country. This was a violation of the promise Stalin had made at Potsdam to help rebuild Germany as a democracy.

Gradually it became clear to Western leaders that the Soviet Union had no intention of giving up control over the German territory it had occupied. This, too, was a violation of promises Stalin had made at Potsdam, where it had been agreed that military occupation of Germany would be only temporary and that, after the occupation, the country would be reunited. Russian behavior caused the prewar distrust of Stalin to come alive again.

Stalin rules with an iron hand. Stalin had consolidated his despotic power in the mid-1930's through a campaign of violence and terror conducted against his own people. On every side, Stalin imagined conspiracies being hatched against him. Between 1936 and 1938 he carried out purges of the Communist Party, ordering the execution of perhaps 800,000 members. Among them were scores of party officials and several hundred senior army commanders, including many leaders of the Bolshevik revolution. Countless others also died. The total number of Stalin's victims has been estimated in the millions.

After the war Stalin became even more autocratic. Having made common cause with the democracies in order to prevent conquest by the Nazis, he now seemed fearful that further cooperation would weaken his control. He was no doubt strengthened in this view as he saw thousands of Soviet citizens and members of the armed forces defect to the West when the fortunes of war gave them the opportunity. Captured Russian soldiers who were returned to the Soviet Union after the peace were thrown into concentration camps — the dreaded *gulags*, cesspools of cruelty and deprivation. Thousands upon thousands of the former prisoners of war were put to death, the fact that they had surrendered to the enemy being "proof" that they were traitors. As he turned his country into a vast prison dominated by his secret police, Stalin felt secure only with a frightened populace.

The Soviet Union sets up a Communist government in Poland. At Yalta, Stalin had agreed to allow free elections in Poland after the war. No such elections were ever held. Truman pointed out at Potsdam how important a free election reported by a free Polish press would be to Americans of Polish heritage.

The majority of Poles were staunch anti-Communists who recalled the role of the Soviet Union in the invasion of their country in 1939 (page 278). The Polish people also recalled the discovery in 1943 of the mass graves of some 14,000 Polish officers who had been prisoners of war in Russian hands. Memories of the Katyn Forest massacre led many Poles to resist Communist domination.

Polish resistance to the Soviet Union, however, was quickly stamped out, and in 1945 a Soviet-backed government was installed. Two years later, when elections were finally held, the opposition to Soviet control had been so completely suppressed in Poland that the Communists polled 90 percent of the vote. Western protests to Stalin fell on deaf ears.

The Soviet Union takes permanent control of Eastern Europe. Because the Red Army had helped roll back the enemy and had then occupied Hungary, Rumania, Bulgaria, Czechoslovakia, and Yugoslavia, the Soviet Union had great power in Eastern Europe. Events in those countries followed a pattern similar to that in Poland. First, Russian-backed Communist groups worked to set up coalition regimes (governments in which various parties were represented). Then they ousted the non-Communist parties and suppressed all political opposition. In the Baltic Sea region three small countries — Latvia, Lithuania, and Estonia — had simply been absorbed into the Soviet Union after the arrival of Russian troops. The countries of Eastern Europe remained independent in name, but in fact they were, by the late 1940's, completely dominated by the Soviet Union.[2] They became known as Russian *satellites.*

In all these lands, people's lives were tightly controlled by their government. No book, magazine, or newspaper critical of

---

[2]Yugoslavia, although a Communist country, was able through the leadership of Marshal Tito to claim a measure of independence from Moscow after 1948.

In an eloquent speech delivered in 1946 at Fulton, Missouri, Winston Churchill described the Soviet threat to Europe.

the Soviet Union or of communism could be published. There was no freedom of speech, assembly, or petition. Those who dared to criticize their rulers risked imprisonment, exile, and even execution. Religion was seen as a harmful influence, so houses of worship were strictly regulated. In all of the satellites, the borders were tightly guarded so that people could not flee to the West and so that non-Communist Westerners could not readily visit, lest they bring with them unwelcome ideas.

The Soviet Union explained its actions on the grounds of self-defense. The Second World War had cost twenty million Russian lives. Russian leaders maintained that from the war they had learned that they must never let down their guard again. They were determined to surround themselves with countries they could control and to maintain a large standing army ever on the alert.

Churchill calls for a policy of strength. The West was alarmed by these developments. In March, 1946, former Prime Minister Winston Churchill was invited by President Truman to speak at Westminster College in Fulton, Missouri. In his address, Churchill said, "A shadow has fallen upon the scenes so lately lighted by Allied victory . . . an iron curtain has descended across the Continent. Behind that line lie all of the capitals of the ancient states of Central and Eastern Europe." The phrase "iron curtain" caught people's imagination; it gave people an image of the world divided in two, with the Soviet-dominated half living in self-imposed isolation. Churchill had helped Americans understand that the United States was involved in a "cold war" with Communist totalitarianism and that the danger of the war years was by no means over.[3]

American policy-makers decide on containment. Many American officials shared the view expressed by Churchill that the expansion of Russian influence was a serious threat to world peace. As early as February, 1946, George F. Kennan, a leading State Department expert on Russia, pointed out that the Soviet Union was growing increasingly hostile to the United States. Kennan argued that the Soviet empire would have to be contained, or restricted, within existing limits. People who favored a policy of *containment* agreed with Churchill's assessment of the Soviet Union's goals: "I do not believe," he had said, "that Soviet Russia desires war. What they want is the fruits of war and the indefinite expansion of their power and doctrines." Backers of the containment policy believed that the Russians were aggressive, but cautious — that the Soviet Union would expand only where its leaders thought they could do so without risking war. American policy-makers be-

---

[3]Immediately after the speech, Truman suggested to Stalin that he respond to Churchill's words from the same platform. Stalin turned down the opportunity.

lieved, with Churchill, that if earlier Western leaders had stood up to Hitler's expansionist aggression in the 1930's, the Second World War might never have taken place, and they drew a parallel to the present. They concluded that the United States must resist Soviet expansion wherever it occurred.

The Truman Doctrine is announced. In the fall of 1946, the government of Greece, which had been receiving aid from Great Britain, came under attack from Communist rebels, who were financed by neighboring Soviet satellite countries. Early in 1947, Britain sent word to the United States that it could no longer afford to support the Greek government's war against the rebels. Neither did it have the means to help Turkey resist Russian demands for a naval base in its territory.

The Truman administration acted quickly. Secretary of State George Marshall worked out an arrangement for sending military and economic aid to the two embattled countries. The President then asked Congress for $400 million to finance Marshall's aid program. Thus was born what became known as the Truman Doctrine. "I believe it must be the policy of the United States," Truman stated, "to support free peoples who are resisting attempted subjugation by armed minorities or by outside pressures." As a result of American aid, both Greece and Turkey were able eventually to withstand the threatened Communist take-overs.

The Marshall Plan aids Europe's recovery. Great Britain's inability to help Greece and Turkey was a symptom of the economic decline into which the Second World War had plunged Europe. Not only were European nations deeply in debt, but they had suffered enormous destruction during the war.

Compassion for the people of Europe, combined with the recognition that a healthy European economy was necessary to the security and prosperity of the United States, led to the adoption of a massive aid program. The Marshall Plan, as it was called, was proposed by Secretary of State Marshall in an address at Harvard University in June, 1947. Under the Marshall Plan, the governments of all the European nations, including Russia, were invited to decide among themselves what aid they would need from the United States in order to restore their economic well-being and stability. "Our policy," said Marshall, "is directed not against any country or doctrine but against hunger, poverty, desperation, and chaos. . . . Any government that is willing to assist in the task of recovery will find full cooperation . . . on the part of the United States government."

The Marshall Plan was vigorously debated in Congress. Most critics argued that the United States could not afford to rebuild Europe. Some people, including former Vice President Henry Wallace, denounced it as somehow aimed against the Soviet Union — indeed, as a "Martial Plan." Following the Communist take-over of democratic Czechoslovakia in February, 1948, however, opposition to the Plan started to fade.

On April 2, 1948, Congress passed an act creating the Economic Cooperation Administration to manage and distribute funds for the European Recovery Program — the official name of the Marshall Plan. Over the next three years, the United States sent $12 billion in assistance to Europe, mostly to Britain, France, and Germany. Poland and Czechoslovakia wished to take part in the Plan, but the Soviet Union stood in the way, refusing to allow them to accept United States aid. In the end, only Western European nations received help. As the economy of Europe improved, a leading British publication said it was plain to see that the Marshall Plan was "the most straightforward generous thing that any country has ever done for others." By 1951 the countries of Western Europe were well on their way to recovery.[4]

---

[4]For his efforts on behalf of the economic reconstruction of Europe, Marshall was awarded the Nobel Peace Prize in 1953.

Berliners watch an American transport plane come in for a landing during the 1948-1949 airlift. Such flights kept West Berlin supplied with food and fuel during the Soviet blockade of land routes.

The effort to reunify Germany strains East-West relations. In apparent resentment at the brightened scene in Western Europe, Soviet leaders became increasingly stubborn when discussing plans for the reunification of Germany. The Soviet Union, moreover, gradually ceased to cooperate with its former allies in the administration of occupied Germany. In the spring of 1948, therefore, France, Britain, and the United States announced plans to join their zones together. By so doing, they brought into existence what became the Federal Republic of Germany, or simply West Germany.[5]

The Russian response, on June 24, 1948, was to shut off all land and water routes through the Soviet zone to Berlin. (Berlin, like the rest of Germany, had been divided among the Allied countries after the war, but the city lay deep inside the Soviet zone.) The Russians hoped that their blockade would drive the Western powers out of West Berlin and force residents to choose between starvation and Communist rule.

President Truman realized that if the Western powers pulled out of the former German capital, they would be handing the Russians a uniquely symbolic prize. Truman stated the West's intention tersely: "We are going to stay, period."

President Truman might have used military force to open the routes to the city. Instead, he chose to try a peaceful way of making the Russians back down. In no time, a gigantic airlift was organized to overcome the Berlin blockade. Day after day an awesome fleet of C-54 Skymasters landed in West Berlin with food and fuel for two million people. At the height of the

---

[5]Shortly the Russians turned their zone into the German Democratic Republic, usually called East Germany.

airlift's operation an average of between four and five thousand tons of supplies, including coal, were being flown daily into the beleaguered city. When the weather prevented flights, it was said, Berlin held its breath, and when the roar was heard overhead again "a hundred thousand sighs of relief" rose from the city.

Finally, after 321 days, Soviet leaders recognized that the Western powers would not be driven out of Berlin. As a result, they finally decided to reopen rail lines, canals, and highways to Berlin on May 12, 1949. The blockade was over.

The airlift had backfired on the Soviet Union. Western nations, now convinced that Russia's activities were a threat to world peace, had been spurred to strengthen their armed forces. They recognized that even more serious military measures might be required to halt Soviet aggression.

NATO is formed. On April 4, 1949, while the Berlin blockade was under way, the United States signed the North Atlantic Treaty with Britain, France, Belgium, the Netherlands, Luxembourg, Italy, Portugal, Denmark, Iceland, Norway, and Canada. (In 1952 Greece and Turkey joined, and in 1954 so did West Germany.) Under the terms of the treaty, an armed attack against one country would be considered an armed attack against all. Moreover, a combined military force would be administered by the North Atlantic Treaty Organization (NATO). The United States, by far the richest of the member-nations, assumed the chief responsibility for NATO's expenses.

Following World War II the Soviet Union imposed Communist governments on neighboring Eastern European countries. To resist Soviet domination of the continent, the United States and Canada joined Western European nations in forming NATO.

Europe After World War II

NATO countries in Europe

Communist countries

FINLAND

NORWAY

SWEDEN

North Sea

Moscow

IRELAND

GREAT BRITAIN

DENMARK

SOVIET UNION

Atlantic Ocean

London

NETH.

Berlin

E. GERMANY

POLAND

BELG. LUX.

Paris

W. GERMANY

CZECH.

SCALE

0   400 mi

0   400 km

FRANCE

SWITZ.

AUSTRIA

HUNGARY

RUMANIA

YUGOSLAVIA

Black Sea

PORTUGAL

SPAIN

ITALY

BULGARIA

Rome

ALB.

TURKEY

Mediterranean Sea

GREECE

Not since 1800, when the alliance with France from revolutionary days had been terminated, had the United States belonged to an alliance in peacetime outside the Americas. Americans had learned, said Secretary of State Dean Acheson, that "if free nations do not stand together, they will fall one by one." The threat of Soviet aggression had, in a short time, profoundly altered American foreign policy. First, it had led to the Truman Doctrine, which modified the Monroe Doctrine's pledge not to intervene in Europe's affairs. Now, in the North Atlantic Treaty, it had broken a long-standing policy of having "no entangling alliances" in time of peace.

SECTION REVIEW

1. Vocabulary: *satellite, containment.*
2. (a) For what reason was the United Nations formed? (b) What are the main bodies of the United Nations? (c) What role did the United Nations play in the founding of Israel?
3. (a) How did the Soviet Union take control of Eastern Europe? (b) What were the Truman Doctrine and the Marshall Plan? (c) Why was each proposed?
4. (a) What was the response of the United States to the blockade of West Berlin? (b) For what reason was the North Atlantic Treaty Organization formed? (c) What nations became members of NATO?

3 The Cold War Leads to a Hot War in Korea

The United States and the Soviet Union were also in contention in Asia, as the Russians aimed to advance communism in that part of the world too. The three main areas of contention were Japan, China, and Korea.

The United States occupies Japan. The competition was mildest in Japan. America's war allies had only an advisory role in the occupation of Japan. Authority lay almost entirely with the United States, represented by General Douglas MacArthur.

Under MacArthur's supervision, Japanese society experienced drastic change. The emperor was stripped of his political role and his claim to divinity; a new constitution was put into effect providing for representative government; the power of the traditional ruling class was weakened through educational and economic reforms; and many laws and customs that discriminated against women were abolished. The purpose of these reforms was to bring democracy to Japan and ensure that the military would never again gain control of the government as it had in the 1930's. The Japanese armed forces were disbanded after 1945 and not allowed to exist again until 1951, when the United States ended its occupation and signed a treaty of peace. Even then, only a small defensive force was authorized.

For decades, Japan had been the most powerful nation in East Asia. When it surrendered to the Allies in 1945, the balance of power in the region shifted, affecting many countries. Two countries that felt this shift most keenly were China, portions of which had spent many years under Japanese occupation, and Korea, which had been governed by Japan.

Communists come to power in China. The Chinese Nationalist government of Chiang Kai-shek had, since the early 1930's, been forced to divide its energies between fighting Japanese invaders and Chinese Communist rebels. During the Second World War, the rebels, led by Mao Tse-tung, joined in the struggle against Japan.

For most Americans and millions of people everywhere, however, Chiang and his sophisticated wife symbolized China and its hopes for the future. When Madame Chiang, a graduate of Wellesley College in Massachusetts, addressed Congress in 1943, she thrilled the audience with her eloquent presentation of China's cause.

After the war, with the Japanese threat gone, civil war again broke out in China. The United States attempted to mediate, urging a Nationalist-dominated coalition government, but negotiators found both sides uncooperative.

As Chinese Communist forces closed in on Nationalist-held Shanghai in 1948, thousands of sampan dwellers sought refuge in the center of the city.

In an attempt to prevent a Communist take-over, the United States sent more than $3 billion in aid to Chiang Kai-shek between 1945 and 1949. Meanwhile, the Soviet Union, which had occupied Manchuria at the end of the war, aided Mao's Communist forces. By the end of 1949, Mao had succeeded in gaining control of the entire Chinese mainland. Chiang and large numbers of his loyal supporters fled to the island of Formosa.

The victory of the Chinese Communists set off a fierce argument in the United States. Critics denounced the Truman administration, accusing it of having betrayed the Nationalists. Truman, they said, had let himself become preoccupied with events in Europe and had ignored the threat to America's former ally in Asia. More aid, they maintained, would have allowed the Nationalists to overcome their foes. Truman's defenders insisted that Chiang's downfall

had been the Chinese leader's own doing. He had permitted corruption to become rampant, they said, and had refused to abolish abuses in his government that would have allowed him to compete with the Communists for popular support. The Nationalists, according to Truman's supporters, had simply lost the will to defeat the Communists, and no amount of money would have saved them from defeat.

The United States continued to grant diplomatic recognition only to the Nationalists on Formosa, saying that they were the legitimate government of all of China. In the United Nations, too, the United States used its veto to ensure that China was represented by the Nationalist government and that the Communists were denied China's seat in the Security Council (page 323).

Korea is divided. China's neighbor, Korea, was also a trouble spot. Long under

Chinese domination, Korea had been annexed by the Japanese in 1910. When Japan surrendered to the Allies in 1945, Russian troops occupied the northern half of Korea, while American troops occupied the southern half. The division of the country was expected to be temporary, because Allied leaders had agreed in 1943 that Korea would be made a unified, independent nation after the surrender of Japan. To that end, the United Nations organized elections

For three years, fighting between Communist and United Nations forces raged back and forth across the Korean peninsula.

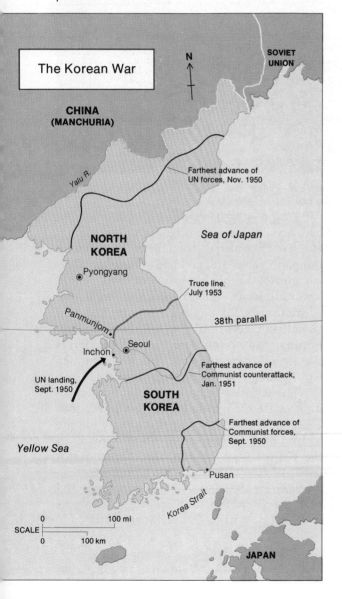

in Korea in 1948, but the Russians refused to allow the north to participate. The elections established the Republic of Korea and placed its capital at Seoul (SOHL), just south of the 38th parallel of latitude, which divided the country.

The United Nations and many of its individual members recognized the Republic of Korea as the legitimate government of all Korea. At the same time, in the north, the Communists called their territory the People's Republic of Korea and claimed that it was the only legitimate government of Korea. By June, 1949, both the United States and the Soviet Union had withdrawn their occupation forces, leaving North and South Korea (as the two nations were commonly called) to defend their own territories.

North Korea invades South Korea. On June 25, 1950, without advance warning, the Communist army of North Korea invaded South Korea. The attack put Truman's policy of containment (page 326) to the test. Secretary of State Acheson warned that the attack was more than an attack on the authority of the United Nations. It was, he declared, "a challenge to the whole system of collective security."

Acheson, at Truman's request, brought the issue before an emergency meeting of the United Nations Security Council. The Security Council promptly passed a resolution ordering the North Koreans to withdraw their forces from south of the 38th parallel. The Soviet Union no doubt would have vetoed this resolution, but its representatives had walked out six months earlier in protest against the United Nations' refusal to recognize the Communist government in China. The North Korean troops, ignoring the order of the Security Council, continued to move south.

On June 27 the Security Council called on UN members to aid South Korea in repelling the invading forces. The United Nations did not have troops of its own, but it invited member nations to take part in a joint "police action" under the command of General MacArthur. Sixteen nations contributed troops to the UN forces, but the majority of the men who took part in the military action were South Koreans and Americans.

During the summer of 1950, the North Koreans were on the offensive. The outnumbered American and South Korean forces gradually retreated south. They were determined to defend their last foothold, the port of Pusan. Then, on September 15 the course of the war turned when MacArthur daringly landed troops behind North Korean lines at Inchon. Shortly, UN forces recaptured Seoul. By October they had driven the North Koreans back to the 38th parallel.

The objectives of the war change. At this point, the original purpose of the UN forces had been accomplished. The General Assembly now debated whether to order its troops into North Korea. On October 8, UN troops, in accordance with the decision of the General Assembly, crossed the 38th parallel. By November, MacArthur's troops had taken over almost all of North Korea.

The Chinese Communists had warned that they would aid the North Koreans if MacArthur's troops moved north of the 38th parallel. MacArthur assured Truman that there was little possibility of such an intervention. Suddenly, late in November, 1951, Chinese forces struck the UN army with devastating power. Greatly outnumbered and overextended, the UN forces were quickly pushed back below the 38th parallel, sustaining heavy casualties and losing the South Korean capital as they retreated.

MacArthur's troops, the general now said, were in "an entirely new war." He demanded that the United States blockade the Chinese coast, bomb China's supply bases in Manchuria, and use Chiang Kai-shek's troops to invade mainland China. General Omar Bradley, chairman of the Joint Chiefs of Staff, argued that to strike China would be to have "the wrong war, in the wrong place, at the wrong time, and with the wrong enemy." President Truman agreed with him and ordered MacArthur to continue to fight a *limited* war aimed only at freeing South Korea from the invaders.

American troops fought in rugged terrain to help repel the Communist invasion of South Korea.

MacArthur denounced the idea of fighting a war with "one hand tied behind our back." Even as the UN forces recovered and began to make plans for a counterattack, MacArthur publicly defied his superiors by calling for an offensive against mainland China. "There is no substitute for victory," he insisted.

Truman dismisses MacArthur. On April 11, 1951, the world was astonished to learn that Truman had dismissed MacArthur for failing to give wholehearted support to United States policy. Truman explained to a friend, "I will undoubtedly create a great furor, but under the circumstances I could do nothing else and still be President of the United States. Even the Chiefs of Staff came to the conclusion that civilian control of the military was at stake, and I didn't let it stay at stake very long." The new commander in Korea was General Matthew B. Ridgway, another distinguished hero of the Second World War.

Following his return to the United States, MacArthur was given triumphal receptions by his supporters. In an address to a joint session of Congress, he ended a moving speech by quoting from a barracks-room tune of his youth: " 'Old soldiers never die, they just fade away.' And like the old soldier of that ballad, I now close my military career and just fade away, an old soldier who tried to do his duty as God gave him the light to see that duty."

Truce talks begin in Korea. Under the new leadership of General Ridgway, UN troops fought a limited war in Korea, in which neither side made much headway. In June, 1951, the Russian ambassador to the UN suggested that a settlement in Korea was possible. Truce talks began in July.

A particularly difficult question arose over the many Chinese and North Korean prisoners of war who did not want to be returned to their homelands to live under communism. Agreement on a cease-fire line and on a means of enforcing the truce also proved difficult to reach. As the talks dragged on, sporadic fighting continued. The American people, who were paying most of the costs of the war, became impatient, and the conflict became an issue in the 1952 presidential election.

Eisenhower is elected President. As the 1952 elections drew near, there was widespread dissatisfaction with the Truman administration. First, the country seemed mired in an expensive war. Second, the public was alarmed by charges that Communist agents had been able to infiltrate the government because of laxness on the part of the Democratic administration. Third, the public was soured by accusations of corruption and influence-peddling among some of the President's friends. In March, 1952, Truman took himself out of the running. The President said, in his characteristically crisp language, "I shall not accept a renomination. I do not feel that it is my duty to spend another four years in the White House."

On the Republican side, Dwight D. Eisenhower, freshly returned from his duties as commander of NATO forces, beat out Senator Taft for the presidential nomination. At the party's convention in Chicago the galleries cheered wildly, "We like Ike!" The general's running mate was Senator Richard M. Nixon of California, who had won national attention through his role in the investigation of Alger Hiss (page 321). Accurately judging the national mood, the Republicans campaigned on the themes of "Korea, communism, and corruption."

The Democrats nominated Governor Adlai E. Stevenson of Illinois, a candidate who had President Truman's strong backing. Stevenson, an eloquent and witty man, bore the same name as his grandfather, who had been Vice President under Grover Cleveland. At first reluctant to seek the presidency, Stevenson was not well-known outside his home state at the beginning of the campaign. As time went on, his effective speeches and agreeable personal style won him heavy support among intellectuals and leaders of organized labor.

In spite of Stevenson's impressive performance, Eisenhower's fame and popularity made his election a certainty. His campaign speeches were often bland and repetitious (causing reporters to joke, "He's crossing the 38th platitude again"). Nevertheless, he displayed a warmth and devotion to traditional values that millions of people found comforting and reassuring. In addition, shortly before the election, Eisenhower made headlines by declaring, "I shall go to Korea." The country took his words to mean that he would end the war.

Eisenhower won by a landslide, the first Republican to break the Democrats' hold on the Solid South since 1928. The victory was proof of Eisenhower's magnetism but not of the drawing power of the Republican Party as a whole. Republicans gained control of Congress, though only by a slim margin.

Along with their wives, Dwight Eisenhower and Richard Nixon celebrate their
nominations as Republican candidates for President and Vice President in 1952.

Truman leaves office. As Truman prepared to return to private life, he delivered a farewell address on television. In it he said, "I suppose that history will remember my term in office as the years when the 'cold war' began to overshadow our lives. I have hardly had a day in office that has not been dominated by this all-embracing struggle . . . and always in the background there has been the atomic bomb."

By the time of Eisenhower's inauguration, Truman and Ike were barely talking to each other. Their strained relations grew out of a clash of personalities. Still, the good of the nation came first. When Eisenhower sat at his desk in the Oval Office on his first day as President, he found one drawer locked. Calling for a key, he opened the drawer and there found a folder of confidential memoranda from Truman on immediate pressing problems. The cold war had been transferred to fresh hands.

SECTION REVIEW

1. (a) What changes were brought about by the American occupation of Japan? (b) What change in power took place in China? (c) What was the reaction in the United States to the news from China?
2. (a) How did war break out in Korea? (b) What was the response of the United Nations? (c) Why did President Truman dismiss General MacArthur in 1951?
3. (a) Who were the candidates for President in 1952? (b) What issues did the Republicans stress? (c) What was the outcome?

Chapter 12 Review

Summary

Thrust into the presidency by Franklin Roosevelt's death, Harry Truman led the nation in the years immediately following the Second World War. At home, the American people were adjusting to peacetime. Programs such as the GI Bill of Rights had been initiated to help veterans. The wartime economy, meanwhile, was quickly converted to peacetime production. The ending of price controls in mid-1946, combined with the pent-up demand for all kinds of consumer goods, caused prices to increase rapidly. Workers, in turn, demanded pay raises, and labor disputes took place in many industries. After a series of crippling strikes, Congress passed the Taft-Hartley Act in June, 1947. This legislation established new rules for collective bargaining.

During his presidency, Harry Truman backed efforts to eliminate racial discrimination. He ordered an end to segregation in the nation's armed forces and asked Congress to create a Commission on Civil Rights.

During the postwar years, problems with the Soviet Union occupied the President's attention. The Russians imposed Communist governments on the nations of Eastern Europe and created what Winston Churchill called an "iron curtain" across Europe. Russian threats against Greece and Turkey prompted Truman to send aid to those countries and to declare a policy that was based on the containment of Soviet expansion. In June, 1947, the Marshall Plan was announced, offering American assistance in rebuilding the war-damaged economies of European countries.

Efforts to reunify Germany led to continued friction between the Soviet Union and its former Allies, as did the unsuccessful Russian attempt to blockade West Berlin. To counter the aggressive actions of the Soviet Union, the North Atlantic Treaty Organization was formed in April, 1949.

In the summer of 1950, the Communist forces of North Korea staged a surprise invasion of South Korea. This action caused the United Nations to take a stand against Communist aggression. The bulk of the fighting during the Korean War fell to the American forces, led by General Douglas MacArthur. Disagreement with Truman over how the war should be fought led to MacArthur's dismissal. Truce talks began in July, 1951, but dragged on into late 1952 with no end to the fighting in sight. The frustrating news from Korea, combined with fear of Communist infiltration into the government, caused voters to turn away from the Democrats. Dwight Eisenhower was elected President in 1952, thus bringing to an end twenty years of Democratic control of the presidency.

Vocabulary and Important Terms

1. GI Bill of Rights
2. Taft-Hartley Act
3. right-to-work laws
4. Twenty-Second Amendment
5. McCarran Internal Security Act
6. Dixiecrats
7. Loyalty Review Board
8. Executive Order 9981
9. Security Council
10. General Assembly
11. satellite
12. "iron curtain"
13. containment
14. Truman Doctrine
15. Marshall Plan
16. Berlin airlift
17. North Atlantic Treaty Organization (NATO)

Discussion Questions

1. (a) After the Second World War, what economic problems beset the country? (b) Why did labor leaders issue calls for strikes? (c) Why did Congress pass the Taft-Hartley Act?

2. (a) What gains were made by black Americans in the years immediately following the Second World War? (b) What actions did President Truman take to end segregation?

3. Compare and contrast the elections of 1948 and 1952. (a) Who were the candidates in each election? (b) What were the main campaign themes? (c) What were the results?

4. (a) What factors and events contributed to concern about internal security in the American government during the postwar era? (b) What was the response of Congress and President Truman to this concern?

5. (a) What were the goals of the United Nations? (b) What responsibilities were assigned to the Security Council? (c) How were the Security Council's actions limited?

6. (a) What steps did the Soviet Union take in Eastern Europe during the postwar era? (b) How did Soviet leaders justify their actions? (c) What was life like for people behind the "iron curtain"?

7. What effect did Soviet aggression have on American foreign policy?

8. (a) To what extent did the United States involve itself in Asian affairs immediately after the Second

World War? (b) After North Korea invaded South Korea in 1950, what role did the United States play in the Korean conflict? (c) What happened after UN forces invaded North Korea?

Relating Past and Present

1. To what extent does the containment of communism remain a major concern of American foreign policy? Have American-Soviet relations fundamentally changed in the years since Truman's presidency? Explain your answer.

2. In 1948 there was a split in the Democratic Party because of differing viewpoints concerning civil rights and American-Soviet relations. What issues have the potential for dividing political parties today? Explain your answer.

Studying Local History

Find out how your state voted in the election of 1948. Then locate a local newspaper story or edito-

rial that contains comments on Truman's surprise victory. What is the tone of the newspaper commentary? What explanation for Truman's victory does the newspaper offer?

Using History Skills

1. *Reading maps.* Study the map on page 329 showing Europe after World War II. (a) What European countries were members of NATO? (b) What countries were behind the "iron curtain"? (c) How does the location of Berlin help explain the Soviet decision to blockade that city?

2. *Reading source material.* Study Eleanor Roosevelt's description on page 323 of the United Nations meeting. How does she convey the high hopes felt by people in 1946 that the United Nations would be able to promote world peace?

3. *Placing events in time.* Look back through the chapter and find five important events of the cold war period. Make a time line showing those events.

WORLD SCENE

Independence in Asia

Many Asians had sought independence for their nations in the years prior to the Second World War. Immediately after the war, patriots in the Philippines and in India achieved their goal.

The Philippine Republic. Preparations for Philippine independence from the United States were interrupted by the Japanese invasion in 1942. After the war the move toward independence was resumed. Elections were held, and Manuel Roxas won the office of president. On July 4, 1946, the Philippines became a republic.

When Roxas died in 1948, his vice president, Elpidio Quirino, succeeded him. Quirino was immediately faced with a challenge to his government from a group of Communist-led rebels. Known as the Huks, the rebels fought a guerrilla war against the Philippine army for several years and were not defeated until the mid-1950's.

Gandhi and the independence of India. One of the leading figures of the twentieth century was Mohandas Gandhi of

India. Beginning in 1915, Gandhi led a movement to persuade the British to grant India its independence. His insistence on nonviolent tactics set an example that was adopted by oppressed groups in many other nations. The protests organized by Gandhi took the form of widespread boycotts and acts of civil disobedience (protests in which British laws were openly defied). British officials repeatedly imprisoned Gandhi but were powerless to halt the unrest.

At the end of the Second World War in 1945, the British government agreed to give India its independence. The British withdrawal, however, was complicated by the demands of the Muslim minority for a separate Islamic state. Gandhi tried to persuade the Muslim leaders to share power with the Hindus in a united India but to no avail. When independence finally came in 1947, two new nations were created: India and the Islamic state of Pakistan. Gandhi, who continued to oppose partition of India, was assassinated in 1948 by a Hindu fanatic infuriated by Gandhi's willingness to cooperate with Muslims.

CHAPTER 13

Tensions Amid Affluence

1953 – 1963

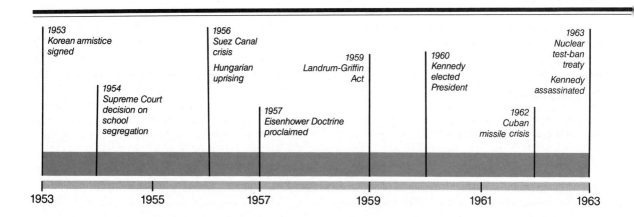

1953
Korean armistice
signed

1954
Supreme Court
decision on
school
segregation

1956
Suez Canal
crisis

Hungarian
uprising

1957
Eisenhower Doctrine
proclaimed

1959
Landrum-Griffin
Act

1960
Kennedy
elected
President

1962
Cuban
missile crisis

1963
Nuclear
test-ban
treaty

Kennedy
assassinated

1953   1955   1957   1959   1961   1963

CHAPTER OUTLINE

1. Cold-war tensions
   remain high.

2. The nation prospers
   under Eisenhower.

3. The Democrats regain
   the White House.

When Dwight Eisenhower became President, he may have been the most widely admired new Chief Executive since George Washington. Fellow Americans believed they saw in Ike a man who stood above politics — a fatherly figure whose sole interest was the good of the country. They knew and admired the fact that he had grown up in a humble home in Abilene, Kansas, and had risen to walk with kings and queens. They also respected him for his patriotism and devotion to service. As a youth, Ike had attended West Point. He later described the feeling that came over him as he took the cadets' oath and uttered the words "the United States of America." "From here on," he said, "it would be the nation I would be serving, not myself. Suddenly the flag itself meant something. I haven't heard other officers speak of their memories of that moment but mine have never left me."

Eisenhower was followed in office by John Kennedy. At his inauguration in 1961, Kennedy proclaimed that "the torch has been passed to a new generation of Americans." By so doing, he helped create the impression that a sharp change was taking place in national life. In fact, the time Eisenhower and Kennedy spent in office may be regarded as a single period. It was a time characterized by general prosperity, public confidence in the judgment of national leaders, and faith in the future.

1 Cold-War Tensions Remain High

At the end of the Korean War, both the Soviet Union and the United States came under new leadership. Joseph Stalin, the ruthless Soviet dictator who had ruled for almost a quarter of a century, died in 1953. His political heirs were vying for power and it was as yet unclear who would emerge the winner. Meanwhile, in the United States, the election of President Eisenhower had ended twenty years of uninterrupted Democratic leadership in the White House. People watched intently to see what effect these changes would have.

The Korean War ends. Eisenhower's first important business as President was to bring the Korean War to a close. In December, 1952, while he was still only President-elect, he had carried out his campaign pledge to go to Korea to seek an end to the hostilities. His trip had no immediate results. The negotiations dragged on for seven more months.

Finally, in July, 1953, an armistice was signed. The negotiators also established a demilitarized zone about two and a half miles wide between the two Koreas. A committee was set up to settle the fate of the Korean prisoners of war who did not wish to return to their home countries, and a military commission was formed to supervise other terms of the armistice. North Korea wound up with about 1,500 fewer square miles of territory than before the war. The United States and South Korea shortly signed a mutual-security treaty,

A symbol of the cold war, the Brandenburg Gate stands at the boundary between East and West Berlin. The sign warns, "Attention! You are leaving West Berlin."

ACHTUNG!
Sie verlassen jetzt
WEST-BERLIN

Dwight Eisenhower, shown here at his desk in the White House, fulfilled a promise made during the 1952 presidential campaign by achieving a negotiated settlement to the Korean conflict.

pledging to consult with each other in case of threatened attack.

The Americans and their UN allies had accomplished their objective. Through prompt military action they had turned back Soviet-supported aggression, thus saving the South Koreans from being swallowed up by the Communist world. Still, Americans found it hard to rejoice. The Korean War had taken the lives of over 33,000 American servicemen, and more than 100,000 had been wounded.

The cold war continues. Although the hot war was over, the cold war went on. The new Secretary of State, John Foster Dulles, was a man of definite ideas. Under his guidance, the incoming administration decided it must no longer wait for Communist aggression to occur before trying to contain it. The resulting "brush-fire wars" — like the one in Korea — were too costly. The Eisen-hower-Dulles position was that in order to discourage Communist aggression, the United States must make clear its determination to retaliate directly against the Soviet Union.

The new American military strategy was known as **massive retaliation.** Dulles boldly declared, moreover, that his diplomatic method was "to get to the verge without getting into war." Critics of this policy called it **brinkmanship,** charging that Dulles's apparent willingness to bring the United States to the brink of war could, through some misunderstanding, lead to war itself. Brinkmanship, they said, was especially unsuitable now that both the United States and the Soviet Union had developed hydrogen bombs. These weapons had been successfully tested by the United States in 1952 and by the Russians less than a year later. They had thousands of times more explosive force than the atomic bombs that had been dropped on Japan in the final days of World War II.

President Eisenhower also expressed concern about the development of these powerful weapons. Speaking at the United Nations in 1953, he said, "Let no one think that the expenditure of vast sums for weapons and systems of defense can guarantee absolute safety. . . . The awful arithmetic of the atomic bomb does not permit of any such easy solution." In this address, known as the Atoms for Peace speech, Eisenhower offered to talk to Soviet leaders, "to seek an acceptable solution to the atomic armaments race, which overshadows not only the peace but the very life of the world."

The Eisenhower administration, meanwhile, did not neglect conventional weapons or defense systems. During the 1950's the United States continued to work closely with its NATO allies to build up military strength sufficient to deter a Russian invasion of Western Europe. It was also decided that the rearming of West Germany was central to the defense of Europe. For this reason, Germany was admitted to NATO in 1955 and allowed to build up an army of half a million men.

The French withdraw from Indochina. Only months after the Korean War was brought to an end, another military crisis arose in Asia. It was destined to have lasting significance for the United States.

Indochina, a French colony in Southeast Asia, was torn by civil war. Rebels, known as Viet Minh, were fighting to drive the French out of the country and to establish a Communist government. The insurgents had the backing of China and the Soviet Union. The United States gave aid to the French and their anti-Communist Indochinese allies, but by 1954 it was clear that the Viet Minh were winning. Late that spring, after suffering defeat in the fierce Battle of Dien Bien Phu, the French decided to pull out of Southeast Asia.

An international conference met at Geneva, Switzerland, to decide the political fate of Indochina. Negotiations led to a political settlement under which the independence of Laos and Cambodia were guaranteed. Vietnam was temporarily divided at the 17th parallel, with the Communists given control of the northern portion. The anti-communist government of President Ngo Dinh Diem (noh din ZEE-em), meanwhile, was given control of the southern portion. Elections were to be held in 1956 with the aim of reuniting the country under one government. The United States participated in the conference but refused to sign the agreements, in protest against the concessions made to the Communists.

A crisis develops in the Middle East. The American public grew accustomed to seeing the focus of the cold war shift constantly from one part of the world to another. The Middle East entered the spotlight in 1956 in an unexpected way. Two years earlier, a nationalist leader named Gamal Abdel Nasser had come to power in Egypt. To obtain Nasser's good will, Secretary of State Dulles offered American help in building a large dam at Aswan, on the Nile River. At the same time, the Soviet Union, bent on wooing Nasser, also held out an offer of a loan for the big project. The Russians, meanwhile, entered into an agreement to trade weapons for Egyptian cotton. Egypt soon used the arms to carry out raids against Israel, which Nasser had pledged to destroy.

In July, 1956, angered by Nasser's dealings with the Soviet Union, Dulles abruptly withdrew the offer of American aid. Nasser lashed back by seizing the Suez Canal, which ran through Egyptian territory but was owned by an international company. He then announced that Israeli ships would no longer be allowed to use the waterway. Britain and France feared that they, too, might soon be denied access to it. They appealed to the United States to join them in taking action against Egypt, but Eisenhower and Dulles were earnestly opposed to military intervention.

The tense situation was heightened when, on October 29, 1956, Israel launched a strike against Egypt. Two days later, without having informed the United States of their intentions, Britain and France joined Israel. When the Soviet Union threatened to send "volunteers" to Egypt to aid Nasser, the world seemed on the threshold of war. Eisenhower decided to place the issue before the United Nations, which quickly passed a resolution calling for the withdrawal of all invading forces. Furious with the United States for its lack of support, Britain, France, and Israel nevertheless complied with the UN resolution.

American commitments grow. One outcome of the 1956 war was a further extension of United States military commitments. In a special message to Congress in January, 1957, the President announced what became known as the Eisenhower Doctrine. He obtained from Congress a resolution permitting him to send troops to any Middle East country whose rulers considered themselves threatened by "international communism."

Three months later, when Egypt's Nasser tried to topple King Hussein of Jordan, the United States Navy was sent to the Mediterranean in a show of force. Then, in July, when the pro-Western government of Lebanon seemed about to be overthrown, Eisenhower sent a contingent of marines to

Hungarians burned pictures of Stalin during the revolt of 1956. Soviet troops soon put down the uprising, crushing hopes for freedom.

restore order in the country. The use of troops in this instance was, however, unusual. The administration mostly relied on the sale of arms and on the distribution of economic aid to maintain its influence in the region.

New crises arise in Europe. At precisely the same time that the world seemed near war in the Middle East, a revolution broke out in Hungary. On October 23, 1956, popular discontent exploded into street fighting in Budapest, the nation's capital. A crowd toppled the immense statue of Stalin that stood in the center of the city and was a hated symbol of Russian domination. The revolution spread quickly throughout the country, with freedom fighters demanding

that Soviet troops be withdrawn and that the Hungarian people be allowed to organize a democratic government.

The Soviet Union moved quickly to quell the Hungarian uprising. While about 200,000 refugees managed to make their way across the Austrian border to freedom, within two weeks the revolution had been crushed by Soviet tanks. In the operation, thousands of people were killed. Once the fighting had ended, the new government, a puppet of the USSR, rounded up all known rebels and imprisoned them, either in Hungary or in the Soviet Union. The inability of the Eisenhower administration to act on a promise it had earlier given to liberate Eastern Europe produced frustration in the United States and disappointment abroad.

Two years after the Hungarian uprising, another crisis arose in Eastern Europe. In November, 1958, Nikita Khrushchev (nih-KEE-tah kroosh-CHOFF), who had emerged as Stalin's successor in the Soviet Union, demanded that the Western powers withdraw from Berlin. Khrushchev threatened that unless they yielded to his demand within six months, he would sign a peace treaty with East Germany and cut off Western access to Berlin. The United States, Britain, and France made it clear that they had no intention of abandoning the city. Meanwhile, thousands of refugees continued to flock to West Berlin to escape the harsh repression in East Germany.

Cold-war tensions are eased. Early in 1959, Khrushchev seemed to back down, saying that he would extend the Berlin deadline if Western leaders agreed to a summit conference. Negotiations to arrange such a meeting began, but no firm agreement was reached. Still, tensions relaxed enough for Vice President Nixon to visit Poland and the Soviet Union during the summer of 1959. That fall, Khrushchev visited the United States and conferred with Eisenhower at Camp David, the presidential retreat in Maryland. The two leaders concluded their meetings by issuing a joint statement in which they said that they would settle all existing disagreements through negotiation. They also said they would soon hold a summit conference that would include European leaders.

Khrushchev cancels the summit conference. In early May, 1960, just as the long-awaited summit conference was about to open, cold-war tensions again took over. Khrushchev announced that on May 1 the Russians had shot down an American U-2 reconnaissance plane flying over their territory. He insisted that the United States apologize, punish those responsible, and promise that such flights would cease. At first, the administration denied that the U-2 had been engaged in spying, but soon the government acknowledged the truth of the Soviet charges. Eisenhower accepted full responsibility for the incident and promised that U-2 flights over Russia would be halted.

He refused, however, to apologize. Other Western leaders supported Eisenhower in his firm stance. Khrushchev would not remain at the summit conference without an apology. He flew back to Moscow, and the summit conference collapsed.

After the U-2 incident, relations between the United States and the Soviet Union seemed to worsen. Khrushchev canceled an invitation he had extended to Eisenhower to visit Russia, and continued to insist that the American President apologize. Eisenhower stood his ground, but nevertheless continued his efforts to reduce tensions. His labors, however, were unsuccessful. Khrushchev continued to denounce American "aggression." In 1960, at a session of the UN in New York, the Soviet leader both alarmed and amused the Western world by taking off his shoe and pounding the table with it to demonstrate his outrage at the United States.

SECTION REVIEW

1. Vocabulary: *massive retaliation, brinkmanship.*
2. (a) What were the terms of the armistice signed in Korea in 1953? (b) How did the Eisenhower administration modify the containment policy? (c) What was the result of the French defeat in Southeast Asia?
3. (a) What factors contributed to the Suez crisis? (b) How was the situation resolved? (c) What was the Eisenhower Doctrine? (d) How was it tested in Lebanon?
4. (a) What was the response of the Soviet Union to the Hungarian uprising? (b) What demands did Nikita Khrushchev make concerning Berlin? (c) Why did he cancel the 1960 Paris summit conference?

2 The Nation Prospers Under Eisenhower

When Dwight Eisenhower later described his election to the presidency, he modestly wrote, "The homely old [saying] had proved to be true: in the United States, any boy *can* grow up to be President." In domestic matters Eisenhower depended upon his forthrightness and his ability, learned during his

Overproduction was the basic problem facing American farmers during the 1950's. Crop output climbed, while farm income declined.

long army career, to work through a trusted staff. He gave his subordinates much leeway. He liked to say, "You do not lead by hitting people over the head."

DOMESTIC POLICIES

The Republicans try to reduce the size of government. Eisenhower had taken office promising to balance the budget. He found it difficult, however, to reduce national expenditures. Eisenhower tried to cut government spending, even allowing about 100,000 civil service jobs to remain unfilled. Still, when a business recession came at the end of his first year in office, the administration resorted to methods formerly used by the Democrats. It cut taxes, increased Social Security payments, and extended unemployment compensation. All of Eisenhower's annual budgets, furthermore, were larger than any of Truman's.

The size of the budgets reflected, in part, the fact that Eisenhower made no attempt to tamper with the main body of social reforms enacted in the previous administrations. Most people probably agreed with Eisenhower's assertion that the path for the nation to take was "down the middle."

Farm problems continue. Notably fewer disputes on domestic economic issues arose during Eisenhower's years in office than in recent administrations. Many farmers, however, were distressed by the proposals of Secretary of Agriculture Ezra Taft Benson.

On American farms overproduction had continued to be a problem. Improvements in all aspects of agriculture — better seed, better cultivation, better storage facilities — had increased the production of crops far beyond national need. As a result, farm prices were dismally low, and many farmers were forced off the land.

Under the existing farm program, the government bought surplus crops from farmers if prices dropped below a certain level. Secretary Benson argued that these fixed payments actually encouraged farmers to overproduce. The solution he proposed was to make price supports flexible. This program was passed by Congress, but it was no more successful than earlier arrangements in reducing farm surpluses.

In 1956 the government made a further attempt to halt overproduction by offering to pay farmers who agreed to cut back their planting. Price-support payments, it was hoped, could be reduced. At the same time, by keeping the soil idle its fertility would be maintained. Even this program, however, failed to prevent mounting farm surpluses.

Americans express concern over internal security. Worry over the loyalty of people employed by the federal government had become widespread during Truman's years in the White House. The same concern confronted Eisenhower when he took office in 1953. In response, he supported strict internal-security laws that provided for the suspension of any government employee accused of being a security risk. He also backed laws that allowed the death penalty for espionage.

The Senate, at this time, was investigating the extent of Communist infiltration into the federal government. A leader of the investigation was Senator Joseph R. McCarthy of Wisconsin. In February, 1950, McCarthy had brought himself to national attention by charging, without substantiation, that the State Department employed more than 200 Communists. The Senate promptly appointed a subcommittee to investigate these and similar accusations. From his position on this subcommittee, McCarthy became one of the most powerful politicians in the country.

The turning point in Senator McCarthy's career came in 1954, when he publicly insisted that there were Communists in the ranks of the United States Army. The Army countercharged that McCarthy was attempting to gain special favors for the recently drafted son of a friend. A special Senate committee held televised hearings on the matter in April and May of 1954. Many supporters, seeing McCarthy in action, turned against him. His manner struck viewers as rude and bullying, and his reckless use of unfounded accusation offended their sense of fair play. From then on, McCarthy's support eroded. In December, 1954, his Senate colleagues formally condemned him for "conduct unbecoming a member." McCarthy's political career never recovered from this blow.

Eisenhower is re-elected. President Eisenhower's remarkable popularity continued undiminished through his first term. His reelection in 1956 seemed sure. The only uncertainty was his health. In September, 1955, he had suffered a heart attack, and less than a year later he underwent abdominal surgery. In each case, however, his recovery was swift and complete.

In running for a second term in 1956, Eisenhower did almost no campaigning. Still, there was little that the Democrats could do. Adlai Stevenson, nominated for a second campaign against Eisenhower, was buried in a Republican landslide. The President won with 35,600,000 votes to slightly over 26,000,000 for Stevenson. In the electoral college the results were even more decisive: 457 votes to 73. In carrying 41 states, the President had won the most overwhelming victory since Roosevelt crushed Landon in 1936. The Democrats had, however, retained control of both houses of Congress. For all his political strength, Eisenhower was unable to transfer his own popularity to his party.

Organized labor faces new problems. As his second term got under way, Eisenhower confronted fresh issues already forming. In 1955 the American Federation of Labor (AFL) and the Congress of Industrial Organizations (CIO), once deadly rivals, had come together in a unified labor organization. At the time of unification, the AFL-CIO represented over fifteen million workers. George Meany of the AFL was named president and Walter Reuther of the CIO became vice president.

The major long-term problem union leaders faced was *automation* — the manufacture of goods by machines controlled electronically rather than by hand. New technology was making it possible for whole factories to be run with only a handful of workers present. The challenge unions faced was how best to serve their members, now subject to loss of jobs owing to technological change rather than economic conditions.

A further problem confronting labor unions during the late 1950's was the corruption of some union leaders. A Senate investigation of the Teamsters, the single largest union in the AFL-CIO, showed that the organization's pension and welfare funds had been used for questionable purposes. The probe also revealed that some Teamster leaders had ties to organized crime and that a large amount of money entrusted to the leadership was missing. Dave Beck, the president of the union, was charged with misappropriating union funds, and eventually he went to jail. When the Teamsters replaced Beck with Jimmy Hoffa, who had also been implicated in criminal activity during the investigation, the AFL-CIO decided to expel the Teamsters from its ranks.

In 1959 Congress passed the Landrum-Griffin Act, the first major piece of labor legislation since the Taft-Hartley Act of 1947 (page 317). The new law was designed to clean up corruption in organized labor. It prohibited Communists and recently convicted felons from serving as union officials; required union elections to be held by secret ballot at least once every five years; and called for union officials to provide the Secretary of Labor with detailed information on the handling of union funds.

Two new states join the Union. In 1959 Alaska and Hawaii, each of which had become United States territories in the nineteenth century, became the 49th and 50th states. They were the first new states to join the Union since New Mexico and Arizona were admitted in 1912. They also shared the distinction of being the first states that did not have a common border with any other state.

THE AFFLUENT SOCIETY

Americans enjoy widespread prosperity. Eisenhower's terms as President coincided with an economic boom unparalleled in the nation's history. The war years had been the launching pad for this unprecedented growth. Between 1949 and 1960, the **gross national product** (the nation's total output of goods and services) nearly doubled. The accompanying good times brought a higher standard of living to most Americans. An economist named John Kenneth Galbraith published an influential book in 1958 that described this prosperity and gave the American scene a name. The book was called *The Affluent Society.*

After enduring the uncertainties of the Depression and the sacrifices of the war years, Americans seemed bent on enjoying their new-found abundance. Countless appliances altered ways of living for practically everybody. Automatic washing machines and clothes driers, for example, simplified one of the oldest household tasks; electric can openers eliminated another nuisance; coffee makers operating on electric timers made preparing breakfast more convenient; power lawn mowers gave countless youths freer weekends; home freezers reduced trips to the store.

The television set was a symbol of the prosperous 1950's. The technology for TV had been known for many years, and experimentation had brought about one improvement after another by the beginning of the Second World War. After the war, commercial television burst on the scene. Suddenly, Americans were viewing everything from Cabinet meetings to World Series games, from religious services to grand opera, from surgical operations to underwater exploration. For the first time, people by the millions were able to watch the same program simultaneously, producing common subjects of conversation in schools, factories, and offices. The advertising that paid for the "free" television served even further to blur local differences in taste as people all across the nation bought the latest gadget or food product shown on the television screen.

Population increases rapidly. While television and other media helped greatly to stimulate consumption, the tremendous leap in population also played a major part. Between 1950 and 1960, the number of Americans increased by more than 18 percent.

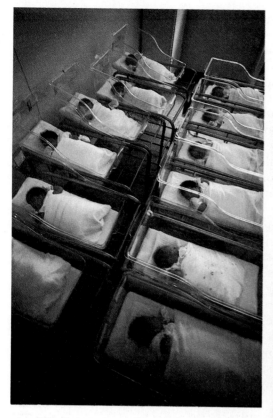

LIFE IN AMERICA

The Prosperous 1950's
Economic advances in the 1950's allowed most Americans to raise their standard of living. Many families moved into suburban houses as soon as they were built and bought their first television sets. Population grew rapidly, partially as the result of a baby boom.

The cause of this increase was the trend toward earlier marriages and larger families, which produced a baby boom during the postwar years. At the same time, advances in medical science had a role in increasing the population by helping people to live longer. By 1960 the average life expectancy was seventy years. A third factor in the population explosion was the arrival in the United States of 2.5 million immigrants.

The United States experiences shifts in population. Along with the growth in population, major changes took place in the geographical distribution of people during the 1950's. The West grew faster than any other part of the country, and by the mid-1960's California had become the most populous state in the Union.

A second major shift in population in the postwar era was the mass migration of middle-class Americans to the suburbs. People who could afford to move began leaving the central cities. Suburban communities were said to offer the best possible setting in which to raise a family — safe streets and open spaces, modern schools and clean air. These were precisely the things that most cities lacked.

The suburbs that grew up in the 1950's were different from those of the 1920's, which had remained dependent on the central city. The newer suburbs were largely self-sufficient communities. They maintained their own school systems, police and fire departments, hospitals, and public health and sanitation services. Many suburban people commuted into the city to work, but increasingly the suburbs themselves were creating local economic opportunities.

Advances in transportation change the way Americans live. One factor shaping the new, emerging society was the widespread ownership of automobiles. Reflecting this fact,

the nation began to build a network of highways extending from one end of the country to another. Unlike public transportation, which is bound to fixed schedules and routes, the private automobile gave its users a sense of personal freedom to come and go at will. One effect was to change shopping habits. The central city, convenient to trains and buses, was no longer the only possible location for major department stores. Branches of downtown stores could now be built outside the cities. Soon, many of these were situated in "shopping centers" that transformed the suburban landscape. Surrounded by acres of parking lots and accessible by highways, shopping centers vastly stimulated consumer spending even as they made shopping more attractive and convenient. Entertainment facilities in the suburbs also began to rival those in the cities as movie theaters, bowling alleys, roller-skating rinks, and restaurants sprang up along the local roadways.

Travel and commuting patterns throughout the United States were affected by the construction of superhighways.

The lives of Americans were also affected by the growth of commercial airline travel. The introduction of commercial jet airliners in the late 1950's added comfort and speed to air travel that propeller-driven planes could not provide. For many people it now became routine to fly to other parts of the country to visit relatives or take a vacation. American business, too, was speeded up by advances in aviation technology. Business meetings to which participants had to travel could now be planned with confidence. Since most airplane passengers were people on business, their needs stimulated a motel-building boom as well as the creation of car-rental agencies.

THE FIGHT AGAINST DISCRIMINATION

The civil rights movement wins an important victory. For black Americans the affluent 1950's was a period both of frustration and dramatic accomplishment. Obstacles to the goal of full civil rights included the continued existence of Jim Crow laws (page 157) and of *de facto* discrimination — discrimination established not by law but by custom and practice.

During the Truman and Eisenhower administrations, civil rights lawyers took a number of cases to the Supreme Court. The most important ruling came in 1954, in a case concerning segregation in primary and secondary schools. Dealing with the issue firmly, the Supreme Court handed down a landmark decision in *Brown v. Board of Education of Topeka.* The unanimous finding of the justices would prove to be a turning point for all Americans, black and white.

In the *Brown* decision, the Court held that state or local laws requiring racial segregation in public schools were unconstitutional. Chief Justice Earl Warren, who wrote the opinion, based it on the Fourteenth Amendment, which says that no state may "deny to any person within its jurisdiction the equal protection of the laws." Fifty-eight years earlier, in *Plessy v. Ferguson* (page 157), the Court had declared that segregation did not violate the Fourteenth Amendment as long as the separate facilities were equal. Now the Court was saying, in effect, that in education the doctrine of "separate but equal" was unconstitutional. Declared Warren, "in the field of public education the doctrine of 'separate but equal' has no place. Separate educational facilities are inherently unequal." In a later decision, the Court ordered local authorities to proceed "with all deliberate speed" to desegregate their schools.

The "Brown" decision meets resistance. Supporters of the civil rights movement were delighted, but they recognized that such an enormous change in society could not be brought about easily. School desegregation was accomplished with relative ease in Washington, D.C., and in some of the border states, but elsewhere public resistance was strong. In Little Rock, Arkansas, opposition to school desegregation was so intense that President Eisenhower sent in federal troops to maintain order while the law was carried out. Under armed guard, nine black students enrolled at Little Rock Central High School in the fall of 1957.

In response to growing protests that black citizens were being denied full rights, Congress in 1957 passed the first civil rights law since Reconstruction. This Civil Rights Act set up a federal Commission on Civil Rights. Its duty was to investigate cases where voting rights were being denied, to examine the effects of federal laws and policies on Americans' civil rights, and to conduct studies on related issues.

The Montgomery bus boycott draws attention. Meanwhile, other developments advanced the movement for civil rights. On December 1, 1955, a seamstress named Rosa Parks took a courageous and fateful step. Her home town, Montgomery, Alabama, was one of the nation's most rigidly segregated cities. Black passengers were required to sit at the back of city buses and were expected to give up their seats to white passengers if a bus was too crowded for everyone to sit down. Mrs. Parks defied this custom. When she refused to give up her place to a white man, she was arrested and jailed. The next day the 50,000 black

Rosa Parks's refusal to give up her seat to a white passenger led to the Montgomery bus boycott of 1955.

citizens of Montgomery began a boycott of the city's buses, choosing to walk rather than ride under humiliating conditions.

The boycott was led by a young Baptist minister named Martin Luther King, Jr. In advocating a policy of passive resistance and nonviolent direct action, King was deeply influenced by the thoughts of two men whose writings he had studied: the Indian nationalist leader Mohandas Gandhi, and the nineteenth-century American philosopher Henry David Thoreau. No matter what violence was done to them, King preached to his followers, they must not fight back, and they must be willing to go to jail for their disobedience of unjust laws. If his people followed this method, he assured them, they would win the attention and sympathy of fellow Americans.

Despite great inconvenience and hardship, the black citizens of Montgomery kept up the boycott for over a year, bringing the bus company close to bankruptcy. In the end, however, it was another court decision that settled the matter. The Supreme Court ruled, late in 1956, that segregation on buses was unconstitutional. The issue had finally been settled. In riding city buses, blacks and whites would at last be treated equally.

Civil rights leaders take direct action. King and other civil rights leaders, encouraged by the boycott and its outcome, formed the Southern Christian Leadership Conference (SCLC) early in 1957. They pledged that they would use nonviolent methods to fight racial discrimination, not only in the South but throughout the United States.

In this spirit, a new desegregation campaign began. On February 1, 1960, in Greensboro, North Carolina, four black students from a local college sat down at a lunch counter in a downtown store. Upon being refused service, they remained seated in protest. Every day, they returned to the lunch counter and sat, their silent presence an eloquent protest against the store's refusal to serve black people. Throughout the country, sympathizers staged demonstrations on behalf of the Greensboro protesters. Finally, in July, the store announced its decision to integrate the lunch counter.

Following the success of the Greensboro "sit-in," thousands of demonstrators, black and white alike, engaged in similar protests — in restaurants, theaters, libraries, churches, and at swimming pools, beaches, and other public places that excluded blacks. This kind of direct action helped bring down the walls of segregation.

SECTION REVIEW

1. Vocabulary: *automation, gross national product.*
2. (a) What were Eisenhower's views about the scope of the federal government's operations? (b) How did his administration tackle the problem of overproduction by the nation's farmers? (c) How successful was the farm policy?
3. (a) Who were the candidates in the 1956 presidential election? (b) What was the outcome?
4. (a) What problems did labor unions face during the 1950's? (b) What was the Landrum-Griffin Act, and what were its main provisions?
5. (a) What evidence was there that by the 1950's the United States had become an affluent society? (b) Describe the major changes in population distribution during the decade. (c) What effect did advances in transportation have on the way Americans lived?
6. (a) What was the importance of the *Brown* decision? (b) What reactions did it provoke? (c) How were nonviolent tactics used in the civil rights movement?

350

3 The Democrats Regain the White House

In July, 1960, the Democrats held their convention in Los Angeles. As their candidate for President, the delegates chose John Fitzgerald Kennedy, a senator from Massachusetts. His running mate was Senator Lyndon B. Johnson of Texas. Kennedy set lofty national goals in his acceptance speech, when he pledged to help conquer a "New Frontier" that consisted of "uncharted areas of science and space, unsolved problems of peace and war, unconquered pockets of ignorance and prejudice, unanswered questions of poverty and surplus."

A NEW PRESIDENT

Kennedy is elected President. At first, the odds seemed to be against Kennedy. For one thing, he faced a formidable Republican opponent — Richard M. Nixon. Nixon was the first Vice President since 1836 to be chosen by his party to succeed his chief. Nixon's running mate was Henry Cabot Lodge, Jr., of Massachusetts, the United States ambassador to the United Nations. Nixon, recognizing the advantage of his connection with Eisenhower, campaigned on the record of the previous eight years. The country was enjoying unprecedented prosperity, peace, and, he insisted, military superiority over its enemies. He offered the nation stability, promising to build on the strong foundations Eisenhower had laid.

Some Democrats feared that Kennedy's youth and religion would prove to be handicaps to his candidacy. Kennedy was the youngest man ever to win his party's nomination for President. Only 43 years old, he had considerably less political experience than his opponent. He was a Roman Catholic as well, and many political observers believed, based on Al Smith's disastrous showing in 1928 (page 134), that a Catholic could not win the presidency. Kennedy

The first President born in the twentieth century, John F. Kennedy won election by a narrow margin. Here, Kennedy greets voters during the 1960 campaign.

faced the religious issue squarely, which proved effective in overcoming concern. "I refuse to believe," he said, "that I was denied the right to be President on the day I was baptized."

The race was extremely close, but the tide turned in Kennedy's favor following a series of four televised debates held late in the campaign. The broadcasts gave voters a chance to see the two candidates side by side and form judgments about them. Many viewers who had previously known little about Kennedy came away from their television sets favorably impressed by him.

On Election Day, a record number of voters went to the polls. Kennedy triumphed with the smallest margin of any President since 1884. Out of a total of 68 million votes, Kennedy won by only 118,000. In the electoral college, he won by 303 to 219.

Kennedy takes office. In his inaugural address, delivered in front of the snow-covered Capitol on January 20, 1961, Kennedy challenged Americans to follow his lead. "Of those to whom much is given, much is required," he declared. ". . . And so, my fellow Americans, ask not what your country can do for you; ask what you can do for your country."

Kennedy was the first American President born in the twentieth century. His youth, thought to be a handicap during the campaign, became an asset to him in office. The public was fascinated by news reports about his young children and his family's zeal for athletics and the out-of-doors. His personal grace and bright wit, moreover, stamped him as an admirable model to copy — especially for young people. The word frequently used to describe the image he projected was "style" — a term suggesting that he was different from his predecessors in the White House, that he was an innovator ready to break loose from established ways without being a radical reformer. John Kennedy and his beautiful wife Jacqueline served French food, wore elegant clothing, and invited leading artists to attend lavish evenings at the White House. The President appreciated the role of intellectuals and serious writers in American life. He once sponsored a dinner for Nobel Prize winners, welcoming them as "the most extraordinary collection of talent, of human knowledge, that has ever been gathered together at the White House, with the possible exception of when Thomas Jefferson dined alone."

New programs are started. The idealism that seemed to accompany Kennedy into office was quickly translated into action. The new administration proposed the establishment of the Peace Corps, an organization designed to provide help for impoverished countries. Peace Corps volunteers — thousands of them — were quickly recruited to serve as teachers, medical aides, agricultural advisers, and technicians in Asia, Africa, and Latin America. Their endeavors and enthusiasm made many fast friends for the United States.

Through a program he called the Alliance for Progress, Kennedy hoped to create in Latin America some of the warm feeling toward the United States that the Good Neighbor Policy had once generated. Under the Alliance, aid was distributed to Latin American countries. It was hoped that this program would raise standards of living, promote economic growth, and help stabilize democratic governments. The results, however, proved to be disappointing. The Alliance did not meet its economic goals. Moreover, the governments of Honduras, Ecuador, and Peru were taken over by military leaders.

COLD-WAR TENSIONS

Communists come to power in Cuba. From the beginning, the Kennedy administration was tied down by the demands of the cold war, which continued unabated. Cuba was a particularly troublesome subject. In 1959, while Eisenhower was President, Cuban rebels had overthrown the dictatorial regime of Fulgencio Batista. At first, most Americans welcomed the new government formed by Fidel Castro, which promised to institute reforms. Their enthusiasm, however, quickly faded. Instead of allowing his people greater liberty than they had known under Batista, Castro declared publicly that

On Assignment with the Peace Corps

Beginning in the early 1960's, the Peace Corps sent volunteers to help teach and train people in countries requesting assistance. The following passage is from a letter written by a Peace Corps volunteer after several months on assignment in the West African nation of Sierra Leone.

A Peace Corps volunteer

For what should Peace Corps volunteers be prepared? They should be prepared for a delightful, warm, friendly, appreciative, and fun-loving people, and for the nerve-racking frustration that arises out of lack of understanding and consistent failure. They should be prepared for a rewarding experience which will live with them as long as they are on the earth.

I know that I have come upon a situation which has caused me to stop and completely re-evaluate myself, my ideas about education, and my ideas about a person's basic relationship with his culture. I have always held that there is a certain "one-ness" about humanity which no amount of difference in skin coloring or cultural uniqueness could hide. The last five months in West Africa have done nothing to alter that view, except to strengthen it.

The need for education in Sierra Leone is desperate, and the appreciation we have been getting from people on all levels is no less than astounding. Some are a little hesitant to believe that we would give up the luxuries of America — the good job, the money, and the conveniences — for that which West Africa has to offer, but they are nonetheless glad to have us. One student said to me, "I really don't understand why you would want to do this, but welcome."

The question "Why did you join the Peace Corps?" that has plagued us all from the beginning becomes increasingly less and less difficult to answer. One no longer has to resort to abstract philosophical arguments, for I now find myself in the midst of the answer, surrounded by a situation which cries out in self-explanation. The poverty, the illiteracy, the substandard educational opportunities which are widespread in this as well as many other countries, are reasons enough for anyone to want to extend his hand and heart in order that these blights might be at least partially erased.

he was a Communist and banned opposition parties, censored the press, refused to hold elections, and murdered or jailed thousands who spoke out against him. In addition, he nationalized the holdings of American companies operating in Cuba and became generally hostile in dealing with the United States.

In 1960, Castro signed a trade agreement with the Soviet Union. The Eisenhower administration responded by suspending American purchases of sugar, Cuba's main export. By the time Kennedy took office, the United States had broken diplomatic relations with Cuba, which was now firmly in the Soviet camp.

The United States aids anti-Castro rebels. This state of affairs disturbed Kennedy, as it had distressed Eisenhower before him. Would Cuba try to export revolution to other Latin American countries? Would it provide the Soviet Union with military bases? When Kennedy came into the White House, he learned of the existence of a secret program begun under Eisenhower to train and equip anti-Castro exiles whose goal was the invasion of Cuba. The new President decided to continue the project.

On April 17, 1961, only three months after Kennedy had taken office, the planned invasion of Cuba was launched. It ended quickly in utter disaster. The little army of

More than three million East Germans fled to West Berlin before Communist authorities ordered the building of the Berlin Wall in 1961.

1,400 men, lacking air cover, was overwhelmed by Castro's forces as it tried to land at a place called the Bay of Pigs. The President, gravely disappointed and dejected, said of the failed scheme, "How could everybody involved have thought such a plan would succeed? I don't know the answer."

Kennedy meets Khrushchev. The costly and humiliating Bay of Pigs episode made the Soviet Union bolder. Russian leaders wondered if the young President would hesitate to resort to force in future crises. In June, 1961, Kennedy flew to Vienna to hold talks with Nikita Khrushchev. The President was stunned when the Soviet premier spoke boldly of ending the United States presence in Berlin. Kennedy made clear his unshakable determination to keep West Berlin from falling into Russian hands. As he left Khrushchev, Kennedy told him bluntly, "It will be a cold winter." Both men returned home ready to seek a build-up of arms. Before long, thousands of Americans were constructing air-raid shelters, and schools and factories were conducting air-raid drills.

A crisis develops in Berlin. In the meantime, as they had since 1945, East Germans continued to risk their lives to flee to West Berlin. This steady exodus was an embarrassment to the Soviet Union. In August, 1961, in order to prevent further loss of population — and prestige — the East German government began constructing a wall across the city. The West quickly dubbed this symbol of Communist repression "the wall of shame."

To help assure the security of West Berlin and to make certain that Western rights were defended, President Kennedy sent additional troops to West Berlin. In the end, the Russians ceased pressuring the United States to pull out.

Kennedy quarantines Cuba. Cuba continued to be a hot spot of anxiety for the United States. During the fall of 1962, American airplanes flying over the island discovered a massive military build-up in

Cuba. Reconnaissance photographs showed that the Soviet Union was equipping Cuba with offensive missiles capable of firing nuclear warheads at most of the major cities in North America.

After a week of secret deliberations with his advisers, Kennedy told the public on October 22, 1962, about the alarming situation in Cuba. He announced, furthermore, his decision to "quarantine," or blockade, Cuba to prevent the importation of more Soviet weapons. He also demanded that the Soviet Union dismantle and remove the missile installations. To underscore the American determination, he placed United States military forces on full alert.

The world held its breath as Russian ships continued to sail toward Cuba and as American ships took up stations to enforce the blockade. On October 24, having reached American-patrolled waters, the Russian ships suddenly stopped dead in the water or simply circled in place. There would be no shoot-out. Secretary of State Dean Rusk observed, "It's eyeball to eyeball, and I think the other fellow just blinked." Four days later, Khrushchev announced that he had ordered the removal of the offending missiles.

A nuclear test-ban treaty is signed. Like his immediate predecessors, Kennedy tried to find a solution to the growing threat of nuclear weapons. Since 1958, the United States and the Soviet Union had informally agreed to halt the testing of atomic weapons in the atmosphere. In 1961, however, the Soviet Union resumed atmospheric testing. Reluctantly, Kennedy authorized the United States to follow suit.

Two years later, in a sudden about-face, the Soviet Union decided to accept a Western offer to ban nuclear testing in the atmosphere, in space, and under water. Representatives of the United States, Britain, and the Soviet Union, meeting in Moscow in July, 1963, signed a treaty embodying this agreement. The good-will between the two superpowers also led to the establishment of a "hot line" — an emergency channel of communication — between the White House and the Kremlin, aimed at preventing an accidental war.

The United States is drawn into conflict in Vietnam. Southeast Asia became another area of concern for President Kennedy. The situation there had its roots in the withdrawal of French forces from Indochina in 1954 (page 341). At the conference which ended French involvement in Indochina, the participants had agreed that Vietnam would be reunited in 1956 through a national election. The election was never held. The South Vietnamese government of Ngo Dinh Diem argued that South Vietnam had not been fairly represented at the conference. In addition, Diem pointed out that the North Vietnamese government had already broken the agreement by building up its armed forces. When the date for the elections passed, the North Vietnamese, along with sympathizers in the south (called the Viet Cong), began to wage guerrilla warfare against the government of South Vietnam. Their aim was to unify Vietnam.

During his last years in office, President Eisenhower had become increasingly concerned about the mounting pressure on South Vietnam. He warned that it was necessary to stop Communist aggression in Southeast Asia. Victory for North Vietnam, he argued, would eventually mean a Communist take-over in every country in that region. This view became known as the "domino theory." Eisenhower explained: "You have a row of dominos set up. You knock over the first one, and what will happen to the last one is the certainty that it will go over very quickly."

By the time Kennedy took office in 1961, the United States had already sent nearly 800 military advisers to South Vietnam. America was also bearing most of the cost of that country's military effort and was helping run Diem's government. Kennedy, who agreed with Eisenhower that South Vietnam must not be allowed to fall to the Communists, decided to send more American military personnel and equipment. Within a year, the number of Americans in Vietnam had increased to 2,700.

Diem is assassinated. Diem, meanwhile, was losing support in his own country. Instead of carrying out reforms, as proposed by his American advisers, he persecuted his political opponents. In 1963, Buddhist monks responded by staging public demonstrations. Then, late in 1963, a group of South Vietnamese generals, displeased by Diem's policies and the corruption in his government, plotted to overthrow Diem. On November 1, 1963, military officers took over the government of South Vietnam, and Diem was assassinated.

Before the year was out, about 17,000 United States military advisers were in Vietnam. Still, most Americans who thought about the war at all regarded it as a matter primarily for the Vietnamese themselves to settle.

DOMESTIC PROGRAMS

Kennedy proposes reform legislation. Kennedy's domestic program was in the tradition of his Democratic predecessors, Truman and Roosevelt. Not having great interest in the legislative process, however, Kennedy never developed a reliable technique for dealing with Congress. Administration members, moreover, were not comfortable with Vice President Johnson, a master of the legislative process, and they never drew significantly on his experience to accomplish domestic goals. An unsympathetic coalition of opponents in Congress defeated many of Kennedy's proposals, including federal aid to public schools, health insurance for the elderly, and the creation of a Department of Urban Affairs. Congress also turned down his proposal for a tax cut and gave him less money for foreign aid than he sought, maintaining that the federal government was too deeply in debt.

Kennedy commits the nation to a massive space program. Kennedy, nevertheless, offered some proposals that met with congressional approval. The Housing Act of 1961 authorized the spending of large sums of money on urban-renewal projects. Public works and job training programs were started in order to aid the unemployed. In addition, minimum wages were raised by 25 percent.

The administration also set a dramatic new goal for the nation: to place an American on the moon before the end of the 1960's. Competition between the United States and the Soviet Union in space exploration had already begun during Eisenhower's second term. In October, 1957, Soviet scientists launched the first space satellite, called *Sputnik*, which circled the earth for three months. Less than four years later, a Soviet air force officer, Yuri Gagarin, became the first human to travel in space.

The United States, meantime, was developing its own space program. In May, 1961, Alan Shepard became the first American launched into space. The first American to orbit the earth was John Glenn, on February 20, 1962. The American people were confident that further successes would follow and that the United States would overtake the Soviet Union's lead in space.

The civil rights movement gains momentum. Kennedy had been elected on a platform containing a strong pledge to end racial discrimination. He did not propose any civil rights legislation, however, until 1963. He had concluded that he could not persuade Congress to follow him, and he feared dividing the country.

Kennedy did issue a number of executive orders to insure equal justice for black Americans. In November, 1962, he signed an executive order prohibiting racial or religious discrimination in housing financed by the federal government. In addition, the President created the Commission on Equal Employment Opportunities, which sought to persuade firms holding government contracts to follow nondiscriminatory hiring practices. Another action taken during his administration was the Interstate Commerce Commission's banning of discrimination on all interstate buses, trains, and airlines. Kennedy also placed a number of black leaders in important positions. Thurgood Marshall was made a judge of the

United States Court of Appeals; Robert Weaver became Home Finance Administrator; Carl Rowan was named ambassador to Finland; and Andrew Hatcher was appointed Kennedy's associate press secretary.

The civil rights movement, meanwhile was acquiring a momentum of its own. In September, 1962, for example, a black air force veteran named James Meredith tried to enroll at the all-white University of Mississippi. Supreme Court Justice Hugo Black ruled that Meredith had to be admitted. When the governor of the state announced that he would go to jail, if necessary, to prevent Meredith (or any other black student) from attending the university, Kennedy ordered federal marshals to escort Meredith to class. Rioting broke out, and Kennedy sent in 5,000 federal troops to restore order. Meredith was admitted to the University of Mississippi and later became the school's first black graduate.

The ratification of two new amendments to the Constitution was applauded by black Americans. The Twenty-Third Amendment, ratified in 1961, made it possible for residents of the District of Columbia, most of them black, to vote in presidential elections. The Twenty-Fourth Amendment, approved by Congress in 1962, prohibited any state from requiring voters to pay a poll tax in order to participate in federal elections. This amendment became part of the Constitution in 1964.

On May 5, 1961, astronaut Alan Shepard became the first American launched into space. Millions of television viewers watched the dramatic moment of recovery as his capsule was hauled out of the sea after the fifteen-minute, suborbital journey.

Martin Luther King, Jr.'s "I Have a Dream" Speech (1963)

... I say to you today, my friends, that in spite of the difficulties and frustrations of the moment, I still have a dream. It is a dream deeply rooted in the American dream. I have a dream that one day this nation will rise up and live out the true meaning of its creed: "We hold these truths to be self-evident: that all men are created equal. . . . "

I have a dream that one day on the red hills of Georgia the sons of former slaves and the sons of former slaveowners will be able to sit down together at the table of brotherhood. . . .

I have a dream that my four children will one day live in a nation where they will not be judged by the color of their skin but by the content of their character. I have a dream today.

I have a dream that one day . . . little black boys and black girls will be able to join hands with little white boys and white girls as sisters and brothers.

I have a dream today. . . .

From every mountainside, let freedom ring. And when we allow freedom to ring, when we let it ring from every village, from every hamlet, from every state and every city, we will be able to speed up the day when all God's children, black men and white men, Jews and Gentiles, Protestants and Catholics, will be able to join hands and sing in the word of the old Negro spiritual: "Free at last! Free at last! Thank God almighty, we are free at last!"

Black Americans make political gains. In 1963, the hundredth anniversary of the Emancipation Proclamation, American civil rights leaders called for a renewal of nonviolent public protest against segregation and against the obstacles faced by black voters in many states. During that year, the nation witnessed scores of demonstrations against racial discrimination.

The peaceful and dignified behavior of most of the demonstrators contrasted favorably with the violence with which their efforts were sometimes met. During a series of demonstrations against segregation in Birmingham, Alabama, for example, a bomb was thrown into a black church, killing 4 children and injuring 21 other people. In Jackson, Mississippi, a civil rights leader, Medgar Evers, was shot to death in front of his home.

By June, 1963, public opinion in many parts of the country had swung sharply in favor of the civil rights demonstrators. Kennedy seized the moment to recommend the passage of strong new civil rights legislation, saying, "We are confronted primarily with a moral issue. . . . The heart of the question is whether all Americans are to be afforded equal rights and equal opportunities." The civil rights legislation Kennedy proposed would (1) prohibit segregation in any public place; (2) ban discrimination in hiring practices; (3) speed school integration; and (4) provide job training for unskilled black workers.

Martin Luther King, Jr., now the undisputed leader of the civil rights movement, called for a "March on Washington" to demonstrate public support for the President's proposed legislation. On August 28, 1963, close to a quarter of a million black and white citizens from all over the country converged on Washington. The enormous demonstration listened as Mahalia Jackson (page 232) sang soaring spirituals and as Martin Luther King delivered an unforgettable speech (page 358). The voice of the crowd then swelled in a heartfelt rendering of the mighty theme song of the civil rights movement: "We Shall Overcome."

Kennedy is assassinated. The Kennedy administration had only a little longer to run. On November 22, 1963, President Kennedy arrived in Dallas, Texas, on a trip designed to build support for his re-election. Kennedy, Vice President Johnson, and Governor John Connally of Texas, accompanied by their wives, rode in open limousines through the downtown area, waving to the large, cheering crowds. Suddenly, shots rang out. The President, struck in the head and neck, was rushed to a hospital where he was shortly pronounced dead. That afternoon, aboard the plane that would carry the President's body back to Washington, United States District Judge Sara T. Hughes administered the presidential oath of office to Lyndon Baines Johnson.

Meanwhile, Dallas police combed the city to find the President's assassin. Within an hour and a half of the shooting, they arrested Lee Harvey Oswald in a Dallas theater. Oswald, a former marine who had once tried to become a Russian citizen, was taken to the city jail. He denied any knowledge of the shootings, but the evidence against him was overwhelming.

Two days later, television cameras were rolling as Oswald was led out of the city jail to be transferred to another facility. Suddenly a local nightclub owner named Jack Ruby stepped forward from the crowd and shot Oswald dead. Millions of Americans witnessed the killing on television.

In Washington, Kennedy's body lay in state at the Capitol rotunda. Hundreds of thousands of people filed past the casket to pay their respects. On Monday, November 25, Kennedy was buried at Arlington National Cemetery in Virginia after a funeral attended by foreign leaders from many parts of the world. They represented grieving people everywhere who had felt the hope for a better tomorrow that the youthful President had inspired in his thousand days in office.

With Mrs. Kennedy on his left and Mrs. Johnson on his right, Lyndon Johnson took the oath of office aboard Air Force One shortly after the assassination of President Kennedy.

SECTION REVIEW

1. (a) Why did the odds seem to be against John Kennedy in the 1960 presidential campaign? (b) When did the tide turn in his favor? (c) What were the results of the election?
2. (a) Why was the Peace Corps established? (b) What was the purpose of the Alliance for Progress?
3. What was the outcome of each of the following? (a) The Bay of Pigs invasion (b) The Berlin crisis (c) The quarantine of Cuba
4. (a) What was the "domino theory"? (b) To what extent had the United States become involved in Vietnam by the end of 1963?
5. (a) Which of President Kennedy's domestic proposals were blocked by Congress? (b) Which of his proposals were passed? (c) What success did the American space program enjoy during the Kennedy administration?
6. (a) What steps were taken by Kennedy in support of civil rights? (b) What civil rights legislation did he propose in 1963? (c) Why was the "March on Washington" organized?

Analyzing Political Cartoons

Political cartoons have appeared in American newspapers and magazines since colonial times. Sometimes they call attention to public issues and problems. Often they make us laugh at our mistakes and misunderstandings. In any event, political cartoons express the viewpoint of the cartoonist and are meant to influence as well as inform.

The cartoon of the snake (below) was drawn by Benjamin Franklin and first appeared in the *Pennsylvania Gazette* in 1754. At that time, French and Indian forces were threatening the English colonies. Through his cartoon, Franklin was suggesting to delegates meeting in Albany that if the colonies remained divided they would be unable to defend themselves.

The symbolism used by Franklin for this cartoon is clear and powerful. A snake is both respected and feared. By labeling the different segments of the snake for various English colonies and including the statement "Join, or Die," Franklin was conveying his belief that union was the only hope for the future of the American colonies.

Showdown

Warren King. *Daily News* (New York), 1962.

The New York *Daily News* published the political cartoon about the Cuban missile crisis (above) in 1962. Cartoonist Warren King showed Soviet leader Nikita Khrushchev, with an armful of nuclear missiles destined for Cuba, being confronted by a powerful American blockade. This image, along with the title "Showdown," conveys the feeling of tension that gripped the world during the crisis.

The political cartoons at the top of the next page were drawn in the late 1920's by Herbert Johnson. The cartoon on the left expresses concern about the effects of industry on the environment. It shows a na-

NATIONAL PARK
AS THE PEOPLE INHERITED IT

THE LOGICAL FINISH
IF WE LET DOWN THE BARS

tional park in its natural state. The second cartoon shows the same setting after a factory has been built. These cartoons make clear the cartoonist's viewpoint on uncontrolled industrial expansion.

Check Your Skill

Use the information presented on these pages to answer the following questions.

1. What is the purpose of a political cartoon?
2. Why is it necessary to analyze political cartoons carefully?

3. Describe the message presented by each of the cartoons shown on these pages. Mention in your answer any symbolism used to help convey the message.

Apply Your Skill

1. Look through the pages of this book and find a political cartoon. Then write a brief description of its purpose.
2. Draw a political cartoon of your own on a local or national issue. Be sure your cartoon has a title and that it expresses your point of view on the issue.

Chapter 13 Review

Summary

President Eisenhower's first goal upon taking office in 1953 was to end the war in Korea. After months of negotiations, an armistice was signed in July, 1953, dividing North and South Korea at the 38th parallel.

Although the Korean War was concluded, cold war tensions continued. Eisenhower's Secretary of State, John Foster Dulles, took a firm stand against the Soviet Union and formulated a policy of massive retaliation to deter Communist aggression. The NATO alliance was strengthened in the 1950's, and when the French withdrew from Indochina in 1954 the United States offered to help South Vietnam.

In 1956 a conflict between Egypt and the forces of Israel, Great Britain, and France created an international crisis that led to strained relations between the United States and its Western allies. Cold-war tensions also flared in Europe in 1956 when a Hungarian revolt against Soviet domination was brutally crushed. Two years later the Soviet leader, Nikita Khrushchev, demanded that the city of Berlin be turned over to the Communists. When the Western powers took a strong stand against such an action, Khrushchev backed down and agreed to a summit conference. Tensions increased again in 1960, when a United States reconnaissance plane was shot down over Soviet territory.

The Eisenhower presidency was a time of unprecedented prosperity and change in America. The population grew dramatically and millions of Americans moved from the eastern states to the West. Meanwhile, thousands of families abandoned the cities for homes in suburban communities.

At the same time, the growth of the civil rights movement was bringing hope to black Americans. The Supreme Court ruled against school segregation in 1954, and a new Civil Rights Act was passed in 1957. Civil rights leaders began organizing boycotts and demonstrations to protest racial discrimination.

The presidential election of 1960 brought John F. Kennedy to the White House. This new President was soon confronted with cold war realities when an American-backed invasion of Cuba ended in failure. The presence of Soviet missiles on the island led to another confrontation — this one with the Soviet Union in 1962. In Europe, tensions over Berlin flared once again; in Southeast Asia, guerrilla war in South Vietnam led to increased American involvement.

At home, Kennedy was largely unsuccessful in his efforts to get legislation through Congress. The government did become more active, however, in safeguarding the rights of all Americans. Tragically, an assassin's bullet ended Kennedy's presidency in November, 1963.

Vocabulary and Important Terms

1. massive retaliation
2. brinkmanship
3. Battle of Dien Bien Phu
4. Eisenhower Doctrine
5. automation
6. Landrum-Griffin Act
7. gross national product
8. baby boom
9. *Brown v. Board of Education of Topeka*
10. Civil Rights Act of 1957
11. Southern Christian Leadership Conference
12. Peace Corps
13. Alliance for Progress
14. Bay of Pigs invasion
15. Cuban missile crisis
16. domino theory

Discussion Questions

1. (a) What incidents contributed to tension between the United States and the Soviet Union during the Eisenhower and Kennedy administrations? (b) What steps were taken to improve relations between the two nations?

2. (a) Why did the Eisenhower administration adopt a policy of massive retaliation? (b) How, at the same time, did President Eisenhower show his concern about the build-up of nuclear weapons?

3. (a) What was the general economic condition of the United States during Eisenhower's presidency? (b) What special problem did farmers face?

4. (a) Why did many Americans move to suburbs during the 1950's? (b) How were those suburbs different from the suburbs of the 1920's?

5. (a) How did the *Brown* decision differ from the *Plessy v. Ferguson* ruling? (b) Why was ratification of the Twenty-Third and Twenty-Fourth amendments important for black Americans? (c) Describe various actions taken by civil rights leaders to fight discrimination. (d) How effective were those actions?

6. (a) What problem did Cuba pose for the United States during the Eisenhower and Kennedy years? (b) What successes and failures did Kennedy have in dealing with Cuba? (c) What step did he take to improve United States relations with Latin America?

7. (a) How did United States involvement in Vietnam begin? (b) What was the extent of this involvement at the end of Eisenhower's presidency? (c) At the time of Kennedy's assassination?

Relating Past and Present

1. Dwight Eisenhower remained highly popular throughout his eight years as President. Could a President maintain a similar degree of popularity today? Explain your answer.

2. John Kennedy's age and religion were considered liabilities when he began campaigning for the presidency. Is either age or religion a characteristic that the American people consider important in presidential candidates today? What other personal characteristics might be considered either assets or liabilities for a modern-day presidential candidate?

Studying Local History

1. The government-funded road construction program of the 1950's resulted in the building of over 40,000 miles of four-lane highways. What highways, if any, were built in your region as part of this program? What impact did these highways have on your community?

2. The 1960 presidential election was one of the closest contests in American history. Which candidate captured the electoral votes of your state? Try to find out the reasons for that candidate's popularity among your state's voters.

Using History Skills

1. *Reading source material.* Study the description of Peace Corps service on page 353. If you were to consider joining the Peace Corps, would you find the letter encouraging or discouraging? Explain your answer.

2. *Analyzing political cartoons.* Do research to find a cartoon that illustrates an event from either the Eisenhower or Kennedy presidency. Write a short report describing the cartoon and the viewpoint of the cartoonist.

WORLD SCENE

New Nations in Africa

In the 1950's and 1960's new nations began to emerge from the African colonial empires.

Ghanaian independence. The movement for African independence got its start in the Gold Coast, a British colony in West Africa. The organizer was Kwame Nkrumah (KWAH-mee en-KROO-mah). As a young man, Nkrumah had studied Western political systems in the United States and Britain. When he returned to the Gold Coast in 1949, he founded a political party dedicated to seeking self-government for his homeland.

After the Second World War, Britain developed a plan to free its African colonies gradually. Britain's timetable, however, was too slow for Nkrumah and his nationalist party. In 1950, inspired by the example of Gandhi in India, he organized a campaign of civil disobedience in the Gold Coast.

Full independence was finally granted in 1957. At that time the former colony was renamed Ghana (after an ancient African kingdom) and Nkrumah was elected president. Some leading black Americans, including W. E. B. Du Bois, later moved to Ghana to show their support for the new country.

Algerian independence. In the hundred years that France had controlled Algeria, the colony became the home of over a million settlers of European descent. The settlers controlled much of the wealth and property in Algeria, which had a Muslim majority.

When widespread demonstrations broke out against French rule in 1945, troops killed more than a thousand Algerians in an effort to restore order. To appease the Muslim population, the French government in 1947 made Algeria formally a part of France and extended French citizenship to all Algerians.

This tactic only briefly restored calm. In 1954, nationalists led another uprising. When European settlers became the target of terrorist attacks, France sent 500,000 troops to Algeria to stop the violence. A ferocious civil war followed.

Dissatisfaction with the government's conduct of the war led French settlers and some army officers to take control of Algeria in 1958 — an action which constituted rebellion against France. The resulting crisis brought General Charles de Gaulle to power in France. De Gaulle moved swiftly to suppress the rebellion and negotiate an end to the war. Peace talks began in 1961, and a year later Algeria was granted independence. This conclusion to the years of struggle was followed by an exodus of the vast majority of Europeans from Algeria.

CHAPTER 14

The Turbulent Johnson Years

1963 – 1968

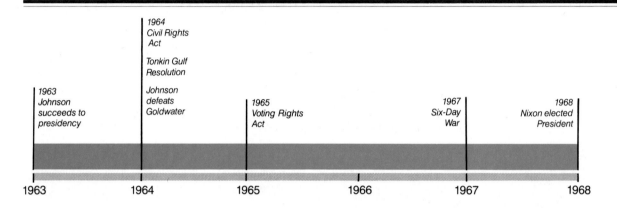

1963 Johnson succeeds to presidency	1964 Civil Rights Act / Tonkin Gulf Resolution / Johnson defeats Goldwater	1965 Voting Rights Act		1967 Six-Day War	1968 Nixon elected President
1963	**1964**	**1965**	**1966**	**1967**	**1968**

CHAPTER OUTLINE

1. Johnson becomes President.

2. The United States confronts problems abroad.

3. The nation elects a new President.

The torch of national leadership had now passed to Lyndon Baines Johnson. "All I have I would have given gladly not to be standing here today," he said in his first address to Congress, five days after the assassination. He pledged to carry out President Kennedy's policies. Where Kennedy had earlier said, as he listed his goals, "Let us begin," Johnson now said, "Let us continue."

The new President, born in 1908 in Texas, had greater experience as a legislator than any previous Chief Executive. His father, a schoolteacher and a farmer, had also served as a state legislator. As a boy, Johnson fell in love with politics, often sitting at his father's side in the Texas House.

Lyndon Johnson was first elected to Congress in a special election in 1937, campaigning as an ardent supporter of Franklin Roosevelt. In 1948 he ran for the Senate and won by 87 votes, thus acquiring the teasing nickname "Landslide Lyndon." Quickly making his mark in the Senate, he was named Democratic whip (assistant leader) while still serving his freshman term.

Johnson became known for his skill at lobbying members and for his ability in getting bills passed. If anyone could obtain passage of Kennedy's domestic legislation, people commented, surely it was Johnson. LBJ's unmatched knowledge of government in general, and of Congress in particular, were reassuring to the grief-stricken American people.

1 Johnson Becomes President

Lyndon Johnson's legislative ability had won him the respect of colleagues in both parties. Now the new President turned to Congress, which responded in the next few months by passing the most far-ranging social programs since those of the New Deal.

The Warren Commission investigates the Kennedy assassination. One of Johnson's first steps was to appoint a special commission to investigate the circumstances of the Kennedy assassination. Chief Justice Earl Warren headed the panel, which examined more than 500 witnesses and reviewed the reports of the FBI and other law-enforcement agencies. The Warren Commission, as the panel came to be called, concluded that Lee Harvey Oswald had assassinated Kennedy and that there was no conspiracy behind either the assassination or the murder of Oswald by Jack Ruby (page 359).

The commission's work was almost immediately criticized and questioned. According to opinion polls, many Americans believed that the full story behind the assassination was not yet known. Public suspicion that there had been some sort of conspiracy behind the assassination remained widespread. In 1979 the investigation was reopened. A House committee found evidence to support charges that more than one assassin had fired at Kennedy. The committee did not, however, draw any conclusions about who the other assassin or assassins might have been.

Lyndon Johnson, assuming leadership after the assassination of President Kennedy, moved with poise and confidence to pull the shocked nation together.

Johnson tackles the nation's economic problems. The unfinished business of the Kennedy administration included a proposed tax cut which had been opposed as inflationary by influential members of Congress. Where Kennedy had failed to bring about its passage, Johnson succeeded. Called the Revenue Act of 1964, it reduced tax rates, giving the economy an important boost. Under its impact, the nation continued to enjoy the long period of economic growth that had begun after the Second World War.

In trying to control inflation, Johnson, like Kennedy, took an interest in the union contracts of the nation's major industries. He tried to talk leaders of business and labor into keeping prices and wages from rising rapidly. In addition, he urged the Federal Reserve Board to limit the loans it made to member banks. Johnson hoped this measure would also help to keep inflation in check.

Congress passes the Civil Rights Act of 1964. One of the most significant laws

A skilled political leader, Johnson persuaded Congress to approve many of the programs Kennedy had proposed, as well as legislation of his own. Some Americans questioned the rapid changes taking place.

"Hope I know where we're goin'."

passed under Johnson's leadership was the Civil Rights Act of 1964. This legislation had been proposed by Kennedy the year before (page 358) but had not yet been taken up by Congress at the time of his death. In his first address to Congress, Johnson urged its passage. "We have talked long enough in this country about equal rights," he said. "We have talked for a hundred years or more. It is time now to write the next chapter — and to write it in the books of law."

The civil rights bill passed the House of Representatives easily, but it ran into trouble in the Senate. Making use of the Senate's traditional policy of allowing unlimited debate on any topic, a number of southern senators attempted to kill the bill by dragging out the debate so long that the supporters of civil rights legislation would give up trying to bring the measure to a vote. This tactic is called a *filibuster.* Opponents of the bill kept up the filibuster for 83 days. By the end of that time, Johnson and his backers in Congress had managed, through tireless effort, to convince the necessary two thirds of the Senate to close debate by imposing *cloture.* The cloture rule, rarely used, limits debate on a matter under consideration. Once administration supporters succeeded in applying cloture, they were able to get a vote on the bill within days. It passed by a wide margin. "Stronger than all the armies," observed Illinois Senator Everett Dirksen, "is an idea whose time has come."

The Civil Rights Act of 1964 was one of the most far-reaching laws ever passed by Congress. Among its most important provisions, it (1) prohibited discrimination in public places such as theaters, restaurants, and hotels; (2) insisted on identical voting requirements for blacks and whites in all states; and (3) prohibited discrimination on the basis of race or sex by all employers, unions, and employment agencies engaged in interstate commerce. The new law also offered financial aid to school districts that needed help in beginning desegregation programs and required that federal funds be denied to districts practicing segregation.

Johnson calls for a war on poverty. In addition to pressing for civil rights, President Johnson sought to bring about yet another social revolution — the elimination of poverty in the United States. In his first State of the Union address, delivered to Congress on January 8, 1964, the President announced, "This administration today, here and now, declares unconditional war on poverty in America." One part of this "war" was an economic policy designed to stimulate growth in the nation's economy as a whole. Johnson also asked Congress to pass legislation aimed at providing direct help to impoverished Americans. "Our task," he said, "is to help replace their despair with opportunity."

The Economic Opportunity Act of 1964, passed by Congress at the President's urging, established an Office of Economic Opportunity to administer a billion-dollar social spending program. The act provided for the creation of the Job Corps, an agency charged with training and finding employment for young people aged sixteen through twenty-one. The act also organized Project Head Start, an effort to provide preschool educational opportunities for disadvantaged children. Other programs instituted under the Economic Opportunity Act included VISTA (Volunteers in Service to America), which created a domestic Peace Corps, and the Community Action Program, which provided federal grants to states and localities for antipoverty programs of their own design. As he signed the act into law, the President declared that "for the first time in all the history of the human race, a great nation is able to make, and is willing to make, a commitment to eradicate poverty." A food-stamp program, designed both to provide food for the needy and to make use of the agricultural surpluses, was also enacted in 1964.

Johnson is elected President. While the administration's efforts to eliminate racial discrimination and poverty were applauded by many Americans, the programs also aroused strong opposition. In July, 1964, one of Johnson's chief critics in Congress

In 1964, Congress set up the Head Start program to provide preschool children with rewarding play and learning activities.

won the Republican presidential nomination. Senator Barry Goldwater of Arizona was chosen on the first ballot and selected as his running mate William Miller, a congressman from New York.

Goldwater opposed Johnson's domestic policies on the ground that the federal government had no constitutional right to undertake social programs like the war on poverty or to enact civil rights laws. Such programs, he argued, if they were undertaken at all, should be the concern of state and local governments. Furthermore, Goldwater maintained that most of the Democrats' social programs were infringements on individual liberty. He criticized what he called the "me-tooism" of many members of his own party — people who, in his view, were practically indistinguishable from the Democrats. He promised to offer the American people "a choice, not an echo."

In August the Democrats, meeting in Atlantic City, quickly nominated Lyndon Johnson. His running mate was Senator Hubert H. Humphrey of Minnesota. Humphrey had first come to national attention during the Democratic convention of 1948, when he fought for a civil rights plank in the party platform. The 1964 convention adopted a platform endorsing the policies of Kennedy and Johnson, and saluted the President for the notable legislative victories of his nine months in office.

Goldwater could not overcome the belief, held by many people, that he was an extremist. He had proclaimed in his acceptance speech, "Extremism in defense of liberty is no vice. And . . . moderation in pursuit of justice is no virtue." There was a widespread perception also that if elected, Goldwater might be too likely to rely on military force, even on the use of nuclear weapons. To the Republican slogan, "In Your Heart, You Know He's Right," the Democrats retorted, "In Your Heart, You Know He Might."

In November, Johnson swamped Goldwater, capturing 61 percent of the popular vote. In the electoral college Johnson received 486 votes compared to Goldwater's 52. The senator carried only his home state and five southern states.

Swept into office with the Johnson landslide was the most lopsidedly Democratic Congress since the days of the New Deal. Democrats outnumbered Republicans by 155 in the House and 38 in the Senate. Johnson interpreted the election results as a "mandate for unity" as well as for his vision of a strong federal government.

Barry Goldwater, defeated in the 1964 race for President, later returned to the United States Senate where he served with distinction.

On the Campaign Trail

The political journalist Theodore H. White won wide acclaim for his book on the 1960 presidential campaign. White also covered the 1964 presidential race, and in the following account describes an exciting day in the campaign of Lyndon Johnson.

Lyndon Johnson campaigning

In every campaign, as politicians know, there can come an unexplained . . . jump of attention when the crowds surge into the streets to cheer their candidate and give him love. It happened to Eisenhower in late September of 1952. It happened to Kennedy the first week in October of 1960. It happened to Lyndon Johnson on Monday, September 18, 1964. His crowds, as I say, had been good and growing throughout September. But on the last weekend of September the Warren Commission issued its massive report. On Sunday afternoon the great television networks devoted hours to it; Monday-morning papers throughout the nation bannered the report, tearing open the scarcely healed wounds in the emotions of the American people. . . . It was as if the nation hungered to see a President, real, live, healthy, in the flesh — as much as the President hungered to see them.

Lyndon Johnson had read the report himself on his ranch in Texas on Saturday and Sunday, September 26th and 27th; had flown back to Washington that night; and had risen early on Monday, September 28th, to give a day to campaigning in New England.

He arrived at the airfield in Providence, Rhode Island, at 9:30 A.M. on a cool fall day, and already some 3,000 people were at the airport, surging against the wire fence,

girls squealing, children crying in the crush, babies held aloft, and boys chanting the particularly New England chant of "Two-four-six-eight, Who-do-we-appreciate?" The President's face suddenly illuminated. It was as if someone had turned the current on in the house. He paused only briefly to hug ninety-seven-year-old ex-Senator Theodore Green . . . and then strode directly to the wire fences. On the trip up, he had complained to the newsmen about their reporting of crowd reaction. Now he hailed them . . . as he grabbed hands . . . and said, "How's that for crowd reaction?"

Johnson launches the Great Society. On Inauguration Day, Lady Bird Johnson, the President's wife, held the Bible as her husband took the oath of office — the first time a woman had participated in the swearing-in ceremony. In his address, President Johnson asked Congress to pass legislation to implement his plan for what he termed the Great Society — a phrase he had introduced the previous year. He had said,

"We have the opportunity to move not only toward the rich society and the powerful society, but upward to the Great Society." The goals of Johnson's crusade went beyond efforts to eradicate poverty and racial discrimination. They also included medical insurance for elderly Americans, immigration reform, federal assistance to education, urban housing projects, and the elimination of pollution.

With Johnson's active urging, Congress approved vast new and expanded undertakings. (1) Over $3 billion was appropriated for aid to the nation's public and parochial schools and for colleges and universities. (2) The Medicare bill, which provided medical insurance for people over 65, was passed, and Social Security taxes were increased to cover the cost. (3) The nation's immigration policy, which had, since 1924, favored immigrants from northern Europe, was replaced by a system that treated all nations equally. Under the new policy, immigration from countries in the Western Hemisphere was restricted for the first time. (4) Over $7 billion was set aside to finance urban-renewal and public-housing programs. The President appointed Robert C. Weaver, the first black American to hold a Cabinet position, as head of the newly created Department of Housing and Urban Development. (5) The amount of money to be spent on federal antipoverty programs was doubled.

This graph shows immigration from 1900 to 1980. During which decade did immigration reach a peak?

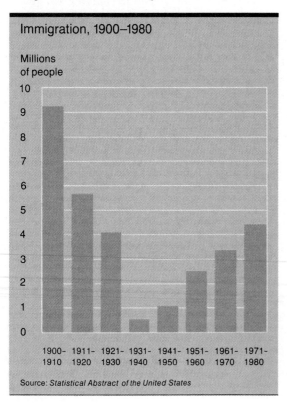

Immigration, 1900–1980

Millions of people

Source: *Statistical Abstract of the United States*

Johnson attained one legislative goal after another: a highway-beautification program (of special interest to Mrs. Johnson); traffic- and highway-safety programs; anti-pollution programs; a model-cities program (to rejuvenate urban communities); and others. The Speaker of the House, John McCormack of Massachusetts, who had been an early New Dealer, said he saw the outpouring of new laws as "realized dreams" of long ago.

The Voting Rights Act of 1965 is passed. One of the most pressing civil rights issues was the denial of suffrage to black voters in some areas of the South. Civil rights legislation had been passed in 1957 and 1960 to protect the right to vote. The procedures specified in those laws had proved too cumbersome, however, to be effective. Another measure removing an impediment to black suffrage — and to that of poor white people — was the ratification in 1964 of the Twenty-Fourth Amendment (page 357).

Recognizing the power of the vote as a key to advancing civil rights, Martin Luther King, Jr., announced his intention of launching a voter-registration drive in the South. King, awarded the 1964 Nobel Peace Prize for his work in promoting nonviolent social change, now had additional prestige. He chose to begin his work in Selma, Alabama, a city in which blacks formed a majority of the population but only a tiny percentage of registered voters. When they met violent resistance, King and his followers decided to march from Selma to Montgomery, the state capital, in protest against this violation of their rights.

To assure the safety of the marchers, President Johnson placed the Alabama National Guard under federal authority and charged it with the responsibility of keeping the peace. On that same evening, March 15, 1965, Johnson addressed a joint session of Congress and lent the full weight of the White House to the Alabama marchers. He appealed to the nation to "overcome the crippling legacy of bigotry and injustice," and asked Congress to pass legislation that became the Voting Rights Act of 1965.

Martin Luther King, Jr., recognized as the leading figure in the civil rights movement, is shown greeting supporters. In his efforts to end segregation and discrimination, King was a devoted advocate of nonviolent methods.

No less than the 1964 Civil Rights Act, the new law had far-reaching effects. It authorized the United States Attorney General to suspend discriminatory voter-registration tests in districts where less than half of the adult population had registered to vote in the 1964 election. It also empowered the Department of Justice to send federal agents to monitor elections and to register qualified black voters in those districts.

After passage of the Voting Rights Act, a wave of enthusiastic voter-registration drives swept across the South. The number of black voters on the rolls increased substantially, and in the next few years black candidates began to be elected to local and state offices. The Voting Rights Act, which originally applied for five years, was renewed by later Congresses and became a powerful symbol of the federal government's determination to protect the civil rights of all Americans.

Riots cause alarm. Although black Americans had made substantial progress by the mid-1960's, they still faced formidable hurdles. Many black people lived in the decaying neighborhoods of the inner city, where good jobs were hard to find. The high unemployment rates angered and discouraged many blacks, who came to believe that they had no chance of escaping poverty.

In the late summer of 1965, only days after the Voting Rights Act was signed into law, resentment and despair erupted into violence in the mostly black area of Los Angeles known as Watts. Rioting and looting raged for six days. Fifteen thousand troops from the National Guard were sent in to quell the uprising, but by the time order was restored 34 people had been killed and 850 wounded. Property damage was estimated to be more than $30 million.

Some Americans were inclined to blame the havoc in Watts on a new generation of black leaders beginning to gain prominence.

Exasperated at what they believed was the slow pace of improvement in American race relations, these leaders had begun to call for fresh ways of achieving better conditions for blacks. They also warned that unless reforms took place, the black ghettos would be breeding grounds for turbulence.

An influential leader in the early 1960's was Malcolm X, born in Omaha, Nebraska. He was an evangelist of the Nation of Islam, a black religious group (commonly known as the Black Muslims) which advocated the separation of the races. A magnetic speaker, Malcolm X preached discipline, self-help, cultural pride, and complete separation from white society. In the last year of his life, Malcolm X changed his mind about black separatism. He began to work with groups favoring integration, but he did not change his insistence that black people must meet violence with violence (not with the passive resistance urged by Martin Luther King and his followers). In February, 1965, Malcolm X was assassinated in a public auditorium in New York City.

The black-power movement attracts attention. Malcolm X was killed before the black militants became prominent in the United States, but he influenced many younger blacks who became leaders of what was called the black-power movement. "Black power" meant different things to different people but, in general, it included the argument that blacks should organize the people in their own communities for political action and should build their own schools and businesses in those communities. There was also a strong feeling that blacks should feel pleasure and satisfaction in their own cultural heritage. Some black militants moved to much more extreme positions, however, advocating the use of violence to achieve their ends and rejecting the goal of racial integration.

Many black leaders opposed the tactics and goals of the black-power movement. They sought to establish a harmonious and "color-blind" society. Martin Luther King and his followers believed that such a society could be established only through non-

violent tactics. Supporters of King's point of view criticized the black-power movement, saying that it stirred up racial hatred, fed people's fears, and threatened to destroy the progress the civil rights movement had made. The vast majority of black Americans supported this more moderate stand. Like the rest of the country, they were shocked by the civil turmoil that broke out in major cities, including Newark, Detroit, Cleveland, Baltimore, and Washington, D.C., in 1966 and 1967.

Republicans do well in the 1966 election. The Democrats' stunning victory in the election of 1964 had been seen by many political observers as a permanent setback for the Republican Party, one from which it might never recover. The mid-term elections of 1966 proved these predictions wrong.

During the campaign, Republican candidates sharply attacked the methods, if not the goals, of the Great Society programs. The Johnson administration, said the critics, was making the federal government too powerful and intrusive. One example often cited was the President's attempt to pass a federal housing law, which would have banned discrimination in the sale or rental of houses and apartments. Many Republicans in Congress opposed the measure, saying that it interfered with people's property rights. Americans, they said, should be able to dispose of their property in any way they saw fit. (Many Democrats agreed with them, and the bill was defeated.)[1] Republican candidates in the 1966 election generally criticized the administration's social programs as ineffective, poorly run, and too expensive.

In November the Republican Party gained 8 new governorships, 47 new seats in the House of Representatives, and 3 new seats in the Senate (including that won by Edward Brooke of Massachusetts, the first black senator since reconstruction). The Democrats did not lose their majority in either the House or the Senate, but President

[1]Not until passage of the Civil Rights Act of 1968 was discrimination in the sale and rental of housing prohibited.

The Saturn V Rocket

During the course of Lyndon Johnson's presidency, American scientists at the National Aeronautics and Space Administration (NASA) developed the Saturn rocket. This large multi-stage launch vehicle, they believed, would enable them to meet the goal of the Apollo space program — to land astronauts on the moon before the end of the decade. The first Saturn rocket was successfully tested in 1964 and was used to place unmanned capsules in orbit around the earth. The improved Saturn IB was introduced soon thereafter, and it launched several manned Apollo spacecraft. The last rocket of the Saturn series — the powerful Saturn V — was ready for testing in 1967. The three-stage Saturn V was designed to lift a manned spacecraft into orbit around the earth and then propel it into a trajectory to the moon. The Saturn V soon made it possible for American astronauts to accomplish the extraordinary feat of exploring the surface of the moon.

Johnson no longer had the wide margin that had allowed his Great Society programs to pass so easily during the previous term.

The youth movement gains national attention. Another concern facing President Johnson during his last years in office was the growth of dissatisfaction among the country's youth. Only a small minority of young people were involved, but their concerns seemed to reveal something amiss in the land. One part of the movement was made up of those who turned their backs on mainstream American culture. Some of these young people moved to remote rural areas to set up utopian communities; others lived in New York's Greenwich Village, San Francisco's Haight-Ashbury district, and similar places elsewhere. In general, they shared certain ideas, including pacifism, the ideal of universal brotherhood, and an aversion to what they saw as Americans' addiction to material possessions and consumerism. They were not politically active, though most were sympathetic with the political protests of the 1960's.

The more politically significant part of the youth movement was centered on the nation's college and university campuses. Beginning with student involvement in the civil rights movement of the early 1960's, protests grew to include demonstrations against American higher education, the arms race, and what these students considered to be America's failure to live up to its ideals at home and abroad. Increasingly, student protests focused on the conflict in Vietnam.

SECTION REVIEW

1. Vocabulary: *filibuster, cloture.*
2. (a) Why was the Civil Rights Act of 1964 such a significant law? (b) What were the provisions of the Economic Opportunity Act of 1964?
3. (a) Who were the candidates in the presidential election of 1964? (b) What was the outcome of the election?
4. (a) What new social legislation was passed by the 89th Congress? (b) What were the provisions of the Voting Rights Act of 1965?
5. (a) What was the black-power movement? (b) Why did many black leaders oppose this movement?

2 The United States Confronts Problems Abroad

Every aspect of the nation's foreign policy — as well as much of domestic policy — eventually was overshadowed by the issue of American involvement in Vietnam. Even as the Vietnam War grew wider, however, dramatic events elsewhere also occupied national attention.

China breaks with the Soviet Union. A remarkable and unheralded turn in world affairs during the 1960's was the growing strain between the Soviet Union and China, the major Communist powers. The two nations had been allied since China's revolution in 1949, and China had accepted massive economic and military aid from the Russians. By the early 1960's, however, the two nations were publicly criticizing each other — the Chinese charging that the Soviet Union had drawn too close to the United States, the Russians denouncing the Chinese as brutal Stalinists. The Sino-Soviet split, as the break between these two countries was called, was of enormous importance because it weakened the Soviet Union's domination of the Communist world and gave the United States the chance to play off one Communist power against the other.

France withdraws its military forces from NATO. At the same time that this promising opportunity came up, tension also developed among the Western powers. This tension placed a strain on the Atlantic alliance, which had been the basis of American foreign policy since the late 1940's.

In 1958, General Charles de Gaulle came to power in France. An ardent nationalist, De Gaulle resented American and British domination of the NATO alliance and sought to increase the power and prestige of his own country. In 1964, France established diplomatic relations with China and broke with the United States and Great Britain over many of the policies they advocated in the United Nations. De Gaulle also strongly criticized the American presence in Vietnam. In 1966, he withdrew French

The Six-Day War of 1967 resulted in a decisive Israeli victory. Israel's fighter-bombers quickly established mastery of the air.

forces from NATO and insisted that NATO military installations be removed from French soil.

The United States intervenes in the Dominican Republic. During the Johnson years, relations between the United States and the Soviet Union were somewhat more relaxed than in the recent past. Nevertheless, a concern of the United States was the possibility of communism taking hold in Latin America. American leaders were determined to block efforts of the Soviet Union — or its ally, Cuba — to sow the seeds for Communist revolution in the Western Hemisphere.

In April, 1965, a revolt broke out in the Dominican Republic, a Caribbean island nation. Fearing that Communists might seize power if the Dominican Republic were left in chaos, Johnson sent more than 22,000 marines to restore order there. Soon afterward, a peacekeeping force established by the Organization of American States brought about a ceasefire and the election of a government in June, 1966.

Johnson's intervention in the Dominican Republic was denounced as high-handed by many people in the United States as well as in Latin America. They insisted that the United States had deprived the Dominican Republic of its right to determine its own form of government.

War breaks out in the Middle East. World tensions increased in 1967 with the third Arab-Israeli war in twenty years. In the spring of 1967, Egypt demanded that United Nations peacekeeping troops be withdrawn from its border with Israel. The Egyptians also closed the vital Gulf of Aqaba to Israeli ships.

On June 5, Israel launched a surprise attack on the airfields of Egypt, Syria, and Jordan, almost completely destroying those nations' air forces. The United States announced that it did not intend to enter the hostilities, but President Johnson immediately placed military forces on alert in case Soviet intervention on the side of the Arab nations made American action necessary. For the first time, the "hot line" — the direct telephone link between Moscow and Washington — was used as Johnson and the Soviet leaders assured each other that they did not wish to enter the war.

By June 10, Israel had defeated the Arab nations, occupying Egyptian, Syrian, and Jordanian territory. The conflict became known as the Six-Day War. Its swift and decisive conclusion, however, was not the end of the strife between Israel and its Arab neighbors. The humiliating defeat only made the Arab world more determined than ever to destroy Israel, which America felt bound to defend.

Communists threaten South Vietnam. All the while, the conflict in Vietnam was increasingly occupying the attention of administration officials. When Johnson took office, there were about 17,000 American military advisers in Vietnam. Reports from South Vietnam suggested that if United States participation were not substantially increased, the Communists would certainly win. Johnson's top advisers, including Secretary of State Dean Rusk and Secretary of Defense Robert S. McNamara, urged him not to abandon the South Vietnamese. Convinced that the domino theory was sound (page 355), they believed America must show its willingness to stop Communist aggression. They were also concerned that if the United States pulled out of Vietnam, the American reputation for reliability as an ally would suffer, seriously affecting the country's foreign policy all over the world.

Many people in the United States and elsewhere called on Johnson to end the war by supporting the establishment of a coalition government in South Vietnam. In such a regime, they said, Vietnam's disagreements could be settled politically rather than by force. The President, however, recalling the history of Eastern Europe after World War II, was concerned that such an arrangement might quickly end in a Communist-dominated government for South Vietnam. He therefore rejected the idea.

Johnson became more and more convinced that further military assistance to South Vietnam was necessary, but he wanted popular and bipartisan support for this commitment. He waited for the right moment, and in the summer of 1964 the time came, just as the presidential election campaign was opening.

This map shows the countries of Southeast Asia at the time of the Vietnam War.

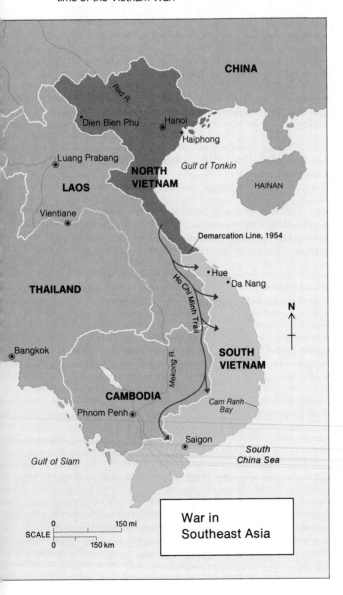

War in
Southeast Asia

Congress passes the Tonkin Gulf Resolution. On August 4, two United States destroyers were attacked by North Vietnamese gunboats in the Gulf of Tonkin, off the coast of North Vietnam. That evening, President Johnson reported the incident on national television. He announced that retaliatory air strikes would be conducted against North Vietnam and called on Congress to authorize him to take whatever further action might be required. His handling of the incident met with broad public support. Johnson did not reveal that South Vietnamese patrol boats, assisted by the United States, had attacked North Vietnamese coastal islands only hours before the American destroyers were hit.

On August 7, 1964, Congress passed the Tonkin Gulf Resolution, which empowered the President to take "all necessary measures to repel any armed attack against the forces of the United States and to prevent further aggression." The vote on the meas-

At Tuesday lunch meetings, President Johnson and his top advisers — the "Tuesday Cabinet" — discussed the situation in Vietnam.

ure was overwhelming — 416–0 in the House and 88–2 in the Senate. Thus, the President was authorized to continue America's military effort in Vietnam.

American involvement in Vietnam grows. During the 1964 presidential campaign, Lyndon Johnson made it clear that he did not wish to broaden the war. He said, "We are not about to send American boys nine or ten thousand miles from home to do what Asian boys ought to be doing for themselves." Shortly after the election, however, Communist gains in South Vietnam caused him to expand the role of the United States. The number of American advisers in the country was increased, reaching 23,000 by the end of 1964. In February, 1965, following Viet Cong attacks on American barracks, Johnson ordered bombing raids against North Vietnamese supply routes and military installations. Shortly, American ground combat troops were sent into action.

American military strategists expected that the escalation of United States military involvement and the heavy bombing of North Vietnam would not only hurt the enemy militarily but destroy the country's morale. That expectation proved false. By mid-1966, 265,000 American troops were on duty in South Vietnam, and the North had endured heavy bombing for over a year. Secretary of Defense McNamara, returning from a visit to Vietnam, reported to the President that the determination of the highly disciplined Communists seemed only to have increased.

Many Americans question Johnson's Vietnam policies. At the time of the Tonkin Gulf Resolution, there was widespread support for Johnson's handling of the Vietnam situation. As the country became more deeply enmeshed in Vietnam, however, criticism of administration policy began to grow. Some people became convinced that the United States had no right to be intervening

377

By the end of President Johnson's term of office, nearly half a million American soldiers were stationed in South Vietnam. Here, American helicopters remove Vietnamese civilians from a combat zone.

in what they said was a civil war. The Vietnamese, they argued, should be left to settle their conflict themselves. Other critics pointed to the corruption and apparent unpopularity of the South Vietnamese government or to the difficulty of judging progress in a guerrilla war. Still others noted that the rising cost of the war was diverting money away from Great Society programs and fueling inflation at home.

Many people, on the other hand, criticized Johnson's handling of the war because they believed the administration was not pressing hard enough for victory. If the full military might of the United States were turned on North Vietnam, they insisted, the Communists could be brought quickly to the bargaining table and the killing would be over. Johnson, calling these critics "hawks," feared that such a policy might

lead to war with China — as had happened during the Korean conflict (page 333).

The administration tried in a number of ways to end the fighting. Although Johnson had rejected the idea of allowing South Vietnam to be ruled by a coalition government, he sought to negotiate a settlement with the North Vietnamese. At Christmastime, 1965, he announced that he was mounting a "peace offensive." As a good-will gesture, he called a halt to the bombing of the North and announced that the United States would work to find a means to begin peace talks. After more than a month, there was no response from the North Vietnamese, and the bombing was resumed.

Another peace effort in February, 1967, met with no greater success. The North Vietnamese refused to negotiate as long as

American troops remained in Vietnam, and the United States government regarded this condition as unreasonable. The North Vietnamese also turned down Johnson's offer of an enormous aid program for Southeast Asia. The fighting, meanwhile, went on. By the end of 1967, almost half a million Americans were on duty in Vietnam.

The Tet offensive is a turning point. In an attempt to strengthen support for the anti-Communist government of South Vietnam both at home and abroad, the United States pressed for elections to establish a representative form of government. In September, 1967, voters in South Vietnam approved a new constitution and elected a new president, General Nguyen Van Thieu (nuh-WIN van TYOO).

Despite increasing opposition at home, Johnson and most of his advisers believed at this point that the war could be won. With the combination of a government that gave an image of democracy and with continued American military aid, they maintained, the South Vietnamese would have both the morale and the strength to defeat their Communist opponents.

The administration's optimism stemmed, in part, from reports that were being sent by General William Westmoreland, the American commander in Vietnam. These reports were passed along to the American public, with the assurance that there was "light at the end of the tunnel." The hope was shattered early in 1968, when the Communists launched the strongest offensive of the war.

During the Vietnamese New Year holiday, called Tet, a truce had traditionally been observed by both sides. For this reason, American and South Vietnamese troops had their guard down when, in January, 1968, the Communists launched surprise attacks on some thirty South Vietnamese cities. The Communists paid dearly for the Tet offensive and soon lost the areas they had taken. The costly battles, nevertheless, had a tremendous psychological impact on the American people.

Military and government leaders were shocked and embarrassed by this demonstration of the Communists' ability to mount a sustained, coordinated assault. General Westmoreland, responsible for the optimistic reports that had recently flowed from his headquarters in Saigon, was soon relieved of his command. In March, 1968, the Senate Foreign Relations Committee held televised hearings on the war, examining closely its conduct and purpose. The President himself was beginning to conclude that the United States would have to find some way of withdrawing its forces from Vietnam.

SECTION REVIEW

1. Describe the significance for the United States of the split between the Soviet Union and China.
2. (a) What steps led to the outbreak of the Six-Day War? (b) Which nations took part in the war? (c) What was the outcome?
3. (a) Why did President Johnson's top advisers urge him to keep American troops in Vietnam? (b) Why did the Johnson administration reject calls for the establishment of a coalition government in South Vietnam? (c) What was the Tonkin Gulf Resolution?
4. What reasons did administration critics give for their belief that the United States should withdraw from Vietnam?
5. (a) What was the Tet offensive? (b) What effects did it have?

3 The Nation Elects a New President

The year 1968, which began so violently in Vietnam, would prove to be the stormiest of a stormy decade. Amid the agony of a foreign war and growing domestic unrest, a presidential election was being conducted at home.

Johnson is challenged in the presidential primaries. Early in January, 1968, Eugene McCarthy, a Democratic senator from Minnesota, announced that he was a candidate for the presidency. To try to take the nomination from a President of one's own party, as the senator was doing, was almost unheard of. An outspoken foe of Johnson's Vietnam policy, McCarthy entered the New Hampshire presidential primary and won an astounding 42 percent of the vote. President Johnson, who had not yet announced his candidacy and had not campaigned, actually won the primary with about 48 percent of the vote. Nonetheless, McCarthy's showing was read by almost everyone as a defeat for the President. A challenge to Johnson's renomination clearly had a chance of success. A few days later, Robert F. Kennedy, brother of the slain President and now a senator from New York, also declared his candidacy for the Democratic nomination. Like McCarthy, Kennedy criticized the President's conduct of the war in Vietnam.

Johnson withdraws from the presidential race. Following the Tet offensive, Johnson had asked his advisers for a full-scale review of American policy in Vietnam. The conclu-

sions they drew were very different from those on which Johnson had earlier based his policy decisions. Far from being close to victory, he now was told, the United States could not hope to gain its objectives in the war without sending another 206,000 American troops to Vietnam. To fail to send them could result in military reverses or in an indefinite continuation of the agonizing struggle. To provide the men, however, would require mobilizing reserve units and making heavy new demands on the public just when protests against the war were becoming more heated.

Johnson reached a momentous decision: the United States must find a way to wind down the war. He would aim again to open negotiations with the North Vietnamese, although he emphasized that the outcome must not be "peace at any price."

On the night of March 31, 1968, Johnson went on national television to announce that as a prelude to peace negotiations, the bombing of North Viet-

Eugene McCarthy's surprise showing in the New Hampshire primary helped persuade President Johnson not to run for re-election in 1968.

nam was to be stopped (except in any area where the enemy was continuing to build up its troops and supplies). Then, in grim tones, he announced his decision to withdraw, for the good of the country, from the presidential race. "I have concluded," he said, "that I should not permit the presidency to become involved in the partisan divisions that are developing in this political year. Accordingly, I shall not seek, and I will not accept, the nomination of my party for another term as President."

Johnson stepped out of the race to help emphasize the sincerity of his wish to end the war. No doubt he also hoped to contribute to restoring an atmosphere of harmony in the country. Possibly he was influenced too by opinion polls suggesting he might not be able to win renomination. Later, he wrote that he had long before decided not to seek re-election. Having suffered a heart attack in 1955, he had a constant fear of being incapacitated in office. He confided, "Whenever I walked through the Red Room and saw the portrait of Woodrow Wilson hanging there, I thought of him stretched out upstairs in the White House, powerless to move, with the machinery of the American government in disarray around him."

Martin Luther King is assassinated. Shortly after Johnson's announcement that he would not run for re-election, the nation was stunned by the assassination of Martin Luther King, Jr., the revered civil rights leader. On the evening of April 4, 1968, he was fatally shot while standing on the balcony of a motel room in Memphis, Tennessee. News that King had been slain touched off rioting in many cities across the country. National leaders pleaded with black rioters not to turn to violence and destruction, but for a time the appeals went unheeded. The rioting continued for a week, at one point coming within two blocks of the White House.

The widespread disorders of the 1960's had led President Johnson in 1967 to appoint a presidential commission, headed by Illinois governor Otto D. Kerner, to investi-

Thurgood Marshall became the first black member of the Supreme Court in 1967. A lawyer best known for winning the *Brown* case (page 349), Marshall served as Solicitor General before being named to the Court.

gate the root causes of urban rioting. The Kerner Commission warned in its report, issued in 1968, that the United States was becoming two societies — one black, one white — "separate and unequal." The Commission proposed increased funding for antipoverty programs as a solution to the festering problem. Many Americans, however, rejected the findings of the Kerner Commission. They believed that tougher law enforcement, not more spending on social programs, was required. The question of how to deal with unrest in America became an important issue as the Democrats and Republicans looked ahead to the 1968 presidential campaign.

Democrats vie for the party's nomination. In late April, Vice President Hubert Humphrey joined the race for the Democratic presidential nomination. He entered too late to participate in the primaries, but his strong support in party organizations at the local level won him delegates in states that did not have primaries. Robert Kennedy and

McCarthy, meanwhile, battled it out in those states that held presidential primaries, moving toward a decisive showdown in California.

Kennedy won the California primary by a 46 to 42 percent margin. As he was leaving a hotel after his victory speech, he was shot. His assassin was Sirhan Sirhan, a Jordanian immigrant who hated Kennedy for his pro-Israel position. The next morning, Kennedy was dead — another shock in a year of shocks for the American people.

After Kennedy's death, some of his supporters decided to support McCarthy while others promoted the candidacy of Senator George McGovern of South Dakota. Neither of these candidates, however, had strong backing at the party convention, which was held in Chicago in late August.

Discord plagues the Democrats. Vice President Humphrey, who had the confidence of most party leaders, easily won the Democratic nomination. He chose as his running mate Senator Edmund Muskie of Maine. The domestic planks of the Democratic platform, basically an endorsement of Great Society programs, caused little discussion within the party.

The most controversial issue at the convention was the party's position on Vietnam. Antiwar delegates, most of whom backed McCarthy or McGovern, sought a platform plank calling for the withdrawal of American troops from Vietnam and the establishment of a coalition government there. Humphrey delegates, on the other hand, supported a platform advocating the holding of peace talks. They argued that the United States could not responsibly withdraw from South Vietnam if the North Vietnamese did not do so at the same time. In the end, the Humphrey position was endorsed by a majority. Nonetheless, the fact that 40 percent of the delegates had voted against it demonstrated the sharp disagreements within the party over Vietnam.

The division in the Democratic Party was reflected in the country as a whole, nowhere more violently than just outside the convention hall, in the streets and parks of Chicago. There, thousands of antiwar protestors had assembled. Irate at the certainty of Humphrey's nomination, some became unruly, taunting the police who were standing guard. Pelted with bricks and bottles, the police struck back, and rioting broke out. Americans watching the convention proceedings on television could hardly believe that the scenes of violence were real. Many people concluded that the police had overreacted; others blamed the demonstrators for having started the fighting. Whatever their opinions about the causes of the rioting, most Americans were deeply concerned about the direction the nation seemed to be taking.

The Republicans nominate Richard Nixon. The chief beneficiary of the divisions within the Democratic Party was the Republican nominee, former Vice President Richard M. Nixon. Nixon had gained the Republican nomination on the first ballot at

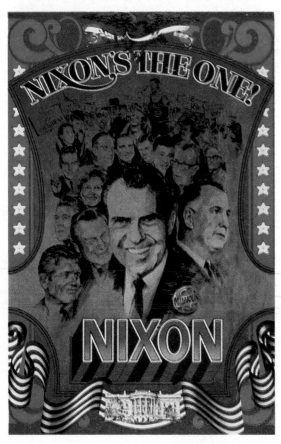

This poster from the 1968 presidential campaign urged the election of Republican candidate Richard Nixon.

the party's convention in Miami, defeating his chief competitors, governors Ronald Reagan of California and Nelson Rockefeller of New York. The apparent peacefulness and unity of the gathering in Florida contrasted sharply and favorably with the scene at Chicago. The picture of calm gave Nixon and his running mate, Governor Spiro T. Agnew of Maryland, an initial advantage that was revealed by their substantial lead in the early opinion polls.

Nixon campaigned as the candidate who could bring the country together again. He called upon those who longed for restoration of American prestige abroad and harmony at home to vote Republicans into office. Nixon argued that many of Johnson's social programs had been expensive failures. He pledged to take personal charge of a law-enforcement campaign to end the street crime and violence that terrified many citizens. Furthermore, he said, he had a plan to end the war in Vietnam honorably. He refused, however, to reveal any specifics, saying that he did not want to upset the peace negotiations then in progress.

The peace talks had opened in Paris in May, 1968, but quickly went nowhere. The North Vietnamese insisted that the United States cease all acts of war, although they themselves were continuing to press the battle against South Vietnam. Some political observers believed that North Vietnam was holding off serious discussions until after the election, hoping that a new President would be easier to deal with.

George Wallace runs as a third-party candidate. A third candidate for the presidency in 1968 was George C. Wallace, an ex-governor of Alabama, who organized his own American Independent Party. Wallace, who had first gained national attention through his opposition to the desegregation of the University of Alabama, campaigned on a states' rights platform. He hoped to benefit from an expected backlash against urban riots, crime, political protest, and the growth of federal social programs.

Nixon is elected President. As the date for the 1968 election approached, Nixon saw

his lead in the opinion polls begin to slip. Humphrey greatly helped his prospects when he broke with the Johnson policy by calling for an end to the bombing of North Vietnam. A month later, only a week before the election, Johnson announced a halt to all air, naval, and artillery bombardment of North Vietnam, adding further impetus to Humphrey's surge.

Nixon, however, held on at the finish. Although he received only 43.4 percent of the popular vote to Humphrey's 42.7, his victory in the electoral college was decisive: 301 to 191. Wallace received 13.5 percent of the popular vote, carrying five states in the Deep South. The narrowness of Nixon's victory was underscored by the fact that the Republicans had failed to win a majority in either house of Congress.

As Lyndon Johnson prepared to return to Texas, he spoke of his pride that a hundred years hence he would be remembered as the "civil rights President" for having placed the nation on the road to racial justice. That he had not been able to attain his goals in Vietnam was a tormenting disappointment to him, denying him a place among America's most admired Chief Executives. He later wrote that every President, deep down, knows that "no living mortal has ever possessed all the required qualifications" to lead the nation. As for his own presidency, "I had given it everything that was in me."

SECTION REVIEW

1. (a) What candidates challenged President Johnson in the 1968 presidential primaries? (b) Who won the Democratic presidential and vice-presidential nominations in 1968? (c) What disagreements arose over the party's official position on Vietnam?

2. (a) Who were the Republican presidential and vice-presidential candidates in 1968? (b) On what issues did the Republican candidates campaign?

3. (a) What was the outcome of the 1968 presidential election? (b) Which party won a majority in both houses of Congress?

Chapter 14 Review

Summary

When Lyndon Johnson succeeded to the presidency in 1963, he took up the unfinished business of the Kennedy administration. A skillful politician, Johnson was able to secure passage of many far-reaching pieces of legislation, including a tax-cut bill and a new civil rights law.

Johnson's landslide victory over Barry Goldwater in the 1964 election provided the President with an opportunity to implement an ambitious program of social legislation. Johnson's goals, in addition to reducing poverty and discrimination, were to provide medical insurance for the elderly, clean up the environment, and improve American education.

The passage of the Voting Rights Act in 1965 was of particular importance to black Americans. This law enabled thousands of black Southerners to register to vote. No law, however, could immediately solve the problems faced by families living in urban slums across the country. The nation was shocked by rioting that broke out in urban ghettos from 1965 to 1967.

At the same time that Johnson was trying to persuade Congress to enact his Great Society program, foreign-policy problems demanded his attention. In Europe, President Charles de Gaulle pulled French forces out of the NATO alliance. In the spring of 1965, Johnson sent American forces to the Dominican Republic to restore order after an outbreak of rioting. When war broke out in the Middle East in June, 1967, United States forces were put on alert.

The most demanding issue that Johnson had to face was American policy in Vietnam. Convinced that the defense of South Vietnam was vital to all of Southeast Asia, Johnson sent large numbers of American combat troops to that nation to try to prevent a Communist take-over. American involvement in Vietnam led to heated debate at home. The presidential election of 1968 provided a forum for opposition to the administration's Vietnam policies. Johnson, faced with challenges for the Democratic nomination by senators Eugene McCarthy and Robert Kennedy, surprised the nation by announcing in March, 1968, that he would not seek re-election.

In the next few months, the nation was shocked by the assassinations of Martin Luther King, Jr., and Robert Kennedy. Vice President Hubert Humphrey won the Democratic presidential nomination, but discord within the party contributed to the victory of the Republican candidate, Richard Nixon, in the 1968 election.

Vocabulary and Important Terms

1. Warren Commission
2. Revenue Act of 1964
3. Civil Rights Act of 1964
4. filibuster
5. cloture
6. Great Society
7. Medicare
8. Voting Rights Act of 1965
9. black power
10. youth movement
11. Sino-Soviet split
12. Six-Day War
13. Tonkin Gulf Resolution
14. Tet offensive
15. Kerner Commission

Discussion Questions

1. (a) What unfinished business did Lyndon Johnson inherit from the Kennedy administration? (b) Which of Kennedy's legislative goals were enacted under Johnson?

2. (a) Through what programs did the Johnson administration attempt to wage war on poverty? (b) On what grounds did Barry Goldwater and other Republican leaders criticize the domestic policies proposed by Lyndon Johnson?

3. (a) Describe the situation of the Republican Party after the 1964 election. (b) To what extent had the Republicans recovered by 1966? (c) What was their standing following the 1968 election?

4. (a) What were the goals of Johnson's Great Society? (b) What social legislation did Congress enact at Johnson's urging?

5. What attempts were made in the 1960's to guarantee the voting rights of black Americans?

6. (a) What obstacles did black Americans face in the mid-1960's? (b) How did the new generation of black leaders differ from earlier civil rights leaders in their efforts to achieve better conditions?

7. (a) During Lyndon Johnson's presidency, what problems did the United States confront in Europe? (b) What problems arose in Latin America? (c) In the Middle East?

8. (a) What factors led to increased American involvement in Vietnam during Johnson's presidency? (b) In what ways was Johnson's handling of the war in Vietnam criticized, and what alternatives did the critics recommend?

9. (a) Why was the Tet offensive regarded as a turning point of the Vietnam War? (b) How had Johnson's perception of American involvement in Vietnam changed by 1968? (c) How did the argument over Vietnam affect the Democratic Party and the election of 1968?

Relating Past and Present

1. By the early 1960's a split had developed between China and the Soviet Union. What is the current status of Sino-Soviet relations? What effect does the relationship between China and the Soviet Union have on the United States today?
2. President Johnson's policies regarding South Vietnam drew criticism both from those who felt the commitment was too great and from those who felt the commitment was not great enough. In what parts of the world does the United States have commitments today, and in what ways, if any, are those commitments criticized by some Americans?

Studying Local History

Find out how the people of your state voted in the presidential election of 1968. What policies of the Johnson administration were widely discussed in your state during the 1968 campaign? Which issues seemed to affect the outcome of the election in your state?

Using History Skills

1. *Reading graphs.* Study the graph on page 370 showing immigration to the United States. (a) Approximately how many people immigrated to the United States in the period from 1970 to 1980? (b) In which decade was immigration at a low point? (c) What factors might explain that decline?
2. *Reading source material.* Study Theodore White's description of the 1964 campaign on page 369. (a) What words would you use to describe Johnson's reception in Rhode Island? (b) What other information would you need to determine accurately Johnson's popularity in that state? (c) What evidence does the account provide concerning President Johnson's relations with reporters?

WORLD SCENE

Communist Repression

In the 1960's the repressive nature of communism was revealed by events in Europe and in Asia.

The invasion of Czechoslovakia. In the decades after World War II, Czechoslovakia had become a satellite of the Soviet Union. The Soviet leadership exercised firm control over the Czech government and used Czechoslovakia's extensive industries to build up the economic strength of the Communist bloc.

Czech discontent grew, and in 1968 reformers managed to install Alexander Dubcek (DOOB-chek) as the party secretary. From his post, Dubcek introduced reforms that promised the Czech people more civil liberties and greater political independence from the Soviet Union. Dubcek did not plan to abandon Communist rule in Czechoslovakia, but he hoped his government could practice what he called "socialism with a human face."

These developments were viewed with alarm by the Soviet rulers in Moscow. When Dubcek refused to curtail his program of reform, the Soviet Union sent an army of 200,000 troops into Czechoslovakia in August, 1968. By the middle of 1969, the Soviet Union had removed Dubcek from office and re-established a tight grip on the Czech Communist Party. For the people of Czechoslovakia, hopes for reform had ended.

The Cultural Revolution in China. The take-over of China by Communist forces in 1949 made Mao Tse-tung the undisputed ruler of that vast land. Mao believed that the Chinese Communist revolution would result in a classless society. Toward that end, and aiming to keep revolutionary fervor high, he devised several economic-development programs. Under one plan, devised in 1958 and known as the Great Leap Forward, the Chinese people were called upon to double industrial production, especially in such key industries as iron- and steel-manufacturing. Hundreds of thousands of small industrial plants requiring substantial hand labor were set up throughout China, but the scheme was a disastrous failure. Workers could not meet production requirements, and the quality of the products was poor.

Influential opponents of the Great Leap Forward denounced Mao's policies. He struck back in 1966 by launching what was called the Cultural Revolution. As part of this movement, Mao unleashed groups of students organized in Red Guards. The Red Guards marched across China, pledging support for Mao's ideas and publicly disgracing officials who were thought to lack proper revolutionary enthusiasm. The resulting turmoil lasted until 1968, when Mao finally called a halt to Red Guard activities.

UNIT 4 REVIEW

Important Dates

1945 United Nations organized.
1947 Marshall Plan adopted.
Taft-Hartley Act passed.
1949 NATO formed.
Communists take control of China.
1950 Korean War begins.
1952 Eisenhower elected President.
1953 Korean armistice signed.
1954 Supreme Court decision on school
segregation.
1955 AFL-CIO formed.
1956 Suez Canal crisis.
Hungarian uprising.
1957 Eisenhower Doctrine proclaimed.
1959 Landrum-Griffin Act passed.
Alaska and Hawaii become states.
1960 Kennedy elected President.
1962 Cuban missile crisis.
1963 Nuclear test-ban treaty signed.
Kennedy assassinated.
1964 Tonkin Gulf Resolution passed.
Johnson wins presidential election.
1965 Voting Rights Act passed.
1966 France withdraws military forces from NATO.
1967 Six-Day War.
1968 Tet offensive.
Nixon elected President.

Review Questions

1. (a) What was Truman's containment policy? (b) Through what programs did the Truman administration attempt to carry out containment? (c) Which efforts at containment proved most successful, and why?
2. (a) Why were there many labor strikes in the years immediately following World War II? (b) What labor legislation was passed during the Truman and Eisenhower administrations? (c) What effect did this legislation have on unions? (d) What new problems did organized labor encounter during the 1950's?
3. What was the response of the United States to each of the following? (a) The creation of Israel (b) The struggle between Nationalist and Communist forces in China (c) The Soviet blockade of Berlin (d) The Suez crisis
4. (a) What similarities were there among the domestic proposals put forth by the Truman, Kennedy, and Johnson administrations? (b) What major social programs were enacted during each administration? (c) What criticism was there of these programs?

5. (a) How did Dwight Eisenhower's foreign and domestic policies differ from those of the Democratic Presidents who preceded and followed him? (b) What were the major characteristics of American society during the Eisenhower years?
6. (a) What was the extent of American involvement in Vietnam during the Eisenhower, Kennedy, and Johnson administrations? (b) Why, by 1968, had the Johnson administration begun to reassess America's role in Vietnam? (c) How did the war affect American society?
7. (a) What civil rights legislation was enacted during the 1950's and 1960's? (b) What court decisions and executive orders also advanced the civil rights movement, and in what ways?

Projects

1. Form a committee to find out more about the Eastern European countries that fell under the control of the Soviet Union after World War II. Each member of the committee might choose one country to study. Use the library to find out how that country came under Soviet domination and the degree to which Soviet domination exists there today. Report your findings to the class.
2. Recreate some of the sights and sounds of the 1940's and 1950's. Begin by finding out more about the music, literature, and other aspects of American society in the period after World War II. Share the information with the class by describing trends in music, reading aloud some of the literature, or telling the class about some of the other ways of living that distinguished American society in the period.
3. Write an essay on this topic: "The civil rights movement of the 1950's and 1960's fulfilled the promise of equality found in the Declaration of Independence." You may either agree or disagree with this statement, but be sure to include evidence to support your point of view.
4. President Johnson prided himself on having "out-Roosevelted Roosevelt" in obtaining social-welfare laws from Congress. Write a report in which you compare the domestic legislation enacted during Franklin Roosevelt's and Lyndon Johnson's administrations. Conclude by stating whether you agree or disagree with Johnson's statement and explain why.
5. Relate past and present by discussing as a class the state of American-Soviet relations today. Recall the reasons why relations between the United States and the Soviet Union were strained after World War II and the degree to which those relations have changed in recent years.

5

TOWARD A NEW CENTURY
1969 – 1980's

We are a powerful force for good. With faith and courage, we can perform great deeds and take freedom's next step.

RONALD REAGAN, STATE OF THE UNION MESSAGE, 1984

UNIT OUTLINE

Crisis in the Presidency

1969 – 1976

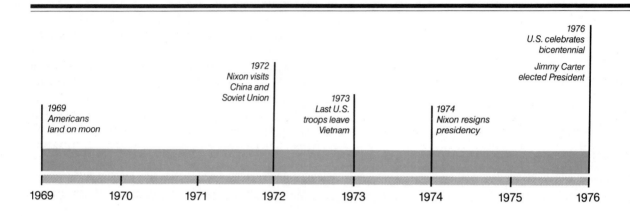

On January 20, 1969, Richard Nixon was inaugurated as the nation's thirty-seventh President. No one in recent American politics had worked harder toward this goal. Born in 1913 in California, Nixon had long been climbing the political ladder. He had long been climbing life's ladder too, for his Quaker parents had struggled constantly to make ends meet for their family of five sons. As a twelve-year-old, Nixon was fascinated and repelled by the corruption of the Harding administration. Nixon's mother remembered the boy's resolve at that time to play a part in public affairs. "I will be an old-fashioned kind of lawyer," he vowed, "a lawyer who can't be bought."

Elected to the House of Representatives in 1946, Nixon attracted national attention soon afterward during the investigation of Alger Hiss. Nixon was elected to the Senate in 1950, and shortly became Vice President, winning on the Republican ticket as Dwight Eisenhower's running mate in 1952 and again in 1956.

An obvious choice as Eisenhower's successor, Nixon was narrowly defeated in the 1960 election by John F. Kennedy. He lost again (more decisively) in a bid for the California governorship in 1962. His political career seemingly over, he moved to New York City to practice law. The allure of politics, however, proved too strong to resist. By 1966, Nixon was making plans that would ultimately bring him to the White House, in a remarkable political comeback.

1 Nixon Tackles Foreign Policy Issues

President Nixon had concluded, as he said in his inaugural, that after the tumultuous presidencies of Kennedy and Johnson, America was suffering from "a fever of words." He declared, "We cannot learn from one another, until we stop shouting at one another." The principal way to lower the national voice appeared to be by finding a solution to the war in Vietnam.

THE VIETNAM WAR

Nixon announces a plan to end the war. Nixon, who had first made his national reputation as a strong anti-Communist, had supported the escalation of United States involvement in Vietnam under Presidents Kennedy and Johnson. By 1968 he believed, however, that the United States was being torn apart by the war and that American troops must be withdrawn. He worked closely with his chief foreign policy adviser, Henry A. Kissinger, a political scientist from Harvard University, to find a way to end the war. Nixon and Kissinger were determined to make an "honorable peace" in Vietnam. The terms under which the United States left Vietnam must not, they maintained, damage America's reputation as a trustworthy ally.

Soon after taking office, Nixon announced his plan for ending American involvement in the war. The United States would pull out its combat forces while South Vietnamese troops would be trained to take over the duties Americans had been performing. This plan came to be called "Vietnamization."

During the next three years, hundreds of thousands of American troops were brought home. By 1972, only 139,000 Americans remained in Vietnam — compared

Richard Nixon took the oath of office as the nation's thirty-seventh President on January 20, 1969. His major goal was settlement of the Vietnam War.

with over 500,000 stationed there when Johnson left office. Nixon also sought to reduce American casualties by ordering United States troops to fight only when under attack or facing the threat of attack.

Vietnamization, nevertheless, presented problems for the Nixon administration. For one thing, the policy did not satisfy those in the United States who demanded the immediate withdrawal of all American troops. In addition, the South Vietnamese were hard-pressed to replace the departing American troops. In order to relieve the pressure on the Saigon government, Nixon ordered intensive bombing raids against the Communist forces, which were gradually extending their control over the South Vietnamese countryside.

Cambodia is invaded. American strategists were becoming increasingly worried about the fate of South Vietnam once United States forces were withdrawn. They feared that as the United States reduced its presence, the enemy would become bolder and less willing to negotiate. Nixon decided to take vigorous action. He would seek to cripple the North Vietnamese by striking at their military sanctuaries.

The Vietnamese Communists' presence in neutral Cambodia (map, page 376) had long concerned American and South Vietnamese policy-makers. Communist troops routinely assaulted South Vietnamese targets from Cambodia and then retreated across the border.

In late April, 1970, President Nixon announced that American and South Vietnamese troops had crossed into Cambodia. Their mission was to destroy enemy camps and supply depots. Nixon explained his belief that this action would shorten the war and save American lives, and he promised to withdraw United States troops within two months.

Most Americans supported the President's decision in this matter, but administration critics charged that instead of ending the war, Nixon was now expanding it. During the next month, antiwar demonstrations were held in a number of cities and on college campuses. At Kent State University, in Ohio, student protests ended in tragic violence. The National Guard, sent to the campus to restore order, fired without warning into a crowd of students on May 4 and killed four people. Violence also erupted at Jackson State College in Mississippi, where two students were killed in a clash with state troopers.

Diplomacy and military force are used in efforts to end the war. Throughout this period the United States, North Vietnam, South Vietnam, and the Viet Cong carried on peace talks in Paris, but made little progress toward reaching an agreement. In the spring of 1972, the Communists attempted to break the stalemate by launching a major offensive in the South. The United States responded with massive bombing raids on enemy positions, a naval blockade of North Vietnam, and the mining of Haiphong harbor. By the end of the summer, the Communist invasion had been halted.

At this point, there was some progress in the negotiations. The North Vietnamese seemed to conclude, as a result of the costly offensive, that the time had come to make concessions at the bargaining table. Beginning in late September, 1972, Henry Kissinger and Le Duc Tho (lee duk TOH), the North Vietnamese negotiator, met in Paris for several weeks. In October an agreement seemed imminent, and Kissinger confidently told reporters, "Peace is at hand."

The announcement proved to be premature. Kissinger had not counted on the strong resistance of South Vietnamese President Thieu, who refused to accept the proposed settlement. Thieu objected to provisions permitting North Vietnamese troops to remain in South Vietnam after a cease-fire had been signed. He objected also to the projected establishment of a coalition government in South Vietnam. Thieu feared that creating such a regime would simply be a prelude to a take-over by the Communists. Talks were again suspended, and the fighting went on.

Following Nixon's re-election in November, 1972, negotiations resumed once more in Paris. In mid-December, however, they again broke down, and a decision was reached to bomb Hanoi and Haiphong in order to force the North Vietnamese back to the bargaining table. This was the first time the United States had bombed North Vietnam since 1968. After absorbing enormous destruction, the Communists agreed to resume the talks, and Nixon ordered the bombing raids halted.

A settlement is reached. Meetings resumed in Paris early in January, 1973. It now took only a short time to reach a final settlement. On January 27, the parties agreed to (1) a cease-fire effective immediately and supervised by an international commission; (2) the withdrawal of all American military personnel from Vietnam within sixty days; and (3) the release of all American prisoners. It was also understood that North Vietnamese forces could remain in South Vietnam, and that the United States would continue to supply the Saigon government with economic and military assistance.

Americans count the costs of the war. Thus ended American participation in the longest and most divisive war in the nation's history. Over 56,000 Americans had died in Vietnam, and more than 300,000 others had been wounded. There was widespread feeling in the country that the war had not been handled correctly but no consensus about what alternative policy should have been followed. There was also no ready agreement on how to deal with the thousands of military deserters or with the young men who had left the United States to avoid being drafted.

One immediate result of the Vietnamese conflict was the enactment of the War Powers Act of 1973, passed over President Nixon's veto. The measure was an attempt by Congress to ensure that it would participate in any future commitment of American troops. The act provides that the President, upon deploying American forces abroad, must notify Congress of the action within 48 hours. If within sixty days Con-

Peace negotiators Le Duc Tho and Henry Kissinger shake hands early in 1973 after the United States and North Vietnam agreed on terms to bring the Vietnam conflict to an end.

gress does not approve the deployment, the troops must be withdrawn.

Vietnam falls to the Communists. As it turned out, the Paris peace treaty did not end the war. Both sides in Vietnam expected the fighting to continue after the American forces were withdrawn, and both sides sought to build up their strength. Then, in the early spring of 1975, North Vietnam launched a powerful military offensive. Meeting only weak resistance from the South Vietnamese armed forces and seeing no threat of renewed United States intervention, the North Vietnamese pushed for final victory.

Gerald R. Ford, the new American President, urged Congress to increase military aid to South Vietnam. (American aid to South Vietnam had fallen from $2.3 billion in 1973 to approximately a billion in 1974.) Congress rejected the President's request, regarding the cause as hopeless. It agreed, however, to appropriate $300 million for "humanitarian" aid.

Late in April, as Communist troops approached Saigon, President Ford ordered a pull-out of all Americans still in South Vietnam. American ships and planes were able also to evacuate approximately 130,000 Vietnamese, most of whom came to live in the United States. On May 1, 1975, Viet Cong soldiers raised their flag over Saigon. After decades of fighting, Vietnam became a single nation under a Communist government. Neighboring Laos and Cambodia also came under Communist control.

CHANGES IN FOREIGN POLICY

President Nixon visits China. Even as the Vietnam War was winding down, the Nixon administration was looking for ways to reduce world tensions. The President and

Henry Kissinger (who became Secretary of State in 1973) saw the quarrel between the Soviet Union and China (page 374) as an opportunity for the United States to win concessions from both countries. The chief fear of each of the Communist giants, American leaders reasoned, was that the other would draw closer to the United States, leaving one of them dangerously isolated. The Nixon administration decided to open negotiations with both countries. It began using a new word to describe its policy of bringing peace to the world: *détente* (day-TAHNT), a French word that means the relaxing of tensions.

The first phase of the administration's policy of détente was the establishment of diplomatic contact with Communist China. In July, 1971, Kissinger secretly flew to China and met with Premier Chou En-lai. Less than a week later, President Nixon astonished the world by announcing that he

Richard Nixon surprised the world by visiting China in 1972. After being greeted upon his arrival by Premier Chou En-lai, the President inspected Chinese troops.

had accepted an invitation to visit China. "I have taken this action," he said, "because of my profound conviction that all nations will gain from a reduction of tensions and a better relationship between the United States and the People's Republic of China."

President and Mrs. Nixon flew to China early in 1972. On February 27, 1972, after a week of meetings in Peking, President Nixon and Premier Chou issued a joint statement. They had agreed to establish trade relations between their two countries and to allow cultural and scientific exchanges. Because of continuing disagreements over the status of the Nationalist government on Taiwan, the establishment of full diplomatic relations between China and the United States was delayed. Clearly, however, a new era in international relations had begun.

Agreements are reached with the Soviet Union. As Nixon and Kissinger had expected, the Soviet Union was alarmed by the prospect of friendship between the United States and China. To reassure the Russians, Nixon announced that he would fly to the Soviet Union in May, 1972, for a summit conference with Leonid Brezhnev, the Soviet premier.

At the conclusion of their talks, Nixon and Brezhnev signed a number of agreements, the most important of them concerning arms limitations. For a five-year period, the two superpowers would freeze the level of offensive missiles and limit the deployment of defensive missiles to two sites in each country. This agreement was the culmination of the Strategic Arms Limitation Talks (SALT) that had been started in November, 1969. The two leaders also agreed to cooperate on various cultural and scientific projects and to establish closer economic ties.

In June, 1973, Brezhnev came to the United States for further talks with Nixon. The two leaders pledged to continue the SALT talks and reaffirmed earlier agreements. This summit meeting was chiefly symbolic, indicating a continuing commitment to détente. Tension between the United States and the Soviet Union appeared to be lower than at any time since the beginning of the cold war.

The Yom Kippur War threatens world peace. Just when the United States was adjusting to the idea of détente, the world was again catapulted into crisis by events in the Middle East. The uneasy peace that had settled over the region after the Six-Day War (page 375) was shattered on October 6, 1973, when Egyptian and Syrian forces attacked Israeli-held territory. The attacks took place on the eve of Yom Kippur, the holiest day in the Hebrew calendar. The Israelis, taken by surprise, fought stubbornly to defend their country and suffered heavy casualties at first. By mid-October, however, they were on the offensive, pushing back the Syrians in the north and crossing the Suez Canal in the south.

Alarmed at the prospect of another Arab defeat in the Middle East, the Soviet Union threatened to intervene. To counter the threat, Nixon placed American military forces on alert throughout the world. Within 24 hours, the Russians backed down, agreeing to the establishment of a United Nations peacekeeping force in the region. Once again, the fighting in the Middle East had been halted, but still no solution had been found to the long-standing antagonism between Israel and its Arab neighbors.

Arab nations impose an oil embargo. The Arab countries were furious with the United States for giving support to Israel during the Yom Kippur War. In retaliation, Saudi Arabia announced in late October, 1973, that it would no longer sell oil to the United States. The other Arab members of the Organization of Petroleum Exporting Countries (OPEC) quickly followed suit.

The United States, dependent on the Middle East for about 12 percent of its oil, suffered from the oil embargo. Fuel prices rose sharply, and long lines of automobiles formed at service stations, waiting for the limited supplies of gasoline.

The oil embargo was not lifted until March, 1974. In the meantime, the American people began making efforts to reduce the country's dependence on Middle East

The Alaska pipeline, built in response to the fuel crisis, carries oil about 800 miles across the state.

oil. Conservation measures were introduced, new oil reserves were sought, and research was stepped up on finding alternative forms of energy. Energy prices, however, never returned to former levels.

SECTION REVIEW

1. Vocabulary: *détente*.
2. (a) What did Nixon hope to achieve by his Vietnamization policy? (b) Why was that policy difficult to carry out?
3. (a) What steps led to the signing of a settlement ending American involvement in Vietnam? (b) Describe what happened to South Vietnam after American troops were withdrawn.
4. (a) Why did Nixon travel to China in 1972? (b) What agreements did the United States and the Soviet Union reach shortly thereafter?
5. (a) What was the Yom Kippur War? (b) Why did the oil-producing countries of the Middle East impose an oil embargo on the United States?

2 Nixon Faces Domestic Concerns

During most of his presidency, Richard Nixon was forced to concentrate on international relations. There were, however, absorbing matters on the home front — among them a shining triumph for America's space program.

Americans land on the moon. Early in Nixon's term, the centuries-old dream of reaching the moon became a reality. President Kennedy's pledge that America would put a man on the moon before 1970 was fulfilled. Apollo 11 was launched on July 16, 1969, with Neil Armstrong, Edwin E. "Buzz" Aldrin, Jr., and Michael Collins aboard. Four days later, the lunar landing ship touched down on the moon. As Armstrong stepped onto the moon's surface, he said, "That's one small step for a man, one giant leap for mankind." Aldrin soon joined him. Perhaps a billion people watched the live telecast of the extraordinary event. They saw the Americans plant the Stars and Stripes and leave a plaque reading: "Here men from planet earth first set foot upon the moon, July 1969, A.D. We came in peace for all mankind."

Nixon appoints four Supreme Court justices. During his campaign in 1968, Nixon had made the Supreme Court an issue, charging that several of its rulings in criminal cases had protected the rights of accused persons at the expense of society at large. In June, 1969, Chief Justice Earl Warren retired. To replace him, Nixon appointed Warren E. Burger of Minnesota, who had publicly supported the President's criticisms of the Warren Court. Burger won quick confirmation by the Senate.

In seeking to fill a second vacancy on the Court, however, the President ran into trouble. The Senate refused to approve the first two men he nominated. The President's third choice, Harry A. Blackmun, also a Minnesotan, won unanimous approval in the Senate.

Later in his term, further vacancies enabled Nixon to put Lewis F. Powell, Jr., of

Americans followed up the 1969 lunar landing with a series of missions, including the Apollo 15 expedition (above), which explored the moon's surface.

Virginia and Assistant Attorney General William H. Rehnquist of Arizona on the Supreme Court. These four appointments led to a significant, though by no means drastic, change in the Court's decisions. The Burger Court did not reverse the decisions of the Warren Court, but it tended to interpret the Constitution more strictly, especially on the issue of the rights of persons accused of crimes.

Americans take steps to end pollution. During the Nixon years, a number of steps were taken that would help reshape American life. None was more important than the fight against pollution.

By the late 1960's, environmental issues had become matters of widespread concern in the United States. The majority of Americans now lived close together in cities and suburbs, and there had been harmful effects on the nation's air, water, and land. As people became aware of pollution problems, local, state, and federal governments began to take measures to clean up the environment. In 1970, President Nixon created the Environmental Protection Agency. The EPA had the responsibility of enforcing the growing number of laws to protect the environment.

Amendments to the Constitution are proposed. Another development during Nixon's presidency was a formal recognition of the role young people were playing in American society. The Twenty-Sixth Amendment to the Constitution was ratified in 1971, lowering the voting age to eighteen in all state and federal elections.

In 1972, Congress passed and then sent to the states a proposed Twenty-Seventh Amendment, which came to be called the Equal Rights Amendment, or ERA. Its first and principal article read, "Equality of rights under the law shall not be denied or abridged by the United States or by any state on account of sex." Unlike the Twenty-Sixth Amendment, the ERA met strong opposition. By the end of Nixon's presidency, it had not been ratified by the required three fourths of the states.

Nixon tries to slow down inflation. As always, most domestic problems did not have easy solutions. One of the most troubling problems was that of inflation. The increases in government spending under the Johnson administration — to finance both Great Society programs and the military effort in Vietnam — had created upward pressure on prices.

In 1970, Congress authorized the President to regulate wages and prices if he thought it necessary. This step had never been taken in peacetime, and Nixon opposed it as incompatible with the free enterprise system. By mid-1971, however, the inflation rate had risen to over 6 percent and showed no sign of slowing down. The President faced increasing pressure to take action. On August 15, 1971, he surprised the nation by announcing a ninety-day freeze on wages, prices, and rents. This step became known as Phase I of the President's economic plan. He also proposed tax reductions designed to stimulate the economy.

The second stage in the President's economic plan went into effect late in 1971. Phase II permitted wage and price increases if they were no greater than the increase in productivity, that is, the stepped-up creation of goods and services. Immediately, however, problems arose. In its very first decision, the federal board overseeing wages authorized a 15 percent boost for coal miners. The price board shortly made similar exceptions, and the floodgates of inflation were reopened.

McGovern challenges Nixon in 1972. In July, 1972, the Democratic National Convention gathered in Miami. The party was badly divided, as it had been since 1968. The major candidates for the nomination were former Vice President Hubert Humphrey, Senator Edmund Muskie of Maine, and Senator George McGovern of South Dakota. Alabama governor George Wallace, who had also been a contender, had withdrawn from the campaign in May

after an assassination attempt left him paralyzed from the waist down.

Owing to changes in party rules, the mix of Democratic delegates had changed significantly since the 1968 convention. For the first time, large numbers of women, blacks, and young people served as delegates. The chief beneficiary of the change was George McGovern, a candidate closely identified with the antiwar movement. McGovern was nominated on the first ballot and chose as his running mate Senator Thomas Eagleton of Missouri. The Democratic platform called for the immediate withdrawal of American troops from Vietnam, amnesty for draft resisters, tax reform, and cuts in military spending.

Doubts about McGovern's ability to lead the nation arose when, only two weeks after the convention, his choice of a running mate was called into question. At that time, Senator Eagleton revealed that he had once been hospitalized for emotional illness. McGovern at first insisted that he was "1,000 percent" behind Eagleton. Within a week, however, McGovern changed his mind and asked Eagleton to step down. He then chose R. Sargent Shriver, former director of the Peace Corps, to be the candidate for Vice President. The episode hurt McGovern, because it led many people to conclude that he was indecisive.

Nixon is re-elected. Nixon easily won renomination at the Republican convention, which was also held in Miami. Confident of victory, he did little personal campaigning, allowing Vice President Agnew and Cabinet officers to make public appearances in his place. Throughout the campaign, he maintained a large lead over McGovern in the opinion polls.

In November, Nixon was re-elected in a landslide. He won 60 percent of the popular vote to McGovern's 37 percent, carrying 49 of the 50 states and winning 520 electoral votes to McGovern's 17. It was the best showing ever made by a Republican presidential candidate. The triumph, however, was a personal one, for the Democrats retained control of both the Senate and the House of Representatives.

The Watergate affair begins to unfold. A seemingly minor campaign event, which attracted only limited attention at the time, soon became the center of a political scandal unmatched in American history. On June 17, 1972, five burglars were arrested at the headquarters of the Democratic National Committee in Washington's Watergate office complex. They had been placing electronic listening devices and were busy copying documents from files. It was later revealed that they were working for officials in Nixon's campaign organization, the Committee to Re-elect the President. At the time, however, the head of the committee, former Attorney General John Mitchell, denied that the burglars had been acting under orders from anyone in the organization. White House officials dismissed the event as a "third-rate burglary."

By early 1973 there was growing suspicion that responsibility for the Watergate break-in did not end with the individuals charged with the crime. Many people believed that officials in the Nixon administration had authorized the burglary and other illegal activities that they were now trying to cover up. Possibly, it was rumored, even the President himself was involved. In response to these suspicions, the Senate voted unanimously to set up a special committee to investigate the matter. Sam J. Ervin, a senator from North Carolina, was appointed chairman of the bipartisan panel, which held televised proceedings in the summer of 1973.

The fight over the tapes begins. On July 16, 1973, testimony was given before the Ervin Committee that, in the end, would undo the President. A White House official, in response to committee questioning, revealed that conversations in Nixon's office had routinely been tape-recorded. This information was important because it meant that the question of whether or not the President was involved in the Watergate cover-up might easily be resolved.

The Senate Select Committee on Watergate was headed by Sam J. Ervin. The televised hearings made the senator from North Carolina a popular figure.

Both the Ervin Committee and Archibald Cox, a Harvard law professor who had been named by the Attorney General as Special Prosecutor in the case, asked to listen to the tapes. The President, however, denied their requests. He argued on the grounds of "executive privilege" that these officials had no constitutional power to force him to reveal the contents of private conversations. To hand over the tapes, he asserted, would forever weaken the presidency. They persisted, however, and went to court to obtain the tapes.

After almost two months of court proceedings, Nixon offered a compromise. He agreed to supply the Special Prosecutor with summaries of the recorded conversations if Cox would seek no more presidential documents. Cox refused the offer on the grounds that summaries were not admissible evidence in courts of law and were therefore of no use to him. Angered by the refusal, Nixon ordered Attorney General Elliot Richardson to fire Cox. Richardson resigned rather than carry out this order. Deputy Attorney General William Ruckelshaus followed suit. Solicitor General Robert Bork, who became acting Attorney General, finally fired Cox. The resignations and the firing took place on the evening of Saturday, October 20, 1973. Known as "the Saturday Night Massacre," the affair prompted public outcry and added to the suspicion that the President had something to hide.

Vice President Agnew resigns. Meanwhile, in the fall of 1973, a separate investigation involving Vice President Agnew was under way. A federal grand jury in Baltimore was examining charges that Agnew, first as governor of Maryland and then as Vice President, had received illegal payments from private firms seeking favored treatment in the awarding of government contracts. Agnew resigned as Vice President on October 10, after pleading *nolo contendere* ("no contest") to a reduced charge of income tax evasion. In return, the court agreed not to sentence him to prison and not to prosecute him for any of the other crimes with which he was charged.

Under the terms of the Twenty-Fifth Amendment, ratified in 1967, President Nixon was empowered to appoint a new Vice President to fill the vacancy in that office. He nominated Congressman Gerald R. Ford of Michigan to replace Agnew as Vice President. Ford, well-liked by his colleagues in Congress, was quickly confirmed by the Senate.

The storm gathers. All the while, the Watergate affair was increasing its hold on the nation's attention. On October 30, 1973, as a result of the firing of Cox, the House Judiciary Committee began preliminary investigations to decide whether President Nixon should be impeached. Two days later, Leon Jaworski, a Houston attorney, was appointed to replace Cox as Special Prosecutor. Both Jaworski and the Judiciary Committee asked the President to supply them with recordings that contained discussions relating to Watergate. The President again refused on the grounds of executive privilege. As a result, in April, 1974, both the Judiciary Committee and the Special Prosecutor issued court orders requesting the White House tapes. Under increasing public pressure, Nixon decided, late in April, to release heavily edited transcripts of 46 tape-recorded conversations. The transcripts were quickly published in the nation's newspapers and in book form.

The release of the transcripts did not improve the President's position. Although they were edited, they contained much embarrassing material. Instead of satisfying public curiosity, the transcripts led to renewed demands for full disclosure and further investigation.

The President resigns. Events moved toward a climax in the last weeks of July, 1974. Jaworski, frustrated by delays in the investigation, asked the Supreme Court to decide, once and for all, whether Nixon could be forced to turn over tapes that had been requested by a federal court. On July 24, the Court unanimously ruled against the President. The decision was written by Chief Justice Burger, who argued that the President could not legally withhold evi-

Newspaper headlines on August 9, 1974, announced that Richard Nixon had resigned from office.

gate break-in. The transcripts clearly showed that Nixon had been a participant in the cover-up effort almost from the beginning. At this point, the calls for his resignation became widespread. It had become clear that, if he did not resign, the Senate would almost certainly remove him from office.

On the evening of August 8, the President announced his decision to leave office. The following day his letter of resignation was delivered to Secretary of State Henry Kissinger. Nixon became the first President to yield his office before the end of his term for any reason other than death. Less than an hour later, Chief Justice Burger administered the oath of office to the new President, Gerald R. Ford.

SECTION REVIEW

1. What success did America's space program enjoy in 1969?
2. (a) What promise did Richard Nixon make during the 1968 campaign concerning the Supreme Court? (b) How successful was he in carrying out that promise?
3. (a) Describe the steps President Nixon took to slow down inflation. (b) What success did he have?
4. (a) What were the results of the 1972 presidential election? (b) What events led to Richard Nixon's resignation?

dence needed in a criminal trial. Within hours, Nixon announced that he would hand over the tapes.

The President's position was further eroded by the action of the House Judiciary Committee. After days of nationally televised debate and discussion, the committee voted to recommend Nixon's impeachment. Republicans as well as Democrats supported the recommendation, prompting observers to predict that the full House would vote to impeach the President. He would then, under the provisions of the Constitution, be tried by the Senate. If found guilty, he would be removed from office.

Despite these severe setbacks, Nixon retained some backing in Congress. On August 5, however, most of this support collapsed. On that day, Nixon released transcripts of three conversations that had taken place only five days after the Water-

3 Ford Completes Nixon's Second Term

Until he became Vice President, Gerald Ford had represented Michigan's Fifth Congressional District for almost a quarter of a century. Minority leader in the House of Representatives since 1965, he once said that his highest ambition in life was to serve as Speaker of the House. Now, through a series of unparalleled events, he had become President of the United States — the first person in the nation's history to become Chief Executive without having been elected President or Vice President.

Ford takes office. Keenly aware of the need to restore public confidence in the national government, President Ford pledged that his administration would be characterized by openness and candor. As his Vice President he quickly nominated Nelson Rockefeller, a four-term governor of New York and a political figure well known to the public. Ford also urged Americans to recognize that the Watergate affair — which he called "our long national nightmare" — had demonstrated the country's strength. "Our Constitution works," he said. "Our great republic is a government of laws and not of men."

Ford seemed to many people to be just the kind of leader the nation needed after the events of the previous two years. The first President to have been an Eagle Scout, he had played center on the University of Michigan football team in the 1930's and had served in the Pacific during the Second World War. Appreciating his unpretentious manner and conciliatory words, Americans rallied around the new Chief Executive.

Nixon is pardoned. On September 8, 1974, a month after Nixon's resignation, Ford made a controversial announcement. He had decided, he said, to grant Richard Nixon a "full, free, and absolute" pardon for all crimes that Nixon "committed or may have committed or taken part in."

Critics of the new President's decision argued that Ford had denied the American people the opportunity to find out, by means of a public trial, the full truth about what the former President had done. Some critics even charged that a deal had been struck — that Ford had guaranteed Nixon a pardon in return for his resignation.

Ford strongly denied these charges. He answered that bringing the former President to trial would create dissension among the American people, who were just beginning to put Watergate behind them. Nonetheless, Ford's popularity declined, and some people never forgave him for the decision to issue the pardon. In the 1974 congressional elections, possibly as a result of Ford's actions, the Democrats scored large gains.

Gerald Ford was sworn in as President shortly after Nixon's resignation. Mrs. Betty Ford watched as Chief Justice Warren Burger administered the oath of office.

Delegations headed by Gerald Ford (right) and Soviet leader Brezhnev (left) met in Helsinki in 1975 to negotiate a treaty that fixed the national boundaries of Europe.

The nation faces economic problems. Another reason for the Democrats' congressional victory in 1974 was the slump in the nation's economy. Convinced that inflation was the nation's chief economic problem, Ford advocated keeping a lid on federal spending and supported a tight monetary policy by the Federal Reserve. He also established a Council on Wage and Price Stability, which had the responsibility of exposing inflationary wage and price increases. Despite these measures, a recession that had begun in the fall of 1973 worsened, and by the spring of 1975 over 9 percent of the nation's workers were unemployed. At the same time, a four-fold increase in oil prices announced by OPEC in early 1974 was putting strong upward pressure on the inflation rate. During 1974 the inflation rate rose to 11 percent; in 1975 it was still above 9 percent.

Ford carries on Nixon's foreign policy. In dealing with other nations, Ford relied on the advice of Secretary of State Kissinger, who kept his Cabinet post in the new administration. As a result, there was a large degree of continuity in the foreign policy of the Nixon and Ford administrations.

In 1975, President Ford and representatives from 34 other countries, including the Soviet Union, gathered in Helsinki, Finland. The outcome was a treaty recognizing the existing boundaries of Europe as permanent and unalterable. The participating nations also pledged to respect and promote basic human rights. Supporters of the treaty saw it as another step in the lessening of tensions between the superpowers. Critics maintained that Western nations, in signing the treaty, were approving of the Soviet Union's domination of Eastern Europe. They also pointed out that, despite the

Impressions of the Bicentennial

The occasion of America's two-hundredth birthday was celebrated in many ways across the nation. The editors of *The New Yorker* magazine published the following account of what they observed in New York City on July 4, 1976.

The Fourth of July, 1976, was unlike any other day we can remember. It was as if a day had descended upon our nation from somewhere else. Yet it was ours. It couldn't be mistaken for anything but an American day. People had been talking about it for months in advance, but when it came, it came unannounced. No one had foreseen this particular day. It had an unplanned, unarranged quality — homemade, do-it-yourself. Government officials took their modest place in the background. Public-relations and promotion people bowed out altogether. Television and press people became self-effacing. People normally drawn to the limelight lay low. And the country's citizens, on their own, took to celebrating a birthday they all shared and suddenly understood. The idea of freedom hung in the air; and the idea of peace. We were at peace with the world, we were at peace with each other, and, unaccountably, we seemed at peace within ourselves. No one was telling us what to think, how to feel, where to go. Mostly, we went outdoors — into the streets, into the parks, down to the riverbanks — just in order to be with one another; and we thought our individual thoughts (thankful ones, very likely) and

A bicentennial celebration in New York City

we felt good. Political rhetoric was held at a minimum, but the words we did hear sounded true. There was little flag-waving, but the flag was once more recognizable and thrilling. Our parades were weak on firepower and strong on high-school bands. It was a blithe day, a gentle day, a curiously lighthearted day. It was a holiday.

promises made in the treaty, the governments of Eastern Europe and the Soviet Union continued to violate the human rights of their citizens.

The nation celebrates the bicentennial. On July 4, 1976, President Ford led the nation in celebrating the two-hundredth anniversary of its declaration of independence. The disappointments and disagreeable events of recent years were still on people's minds. Nevertheless, in every corner of the land

the bicentennial brought satisfaction that the freest country on earth, living under the oldest continuous government in the world, had safely weathered fierce storms.

The parties choose their presidential nominees. In 1976, Gerald Ford decided to seek election to a full term as President. He had a difficult time, however, winning his party's nomination. His challenger in the primaries was Ronald Reagan, who had served two terms as governor of California.

At the Republican convention in Kansas City, Missouri, Ford narrowly defeated Reagan for the party's nomination. As his running mate, Ford chose Senator Robert Dole of Kansas.

Republican fortunes were at a low point in 1976 because of the recession and the lingering effects of the Watergate affair. Many prominent Democrats, therefore, sought their party's nomination, believing it would be a sure ticket to the White House. Instead of a familiar name, however, a newcomer to national politics gained a first-ballot victory at the July convention in New York City. He was Jimmy Carter.

Carter, a graduate of the United States Naval Academy, was a peanut farmer and businessman who had served one term as governor of Georgia. He had begun planning to run for the presidency as early as 1972, and with excellent organizational work and tireless campaigning was able to score well in the first events of the 1976 presidential campaign. By winning the Iowa caucuses and the New Hampshire primary he attracted wide attention, leading to his victory in New York.

Jimmy Carter is elected President. Immediately after the Democratic convention, Carter and his running mate, Senator Walter Mondale of Minnesota, held a substantial lead over their Republican rivals. As the campaign shifted into full gear, however, the gap between the two candidates narrowed considerably. Ford and his fellow Republicans argued that Carter lacked the necessary experience to be President and that his positions on particular issues were difficult to pin down. Carter, on the other hand, charged that Ford's policies had failed to end the recession. He promised to boost the economy through increased government spending, to streamline the federal bureaucracy, and to develop alternative sources of energy to reduce dependence on foreign oil. As Election Day neared, neither candidate had a significant lead in the opinion polls.

By a narrow margin, the voters favored the outsider. Carter won 51 percent of the vote to Ford's 48 percent and carried the

Jimmy Carter, a newcomer to national politics, defeated Gerald Ford in the presidential election of 1976.

electoral college by a margin of 297 to 241. The Democrats once again maintained control of both houses of Congress.

As President Ford prepared to leave the White House after less than two and a half years in office, he was satisfied with the historic role he had played. He would be remembered for having helped the nation put behind it two of its most distressing experiences: the war in Vietnam and the Watergate affair.

SECTION REVIEW

1. (a) Why did President Ford pardon Richard Nixon? (b) On what grounds was Ford's decision criticized?
2. (a) What steps did Ford take to fight inflation? (b) How effective were they?
3. How did Ford carry on the Nixon administration's policy of détente?
4. (a) Who were the nominees for President in the 1976 election? (b) What issues were debated in that campaign? (c) What was the outcome?

Analyzing News Reports

People get their information about current news events from a variety of sources—newspapers, television, radio, news magazines. To understand current events, you need both to be aware of the different sources of news and to analyze the information that these *news media* present. Because current news is history in the making, you can use many of the same skills of analysis that you have learned to apply to historical sources (pages 146–147). You need to be able to distinguish fact from opinion, recognize the writer's or speaker's bias, and decide whether the facts are complete and accurate.

Sources of News

Newspapers. The greatest amount and variety of current news coverage is found in large daily newspapers. In addition to news stories, newspapers carry several kinds of articles that should not be read as if they were objective, factual accounts. These include *editorials*, which express the views of the newspaper's management, and *columns*, which give the thoughts and opinions of writers and experts on specific subjects. Such articles are intended to present a personal point of view, and so their writers often do not try to be objective.

Television. Television is the most important source of news for many people. TV news programs in some ways resemble newspapers in their arrangement and presentation of the news. On the other hand, because so much news must be covered in a limited time, TV news cannot be as complete or detailed as a newspaper. For the same reason, a TV news show cannot cover as many events. Also, television news tends to emphasize the kinds of events that can be shown quickly and dramatically through pictures.

Like the editorial pages of a newspaper, some television news programs present opinions in the form of discussions or debates. These programs can be valuable in understanding an issue, but it is important to keep in mind that the participants usually are expressing their individual points of view.

Radio. Many radio stations carry only short news broadcasts giving highlights of major happenings, weather, and sports news. Some stations, however, are "all-news" stations — which usually means a mixture of news stories, background information, and opinion. Radio, like TV, also presents debates, discussions, and programs that analyze the news.

News magazines. The major news magazines take a different approach to the news. Long articles are focused on a few major events or long-term developments; the magazine's staff members do extensive research to provide detailed information. Other sections give highlights of events in various fields such as sports, entertainment, and business.

News magazines, too, contain signed articles expressing the writer's opinion. Some magazines have an overall "slant" or philosophy that is designed to appeal to their readers. This may influence both the choice of subject matter and the way facts are presented.

Analyzing the News

What skills can you use to get the most from these different types of news reports? To begin, try to become aware of the way the news is presented. Is it a detailed story written in a newspaper? Is it a short, action-filled report on television? Does the report appear in an editorial or column?

Once you have thought about the source of a news report, recall what you have learned about distinguishing fact from opinion. As you read an article or listen to a report, ask, "Can that statement be checked or verified?" Remember that opinion can also be conveyed by the choice of words and the choice of which facts to include. While an opinion is not necessarily untrue, you should be aware that it *is* an opinion.

Read the two paragraphs below, each of which reports on an imaginary election campaign. Which one is more factual and objective?

Ann Johnson, the People's Party candidate for state senator, presented her proposals for tax reform at a press conference today. She answered questions from critics of the plan and outlined a proposal for cutting costs by combining several state agencies into one with fewer staff members.

With elections only a week away, senatorial candidate George Cromwell made a desperate bid for voter support with his plan for tax reform. Cromwell's program would cut the state budget harshly, combining several agencies and leading to the firing of many employees. The candidate, who has no previous experience in government, responded angrily when reporters asked questions critical of his proposal.

The second paragraph not only reflects the writer's opinion but also shows bias against the candidate. Notice the choice of words like *desperate, harshly,* and *angrily.* Notice also that in telling about two similar tax programs, the second article emphasizes the negative results.

The second paragraph also contains a statement that should lead the reader to question whether this story is presenting all the facts or only one side of the issue. Perhaps it is true that Cromwell has no previous experience in government. It may also be true, however, that he has other experience that would be valuable in office. The reporter has shown bias by giving only half the facts.

Analyzing news reports takes time and thought. It is probably easier to analyze a written news report in a newspaper or magazine, because you have time to reread passages and consider whether they are objective or not. With careful and attentive listening, however, you can apply the same analytical skills to radio and television news.

Check Your Skill

Use the information presented on these pages to answer the following questions.
1. Which of the news media gives you the most information about many different events?
2. Why does television coverage of the news differ from a newspaper report?
3. How can you distinguish fact from opinion in reading a newspaper or magazine story?
4. How may the writer's choice of words show bias or opinion?

Apply Your Skill

1. Compare the way in which a daily newspaper and an evening television news program cover the same event. As part of your comparison, list the facts and details each one gives.
2. Read the editorials in a daily newspaper and write a short paragraph describing the point of view expressed in one editorial.
3. Compare two television reporters' programs on the same event. How are their reports alike or different?

Chapter 15 Review

Summary

Richard Nixon's overriding concern upon taking office as President in 1969 was to end American involvement in the Vietnam War. With the aid of his foreign policy adviser, Henry Kissinger, Nixon formulated a plan to withdraw American combat forces and train Vietnamese troops to take over the fighting. A peace settlement was finally reached in January, 1973, but not before Nixon ordered an invasion of Cambodia, renewed the bombing of North Vietnam, and witnessed bitter antiwar demonstrations at home.

At the same time that American involvement in the Vietnam War was being concluded, Nixon was pursuing other means of easing international tensions. In a historic move, he journeyed to China early in 1972 and established trade and cultural ties. In May, 1972, Nixon visited the Soviet Union and met with Soviet leader Leonid Brezhnev to work out an arms-limitation agreement.

Although Nixon concentrated on foreign policy, domestic issues also demanded his attention. During his presidency, Nixon had the opportunity to appoint four justices to the Supreme Court. Nixon addressed the growing concern over pollution by creating the Environmental Protection Agency. The agency's duty was to enforce laws designed to protect the environment. The pressing issue of inflation prompted Nixon to regulate wages and prices, an effort that was largely unsuccessful.

Nixon easily defeated George McGovern in the 1972 presidential election, but an incident during the campaign set in motion a sequence of events that proved to be the President's undoing. Men associated with the Committee to Re-elect the President were arrested during a break-in at Democratic Party headquarters in Washington. Evidence of White House involvement in a cover-up of the so-called "Watergate affair" was eventually disclosed by a congressional investigation. Faced with impeachment proceedings, Nixon chose to resign, leaving office on August 9, 1974. Vice President Gerald Ford was sworn in as President and completed Nixon's second term.

One of Ford's first acts as President was to issue a pardon freeing Nixon from any possible criminal prosecution, growing out of the Watergate affair. Ford continued Nixon's foreign-policy initiatives, while at home he faced increases in the inflation and unemployment rates. In the 1976 presidential election, the Democratic candidate, Jimmy Carter, defeated Ford by a narrow margin.

Vocabulary and Important Terms

1. Vietnamization
2. War Powers Act
3. détente
4. Strategic Arms Limitation Talks
5. Yom Kippur War
6. Environmental Protection Agency
7. Twenty-Fifth Amendment
8. Twenty-Sixth Amendment
9. Equal Rights Amendment
10. Watergate affair
11. "Saturday Night Massacre"
12. Council on Wage and Price Stability
13. bicentennial

Discussion Questions

1. (a) What was President Nixon's plan for ending American involvement in the Vietnam War? (b) Why did Nixon send troops into Cambodia? (c) What was the reaction at home? (d) Why did the Paris peace treaty not end the war? (e) How did the Vietnamese conflict spill over into the Ford administration, and what was the eventual fate not only of Vietnam but also of Laos and Cambodia?

2. (a) What were the costs of the Vietnam War for the United States? (b) What aspects of the war did Americans continue to debate even after the conflict had ended?

3. (a) What steps did President Nixon take as part of his détente policy? (b) To what extent was the United States committed to détente during Gerald Ford's tenure as President?

4. (a) What were some of the most pressing domestic issues facing the nation during Nixon's presidency, and what steps were taken to deal with those issues? (b) What factors contributed to Nixon's landslide victory in the election of 1972?

5. (a) What caused inflation to be a major domestic problem for both the Nixon and Ford administrations? (b) How similar were their proposed solutions to the problem? (c) To what extent was either successful in bringing inflation under control?

6. (a) During the Watergate investigation, on what grounds did Nixon argue that neither members of Congress nor the special prosecutors should have access to the White House tapes? (b) How did the Supreme Court respond to the President's argument? (c) What happened when the transcripts of the tapes were released?

7. (a) What political experience and personal qualities did Gerald Ford bring to the presidency? (b) How did he try to restore public confidence?

8. What factors contributed to Jimmy Carter's election as President in 1972?

Relating Past and Present

1. One of the most pressing concerns of the Nixon administration was the effort to halt pollution. To what extent is pollution a problem today? What other environmental concerns receive attention today?

2. What is the state of American-Soviet relations today compared to the relations that existed during the Nixon administration? What factors have caused American-Soviet relations to change? What has happened to the policy of détente?

Studying Local History

1. How did your community respond to the concern about environmental issues in the late 1960's? What measures, if any, did your local and state governments take to deal with air, water, and land pollution and with other environmental concerns? What measures are being taken today?

2. Find out how your community celebrated the bicentennial and report on it to the class.

Using History Skills

1. *Using the index.* In the index find the entry for Vietnam. On what pages of your book is Vietnam mentioned or discussed? Look up each of these references. Based on the information you find, write a brief history of American involvement in Vietnam from its beginnings to the withdrawal of the last American troops.

2. *Analyzing news reports.* Find accounts in two news magazines of President Nixon's trip to China in 1972. Compare the background information presented in each account.

WORLD SCENE

Political Changes in Europe

In the early 1970's, the long-established authoritarian regimes of Spain and Portugal came to an end. Both countries gained new, democratic governments.

A constitutional monarchy in Spain. In 1939, General Francisco Franco led his forces to victory in the Spanish Civil War. With the backing of the army, Franco set up a dictatorship and established himself as Spain's all-powerful leader.

Franco's economic reforms in the 1950's and 1960's brought industry to Spain and provided a higher standard of living for most of the Spanish people. By the end of the 1960's, Franco began to ease some of his restrictions on personal freedom. Soon, protests against his rule broke out. Student demonstrations forced the closing of several universities in 1969, and labor strikes in the early 1970's were further proof of the extent of popular dissatisfaction.

Franco managed to retain power until his death in 1975. When Prince Juan Carlos succeeded Franco, he announced that Spain would become a constitutional monarchy. Elections were held two years later to select a parliament. These were the first free elections held in Spain in more than forty years.

A new Portuguese republic. In 1926 military leaders overthrew Portugal's democratic government. To deal with severe economic problems, an economics professor named Antonio Salazar was appointed minister of finance. Before long, Salazar extended his influence beyond economic matters and took control of the Portuguese government.

Salazar ruled Portugal as a dictator. He remained in power for nearly forty years with the help of a powerful secret-police organization which assured obedience to his repressive laws. During Salazar's rule, little improvement took place in the living standards of the people, and Portugal remained the poorest country in Western Europe.

Inspired by memories of past Portuguese empires, Salazar was determined to maintain his nation's hold on its African colonies. In the 1960's, when rebellions erupted in Angola, Mozambique, and Portuguese Guinea, Salazar sent large numbers of troops to deal with the trouble.

Salazar fell seriously ill in 1968 and was forced to retire. His followers tried to maintain the dictatorship, but young army officers overthrew the hated regime in 1974. Reforms were rapidly introduced that abolished the secret police, restored civil liberties, and allowed the formation of political parties. Arrangements were made to grant Portugal's African possessions their independence, and in 1976 elections led to the formation of a new Portuguese republic.

Challenging Years

1977 – 1980's

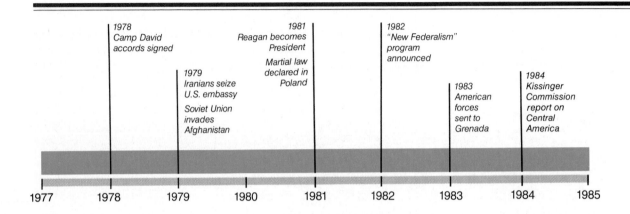

| 1978 Camp David accords signed | 1979 Iranians seize U.S. embassy | Soviet Union invades Afghanistan | 1981 Reagan becomes President | Martial law declared in Poland | 1982 "New Federalism" program announced | 1983 American forces sent to Grenada | 1984 Kissinger Commission report on Central America |

1977   1978   1979   1980   1981   1982   1983   1984   1985

CHAPTER OUTLINE

1. Jimmy Carter faces critical problems.

2. New patterns of population growth affect ways of living.

3. Ronald Reagan proposes new directions.

The 1976 election was the first presidential contest following the Watergate affair. Many voters, distrustful of politicians whose base was Washington, D.C., seemed ready to accept a candidate whose service was not associated with the capital. The Democrats had emphasized that Jimmy Carter was an outsider to Washington, whose political know-how came from state rather than federal experience. Carter thought of himself as a citizen who was reviving the ideal of plain goodness in national politics. He pledged: "I'll never tell a lie." At his inauguration, Carter presented himself as an ordinary man by wearing a business suit rather than the traditional formal attire. Instead of the usual limousine ride back to the White House from the Capitol, he chose to walk the route with his wife and children.

Ronald Reagan, the Republican candidate who ran against Carter in the 1980 presidential campaign, also adopted an anti-Washington stance. Reagan, long a motion-picture and television star, was a familiar name and face to millions of Americans. Twice elected governor of California, he had never held national office. An admirer of Franklin D. Roosevelt, Reagan had once been a Democrat. He changed his mind, however, as he grew older. "I didn't desert my party," he liked to explain. "It deserted me." His campaign promise to reduce the federal government's involvement in many areas of American life appealed to voters.

1 Jimmy Carter Faces Critical Problems

When Jimmy Carter came to office, he announced that he was eager to usher in "a new national spirit of unity and trust." One of his first official acts was to issue an unconditional pardon to all draft resisters from the Vietnam War period. He hoped that this measure would help erase some of the resentfulness the war had aroused and allow the country to face the future with a clean slate.

CONCERNS AT HOME

The administration proposes an energy program. A major problem requiring attention when President Carter took office was the country's dependence on imported oil. Ever since the Arab oil embargo of 1973 (page 393), Americans had been well aware of the

danger of this kind of dependence. Even though conservation measures had been instituted, the proportion of the country's oil needs filled by imported supplies had actually increased during the 1970's.

Carter began his efforts to solve the energy problem by creating the Department of Energy. The department's duty was to develop and coordinate national energy programs and policies. Next, Carter proposed new legislation that he believed would reduce — and, ultimately, eliminate — America's dependence on foreign oil. His program sought to increase the prices of domestically produced oil and natural gas by removing federal controls from the price of these fuels. He also called for additional taxes on gasoline to discourage its wasteful use. Revenue from the new taxes would be used to support research on the development of alternative sources of energy.

Not until 1978 did Congress pass a modified version of Carter's energy pro-

Washington, D.C., is not only the capital of the United States but also a symbol of the nation's unity, history, and traditions.

gram. The legislation encouraged some industries to use coal as a fuel despite the likely adverse effect on the environment. Government controls over natural gas prices were relaxed, and new taxes were passed to encourage conservation.

Relations with Congress are strained. The prolonged debate over President Carter's energy program was typical of his relations with Congress, which often were rocky, especially on domestic issues. After the events of the Vietnam War and Watergate, Congress was mistrustful of the executive branch of government. One effect was that a President could no longer count on near-automatic support of his programs from members of his own party. Party loyalty, too, had declined. In running for office, many candidates relied heavily on personal television advertising, leading some of them to conclude that they had been elected on their own, rather than through identification with a particular party.

Carter's lack of experience in Washington's ways soon was viewed by many Americans as a handicap. Members of Congress complained that the White House was ignoring their concerns. A number of minor controversies reinforced this impression. Early in his administration, for instance, the President vowed to fight what he considered to be "pork-barrel" public works projects. He neglected, however, to consult with members of Congress in whose districts those projects were to be located. The result, almost from the beginning, was strained relations between the executive and legislative branches.

Although the administration worked at improving relations with Congress, the effort was only moderately successful. Many members of Congress — even fellow-Democrats — never forgave Carter and his staff for those early mistakes.

Economic problems continue. When Carter took office, unemployment was on the upswing. Approximately seven million Americans were out of work. The new President's economic program, designed to create jobs, included proposals to reduce government spending, initiate public works projects, and cut taxes. By the end of 1978, the unemployment rate was on the way down. Inflation, however, had become a serious problem. In January, 1977, the inflation rate was running at 4.8 percent annually. By the fall of 1978, it had climbed to 10 percent.

In October, the administration announced the establishment of voluntary wage and price guidelines as part of an anti-inflation program. A Council on Wage and Price Stability was created to monitor compliance with these guidelines. The administration announced that businesses failing to follow the guidelines would be ineligible for government contracts. Overall, however, the necessary strong incentives for compliance were lacking, and the guidelines were not widely followed.

Owing partly to domestic causes and partly to enormous increases in the price of oil, inflation continued to soar. By 1979 the rate had reached 11.3 percent. The alarming rise in inflation became a major political liability for the President as the 1980 election drew near.

Carter's popularity declines. By the spring of 1979, administration officials were uneasy about Carter's prospects for re-election. The administration laid much of the blame for the President's difficulties on Congress, which had failed to pass many of Carter's legislative proposals. The overriding issue for Americans, however, continued to be oil. During the early months of 1979, political turmoil in the Middle East had resulted in reduced oil supplies and an OPEC price hike. Once again, Americans were lining up to pay high prices for gasoline, and many people, in their irritation, held the White House responsible.

On July 4, 1979, the President abruptly canceled a planned television address on the subject of energy and journeyed to the presidential retreat at Camp David in Maryland. There, for the next ten days, more than a hundred American leaders from various fields met with Carter and his top advisers, suggesting ways of increasing the administration's effectiveness.

Following the Camp David meetings, Carter addressed the country. He admitted that he had made mistakes and promised to provide stronger leadership. He also warned of a national "crisis of confidence" and passionately repeated his calls for the enactment of a massive federal energy program. Two days later, the President announced that the resignations of a number of Cabinet officers had been accepted.

The dramatic "crisis-of-confidence" speech and the Cabinet shuffle did not achieve the desired goal of restoring public faith in the Carter presidency. In the following months, the President's prospects for re-election seemed bleaker than ever.

FOREIGN POLICY

Carter supports human rights. In foreign affairs, President Carter made human rights a cornerstone of his foreign policy. He declared in his inaugural address that he would work to guarantee "the basic right of every human to be free of poverty, disease, and political repression." He criticized nations that denied these rights to their people, and he encouraged people living under repression to speak out against it. He even tried to persuade American allies in Asia, Africa, and South America to cease their violations of human rights. In some cases, Carter threatened to withdraw American aid if such offenses continued.

Carter mediates an agreement between Israel and Egypt. Like his predecessors, Carter worked hard to reduce tension in the Middle East. Taking advantage of startling new developments, he was able to play the role of peacemaker.

The Egyptian president, Anwar Sadat, had stunned the world by flying to Jerusalem in November, 1977, to meet with the Israeli prime minister, Menachem Begin. Up to that time, no Arab leader had ever visited Israel or even formally recognized its existence. Addressing the Israeli parliament, Sadat called for the normalization of Egyptian-Israeli relations, the negotiation of a peace treaty, and the withdrawal of Israeli forces from all occupied Arab lands.

President Carter's mediation of an agreement between President Sadat of Egypt (left) and Prime Minister Begin of Israel (right) boosted hopes for peace in the Middle East.

American diplomats, delighted with this turn of events, redoubled their efforts to bring about peace in the Middle East. When the talks between Sadat and Begin seemed to be at a stalemate, President Carter intervened, inviting the two leaders to meet with him in the United States.

Early in September, 1978, the three leaders went into seclusion at Camp David. Carter started by holding individual sessions with Sadat and Begin in order to probe their positions. When he brought them together, however, the meetings proved unproductive, and the two foreign leaders were soon barely talking to each other. Carter thereupon resumed the one-on-one arrangement, going back and forth between the two men, slowly nudging them off their fixed stands.

After twelve tense days Carter produced a diplomatic "miracle" — the Camp David accords. Under the accords, signed in a dramatic ceremony at the White House on September 17, 1978, an Israeli-Egyptian peace treaty was to be drawn up, and Israel would withdraw from Egyptian territories it had occupied. The Camp David accords included arrangements to discuss self-government for other occupied territories and Palestinian representation in later stages of the peace talks.

Sadat paid a high price for what he had done. Other Arab leaders denounced him for "selling out" the cause of the Palestinian Arabs, and they immediately subjected Egypt to a diplomatic and economic boycott. For Israel, removing its forces from the Sinai Peninsula was also a hard concession to make. Many Israelis criticized Begin, fearing that a withdrawal from the occupied territory would endanger their country's security.

The formal treaty was signed at the White House in March, 1979. Although little progress was made in later discussions on the other territories or on the Palestinian question, the "spirit of Camp David" generated hope for eventual peace between Israel and the Arab world. For President Carter,

his success as a mediator boosted the public's confidence in his leadership.

The United States establishes formal relations with China. American recognition of the People's Republic of China was another milestone of the Carter administration. The United States took this action on January 1, 1979, having received informal assurances from the mainland Chinese that they would not invade Taiwan, the offshore island which remained under Nationalist control (page 393).

In 1980 the United States and China signed a trade agreement. Soon, American commerce with the Chinese, especially in agricultural produce, outstripped trade with Russia. The continuation of American arms sales to Taiwan, however, remained a point of controversy between the United States and China.

Following the establishment of formal relations between the United States and China, Deputy Chairman Deng Xiaoping visited Washington, D.C. After productive talks, the two leaders attended a theater performance with their families.

Massive demonstrations forced the shah to leave Iran in 1979 and led to the return from exile of the Ayatollah Khomeini, a fiercely anti-American religious leader.

A pro-Western government is overthrown in Iran. United States relations with Iran were close when Carter came to office. In an unlikely way, however, they became so strained that they eventually undermined Carter's presidency. Iran had long been of interest to the West because of its strategic location between Russia and the oil fields of Saudi Arabia and because of its own important oil deposits. The Iranian monarch, Shah Mohammed Reza Pahlevi, who had come to the throne in 1941, was closely allied with the United States. His program of modernization, which included land reform and greater freedom for women, won praise from many quarters. In the 1970's, however, the shah faced increasing opposition from his subjects. Many Iranians who supported modernization criticized the shah's harsh repression of political dissent. Muslim extremists, on the other hand, opposed modernization, claiming that it violated sacred religious rules. This group, which grew rapidly during the late 1970's, advocated the installation of a government that would strictly enforce Islamic law.

Successive waves of angry protest forced the shah to leave Iran in January, 1979. Soon a religious leader, the Ayatollah Khomeini (AH-yah-tol-ah koh-MAY-nee), took over the government. His followers demanded that the shah, who had sought asylum in a number of countries, be returned to Iran for trial. They were outraged when President Carter allowed the former ruler to enter the United States in October, 1979, to undergo medical treatment at a New York hospital.

The American embassy is seized. On November 4, 1979, in an apparent attempt to force the United States to return the shah, an Iranian mob stormed the American embassy in Tehran, the Iranian capital, and took hostage Americans who worked there. Even though the United Nations Security Council and the International Court of Justice unanimously demanded the immediate release of the hostages, the Khomeini government, which had announced its support of the embassy take-over, remained unmoved.

In deciding what action to take, Carter placed the highest value on the safety of the hostages. For this reason, he said, he would order no military action against Iran. He instead pursued a variety of avenues in seeking the hostages' release, including

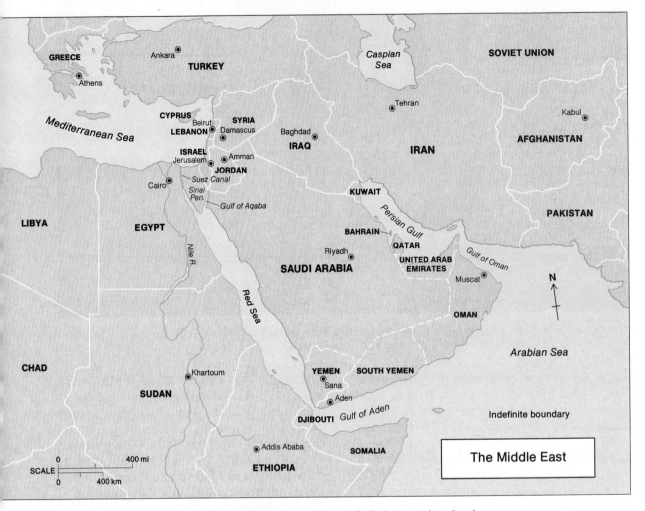

The Middle East has been a region of tension in recent years. Strife between Israel and its Arab neighbors continues, while events in Iran and Afghanistan have posed threats to world peace.

economic sanctions, diplomatic pressure, and secret negotiations.

As the months of frustration dragged on, Carter came under intense pressure to resolve the crisis. Five months after the embassy seizure, he ordered a secret military mission to rescue the hostages. Eight helicopters left an American aircraft carrier in the Gulf of Oman and headed for a desert area of Iran. From the desert, they were to proceed to Tehran. Mechanical difficulties in the desert, however, caused the operation to be canceled. As the American forces began their pull-out, a helicopter collided with a transport plane, killing eight servicemen and wounding five others.

The hostages are released. After the failure of the rescue mission, the United States renewed its efforts to gain the release of the hostages through negotiation. Again, months passed without significant progress. Even the death of the shah, who was then in exile in Egypt, brought no change in the Iranian position.

Finally, late in 1980, the Algerian government helped the two sides reach a settlement. The United States agreed not to interfere in Iranian affairs. The United States also promised to release most of the Iranian funds that President Carter had "frozen" in American banks in November, 1979, and agreed to drop financial claims

Homecoming for the Hostages

On January 20, 1981, the American hostages in Iran were released and began their journey back to the United States. Ed Magnuson, a writer for *Time*, described how people throughout the country reacted to the return of the hostages.

America's joy pealed from church belfries, rippled from flagstaffs, and wrapped itself in a million miles of yellow ribbon, tied around trees, car antennas, and even the 32-story Foshay Tower in Minneapolis. Barbara Deffley, wife of the Methodist minister in Holmer, Illinois, rang the church bell 444 times, once for each day of captivity. "At about 200 pulls, I thought I'd never make it," she gasped. "Then at about 300 pulls, I got my second wind and kept going all the way." Massachusetts House Speaker Thomas W. McGee, 56, was too impatient to wait for a ladder, so he shinnied ten feet up a pole to . . . hoist the U.S. flag over the statehouse in Boston. In Mountain Home, Idaho, some 200 townspeople staged an impromptu parade, driving their cars three abreast, headlights on and horns blaring. Patrolman Joseph McDermott coasted his cruiser to the side of a street in Rochester, New Hampshire, fighting back tears. Said he: "I am overjoyed. I feel proud again."

Joy at the restoration of pride to a nation that had been humbled for so long by [Iran] was but one of the many reactions of Americans to the release of the 52 U.S.

The American hostages are welcomed home.

hostages last week. There was a sense of relief too. And scorn for Iran. But above all the initial dominant mood was one of continuing celebration, from the moment the first plane carrying the former captives cleared Iranian airspace to the climactic touchdown on U.S. soil . . . at Stewart Airport, 50 miles north of New York City. There in privacy that not even the longest lens of press and TV cameras could penetrate, the returnees from Iran at long last were tearfully reunited with their families. . . .

against Iran. On January 21, 1981, just as Ronald Reagan was taking the oath of office, a plane containing the hostages left Tehran, bringing the Americans back to a hero's welcome.

The United States responds to the Russian invasion of Afghanistan. Late in 1979, while the American negotiations with Iran were still under way, the Soviet Union alarmed the world by sending troops southward into Afghanistan. The Soviet troops were or-

dered to support Afghanistan's Communist government, which was under attack from Muslim guerrillas. Within days, the Soviet forces had taken control of the capital city of Kabul and set about crushing resistance in the countryside.

President Carter, concerned that the Soviet Union might invade Iran as well, decided that immediate action was necessary. Declaring that "aggression unopposed becomes a contagious disease," the President announced sanctions against the Soviet

Union. A major arms-limitation treaty (SALT II) was withdrawn from consideration by the Senate; an embargo was placed on sales of grain to the Soviet Union; and the United States announced that it would boycott the 1980 Olympic Games, which were to be held in Moscow. In addition, the President asked Congress to enact a new draft-registration law which would enable the armed forces to mobilize quickly in the event of war. Congress complied.

Other nations were unwilling to join in economic sanctions against the Soviet Union, but international disapproval of the Soviet invasion was widespread. Both the United Nations Security Council and the General Assembly condemned the Soviet action and demanded the immediate withdrawal of the Red Army. Such protests, however, had no apparent effect. Instead of withdrawing, the Soviet Union built up its troop strength in Afghanistan. There, Soviet forces faced continuing resistance from anti-Communist guerrillas.

For Americans, the invasion of Afghanistan aroused fresh concern over Soviet aggression. In combination with the failure of the American rescue mission in Iran, it led many Americans to place renewed emphasis on the need for strong national defenses.

THE 1980 ELECTION

Carter is challenged by fellow Democrats. The crises in Iran and Afghanistan coincided with the 1980 presidential campaign. President Carter found himself under attack not only from the Republicans but from members of his own party as well.

On November 7, 1979 — just three days after the seizure of the American embassy in Tehran — Senator Edward Kennedy of Massachusetts, youngest brother of President Kennedy, announced his decision to challenge Carter for the Democratic presidential nomination. The governor of California, Jerry Brown, soon entered the race too. In their quest for support, Kennedy and Brown both argued that the United States faced difficult problems and that Carter had

been unable to exert the strong leadership the country required.

Carter did not actively campaign during the first four months of the year because, he maintained, the hostage crisis made it necessary for him to remain in Washington. His Democratic opponents scornfully condemned his behavior. They charged that he was using the episode in Iran as an excuse to avoid the political risks of campaigning and open debate.

As the incumbent, the President had an advantage over Kennedy and Brown. Many Democrats, furthermore, were convinced that neither Kennedy nor Brown could win the support of the majority of the American people. In addition, the crises in Iran and Afghanistan had caused many Americans to rally around the President, regarding his restraint during the early months of 1980 as worthy of support.

By the end of the primary season, Carter had won more than enough delegates to capture the party's nomination. At the Democratic National Convention in New York City, the Carter-Mondale team was again chosen to face the Republicans in the November election. The party platform, which had been heavily influenced by Kennedy and his supporters, called for an expanded federal jobs program, opposition to any anti-inflation measure that would tend to increase unemployment, détente with the Soviet Union, and extensive revamping of the nation's armed forces.

Ronald Reagan wins the Republican nomination. At the beginning of 1980, Ronald Reagan appeared to be the leading Republican contender for the presidential nomination. Reagan's main rival was George Bush, who had served as a congressman from Texas, ambassador to the United Nations, director of the Central Intelligence Agency, and diplomatic representative to China. Bush ran a strong campaign, but by the end of May, Reagan clearly had locked up enough delegates to gain the Republican nomination. At that point, Bush withdrew from the race, asking his delegates to support Reagan.

At the Republican convention, which was held in Detroit, the major question centered around the vice-presidential nomination. There was speculation that former President Gerald Ford might accept the spot. Many Republicans believed that Reagan and Ford would make an unbeatable combination — a "dream ticket." In the end, however, Ford decided not to seek the nomination. Reagan then announced that he had chosen George Bush as his running mate.

The Republican platform reflected Reagan's views. On economic matters, the platform called for a major tax cut, limits on federal spending, and a reduction in government regulation of American business. In foreign policy, it called for increased emphasis on national defense and a firm policy toward the Soviet Union.

John Anderson runs as an independent. Polls showed that a significant number of Americans were disappointed in the nominees of both major parties. It was to this group of voters that Representative John Anderson of Illinois attempted to appeal. Having lost his bid for the Republican nomination, Anderson ran as an independent candidate for President. Despite some interest in Anderson as a new man in the race, significant support for his candidacy failed to materialize.

Reagan wins by a landslide. The contest between Carter and Reagan was widely considered to be close. Polls were inconclusive — some giving a slight edge to Carter, some to Reagan. In the final weeks of the campaign, each candidate tried to concentrate on what he believed to be his opponent's major weakness. Reagan emphasized what he called the nation's "misery index" — the combination of high unemployment and double-digit inflation that had plagued the country under the Carter administration. Carter, on the other hand, pointed to his foreign-policy achievements — especially the Camp David agreements — saying that his administration had succeeded in reducing world tensions. He argued that the

Ronald Reagan stands before the delegates at the 1980 Republican convention, having just won his party's nomination for President.

hard-line foreign policy advocated by Reagan and the Republicans might lead the country into war.

Late in October, an audience of over 100 million people watched as the two candidates met in a televised debate. In the course of his exchanges with the President, Reagan displayed his personal warmth and did much to defuse the Democrats' charges that he was a dangerous extremist.

On Election Day, the American voters chose Reagan in a landslide — defying the predictions of a close race. The vote was the most sweeping repudiation of an incumbent President since Hoover's loss to Roosevelt in 1932 (page 235). Reagan won 51 percent of the popular vote compared to Carter's 41 percent. In the electoral college, Reagan's triumph was even more overwhelming: 489 votes to 49. Anderson, who captured less than 7 percent of the popular vote, received no electoral votes.

In winning so convincingly, Reagan carried many other Republican candidates into office. For the first time since 1952, the Republicans emerged with a majority in the Senate. They also gained 32 seats in the House, which remained under Democratic control but by a significantly narrower margin. In addition, Republicans won four new governorships.

SECTION REVIEW

1. (a) For what reason did Carter propose a new energy program? (b) What steps did he take?
2. Why did Carter find it difficult to work with Congress?
3. (a) How did Carter try to combat unemployment and inflation? (b) How effective were his efforts?
4. (a) What were the Camp David accords? (b) Why were they important?
5. (a) What problem developed as the result of the seizure of the American embassy in Tehran? (b) What steps did Carter take to secure the release of the American hostages? (c) On what terms were the hostages released?
6. (a) Why did the Soviet Union send troops to Afghanistan? (b) What was the reaction of the United States?
7. (a) Who were the candidates in the 1980 election? (b) What were their main campaign themes? (c) What was the election result?

2 New Patterns of Population Growth Affect Ways of Living

As it has done at the start of each decade since 1790, the United States government took an inventory of the nation's population in 1980. The statistics tabulated from the 1980 census showed that some 226 million people lived in the United States. The census also provided new insights into the nature of the American population.

Population growth slows down. One of the most notable findings of the Census Bureau was that the rate of population growth in the 1970's was the lowest it had been since the Great Depression. A major cause for this slowdown was the increase in the proportion of Americans aged 65 and older. The 1980 census found that there were 25 million Americans in this category. During the 1970's this group grew twice as fast as the rest of the population and in the future seemed likely to continue growing at a similar rate.

The "graying of America" can be attributed in part to the simple fact that more people in the United States are living longer. Medical advances have raised the average lifetime in the United States from 70.8 years in 1970 to 73.8 in 1980. This greater longevity produced a large constituency of elderly Americans whose concerns about health care, housing, and social security make them a powerful political force. In the 1980 presidential election, for example, one third of those who voted were 55 years old or older.

The population of America continues to shift. The results of the 1980 census also reconfirmed a trend that had begun after World War II. This trend had to do with where Americans preferred to live. Many people, seeking to escape the harsh winter weather and high heating bills of the North, moved to the *sunbelt,* a region stretching across the country from the southeastern Atlantic coast to southern California. Industries also relocated to the sunbelt, prompting people unable to find jobs in the Northeast and Upper Midwest to flock to this region in search of employment.

Statistics from the census showed a sharp contrast between population growth in the South and West as compared with the Northeast and Upper Midwest. Nearly 90 percent of the increase in population in the 1970's took place in the South and West, with many states in those regions growing at a rate of over 20 percent. The population of most states in the Northeast and Upper Midwest, on the other hand, grew by only about 2 percent. By 1980 more than half of all Americans lived in the South and West.

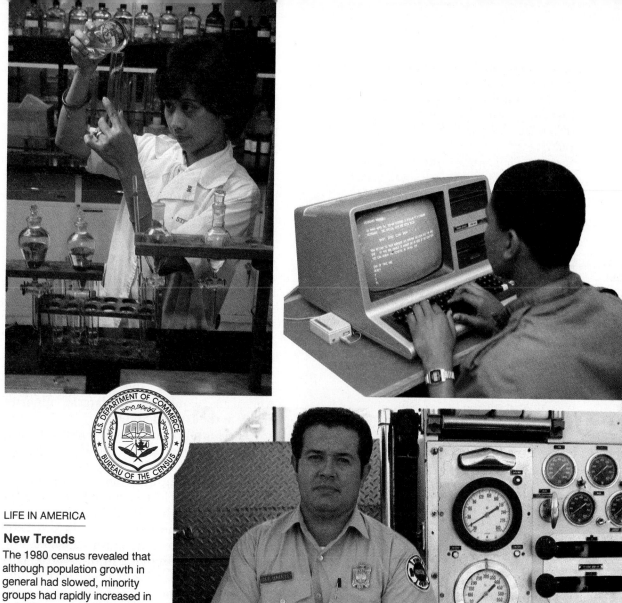

New Trends

The 1980 census revealed that although population growth in general had slowed, minority groups had rapidly increased in size. The census also reported on employment trends, finding that more and more Americans were employed in service occupations — such as computer operations and programming — and that large numbers of women were entering the work force.

The shifting of population had important political consequences because the census is used to determine the number of members a state sends to the House of Representatives. After the 1980 census, 17 congressional seats were lost by northern and midwestern states to states in the sunbelt.

The 98th Congress, which was elected in 1982, was the first in American history to have a majority of its members come from the South and West.

Urban centers lose population. Another trend revealed by the 1980 census was the

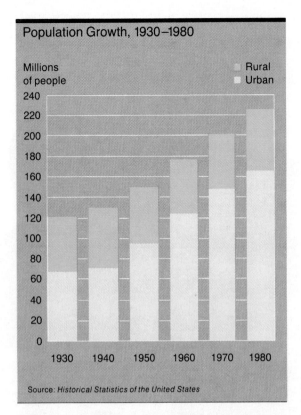

Population Growth, 1930–1980

Millions of people

■ Rural
□ Urban

240
220
200
180
160
140
120
100
80
60
40
20
0

1930 1940 1950 1960 1970 1980

Source: *Historical Statistics of the United States*

Population growth from 1930 to 1980 is shown in this graph. The 1980 census indicated that the United States population has passed the 225-million mark.

large-scale migration out of older urban areas. This was an historic shift because for well over a century most Americans had preferred to live in or near large metropolitan centers. In the 1970's, rural areas and small towns, which for years had been losing population, grew at a rate of approximately 15 percent.

The older cities of the Northeast and Upper Midwest suffered the greatest loss of population. Between 1970 and 1980, for instance, the New York metropolitan area lost over 850,000 inhabitants. During those same years, the population of the Cleveland metropolitan area declined by nearly 200,000. Of the 32 urban centers that suffered decreases in population during the 1970's, all but two were in the Northeast and Upper Midwest. The loss of population led to a reduction in tax revenues, severely hurting urban areas.

Minority groups gain in population. Due to improved methods of gathering population figures, the Census Bureau in 1980 was able to tabulate the growth of minorities in the United States more accurately than ever before. The results showed that the percentage of Hispanics, black Americans, Asian Americans, and American Indians was increasing dramatically.

The Hispanic population was the fastest-growing segment of American society. People of Spanish origin had increased nearly 60 percent since 1970 and by 1980 made up over 6 percent of the total population of the United States. Increases in immigration contributed to this rapid rise. At the time of the census, the great majority of Spanish-speaking people was concentrated in California, Texas, New York, and Florida. The Census Bureau predicted that before the end of the decade Hispanic Americans would be the largest minority group in the United States.

The number of black Americans increased by 17 percent in the 1970's and by 1980 constituted 11.7 percent of the national population, up from 11.1 percent in 1970. One notable fact brought to light by the census was that for the first time since the Civil War the number of black Americans moving to the South equalled the number of those moving to the North. This was another indication that northern industrial cities were no longer providing the employment opportunities that once had attracted millions of workers, both black and white.

The continent from which the largest number of immigrants arrived during the 1970's was Asia. Nearly two million Asian immigrants came to the United States. Many were fleeing the unrest that was convulsing the Southeast Asian countries of Vietnam, Laos, and Cambodia, while others were leaving the Philippines, Korea, and Taiwan. Three fourths of all Asian Americans made their homes in the following seven states: California, Hawaii, New York, Illinois, Texas, Washington, and New Jersey.

The size of households decreases. Another finding of the 1980 census was that the average size of households in the United States was becoming considerably smaller. Even though the number of households increased by nearly 30 percent between 1970 and 1980, the number of people living in households grew by only 12 percent. As a result, the average household fell in size from 3.11 people in 1970 to 2.75 in 1980. The sharp decline reflected changes in the way Americans lived — more divorces, fewer marriages, couples having only one child or none at all, and more elderly people living alone.

The nature of work changes. Over the decades, the types of jobs Americans have held have changed dramatically. At first an agricultural nation and then an industrial one, the United States by the late twentieth century was experiencing yet another transformation in the nature of the work its citizens do. This change was in the growth of service occupations. Instead of working in mills and factories, where they produced goods, more and more Americans were employed as teachers, salespeople, lawyers, writers, computer operators, government workers, restaurant and hotel personnel, repair workers, and so on. By 1980 more than half of all American jobholders were working in what is called the service sector, and the probable trend was for that number to continue to increase.

During the 1970's an increasing number of women in the United States were seeking employment outside the home. Compared with 1950, when only about 30 percent of women held jobs, the figure in 1980 had risen to nearly 50 percent.

As more and more women found work outside the home, the campaign for women's rights was renewed. Women demanded equal treatment in business, education, and in other professions. National groups were also formed to get more women elected to public office. Among these groups was the National Organization of Women (NOW), formed in 1966. By

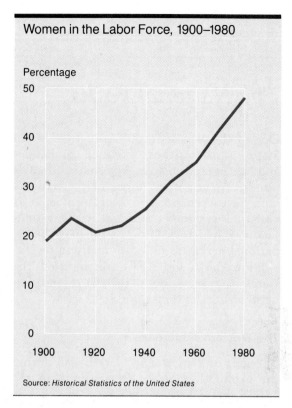

Women in the Labor Force, 1900–1980

Percentage

Source: *Historical Statistics of the United States*

In the 1960's and 1970's women entered the work force in large numbers and were employed in nearly every occupation. By 1980 almost 50 percent of American women held jobs outside the home.

1975, 4 percent of all the elected officials in the United States were women; just six years later that figure had risen to nearly 10 percent.

SECTION REVIEW

1. Vocabulary: *sunbelt.*
2. (a) What information did the 1980 census provide concerning the rate of population growth? (b) What information did it provide concerning the number of Americans aged 65 and over? (c) The shift of population distribution? (d) The population of urban centers?
3. (a) What was the fastest growing minority group in the United States during the 1970's? (b) From what continent did the largest number of immigrants come in that same decade?
4. (a) What changes took place in the nature of work in the United States? (b) In the number of women in the work force?

421

The National Parks

One of the richest resources of the United States is its heritage of varied landscapes and natural wonders. For more than a hundred years, many areas of the nation's land have been preserved and protected as part of a system of national parks, monuments, and historic sites. As the map shows, national parks are found in many states, including Alaska and Hawaii. In addition, the states have set aside historic sites and wilderness areas of their own.

The Western Wilderness

The idea of a "national" park began during the exploration of the West. Early in the 1800's, trappers and explorers in what is now Wyoming discovered a remarkable area of canyons, valleys, geysers, hot springs, and bubbling mud volcanoes. The local Indians had long regarded this spot as strange and mysterious. The reports that were brought to the East were almost too amazing to be believed, and a number of expeditions were sent to investigate.

Some of the explorers originated the idea that a place of such natural beauty and scientific importance should remain the property of all the people. In 1870 the federal government sent out an official survey party led by a well-known geologist, F. V. Hayden. A pioneer photographer, William H. Jackson, accompanied the group. At that time, photographs were made on huge glass plates, which Jackson had to carry across the rugged mountains on mule-back. To develop the glass-plate negatives, he washed them in the boiling water of a geyser. Jackson's photographs portrayed the landscape with such drama and beauty that many influential people and members of Congress were convinced of the wonders of this distant part of the nation.

Officially named Yellowstone, the area became the first national park in 1872. President Ulysses S. Grant signed the bill declaring Yellowstone under federal government protection as "a public park or pleasuring ground for the benefit and enjoyment of the people." Yellowstone eventually included more than two million acres, mostly in northwestern Wyoming.

Dedicated and enthusiastic explorers and naturalists also worked for the protection of other scenic areas in the West during the late 1800's. Yosemite Valley, in the Sierra Nevada of California, drew people's attention in the early 1860's for its granite rock formations, high waterfalls, and the variety of plant and animal life. To preserve the landscape of the valley and the towering sequoia trees, President Abraham Lincoln in 1864 approved granting the area to the state of California as a public park. The efforts of naturalist John Muir and other conservationists eventually brought Yosemite into the national park system.

The Growth of the National Parks

Under President Theodore Roosevelt, interest and support for public parks and wilderness areas grew (page 133). Other remote areas in the West were designated as public land in the early 1900's. These included the desert rock formations of Zion Canyon, the spectacular Grand Canyon, and the ancient Indian cliff dwellings at Mesa Verde in Colorado. Hawaii was not yet a state, but its active volcanoes were made part of a national park. To manage the parks, the National Park System was set up in 1916.

The idea of national parks had been inspired by the western wilderness. By the early 1920's, there was only one national park in the eastern part of the country — the rugged coastline and islands of Acadia National Park in Maine. Many more eastern parks were added in the 1920's and 1930's,

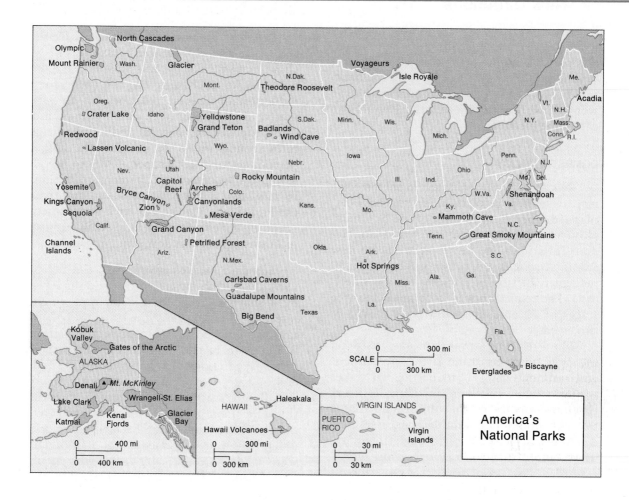

America's National Parks

however. They included such varied land-scapes as the Florida Everglades and the Great Smoky Mountains.

When the idea of national parks was new, the United States still had millions of acres of unclaimed, unexplored wilderness land. Although this is no longer true, new parks are still being added. One, the Guadalupe Mountains in western Texas, includes a range of mountains that rise steeply from the surrounding desert and salt flats. Geologists believe that the sheer cliffs in the park were once part of a huge underwater reef of limestone.

Many national parks, like the Guadalupe Mountains, preserve landforms in iso-lated areas. Many others, however, are near densely populated areas and draw huge crowds of visitors. These uses sometimes conflict with the ideal of preserving wilderness but still carry out the ideal of keeping the land available for all the people.

---

1. What was the idea behind the establishment of national parks?
2. (a) What was the first national park? (b) How was it established?
3. (a) Why were the earliest parks in the West? (b) When were more parks established in the eastern United States?

3 Ronald Reagan Proposes New Directions

President Reagan's first months in office were so full of activity that they were often compared with Franklin Roosevelt's "Hundred Days" (page 238). With the backing of Congress, the new administration went to work carrying out the Republican campaign pledges.

DOMESTIC POLICY

Reagan proposes legislation to aid the economy. The top priority was the economy, plagued when Reagan took office by unemployment, high interest rates, and double-digit inflation. The centerpiece of the new administration's program was a call for a 30 percent reduction in tax rates for all Americans. The reduction was to be made in three stages of 10 percent each, over a period of three years.

The President's program was based on the idea that, by stimulating investment and productivity, a reduction in taxes would actually result in an increase in tax revenues. Critics of the bill argued that a tax cut would not stimulate enough new economic activity to yield such revenues. They feared that the tax reduction would lead to a shortage of funds for government programs they regarded as indispensable. Many critics, opposed to what they called "Reaganomics," also charged that the tax cuts unfairly favored those in higher income brackets. Economists who supported the Reagan proposal responded by saying that tax cuts for wealthier people were essential to economic recovery. They claimed that from these reductions would come the capital for new investments which, in turn, would make new jobs.

Early in 1981 the nation's attention was diverted from the administration's economic proposals by an attempt on the President's life. On March 30, as he left a Washington hotel, Reagan was wounded by a would-be assassin's bullet. He was rushed to a nearby hospital to undergo emergency surgery. Reagan's courage won him widespread sympathy and admiration. Two weeks later, he was back in the White House on the road to complete recovery.

Congress approves the President's legislation. Late in July, Reagan's tax-cut bill — slightly modified — was passed by Congress. In its final form, the bill called for a reduction of federal revenues by an estimated $750 billion over a five-year period. The proposed 30 percent reduction in tax rates wound up as 25 percent, the first 5 percent coming in October, 1981, to be followed by successive 10 percent reductions in 1982 and 1983. Congress also approved the President's plan to cut back government spending by eliminating or reducing appropriations for certain domestic programs.

Economic troubles worsen. In the fall of 1981 the nation entered a recession marked by a sharp increase in the unemployment rate. By April, 1982, the unemployment rate had reached 9.4 percent — the highest it had been in the postwar era. The recession placed enormous demands on the federal budget. Government outlays for many so-called "entitlement programs," such as those for unemployment insurance and welfare benefits, could not be limited to any dollar amount. Payments to individuals were made automatically to all who qualified. Because of the hardships caused by the recession, large numbers of people were eligible for federal aid.

In addition to causing these unexpectedly high outlays, the recession contributed to a budgetary crisis by decreasing the government's tax receipts. Many American businesses were cutting back production, closing down plants, and even declaring bankruptcy. Individuals, too, had less income because of lay-offs and pay cuts. As their incomes decreased, they paid less in taxes. If it could not cut its spending, the government had only two choices: to increase taxes or go deeper into debt.

The administration proposes a new budget. In February, 1982, the Reagan administration presented its 1983 budget to Congress.

President and Mrs. Reagan appear at a Texas campaign rally for congressional supporters of the administration's economic program.

The budget called for new cuts in domestic spending, increased military spending, and no tax increases. It projected a deficit of $91.5 billion.

The proposed budget met with criticism from all sides. Many critics were concerned with the size of the deficit. To reduce the government's debt, some wanted further cuts in spending. Others wanted a tax increase. Republicans in Congress warned the President that his budget could not be passed in its original form, and they urged him to reconsider his demands.

Negotiations between administration officials and members of Congress finally produced a compromise package. This compromise, which Reagan accepted, called for further reductions in both defense and social-welfare spending and for a tax increase. President Reagan and Speaker of the House Thomas P. O'Neill joined in an unusual bipartisan effort to secure passage of the new tax bill. The bill, which approved a three-year round of tax increases totalling $98.3 billion, was passed by a narrow margin, and President Reagan signed it into law.

The inflation rate drops rapidly. The recession created many problems, but it also helped to solve one. Inflation, which had been running at well over 10 percent in 1980, had dropped by mid-1982 to an annual rate of about 5 percent. In the next years, it fell even lower. One effect was a desired leveling-off of the cost of living. Another restraining influence on the cost of living was the "tight-money" policy of the Federal Reserve Board. By controlling the amount of money available for private loans, the Federal Reserve forced interest rates to rise, which decreased demand for goods and services. The drop in demand resulted in lower prices.

Democrats make gains in the mid-term elections. Inflation continued to decline at a much faster pace than most observers had expected, and even interest rates began to fall. Unemployment, nevertheless, continued to be a serious problem and was a handicap for the Republicans in the 1982 elections. In October, 1982, the Labor Department announced that the unemploy-

Industrial Robots

Advances in electronic technology have made robots available for use in industry. These self-operating mechanical units, directed by microcomputer "brains," perform a wide range of manufacturing operations. Depending on how they are programmed, or instructed, industrial robots can use their claw-like "hands" to weld, drill, rivet, paint, assemble, inspect, and load.

The development of robots for industry holds out the promise of increased efficiency and greater productivity. At the same time, jobs will be created for highly skilled workers to build, program, and service these devices. To insure that the United States remains competitive in the world economy, robots have already been introduced in the automobile industry, where they have demonstrated their many capabilities and have proved their value in reducing operating costs.

ment rate had climbed to 10.1 percent. Democrats blamed the administration's economic policies for the recession. The President and his allies, on the other hand, asked the public to "stay the course," arguing that the new policies had not had time to prove their worth. In November, the Republicans lost 26 seats in the House of Representatives — about the average loss the party in power suffers in a mid-term election. They maintained control of the Senate.

Economic recovery begins. In November, 1982, the recession reached what proved to be its bottom, and an economic recovery began. Production indexes rose, and inflation remained under control. The unemployment rate held steady and within a few months began to drop. With the recovery under way, the President remarked of his critics, "They don't call it 'Reaganomics' any more."

Meanwhile, Reagan proposed other solutions to long-standing domestic concerns. The President's major new domestic pro-

gram became known as the "New Federalism." This plan called for a reduction in the size, power, and cost of running the federal government by gradually turning over responsibility for many of its social programs to state and local governments. In return, the federal government would assume full responsibility for Medicaid, a health-care program for needy Americans.

The President argued that his plan would make government more responsive to the needs of citizens by allowing programs to be tailored to the needs of each locality. State and local governments, on the other hand, were wary of accepting responsibility for funding more programs, especially in the midst of a recession. As a result, the New Federalism program did not win significant support.

The space shuttle is a success. A major domestic achievement in space exploration brightened the early days of the Reagan administration. In April, 1981, the spaceship *Columbia* completed 36 orbits of the earth

Having completed a successful mission, the space shuttle *Columbia* is placed aboard a jumbo jet for the flight back to the Kennedy Space Center in Florida.

and made a perfect landing at Edwards Air Force Base in California. The remarkable *Columbia* was the world's first reusable spacecraft. Whereas every previous space flight had required the enormous expense of building a new craft and new launching equipment, the *Columbia* and other shuttles, as these spaceships were called, could be used over and over. The comparatively frequent flights would make it possible for private industry to lease room on the spacecraft to conduct experiments, which, it was predicted, would lead to advances in industrial technology. Regular flights of the shuttle spacecraft soon began to fulfill the expectations of the planners that shuttle flights would play a part in America's future.

The Equal Rights Amendment fails to be ratified. For a number of years the Equal Rights

Sandra Day O'Connor, shown with Chief Justice Warren Burger, was named by President Reagan to serve on the Supreme Court.

Amendment (page 395) had been the focus of national attention. Supporters argued that the amendment was necessary to halt what they said was flagrant discrimination against women in areas such as taxation, insurance, marriage law, and Social Security. Opponents of ERA, who included President Reagan in their ranks, countered that the amendment was unnecessary because the Constitution and existing federal laws already guaranteed equal rights. The ERA, opponents maintained, would abolish many benefits enjoyed by women, such as alimony and child-support laws.

In June, 1982, time ran out for ERA. Only 35 of the required 38 state legislatures had ratified the amendment — and five of those states had later voted to reverse their decision. Pro-ERA forces immediately reintroduced the amendment in Congress, but in 1983 it failed to pass in the House.

Women's rights leaders, though angered by the President's opposition to the ERA, had applauded his appointment in 1981 of Sandra Day O'Connor to the Supreme Court. Following her unanimous confirmation by the Senate, Mrs. O'Connor, a former Arizona state senator and judge, became the first woman member of the Supreme Court.

FOREIGN AFFAIRS

The United States strengthens its armed forces. During the 1980 campaign, Reagan had argued that because of the Soviet Union's threat to world peace, American foreign policy needed to be based on a strong national defense. Under his administration, the nation expanded the arms build-up that had been started in the last year of Carter's presidency. Reagan's concern about defense was demonstrated in his budget proposals. While recommending cuts in spending in nearly all other sectors of government, Reagan asked for large increases in expenditures for the defense budget.

Reagan responds to a crisis in Poland. In addition to an arms build-up, the President relied on diplomatic and economic pressure to influence the actions of the Soviet government. In Soviet-dominated Poland, a

World tensions mounted in 1981 when Polish officials declared a state of martial law and suspended the operations of the independent trade union Solidarity.

crisis arose late in 1981. Polish workers had, the year before, formed a labor union called Solidarity, and had begun to demand a voice in government policy-making. They had wide support from the Polish people, who resented the Soviet Union's strangle hold on their country.

In December, 1981, Solidarity leaders called for a national referendum on whether Poland should continue its alliance with the Soviet Union and whether Poland itself should maintain a Communist form of government. In response, the Polish government declared martial law. The Soviet Union, claiming that its own security was being threatened by the Polish crisis, began to build up troop strength along the Polish border.

Western leaders feared that the Red Army would invade Poland to put an end to demands for reform. Through diplomatic channels and in public, the Reagan administration warned the Soviet Union not to interfere in Poland. Blaming the Soviet Union for the repression of Solidarity, Reagan also announced a number of sanctions. He placed an embargo on the sale of electronic equipment to the Soviet Union; postponed

discussions on the lifting of the Carter grain embargo (page 416); suspended American landing rights for Aeroflot, the Soviet airline; and halted the sale of American equipment that was to have been used in constructing a natural-gas pipeline between the Soviet Union and Western Europe.

The Soviet Union did not invade Poland, but the Communist government of Poland did not relax its political repression either. Even the minimal civil liberties granted to citizens under the Polish constitution were suspended. Private meetings were banned, identity papers had to be carried at all times, and a curfew was strictly enforced. Many Poles, furthermore, were jailed for their support of Solidarity. Among these was the immensely popular leader of the movement, Lech Walesa, who was imprisoned for eleven months. For his efforts on behalf of the Polish people, Walesa was awarded the Nobel Peace Prize in 1983.

Many of America's European allies, meanwhile, objected to President Reagan's efforts to halt construction of the gas pipeline. They complained that they had not been consulted on the equipment embargo and that contracts for construction of the pipeline, which had been signed long before the Polish crisis, could not legally be broken. As a result of the protests, the Reagan administration afterwards decided to lift the embargo.

The arms race stirs controversy. During the Carter presidency, the Soviet Union had installed hundreds of long-range missiles in Eastern Europe, aimed at targets in Western Europe. In response, the United States and its NATO allies moved ahead with the production of new weapons designed to counter the Soviet missiles.

As the new missiles went into production, public concern that the arms race might lead to nuclear war was heightened. In Western Europe and the United States, a movement arose that demanded a "freeze" in the existing levels of nuclear weapons possessed by both the United States and the Soviet Union. Advocates of a nuclear freeze saw it as a first step in bringing the arms race under control, to be followed by negotiations leading to further reductions in armaments. Reagan administration officials favored arms-reduction talks but opposed an immediate freeze. Two sets of arms-limitations talks proceeded simultaneously in Geneva, Switzerland — the strategic arms reduction talks (START), which involved intercontinental missiles, and the intermediate-range nuclear forces talks (INF), which focused on the missiles being placed in Europe. As these negotiations went on, so did planning for deployment of the new NATO missiles. When the first of those missiles were put in place late in 1983, the Soviet Union halted the arms-control talks.

The Soviet air force shoots down a Korean plane. Tension between the United States and the Soviet Union was heightened in September, 1983, when a South Korean commercial airliner was shot down over Soviet territory. In the incident, 269 people were killed — 61 of them American. World reaction was highly critical, especially because Soviet leaders refused at first even to admit that their pilots had shot down the

plane and later because of their claims that they had been within their rights to do so. Investigations eventually revealed that the Soviet pilot had erred in destroying the jetliner, apparently having mistaken it for an American reconnaissance plane. Nevertheless, the Soviet Union did not take responsibility for the tragedy.

The United States seeks peace in the Middle East. The Middle East offered the Reagan administration perhaps its greatest challenge in foreign policy. The framework of the administration's efforts to achieve a lasting peace in the region was the Camp David accords (page 411). The durability of these agreements was called into question in October, 1981, when President Sadat of Egypt was assassinated by extremists.

Relations between the United States and Israel, meanwhile, were strained in December, 1981, when Israel annexed the Golan Heights, strategically located on its border with Syria. Israel defended its action as necessary to its security. The United States, on the other hand, charged that the annexation was a direct violation of the Camp David agreements.

Israel invades Lebanon. In 1982 the focus of trouble in the Middle East shifted to Lebanon. The Palestine Liberation Organization (PLO), a terrorist group pledged to the destruction of Israel, had long used southern Lebanon as a base for attacks on Israel. Israel appealed to the Lebanese government to put a stop to these assaults, but the government, plagued by years of civil strife, was unable to control the PLO guerrillas.

Determined to rid themselves of the constant harassment and loss of life, Israeli forces invaded Lebanon early in June, 1982. The Israelis quickly moved northward, and within a week they had pushed the PLO back to Lebanon's capital city of Beirut (bay-ROOT). There the guerrillas mingled with the civilian population, while continuing to fire on the Israeli troops that surrounded the city.

More than any previous incident, the invasion of Lebanon strained Israeli-American relations. The United States attempted to persuade Israel to withdraw from Lebanon, but the Israelis, clearly victorious, refused to withdraw before certain security conditions were met. The most important of these were the withdrawal of the PLO and of Syrian forces that had occupied parts of Lebanon since 1976; the introduction of a strong, multinational peacekeeping force; and the creation of a government sympathetic to Israel's concerns. Through the tireless efforts of United States diplomats, Israel's conditions were largely met, and in August, 1982, units of troops from the United States, France, and Italy arrived in Beirut to supervise the evacuation of the PLO guerrillas.

Reagan proposes a new Middle East peace plan. Responding to these events and sensing an opportunity, President Reagan in a major speech on September 1, 1982, made public a new plan for ending the strife in the Middle East. Linking his proposals directly to the recently halted war in Lebanon, he called for the cooperation of all parties to make a fresh start toward the achievement of a lasting peace not only in Lebanon but throughout the region. First, he called on the international community to help in the rebuilding of Lebanon, which had been devastated by years of warfare. Second, he called on Israel to reverse its policy of building new settlements in the occupied territories of the West Bank and the Gaza Strip, which had been won in the 1967 war. In return, he called upon Arab and Palestinian leaders to recognize Israel's right to exist and to begin peace negotiations. Finally, as a solution to the problem of the Palestinians' demands for a homeland, he proposed a five-year transition period after which the Palestinians on the West Bank and in the Gaza Strip would be granted self-government under the supervision of Jordan.

Tanks and armored personnel carriers spearheaded the Israeli drive into Lebanon in 1982, as Israel sought to destroy Palestine Liberation Organization strongholds.

Reaction to the President's plan was mixed. Before it was thoroughly debated, however, events in Lebanon again chilled hopes for peace in the Middle East. Just two weeks after Reagan's speech, the president-elect of Lebanon was assassinated. Shortly thereafter, there was more shocking news, this time of mass killings in two Palestinian refugee camps in Beirut. As a result of these incidents, the Lebanese government asked for the return of the peacekeeping force (which had left the city following the evacuation of the PLO).

During the next months, sporadic fighting continued among the Israelis, the Syrians, and the many Lebanese factions that had developed during years of civil war. Meanwhile, agreement was finally reached on the withdrawal of Israeli troops from their positions around Beirut to fortified positions in southern Lebanon. As the time for their departure approached, however, fighting among various Lebanese groups intensified. Each group sought to gain control of the areas the Israelis were about to abandon. Twice, the Israelis agreed to postpone their pullback in order to give the Lebanese army more time to arrange a cease-fire with rebel groups, but these efforts failed. When the Israelis finally departed, Lebanon seemed to be on the brink of full-scale civil war.

The search for peace in the Middle East continues. The peacekeeping force stationed in Beirut faced a dangerous assignment. They constantly found themselves under sniper fire. Then, on October 23, 1983, a terrorist drove a truck filled with explosives into barracks that were used for housing American marines. The massive explosion left 241 dead and more than 80 wounded. A similar attack on French barracks resulted in 56 dead and 15 wounded.

The American people were outraged by the bombings. Meanwhile, in the next few months the situation in Lebanon deteriorated into a chaotic, bloody struggle between Muslim militiamen and the shaky Lebanese army. Early in 1984 the multinational peacekeeping force withdrew from Beirut.

The departure of the peacekeeping force did not put an end to the United States troubles in Lebanon, however. On September 20, 1984, terrorists struck again, this time bombing an American embassy building in Beirut. Twelve people were killed and 35 wounded. United States officials found the incident deeply disturbing. Not only did it show that American embassies were still vulnerable to terrorist attacks; it also indicated the continuing difficulty in bringing peace to the Middle East.

War in the Falklands strains relations with Latin America. Reagan was confronted with problems not only in Europe, Asia, and the Middle East but in the Western Hemisphere as well. Early in his administration the United States was caught in the middle of a dispute between two of its allies — Argentina and Great Britain. In April, 1982, Argentina seized the Falkland Islands, a British possession lying 300 miles off the Argentine coast. Outraged, the British government sent naval forces to retake the islands.

The United States wanted to avoid angering either party in the dispute, but neutrality proved to be impossible. Because Argentina had been the aggressor in the incident, Secretary of State Alexander Haig announced that the United States was backing Britain. Along with a number of European countries, the United States imposed economic sanctions on Argentina. This action angered many Latin Americans who, while disapproving of Argentina's resort to force, believed its claim to the islands to be legitimate.

By mid-June, British forces had defeated the Argentinians and retaken the Falklands. Relations between the United States and Latin America, however, had been severely strained.

Unrest in Central America causes concern. The ire felt by many Latin Americans was soon fed by events in Central America. Communist-backed revolutionaries had come to power in Nicaragua in 1979. Nicaraguan officials, assuming a harsh anti-American position, seemed to be moving relentlessly toward the establishment of a one-party Marxist state. They were also, the Reagan administration had concluded, mounting a major Soviet-backed arms build-up and supplying arms and ammunition to guerrillas who were trying to overthrow the government of neighboring El Salvador.

In light of this situation, administration officials sought to remove the immediate threat to El Salvador by sending military aid and by trying to halt the flow of arms to the rebels. They also attempted to address the underlying causes of popular discontent in Central America by pressing for economic and political reforms in countries receiving American assistance.

The flow of American arms to El Salvador gave rise to controversy in the United States. Opponents of the administration's policy argued that the role of outsiders in the civil war there was being exaggerated and that the causes of the war were internal. In addition, they criticized the Salvadorian government for serious human-rights violations, including political killings.

To answer the criticism, the President appointed a commission, headed by former Secretary of State Henry Kissinger, to analyze United States policy in Central America. In its report, issued early in 1984, the National Bipartisan Commission on Central America strongly endorsed administration policies. It asserted that the Soviet-Cuban backing of Nicaragua posed a threat to the security of the region, and it insisted on changes toward democracy in Nicaragua. It also proposed that the United States provide Central America with $8 billion in economic aid from 1985 to 1989.

Reagan sends American troops to Grenada. The Caribbean island of Grenada was the setting for another crisis for the United States. American and various Latin American and Caribbean officials had been watching for months the involvement of Cuba

Within a few weeks of restoring order in Grenada, American combat troops were withdrawn from the island.

and other Soviet allies in Grenadian life. The Marxist government of Grenada was constructing an international airport with Cuban money and hundreds of Cuban workers. American observers believed that the airport was to be used as a staging point for Cuban and Soviet military aircraft.

On October 20, 1983, the Grenadian prime minister was assassinated. His slayers, acting for a hard-line Marxist faction in the government, immediately took full control of the island.

Three days later, leaders of several Caribbean nations asked President Reagan for American assistance in restoring order and democracy to Grenada. The President, who shared their concern about the situation on the island, also wanted to ensure the safety of Americans living in Grenada. On October 25, military forces from the United States and six Caribbean nations landed on Grenada. They quickly secured their military objectives and safely evacuated all the Americans who wanted to leave. In the course of the fighting, they discovered supplies of Soviet-made weapons and a number of Communist-bloc "advisers." The weapons were confiscated and the foreign nationals were allowed to return home.

Geraldine Ferraro was the first woman to win the nomination of a major party for Vice President.

In the United States, reaction to this incident was overwhelmingly on the President's side. Within a few days, all reports indicated clearly that the Grenadians had welcomed the international force that had rid them of an unwanted dictator. Moreover, the enthusiastic gratitude of the rescued American nationals was enough to persuade the majority of Americans that Reagan had made the right decision.

THE ELECTION OF 1984

The 1984 presidential campaign gets under way. Confident that the American people were feeling more prosperous and optimistic than four years earlier, President Reagan announced that he would seek re-election in 1984. Again he chose George Bush to be his Vice President. As their candidate, the Democrats nominated former Vice President Walter Mondale, who won out at the party's convention in San Francisco over a field that included Senator Gary Hart of Colorado and Jesse Jackson. Jackson had mounted the first significant run for the White House by a black candidate.

Mondale selected Congresswoman Geraldine A. Ferraro of New York as his vice-presidential running mate. The choice of a woman to share for the first time the leadership of a major-party ticket stirred the nation. Observers suggested that the Democrats hoped to influence women voters, who in 1980 had cast six million more votes than men. Mondale replied simply, "I looked for the best Vice President and I found her in Gerry Ferraro."

During the campaign the Democratic standard-bearer denounced the President for failing to sit down with Soviet leaders to discuss nuclear-arms control—a charge that lost force when Reagan met with the Soviet foreign minister shortly before the election. Mondale also declared that, if elected, he would raise taxes in order to reduce the enormous federal budget deficit of $175 billion—the largest in the nation's history. Reagan derided Mondale's proposal. "Why raise our taxes when we can raise our sights?" he said, pointing to the booming economy and the reduction in inflation.

Ronald and Nancy Reagan acknowledge the cheers of supporters on election night, 1984, after receiving news of his landslide re-election.

Reagan wins re-election. Two televised debates between the candidates resulted in much discussion of the President's age (Reagan was 73 years old), and whether he had full command of the details of government. The voters gave a resounding judgment. On Election Day, 1984, Reagan swept 49 states, giving him 525 electoral votes, the highest total in history. He had captured 59 percent of the popular vote. Mondale, with 41 percent of the vote, carried only his home state of Minnesota and the District of Columbia. The Republicans retained control of the Senate, although the Democrats still held a majority in the House of Representatives. Ronald Reagan's overwhelming personal triumph marked the first time a presidential candidate had won two landslide victories in a row since Dwight D. Eisenhower.

_____

In setting a course for tomorrow, nations gaze backward as well as forward. They search in their history for guidelines, if not for directions. Americans have the satisfaction of finding in their past, for instruction and inspiration, an incomparable story of high achievement and steady devotion to the ideal of freedom for all. Each succeeding generation of the Glorious Republic takes on the obligation to write a bright new chapter in this grandest of unfinished epics. Every patriotic voice — young and old alike — echoes the poet's proud salute penned long ago:

> . . . Sail on, O Ship of State!
> Sail on, O Union, strong and great!
> Humanity with all its fears,
> With all the hopes of future years,
> Is hanging breathless on thy fate!

SECTION REVIEW

1. (a) What economic problems did the nation face when Ronald Reagan took office? (b) How did Reagan attempt to solve those problems? (c) What were the results?
2. (a) What happened to the Equal Rights Amendment? (b) What historic appointment did President Reagan make?
3. (a) How did Reagan respond to the crackdown on Solidarity in Poland? (b) What caused the nuclear-freeze movement to gain strength?
4. (a) What events in the Middle East upset the progress toward peace that had earlier been made at Camp David? (b) Why did Israel invade Lebanon? (c) What role has the United States played in the Middle East in recent years?
5. (a) Why did the Reagan administration send aid to El Salvador? (b) Why were American troops sent to Grenada?
6. (a) Who were the candidates for President in 1984? (b) What was the outcome of the election?

Chapter 16 Review

Summary

When Jimmy Carter took the oath of office as President in 1977, he faced many challenges. To try to heal the disunity caused by the Vietnam War, he granted an amnesty to all Vietnam-era draft resisters. In an attempt to ensure that there would be no repeat of the 1973 energy crisis, Carter introduced a comprehensive energy program designed to develop American independence from foreign energy sources. Alarming rates of unemployment and inflation also confronted the Carter administration, and efforts were made to stabilize wages and prices as well as reduce the jobless rate.

Carter's greatest achievement was to bring Israel's Menachem Begin and Egypt's Anwar Sadat together at Camp David to mediate agreements that were seen as a first step toward peace in the Middle East. His most difficult challenge came after Iranians seized the American embassy in Tehran and made hostages of the embassy staff. Unable to negotiate a release of the hostages, Carter authorized a military rescue mission that ended in failure. The hostages were finally released early in 1981, on the last day of Carter's presidency.

In the presidential campaign of 1980, Carter again won the Democratic nomination, while Ronald Reagan became the Republican candidate. The election resulted in an overwhelming victory for Reagan, and the Republican Party gained control of the Senate for the first time since 1952.

The 1980 census provided the American people with an opportunity to examine a number of trends that had been developing in their country. The population growth rate was slowing considerably, while the average age of the nation's citizens was steadily increasing. Minority population in the United States grew rapidly during the 1970's, while many people continued to leave the Northeast and the Upper Midwest for the sunbelt.

The most pressing issue facing Ronald Reagan when he came to office in 1981 was the state of the economy. High unemployment and inflation were crippling the nation. Reagan proposed legislation designed to stimulate the economy through a series of tax cuts. By the end of 1982 the economy had begun to recover, and the rate of inflation had notably declined.

Reagan's main position in foreign affairs was to take a firm stand against the Soviet Union by building up America's military power. Tension between the two superpowers heated up following unrest in Poland, the installation of new Soviet missiles in Eastern Europe, and the shooting down of a Korean airliner that strayed over Soviet territory. Reagan showed his readiness to display strength by sending advisers and arms to Central America, stationing a contingent of marines in Lebanon, and sending troops to the Caribbean island of Grenada.

Vocabulary and Important Terms

1. Department of Energy
2. Council on Wage and Price Stability
3. "crisis-of-confidence" speech
4. human rights
5. Camp David accords
6. sunbelt
7. New Federalism
8. *Columbia*
9. Solidarity

Discussion Questions

1. (a) To what extent were inflation and unemployment problems during the Carter administration? (b) During the Reagan administration? (c) How did Carter and Reagan differ in their proposals to aid the economy, and what successes, if any, did each have?

2. (a) What role did Carter play in helping Israel and Egypt reach a peaceful agreement? (b) What events after the Camp David accords strained relations between the United States and Israel? (c) How did Reagan propose to bring peace to the Middle East? (d) What happened to Reagan's peace plan, and why?

3. (a) On what grounds was Carter challenged for the Democratic presidential nomination in 1980? (b) Why were the challenges of his Democratic opponents unsuccessful? (c) What factors contributed to Carter's defeat in the election?

4. (a) What events caused a deterioration in American-Soviet relations during Carter's presidency? (b) During Reagan's years in office? (c) How did this deterioration in relations affect the arms race?

5. (a) What areas of the country have experienced the fastest rate of growth in recent years? (b) How has the percentage of elderly Americans changed? (c) What factor helps explain that change?

6. (a) Why did the Falklands War strain relations between Latin America and the United States? (b) What was the Reagan administration's policy regarding El Salvador? (c) Why did that policy give rise to controversy? (d) Why did Reagan send American troops to Grenada? (e) What was the reaction of the American people?

Relating Past and Present

1. Unrest in Central America in the early 1980's caused concern among Reagan administration officials. Does unrest in Central America continue to be a problem for the United States? What is the current policy regarding Central America?

2. What economic problems does the United States face today? To what extent are inflation, unemployment, and deficit spending cause for concern, and what is the current economic policy?

Studying Local History

Find out what shifts in population occurred in your region during the 1970's. Account for any local population gains or losses. Explain how shifts in population affected your region.

Using History Skills

1. *Using reference books.* Find the population figures for the 1980 census in library reference books. (a) Which regions of the United States showed the greatest gains in population between 1970 and 1980? (b) Which regions showed the smallest gains? (c) What were the ten largest states by 1980, and by what percentages did their population change between 1970 and 1980? (d) Which states actually lost population during that same decade, and by what percentages?

2. *Reading graphs.* Study the graph on page 421 showing the percentage of women in the labor force. (a) Approximately what percentage of women worked outside the home in 1900? (b) In 1940? (c) In 1980? (d) What factors help explain the growing percentage of working women?

WORLD SCENE

The Quest for Human Rights

The right of individuals to express their opinions is a fundamental freedom for which people throughout history have fought. In many nations today, the struggle to gain this freedom continues.

Soviet dissidents. The Communist government of the Soviet Union demands absolute obedience and loyalty from its citizens. Dissidents who defy the government by speaking out against injustice are considered by Soviet officials to be traitors who threaten the security of the state.

Opposition to Communist rule comes from various sectors of Soviet society. Many dissidents are intellectuals who oppose control of what they may write and teach; others represent religious and ethnic minorities who resist government efforts to deny them freedom to worship and live as they desire; still others are individuals who object to the Soviet Union's participation in the nuclear arms build-up.

All opposition to official policy is regarded by Soviet authorities as criminal activity. The notorious KGB, the Soviet secret police, harasses dissidents and their families. Many Soviet dissidents have been sentenced to years in forced-labor camps. Some dissidents have been confined to mental hospitals and treated as if they were ill. A number of dissidents have been forced into exile.

Novelist Alexander Solzhenitsyn (sohl-zhuh-NEET-sihn) was one well-known Soviet dissident. After being forced to spend years in labor camps and mental hospitals, Solzhenitsyn wrote about his experiences in books that were eventually published in Europe and the United States. Solzhenitsyn's novels and insistent calls for greater freedom in the Soviet Union led to even more trouble with Communist authorities. Shortly after receiving the Nobel Prize for literature in 1970, Solzhenitsyn and his family were forced to leave the Soviet Union. They finally settled in the United States, where he continued to write about the denial of freedom in Communist Russia.

Another prominent dissident was Andrei Sakharov. A highly honored scientist who had helped develop the Soviet Union's hydrogen bomb, Sakharov publicly challenged his government's human-rights violations. He also organized a movement in the Soviet Union to protest the deployment of nuclear missiles. For his courageous efforts, Sakharov was awarded the Nobel Peace Prize in 1975.

Sakharov was arrested in 1980 on the charge that he was a threat to the security of the state. His Soviet honors were revoked, and he was exiled to the remote city of Gorky. His banishment caused governments and civil-liberties groups around the world to protest this outrage.

UNIT 5 REVIEW

Important Dates

1969 Americans land on moon.
1970 Environmental Protection Agency created.
1972 Nixon visits China and Soviet Union.
Watergate break-in.
1973 Last American troops leave Vietnam.
Yom Kippur War.
Ervin Committee investigates
Watergate affair.
1974 Nixon resigns presidency.
Ford pardons Nixon.
1976 Carter elected President.
1978 Camp David accords signed.
1979 American embassy in Iran seized.
Soviet Union invades Afghanistan.
1980 United States boycotts Olympic Games.
Reagan elected President.
1981 American hostages released by Iran.
American space shuttle completes first
successful flight.
First woman named to Supreme Court.
1983 American forces sent to Grenada.
1984 First woman nominated to run for
vice presidency.

Review Questions

1. (a) Upon taking office, every President faces important challenges. What, in your opinion, were the most important challenges facing President Nixon, Ford, Carter, and Reagan? (b) How successful was each at achieving his goal? Explain your answer.
2. (a) What have been the major economic concerns of recent years? (b) What proposals have various administrations made to solve those economic problems?
3. (a) What events led to President Nixon's resignation? (b) Why did Gerald Ford pardon Nixon? (c) Why did some Americans criticize that action?
4. (a) What factors contributed to the defeat at the polls of Presidents Ford and Carter? (b) In what ways were the reasons for each incumbent's defeat similar? (c) How were they different?
5. (a) What were America's notable achievements in space during the 1970's and 1980's? (b) Why were these achievements important?
6. (a) What was the state of relations between the United States and Soviet Union during the Nixon administration? (b) What actions by the United States brought about this relationship?
7. (a) What events affected American-Soviet relations during the Carter and Reagan administrations?

(b) What effect did these events have on American defense spending and on the arms race? (c) During the same span of years, what changes took place in United States relations with China?
8. (a) How did the Yom Kippur War of 1973 threaten world peace? (b) What approach did the Camp David accords of 1978 take in laying the foundation for peace in the Middle East? (c) What factors contributed to a renewal of tension in that region?

Projects

1. Play the part of a newspaper editor whose job it was to write headlines regarding the end of American involvement in Vietnam. Your first headline should announce Nixon's Vietnamization policy. Your subsequent headlines should focus on American diplomatic and military efforts to end the war. Your final headline should indicate what happened to Vietnam once American troops were withdrawn.
2. Make a model of one of the spacecraft that projected the United States into the forefront of the space race. You might make a model of an Apollo command module, an Apollo lunar module, the space shuttle, or some other American contribution to space exploration. Include a brief description of how the innovation represented by your model helped advance space exploration.
3. Form a committee to find out more about the impact of pollution on the nation's environment. Each member of the committee might choose one type of pollution (air, water, or land pollution) and use the library and other resources to find information about it. Report your findings to the class.
4. Participate in a classroom panel discussion of the current situation in the Middle East. The panel should identify the countries that are located in the Middle East, the ways in which these countries interact with one another, and the extent of American and Soviet involvement in that area of the world. Panel members might also discuss possible solutions to the issues that divide the countries of the Middle East.
5. Write an essay relating United States concern over Central America during the 1980's to the concern expressed in 1823 when the Monroe Doctrine was proclaimed. First, review the circumstances under which the Monroe Doctrine was issued and the steps by which it became the cornerstone of American foreign policy. Then, write a paragraph or two in which you discuss whether or not United States concern about Central America today is an application of the Monroe Doctrine.

Readings

The readings that follow are all primary sources. The most common kind of primary source is a document that was written at the same time as the events it describes. Primary sources include letters, diaries, newspaper articles, public records, or official documents that have survived from the past. It is by using the information found in primary sources that historians are able to view the past and then write their interpretation of what happened.

In some instances, primary sources may be difficult to understand because of unfamiliar words or the absence of needed information. To improve comprehension, some of the readings in this volume have been adapted. In adapted material two special kinds of punctuation are used. Brackets ([ ]) are inserted to indicate where a word or phrase has been changed or when an explanation has been added. Ellipses (. . .) appear when a word or phrase has been omitted to improve the clarity of a reading or to condense it.

The Last Great West
1860–1900

CHAPTER

1

In 1860, the Pony Express carried the news of Lincoln's election from St. Louis to Sacramento in ten days. The vast stretch of land over which the riders spurred their horses was still the West of the frontier scout and the Plains Indians.

By 1890, this western frontier had vanished. Miners, ranchers, farmers, and merchants flooded into the territories west of the Mississippi River. One observer, William M. Thayer, wrote a book in 1888 entitled *Marvels of the West* in which he described the transformation of the West:

> The wildest dream has become reality. . . . Nothing is too large for belief. Twenty- and even thirty-thousand-acre farms, and a hundred bushels to the acre is not an extravagant story now. . . .
>
> The New West . . . is a veritable "Wonderland," as crowded with OPPORTUNITIES as it is with marvels. . . . The changes wrought . . . have been about as startling as transformations under the wand of a magician. . . .

Not all those who came to the West to seek opportunity shared in the prosperity. The Plains presented a difficult challenge to those farmers who tried to homestead there. Droughts, insect plagues, and the loneliness of the vast unsettled area were problems that many pioneer families struggled to overcome.

A train can be seen traveling westward across the continent in this 1868 Currier and Ives picture entitled "Westward the Course of Empire Takes Its Way."

1 Chester Arthur Proposes a New Indian Policy

Beginning in 1867, the United States settled large numbers of Plains Indians on reservations. In light of the mixed success of this policy, President Chester Arthur in 1881 offered the following suggestions. Six years later, many of the ideas in his proposal were incorporated in the Dawes Act.

Prominent among the matters which challenge the attention of Congress at present is the management of our Indian affairs.

While this question has been a cause of trouble and embarrassment from the infancy of the government, it is [only] recently that any effort has been made for its solution. . . .

It was natural, at a time when the national territory seemed almost [limitless] . . . that a policy should have been initiated which more than [anything] else has been the fruitful source of our Indian complications.

I refer, of course, to the policy of dealing with the various Indian tribes as separate nationalities, of relegating them by treaty stipulations to the occupancy of immense reservations in the West, and of encouraging them to live . . . undisturbed by any earnest and well-directed efforts to bring them under the influences of civilization.

The unsatisfactory results which have sprung from this policy are becoming apparent to all.

As the white settlements have crowded the borders of the reservations, the Indians, sometimes contentedly and sometimes against their will, have been transferred from their hunting grounds, from which they have again been dislodged whenever their new-found homes have been desired by the adventurous settlers.

These removals and the frontier collisions by which they have often been preceded have led to frequent and disastrous conflicts between the races. . . .

We have to deal with the appalling fact that though thousands of lives have been sacrificed and hundreds of millions of dollars expended in the attempt to solve the Indian problem, it has until within the past few years seemed scarcely nearer a solution than it was half a century ago. . . .

For the success of the efforts now [under way] to introduce among the Indians the customs and pursuits of civilized life and gradually to absorb them into the mass of our citizens, sharing their rights and . . . responsibilities, there is imperative need for legislation.

First. I recommend the passage of an act making the laws of the various states and territories applicable to the Indian reservations within their borders. . . .

The Indian should receive the protection of the law. He should be allowed to maintain in court his rights of person and property. He has repeatedly begged for this privilege. Its exercise would be very valuable . . . in his progress toward civilization.

Second. Of even greater importance is . . . [the] enactment of a general law permitting the allotment . . . to such Indians . . . as desire it, of a reasonable quantity of land secured to them by [legal grant], and for their own protection made [non-transferable] for twenty or twenty-five years. . . .

In return for such considerate action on the part of the Government, there is reason to believe that the Indians in large numbers would be persuaded to sever their tribal relations and to engage at once in agricultural pursuits. . . .

Third. I advise a liberal appropriation for the support of Indian schools, because of my confident belief that such a course is consistent with the wisest economy.

From James A. Richardson, ed., *A Compilation of the Messages and Papers of the Presidents* (New York, 1897), Vol. 11.

1. What were President Arthur's objections to the Indian policy of that time?
2. What specific recommendations did he make?

2 Custer's Last Stand

One of the best-known battles of the Indian wars took place in 1876 at the Little Bighorn. Years later, a Cheyenne warrior named Two Moons described George Custer's defeat to a journalist.

About May, when the grass was tall and the horses strong, we broke camp and started across the country to the mouth of the Tongue River. Then Sitting Bull and Crazy Horse and all went up the Rosebud [River]. There we had a big fight with General Crook and whipped him. Many soldiers were killed—few Indians. It was a great fight, much smoke and dust.

From there we all went over the divide, and camped in the valley of Little Horn. Everybody thought, "Now we are out of the white man's country. He can live there, we will live here." After a few days . . . a messenger rode up and said, "Let everybody paint up, cook, and get ready for a big dance." . . . We were very glad to think we were far away from the white man.

I went to water my horses at the creek . . . then took a swim myself. I came back to the camp afoot. When I got near my lodge, I looked up the Little Horn toward Sitting Bull's camp. I saw a great dust rising. It looked like a whirlwind. Soon Sioux horsemen came rushing into camp shouting: "Soldiers come! Plenty white soldiers. . . ."

Outside, far up the valley, I heard a battle cry. . . . After I had caught my horse, a Sioux warrior came again and said, "Many soldiers are coming. . . ."

I rode swiftly toward Sitting Bull's camp. There I saw the white soldiers fighting in a line. Indians covered the flat. They began to drive the soldiers all mixed up—Sioux, then soldiers, then more Sioux, and all shooting. The air was full of smoke and dust. I saw the soldiers fall back and drop into the river-bed like buffalo fleeing. They had no time to look for a crossing. The Sioux chased them up the hill. . . .

While I was sitting on my horse I saw flags come up over the hill to the east. . . . Then the soldiers rose all at once, all on horses. . . . They formed into three bunches [squadrons] with a little ways between. Then a bugle sounded, and they all got off horses, and some soldiers led the horses back over the hill.

Then the Sioux rode up the ridge on all sides, riding very fast. The Cheyennes went up the left way. Then the shooting was quick, quick. Pop—pop—pop very fast. Some of the soldiers were down on their knees, some standing, officers all in front. The smoke was like a great cloud, and everywhere the Sioux went the dust rose like smoke. We circled all round. . . . We shoot, we ride fast, we shoot again. Soldiers drop, and horses fall on them. Soldiers in line drop, but one man rides up and down the line—all the time shouting. He rode a sorrel horse with white face and white forelegs. I don't know who he was. He was a brave man.

Indians keep swirling round and round, and the soldiers killed only a few. Many soldiers fell. At last all horses killed but five. Once in a while some man would break out and run toward the river, but he would fall. At last about a hundred men and five horsemen stood on the hill all bunched together. All along the bugler kept

This pictograph, painted by an Oglala Sioux artist, depicts the Battle of the Little Bighorn.

blowing his commands. He was very brave too. Then a chief was killed. I hear it was Long Hair [Custer], I don't know; and then the five horsemen and the bunch of men . . . started toward the river. The man on the sorrel horse led them, shouting all the time. He wore a buckskin shirt, and had long black hair and mustache. He fought hard with a big knife. His men were all covered with white dust. I couldn't tell whether they were officers or not. One man all alone ran far down toward the river, then round up over the hill. I thought he was going to escape, but a Sioux fired and hit him in the head. He was the last man. . . .

Next day four Sioux chiefs and two Cheyennes and I . . . went upon the battlefield to count the dead. . . . There were 388. There were 39 Sioux and 7 Cheyennes killed, and about 100 wounded.

From *McClure's Magazine*, September, 1898.

1. Why were the Indians camped in what Two Moons called "the valley of Little Horn"?
2. Summarize the events of the battle.

3 Chief Joseph Pleads for Justice

In 1877, Chief Joseph led the Nez Perce toward Canada in an attempt to escape reservation life. After his capture the Nez Perce were transferred to the Indian Territory, where many died of malaria. Chief Joseph was allowed to visit Washington in 1879, where he met with officials of the Hayes administration. Portions of his impassioned appeal for justice follow.

I have heard talk and talk, but nothing is done. Good words do not last long unless they amount to something. Words do not pay for my dead people. They do not pay for my country, now overrun by white men. They do not protect my father's grave. They do not pay for my horses and cattle.

Good words do not give me back my children. Good words will not make good the promise of your war chief, General Miles. Good words will not give my people good health and stop them from dying. Good words will not get my people a home where they can live in peace and take care of themselves.

I am tired of talk that comes to noth-ing. . . . If the white man wants to live in peace with the Indian, he can live in peace. There need be no trouble. Treat all men alike. Give them the same laws. Give them all an even chance to live and grow.

All men are made by the same Great Spirit Chief. They are all brothers. The earth is the mother of all people, and all people should have equal rights upon it. You might as well expect all rivers to run backward as that any man who was born a free man should be contented penned up and denied liberty to go where he pleases. If you tie a horse to a stake, do you expect he will grow fat? If you pen an Indian up on a small spot of earth and compel him to stay there, he will not be contented nor will he grow and prosper.

I have asked some of the Great White Chiefs where they get their authority to say to the Indian that he shall stay in one place, while he sees white men going where they please. They cannot tell me.

I only ask of the government to be treated as all other men are treated. If I cannot go to my own home, let me have a home in a country where my people will not die so fast. I would like to go to Bitter Root Valley [in western Montana]. There my people would be healthy; where they are now, they are dying. . . . When I think of our condition, my heart is heavy. I see

Chief Joseph was moved from the Indian Territory to a reservation in the state of Washington in 1885. Here he is visited by Alice Fletcher, a government agent.

men of my own race treated as outlaws and driven from country to country, or shot down like animals.

I know that my race must change. We cannot hold our own with the white men as we are. We only ask an even chance to live as other men live. We ask to be recognized as men. We ask that the same law shall work alike on all men. If an Indian breaks the law, punish him by the law. If a white man breaks the law, punish him also.

Let me be a free man—free to travel, free to stop, free to work, free to trade where I choose, free to choose my own teachers, free to follow the religion of my fathers, free to think and talk and act for myself—and I will obey every law or submit to the penalty.

Whenever the white man treats the Indian as they treat each other, then we shall have no more wars. We shall all be alike— brothers of one father and mother.... Then the Great Spirit Chief who rules above will smile upon this land and send rain to wash out the bloody spots made by brothers' hands upon the face of the earth. For this time the Indian race are waiting and praying. I hope no more groans of wounded men and women will ever go to the ear of the Great Spirit Chief above, and that all people may be one people.

From *North American Review*, Vol. 128 (April, 1879).

1. What did Chief Joseph say were the causes of the Indians' distress?
2. What was the main request Chief Joseph asked of white Americans?

4 Memoirs of a Black Cowboy

Ranchers, miners, and farmers were moving onto the Plains at the same time Indians were being forced onto reservations. Among them were black Americans, hoping to build a better life. Some became cowboys, including Nat Love, who left Tennessee in 1869 at the age of fifteen and headed for Kansas. Love, who won the title "Deadwood Dick" at an 1876 rodeo, later published his autobiography in which he described his adventures as a cowboy.

The outfit of which I was a member was called the Duval outfit, and their brand was known as the Pig Pen brand....

The home ranch was located on the Palo Duro River in the western part of the Panhandle, Texas.... I remained in the employ of the Duval outfit for three years, making regular trips to Dodge City every season and to many other places in the surrounding states with herds of horses and cattle for market and to be delivered to other ranch owners all over Texas, Wyoming, and the Dakotas. By strict attention to business, born of a genuine love of the free and wild life of the range, and absolute fearlessness, I became known throughout the country as a good all-around cowboy and a splendid hand in a stampede.

After returning from one of our trips north . . . in the fall of 1872, I received and accepted a better position with the Pete Gallinger company, whose immense range was located on the Gila River in southern Arizona. . . . I stayed with the Pete Gallinger company for several years and soon became one of their most trusted men, taking an important part in all the big round-ups and cuttings throughout western Texas, Arizona, and other states where the company had interests to be looked after, sometimes riding eighty miles a day for days at a time over the trails of Texas and the surrounding country. . . . I soon became well known among the cowboys, rangers, scouts, and guides it was my pleasure to meet in my wanderings over the country. . . . Many of these men . . . have since become famous in story and history, and a braver, truer set of men never lived than these wild sons of the plains whose home was in the saddle and their couch, mother earth, with the sky for a covering. They were always ready to share their blanket and their last ration with a less fortunate fellow companion and always assisted each other in the many trying situations that were continually coming up in a cowboy's life.

When we were not on the trail taking large herds of cattle or horses to market to be delivered to other ranches, we were engaged in range riding, moving large numbers of cattle from one grazing range to another, keeping them together, and hunting up strays which, despite the most earnest efforts of the range riders would get away from the main herd and wander for miles over the plains before they could be found, overtaken, and returned to the main herd.

Then the Indians and the white outlaws who infested the country gave us no end of trouble, as they lost no opportunity to cut out and run off the choicest part of a herd of longhorns, or the best of a band of horses, causing the cowboys a ride of many a long mile over the dusty plains in pursuit. . . . [Many] are the fierce engagements we had, when after a long chase of perhaps hundreds of miles over the ranges we overtook the thieves. It then became a case of "to the victor belongs the spoils," as there was no law respected in this wild country, except the law of might and the persuasive qualities of a 45 Colt pistol.

Accordingly it became absolutely necessary for a cowboy to understand his gun and know how to place its contents where it would do the most good. . . . [Therefore] I in common with my other companions never lost an opportunity to practice with my 45 Colts. . . . [The] opportunities were not lacking by any means and so in time I became fairly proficient and able in most cases to hit a barn door, providing the door was not too far away. . . . [I] was steadily improving in this as I was in experience and knowledge of the other branches of the business which I had chosen as my life's work and which I had begun to like so

In his autobiography, written in 1907, Nat Love told of his many adventures on the frontier.

well. . . . [While] the life was hard and in some ways exacting, yet it was free and wild and contained the elements of danger which my nature craved and which began to manifest itself when I was a . . . youngster on the old plantation in our rock battles and the breaking of the wild horses. I gloried in the danger, and the wild and free life of the plains, the new country I was continually traversing, and the many new scenes and incidents continually arising in the life of a rough rider.

From Nat Love, *The Life and Adventures of Nat Love, Better Known in the Cattle-Country as "Deadwood Dick"* (Los Angeles: Ayer Co., 1907).

1. Describe the work Nat Love did for the Pete Gallinger company. What were some of the challenges of a trail drive?
2. How did Nat Love characterize his fellow cowboys?
3. What personal qualities appear to have contributed to Nat Love's success as a cowboy?

5 The Arid Regions of the West

John Wesley Powell, a Civil War hero, explorer of the West, and conservationist, became director of the United States Geological Survey in 1880. The year before, while on the Survey staff, he wrote a report on the "Arid Region" of the American West. His recommendations were eventually incorporated into the national land policy.

The general subject of water rights is one of great importance. In many places in the Arid Region irrigation companies are organized [by those] who obtain vested rights in the waters they control, and consequently the rights to such waters do not inhere in any particular tracts of land. . . .

In general the lands greatly exceed the capacities of the streams. Thus the lands have no value without water. If the water rights fall into the hands of irrigating companies and the lands into the hands of individual farmers, the farmers then will be dependent upon the stock companies, and eventually the monopoly of water rights will be an intolerable burden to the people.

The magnitude of the interests involved must not be overlooked. All the present and future agriculture of more than four-tenths of the area of the United States is dependent upon irrigation, and practically all values for agricultural industries inhere, not in the lands, but in the water. Monopoly of land need not be feared. The question for legislators to solve is to devise some practical means by which water rights may be distributed among individual farmers and water monopolies prevented. . . .

The pioneer is fully engaged in the present with its hopes of immediate remuneration for labor. The present development of the country fully occupies him. For this reason every effort put forth to increase the area of the agricultural land by irrigation is welcomed. Every man who turns his attention to this department of history is considered a public benefactor. But if in the eagerness for present development a land and water system shall grow up in which the practical control of agriculture shall fall into the hands of water companies, evils will result therefrom that generations may not be able to correct, and the very men who are now lauded as benefactors to the country will, in the ungovernable reaction which is sure to come, be denounced as oppressors of the people.

The right to use water should inhere in the land to be irrigated, and water rights should go with land titles. . . .

Practically, in that country the right to water is acquired by priority of utilization, and this is as it should be from the necessities of the country. But two important qualifications are needed. The *user right* should attach to the *land* where used, not to the individual or company constructing the canals by which it is used; the priority of usage should secure the right. But this needs some slight modification. A farmer settling on a small tract, to be redeemed by irrigation, should be given a reasonable length of time in which to secure his water right by utilization, that he may secure it by his own labor, either directly by constructing the waterways himself, or indirectly by cooperating with his neighbors in constructing systems of waterways. Without this provision there is little inducement for poor men to commence farming operations, and men of ready capital only will engage in such enterprises. . . .

If there be any doubt of ultimate legality of the practices of the people in the arid country relating to water and land rights,

all such doubt should be speedily quieted through the enactment of appropriate laws by the national legislature. Perhaps an amplification by the courts of what had been designated as the *natural right* to use of water may be made to cover the practices now obtaining; but it hardly seems wise to imperil interests so great by entrusting them to the possibility of some future court-made law.

From John W. Powell, "Report on the Lands of the Arid Region of the United States" in *Documents of American History*, edited by Henry Steele Commager, © 1963, p. 552. Reprinted by permission of Prentice-Hall, Inc., Englewood Cliffs, N.J.

1. Why, according to Powell, was the question of water rights so important in the West?
2. What did Powell believe would be the consequences if water rights were held by a few people of wealth and power?

6 The Closing of the Frontier

By 1890, so many people had settled in so many parts of the West that the Census Bureau reported the disappearance of the frontier line. Three years later a young historian, Frederick Jackson Turner, presented a paper to the American Historical Association in which he examined the effect on the American character of the availability of almost endless stretches of land.

From the conditions of frontier life came intellectual traits of profound importance. The works of travelers along each frontier from colonial days describe certain common traits, and these traits have, while softening down, still persisted as survivals in the place of their origin, even when a higher social organization succeeded. The result is that to the frontier the American intellect owes its striking characteristics.

That coarseness and strength combined with acuteness and inquisitiveness; that practical, inventive turn of mind, quick to find expedients; that masterful grasp of material things, lacking in the artistic but powerful to effect great ends; that restless, nervous energy; that dominant individualism, working for good and for evil, and withal that buoyancy and exuberance which comes with freedom—these are traits of the frontier, or traits called out elsewhere because of the existence of the frontier. Since the days when the fleet of Columbus sailed into the waters of the New World, America has been another name for opportunity, and the people of the United States have taken their tone from the incessant expansion which has not only been open but has even been forced upon them. He would be a rash prophet who would assert that the expansive character of American life has now entirely ceased. Movement has been its dominant fact, and, unless this training has no effect upon a people, the American energy will continually demand a wider field for its exercise. But never again will such gifts of free land offer themselves. For a moment, at the frontier, the bonds of custom are broken and unrestraint is triumphant. . . . The stubborn American environment is there with its imperious summons to accept its conditions; the inherited ways of doing things are also there; and yet, in spite of environment, and in spite of custom, each frontier did indeed furnish a new field of opportunity, a gate of escape from the bondage of the past; and freshness, and confidence, and scorn of older society, impatience of its restraints and its ideas, and indifference to its lessons, have accompanied the frontier. What the Mediterranean Sea was to the Greeks, breaking the bond of custom, offering new experiences, calling out new institutions and activities, that, and more, the ever-retreating frontier has been to the United States directly, and to the nations of Europe more remotely. And now, four centuries from the discovery of America, at the end of a hundred years of life under the Constitution, the frontier has gone, and with its going has closed the first period of American history.

From Frederick Jackson Turner, "The Significance of the Frontier in American History," American Historical Association, *Annual Report for 1893* (Washington, D.C.: Government Printing Office, 1894).

1. What American values and ways of thinking did Turner believe grew out of the conditions of life on the frontier?
2. Did Turner believe that "the expansive character of American life" had come to an end? Explain.

Analysis

1. Both President Arthur and Chief Joseph declared that they wanted Indians and whites to live in peace. Compare and contrast the ways in which these two leaders sought to reach this goal.

2. In his plea for his people, Chief Joseph stated that he wanted to be "a free man—free to travel, free to stop, free to trade where I choose . . . free to think and talk and act for myself. . . ." What objections might the homesteaders of the West have had to Chief Joseph's goal?

3. Frederick Jackson Turner wrote that life on the frontier had given Americans a number of "striking characteristics." Which of those characteristics are exhibited in the selection written by Nat Love? Support your answer with statements from Nat Love's writings.

4. John Wesley Powell maintained that the right to use water for irrigation should be included in the title to land. What arguments might an irrigation company have offered against this principle?

The Making of Big Business
1865–1900

CHAPTER

2

In the years following the Civil War, railroads played a vital role in the economic growth of the United States. The completion of the first transcontinental railroad in 1869 was an event heralded throughout the nation. Alexander Toponce, a pioneer traveling through the West at that time, wrote the following account:

> I saw the Golden Spike driven at Promontory, Utah, on May 10, 1869. . . . On the last day, only about a hundred feet of rail were laid, and everybody tried to have a hand in the work. I took a shovel from an Irishman and threw a shovelful of dirt on the ties just to tell about it afterward.
>
> When they came to drive the last spike, Governor Stanford, president of the Central Pacific, took the sledge, and the first time he struck he missed the spike and hit the rail. . . . Then Stanford tried it again and tapped the spike, and the telegraph operators had fixed their instruments so that the tap was reported in all the offices east and west, and this in turn, set bells tapping in hundreds of towns and cities.

Soon railroads crisscrossed the land, tying together the fields and factories of the nation. Abundant natural resources, a rapidly growing labor force, and new sources of power contributed to a tremendous increase in manufacturing. This mushrooming growth provided new opportunities for millions of Americans and altered their lives in significant ways.

The Bessemer steel-manufacturing process was used at Andrew Carnegie's steelworks in Pittsburgh, Pennsylvania.

1 The Impact of War on Invention

In 1861, as American industry began to feel the full impact of the Civil War, the Scientific American *took stock of some of the advances in technology brought about by the conflict.*

At the close of the year 1860, we congratulated our readers upon a year of unexampled national prosperity. . . . It would have afforded us intense pleasure had we been able to close our present volume in the same tones of peaceful gladness; but in thousands of workshops, factories, and farms, the hammer, the saw, and the plow have been laid aside for the sword, the rifle, and the cannon, and our country has become one vast camp of armed men. Fierce battles have been fought, and many brave men have fallen and now "sleep the sleep which knows no waking." Still there is much to cheer and awaken faith and hope for the future. Many philosophers believe that wars are tribulations which exert similar influences among the nations that thunderstorms do upon the atmosphere. They are evils while they exist, but when the clouds are dispersed, men breathe a purer and more serene atmosphere. May this be the happy consummation of our national troubles!

Although the vast insurrection has exerted a disorganizing influence upon many manufacturers and other branches of business, it is really wonderful to witness the elasticity of our people and the facility with which they have adapted themselves to altered circumstances. Many old branches of industry have been destroyed, but new ones have sprung up, and there is now a great amount of industrial prosperity enjoyed in most of the manufacturing sections of our country.

The war has stimulated the genius of our people and directed it to the service of our country. Sixty-six new inventions relating to engines, implements, and articles of warfare have been illustrated in our columns, with no less than 147 figures. These embrace a great variety of cannon, rifle, shells, shot, tents, kits, and almost all articles found in the military vocabulary. . . . No man can really be intelligent in matters relating to modern warfare unless he has made himself acquainted with these inventions.

Other departments of industry have also been represented. Our inventors have not devoted themselves exclusively to the invention of destructive implements; they have also cultivated the arts of peace. In the present volume of the *Scientific American*—extending only over six months—160 different subjects have been illustrated, averaging from three to four figures each. It would take up too much space to enumerate all these; but in thus summing up our yearly progress in a general way, we can safely assert that for original and well-studied efforts of genius, they equal if they do not surpass the inventions of any former year. And as the number of patents issued is a very good exponent of the progress of our country, we can point to no less than 2,919, which is equal to the number (2,910) issued in 1857—four years ago. When the defection of eleven states and the distractions of our country are taken into consideration, it is not too much to assert that our inventors have done better last year than ever before, and that inventions are perhaps the most safe and profitable sources of investment in times of war as well as peace.

Considering the nature and extent of the tremendous struggle in which our country is engaged, we have really great reason as a people to feel grateful and call this a prosperous year after all. Never before have our fields yielded so bountifully. The great West is [overflowing] with wheat and corn, and we are in the happy condition of enjoying a surplus of the necessaries of life. In thus viewing the past, we can still say with cheerfulness, "Thy face, old year, has been deeply furrowed by scars and tears, but it has also been illuminated with many sunny smiles."

From "The Old Year's Progress," *Scientific American*, December 28, 1861.

1. What new types of inventions did the article from the *Scientific American* say had come about in 1861?

2. What reasons did the writer give for his optimism about the future?

2 The Importance of Technology

In the years after the Civil War, technological advances continued to spur rapid industrial growth. In The Progress of Invention in the Nineteenth Century, *written in 1900, Edward Byrn emphasized the changes technology had brought to the United States.*

Standing on the threshold of the Twentieth Century, and looking back a hundred years, the Nineteenth Century presents in the field of invention a magnificent museum of thoughts crystallized and made immortal. . . . The philosophical mind is ever accustomed to regard all stages of growth as proceeding by slow and uniform processes of evolution, but in the field of invention the Nineteenth Century has been unique. It has been something more than a merely normal growth or natural development. It has been a gigantic tidal wave of human ingenuity and resource, so stupendous in its magnitude, so complex in its diversity, so profound in its thought, so

This sewing machine company's advertisement pictured one of the technological wonders of the day—the Brooklyn Bridge.

fruitful in its wealth, so beneficent in its results, that the mind is strained and embarrassed in its effort to expand to a full appreciation of it. . . .

Even up to the beginning of this century so strong a hold had superstition on the human mind, that inventions were almost synonymous with the black arts, and the struggling genius had not only to contend with the natural laws and the thousand and one expected difficulties that hedge the path of the inventor, but had also to overcome the far greater obstacles of ignorant fear and bigoted prejudice. A labor-saving machine was looked upon askance as the enemy of the working man, and many an earnest inventor, after years of arduous thought and painstaking labor, saw his cherished model broken up and his hopes forever blasted by the animosity of his fellow men. But with the Nineteenth Century a new era has dawned. The legitimate results of inventions have been realized in larger incomes, shorter hours of labor, and lives so much richer in health, comfort, happiness, and usefulness, that today the inventor is a benefactor whom the world delights to honor. So crowded is the busy life of modern civilization with the evidences of his work, that it is impossible to open one's eyes without seeing it on every hand, woven into the very fabric of daily existence.

From Edward W. Byrn, *The Progress of Invention in the Nineteenth Century* (New York: Munn & Co., 1900).

1. According to Byrn, what obstacles had inventors faced throughout history?
2. What benefits did Byrn believe had come from inventions during the nineteenth century?

3 John D. Rockefeller on Industrial Combinations

One of the most successful nineteenth-century business leaders was John D. Rockefeller, founder of the powerful Standard Oil Company. In 1899, Rockefeller testified before a congressional commission that was investigating industrial combinations. Portions of his testimony follow.

Question. What are the chief advantages from industrial combinations [trusts, monopolies, and so on]—*(a)* financially to stockholders; *(b)* to the public?
Answer. All the advantages which can be derived from a cooperation of persons and aggregation of capital. Much that one man cannot do alone two can do together, and once one admits that cooperation, or, what is the same thing, combination, is necessary on a small scale, the limit depends solely upon the necessities of business.

It is too late to argue about advantages of industrial combinations. They are a necessity if Americans are to have the privilege of extending their business in all the states of the Union, and into foreign countries as well. Their chief advantages are:
(1) Command of necessary capital.
(2) Extension of limits of business.
(3) Increase of number of persons interested in the business.
(4) Economy in the business.
(5) Improvements and economies which are derived from knowledge of many interested persons of wide experience.
(6) Power to give the public improved products at less prices and still make profit for stockholders.
(7) Permanent work and good wages for labor.

Question. What are the chief disadvantages or dangers to the public arising from them?
Answer. The dangers are that the power conferred by combination may be abused; that combinations may be formed for speculation in stocks rather than for conducting business, and that for this purpose prices may be temporarily raised instead of being lowered. These abuses are possible in

all combinations, large or small, but this fact is no more of an argument against combinations than the fact that steam may explode is an argument against steam. Steam is necessary and can be made comparatively safe. Combination is necessary and its abuses can be minimized.

Question. What legislation, if any, would you suggest regarding industrial combinations?
Answer. First. Federal legislation under which corporations may be created and regulated, if that be possible. Second. In lieu thereof, state legislation as nearly uniform as possible encouraging combinations of persons and capital for the purpose of carrying on industries, but permitting state supervision, not of a character to hamper industries, but sufficient to prevent frauds upon the public.

Adapted from U.S. Industrial Commission, *Preliminary Report on Trusts and Industrial Combinations*, 56th Congress, 1st Session (December 30, 1899), Document No. 476, Part 1.

1. What advantages did Rockefeller say industrial combinations offered? What disadvantages did he mention?
2. What was Rockefeller's attitude concerning regulation of combinations by the federal and state governments?

4 Horatio Alger on How to Get Ahead

Stories which told of young people rising from "rags to riches" won a national reputation for the author Horatio Alger. The following passages from a typical Alger story, reflect the optimism of the post-Civil War period.

When Micky had gone out, Mr. Rockwell said, "Well Richard, I have lost my bookkeeper."

"Yes, sir," said Dick.

"And I can't say I am sorry. . . . Now I suppose I must look for a successor."

"Yes, sir, I suppose so."

"I know a very competent bookkeeper, who is intending to go into business for himself at the expiration of six months. Until that time I can secure his services. Now, I have a plan in view which I think you will approve. You shall at once commence the study of bookkeeping in a commercial school in the evening, and during the day I will direct Mr. Haley to employ you as his assistant. I think in that way you will be able to succeed him at the end of his term."

Dick was taken completely by surprise. The thought that he, so recently plying the trade of a bootblack in the public streets, could rise in six months to the responsible post of a bookkeeper in a large wholesale house, seemed almost incredible.

"I should like nothing better," he said, his eyes sparkling with delight, "if you really think I could discharge the duties satisfactorily."

"I think you could. I believe you have the ability, and of your fidelity I feel assured."

"Thank you, sir; you are very kind to me," said Dick, gratefully.

"I have reason to be," said Mr. Rockwell, taking his hand. . . .

And now, almost with regret, I find myself closing up the record of Dick's checkered career. The past with its trials is over; the future expands before him, a bright vista of merited success. . . .

In six months, at the age of seventeen, Dick succeeded to Mr. Gilber's place with a salary, to commence with, of $1,000. To this an annual increase was made, making his income at twenty-one, $1,400. Just about that time he had an opportunity to sell his uptown lots, to a gentleman who had taken a great fancy to them, for five times the amount he paid, or $5,000. His savings from his salary amounted to about $2,000.

Meanwhile, Mr. Rockwell's partner, Mr. Cooper, from ill health felt obliged to withdraw from business, and Richard . . . was admitted to the post of junior partner, embarking the capital he had already accumulated, and receiving a corresponding share of the profits. These were so large that Richard was able to increase his interest yearly by investing his additional savings, and three years later he felt justified in offering his hand to Ida Greyson, whose partiality to Dick had never wavered. He was no longer Ragged Dick now, but Mr. Richard Hunter, junior partner in the large firm of Rockwell & Hunter. Mr. Greyson felt that even in a worldly way Dick was a good match for his daughter; but he knew and valued still more his good heart and conscientious fidelity to duty, and excellent principles, and cheerfully gave his consent. . . .

So Dick has achieved FAME and FORTUNE—the fame of an honorable and enterprising man of business, and a fortune which promises to be very large. But I am glad to say that Dick has not been spoiled by prosperity. He never forgets his humble beginnings, and tries to show his sense of God's goodness by extending a helping hand to the poor and needy boys, whose trials and privations he understands well from his own past experience.

From Horatio Alger, Jr., *Fame and Fortune; or, The Progress of Richard Hunter* (Philadelphia: Porter & Coates, 1868).

1. What plan did Mr. Rockwell offer Dick? What was Dick's reaction?
2. Trace the steps whereby Dick achieved fame and fortune.

5 "Acres of Diamonds"

During the late nineteenth century, a number of clergymen preached that great wealth was a great blessing. No one expressed this view more explicitly than Russell Conwell, a Baptist minister from Philadelphia and the founder of Temple University (1888). Conwell's philosophy was contained in his famous "Acres of Diamonds," a sermon that he preached over 6,000 times.

Now then, I say again that the opportunity to get rich, to attain . . . great wealth, is here in Philadelphia now, within the reach of almost every man and woman who hears me speak tonight, and I mean just what I say. . . . I have come to tell you what in God's sight I believe to be the truth, . . . that the men and women sitting here, who found it difficult perhaps to buy a ticket to this lecture, . . . have within their reach "acres of diamonds," opportunities to get largely wealthy. . . .

I say that you ought to get rich, and it is your duty to get rich. How many of my pious brethren say to me, "Do you, a Christian minister, spend your time going up and down the country advising young people to get rich, to get money?" "Yes, of course I do." They say, "Isn't that awful! Why don't you preach the gospel instead of preaching about man's making money?" "Because to make money honestly is to preach the gospel." That is the reason. The men who get rich may be the most honest men you find in the community. . . .

Let me say here clearly, and say it briefly, . . . that ninety-eight out of one hundred of the rich men in America are honest. That is why they are rich. That is why they are trusted with money. That is why they carry on great enterprises and find plenty of people to work with them. It is because they are honest men. . . .

Money is power, and you ought to be reasonably ambitious to have it. You ought because you can do more good with it than you could without it. Money printed your Bible, money builds your churches, money sends your missionaries, and money pays your preachers, and you would not have many of them either, if you did not pay them. I am always willing that my church should raise my salary, because the church that pays the largest salary always raises it the easiest. You never knew an exception to it in your life. The man who gets the largest salary can do the most good with the power that is furnished to him. Of course he can if his spirit be right to use it for what is given to him.

I say, then, you ought to have money. If you can honestly attain unto riches in Philadelphia, it is your Christian and godly duty to do so. It is an awful mistake of these pious people to think you must be awfully poor in order to be pious.

Some men say, "Don't you sympathize with the poor people?" Of course I do, or else I would not have been lecturing these years. I won't give in but what I sympathize with the poor, but the number of poor who are to be sympathized with is very small. To sympathize with a man whom God has punished for his sins, thus to help him when God would still continue a just punishment, is to do wrong, no doubt about it, and we do that more than we help those who are deserving. While we should sympathize with God's poor—that is, those who cannot help themselves—let us remember there is not a poor person in the United States who was not made poor by his own shortcomings, or by the shortcomings of someone else. It is all wrong to be poor anyhow. Let us give in to that argument and pass that to one side.

1. What did the Reverend Conwell mean by the expression "acres of diamonds"?
2. What was his view of wealthy Americans? What did he think about poor people?

Analysis

1. Both Edward Byrn and the editors of the *Scientific American* wrote that invention and technology were improving the quality of American life. What aspects of American life did they believe were improving and why did they think this was happening?

2. What arguments might a critic of industrial combinations have put forward in opposition to John D. Rockefeller's analysis?

3. Horatio Alger argued that Americans could readily rise from poverty to wealth and power. What personal qualities and abilities did he believe enabled people to do this?

4. Russell Conwell argued that anyone in America who was poor was "made poor by his own shortcomings, or by the shortcomings of someone else." Would John D. Rockefeller and Horatio Alger have agreed with this? Explain your answer.

An Urban Industrial Society
1865–1900

CHAPTER

3

The great majority of immigrants who came to the United States between 1860 and 1900 settled in urban centers. For those immigrants, America was the land of opportunity and hope—a chance to be a part of a new society.

One immigrant who came to the United States in the 1890's was Mary Antin. Arriving as a young girl from Russia, Mary Antin later became a well-known American writer. In her book *The Promised Land,* she related what public education meant to new immigrants:

> Education was free. That subject my father had written about repeatedly, as comprising his chief hope for us children, the essence of American opportunity, the treasure that no thief could touch. . . . It was the one thing that he was able to promise us when he sent for us; surer, safer than bread or shelter. On our second day I was thrilled with the realization of what this freedom of education meant. A little girl from across the alley came and offered to conduct us to school. . . . No application made, no questions asked, no examinations, rulings, exclusions; . . . no fees. The doors stood open for every one of us. The smallest child could show us the way.

The fortunes of the immigrants who came to the United States were as varied as the countries from which they came. Over time, the vast majority of the immigrants adapted to America and enriched its culture with their own ethnic contributions.

Throughout the second half of the nineteenth century, the percentage of Americans living on farms decreased. At the same time, cities grew steadily larger. This picture shows a busy street in New York City in the 1880's.

459

1 The Melting Pot

Israel Zangwill, a British playwright and novelist, was a frequent traveler to the United States in the late 1800's and early 1900's. In 1908, he gained immense popular success with his play The Melting Pot. *The following passages from that work describe the way immigrant traditions were being blended in this country.*

America is God's Crucible, the great Melting Pot where all the races of Europe are melting and re-forming! Here you stand, good folk, think I, when I see them at Ellis Island [where immigrants arrived in New York City], here you stand in your fifty groups, with your fifty languages and histories, and your fifty blood hatreds and rivalries. But you won't be long like that, brothers, for these are the fires of God you've come to—these are the fires of God. A fig for your feuds and vendettas! Germans and Frenchmen, Irishmen and Englishmen, Jews and Russians—into the Crucible with you all! God is making the American. . . .

There she lies, the great Melting Pot—listen! Can't you hear the roaring and the bubbling? There gapes her mouth—the harbour where a thousand mammoth feeders come from the ends of the world to pour in their human freight. Ah, what a stirring and a seething! Celt and Latin, Slav and Teuton, Greek and Syrian—black and yellow—Jew and Gentile . . . East and West, North and South . . . how the great Alchemist melts and fuses them with his purging flame! Here shall they all unite to build the Republic of Man. . . . What is the glory of Rome and Jerusalem where all nations and races come to worship and look back compared with the glory of America, where all races and nations come to labor and look forward!

From Israel Zangwill, *The Melting Pot, A Drama in Four Acts* (New York: The Macmillan Company, 1909).

1. What future did Zangwill foresee for people coming to America?
2. What contrast did Zangwill make between America and the cities of Rome and Jerusalem?

2 An Immigrant's Experience

Abraham Rihbany came to the United States from Syria in 1891. In the following passages from his autobiography, he described what life was like in his Syrian neighborhood in New York City.

My friend, Moses, did not forget his promise to be on the lookout for a position for me in some Syrian store, for on my tenth day in New York he told me of a merchant who needed a *katib*—a bookkeeper. Realizing that I had never had any experience in bookkeeping, he instructed me not to be overconscientious in confessing my ignorance. The customers of the store were peddlers of "jewelry and notions," and almost all the transactions were carried on in the Arabic language.

In company with my beneficent friend I proceeded to the store of Khawaja Maron. Moses introduced me to the proprietor and departed. Maron told me that the salary of the position I was seeking was $20 per month. Recalling the time when as a schoolteacher in Syria my salary was $3 a month and my board, $20 seemed to me a species of "frenzied financiering." I had

Open-air markets like this one on Orchard Street in New York City were common in the late 1800's.

every reason to imagine that my new position was the gateway to riches and honor. . . .

The Syrian colony in New York seemed to me to be simply Syria on a smaller scale. During my stay of nearly eighteen months in it I did not have occasion to speak ten sentences in English. We ate the same dishes, spoke the same language, told the same stories, indulged in the same pleasures, and were torn by the same feuds, as those that had filled our lives on the eastern shores of the Mediterranean. . . .

The Syrian colony in New York rendered me all the service it could by providing me with a home for about eighteen months among those whose language was my language and whose habits were my habits. Its Oriental atmosphere with its slight Occidental tinge protected me from the dangers of an abrupt transition. Had I been thrust into American society upon my arrival in this country, penniless and without serviceable knowledge of the English language,

the change in environment might have proved too violent for me to endure with any comfort. To me the colony was a habitat so much like the one I had left behind me in Syria that its home atmosphere enabled me to maintain a firm hold on life in the face of the many difficulties which confronted me in those days, and just different enough to awaken my curiosity to know more about the surrounding American influences.

1. What help did Rihbany receive soon after his arrival in America?
2. In what ways did he find life in the Syrian community of New York similar to life in Syria?
3. How did life in the Syrian community ease the transition to life in America?

3 Josiah Strong on Cities

Many Americans viewed the nation's cities as threats to traditional values. In his widely read Our Country, *Josiah Strong issued the following warning.*

The city is the nerve end of our civilization. It is also the storm center. . . . The city has become a serious menace to our civilization. . . . It has a peculiar attraction for the immigrant. . . . The saloon, together with the intemperance and the liquor problem which it represents, is multiplied in the city. . . . Of course, the demoralizing and pauperizing power of the saloons and their debauching influence in politics increase with their numerical strength.

It is in the city where wealth is massed; and here are the tangible evidences of it piled many stories high. . . . Here are luxuries gathered—everything that dazzles the eye, or tempts the appetite; here is the most extravagant expenditure. Here, also, is the *congestion* of wealth the severest.

Here is heaped the social dynamite; here roughs, gamblers, thieves, robbers, lawless and desperate men of all sorts, congregate; men who are ready on any pretext to raise riots for the purpose of destruction and plunder; here gather foreigners and wage-workers; here skepticism and irreligion abound. . . .

As a rule, our largest cities are the worst governed. It is natural, therefore, to infer that, as our cities grow larger and more dangerous, the government will become more corrupt, and control will pass completely into the hands of those who themselves most need to be controlled.

From Josiah Strong, *Our Country* (New York: Baker & Taylor, 1885).

1. What dangers did Strong see in the cities of America?
2. What was Strong's probable stand on immigration restriction? On temperance?

4 The Tenement House

Many newcomers to American cities lived and worked in crowded tenements. Jacob Riis, who had emigrated to the United States from Denmark at the age of 21, described New York City tenement life in 1890 in his book How the Other Half Lives.

Let us . . . see how Sunday passes in a Ludlow Street tenement.

Up two flights of dark stairs, three, four, with new smells of cabbage, of onions, of frying fish, on every landing, whirring sewing machines behind closed doors betraying what goes on within, to the door that opens to admit the bundle and the man. A sweater [a sweatshop operator] this, in a small way. Five men and a woman, two young girls, not fifteen, and a boy who says unasked that he is fifteen, and lies in saying it, are at the machines sewing knickerbockers, "knee-pants" in the Ludlow Street dialect. The floor is littered ankle-deep with half-sewn garments. In the alcove, on a couch of many dozens of "pants" ready for the finisher, a bare-legged baby with pinched face is asleep. The faces, hands, and arms to the elbows of everyone in the room are black with the color of the cloth on which they are working. The boy and the woman alone look up at our entrance. The girls shoot sidelong glances, but at a warning look from the man with the bundle they tread their machines more energetically than ever. The

Many immigrant families got a start in America by doing garment work.

men do not appear to be aware even of the presence of a stranger.

They are "learners," all of them, says the woman, who proves to be the wife of the boss, and have "come over" only a few weeks ago. She is disinclined to talk at first, but a few words in her own tongue from our guide set her fears . . . at rest, and she grows almost talkative. . . . There are ten machines in the room; six are hired at $2 a month. For the two shabby, smoke-begrimed rooms, one somewhat larger than ordinary, they pay $20 a month. She does not complain, though "times are not what they were, and it costs a good deal to live." Eight dollars a week for a family of six and two boarders? How do they do it? She laughs, as she goes over the bill of fare. . . . Bread, fifteen cents a day, of milk, two quarts a day at four cents a quart, one pound of meat for dinner at twelve cents, butter, one pound a week at "eight cents a quarter of a pound." Coffee, potatoes, and pickles complete the list. At the last calculation, probably, this sweater's family hoards up $30 a month, and in a few years will own a tenement somewhere and profit by the example set by their landlord in rent-collecting.

On the next floor, in a dimly lighted room with a big red-hot stove to keep the pressing irons ready for use, is a family of man, wife, three children, and a boarder. . . . The boarder pays sixty-five cents a week. He is really only a lodger, getting his meals outside. The rent is $2.25 a week, cost of living $5. Every floor has at least two, sometimes four, such shops. Here is one with a young family for which life is bright with promise. Husband and wife work together; just now the latter, a [pretty] young woman, is eating her dinner of dry bread and green pickles. . . . [The pickles] are filling, and keep the children from crying with hunger. Those who have stomachs like ostriches thrive in spite of them and grow strong—plain proof that they are good to eat. The rest? "Well, they die," says our guide, dryly. No thought of untimely death comes to disturb this family with life all before it. In a few years the man will be a prosperous sweater. Already he employs an old man as ironer at $3 a week, and a sweet-faced little Italian girl as finisher at $1.50. She is twelve, she says, and can neither read nor write, will probably never learn. How should she? The family clears from $10 to $11 a week in brisk times, more than half of which goes into the bank. . . .

The majority of the children seek the public schools, where they are received sometimes with misgivings on the part of the teachers, who find it necessary to inculcate lessons of cleanliness in the worst cases by practical demonstration with wash-bowl and soap. . . . In the Allen Street public school the experienced principal has embodied among the elementary lessons . . . a characteristic exercise. The question is asked daily from the teacher's desk: "What must I do to be healthy?" and the whole school responds:

"I must keep my skin clean,
Wear clean clothes,
Breathe pure air,
And live in the sunlight."

From Jacob Riis, *How the Other Half Lives* (New York: Scribner, 1890).

1. How did the people in the Ludlow Street tenement make a living? What hopes did they have for the future?
2. What question did the teachers in the Allen Street public school ask their students every day? For what purpose did they ask that question?

5 Samuel Gompers Asks for Government Action

Labor strife increased dramatically during the 1880's. In 1881, there were 500 strikes involving 130,000 workers; by 1886, there were more than 1,000 strikes involving more than 600,000 workers. Deeply concerned, Congress held a series of hearings to explore the issue. Samuel Gompers, soon to become head of the American Federation of Labor, gave the following testimony to the Senate Committee on Education and Labor in 1885.

I say that the government of the United States ought to be in advance of its people. It is the duty of a legislator, as I understand it, to frame and adopt measures for the welfare of the people. The Constitution of the country, I believe, does not give our national government the right to adopt a law which would be applicable to private employments; yet for its own employees, it ought to be in advance; it ought not to enter the labor market, as you have suggested, Mr. Chairman, in competition with all other employers, but ought to be in advance. The selfish, mercenary, or other such motives which govern individuals in their struggle to accumulate wealth ought not to exist in our government, although they do exist to a morbid degree in too many of our employers.

Let the question of endeavoring to enforce a reduction of hours of labor among private employers be a question to be settled amicably, if possible, between ourselves and our employers, and I think it will not be many years before it will be generally settled. This seems to me to be the question of questions, the reduction of the hours of labor. . . .

The remedies that I suggest, and which I think the government can and ought to adopt, are the following:

1. Strict enforcement of the national eight-hour law. The workingmen of this country, in all their organizations where they have come together, either in private or in public, either as local, state, national, or confederated unions, have set forth that demand for the enforcement of the national eight-hour law.

2. The passage of a law by Congress giving the trades and labor unions the right to become chartered under the general laws of our government. The laws written and now in operation to protect the property of

the capitalist and the moneyed class generally are almost innumerable, yet nothing has been done to protect the property of the workingmen, the only property that they possess, their school, and trades union; and we ask that our existence as organizations may be legalized. . . .

3. We ask also, for the purpose of procuring information for the legislators of our country (who frequently find a very good excuse for nonaction by saying that they are ignorant as to the true condition of the working people), the establishment of a national bureau of labor statistics. Such a bureau would give our legislators an opportunity to know, not from mere conjecture but actually, the condition of our industries, our production and consumption, and what could be done by law to improve both. Our state governments would undoubtedly follow the lead of the national Congress and legislate in the interest of labor; but we see that so long as our national legislators have an excuse for saying that they do not know the condition of labor, there is very little chance of obtaining legislation. . . .

There are several other measures to which I might call attention and which I might suggest as remedies, but the best organized trades unions of the world are eminently practical. They are composed of men who are desirous of obtaining reforms by gradual means, and in that spirit we ask the adoption of these measures which I have set forth here, because we believe and know that they will [contribute] to our benefit as workingmen and to the benefit of society. If the legislators of this country are desirous of acting in this matter and alleviating the distress that is too prevalent, and if they desire to assist those who are working in this cause to mount a step higher, let them adopt these measures and they will receive the thanks of the working people of the world and of all posterity.

Adapted from U.S. Congress, Senate Committee on Education and Labor, *Report*, 1885, Vol. 1.

1. What, according to Gompers, was the most important aim of organized labor?
2. What specific actions did he recommend that the federal government take on behalf of workers?

Analysis

1. To what extent did the experiences of Abraham Rihbany confirm the ideas about Americans put forth in Israel Zangwill's "melting pot" theory?

2. Both Josiah Strong and Jacob Riis condemned conditions in American cities. Compare and contrast their attitudes.

3. Cite evidence from Samuel Gompers's testimony before Congress to prove that he disagreed with the revolutionary tactics of some American labor leaders.

4. Do the selections in this chapter convey a mood of optimism or pessimism? Cite specific examples to support your answer.

Politicians and Protest
1865–1900

CHAPTER

4

In the years after the Civil War, political campaigns were often showy events that tended to focus on the personalities of the candidates rather than on issues. An article published in the New York *Tribune* in 1876 described a typical campaign rally:

> We newsmen arrived about noon with the orator of the day. At the railway station a company of men in continental cocked hats and black oilcloth capes, trimmed with white, headed by a brass band, waits in line to receive him. While the band plays, the local committeemen put us in a carriage drawn by four white horses with tall plumes nodding on their heads, and we move off in quite a triumphal fashion.
>
> Only a small part of the throng can get within range of the orator's voice, but the rest seem nonetheless happy, for it is the holiday diversion, the crowds, the bravery of the procession, the music, and the fun of the occasion they came chiefly to enjoy.

The neglect of pressing social and economic problems by the politicians of both major parties gave rise, in time, to a third party. Called the Populist Party, it represented farmers, industrial workers, and others who were seeking reforms.

This Currier and Ives lithograph shows Washington, D.C., in 1880.

1 James Bryce on the Quality of Public Life in America

The British historian James Bryce, who later became ambassador to the United States, published The American Commonwealth *in 1888. In this classic work on government in the United States, Bryce expressed reservations about the quality of American public life.*

The tone of public life is lower [in the United States] than one expects to find it in so great a nation. Just as we assume that an individual man will at any supreme moment in his own life rise to a higher level than that on which he usually moves, so we look to find those who conduct the affairs of a great state inspired by a sense of the magnitude of the interests entrusted to them. Their horizon ought to be expanded, their feeling of duty quickened, their dignity of attitude enhanced. Human nature with all its weaknesses does show itself capable of being thus roused on its imaginative side; and in Europe, where the traditions of aristocracy survive, everybody condemns . . . acts done or language held by a great official which would pass unnoticed in a private citizen. It is the . . . sense of duty and trust substituted for that of mere hereditary rank.

Such a sentiment is comparatively weak in America. A Cabinet minister, or senator, or governor of a state, sometimes even a President, hardly feels himself more bound by it than the director of a railway company or the mayor of a town does in Europe. Not assuming himself to be individually wiser, stronger, or better than his fellow-citizens, he acts and speaks as though he were still simply one of them, and so far from magnifying his office and making it honorable, seems anxious to show that he is the mere creature of the popular vote, so filled by the sense that it is the people and not he who governs. . . . There is in the United States an abundance of patriotism, that is to say, of a passion for the greatness and happiness of the Republic, and a readiness to make sacrifices for it. . . . There is no [lack] of an appreciation of the collective majesty of the nation, for this is the theme of incessant speeches, nor even of the past and future glories of each particular state in the Union. But these sentiments do not bear their appropriate fruit in raising the conception of public office, of its worth and its dignity. The newspapers assume public men to be selfish and cynical. Disinterested virtue is not looked for, is perhaps turned into ridicule where it exists. The hard commercial spirit which pervades the meetings of a joint-stock company is the spirit in which most politicians speak of public business, and are not blamed for speaking. Something, especially in the case of newspapers, must be allowed for the humorous tendencies of the American mind, which likes to put forward the absurd and even vulgar side of things for the sake of getting fun out of them. But after making such allowances, the fact remains that, although no people is more emotional, and even in a sense more poetical, in no country is the ideal side of public life . . . so ignored by the mass and repudiated by the leaders. This affects not only the elevation but the independence and courage of public men; and the country suffers from the [lack] of what we call distinction in its conspicuous figures.

From James Bryce, *The American Commonwealth* (New York: Macmillan, 1893), Vol. 2.

1. Why was Bryce surprised to find that the "tone of public life" in the United States was so low?
2. What particular weaknesses and failings among American public officials did Bryce identify?

2 Senator Morton and Civil Service Reform

As part of the movement of political reform in the 1870's and 1880's, critics of the spoils system backed the creation of a civil service based on a merit system. Many officials, however, defended the existing spoils system. The following speech by Senator Oliver Morton, an honest and able Republican from Indiana, was typical of such defenses.

The senator [Trumbull from Illinois] praises the civil service system of Great Britain. A system that might be appropriate to Great Britain would not be appropriate here; our institutions are different. In England the tenure of office in the civil service is for life. They hold their offices during good behavior; that is to say, during life. Can we adopt the life tenure?

Why, sir, ten thousand men in this city [Washington] holding office for life would form a privileged class that would revolutionize the very foundation principle of this government. . . . If a man has an office for life, it takes a very serious cause to get him out. An ordinary delinquency, an ordinary neglect or abuse or failure, is never sufficient to oust a man who holds an office for life.

No, sir, we cannot afford to adopt the English system under any circumstances; it

People seeking federal jobs are seen waiting outside of President-elect Hayes's office.

is anti-republican; it is contrary to the fundamental principles of this government. . . .

I am not arguing against competitive examinations. I am in favor of them; but they are not infallible by any means. Men may pass an examination, and a first-rate examination, and yet be utterly unqualified for the position. . . .

But the senator says that officers ought to be appointed without regard to politics. Whenever you can carry on this government without regard to politics, that doctrine will do. But this is a government of the people and a government of public opinion, in which the mass of the people take a deep interest, as they do not in England and in countries on the continent of Europe. Just so long as the character of this government continues as it is, appointments will continue to be made with reference to politics; and no system can be devised to prevent it. I do not care how many competitive examinations you institute, or whether you make the tenure for life or a tenure for ten years, you cannot change that thing unless you change the character of the government. . . .

I have been in the Senate now nearly four years, and, so far as I know, there have been three clerks appointed upon my recommendation. . . . As far as I am personally concerned, I would be glad to be relieved of all this labor. But what right have I to be relieved? My friends have the same right to call upon me that I have had in times past to call upon them, and, if they are respectable, and capable, and honest, why should I refuse to give them that legitimate aid which may be within my power? Why, sir, men act upon this principle in all conditions of life, whether in regard to politics or in regard to business; and you cannot change it by any enactment which you can make.

From a speech by Oliver Morton, *Congressional Globe*, 41st Congress, 3rd Session (January 12, 1871).

1. What arguments did Morton give for opposing civil service reform?
2. What response might a supporter of civil service reform have made to Morton's arguments?

3 Carl Schurz—The Impact of Civil Service Reform

After years of agitation, reformers such as Carl Schurz welcomed the passage in 1883 of the Pendleton Act. Ten years later Schurz, serving as president of the Civil Service Reform League, gave the following assessment of the impact of civil service reform.

The Fourth of March last [1893] a new administration went into power. Untold thousands of men poured into the national capital clamoring for office; not for offices that were vacant, but to be vacated. . . . No matter whether he was ever so good a public servant, the man who was in was to be kicked out, to let him in who was out, no matter whether he would be not half so good a public servant. . . .

But there is one part of the public service which now remains untouched by the tumultuous debauch of the spoils carnival. It is like a quiet, peaceable island, with a civilized, industrious population, surrounded by the howling sea. The President and the chiefs of the government departments contemplate this part of the service with calmness and contentment, for it gives them no trouble while the turmoil of the office hunt rages all around it. The good citizen, anxious for the honor of his country, beholds it with relief and satisfaction, for here he finds nothing to be ashamed of, and much that is worthy of

Following passage of the Pendleton Act in 1883, candidates for some federal jobs were required to take special examinations.

this free and great nation. This is the "classified service," covered by the Civil Service Law, the creation of Civil Service Reform. On the portals the words are written: "Nobody enters here who has not proved his fitness for the duties to be performed." The office-hunting mob reads this and recoils. The public servant within it calmly walks the paths of his duty, undisturbed by the thought of the greedy . . . hungering for his place. He depends upon his merit for his security and advancement, and this consciousness inspires his work. This is the application of common sense and common honesty to the public service. It is Civil Service Reform. . . .

As the whole number of places under the national government amounts to about 180,000, we may say that more than one fourth of the service of the national gov-

ernment has ceased to be treated as mere spoils of party warfare. In one fourth the party boss has lost his power. One fourth is secure from the quadrennial loot. . . . So much Civil Service Reform has accomplished in the time of three presidential terms.

But great and encouraging as its progress has been, Civil Service Reform, having conquered only one fourth of the service, has done only one fourth of its work. . . . Civil Service Reform has undertaken to open the offices to all according to their ability to serve the people. . . .

On the one side, under the spoils system, [is] the aristocracy of influence—and a very vulgar aristocracy it is—robbing a man who has only merit, unbacked by power, of his rightful chance. On the other hand [is] Civil Service Reform, inviting all freely to compete, and then giving the best chance to the best man, be that man ever so lowly, and be his competitor ever so great a favorite of wealth and power. On that side the aristocracy of "pull"; on this the democracy of merit. . . .

The spoils politician is fond of objecting that civil service examinations do not always point out the fittest man for the place. Perhaps not always. The best marksman does not hit the bulls-eye every time; but he misses it rarely. The civil service examinations may have a small record of failures. But what the system, fairly conducted, *always* does is to snatch public office from the undemocratic control of influence and favoritism. And there is the point which stings the spoils politician.

From National Civil Service Reform League, *Proceedings* (1893).

1. What contrast did Schurz draw between jobs filled by merit and those filled by the spoils system?
2. What percentage of federal jobs were covered by the merit system in 1893?
3. What did Schurz see as the advantages of the merit system?

4 Jacob Coxey's Proposal for a Federal Public Works Program

Large numbers of factory workers lost their jobs during the depression of 1893. One proposal for dealing with the hard times that followed came from Jacob Coxey, a businessman who gained attention by leading an "army" of unemployed workers to Washington. Coxey recommended the following public works legislation, but his proposal was rejected by Congress.

Section 1. Be it enacted. . . . That the Secretary of the Treasury of the United States is hereby authorized and instructed to have engraved and printed . . . five hundred millions of dollars of treasury notes, as legal tender for all debts, public and private, said notes to be in denominations of one, two, five, and ten dollars, and to be placed in a fund to be known as the "General County Road Fund System in the United States," and to be expended solely for the said purpose.

Section 2. . . . That it shall be the duty of the Secretary of War to take charge of the construction of the General County Road System in the United States, and said construction to commence as soon as . . . said fund is available . . . when it shall be the duty of the Secretary of War to inaugurate the work and expend the sum of twenty millions of dollars per month, pro rata with the number of miles of roads in each state and territory in the United States.

Section 3. . . . That all labor other than that of the Secretary of War . . . shall be paid by the day, and that the rate be not less than $1.50 per day for common labor, and $3.50 per day for teams and labor, and that eight hours shall constitute a day's labor under the provisions of this bill.

From H. Vincent, *The Story of the Commonweal* (Chicago: W. K. Conkey Company, 1894).

1. How was Coxey's program to be financed?
2. Who would administer the program? What was to be constructed? What was the rate of pay to be?
3. What arguments might Coxey have made to support these proposals?

5 The Farmers' Plight

By the late 1800's, the economic position of American farmers had worsened. Washington Gladden, an influential Congregational minister who preached the application of religious principles to social problems, described the plight of farmers in the following magazine article in 1890.

The farmers of the United States are up in arms. They are the bone and sinew of the nation; they produce the largest share of its wealth; but they are getting, they say, the smallest share for themselves. The American farmer is steadily losing ground. His burdens are heavier every year and his gains are more meager; he is beginning to fear that he may be sinking into a servile condition. He has waited long for the redress of his grievances; he [intends] to wait no longer. Whatever he can do by social combinations or by united political action to remove the disabilities under which he is suffering, he intends to do at once and with all his might.

There is no doubt at all that the farmers of this country are tremendously in earnest just now, and they have reason to be. Beyond question they are suffering sorely. The business of farming has become, for some reasons, extremely unprofitable. With the hardest work and with the sharpest economy, the average farmer is unable to make both ends meet; every year closes with debt, and the mortgage grows till it devours the land. The Labor Bureau of Connecticut has shown, by an investigation of 693 representative farms, that the average annual reward of the farm proprietor of that state for his expenditure of muscle and brain is $181.31, while the average annual wages of the ordinary hired man is $386.36. Even if the price of board must come out of the hired man's [wages], it still leaves him a long way ahead of his employer. In Massachusetts the case is a little better; the average farmer makes $326.49, while his hired man gets $345.

In a fertile district in the state of New York, a few weeks ago, an absentee landlord advertised for a man to manage his farm. The [pay] offered was not princely. The farm manager was to have his rent, his garden, pasturage for one cow, and a salary of $250 a year for his services and those of his wife. There was a rush of applicants for the place. Who were they? Many of them were capable and intelligent farmers who had lost their own farms in the hopeless struggle with adverse conditions and who were now well content to exchange their labor and their experience against a yearly reward of $250. The instance is typical. . . .

The same story is heard in the central states. In Ohio, farms are offered for beggarly rents, and even on these favorable terms farming does not pay. Tenant farmers are throwing up their leases and moving into the cities, well content to receive as common laborers $1.25 a day, and to pay such rents and to run such risks of enforced idleness as the change involves. At the South the case is even worse. Under a heavy burden of debt the farmer struggles on from year to year, the phenomenal growth of the manufacturing interests in his section seeming to bring him but slight relief. And even in the West we find the same state of things. . . . From Kansas and Nebraska and Dakota the cry is no less loud and bitter than from Connecticut and New York and North Carolina.

From Washington Gladden, "The Embattled Farmers," *Forum*, Vol. 10 (November, 1890).

1. What difficulties, according to the Reverend Gladden, were American farmers confronting?
2. What actions were American farmers taking to overcome these problems?
3. Why does the Reverend Gladden compare the wages of hired hands to the earnings of farm owners?

6 Mary Elizabeth Lease and the Populist Movement

The farmers' struggle came to a climax with the founding of the Populist Party in 1892. One well-known Populist leader was Mary Elizabeth Lease of Kansas. In her speeches she expressed the farmers' frustrations.

Wall Street owns the country. It is no longer a government of the people, by the people, and for the people, but a government of Wall Street, by Wall Street, and for Wall Street.

The great common people of this country are slaves, and monopoly is the master. The West and South are bound and prostrate before the manufacturing East. . . .

The parties lie to us, and the political leaders mislead us. We were told two years ago to go to work and raise a big crop, that was all we needed. We went to work and plowed and planted; the rains fell, the sun shone, nature smiled, and we raised the big crop that they told us to; and what came of it? Eight-cent corn, ten-cent oats, two-cent beef, and no price at all for butter and eggs —that's what came of it.

Then the politicians said we suffered from overproduction. Overproduction, when 10,000 little children, so statistics tell us,

A farm family stands next to a steam tractor in this photograph taken at harvest time in 1883.

starve to death every year in the United States. . . .

Tariff is not the paramount question. The main question is the money question. . . . Kansas suffers from two great robbers, the Santa Fe Railroad and the loan companies. The common people are robbed to enrich their masters. . . .

We want money, land, and transportation. We want the abolition of the national banks and we want the power to make loans direct from the government. We want the accursed foreclosure system wiped out. . . .

We will stand by our homes and stay by our fireside by force if necessary, and we will not pay our debts to the loan-shark companies until the government pays its debts to us. The people are at bay; let the bloodhounds of money who have dogged us thus far beware.

From Elizabeth N. Barr, "The Populist Uprising," in W. E. Connelly, ed., *History of Kansas, State and People* (Chicago: American Historical Society, 1928), Vol. 2.

1. Who did Mary Elizabeth Lease say was to blame for the nation's problems?
2. What measures did she propose in response to the situation?

Analysis

1. Compare the views of James Bryce and Carl Schurz concerning the quality and performance of American public officials during the latter part of the nineteenth century.

2. What reasons might Congress have offered for rejecting Jacob Coxey's proposals to use public works as a means of relieving unemployment during the depression of 1893?

3. Compare the descriptions of the problems of farmers given in Selections 5 and 6. Do the measures proposed by Mary Elizabeth Lease offer a solution to the problems raised by Reverend Gladden? Explain your answer.

4. To what extent did Mary Elizabeth Lease, in her description of the difficulties facing American farmers, appeal to the emotions of her audience? Cite specific examples to support your answer.

5. The enormous economic advances that came about in the years following the Civil War brought with them new problems and challenges. Based on your reading of Chapters 3 and 4, what major social and economic problems were facing the United States at the end of the nineteenth century?

A Force in the World
1865–1900

5

Absorbed in the rebuilding of the Union and the development of vast resources within the nation, Americans paid little attention to international issues in the 1870's and 1880's. Then, as the economy of the United States expanded and as systems of transportation and communications improved, many American businesses began to look abroad for new markets and reliable sources of raw materials. To insure that the sea lanes to foreign markets and resources remained open, the American government built a modern navy to compete with the European powers.

An article printed in the *Washington Post* in 1898 reflected this growing international outlook:

> A new consciousness seems to have come upon us —the consciousness of strength—and with it a new appetite, the yearning to show our strength. . . . Ambition, interest, land hunger, pride, the mere joy of fighting, whatever it may be, we are animated by a new sensation.

An emerging sense of confidence in the ability of America to deal forcefully with the world was everywhere evident. During the Spanish-American War, the United States demonstrated the power it could exert in the international arena.

This painting commemorates the United States Navy's victory over the Spanish at the Battle of Santiago.

1 Alfred Mahan — The Importance of Sea Power

By the mid-1880's, as more Americans grew interested in expansion, a campaign in the United States for a larger merchant marine and navy began to emerge. Indeed, Captain Alfred Thayer Mahan, a lecturer at the Naval War College in Newport, Rhode Island, argued that naval power was the key element for success in international politics and military power. Some of Mahan's ideas are contained in the following passages from his book The Interest of America in Sea Power, *published in 1897.*

Whether they will or no, Americans must begin to look outward. The growing production of the country demands it. An increasing volume of public sentiment demands it. The position of the United States, between the two Old Worlds and the two great oceans, makes the same claim. . . . The tendency will be maintained and increased by the growth of the European colonies in the Pacific, by the advancing civilization of Japan, and by the rapid peopling of our Pacific states with men who have all the aggressive spirit of the advanced line of national progress. Nowhere does a vigorous foreign policy find more favor than among the people west of the Rocky Mountains. . . .

The military needs of the Pacific states, as well as their supreme importance to the whole country, are yet a matter of the future, but of a future so near that provision should begin immediately. To weight their importance, consider what influence in the Pacific would be attributed to a nation comprising only the States of Washington, Oregon, and California, when filled with such men as now people them and still are pouring in, and which controlled such maritime centers as San Francisco, Puget Sound, and the Columbia River. . . . But

such influence, to work without jar and friction, requires underlying military readiness, like the proverbial iron hand under the velvet glove. To provide this, three things are needful: First, protection of the chief harbors, by fortifications and coast-defense ships. . . . Secondly, naval force, the arm of offensive power, which alone enables a country to extend its influence outward. Thirdly, it should be an inviolable resolution of our national policy, that no foreign state should henceforth acquire a coaling [refueling] position within three thousand miles of San Francisco — and a distance which includes the Hawaiian and Galápagos islands and the coast of Central America. . . .

In conclusion, while Great Britain is undoubtedly the most formidable of our possible enemies, both by her great navy and by the strong positions she holds near our coasts, it must be added that a cordial understanding with that country is one of the first of our external interests. Both nations doubtless, and properly, seek their own advantage; but both also are controlled by a sense of law and justice, drawn from the same sources, and deep-rooted in their instincts. Whatever temporary [problems] may occur, a return to mutual standards of right will certainly follow. Formal alliance between the two is out of the question, but a cordial recognition of the similarity of character and ideas will give birth to sympathy, which in turn will facilitate a cooperation beneficial to both.

From Alfred T. Mahan, *The Interest of America in Sea Power* (Boston: Little, Brown and Company, 1897).

1. Why, according to Mahan, must Americans "begin to look outward"?
2. What recommendations did Mahan make concerning the military readiness of the Pacific states?
3. What policy did Mahan believe the United States should maintain with Great Britain? Why?

2 Joseph Pulitzer and the Cuban Rebellion

Following the outbreak of a rebellion in Cuba in 1895, many American newspapers, in an effort to boost circulation, carried exaggerated stories of atrocities that they blamed on Spanish authorities. William Randolph Hearst's New York Journal *and Joseph Pulitzer's* New York World *were two of the best known of these newspapers. The following editorial, which is typical of the journalism of the era, is from Pulitzer's* World.

Joseph Pulitzer established the Pulitzer prizes "for the encouragement of public service, public morals, American literature, and the advancement of education."

How long are the Spaniards to drench Cuba with the blood and tears of her people?

How long is the peasantry of Spain to be drafted away to Cuba to die miserably in a hopeless war, that Spanish nobles and Spanish officers may get medals and honors?

How long shall old men and women be murdered by the score, the innocent victims of Spanish rage against the patriot armies they cannot conquer?

How long shall the sound of rifles in Castle Morro [in Havana] at sunrise proclaim that bound and helpless prisoners of war have been murdered in cold blood?

How long shall Cuban women be the victims of Spanish outrages and lie sobbing and bruised in loathsome prisons?

How long shall women passengers on vessels flying the American flag be unlawfully seized and searched by brutal, jeering Spanish officers, in violation of the laws of nations and of the honor of the United States?

How long shall American citizens, arbitrarily arrested while on peaceful and legitimate errands, be immured [shut up] in foul Spanish prisons without trial? . . .

How long shall the United States sit idle and indifferent within sound and hearing of . . . murder?

How long?

From New York *World*, February 13, 1897.

1. What specific charges did the editorial make against Spain? Which of these charges involved Americans?
2. What policy regarding Spain and Cuba would the New York *World* most likely have urged the United States to follow?

3 Life in the Army

When the United States declared war against Spain in 1898, the War Department found that it was not prepared to provide American troops with proper equipment or supplies. The following passages, from a letter written by an American veteran more than fifty years after the war, suggest how this situation affected the soldiers.

It's remarkable what our bodies can stand, when I think back on our Picnic Island days in Tampa, Florida [the departure point for the American forces]—raw men in a heavy rain, a fierce storm blowing our pup tents out into the sea, no protection, our clothing soaked to the skin. Then came the issue of canned corned beef at sea that stunk so that we had to throw it into the sea—our landing at Sebony in Cuba, camping at the foot of a hill, large land crabs crawling over us at night, our long march toward San Juan Hill through jungles and swamps, joining up with the Rough Riders on Kettle Hill, heavy rains pouring down, no tents for cover, every man for himself, standing in trenches in a foot of water and mud, day and night. When off duty we kneaded our feet to get them back in shape. When the sun came out our boys would help each other by wringing out our wet clothes and blankets, quickly cutting down limbs of trees, and constructing an overhead protection by laying on palm leaves. . . .

In this painting, American soldiers are shown in combat in Cuba during the Spanish-American War.

For lack of proper nourishment men were becoming weak, ration issue consisting of a slice of sow belly, hardtack, and some grains of coffee that we had to crack between stones or rocks. Then came the issue of fleece-lined underwear in a 132° climate, and orders to burn the underwear we brought from home—result, you would see the boys in the river streams, backs covered with boils. Fleece-lined underwear and sow belly do not go in a 132° climate. Then came on malaria. It was my duty on mornings to take our sick boys to the Division hospital. There were no doctors in attendance, just a hospital corps sergeant who issued pills out of one bottle for all ailments. Sick men laying on cots, their mouths, ears, and noses full of flies. I would go over to these poor boys and with my finger clear their mouths of flies—not so much as a piece of paper to cover their faces. . . .

Colonel Teddy Roosevelt said to his daughter-in-law, Mrs. Teddy Roosevelt, Jr.: "The Spanish War was but a drop in the bucket as compared with the war following." This statement was no doubt true; the war following [First World War] had troops spread all over Europe, but the soldier had full modern equipment, was properly clothed, had healthy, nourishing food and the very best medical care, none of which was given the Spanish War soldier.

So when the war ended and we landed at Montauk, Long Island, our boys were thin, underweight, yellow as lemons, and it took us years to recover. So I say: Let us thank God for taking care of us all these years.

From letter of Jacob Judson, Captain, Company E, First Regiment, Illinois National Guard, April 15, 1956, in *The American Reader*, Paul Angle, ed. Used by permission of Rand McNally & Company.

1. What problems did American soldiers face in 1898?
2. What comparison did the writer make between supplies and equipment available to American soldiers in 1898 and in the First World War?

4 Mark Twain and the Debate over Annexation

Following the signing of the peace treaty with Spain, the United States was faced with the problem of what to do with its new possessions. Mark Twain, one of the country's leading writers and social commentators, opposed the holding of colonies. In the following essay, he satirized the desire of some Americans to bring the "light of civilization" to people living in "darkness."

Shall we go on conferring our Civilization upon the People that Sit in Darkness, or shall we give those poor things a rest? Shall we bang right ahead in our old-time, loud, pious way, and commit the new century to the game; or shall we sober up and sit down and think it over first? . . .

Extending the Blessings of Civilization to our Brother Who Sits in Darkness has been a good trade and has paid well, on the whole; and there is money in it yet, if carefully worked—but not enough, in my judgment, to make any considerable risk advisable. The People that Sit in Darkness are getting to be too scarce—too scarce and too shy. And such darkness as is now left is really of but an indifferent quality, and not dark enough for the game. The most of those People that Sit in Darkness have been furnished with more light than was good for them or profitable for us. We have been injudicious.

The Blessings-of-Civilization Trust, wisely and cautiously administered, is a Daisy. There is more money in it, more territory, more sovereignty, and other kinds of emolument [payment], than there

is in any other game that is played. But [the West] has been playing it badly of late years, and must certainly suffer by it, in my opinion. [The West] has been so eager to get every stake that appeared on the green cloth, that the People Who Sit in Darkness have noticed it—they have noticed it, and have begun to show alarm. They have become suspicious of the Blessings of Civilization.

From Mark Twain, "To the Person Sitting in Darkness," *North American Review*, Vol. 172 (February, 1901).

1. Who did Twain have in mind when he spoke of the "People that Sit in Darkness"? What did he mean by the "Blessings-of-Civilization Trust"?
2. What did Twain probably think about America's role in the war with Spain?
3. What motives might Twain have seen for American involvement in the war?

Mark Twain sought to rally public opinion against annexation of the Philippines.

5 Theodore Roosevelt on Annexation

The decision of the United States to declare war on Spain had been strongly supported by Theodore Roosevelt, who gained fame in Cuba as head of the Rough Riders. The following passages, from a speech given in 1899, suggest how Roosevelt linked his idea of "the strenuous life" with an active role for the United States in world affairs.

In speaking to you . . . I wish to preach, not the doctrine of ignoble ease, but the doctrine of the strenuous life, the life of toil and effort, of labor and strife; to preach that highest form of success which comes, not to the man who desires mere easy peace, but to the man who does not shrink from danger, from hardship, or from bitter toil, and who out of these wins the splendid ultimate triumph. . . .

If we are to be a really great people, we must strive in good faith to play a great part in the world. We cannot avoid meeting great issues. All that we can determine for ourselves is whether we shall meet them well or ill. In 1898 we could not help being brought face to face with the problem of war with Spain. All we could decide was whether we should shrink like cowards from the contest, or enter into it as beseemed a brave and high-spirited people; and, once in, whether failure or success should crown our banners. So it is now. We cannot avoid the responsibilities that confront us in Hawaii, Cuba, Puerto Rico, and the Philippines. All we can decide is whether we shall meet them in a way that will [contribute] to the national credit, or whether we shall make of our dealings with these new problems a dark and shameful page in our history. To refuse to deal with them at all merely amounts to dealing with them badly. We have a given problem to solve. If we undertake the solution, there is, of course, always danger that we may not solve it [correctly]; but to refuse to undertake the solution simply renders it certain that we cannot possibly solve it [correctly]. The timid man, the lazy man, the man who distrusts his country, the overcivilized man, who has lost the great fighting, masterful virtues, the ignorant man, and the man of dull mind, whose soul is incapable of feeling the mighty life that thrills "stern men with empires in their brains"—all these, of course, shrink from seeing the nation undertake its new duties; shrink from seeing us build a navy and an army adequate to our needs; shrink from seeing us do our share of the world's work, by bringing order out of chaos in the great, fair tropic islands from which the valor of our soldiers and sailors has driven the Spanish flag. . . .

I preach to you . . . that our country calls not for the life of ease but for the life of strenuous endeavor. The twentieth century looms before us big with the fate of many nations. If we stand idly by, if we seek merely swollen, slothful ease and ignoble peace, if we shrink from the hard contests where men must win at hazard of their lives and at the risk of all they hold dear, then the bolder and stronger peoples will pass us by, and will win for themselves the domination of the world. Let us therefore boldly face the life of strife, resolute to do our duty well. . . . Above all, let us shrink from no strife, moral or physical, within or without the nation, provided we are certain that the strife is justified, for it is only through strife, through hard and dangerous endeavor, that we shall ultimately win the goal of true national greatness.

From Theodore Roosevelt, *The Strenuous Life: Essays and Addresses* (New York: Century, 1901).

1. From what, according to Roosevelt, does the highest form of success come?
2. What role in world affairs did Roosevelt envision for the United States? What position would he most likely have taken on the question of annexation?

Analysis

1. Compare the views of Alfred T. Mahan and Theodore Roosevelt on the role of the United States in world affairs.

2. The editorial writer in the New York *World* sought to arouse American hostility against Spain. To what emotions did the writer appeal? What effect might this appeal have had on the readers of the newspaper?

3. What reasons might explain the lack of American preparation for the military campaign against Spain in Cuba?

4. Mark Twain chose to use satire, rather than direct statements, in his criticism of American policy. What reasons might he have had for using this method, and what effect might this method have had on his readers?

The Progressive Presidents
1900–1920

CHAPTER

6

The spirit of reform that had been gathering force in the United States during the late 1800's received national attention with the swearing in of Theodore Roosevelt as President in 1901. Many of the economic and political injustices being given broad public exposure by a group of dedicated writers and journalists were soon addressed by national legislation.

An article printed in *Everybody's* magazine in 1909 described the changes that had taken place in American society during Roosevelt's terms in office:

> The hour of the old-time political boss has struck. States and municipalities are insisting upon clean administrations. The people are naming their own candidates. Independent voters, and that means thinking men, are numerous. The children are having their day in court. Protection is offered to the weak against the gambling shark and the saloon. Our public resources are being conserved. New standards of life have been raised up. The money god totters. . . . It is a new era. A new world.

The progressive reform movement continued in the administration of William H. Taft. It reached its height during the first term of Woodrow Wilson.

The American artist Childe Hassam called his painting of New York City "Winter in Union Square."

1 Lincoln Steffens—The Shame of the Cities

One of the leading journalists of the Progressive Era was Lincoln Steffens. A fearless reporter, Steffens gained fame for his articles in McClure's *on misgovernment in American cities. In 1904 he brought together these articles in a book, entitled* The Shame of the Cities. *The following passages are from that work.*

Now, the typical American citizen is the businessman. The typical businessman is a bad citizen; he is busy. . . . He is too busy, he is the one that has no use and therefore no time for politics. When his neglect has permitted bad government to go so far that he can be stirred to action, he is unhappy, and he looks around for a cure that shall be quick, so that he may hurry back to the shop. Naturally, too, when he talks politics, he talks shop. His patent remedy is quack; it is business.

"Give us a businessman," he says ("like me," he means). "Let him introduce business methods into politics and government; then I shall be left alone to attend to my business."

There is hardly an office from United States senator down to alderman in any part of the country to which the businessman has not been elected; yet politics remains corrupt, government pretty bad. . . . The businessman has failed in politics as he has in citizenship. Why?

Because politics is business. That's what's the matter with it. That's what's the matter with everything—art, literature, religion, journalism, law, medicine—they're all business. . . . But don't try to reform politics with the banker, the lawyer, and the dry-goods merchant, for these are businessmen and there are two great hindrances to their achievement of reform: one is that they are different from, but no

better than, the politicians; the other is that politics is not "their line." . . .

But there is hope, not alone despair, in the commercialism of our politics. If our political leaders are to be always a lot of political merchants, they will supply any demand we may create. All we have to do is to establish a steady demand for good government. The bosses have us split up into parties. To him parties are nothing but means to his corrupt ends. He "bolts" his party, but we must not. . . . Why? Because if the honest voter cared no more for his party than the politician and the grafter, then the honest vote would govern, and that would be bad—for graft. . . . If we would leave parties to the politicians, and would vote not for the party, not even for men, but for the city, and the state, and the nation, we should rule parties, and cities, and states, and nation. If we would vote in mass on the more promising ticket, or, if the two were equally bad, would throw out the party that is in, and wait till the next election and then throw out the other party that is in—then . . . the commercial politician would feel a demand for good government and he would supply it. . . . If [bad government] would not "go," they would offer something else, and, if the demand were steady, they, being so commercial, would "deliver the goods."

But do the people want good government? Tammany [the New York political machine] says they don't. Are the people honest? Are the people better than Tammany? . . .

No, . . . the corruption that shocks us in public affairs we practice ourselves in our private concerns. There is no essential difference between the pull that gets your wife into society or your book a favorable review, and that which gets a heeler [a worker for a political machine] into office, a thief out of jail, and a rich man's son on the board of directors of a corporation; none between the corruption of a labor union, a bank, and a political machine. . . .

And it's all a moral weakness; a weakness right where we think we are strongest. Oh, we are good—on Sunday—and we are "fearfully patriotic" on the Fourth of July. But the bribe we pay to the janitor to prefer our interests to the landlord's, is the little brother of the bribe passed to the alderman to sell a city street, and the father of the air-brake stock assigned to the president of a railroad to have this life-saving invention adopted on his road. . . . We are a free and sovereign people, we govern ourselves and the government is ours. But that is the point. We are responsible, not our leaders, since we follow them. We *let* them divert our loyalty from the United States to some "party"; we *let* them boss the party and turn our municipal democracies into autocracies [governments run by one person] and our republican nation into a plutocracy [a government run by those of wealth]. We cheat our government and we let our leaders loot it, and we let them wheedle and bribe our sovereignty from us. . . .

We Americans may have failed. We may be mercenary and selfish. Democracy with us may be impossible and corruption inevitable, but these articles, if they have proved nothing else, have demonstrated beyond doubt that we can stand the truth; that there is pride in the character of American citizenship; and that this pride may be a power in this land. So this little volume, a record of shame and yet of self-respect, a disgraceful confession, yet a declaration of honor, is dedicated, in all good faith, to the accused—to all the citizens of all the cities in the United States.

From Lincoln Steffens, *The Shame of the Cities* (New York: McClure, Phillips & Company, 1904).

1. What, according to Steffens, was the reason for corruption in government?
2. What view did Steffens hold regarding loyalty to political parties? Explain.
3. What hope did Steffens see for the future?

2 Child Labor

A British reformer who moved to the United States in 1901, John Spargo became an influential muckraker. His book The Bitter Cry of the Children *(1906), passages of which follow, addressed the controversial subject of child labor.*

Work in the coal breakers is exceedingly hard and dangerous. Crouched over the chutes, the boys sit hour after hour, picking out the pieces of slate and other refuse from the coal as it rushes past to the washers. From the cramped position they have to assume, most of them become more or less deformed and bent-backed like old men. . . .

The coal is hard, and accidents to the hands, such as cut, broken, or crushed fingers, are common among the boys. Sometimes there is a worse accident: a terrified shriek is heard, and a boy is mangled and torn in the machinery, or disappears in the chute to be picked out later smothered and dead. Clouds of dust fill the breakers and are inhaled by the boys, laying the foundations for asthma and miners' consumption.

I once stood in a breaker for half an hour and tried to do the work a twelve-year-old boy was doing day after day, for ten hours at a stretch, for sixty cents a day. The gloom of the breaker appalled me. Outside the sun shone brightly, the air was [clear], and the birds sang in chorus with the trees and the rivers. Within the breaker there was blackness, clouds of deadly dust enfolded everything, the harsh, grinding roar of the machinery and the ceaseless rushing of coal through the chutes filled the ears. I tried to pick out the pieces of slate from the hurrying stream of coal, often missing them; my hands were bruised and cut in a few minutes; I was covered from head to foot with coal dust. . . .

I could not do that work and live, but there were boys of ten and twelve years of age doing it for fifty and sixty cents a day. Some of them had never been inside of a school; few of them could read a child's primer. True, some of them attended the night schools, but after working ten hours in the breaker the educational results from attending school were practically nil. . . .

From the breakers the boys graduate to the mine depths, where they become door tenders, switch boys, or mule drivers. Here, far below the surface, work is still more dangerous. At fourteen or fifteen the boys assume the same risks as the men, and are surrounded by the same perils. Nor is it in Pennsylvania only that these conditions exist. In the bituminous mines of West Virginia, boys of nine or ten are frequently employed. I met one little fellow ten years old in Mt. Carbon, W. Va., last year, who was employed as a "trap boy." Think of what it means to be a trap boy at ten years of age. It means to sit alone in a dark mine passage hour after hour, with no human soul near; to see no living creature except the mules as they pass with their loads, or a rat or two seeking to share one's meal; to stand in water or mud that covers the ankles, chilled to the marrow by the cold drafts that rush in when you open the trap door for the mules to pass through; to work for fourteen hours—waiting—opening and shutting a door—then waiting again—for sixty cents; to reach the surface when all is wrapped in the mantle of night, and to fall to the earth exhausted and have to be carried away to the nearest "shack" to be revived before it is possible to walk to the farther shack called "home."

Boys twelve years of age may be *legally* employed in the mines of West Virginia, by day or by night, and for as many hours as the employers care to make them toil or their bodies will stand the strain. Where the disregard of child life is such that this may be done openly and with legal sanc-

These boys are picking out pieces of slate from coal in a Pennsylvania mine in 1913.

tion, it is easy to believe what miners have again and again told me—that there are hundreds of little boys of nine and ten years of age employed in the coal mines of this state.

From John Spargo, *The Bitter Cry of the Children* (New York: Macmillan, 1906), pp. 163–165.

1. What accidents did children suffer in the coal mines? What other dangers were there?
2. What reforms might have been offered to correct the abuses described in this selection?

3 Carrie Chapman Catt on Women's Suffrage

The women's suffrage movement began in the middle of the nineteenth century and grew in intensity during the early 1900's. The following passages are from a speech given in 1902 by Carrie Chapman Catt, an Iowa educator and president of the National American Woman Suffrage Association.

The question of women's suffrage is a very simple one. The plea is dignified, calm, and logical. Yet, great as is the victory over conservatism which is represented in the accomplishment of male suffrage, infinitely greater will be the attainment of women's suffrage. Male suffrage exists through the surrender of many a stronghold of ancient thought.

Women's suffrage must meet precisely the same objections which have been urged against male suffrage, but in addition, it must combat prejudice, the oldest, the most unreasoning, the most stubborn of all human characteristics. Such prejudice is a pre-judgment against the rights, liberties, and opportunities of women. It is a belief, without proof, in the incapacity of women to do that which they have never done. This prejudice has been the chief hindrance in the rapid advance of the women's rights movement to its present status, and it is still a stupendous obstacle to be overcome.

Elizabeth Blackwell, the first woman licensed to practice medicine in the United States, rode in this suffragist parade in 1911.

Prejudice against women is the outgrowth of a theory practically universal throughout the world for many centuries past. It may be briefly stated as a belief that men were the units of the human race. They performed the real functions of the race; all the responsibilities and duties of working out the destiny of the race were theirs. Women were auxiliaries, or dependents, with no responsibilities of their own. In the perpetuation of the race the contribution of the mother was negative and insignificant; that of the father vital and all-important. Man was considered the real creator of the race.

Four chief causes led to the subjection of women, each the logical deduction from the theory that men were the primary units of the race—obedience, ignorance, the denial of personal liberty, and the denial of right to property and wages. These forces united in cultivating a spirit of egotism and tyranny in men and weak dependence in women. The perpetual tutelage and subjection robbed women of all freedom of thought and action, and all incentive for growth, and they logically became the inane weaklings the world would have them, and their condition strengthened the universal belief in their incapacity. This world taught woman nothing skillful and then said her work was valueless. It permitted her no opinions and said she did not know how to think. It forbade her to speak in public, and said there were no orators. It denied her the schools, and said women had no genius. It robbed her of every vestige of responsibility, and then called her weak. It taught her that every pleasure must come as a favor from men, and when to gain it she decked herself in paint and fine feathers, as she had been taught to do, it called her vain.

When at last the New Woman came, bearing the torch of truth, and with calm dignity asked a share in the world's education, opportunities, and duties, it is no wonder that man should arise to defend the woman of the past, whom he had learned to love and cherish. Her very weakness and dependence were dear to him, and he loved to think of her as the tender clinging vine, while he was the strong and sturdy oak.

The fate of the woman question turns upon the truth or falsity of the premise from which the world has reasoned throughout the ages past. Women are either inferior to men, or they are not.

The whole aim of the women's movement has been to destroy the idea that obedience is necessary to women; to train women to such self-respect that they would not grant obedience and to train men to such comprehension of equity they would not exact it. The opposition to the enfranchisement of women is the last defense of the old theory that obedience is necessary for women, because man alone is the creator of the race.

The whole effort of the women's movement has been to destroy obedience of woman in the home. That end has been very generally attained, and the average civilized woman enjoys the right of individual liberty in the home of her father, her husband, and her son. The individual woman no longer obeys the individual man. She enjoys self-government in the home and in society. The question now is, shall all women as a body obey all men as a body? Shall the woman who enjoys the right of self-government in every other department of life be permitted the right of self-government in the state? It is no more right for all men to govern all women than it was for one man to govern one woman. It is no more right for men to govern women than it was for one man to govern other men.

Adapted from Carrie Chapman Catt, *The President's Annual Message* (National American Woman Suffrage Association, 1902).

1. What did Carrie Chapman Catt see as the main reason why women were denied the vote?
2. What did she see as the effects of this on women in the past?
3. What did she say the New Woman was demanding?

4 Booker T. Washington— "Cast Down Your Bucket"

At the turn of the century, Booker T. Washington was probably the best-known black leader in the United States. He maintained that black Americans would make greater progress if they avoided protests against segregation and instead emphasized vocational education. A speech given in Atlanta, in 1895, illustrates his view.

A ship lost at sea for many days suddenly sighted a friendly vessel. From the mast of the unfortunate vessel was seen a signal, "Water, water; we die of thirst!" The answer from the friendly vessel at once came back, "Cast down your bucket where you are." [After this was repeated several times, the] captain of the distressed vessel . . . cast down his bucket, and it came up full of fresh, sparkling water from the mouth of the Amazon River. To those of my race who depend on bettering their condition in a foreign land or who underestimate the importance of cultivating friendly relations with the southern white man, who is their next-door neighbor, I would say: "Cast down your bucket where you are"—cast it down in making friends in every manly way of the people of all races by whom we are surrounded.

Cast it down in agriculture, mechanics, in commerce, in domestic service, and in the professions. And in this connection it is well to bear in mind that whatever other sins the South may be called to bear, when it comes to business, pure and simple, it is in the South that the Negro is given a man's chance in the commercial world. . . . Our greatest danger is that in the great leap from slavery to freedom we may overlook the fact that the masses of us are to live by the productions of our hands, and fail to keep in mind that we shall prosper in proportion as we learn to dignify and glorify common labor and put brains and skill into the common occupations of life. . . . No race can prosper till it learns that there is as much dignity in tilling a field as in writing a poem. It is at the bottom of life we must begin, and not at the top. Nor should we permit our grievances to overshadow our opportunities.

To those of the white race who look to the incoming of those of foreign birth and strange tongue and habits for the prosperity of the South, were I permitted I would repeat what I say to my own race, "Cast down your bucket where you are." Cast it down among the eight millions of Negroes whose habits you know, whose fidelity and love you have tested. . . . Cast down your bucket among these people who have, without strikes and labor wars, tilled your fields, cleared your forests, [built] your railroads and cities, and brought forth treasures from the bowels of the earth. . . . As we have proved our loyalty to you in the past, in nursing your children, watching by the sickbed of your mothers and fathers, and often following them with tear-dimmed eyes to their graves, so in the future, in our humble way, we shall stand by you with a devotion that no foreigner can approach, ready to lay down our lives,

In attendance at Tuskegee Institute's fifteenth anniversary celebration in 1906 were [right to left] Andrew Carnegie, Booker T. Washington, William Howard Taft, and Robert C. Ogden (a trustee).

if need be, in defense of yours . . . in a way that shall make the interests of both races one. In all things that are purely social we can be separate as the fingers, yet one as the hand in all things essential to mutual progress. . . .

The wisest among my race understand that the agitation of questions of social equality is the extremest folly, and that progress in the enjoyment of all the privileges that will come to us must be the result of severe and constant struggle rather than an artificial forcing. No race that has anything to contribute to the markets of the world is long in any degree ostracized [kept out]. It is important and right that all privileges of the law be ours, but it is vastly more important that we be prepared for the exercises of these privileges. The opportunity to earn a dollar in a factory just now is worth infinitely more than the opportunity to spend a dollar in an opera house.

From Booker T. Washington, *Up From Slavery: An Autobiography* (New York: Doubleday, Page, 1901).

1. What arguments did Washington use to support his belief that southern whites would be better off hiring black workers than immigrant workers?
2. What hope for a better economic future did this speech offer black Americans?

5 W. E. B. Du Bois—The Souls of Black Folk

One of the most outspoken critics of Booker T. Washington was historian W. E. B. Du Bois. In his book The Souls of Black Folk *(1903), Du Bois had this to say about Washington's policies.*

W. E. B. Du Bois studied in German universities and earned his Ph.D. at Harvard in 1895.

Mr. Washington represents in Negro thought the old attitude of adjustment and submission; but adjustment at such a peculiar time as to make his program unique. This is an age of unusual economic development, and Mr. Washington's program naturally takes an economic cast, becoming a gospel of Work and Money, to such an extent as apparently almost completely to overshadow the higher aims of life. . . . Moreover, this is an age when the more advanced races are coming in closer contact with the less developed races, and the race feeling is therefore intensified; and Mr. Washington's program practically accepts the alleged inferiority of the Negro races. . . .

Mr. Washington distinctly asks that black people give up, at least for the present, three things—

First, political power,

Second, insistence on civil rights,

Third, higher education of Negro youth —and concentrate all their energies on industrial education, the accumulation of wealth, and the conciliation of the South. . . . As a result of this tender of the palm-branch, what has been the return? . . .

1. The disfranchisement of the Negro.
2. The legal creation of a distant status of civil inferiority for the Negro.
3. The steady withdrawal of aid from institutions for the higher training of the Negro.

These movements are not, to be sure, direct results of Mr. Washington's teachings; but his propaganda has, without a shadow of doubt, helped their speedier accomplishment. The question then comes: Is it possible, and probable, that nine millions of men can make effective progress in economic lines if they are deprived of political rights, made a servile caste, and allowed only the most meager chance for developing their exceptional men? If history and reason give any distinct answer to these questions, it is an emphatic *No.* . . .

[Black Americans] do not expect that the free right to vote, to enjoy civic rights, and to be educated, will come in a moment; they do not expect to see the bias and prejudices of years disappear at the blast of a trumpet; but they are absolutely certain that the way for a people to gain their reasonable rights is not by voluntarily throwing them away and insisting that they do not want them; that the way for a people to gain respect is not by continually belittling and ridiculing themselves; that, on the contrary, Negroes must insist continually, in season and out of season, that voting is necessary to modern manhood, that color discrimination is barbarism, and that black boys need education as well as white boys.

From W. E. B. Du Bois, *The Souls of Black Folk* (Chicago: A. C. McClurg and Co., 1903).

1. What did Du Bois see as the major effects of Washington's policies?
2. What goals did Du Bois think black people should seek?

Analysis

1. How might American business leaders have reacted to the criticisms made by Lincoln Steffens? With what arguments might they have responded?

2. Do the writings of Lincoln Steffens and John Spargo seem sensational or slanted? Explain your answer.

3. How have the aims of the women's rights movement changed since the time of Carrie Chapman Catt? How have they remained the same?

4. Compare the goals and arguments of Booker T. Washington and W. E. B. Du Bois.

5. What evidence is there in these selections that the demand for reform was widespread in the early 1900's?

Defending Democracy
1914–1920

CHAPTER

7

In the spring of 1917, President Wilson asked Congress to declare war against Germany. Having joined the Allied cause, the United States was then faced with the challenging task of transporting troops to the battlefront in France.

Grouped together for protection against German submarines, American troop ships made their way across the Atlantic Ocean. The commander of one such convoy, Yates Sterling, wrote an account of the arrival of an American convoy at the French port of St. Nazaire:

> The populace were out in full force to welcome the troops. There was no more soul-stirring sight than those six huge ships loaded down with khaki-clad men, . . . passing each other close aboard as one after another was docked into the small harbor and berthed alongside the pier. Bands were playing "Over There," "It's a Long, Long Trail," "Keep the Home Fires Burning," and so forth. Each ship, as it entered the harbor, cheered those it passed, until there was a continuous roar of young American voices mingled with stirring music and song. They were "over there"!

In the months that followed, American soldiers took part in battles that led to the Allied victory. The United States had been thrust squarely into the forefront of world affairs.

In 1918, illustrator James Montgomery Flagg created this memorable recruiting poster for the United States Army.

I WANT YOU
FOR U.S. ARMY
NEAREST RECRUITING STATION

1 Woodrow Wilson—War Message

On April 2, 1917, President Wilson went before Congress to deliver his war message. Passages from his address follow.

I have called the Congress into extraordinary session because there are serious, very serious, choices of policy to be made, and made immediately, which it was neither right nor constitutionally permissible that I should assume the responsibility of making.

On the third of February last I officially laid before you the extraordinary announcement of the Imperial German Government that on and after the first day of February it was its purpose to put aside all restraints of law or of humanity and use its submarines to sink every vessel that sought to approach either the ports of Great Britain and Ireland or the western coasts of Europe or any of the ports controlled by the enemies of Germany within the Mediterranean. . . . The new policy has swept every restriction aside. Vessels of every kind, whatever their flag, their character, their cargo, their destination, their errand, have been ruthlessly sent to the bottom without warning and without thought of help or mercy for those on board, the vessels of friendly neutrals along with those of belligerents. Even hospital ships and ships carrying relief to the sorely bereaved and stricken people of Belgium . . . have been sunk with the same reckless lack of compassion or of principle. . . . I am not now thinking of the loss of property involved. . . . Property can be paid for; the lives of peaceful and innocent people cannot be. The present German submarine warfare against commerce is a warfare against mankind.

It is a war against all nations. American ships have been sunk, American lives taken, in ways which it has stirred us very deeply to learn of, but the ships and people of other neutral and friendly nations have been sunk and overwhelmed in the waters

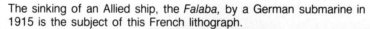
The sinking of an Allied ship, the *Falaba*, by a German submarine in 1915 is the subject of this French lithograph.

in the same way. There has been no discrimination. The challenge is to all mankind. . . .

With a profound sense of the solemn and even tragical character of the step I am taking and of the grave responsibilities which it involves, but in unhesitating obedience to what I deem my constitutional duty, I advise that the Congress declare the recent course of the Imperial German Government to be in fact nothing less than war against the government and people of the United States; that it formally accept the status of belligerent which has thus been thrust upon it; and that it take immediate steps not only to put the country in a more thorough state of defense but also to exert all its power and employ all its resources to bring the government of the German Empire to terms and end the war.

What this will involve is clear. It will involve the utmost practicable cooperation in counsel and action with the governments now at war with Germany, and . . . the extension to those governments of the most liberal financial credits, in order that our resources may so far as possible be added to theirs. It will involve the organization and mobilization of all the material resources of the country to supply the materials of war and serve the incidental needs of the nation. . . . It will involve the immediate full equipment of the navy. . . . It will involve the immediate addition to the armed forces of the United States . . . of at least five hundred thousand men, who should, in my opinion, be chosen upon the principle of universal liability to service, and also the authorization of subsequent additional increments of equal force as soon as they may be needed and can be handled in training. . . .

While we do these things, these deeply momentous things, let us be very clear, and make very clear to all the world what our motives and our objects are. . . . Our object . . . is to vindicate the principles of peace and justice in the life of the world as against selfish and autocratic power. . . . Neutrality is no longer feasible or desirable where the peace of the world is involved and the freedom of its peoples, and the menace to that peace and freedom lies in the existence of autocratic governments backed by organized force which is controlled wholly by their will, not by the will of their people. We have seen the last of neutrality in such circumstances. We are at the beginning of an age in which it will be insisted that the same standards of conduct and of responsibility for wrong done shall be observed among nations and their governments that are observed among the individual citizens of civilized states. . . .

It is a distressing and oppressive duty, Gentlemen of the Congress, which I have performed in thus addressing you. There are, it may be, many months of fiery trial and sacrifice ahead of us. It is a fearful thing to lead this great peaceful people into war, into the most terrible and disastrous of all wars, civilization itself seeming to be in the balance. But the right is more precious than peace, and we shall fight for the things which we have always carried nearest our hearts—for democracy, for the right of those who submit to authority to have a voice in their own governments, for the rights and liberties of small nations, for a universal dominion of right by such a concert of free peoples as shall bring peace and safety to all nations and make the world itself at last free. To such a task we can dedicate our lives and our fortunes, everything that we are and everything that we have, with the pride of those who know that the day has come when America is privileged to spend her blood and her might for the principles that gave her birth and happiness and the peace which she has treasured. God helping her, she can do no other.

From Woodrow Wilson, Message to Congress, *Congressional Record*, 65th Congress, 1st Session (April 2, 1917).

1. What German policy led to Wilson's war message?
2. What goals did Wilson say the United States would fight for in the struggle against Germany?

2 George Norris—Opposition to the War

Four days after Wilson's speech, Congress declared war on Germany. Six senators and fifty representatives, however, voted against the war resolution. Among them was George Norris, an influential Republican senator from Nebraska. Norris described his opposition in a Senate speech.

The resolution now before the Senate is a declaration of war. Before taking this momentous step, . . . we ought to pause and calmly and judiciously consider the terrible consequences of the step we are about to take. . . .

No close student of recent history will deny that both Great Britain and Germany have, on numerous occasions since the beginning of the war, flagrantly violated in the most serious manner the rights of neutral vessels and neutral nations. . . .

[We] have the two declarations of the two governments, each declaring a military zone and warning neutral shipping from going into the prohibited area. England sought to make her order effective by the use of submerged mines. Germany sought to make her order effective by the use of submarines. Both of these orders were illegal and contrary to all international law as well as the principles of humanity. . . . In carrying out these two policies, both Great Britain and Germany have sunk American ships and destroyed American lives without provocation and without notice. There have been more ships sunk and more American lives lost from the action of submarines than from English mines . . . for the simple reason that we finally acquiesced in the British war zone and kept our ships out of it, while in the German war zone we have refused to recognize its legality and have not kept either our ships or our citizens out of its area. . . .

There are a great many American citizens who feel that we owe it as a duty to humanity to take part in this war. Many instances of cruelty and inhumanity can be found on both sides. Men are often biased in their judgment on account of their sympathy and interests. To my mind, what we ought to have maintained from the beginning was the strictest neutrality. If we had done this I do not believe we would have been on the verge of war at the present time. We had a right as a nation, if we desired, to cease at any time to be neutral. We had a technical right to respect the English war zone and to disregard the German war zone, but we could not do that and be neutral. I have no quarrel to find with the man who does not desire our country to remain neutral. While many such people are moved by selfish motives and hopes of gain, I have no doubt but that in a great many instances . . . there are many honest, patriotic citizens who think we ought to engage in this war and who are behind the President in his demand that we should declare war against Germany. I think such people err in judgment and to a great extent have been misled as to the real history and the true facts by the almost unanimous demand of the great combination of wealth that has a direct financial interest in our participation in the war. . . .

To whom does war bring prosperity? . . . War brings prosperity to the stock gambler on Wall Street—to those who are already in possession of more wealth than can be realized or enjoyed. . . .

Their object in having war and in preparing for war is to make money. Human suffering and the sacrifice of human life are necessary, but Wall Street considers only the dollars and the cents. The men who do the fighting, the people who make the sacrifices, are the ones who will not be counted in the measure of this great prosperity. . . .

We are taking a step today that is fraught with untold danger. We are going into war upon the command of gold. We are going to run the risk of sacrificing millions of our countrymen's lives in order that other countrymen may coin their lifeblood into money.... By our act we will make millions of our countrymen suffer, and the consequences of it may well be that millions of our brethren must shed their lifeblood, millions of broken-hearted women must weep, millions of children must suffer with cold, and millions of babes must die from hunger, and all because we want to preserve the commercial right of American citizens to deliver munitions of war to belligerent nations.

From George Norris, Speech to Congress, *Congressional Record*, 65th Congress, 1st Session (April 4, 1917).

1. Why did Norris believe that Great Britain was as guilty as Germany in violating America's neutral rights?
2. Who did Norris think would benefit most from American entry into the war?

3 Conservation on the Home Front

Once the United States had entered the war, the country began working at top speed to supply the needs of its armed forces as well as those of the other Allied powers. The Food Administration, a government agency set up to insure the most efficient use of food, took the following approach to conservation.

The United States [has] always been the greatest granary, food store, and butcher shop in the world, and our resources have by no means reached the limit of our development. Food ... sufficient for our mighty fighting armies—our own and our allies— for the working men and women behind the trench lines, for the old people, women and children, must be supplied if the war is to be won, and we can supply it.

Millions of men in Europe have been withdrawn from farm and field to fight, and many thousands have been sent into factories to equip the fighters with munitions of war. This means that less food is produced in the countries of our allies. Moreover, the hard work of war activities has meant an increased demand upon food supply. The decreased food production and increased food demand have made a yawning chasm in Europe which only America can bridge....

During World War I, government posters encouraged citizens to support the American war effort by conserving food.

France, Great Britain, Italy, and Belgium need for their normal use six million bushels of wheat more than they can produce. The Central Powers control the grain available in Russia, Bulgaria, and Rumania,

499

so that our allies cannot draw upon these supplies. Australia and India are practically cut off. . . . The South American crop was a failure, and the new harvest cannot reach Europe until next spring.

In short, the Allies need 577,000,000 bushels of wheat and we have a surplus of 208,000,000 bushels. Out of this surplus a certain amount must be kept for friendly neutrals. Therefore, if we continue to consume as much wheat as usual, there will be a deficit in round figures of 400,000,000 bushels. . . .

Meat is another food especially needed that we must export in larger quantity. The people who are fighting and making war supplies need more meat than they would in peace times. But the reproduction of cattle, sheep, and hogs has lessened by 33,000,000 in Europe, and they have been compelled to "eat into the herd" to an alarming extent. Also an extra demand for wool and leather clothing for soldiers has meant a decrease of animals.

From the 1st of July, 1915, to the 30th of June, 1916, we exported more than 1,500,000,000 pounds of animal products and fats. We are selling faster than we can produce them. Of course this condition calls for increased production, but it also means that for the present conservation is of the gravest importance. . . .

Another necessary food staple that our allies must have is sugar. They formerly got it from Russia, Germany, Austria, and Java. Now they are dependent upon us and the sources which supply us.

One other aspect of food conservation as a war measure should be mentioned. Wars are paid for out of the people's pocket. If we wish to avoid financial troubles we ought to carry on this war to a great extent paying "as we go." If we reduce the waste and unwise use of food by only six cents a day for each person in our population we shall have saved more than two billion dollars a year.

Each one of us wants to help, but sometimes we feel stunned by these huge sums and amounts. A million dollars, a million bushels! We gasp, "But how can I do anything? I am only one, and I have no millions to give or save." Then is the time to recall the old rhyme about the "little drops of water, little grains of sand." These vast amounts are composed of shovelfuls, basketfuls, cupfuls, teaspoonfuls. Just remember that if each individual saves one pound of wheat flour a week and six cents' worth of meat, fats, and sugar a day, it will mean enough to win through. . . .

Every single person in this democracy has the opportunity of the centuries to take part in the greatest adventure for democracy ever known. Democracy is worth it. Your right to your own life, to liberty, and to the pursuit of happiness is worth your service, your cooperation, your devotion.

From "America's Food Problem," *Independent*, Vol. 92 (1917).

1. What were the chief food products needed by the Allies?
2. How much food was each citizen asked to conserve?

4 The Committee on Public Information

The Committee on Public Information was set up to mobilize public support for the war effort. The following passages appeared in a pamphlet published by that agency.

Now let us picture what a sudden invasion of the United States by these Germans would mean: sudden, because their settled way is always to attack suddenly.

First, they set themselves to capture New York City. While their fleet blockades the harbor and shells the city and the forts from far at sea, their troops land somewhere near and advance toward the city in order to cut its rail communications, starve it into surrender, and then plunder it.

One body of from 50,000 to 100,000 men lands, let us suppose, at Barnegat Bay, New Jersey, and advances without meeting resistance, for the brave but small American army is scattered elsewhere. They pass through Lakewood, a station on the Central Railroad of New Jersey. They first demand wine for the officers and beer for the men. Angered to find that an American town does not contain large quantities of either, they pillage and burn the post office and most of the hotels and stores. Then they demand $1,000,000 from the residents. One feeble old woman tries to conceal $20 which she has been hoarding in her desk drawer; she is taken out and hanged (to save a cartridge). Some of the teachers in two district schools meet a fate which makes them envy her. The Catholic priest and Methodist minister are thrown into a pig-sty, while the German soldiers look on and laugh. Some of the officers quarter themselves in a handsome house on the edge of town, insult the ladies of the family, and destroy and defile the contents of the house.

By this time some of the soldiers have managed to get drunk; one of them discharges his gun accidentally, the cry goes up that the residents are firing on the troops, and then [fighting] breaks loose. Robbery, murder, and outrage run riot. Fifty leading citizens are lined up against the First National Bank Building and shot. Most of the town and the beautiful pine-woods are burned, and then the troops move on to treat New Brunswick in the same way—if they get there.

This is not just a snappy story. It is not fancy. The general plan of campaign against America has been announced repeatedly by German military men. *And every horrible detail is just what the German troops have done in Belgium and France.*

From J. S. P. Tatlock, *Why America Fights Germany*, War Information Series No. 15, Cantonment Edition (1918).

1. What image of the German troops was given in this pamphlet?
2. How did the pamphlet appeal to emotion? Cite specific examples to support your answer.

5 "Lafayette, We Are Here"

In June, 1917, the vanguard of the American Expeditionary Force began arriving in France. A correspondent for the Chicago Tribune *wrote this highly dramatic account of the reception in Paris accorded General John J. Pershing and his staff.*

At the conclusion of the train-side greetings and introductions, Marshal Joffre [French commander-in-chief from 1911 to 1916] and General Pershing walked down the platform together. . . .

A minute later, there was a terrific roar from beyond the walls of the station. The crowds outside had heard the cheering within. They took it up with thousands of throats. They made their welcome a ringing one. Paris took Pershing by storm. . . .

General Pershing and M. Painlevé, Minister of War, took seats in a large automobile. . . . The procession started to the accompaniment of martial music by massed military bands in the courtyard of the station.

The crowds overflowed the sidewalks. They extended from the building walls out beyond the curbs and into the streets. . . . From the crowded balconies and windows overlooking the route, women and children tossed down showers of flowers and bits of colored paper. . . .

President Wilson selected Major General John J. Pershing, shown here arriving in France, to command the American Expeditionary Force in Europe.

Old grey-haired fathers of French fighting men bared their heads and with tears streaming down their cheeks shouted greetings to the tall, thin, grey-moustached American commander who was leading new armies to the support of their sons. Women heaped armfuls of roses into the General's car and into the cars of other American officers that followed him. . . .

Through such scenes as these, the procession reached the great Place de la Concorde. In this wide, paved, open space an enormous crowd had assembled. As the autos appeared the cheering, the flower throwing, the tumultuous kiss-blowing began. It increased in intensity as the motors stopped in front of the Hotel Crillon into which General Pershing disappeared, followed by his staff. . . .

General Pershing stepped forth on the balcony. . . . A soft breeze . . . touched the cluster of flags on the General's right and . . . selected one flag.

The breeze tenderly caught the folds of this flag and wafted them across the balcony on which the General bowed. He saw and recognized that flag. He extended his hand, caught the flag in his fingers and pressed it to his lips. All France and all America represented in that vast throng that day cheered to the mighty echo when Pershing kissed the [flag] of France.

It was a tremendous, unforgettable incident. It was exceeded by no other incident during those days of receptions and ceremonies, except one. . . . This happened several days after the demonstration in the Place de la Concorde.

On that day of bright sunshine, General Pershing and a small party of officers, French and American, walked through the gravel paths of Picpus Cemetery in the sub-

urbs of Paris, where the bodies of hundreds of those who made the history of France are buried.

Several French women in deep mourning curtsied as General Pershing passed. His party stopped in front of two marble slabs that lay side by side at the foot of a granite monument. . . .

General Pershing advanced to the tomb and placed upon the marble slab an enormous wreath of pink and white roses. Then he stepped back. He removed his cap and held it in both hands in front of him. The bright sunlight shone down on his silvery grey hair. Looking down at the grave, he spoke in a quiet, impressive tone four simple, all-meaning words:

"Lafayette, we are here."

From Floyd Gibbons, *And They Thought We Wouldn't Fight*. (New York: Doran & Company, 1918).

---

1. How did the people of Paris greet General Pershing and his staff?
2. What did Pershing mean by his statement, "Lafayette, we are here"?

Analysis

1. Woodrow Wilson argued that American involvement in World War I was based on a need to defend key principles and rights. What principles and rights did he have in mind? Support your answer with statements from this chapter.

2. Why did the United States find it so difficult to remain neutral even though it was thousands of miles from the warring European nations?

3. What was the aim of the pamphlet issued by the Committee on Public Information? How effective was the pamphlet in achieving that aim?

4. How do you explain the reaction of the people of France to the arriving American forces in 1917?

A Roaring Decade
1919–1929

CHAPTER

8

The prosperity that swept the United States in the 1920's brought a better life to most Americans. Improved technology and innovations in production provided an abundance of consumer goods.

The new affluence came under the critical examination of America's leading literary figures. Labeled the Lost Generation, these writers and poets wrote about the disillusionment and discontent that existed beneath the prosperous exterior of American society.

One of the most celebrated of the young writers was F. Scott Fitzgerald. In his essay *Commentary on New York, 1926*, Fitzgerald depicted the mood of the mid-1920's:

> The restlessness approached hysteria. The parties were bigger. The pace faster, the shows broader, the buildings were higher, . . . but all these benefits did not really bring about much delight. Young people wore out early—they were harder and languid at twenty-one. . . . The city was bloated, glutted, stupid with cake and circuses, and a new expression 'Oh yeah?' summed up all the enthusiasm evoked by the announcement of the last super-skyscrapers.

Most people did not see the American scene as Fitzgerald did. As the decade progressed, the pursuit of quick wealth and good times seemed increasingly important to the American public.

American illustrator and cartoonist John Held, Jr., poked fun at American college students of the 1920's in this cover for *Life* magazine.

1 The Business of America Is Business

Throughout the 1920's, business activity and profits increased, and the incomes of many people rose. Most Americans looked to business to provide national direction. Nowhere was the faith in American business better expressed than in the following magazine article.

What is the finest game? Business. The soundest science? Business. The truest art? Business. The fullest education? Business. The fairest opportunity? Business. The cleanest philanthropy? Business. The sanest religion? Business.

You may not agree. That is because you judge business by the crude, mean, stupid, false imitation of business that happens to be located near you.

The finest game is business. The rewards are for everybody, and all can win. There are no favorites—Providence always crowns the career of the man who is worthy. And in this game there is no "luck"—you have the fun of taking chances but the sobriety of guaranteeing certainties. The speed and size of your winnings are for you alone to determine; you needn't wait for the other fellow in the game—it is always your move. . . . The great sportsmen of the world are the great businessmen.

The soundest science is business. All investigation is reduced to action, and by action proved or disproved. . . . Hearts as well as minds are open to the truth. Capital is furnished for the researches of "pure science"; yet pure science is not regarded pure until practical. Competent scientists are suitably rewarded. . . .

The truest art is business. The art is so fine, so exquisite, that you do not think of it as art. Language, color, form, line, music, drama, discovery, adventure—all the components of art must be used in business to make it of superior character.

The fullest education is business. A proper blend of study, work, and life is essential to advancement. The whole man is educated. Human nature itself is the open book that all businessmen study; and the mastery of a page of this educates you more than the memorizing of a dusty tome [book] from a library shelf. In the school of business, moreover, you teach yourself and learn most from your own mistakes. What you learn here, you live out, the only real test.

The fairest opportunity is business. You can find more, better, quicker chances to get ahead in a large business house than anywhere else on earth. The biographies of champion businessmen show how they climbed, and how you can climb. Recognition of better work, of keener and quicker thought, of deeper and finer feeling, is gladly offered by the men higher up, with early promotion the rule for the man who justifies it. There is, and can be, no such thing as buried talent in a modern business organization.

The cleanest philanthropy is business. By "clean" philanthropy I mean that [which is] devoid of graft, inefficiency, and professionalism. . . . Savings and loan funds; pension and insurance provisions; health precautions, instructions, and safeguards; medical attention and hospital care; libraries, lectures, and classes; musical, athletic, and social features of all kinds; recreational facilities and financial opportunities—these types of "charitable institutions" for employees add to the worker's self-respect, self-knowledge, and self-improvement by making him an active partner in the welfare program, a producer of benefits for his employer and associates quite as much as a recipient of bounty from the company. . . .

The sanest religion is business. Any relationship that forces a man to follow the Golden Rule rightfully belongs amid the ceremonials of the church. A great business enterprise includes and presupposes this relationship. . . . I would make every business house a consultation bureau for the guidance of the church whose members were employees of the house.

I am aware that some of the preceding statements will be challenged by many readers. I should not myself have made them, or believed them, twenty years ago. . . . A thorough knowledge of business has implanted a deep respect for business and real businessmen.

From Edward E. Purinton, "Big Ideas from Big Business," *Independent*, April 16, 1921.

1. According to the author, why was business the best source of opportunity?
2. How did he say business acted as a philanthropy?
3. Why did he believe business provided a more complete education than mere schooling?

2 Marcus Garvey—A Free Africa for Africans

During the 1920's, most black Americans hoped to win equal rights through legal action and through enlightened public opinion. Marcus Garvey attracted widespread support, however, for his "back-to-Africa" movement.

As far as Negroes are concerned, in America we have the problem of lynching, peonage, and disfranchisement.

In the West Indies, and South and Central America, we have the problem of peonage, serfdom, and industrial and political inequality.

In Africa we have, not only peonage and serfdom, but outright slavery, racial exploitation, and alien political monopoly.

We cannot allow a continuation of these crimes against our race. As four hundred million men, women, and children, worthy of the existence given us by the Divine Creator, we are determined to solve our own problem, by redeeming our Motherland Africa from the hands of alien exploiters and found there a government, a nation of our own, strong enough to lend protection to the members of our race scattered all over the world, and to compel the respect of the nations and races of the earth.

Do they lynch Englishmen, Frenchmen, Germans, or Japanese? No. And why? Because these people are represented by great governments, mighty nations and empires, strongly organized. Yes, and ever ready to shed the last drop of blood and spend the last penny of the national treasury to protect the honor and integrity of a citizen outraged anywhere.

Until the Negro reaches this point of national independence, all he does as a race will count for naught, because the prejudice that will stand out against him even with his ballot in his hand, with his industrial progress to show, will be of such an overwhelming nature as to perpetuate mob violence and mob rule, from which he will suffer, and which he will not be able to stop with his industrial wealth and with his ballot.

You may argue that he can use his industrial wealth and his ballot to force the government to recognize him, but he must understand that the government is the people. That the majority of the people dictate the policy of governments, and if the majority are against a measure, a thing, or a race, then the government is [helpless] to protect that measure, thing, or race.

If the Negro were to live in this Western Hemisphere for another five hundred years he would still be outnumbered by other races who are prejudiced against him. He cannot resort to the government for protection, for government will be in the hands of the majority of the people who are prejudiced against him; hence for the Negro to depend on the ballot and his industrial progress alone will be hopeless as it does not help him when he is lynched, burned . . . and segregated. The future of the Negro, therefore, outside of Africa, spells ruin and disaster.

From Amy Jacques-Garvey, ed., *Philosophy and Opinions of Marcus Garvey* (New York: Universal, 1925). Reprinted by permission of the publishers, Frank Cass and Co. Limited, London.

1. What problems did Marcus Garvey say that blacks faced throughout the world?
2. Why did he think the future for his race lay in Africa?

3 How to Quench Flaming Youth

Throughout the 1920's, much concern was voiced about the much-discussed changes in American morality and behavior. The following article, published in the Literary Digest *in 1922, reported on a program designed to improve the situation.*

Sensational criticism of our young people has been reaching us from time to time from the churches, the colleges, and numerous scandalized members of the younger generation itself. If the newspapers are less outspoken than a year ago, when the *Digest* investigated these matters by questionnaire, the change appears to be not so much a result of improvement in our young people as of indifference toward conditions that have lost their "news punch." To many . . . this indifference is alarming, as it seems to indicate that we are acquiescing in what such observers call a moral and spiritual revolution. . . .

Perhaps the crux of the question may be stated in this way: Is society, especially the younger part of it, undergoing a revolution in morals, in manners, or both?

In so broad and diverse a land as America, conditions, of course, are not everywhere the same, and the replies fall naturally into two classes, those revealing conditions that are deplorable, and those which show that the young folks are returning to normalcy. . . .

In view of [this], one asks, not unnaturally, "What are we going to do about it?" The questionnaire [of last year] has brought in a uniform array of answers. While many of them emphasize the need for a revival of old-fashioned religious instruction and many more demand a reform of the movies and of current fiction, an overwhelming majority declare that improvement can come only from influences brought to bear in the home. If girls dress indecently, dance shockingly, go traveling around the country at night in chaperonless automobiles, . . . and talk freely of things they ought to leave unmentioned, our correspondents ask, "Where are their mothers?" If boys are wild, where are their fathers? All through the mass of replies from horrified onlookers runs this censure of the American home. The great need, we are told, is a reassertion of parental authority. . . .

In the meantime, members of the Parents League of Brooklyn have decided not only that conditions are capable of improvement but also that a certain set of [rules] may help in the process. . . .

1. Hours for evening parties are limited to 8:30 to 12. It's curfew after midnight.

2. Parties are to be held only on Friday and Saturday nights.

3. Simple, refined clothes are to be worn at all times.

4. Chaperons must be present at all parties.

5. Chaperons will accompany the girls home.

6. Censorship over the plays and movies to be attended.

7. Improper dancing forbidden.

8. No refreshments served after dances.

9. Not more than one party to be attended on the same evening.

Here are the rules which the smaller boys and girls, those of primary school age, must observe:

1. Entertain in small groups.

2. Serve very simple refreshments at parties.

3. All games must be supervised.

4. Use simple favors and no prizes.

5. Parties must end at 8:30 P.M.

6. Simple afternoon dress is to be worn on all occasions.

7. No movies or theaters, except those recommended by the school or investigated and approved by parents.

From ''The Case Against the Younger Generation,'' *Literary Digest* (June 17, 1922).

1. According to the *Literary Digest*, what did most people see as the reason for the change in behavior of American youth?
2. What solution did the Parents League of Brooklyn propose? How might young people have responded?

This cartoon sketch shows a young woman of the 1920's dressed in the ''flapper'' style.

4 Charles Lindbergh's Triumph

Charles Lindbergh captured the imagination of the American people when he flew nonstop from New York to Paris. The public response to Lindbergh's solo flight is analyzed in the following selection.

No sooner had the word been flashed along the wires that Lindbergh had started than the whole population of the country became united in the exaltation of a common emotion. Young and old, rich and poor, farmer and stockbroker, fundamentalist and skeptic, highbrow and lowbrow, all with one accord fastened their hopes upon the young man in the *Spirit of St. Louis*. To give a single instance of the intensity of their mood: at the Yankee Stadium in New York, where the Maloney-Sharkey fight was held on the evening of the 20th, forty thousand hard-boiled boxing fans rose as one man and stood with bared heads in impressive silence when the announcer asked them to pray for Lindbergh. The next day came the successive reports of Lindbergh's success— he had reached the Irish coast, he was crossing over England, he was over the Channel, he had landed at Le Bourget to be enthusiastically mobbed by a vast crowd of Frenchmen—and the American people went almost mad with joy and relief. And when the reports of Lindbergh's first few days in Paris showed that he was behaving with charming modesty and courtesy, millions of his countrymen took him to their hearts as they had taken no other human being in living memory. . . .

Upon his return to the United States, a single Sunday issue of a single paper contained one hundred columns of text and pictures devoted to him. No one appeared to question the fitness of President Coolidge's action in sending a cruiser of the United States Navy to bring this young private citizen and his plane back from France. . . .

Lindbergh was commissioned Colonel, and received the Distinguished Flying Cross, the Congressional Medal of Honor, and so many foreign decorations and honorary memberships that to repeat the list would be a weary task. . . .

To appreciate how extraordinary was this outpouring of admiration and love— for the word love is hardly too strong—one must remind oneself of two or three facts.

Lindbergh's flight was not the first crossing of the Atlantic by air. . . . The novelty of Lindbergh's flight lay only in the fact that he went all the way from New York to Paris instead of jumping off from Newfoundland, that he reached his precise objective, and that he went alone.

Furthermore, there was little practical advantage in such an exploit. It brought about a boom in aviation, to be sure, but a not altogether healthy one, and it led many a flyer to hop off blindly for foreign shores in emulation of Lindbergh and be drowned. Looking back on the event after a lapse of years, and stripping it of its emotional connotations, one sees it simply as a daring stunt flight—the longest trip up to that time—by a man who did not claim to be anything but a stunt flyer. Why, then, this idolization of Lindbergh?

The explanation is simple. A disillusioned nation fed on cheap heroics and scandal and crime was revolting against the low estimate of human nature which it had allowed itself to entertain. For years the American people had been spiritually starved. They had seen their early ideals and illusions and hopes one by one worn away by the corrosive influence of events and ideas—by the disappointing aftermath of the war, by scientific doctrines and psychological theories which undermined their religion and ridiculed their sentimental notions, by the spectacle of graft in politics and crime in the city streets, and finally by their recent newspaper diet of smut and murder. Romance, chivalry, and self-dedi-

Charles Lindbergh became an American hero when he flew his plane, *The Spirit of St. Louis*, nonstop from New York to Paris.

cation had been debunked. . . . There was the god of business to worship—but a suspicion lingered that he was made of brass. Ballyhoo had given the public contemporary heroes to bow down before—but these contemporary heroes, with their fat profits from moving-picture contracts and ghost-written syndicated articles, were not wholly convincing. Something that people needed, if they were to live at peace with themselves and with the world, was missing from their lives. And all at once Lindbergh provided it. Romance, chivalry, self-dedication—here they were. . . . Lindbergh did not accept the moving-picture offers that came his way, he did not sell testimonials, did not boast, did not get himself involved in scandal, conducted himself with unerring tact—and [in addition] was handsome and brave. . . .

Pretty good, one reflects, for a stunt flyer. But also, one must add, pretty good for the American people. They had shown that they had better taste in heroes than anyone would have dared to predict during the years which immediately preceded the 20th of May, 1927.

1. How did the public react to the news of Lindbergh's flight? To the news of his arrival in Paris?
2. Why, if Lindbergh had only made a "daring stunt flight," was he welcomed home so enthusiastically by the American people?

5 Herbert Hoover—Rugged Individualism

In his 1928 campaign for President, Herbert Hoover stressed the success of the Republicans in leading the country throughout the 1920's. Much of that success was due, he believed, to his party's refusal to allow government to interfere with the free enterprise system. In the final speech of his campaign, portions of which follow, he urged the voters not to abandon that principle.

The campaign now draws near a close. The platforms of the two parties defining principles and offering solutions of various national problems have been presented and are being earnestly considered by our people. . . .

During the war we necessarily turned to the government to solve every difficult economic problem. The government having absorbed every energy of our people for war, there was no other solution. . . .

When the war closed, the most vital of all issues both in our own country and throughout the world was whether governments should continue their wartime ownership and operation of many instruments of production and distribution. We were challenged with a peacetime choice between the American system of rugged individualism and a European philosophy of diametrically opposed doctrines—doctrines of paternalism and state socialism. The acceptance of these ideas would have meant the destruction of self-government through centralization of government. It would have meant the undermining of the individual initiative and enterprise through which our people have grown to unparalleled greatness. . . .

There has been revived in this campaign, however, a series of proposals which, if adopted, would be a long step toward the

Herbert Hoover led the Republicans to a substantial victory in the election of 1928.

abandonment of our American system and a surrender to the destructive operation of governmental conduct of commercial business. Because the country is faced with difficulty and doubt over certain national problems—that is, prohibition, farm relief, and electrical power—our opponents propose that we must thrust government a long way into the businesses which give rise to these problems. . . .

There is, therefore, submitted to the American people a question of fundamental principle. That is: shall we depart from the principles of our American political and economic system, upon which we have advanced beyond all the rest of the world, in order to adopt methods based on principles destructive of its very foundations? . . .

By adherence to the principles of decentralized self-government, ordered liberty, equal opportunity, and freedom to the individual, our American experiment in human welfare has yielded a degree of well-being unparalleled in all the world. It has come nearer to the abolition of pov-

erty, to the abolition of fear of want, than humanity has ever reached before. Progress of the past seven years is proof of it. This alone furnishes the answer to our opponents, who ask us to introduce destructive elements into the system by which this has been accomplished. . . .

And I again repeat that the departure from our American system by injecting principles destructive to it which our opponents propose, will jeopardize the very liberty and freedom of our people, and will destroy equality of opportunity not alone to ourselves but to our children.

From *The New Day: Campaign Speeches of Herbert Hoover, 1928* (Stanford, California: Stanford University Press, 1928).

1. What did Hoover view as the reasons for America's prosperity?
2. What changes in the American system did he believe were being suggested by his political opponents?
3. What did he say the effects of this would be?

Analysis

1. In 1920, Warren G. Harding said, "What we want in America is less government in business and more business in government." How is that view reflected in the selections in this chapter?

2. How might Booker T. Washington have replied to Marcus Garvey's call for the establishment of black nations in Africa? Use examples from Garvey's statement in this chapter and from Washington's speech in Chapter 6 to support your answer.

3. In what ways are the concerns about youth expressed in the *Literary Digest* similar to present-day concerns? In what ways are they different?

4. What factors help to explain Charles Lindbergh's status as a hero? Is it possible for a similar hero to arise today? Explain.

Fashioning the New Deal
1929–1940

CHAPTER

9

On October 29, 1929, a sharp decline in the stock market marked the end of the speculation that had inflated stock prices in the late 1920's. Frederick Lewis Allen, in a popular book about the decade, described anxious stockholders gathering in stockbrokers' offices during the crash:

> At ten-minute intervals the bond ticker over in the corner would hammer off a list of selected prices direct from the floor of the stock exchange. A broker's clerk would grab the uncoiling sheet of paper and . . . read the figures aloud in a mumbling expressionless monotone to the white-faced men who occupied every seat on the floor. . . .
>
> In that broker's office one saw men looking defeat in the face. One of them was slowly walking up and down, mechanically tearing a piece of paper into tiny and still tinier fragments. . . . And still another was sitting motionless, as if stunned, his eyes fixed blindly on the moving figures on the screen, those innocent-looking figures that meant the smash-up of the hope of years.

Bankruptcies, bank closings, and factory shutdowns followed, putting people out of work across the United States. The Great Depression affected the lives of all Americans and prompted President Franklin Roosevelt to offer bold measures to put the country on the road to recovery.

American artist Ben Shahn's paintings, which reflected his concern for social and political justice, include this poster entitled "Years of Dust."

RESETTLEMENT ADMINISTRATION
Rescues Victims
Restores Land to Proper Use

1 The Impact of Unemployment

On July 21, 1932, as the economic crisis deepened, Congress passed the Emergency Relief Act. Recommended by President Hoover, this measure provided $300 million to states whose relief funds were exhausted. Fortune magazine, in an article describing the hardships caused by unemployment, examined the significance of this shift in government policy.

Dull mornings last winter the sheriff of Miami, Florida, used to fill a truck with homeless men and run them up to the county line. Where the sheriff of Fort Lauderdale used to meet them and load them into a second truck and run them up to *his* county line. Where the sheriff of Saint Lucie's would meet them and load them into a third truck and run them up to *his* county line. Where the sheriff of Brevard County would *not* meet them. And whence they would trickle back down the roads to Miami. To repeat. . . .

That was last winter.

Next winter there will be no truck. And there will be no truck, not because the transients will have disappeared from Miami . . . [but] because the sheriff of Miami, like the President of the U.S., will next winter think of transients and unemployed miners and jobless mill workers in completely different terms.

The difference will be made by the Emergency Relief Act. Or rather by the fact that the Emergency Relief Act exists. . . . [Passage of the Emergency Relief Act] marks a turning point in American political history. And the beginning of a new chapter in American unemployment relief. It constitutes an open and legible acknowledgment of governmental responsibility for the welfare of the victims of industrial unemployment. And its ultimate effect must be the substitution of an ordered, realistic, and intelligent relief program for the wasteful and uneconomic methods (of which the Miami truck is an adequate symbol) employed during the first three years of the Depression.

There can be no serious question of the failure of those methods. For the methods were never seriously capable of success. They were diffuse, unrelated, and unplanned. The theory was that private charitable organizations and semi-public welfare groups, established to care for the old and the sick and the indigent, were capable of caring for the casuals [victims] of a worldwide economic disaster. And the theory in application meant that social agencies manned for the service of a few hundred families, and city shelters set up to house and feed a handful of homeless men, were compelled by the brutal necessities of hunger to care for hundreds of thousands of families and whole armies of the displaced and the jobless. . . . The result was the picture now presented in city after city and state after state—heterogeneous groups of official and semi-official and unofficial relief agencies struggling under the earnest and untrained leadership of the local men of affairs against an inertia of misery and suffering and want they are powerless to overcome. . . .

But the individual localities present their own picture:

New York City

About 1,000,000 of the city's 3,200,000 working population are unemployed. Last April, 410,000 were estimated to be in dire want. Seven hundred and fifty thousand [people in] 150,000 families were receiving emergency aid while 160,000 more in 32,000 families were waiting to receive aid not then available. Of these latter families —families which normally earn an average of $141.50 a month—the average income from all sources was $8.20. Of families receiving relief, the allowance has been anything from a box of groceries up to $60 a month. . . . It is impossible to estimate the number of deaths in the last year in which

During the Depression years, sidewalk apple-stands were a familiar sight in large cities.

Chicago

Unemployed in Chicago number somewhere between 660,000 and 700,000 or 40 percent of its employable workers while the number for the state at large is about one in three of the gainfully employed. About 100,000 families have applied down to July for relief in Cook County. The minimum relief budget has been $2.40 per week for an adult and $1.50 per week for a child for food, with $22 to $23 per month to a family. But these figures have since been cut to $2.15 weekly for a man, $1.10 for a child. And persons demanding relief must be completely destitute to receive it.

starvation was a contributing cause. But 95 persons suffering directly from starvation were admitted to the city hospitals in 1931, of whom 20 died; and 143 suffering from malnutrition, of whom 25 died. . . .

From "No One Has Starved," *Fortune* (September, 1932), copyright © Time Inc. All rights reserved.

1. Why did *Fortune* see passage of the Emergency Relief Act as "the beginning of a new chapter"?
2. What examples did the magazine cite to point out the impact of the Depression?

2 The "Dust Bowl"

The impact of the Depression was heightened by the severe drought and dust storms that struck the Great Plains during the early 1930's, turning much of the area into a "Dust Bowl." A Texas newspaper described conditions in the summer of 1933.

Not a blade of wheat in Cimarron County, Oklahoma; cattle dying there on the range; a few bushels of wheat in the Perryton [Texas] area against an average yield of from four to six million bushels; . . . 90 percent of the poultry dead because of the sand storms; sixty cattle dying Friday between Guymon [Oklahoma] and Liberal [Kansas] from some disease induced by dust—humans suffering from dust fever—milk cows going dry, turned onto pasture to starve, hogs in such pitiable shape that buyers will not have them; . . . no wheat in Hartley County [Texas]; new crops a remote possibility, cattle facing starvation; Potter [Texas], Seward [Kansas], and other Panhandle counties with one third of their populations on charity or relief work; 90 percent of the farmers in most counties have had to have crop loans, and continued drought forcing many of them to use the money for food, clothes, medicine, shelter.

From *Dalhart Texan*, June 17, 1933.

1. What words would you use to describe conditions in the "Dust Bowl"?
2. How had the hard times affected the people in these states?

3 Franklin Roosevelt Takes Office

Franklin Roosevelt led the Democrats to a resounding victory in November, 1932. Thomas L. Stokes, a reporter for the United Press, described the scene when Roosevelt was sworn in as President four months later.

He stood, bareheaded, as the raw wind pecked at his hair.

He spoke and his voice had an electric, vibrant quality that magnetized the multitudes before him.

"This nation asks for action and action now," he cried.

The crowd thundered back its acclaim. Little boys, hanging from trees and lamp posts, unknowing, clapped their hands and whistled shrilly.

His face was stern. Tightly he gripped the sides of the reading stand. He knew . . . the gigantic task which had been imposed upon him a few minutes before he took the oath of office.

To millions of Americans in despair his voice was the symbol of hope. As we listened, it seemed that the pall of gloom was lifting a bit. It was an overwhelming gloom. The newspapers brought word of banks closing all over the country. The structure seemed to be giving away at every point. Desolate men . . . trailed in gaunt lines about windy corners to get a bowl of soup and a piece of bread. Farmers looked out across their acres and wondered how they would meet the mortgage. Families in financial straits watched neighbors evicted and wondered how long before they would be on the streets. Businessmen scanned their balance sheets and knew not how they would survive. America was in panic.

This *must* be the Deliverer from the troubles which encompassed us on every side.

In March, 1933, Franklin Delano Roosevelt delivered a stirring inaugural address and began the longest presidential administration in American history.

Certainly it was a complete change of management. The old order had been swept out in the election the previous November. . . .

[The people] wanted to forget the name Hoover and everything it connoted.

There was no mention of him, except derisively, that night in the buzz of conversation about Washington. Franklin D. Roosevelt was the man of the hour, his name the charmed sesame to open the door of hope and new life. . . . Washington was ready to believe, to have faith. . . . If Washington reacted thus to a man and a voice, what must be happening out in the country where people were crushed and desperate? . . . Washington was ready for the drama. Eagerly it waited for the play to begin.

From Thomas L. Stokes, *Chip Off My Shoulder* (Princeton: Princeton University Press, 1940).

1. What was the mood of the country as Roosevelt took office? Why was he viewed as a "symbol of hope"?
2. What was the public's attitude toward Hoover and his administration? How can this attitude be explained?

4 "The Hundred Days"

On the day after his inauguration, President Roosevelt called a special session of Congress to begin on March 9, 1933. During that session, later known as the "Hundred Days," Congress launched some of the New Deal's most important programs. Thomas Stokes described some of what happened during those days.

The gloom, the tenseness, the fear of the closing months of the Hoover administration had vanished. . . . We were so confident. . . .

So, too, were the young men who descended upon Washington from college [classrooms] and lawyers' offices and quickly found themselves places behind hundreds of desks and began to explore every cranny of the national economy, to probe its faults, and to draw diagrams and blueprints of a new world. They were going to make the world over. We talked then of a planned economy. We learned new [terms]. In time there were agencies with initials which gave the whole task the aspects of revolution. We spoke of "The Roosevelt Revolution."

They were exciting, exhilarating days. . . . We came alive, we were eager.

We were infected with a gay spirit of adventure, for something concrete and constructive finally was being done about the chaos which confronted the nation. The buoyancy and informality of the New Deal, the roll-up-your-sleeves and go-to-it attitude percolated out from the conferences at the White House, from conferences in other government buildings, from conferences at the Capitol where congressmen were caught up in the enthusiasm. . . .

Roosevelt could have become a dictator in 1933. He did not. . . . His first job was to do something, and do it quickly to save the nation's banking structure. . . .

Roosevelt's calm and optimism carried us through those trying days, so that we could joke about our individual plights as he closed the banks. That was ordered in a proclamation issued at the White House at one o'clock in the morning of Monday, March 6, less than two days after he had been in the White House. Most of the banks were shut down already. The bank holiday he proclaimed stopped all financial transactions. Working day and night, he and his experts drew up a plan for their reopening. He called in the heads of the press associations and explained the plan to them. . . .

The next night the President talked to the people in their homes [gathered] about the radio in the first of his "fireside chats." He explained the banking dilemma in simple language and told what was being done about it. It was a masterpiece of exposition. His voice inspired confidence. The effect was just as if he were sitting in the room with the family. He displayed in that talk the insight into public psychology which made him the idol of the masses.

From Thomas L. Stokes, *Chip Off My Shoulder* (Princeton: Princeton University Press, 1940).

1. Where did the President's young advisers come from? What was their attitude about what they were doing?
2. How did the President go about handling the banking crisis?

5 Frances Perkins on the Federal Relief Program

From the very first, the Roosevelt administration sought ways to provide relief for the millions of unemployed workers in the country. In the following passages, Frances Perkins, Secretary of Labor and the first woman to hold a Cabinet office, describes the administration's efforts.

The fortunes of the unemployed took a turn for the better the day FERA [the Federal Emergency Relief Administration] began to operate. The original appropriation [$500 million] and an additional $850 million were expended by March, 1934, including the Civil Works Program. Congress, surveying the results at that time, was generous with FERA.

In its brief span of life, FERA received and spent $4 billion on all projects. It was the first step in the economic pump priming that was to break the back of the Depression. FERA spent money for many things, all necessities of life—food, clothing, fuel, shelter, medicine. In an analysis of how the money was spent, Harry Hopkins [administrator of FERA] said, "We can only say that out of every dollar entrusted to us for lessening of distress, the maximum amount humanly possible was put into the people's hands. The money, spent honestly and with constant remembrance of its purpose, bought more of courage than it ever bought of goods. . . ."

American labor leaders William Greene (left) and John L. Lewis (right) met with Secretary of Labor Frances Perkins at the White House in 1935.

The Civil Works Program was intended originally to give employment to about four million unemployed, anticipating that others in distress would have help through direct relief. It was never intended that Civil Works would offer permanent employment. For many families, however, it was the sole source of occupation and income for a considerable period of time. Brief experience with it convinced most observers that it should be continued with careful attention and planning. The effect upon people of having their own money to spend rather than having it doled out to them was good, and their ingenuity in making ends meet was better than that of any social work adviser in a vast majority of cases. . . .

Roosevelt supported the Civil Works Administration and later became a great advocate of the Works Progress Administration which grew out of it. The Works Progress Administration, at its peak in the fiscal year July, 1938–July, 1939, took care of 3,325,000 people, and in the fiscal year 1939, its largest year of expenditure, spent $2,067,972,000 in both federal and sponsor's funds.

The President was always annoyed that so much complaint was made about the WPA. It is granted that there were ridiculous aspects to some of the enterprises and that some parts of the program got out of control. The freedom encouraged in this country led to the selection of some strange plays by local groups, and some congressmen and other citizens protested that the public money was being used to circulate subversive propaganda or to challenge the moral code. Roosevelt bore these accusations without being too disturbed. . . .

As times grew better the relief projects were gradually slowed down and closed off. WPA became unpopular in Congress and there was constant protest against further relief appropriations. There remained in this country, however, a core of people, not too many in number, who did better on WPA than ever before in their lives and perhaps better than they are ever likely to. Among these were the handicapped. . . .

The President, I repeat, never regretted the relief program. He never apologized for it. He was proud of what it had done.

From *The Roosevelt I Knew* by Frances Perkins. Copyright 1946 by Frances Perkins. Copyright renewed © 1974 by Susanna W. Coggeshall. Reprinted by permission of Viking Penguin Inc.

1. What specific projects did Frances Perkins describe? What were the goals of those programs?
2. What was President Roosevelt's attitude toward the relief projects?

6 A Family Lives Through the Depression

Government officials compiled reports of the impact of relief on selected families. The following selection is from a study of one WPA worker's experiences.

His next job was as timekeeper on a WPA project; he was assigned on a nonrelief basis through the employment office. Mr. Donner attributes his assignment to one of the better jobs to his "good education" and to his experience as a bookkeeper when he had his own business. For the past two years he has been working as timekeeper on WPA projects.

Mr. Donner feels that the Depression really hit hardest the families like his, who had been used to a relatively "high standard of living." For 25 years Mr. Donner's earnings had averaged not less than $300 a month. Since he now earns only about $90 a month, he thinks that his income has been reduced, proportionately, more than that of the average WPA worker. He is nevertheless sympathetic with relief clients and especially with the WPA workers who earn "a few dollars a month" less than he.

These past several years, the Donners have heard a great deal about the unemployed men who don't want to work and won't look for jobs and about the "shovel-leaners" on WPA jobs. "Of course," Mr. Donner says, "there are a few loafers on WPA projects; but there are also a few loafers on jobs in private industry." But on the whole, as Mr. Donner knows from having seen hundreds of WPA workers come and go, they are most eager to have employment and to do what is expected of them, or even "more than is expected.". . .

Mr. Donner does not see any immediate prospect of his leaving the WPA rolls. Business today is little better than when Mr. Donner returned to Dubuque more than three years ago, and "numbers of WPA rolls in the county are increasing." From his correspondence with friends in Chicago and other cities Mr. Donner gathers that conditions elsewhere are much the same as in Dubuque. . . .

What Mr. Donner would really like is to return to Chicago and go into the printing business again. If business is again "as good as it was last summer when most of the Dubuque factories were working 24 hours a day," there may be some possibility of his returning to Chicago; in the meantime, there is none. He has done everything he can to find a job other than on WPA projects: he has taken four civil service examinations, and has kept applications on file with the state employment office and with all of the local factories. There is nothing more to be done. He is not particularly hopeful of finding work; neither is he particularly discouraged. There is no bitterness or resentment evident in his expression of attitudes and opinion.

From J. N. Webb, with J. A. Bloodworth and E. J. Greenwood, *The Personal Side* (Washington: WPA Division of Research, 1939).

1. How had the Depression affected Mr. Donner?
2. How did Mr. Donner respond to criticism of the work habits of some WPA employees?
3. What would Mr. Donner's opinion of relief programs most likely have been?

7 The Impact of New Deal Programs

Federal projects not only provided employment but brought changes to the communities in which they operated. The following passages describe how these federal programs affected the typical, medium-size city of Muncie, Indiana (called "Middletown" by the authors).

When, on November 15, 1933, the blessed rain of federal CWA [Civil Works Administration] funds began to fall upon the parched taxpayers, the straining city brought out projects big and little to catch the golden flood. . . .

The first week's shower of $6,000 reached less than 500 workers, but by mid-December of 1933 the workers had increased to 1,750 and by mid-January, 1934, $33,500 of federal funds were pouring in each week to 1,840 workers. . . . Then, after $350,000 of CWA funds had been expended locally, the FERA took up the load, and, operating on a more economical basis and hiring only persons on relief, paid in sums ranging up to $16,000 to $17,000 a week. The peak number of men carried under the FERA funds was 1,100 in January and February, 1935, and, with increasing employment, this total dropped to 900 in mid-June, 1935.

In returning to Middletown in 1935 one got an impression of external improvement and sprucing up at a number of points. . . .

The local projects began as rather obvious jobs such as redecorating public schools and improving their grounds but quickly spread to such things as the following:

A riverside boulevard across the city.

The dredging and cleaning of the river, looking toward its use for recreational purposes when the new sewage system is secured.

New bridges across the river.

A park and $90,000 municipal swimming pool replacing an unsightly city dump near the center of town.

Draining and reclaiming of swamp areas.

Widening, repairing, and paving of streets and construction of traffic signs.

A handsome $350,000 arts building, . . . a swimming pool, and other extensive improvements . . . at the college.

Drainage and grading of the airport. . . .

An extensive . . . recreational program for adults and children in the city parks.

School athletic fields. . . .

As this is being written, in the summer of 1936, other large improvements are going forward with the help of federal and state funds:

Part of the long-planned new sewer system is actually under construction, with the WPA paying for the labor and the city supplying the materials and equipment.

A three-state highway through the city. . . .

Favorable action was also expected on a $500,000 project to build five additional modern bridges over the river that crosses the city.

The city was congratulating itself over the prospect. . . . And, sensing the fact that such a Cinderella existence will not go on forever, a press comment on the new bridges stated: "It is unlikely that ever again will there be an opportunity for the county to build new bridges here at a little more than half of their cost to the local taxpayers."

Abridged from *Middletown in Transition* by Robert S. Lynd and Helen Merrell Lynd, copyright 1937 by Harcourt Brace Jovanovich, Inc.; renewed 1965 by Robert S. and Helen M. Lynd. Reprinted by permission of the publisher.

1. What was the peak number of people being paid by the FERA?
2. What were some of the ways in which Middletown benefited from New Deal projects? What additional projects were being planned in 1936?
3. How did the people of Middletown feel about the programs?

Analysis

1. How might Herbert Hoover have responded to the attitudes of Roosevelt's supporters as expressed in Thomas Stokes's descriptions of the early days of the New Deal?

2. In what ways did the New Deal programs change how state and local governments dealt with the problems of providing relief for the unemployed? Use examples from this chapter to support your answer.

3. How do the selections in this chapter provide you with a picture of the scope of the hardships caused by the Depression? Cite specific examples to support your answer.

4. How might a critic of New Deal policies have responded to Frances Perkins's arguments in support of FERA, CWA, and the WPA?

From Isolation to Involvement
1920–1941

10

The republic that was established in Germany at the end of the First World War had to contend with serious economic problems as well as the criticism of political enemies. One charge made against the republic was that it had been too quick to accept defeat and the terms of the Treaty of Versailles. As economic chaos and political turmoil engulfed Germany in the early 1930's, Adolf Hitler was able to take control of the German government.

In an article published in *Collier's* magazine in 1938, Winston Churchill—soon to become the British prime minister—described Hitler's rise to power:

> The tale Hitler had to tell of a Germany betrayed, her soldiers stabbed in the back . . . was more pleasant to German ears than the truth. And the dream of a greater Germany, which only Hitler then dared to voice, thrilled the fighting men whose world had fallen into ruin. He revived the strong by leading them to the attack of the weak and unpopular. . . . He harnessed all prejudices and all difficulties to the wagon of . . . hate.

Hitler quickly led Germany on the path to rearmament and aggression. At the same time that clouds of war were gathering in Europe, Japan was engaged in acts of military conquest in Asia. These developments sparked a heated debate in Congress over what steps the United States should take to oppose threats to world peace.

In 1933, Adolf Hitler came to power in Germany and quickly established a totalitarian dictatorship. On April 20, 1939, a military demonstration was held in Berlin, Germany, in honor of Hitler's birthday.

1 Franklin Roosevelt on Quarantining the Aggressors

In 1937, President Roosevelt warned the American people of the growing danger of war. In the following speech, delivered in Chicago, he urged that aggressor nations be "quarantined."

The peace, the freedom, and the security of 90 percent of the population of the world is being jeopardized by the remaining 10 percent who are threatening a breakdown of all international order and law. Surely the 90 percent who want to live in peace under law and in accordance with moral standards that have received almost universal acceptance through the centuries can and must find some way to make their will prevail. . . .

Military rallies were staged in Germany to build support for Hitler at home and to impress the rest of Europe with Germany's power.

Anti-Semitism in Germany included Nazi-organized boycotts against Jewish merchants. The banner in this 1936 photograph advised Germans not to buy from Jews.

It seems to be unfortunately true that the epidemic of world lawlessness is spreading. When an epidemic of physical disease starts to spread, the community approves and joins in a quarantine of the patients in order to protect the health of the community against the spread of the disease.

It is my determination to pursue a policy of peace and to adopt every practicable measure to avoid involvement in war. It ought to be inconceivable that in this modern era, and in the face of experience, any nation could be so foolish and ruthless as to run the risk of plunging the whole world into war by invading and violating, in contravention of solemn treaties, the territory of other nations that have done them no real harm and which are too weak to protect themselves adequately. Yet the peace of the world and the welfare and security of every nation is today being threatened by that very thing.

No nation which refuses to exercise forebearance and to respect the freedom and rights of others can long remain strong and retain the confidence and respect of other nations. No nation ever loses its dignity or good standing by conciliating its differences and by exercising great patience with, and consideration for, the rights of other nations.

War is a contagion, whether it be declared or undeclared. It can engulf states and peoples remote from the original scene of hostilities. We are determined to keep out of war, yet we cannot insure ourselves against the disastrous effects of war and the dangers of involvement. We are adopting such measures as will minimize our risk of involvement, but we cannot have complete protection in a world of disorder in which confidence and security have broken down.

If civilization is to survive, the principles of [peace] must be restored. Shattered trust between nations must be revived. Most important of all, the will for peace on the part of peace-loving nations must express itself to the end that nations that may be tempted to violate their agreements and the rights of others will desist from such a cause. There must be positive endeavors to preserve peace.

America hates war. America hopes for peace. Therefore, America actively engages in the search for peace.

From address by Franklin D. Roosevelt, October 5, 1937. United States Department of State, *Peace and War: United States Foreign Policy, 1931–1941* (Washington, D.C., 1943).

1. Why was President Roosevelt concerned about the prospects of world peace?
2. What did he mean when he suggested that the world community should join in a "quarantine of the patients"?

2 The Growing Nazi Threat

Throughout the 1930's, concerned Americans spoke out about the actions of the aggressive dictatorships in Germany, Italy, and Japan. One such person was the American journalist Dorothy Thompson. Named as head of the Berlin office of the Philadelphia Public Ledger *and* New York Evening Post *in 1925, she was expelled from Germany in 1934 for writing articles critical of Hitler. The following article was published shortly after Hitler's take-over of Austria, in February, 1938.*

Write it down. On Saturday, February 12, 1938, Germany . . . dictated, at Hitler's mountain retreat, a peace treaty to make the Treaty of Versailles look like one of the great humane documents of the ages.

Write it down. On Saturday, February 12, 1938, nazism started on the march across all of Europe east of the Rhine.

Write it down that the world revolution began in earnest—and perhaps the world war.

Write it down that the democratic world broke its promises . . . and capitulated, not before strength, but before terrible weakness. . . .

What happened?

On February 4, Hitler ousted his chief of staff and fourteen other generals. Why? Because the army leadership refused to move against an unarmed, friendly country— their German-speaking neighbor, Austria. Why did they refuse? Because of squeamishness? Hardly. Because they thought that Britain and France would interfere? Perhaps. Or because they themselves feared the ultimate catastrophe the future would bring as a result of this move? I think this is the best guess.

A week later, Hitler, with his reorganized army, made his move. How did he make it? He called in the chancellor of Austria, Doctor von Schuschnigg, and gave him an ultimatum. Sixty-six million people against six million people. German troops were ready at Austria's borders. Hitler's generals stood behind him as he interviewed the Austrian chancellor. Hitler taunted his victim. "You know as well as I know that France and Britain will not move a hand to save you." Hitler will doubtless hail this meeting as a friendly reconciliation between two German-speaking peoples and the strengthening of peace in eastern Europe. . . .

Why does Germany want Austria? For raw materials? It has none of any importance. To add to German prosperity? Austria is a poor country with serious problems. But strategically it is the key to the whole of central Europe. Czechoslovakia is now surrounded. The wheat fields of Hungary and the oil fields of Rumania are now open. Not one of them will be able to withstand the pressure of German domination. . . .

It is horror walking. Not that "Germany" joins with Austria. We are not talking of "Germany." We see a new Crusade, under a pagan symbol, worshipping "blood" and "soil," preaching the holiness of the sword and glorifying conquest. It hates the Slavs, whom it thinks to be its historic "mission" to rule. It subjects all of life to a militarized state. It persecutes men and women of Jewish blood. Now it moves against the historic stronghold of Catholic Christianity, into an area of mixed races and mixed nationalities, which for a thousand years the Austro-Hungarian Empire could rule only with tolerance. Adolf Hitler's first hatred was not communism, but Austria-Hungary. Read *Mein Kampf* [Hitler's autobiography]. And he hated it for what? For its tolerance? He wanted eighty million Germans to rule with an iron hand an empire of eighty million "inferiors"—Czechs, Slovaks, Magyars, Jews, Serbs, Poles, and Croats.

Today, all of Europe east of the Rhine is cut off completely from the western world.

Copies of this poster were hung in Germany during the 1932 election. The poster called on workers to vote for candidate Hitler, the "front-line soldier."

The swastika banner, we are told, is the crusader's flag against Bolshevism! Madness! Only the signs on the flags divide them [communism and nazism].

And it never needed to have happened. One strong voice of one strong power could have stopped it.

Tomorrow, one of two things can happen. Despotism can settle into horrible stagnation, through the lack of real leadership and creative brains. For the law of despotisms is that they decapitate the good, and the brave, and the wise. . . . Perhaps all of Europe east of the Rhine will become, eventually, a no-man's land of poverty, militarism, and futility. . . .

More likely the other law of despotism's

nature—the law of constant aggressiveness—will cause it to move farther and onward, made bolder and stronger by each success.

To the point where civilization will take a last stand. For take a stand it will. Of that there is not the slightest doubt.

Too bad that it did not take it this week.

1. Why, according to Dorothy Thompson, did Germany take over Austria?
2. What did she believe was likely to happen next in Europe?

3 The United States as the Arsenal of Democracy

Following the German defeat of France and other Western European nations in 1940, President Roosevelt resolved to strengthen American defenses and give all possible aid to Great Britain. He explained his policy to the American people in a radio address on December 29, 1940.

On September 27, 1940, by an agreement signed in Berlin, three powerful nations, two in Europe and one in Asia, joined themselves together in the threat that if the United States interfered with or blocked the expansion program of these three nations—a program aimed at world control—they would unite in ultimate action against the United States.

The Nazi masters of Germany have made it clear that they intend not only to dominate all life and thought in their own country but also to enslave the whole of Europe, and then to use the resources of Europe to dominate the rest of the world. . . .

Some of our people like to believe that wars in Europe and in Asia are of no concern to us. But it is a matter of most vital concern to us that European and Asiatic war-makers should not gain control of the oceans that lead to this continent. . . .

If Great Britain goes down, the Axis powers will control the continents of Europe, Asia, Africa, Australia, and the high seas—and they will be in a position to bring enormous military and naval resources against this hemisphere. It is no exaggeration to say that all of us in the Americas would be living at the point of a gun—a gun loaded with explosive bullets, economic as well as military. . . .

The experience of the past two years has proven beyond doubt that no nation can appease the Nazis. . . . There can be no appeasement with ruthlessness. There can be no reasoning with an incendiary bomb. We know now that a nation can have peace with the Nazis only at the price of total surrender. . . .

Thinking in terms of today and tomorrow, I make the direct statement to the American people that there is far less chance of the United States getting into war if we do all we can now to support the nations defending themselves against attack by the Axis than if we acquiesce in their defeat, submit tamely to an Axis victory, and wait our turn to be the object of attack in another war later on. . . .

The people of Europe who are defending themselves do not ask us to do their fighting. They ask us for the implements of war, the planes, the tanks, the guns, the freighters, which will enable them to fight for their liberty and our security. Emphatically we must get these weapons to them in sufficient volume and quickly enough, so that we and our children will be saved the agony and suffering of war which others have had to endure. . . .

Nine days ago I announced the setting up of a more effective organization to direct our gigantic efforts to increase the production of munitions. The appropriation of vast sums of money and a well-coordinated executive direction of our defense efforts are not in themselves enough. Guns, planes, and ships have to be built in the factories and arsenals of America. They have to be produced by workers and managers and engineers with the aid of machines, which in turn have to be built by hundreds of thousands of workers throughout the land. . . .

We must be the great arsenal of democracy. For us this is an emergency as serious as war itself. We must apply ourselves to our task with the same resolution, the same sense of urgency, the same spirit of patriotism and sacrifice, as we would show were we at war. . . .

As President of the United States I call for that national effort. I call for it in the name of this nation which we love and honor and which we are privileged and proud to serve. I call upon our people with absolute confidence that our common cause will greatly succeed.

From address by Franklin D. Roosevelt, December 29, 1940. United States Department of State, *Peace and War: United States Foreign Policy, 1931–1941* (Washington, D.C., 1943).

1. What did President Roosevelt say would happen if Great Britain were defeated?
2. What did he mean when he spoke of the United States becoming an "arsenal of democracy"?

4 Charles Lindbergh on Intervention

Charles Lindbergh was a prominent member of the America First Committee, an organization that favored strengthening the nation's defenses but argued that the United States could not prevent an Allied defeat. Passages from a speech he gave in 1941 follow.

In time of war, truth is always replaced by propaganda. I do not believe we should be too quick to criticize the actions of a belligerent nation. There is always the question whether we, ourselves, would do better under similar circumstances. But we in this country have a right to think of the welfare of America first, just as the people in England thought first of their own country when they encouraged the smaller nations of Europe to fight against hopeless odds. When England asks us to enter this war, she is considering her own future and that of her Empire. In making our reply, I believe we should consider the future of the United States and that of the Western Hemisphere.

It is not only our right but it is our obligation as American citizens to look at this war objectively and to weigh our chances for success if we should enter it. I have attempted to do this, especially from the standpoint of aviation; and I have been forced to the conclusion that we cannot win this war for England, regardless of how much assistance we extend.

I ask you to look at the map of Europe today and see if you can suggest any way in which we could win this war if we entered it. Suppose we had a large army in America, trained and equipped. Where would we send it to fight? The campaigns of the war show only too clearly how difficult it is to force a landing, or to maintain an army, on a hostile coast.

Suppose we took our navy from the Pacific and used it to convoy British shipping. That would not win the war for England. It would, at best, permit her to exist under the constant bombing of the German air fleet. Suppose we had an air force that we could send to Europe. Where could it operate? Some of our squadrons might be based in the British Isles, but it is physically impossible to base enough aircraft in the British Isles alone to equal in strength the aircraft that can be based on the continent of Europe.

I have asked these questions on the supposition that we had in existence an army and an air force large enough and well enough equipped to send to Europe; and that we would dare to remove our navy from the Pacific. Even on this basis, I do not see how we could invade the continent of Europe successfully as long as all of that continent and most of Asia is under Axis domination. But the fact is that none of these suppositions are correct. We have only a one-ocean navy. Our army is still untrained and inadequately equipped for foreign war. Our air force is deplorably lacking in modern fighting planes.

When these facts are cited, the interventionists shout that we are defeatists, that we are undermining the principles of democracy, and that we are giving comfort to Germany by talking about our military weakness. But everything I mention here has been published in our newspapers and in the reports of congressional hearings in Washington. Our military position is well known to the governments of Europe and Asia. Why, then, should it not be brought to the attention of our own people?

I say it is the interventionists in America, as it was in England and in France, who give comfort to the enemy. I say it is they who are undermining the principles of democracy when they demand that we take a course to which more than 80 percent of our citizens are opposed. I charge them with being the real defeatists, for their policy has led to the defeat of every country that followed their advice since this war began. There is no better way to give comfort to an enemy than to divide the people of a nation over the issue of foreign war. There is no shorter road to defeat than by entering a war with inadequate preparation. Every nation that has adopted the interventionist policy of depending on someone else for its own defense has met with nothing but defeat and failure.

From speech by Charles A. Lindbergh, April 23, 1941, *Congressional Record, Appendix*, 77th Congress, 1st Session.

1. What policy did Lindbergh favor regarding the sending of aid to Great Britain? How did he justify this position?
2. On what basis did Lindbergh claim that the interventionists were "undermining the principles of democracy"?

Analysis

1. Why did many Americans become concerned about the actions of Germany in the 1930's? Use statements from Dorothy Thompson and Franklin Roosevelt to support your answer.

2. What arguments might an isolationist have put forward in opposition to Dorothy Thompson's view that conflict with the Axis was inevitable?

3. What response might Dorothy Thompson have given to Charles Lindbergh's arguments against American assistance for the Allies?

4. In what ways might America's experience in World War I have influenced those who opposed United States economic and military assistance for the Allies during the 1930's and early 1940's?

Global War
1941–1945

CHAPTER

11

On December 8, 1941, the day after the attack by Japanese forces on Pearl Harbor, Congress declared that a state of war existed with Japan. That evening President Roosevelt spoke to the nation:

> We are now in the midst of a war, not for conquest, not for vengeance, but for a world in which this nation and all that this nation represents will be safe for our children. We expect to eliminate the danger from Japan, but it would serve us ill if we accomplished that and found that the rest of the world was dominated by Hitler and Mussolini.
>
> We are going to win the war, and we are going to win the peace that follows. And in the dark hours of this day—and through dark days that may be yet to come—we will know that the vast majority of the members of the human race are on our side.

After nearly four years of fighting, the Allies defeated the Axis forces. The United States emerged from the Second World War as the leader of the Western powers.

The Japanese attack on Pearl Harbor on December 7, 1941, brought war between the United States and Japan. This poster aimed at rallying the American spirit.

...we here highly resolve that these dead shall not have died in vain...

REMEMBER DEC. 7th!

1 Attack on Pearl Harbor

On December 7, 1941, Japanese airplanes bombed American airstrips and the naval base at Pearl Harbor in Hawaii. Rear Admiral William Furlong of the United States Navy dictated the following report within three hours of the surprise attack.

At about [8:00 A.M.] this morning, Sunday, December 7, 1941, I was on the deck of my flagship and saw the first enemy bomb fall on the seaward end of Ford Island close to the water. This one did not hit the planes parked there. Another fell immediately afterward in the same vicin-

On December 8, 1941, Americans read in their local newspapers about Japan's attack on Pearl Harbor. In this photograph, a Californian is reading the *San Francisco Chronicle.*

ity and caused fires near the water. U.S. planes were on the ground nearby and later flames flared up from the structures at the south end of the island. The next bombs fell alongside or on board the seven battleships moored on the east side of Ford Island.

Japanese planes flew within fifty and one hundred feet of the water and dropped three torpedoes or mines in the channel. . . . A torpedo hit *Oglala* and *Helena.* . . . Fire was opened by *Oglala* and *Helena* anti-aircraft battery. . . .

One Japanese plane was shot down over the harbor and came down in flames to seaward of Ford Island but probably on land. There was no trouble distinguishing Japanese planes because the red sun painted on the side showed plainly.

Meanwhile planes were strafing as well as bombing. Planes kept coming for quite some time, making it difficult to estimate numbers. I saw four battleships hit with bombs and fires broke out. I saw one battleship turn over. There were six to ten enemy planes visible at any one time over the harbor.

The *Nevada* got under way and passed out of the channel near where I had seen the three mines or torpedoes fall. When she arrived in this vicinity her bow apparently hove up as if she had passed over a mine, and about a minute later two bombs fell, one of which hit her . . . , throwing up flame and smoke. . . .

On the second attack I saw a bomb drop which hit the forward part of the *Pennsylvania* or the dry-dock ahead of the *Pennsylvania.* Two destroyers of Destroyer Division Five were in the dock ahead of the *Pennsylvania,* and flames went up from them. . . .

Following the bombing of the *Pennsylvania,* I saw a bomb fall near or on the destroyer *Shaw* in the floating dry-dock. This destroyer was later in flames.

Meanwhile the *Oglala* had taken a list of about 40 degrees. The wire lines to the deck parted and her port upper deck rail was so far under that she might sink suddenly at any moment. I ordered all hands to abandon the ship shortly after 9:00 A.M., the only ones remaining being the guns' crews and myself. The *Oglala* kept up the anti-aircraft fire until the ship's list was at such an angle that the men on the machine guns were sliding off the deck. . . . During this last period the Japanese planes were strafing us, not bombing. As the ship was about to turn over, I ordered the guns' crews to leave the ship, and left with them. The machine guns were slid off the top of the deckhouse to the pier as the ship went over and were set up on the pier.

From *Battle Report, Pearl Harbor to Coral Sea*, Prepared from official sources by Commander Walter Karig and Lieutenant Welbourn Kelley (New York: Rinehart & Co., 1944).

---

1. What evidence was there in Furlong's report that the attack came as a surprise to the American forces?
2. What actions did the Americans take to defend themselves and protect their warships?

2 The Last Days on Corregidor

United States bases on the Philippines were hit by Japanese bombers just ten hours after the raid on Pearl Harbor. When Japanese troops landed in the Philippines, they met stiff resistance from American and Filipino troops under General Douglas MacArthur. Nevertheless, early in January, 1942, Manila surrendered, and the American forces retreated to Bataan Peninsula and the island of Corregidor in Manila Bay. An army nurse described the last days of resistance on Corregidor.

We left the hospital [on Bataan] at nine that night—got to Corregidor at three in the morning. The trip usually took a little over an hour. As we drove down to the docks, the roads were jammed. Soldiers were tired, aimless, frightened. Cars were overturned; there were bodies in the road. Clouds of dust made it hard to breathe. At midnight on the docks we heard the Japanese had burned our hospital to the ground.

Bombers were overhead, but we were too tired to care. We waited on the docks while the [ammunition dumps] were blown up. Blasting explosions, blue flares, red flares, shrapnel, tracers, gasoline exploding—it was like a hundred Fourths of July and Christmases all at once, but we were too frightened to be impressed. As we crossed the water with Corregidor's big guns firing over our heads and shells from somewhere landing close by, the boat suddenly shivered and the whole ocean seemed to rock. We thought a big shell had hit the water in front of us—it wasn't until we landed that we found an earthquake had come just as Bataan fell.

Corregidor seemed like heaven that night. They fed us and we slept, two to an army cot. We went to work the following morning. . . .

Months before, patients on Corregidor had filled a few [beds] only. Now they were in double-decked beds all along the halls and in the main tunnel. There was constant bombing and shelling—sometimes concussion from a bomb outside would knock people down at the opposite end of the tunnel. Emperor Hirohito's birthday, April 29th, was a specially bad day. The bombing began at 7:30 A.M. and never stopped. Shelling was heavy; soldiers counted over a hundred explosions per minute. Dive bombers were going after the gun on the hill directly above our heads and the concussion inside was terrific. . . .

Through all those weeks on Corregidor everyone was grand. At 6 o'clock one evening, after the usual bombing and shelling, twenty-one of us were told we were leaving Corregidor by plane with ten pounds of luggage apiece. We don't know how we were selected. Everyone wanted to leave, of course, but morale was splendid. Everyone realized the end was getting close, but none gave up hope.

All Corregidor was under shellfire. . . . The pilot hustled us aboard—said to pile in quickly, not to bother to find seats. He was anxious to get off because we were . . . directly in the range of artillery. On that trip we almost skimmed the water. . . .

[After stopping on Mindanao,] we left for Australia. . . . There is no joy in escaping when all one's best friends are prisoners or dead. But we reached Australia dirty, tired, dressed in overalls we'd worn for four days.

Now we're safe, but the only reaction we notice is wanting to make up somehow, anyhow, for those who didn't get away.

From "An Army Nurse at Bataan and Corregidor," as told to Annalee Jacoby; from *History in the Writing* by Gordon Carroll. Copyright 1945 by Time Inc. Reprinted by permission of Time Inc.

1. Describe conditions for the wounded on Corregidor.
2. What was the state of American morale during this period of the battle for the Philippines?
3. How did the nurse escape from Corregidor? What was her reaction upon reaching safety in Australia?

3 Eisenhower Receives His Orders

Following the Allied landings in Italy in 1943, President Roosevelt and Prime Minister Churchill began to make plans for an invasion of France. In February, 1944, the Allied Chiefs of Staff sent the following orders to Dwight Eisenhower, making him Supreme Commander of that invasion.

1. You are hereby designated as Supreme Allied Commander of the forces placed under your orders for operations for liberation of Europe from Germans. Your title will be Supreme Commander Allied Expeditionary Force.

2. *Task.* You will enter the continent of Europe and, in conjunction with the other United Nations [Allies], undertake operations aimed at the heart of Germany and the destruction of her armed forces. The date for entering the continent is the month of May, 1944. After adequate channel ports have been secured, exploitation will be directed toward securing an area that will facilitate both ground and air operations against the enemy.

3. Notwithstanding the target date above you will be prepared at any time to take immediate advantage of favorable circumstances, such as withdrawal by the enemy on your front, to effect a re-entry into the continent with such forces as you have available at the time; a general plan for this operation when approved will be furnished for your assistance.

4. *Command.* You are responsible to the Combined Chiefs of Staff. . . . Direct communication with the United States and British Chiefs of Staff is authorized in the interest of facilitating your operations and for arranging necessary logistic support.

5. *Logistics.* In the United Kingdom the responsibility for logistics organization, concentration, movement, and supply of forces to meet the requirements of your plan will rest with British Service Ministries so far as British forces are concerned. So far as United States forces are concerned, this re-

sponsibility will rest with the United States War and Navy Departments. You will be responsible for coordinating the requirements of British and United States forces under your command.

6. *Coordination of operations of other forces and agencies.* In preparation for your assault on enemy-occupied Europe, . . . sabotage, subversion, and propaganda . . . are now in action. You may recommend any variation in these activities which may seem to you desirable.

7. *Relationship to United Nations forces in other areas.* Responsibility will rest with the Combined Chiefs of Staff for supplying information relating to operations of the forces of the USSR for your guidance in timing your operations. It is understood that the Soviet forces will launch an offensive at about the same time as OVERLORD [the code name for the Allied invasion of France] with the object of preventing the German forces from transferring from the eastern to the western front. The Allied Commander-in-Chief, Mediterranean Theater, will conduct operations designed to assist your operation, including the launching of an attack against the south of France at about the same time as OVERLORD. The scope and timing of his operations will be decided by the Combined Chiefs of Staff. . . . The Combined Chiefs of Staff

Just before "D-Day"—June 6, 1944—General Dwight Eisenhower gives a pep talk to a group of paratroopers.

will place under your command the forces operating in Southern France as soon as you are in a position to assume such command.

From directive to Supreme Commander, Allied Expeditionary Force, issued by Combined Chiefs of Staff, February 11, 1944, Office of the Chief of Military History, Department of the Army.

1. According to this directive, what was Eisenhower's primary task?
2. What support was Eisenhower promised from Allied forces in other areas?

4 The Allies Advance

The long-planned Allied invasion of France took place on June 6, 1944—D-Day. Ernie Pyle, one of the most famous correspondents covering the war, described what had happened on the Normandy beaches.

I didn't arrive on the beachhead until the morning after D-Day, after our first wave of assault troops had hit the shore.

By the time we got there the beaches had been taken and the fighting had moved a couple of miles inland. All that remained on the beach was some sniping and artillery fire, and the occasional startling blast of a mine [showering] brown sand into the air. That plus a gigantic and pitiful litter of wreckage along miles of shoreline. . . .

After it was all over it seemed to me a pure miracle that we ever took the beach at all. For some of our units it was easy, but in the special sector where I landed our troops faced such odds that our getting ashore was like my whipping [heavyweight champion] Joe Louis down to a pulp. The men who did it on that beach were men of the First and Twenty-Ninth Divisions. . . .

Ashore, facing us, were more enemy troops than we had in our assault waves. The advantages were all theirs, the disadvantages all ours. The Germans were dug into positions they had been working on for months, although they were not entirely complete. A 100-foot bluff a couple of hundred yards back from the beach had great concrete gun emplacements built right into the hilltop. These opened to the sides instead of to the front, thus making it hard for naval fire from the sea to reach them. They could shoot parallel with the shore and cover every foot of it for miles with artillery fire.

Then they had hidden machine-gun nests on the forward slopes, with crossfire taking in every inch of the beach. These nests were connected by networks of trenches, so that the German gunners could move about without exposing themselves.

Throughout the length of the beach, running zigzag a couple of hundred yards back from the shoreline, was an immense V-shaped ditch fifteen feet deep. Nothing could cross it, not even men on foot, until [it had been filled]. And in other places at the far end of the beach, where the ground was flatter, they had great concrete walls. These were blasted by our naval gunfire or by explosives set by hand after we got ashore. . . .

All this was on the shore. But our men had to go through a maze nearly as deadly before they even got ashore. Underwater obstacles were terrific. Under the water the Germans had whole fields of evil devices to catch our boats. Several days after the landing we had cleared only channels through them and still could not approach the whole length of the beach with our ships. Even then some ship or boat would hit one of those mines and be knocked out of commission. . . .

In addition to these obstacles they had floating mines offshore, land mines buried in the sand of the beach, and more mines in checkerboard rows in the tall grass beyond the sand. And the enemy had four men on shore for every three men we had approaching the shore.

And yet we got on. . . .

The first crack in the beach defenses was finally accomplished by terrific and wonderful naval gunfire, which knocked out the big emplacements. Epic stories have been told of destroyers that ran right up into shallow water and had it out point-blank with the big guns in those concrete emplacements ashore. . . .

Our men were pinned down for a while, but finally they stood up and went through, and so we took that beach and accomplished our landing. In the light of a couple of days of retrospection, we sat and talked and called it a miracle that our men ever got on at all or were able to stay on.

They suffered casualties. And yet considering the entire beachhead assault, including other units that had a much easier time, our total casualties in driving that wedge into the continent of Europe were remarkably low—only a fraction, in fact, of what our commanders had been prepared to accept.

And those units that were so battered . . . pushed on inland without rest, their spirits high, their egotism in victory almost reaching the smart-alecky stage.

Their tails were up. "We've done it again," they said. They figured that the rest of the army wasn't needed at all. Which proves that, while their judgment in this respect was bad, they certainly had the spirit that wins battles, and eventually wars.

1. What defenses had the Germans prepared?
2. How did the Allied troops go about taking the beaches?
3. What was the state of the morale of the troops who had fought on the beaches?

5 Bravery in Battle

Throughout most of World War II, black and white troops served in separate military units. As the Allied forces pushed toward Germany late in 1944, however, the Nazi counteroffensive created a special crisis. In response, black troops—many of them from service units assigned to supply depots and maintenance and repair centers—volunteered to fight alongside white units during the Battle of the Bulge. Walter White, secretary of the NAACP, described the experience in his autobiography.

American infantrymen wearing snow camouflage advance in Belgium during the Battle of the Bulge.

The Germans' sudden, effective breakthrough threatened disaster. . . .

Every available man was thrown into the fight to stop the German advance. But even then there were not enough. Desperate appeals were sent to the United States to rush more combat troops as quickly as possible. Many were sent by plane, but even these were not enough. It was at this point, during some of the fiercest fighting, that General John C. H. Lee issued an appeal to colored Service of Supply troops to volunteer for combat.

"It is planned to assign you without regard to color or race to units where assistance is most needed," General Lee promised. He made no effort to minimize the desperate nature of the fighting nor the great number of casualties caused by the German breakthrough. He pointed out that all noncommissioned officers would have to give up their ratings [ranks] to qualify for service as combat troops.

Great numbers of volunteers answered General Lee's appeal. In some units 80 percent of the soldiers offered their services. In one engineer unit, 171 out of 186 men volunteered. One private in an ordnance company declared: "We've been giving a lot of sweat. Now I think we'll mix some blood with it."

Negroes were delighted at this . . . opportunity to function as "real" soldiers. The response was so great that the army had to set up a quota to prevent complete disorganization of its service units.

Generals George Patton, Omar Bradley, and Courtney Hodges gave their approval to the use of Negro soldiers in completely unsegregated units. General Eisenhower was enthusiastic. But Eisenhower's chief-of-staff, W. Bedell Smith, insisted that the plan be submitted to General George C. Marshall, army chief of staff.

Washington was alarmed at the idea of an unsegregated, genuinely democratic army. It ordered the plan abandoned. But the need for combat troops was so critical that the high command in Washington was forced to agree to a compromise—the use of all-Negro platoons in white regiments, instead of a mixture of whites and Negroes throughout the regiments. Although Negro soldiers felt that they had been let down, they were still enthusiastic. The Negro platoons were distributed among the eleven combat divisions of the First and Seventh Armies. They fought in the crucial stages of the Battle of the Bulge and through the later Allied drive across Germany.

Several of the Negro volunteers won the Distinguished Service Cross or Silver Star. Others were cited for bravery beyond the call of duty. . . .

General Patton highly praised the black volunteers. General Eisenhower declared: "All my commanders reported that these volunteers did excellent work." General Charles Lanham of the 104th Division, presenting combat decorations to eleven Negroes, went even further to declare: "I have never seen any soldiers who have performed better in combat than you have."

1. What was the response of the black troops to the call for volunteers?
2. What evidence is there in this selection of the accomplishments and courage of the black troops?

6 War Industries at Home

During World War II, American industry produced enormous quantities of war equipment and material needed by the armed forces. The following description of war work is from the diary of Augusta Clawson, a welder in a shipyard.

I, who hate heights, climbed stair after stair after stair till I thought I must be close to the sun. I stopped on the top deck. I, who hate confined spaces, went through narrow corridors. . . . I went into a room about four feet by ten where two shipfitters, a shipfitter's helper, a chipper, and I all worked. I welded . . . lying on the floor while another welder spattered sparks from the ceiling and chippers like giant woodpeckers shattered our eardrums. I, who've taken welding, and have sat at a bench welding flat and vertical plates, was told to weld braces along a baseboard below a door opening. On these a heavy steel door was braced while it was hung to a fine degree of accuracy. I welded more braces along the side, and along the top. I did overhead welding, horizontal, flat, vertical. . . . I made some good welds and some frightful ones. But now a door in . . . an oil tanker is

Throughout the war years, women filled jobs that had previously been unavailable to them. This woman worked as a riveter.

hanging, four feet by six of solid steel, by *my* welds. Pretty exciting! . . .

I had a good taste of summer today, and I am convinced that it is going to take backbone for welders to stick to their jobs through the summer months. It is harder on them than on any of the other workers —their leathers are so hot and heavy, they get more of the fumes, and their hoods become instruments of torture. There were times today when I'd have to stop in the middle of a tack and push my hood back just to get a breath of fresh air. It grows unbearably hot under the hood, my glasses fog and blur my vision, and the only thing to do is to stop. . . .

My work was . . . where the last crew had put brackets in place *upside down.* The burner had to burn off six of them completely. For me, this meant climbing halfway up the wall and tacking them in place with horizontal, vertical, and overhead tacks. One's position is often so precarious at such an angle that it is hard to maintain a steady arc. Add to this that often I could not stand straight or kneel. The result was that trying to hold a position halfway between would start some contrary nerve quivering so that my hand would carry out the "jiggle" and affect the weld. Yet the job confirmed my strong conviction . . . [that] what exhausts the woman welder is not the work, nor the heat, nor the demands upon physical strength. It is the apprehension that arises from inadequate skill and consequent lack of confidence; and this *can* be overcome by the right kind of training. I've mastered tacking now, so that [doesn't] bother me. I know I can do it if my machine is correctly set, and I have learned enough of the [ways] of machines to be able to set them. And so, in spite of the discomforts of climbing, heavy equipment, and heat, I enjoyed the work today because I *could do it.*

From Augusta Clawson, *Shipyard Diary of a Woman Welder* (New York: Penguin, 1944).

1. What difficulties did Augusta Clawson encounter in welding? What difficulties did she think women in general faced?
2. Describe the way Augusta Clawson felt about her work.

Analysis

1. What effect might news of the American setbacks at Pearl Harbor and the Philippines have had on the resolve of American troops and civilians?

2. In his report on the Allied landing at Normandy, Ernie Pyle described the taking of the beach as a "pure miracle." What evidence did he give to support this view?

3. During World War II, women and black Americans assumed responsibilities that had often been denied them in peacetime. How might this have affected their attitudes once the war was over?

4. Many strategists believe that "morale" is one of the key elements of military success. In what ways did America's experience in World War II justify this view? Use statements from the selections in this chapter in your answer.

Cold War and Hot
1945–1952

CHAPTER

12

When the Second World War came to an end in 1945, Americans hoped that a period of peace and international cooperation would follow. Some officials in the United States government were growing concerned at this time about the aggressive stance of the Soviet Union. In May, 1945, Acting Secretary of State Joseph C. Grew set down his impression of the situation in a memorandum:

> This war, so far as the interests of the United States are concerned, will have achieved one purpose and one purpose only, namely protection from the military expansion of Germany and Japan. For that purpose we had to fight, for had we not fought, our nation itself would have been in direct peril. . . .
>
> But as "a war to end wars," the war will have been futile, for the result will be merely the transfer of totalitarian dictatorship and power from Germany and Japan to Soviet Russia which will constitute in the future as grave a danger to us as did the Axis.

The increasing tensions between the Soviet Union and the Western democracies dashed any hope for cooperation in the postwar era. Mindful of the failure of appeasement to control Hitler's advances, the United States was determined to oppose forcefully any power that threatened to dominate other nations.

The cold war turned hot in 1950 when North Korean forces invaded South Korea. Here, American soldiers stationed in Korea defend an entrenched position.

1 An Iron Curtain Descends over Europe

In the months after the end of World War II, the actions of the Soviet Union increasingly alarmed the leaders of the Western powers. In a speech delivered at Fulton, Missouri, in 1946, Winston Churchill stressed the need for a policy of strength in dealing with the Soviet Union.

A shadow has fallen upon the scenes so lately lighted by the Allied victory. Nobody knows what Soviet Russia and its Communist international organization intends to do in the immediate future, or what are the limits, if any, to their expansive . . . tendencies. . . . We understand the Russian need to be secure on her western frontiers by the removal of all possibility of German aggression. We welcome Russia to her rightful place among the leading nations of the world. We welcome her flag upon the seas. Above all, we welcome constant, frequent, and growing contacts between the Russian people and our own people on both sides of the Atlantic. It is my duty however . . . to place before you certain facts about the present position in Europe.

From Stettin in the Baltic to Trieste in the Adriatic, an iron curtain has descended across the Continent. Behind that line lie all the capitals of the ancient states of Central and Eastern Europe. Warsaw, Berlin, Prague, Vienna, Budapest, Belgrade, Bucharest, and Sofia, all of these famous cities and the populations around them lie in what I must call the Soviet sphere, and all are subject in one form or another, not only to Soviet influence but to a very high, and in many cases, increasing measure of

Canadian photographer Yousuf Karsh took this memorable portrait of Winston Churchill in 1941.

control from Moscow. . . . The Communist parties, which were very small in all these Eastern states of Europe, have been raised to pre-eminence and power far beyond their numbers and are seeking everywhere to obtain totalitarian control. Police governments are prevailing in nearly every case, and so far, . . . there is no true democracy. . . .

I repulse the idea that a new war is inevitable; still more that it is imminent. It is because I am sure that our fortunes are still in our own hands and that we hold the power to save the future, that I feel the duty to speak out now. . . . I do not believe that Soviet Russia desires war. What they desire is the fruits of war and the indefinite expansion of their power and doctrines. But what we have to consider here today, while time remains, is the permanent prevention of war and the establishment of conditions of freedom and democracy as rapidly as possible in all countries. Our difficulties and dangers will not be removed by closing our eyes to them. They will not be removed by mere waiting to see what happens; nor will they be removed by a policy of appeasement. What is needed is a settlement, and the longer this is delayed, the more difficult it

will be and the greater our dangers will become.

From what I have seen of our Russian friends and allies during the war, I am convinced that there is nothing they admire so much as strength, and there is nothing for which they have less respect than for weakness, especially military weakness. For that reason the old doctrine of a balance of power is unsound. We cannot afford . . . to work on narrow margins, offering temptations to a trial of strength. If the Western democracies stand together in strict adherence to the principles of the United Nations Charter, their influence for furthering those principles will be immense and no one is likely to molest them. If however they become divided or falter in their duty and if these all-important years are allowed to slip away then indeed catastrophe may overwhelm us all.

From address by Winston Churchill at Fulton, Missouri, March 5, 1946. *Vital Speeches*, Vol. 12.

1. According to Churchill, what were the goals of the Soviet Union?
2. What specific policies did he suggest the Western powers follow to prevent another war?

2 The Truman Doctrine

In February, 1947, President Truman received word that the British could no longer afford to support the Greek government, then under attack by Communist rebels. This withdrawal would almost certainly have meant the triumph of communism in Greece and probably in neighboring Turkey as well. In his memoirs, Truman described how the decision was then made to issue the Truman Doctrine.

Greece needed aid, and needed it quickly and in substantial amounts. The alternative

was the loss of Greece and the extension of the iron curtain across the eastern Mediterranean. . . .

But the situation had even wider implications. Poland, Rumania, and the other satellite nations of Eastern Europe had been turned into Communist camps because, in the course of the war, they had been occupied by the Russian Army. We had tried, vainly, to persuade the Soviets to permit political freedom in these countries, but we had no means to compel them to relinquish their control, unless we were prepared to wage war.

Greece and Turkey were still free countries being challenged by Communist threats both from within and without.

President at one of the most crucial periods in American history, Harry Truman established a policy of containment of Soviet power.

These free peoples were now engaged in a valiant struggle to preserve their liberties and their independence.

America could not, and should not, let these free countries stand unaided. To do so would carry the clearest implications in the Middle East and in Italy, Germany, and France. The ideals and the traditions of our nation demanded that we come to the aid of Greece and Turkey and that we put the world on notice that it would be our policy to support the cause of freedom wherever it was threatened. . . .

On Wednesday, March 12, 1947, at one o'clock in the afternoon, I stepped to the rostrum in the hall of the House of Representatives and addressed a joint session of the Congress. I had asked the senators and representatives to meet together so that I might place before them what I believed was an extremely critical situation.

To cope with this situation, I recom-

mended immediate action by the Congress. But I also wished to state, for all the world to know, what the position of the United States was in the face of the new totalitarian challenge. This declaration of policy soon began to be referred to as the "Truman Doctrine." This was, I believe, the turning point in America's foreign policy, which now declared that wherever aggression, direct or indirect, threatened the peace, the security of the United States was involved.

From Harry S. Truman, *Memoirs of Harry S. Truman: Years of Trial and Hope*, Doubleday & Co. Inc., Publishers, 1956, by permission of Margaret Truman Daniel.

1. How was the case of Greece and Turkey different from that of the Eastern European satellite countries?
2. How did President Truman define the "Truman Doctrine"?

3 President Truman on the Invasion of South Korea

On June 25, 1950, President Truman received word at his family home in Independence, Missouri, that the Communist forces of North Korea had invaded South Korea. The next day, the President flew to Washington to meet with his Cabinet and military advisers. In his memoirs, Truman described his thoughts during the trip and the meeting he had with his advisers upon his arrival.

The plane left the Kansas City Municipal Airport at two o'clock, and it took just a little over three hours to make the trip to Washington. I had time to think aboard the plane. In my generation, this was not the first occasion when the strong had attacked the weak. I recalled some earlier instances: Manchuria, Ethiopia, Austria. I remembered how each time that the democracies failed to act it had encouraged the aggressors to keep going ahead. Communism was acting in Korea just as Hitler, Mussolini, and the Japanese had acted ten, fifteen, and twenty years earlier. I felt certain that if South Korea was allowed to fall Communist leaders would be emboldened to override nations closer to our own shores. If the Communists were permitted to force their way into the Republic of Korea without opposition from the free world, no small nation would have the courage to resist threats and aggression by stronger Communist neighbors. If this was allowed to go unchallenged it would mean a third world war, just as similar incidents had brought on the second world war. It was also clear to me that the foundations and the principles of the United Nations were at stake unless this unprovoked attack on Korea could be stopped.

I had the plane's radio operator send a message to [Secretary of State] Dean Acheson asking him and his immediate advisers and the top defense chiefs to [assemble] for a dinner conference. . . .

It was late, and we went at once to the dining room for dinner. I asked that no discussion take place until dinner was served and over. . . . I called on Dean Acheson first to give us a detailed picture of the situation. . . .

I then called on Acheson to present the recommendations which the State and Defense Departments had prepared. He presented the following recommendations for immediate action:

1. That [General] MacArthur should evacuate the Americans from Korea—including the dependents of the military mission—and, in order to do so, should keep open the . . . airports, repelling all hostile attacks thereon. In doing this, his air forces should stay south of the 38th parallel [the border between North and South Korea].
2. That MacArthur should be instructed to get ammunition and supplies to the Korean army by airdrop and otherwise.
3. That the Seventh Fleet should be ordered into the Formosa Strait to prevent the conflict from spreading to that area. . . . We should make a statement that the fleet would repel any attack on Formosa and that no attacks should be made from Formosa on the mainland. . . .

As we continued our discussion, I stated that I did not expect the North Koreans to pay any attention to the United Nations. This, I said, would mean that the United Nations would have to apply force if it wanted its order [for the North Koreans to withdraw] obeyed.

From Harry S. Truman, *Memoirs of Harry S. Truman: Years of Trial and Hope,* Doubleday & Co. Inc., Publishers, 1956, by permission of Margaret Truman Daniel.

1. To what earlier actions did Truman compare the North Korean attack?
2. What recommendations did the State and Defense Departments make?

4 Reporting from the Front in Korea

In the early days of fighting in Korea, United Nations forces were pushed back to the southeastern part of the peninsula, around Pusan. Marguerite Higgins, a correspondent for the New York Herald Tribune, *reported on the situation facing the 27th (Wolfhound) Infantry, a regiment commanded by Colonel John ("Mike") Michaelis, former aide to General Eisenhower.*

On [my] first night at Chindongni, I found Colonel Michaelis in a state of tension. Mike Michaelis is a high-strung, good-looking officer with much of the cockiness of an ex-paratrooper. . . .

That night Mike Michaelis felt he had made a bad [mistake]. His very presence in Chindongni was technically against orders. He had turned his troops around and rushed them away from assigned positions when he heard the Reds had seized the road junction pointing along the southern coast straight at Masan and Pusan. . . . But, reaching Chindongni, his patrols could find no enemy. There were only swarms of refugees pumping down the road. And at the very point Michaelis had left, heavy enemy attacks were reported.

Miserably, Michaelis had told his officers: "I gambled and lost. I brought you to the wrong place."

But depression did not subdue him for long. He decided he would find the enemy by attacking in battalion strength. If the road really was empty, his men might recapture the critical road junction some twenty miles to the east.

Michaelis asked the 35th Regiment some miles to the north to send a spearhead to link up with his troops approaching the junction on the coastal route, and ordered Colonel Gilbert Check to push forward the twenty miles. The advance turned into the first major counterattack of the Korean campaign.

Michaelis told me about it in the lamplit headquarters room. . . . Again he was unhappily belaboring himself for having made a bad gamble.

It appeared that the Reds had been on the coastal road after all. Disguised in the broad white hats and white linen garb of the Korean farmer, they had filtered unhindered in the refugee surge toward Chindongni. Then, singly or in small groups, they had streamed to collecting points in the hills, some to change into uniform and others simply to get weapons.

From their mountainous hiding places they had watched Colonel Check's battalion plunge down the road. Then they had struck from the rear. . . . The regiment was split in two; the line of supply cut. . . .

The fate of Colonel Check's battalion showed that the enemy was here in force and proved that Michaelis had been right to wheel his forces south to block this vital pathway to Pusan. But he felt he had bungled in ordering the battalion to advance so far.

"I overcommitted myself," Michaelis said miserably. "Now Check's men are stranded eighteen miles deep in enemy territory. From early reports, they've got a lot of wounded. But we've lost all contact. I sent a liaison plane to drop them a message to beat their way back here. I'm afraid we've lost the tanks."

Colonel Check's tanks took a pummeling, all right, from enemy antitank guns. But the tanks got back. Colonel Check himself told us the remarkable story as his weary battalion funneled into Chindongni at one o'clock in the morning.

"Antitank guns caught us on a curve several miles short of our objective," Check said. . . . "The tanks caught partially afire and the crews were wounded. But three of the tanks were still operable. . . . I was [not] going to let several hundred thousand dollars' worth of American equipment sit back there on the road. I

In the winter of 1950, United Nations forces withdrew along mountain trails following China's entry into the war.

yelled, 'Who around here thinks he can drive a tank?' A couple of ex-bulldozer operators and an ex-mason volunteered. They got about three minutes' checking out and off they went.''

One of the ex-bulldozer operators was Private Ray Roberts. His partly disabled tank led Check's column through ambush after ambush back to safety. Men were piled all over the tanks, and the gunners— also volunteers—had plenty of practice shooting back at Reds harassing them from ridges.

From *War in Korea* by Marguerite Higgins. Copyright 1951 by Marguerite Higgins, copyright 1951 by Time Inc. Reprinted by permission of Doubleday & Co., Inc.

1. When Marguerite Higgins first encountered Colonel Michaelis, why was he "in a state of tension"?
2. What happened to Colonel Check's battalion?
3. What peacetime skill did Private Ray Roberts have that enabled him to lead the men of his battalion back to safety?

5 Douglas MacArthur on His Removal

After President Truman relieved him of his command in Korea in April, 1951, General Douglas MacArthur returned to the United States, where he received a hero's welcome. Speaking before a joint session of Congress on April 19, MacArthur explained his position.

I now turn to the Korean conflict. While I was not consulted prior to the President's decision to intervene in the support of the Republic of Korea, that decision from a military standpoint proved a sound one as we hurled back the invader and decimated his forces. Our victory was complete and our objectives within reach when Red China intervened with numerically superior ground forces. This created a new war and an entirely new situation, a situation not contemplated when our forces were committed against the North Korean invaders; a situation which called for new decisions in the diplomatic sphere to permit the realistic adjustment of military strategy. Such decisions have not been forthcoming.

While no man in his right mind would advocate sending our ground forces into continental China, and such was never given a thought, the new situation did urgently demand a drastic revision of strategic planning if our political aim was to defeat this new enemy as we had defeated the old.

Apart from the military need, as I saw it, to neutralize the sanctuary protection given the enemy north of the Yalu, I felt

General Douglas MacArthur led the Inchon landing, a surprise move that changed the course of the fighting in Korea. After the landing, MacArthur and his aides inspected the area north of Seoul.

that military necessity in the conduct of the war made mandatory—

(1) The intensification of our economic blockade against China.

(2) The imposition of a naval blockade against the China coast.

(3) Removal of restrictions on air reconnaissance of China's coastal area and of Manchuria.

(4) Removal of restrictions on the forces of the Republic of China on Formosa, with [supply] support to contribute to their effective operations against the common enemy. . . .

Efforts have been made to distort my position. It has been said in effect that I was a warmonger. Nothing could be further from the truth.

I know war as few other men living know it, and nothing to me is more revolting. I have long advocated its complete abolition, as its very destructiveness on both friend and foe has rendered it useless as a means of settling international disputes. . . .

But once [war] was forced upon us, there is no other alternative than to apply every available means to bring it to a swift end.

War's very object is victory, not prolonged indecision.

In war there can be no substitute for victory.

There are some who for varying reasons would appease Red China. They are blind to history's clear lesson, for history teaches with unmistakable emphasis that appeasement but begets new and bloodier war. It points to no single instance where the end has justified that means, where appeasement has led to more than a sham peace.

Like blackmail, it lays the basis for new and successively greater demands until, as in blackmail, violence becomes the only other alternative. Why, my soldiers asked of me, surrender military advantages to an enemy in the field? I could not answer.

From General Douglas MacArthur, Address to Congress, April 19, 1951. *Congressional Record*, 82nd Congress, 1st Session.

---

1. What circumstances, according to MacArthur, created an entirely new situation in Korea?
2. What steps did MacArthur favor for winning the war in Korea?

Analysis

1. Why was the Truman Doctrine a turning point in American history?

2. In the postwar era, leaders such as Winston Churchill, Harry Truman, and Douglas MacArthur all warned of the dangers of trying to appease aggressors. What evidence did they present to support this position?

3. What did General MacArthur mean when he said, "In war there can be no substitute for victory"? How did this apply to the situation in Korea?

4. How might a defender of President Truman have responded to General MacArthur's position?

Tensions Amid Affluence
1953–1963

CHAPTER

13

Widespread economic advances in the 1950's and early 1960's brought prosperity to many Americans. One example of this new affluence was the ability of families to purchase homes in the new suburban developments that were being constructed during this period. *Time* magazine printed a description of how a typical suburb was built:

> On 1,200 flat acres of potato farmland . . . an army of trucks sped over new-laid roads. Every 100 feet, the trucks stopped and dumped identical bundles of lumber, pipes, bricks, shingles, and copper tubing. . . . Near the bundles giant machines with an endless chain of buckets ate into the earth, taking just thirteen minutes to dig a narrow, four-foot trench around a 25-by-32 foot rectangle. . . . After the machines came the men. Under the skilled combination of men and machines, new houses rose . . . a new one was finished every fifteen minutes.

American society, during this period, also faced a number of challenges. Fears of Communist infiltration in government, the movement to desegregate public schools, and the existence of severe poverty in some areas of the country were issues which confronted the nation.

During the 1950's and 1960's, extensive housing developments were built on the outskirts of many American cities. Standardized construction methods reduced developers' building costs and, consequently, helped keep the price of homes at an affordable level for many American families.

1 Joseph McCarthy on the Communist Threat

On February 9, 1950, Senator Joseph R. McCarthy of Wisconsin, speaking in Wheeling, West Virginia, charged that 205 known Communists were "working and shaping State Department policy." The next night he repeated his charges in Reno, Nevada, where he mentioned a list of 57 Communists. In Salt Lake City, a week later, the number was 81. Whatever the number, the attention given to McCarthy's charges paved the way for his rise to political prominence. Portions of the Nevada speech follow.

Senator Joseph R. McCarthy charged that Communists had infiltrated the government.

This is a time of the "cold war." This is a time when all the world is split into two vast, increasingly hostile armed camps—a time of a great armaments race. . . .

Today we are engaged in a final, all-out battle between communistic atheism and Christianity. The modern champions of communism have selected this as the time. And, ladies and gentlemen, the chips are down—they are truly down. . . .

The reason why we find ourselves in a position of impotency is not because our only powerful potential enemy has sent men to invade our shores, but rather because of the traitorous actions of those who have been treated so well by this nation. It has not been the less fortunate or members of minority groups who have been selling this nation out, but rather those who have had all the benefits that the wealthiest nation on earth has had to offer—the finest homes, the finest college education, and the finest jobs in government we can give.

This is glaringly true in the State Department. There the bright young men who are born with silver spoons in their mouths are the ones who have been the worst. . . . In my opinion the State Department, which is one of the most important government departments, is thoroughly infested with Communists.

I have in my hand 57 cases of individuals who would appear to be either card-carrying members or certainly loyal to the Communist Party, but who nevertheless are still helping to shape our foreign policy. . . .

I know that you are saying to yourself, "Well, why doesn't the Congress do something about it?" Actually, ladies and gentlemen, one of the important reasons for the graft, the corruption, the dishonesty, the disloyalty, the treason in high government positions—one of the most important reasons why this continues is a lack of moral uprising on the part of the 140,000,000

American people. In the light of history, however, this is not hard to explain.

It is the result of an emotional hangover and a temporary moral lapse which follows every war. . . . It has always been thus after war.

However, the morals of our people have not been destroyed. They still exist. This cloak of numbness and apathy has only needed a spark to rekindle them. Happily, this spark has finally been supplied.

From *Congressional Record*, 81st Congress, 2nd Session.

1. Why, according to McCarthy, had Congress done nothing about Communist subversion?
2. What evidence did McCarthy offer to support his contention that the government was being subverted by Communists?

2 Margaret Chase Smith's "Declaration of Conscience"

Senator Margaret Chase Smith of Maine was the first of Joseph McCarthy's fellow Republicans to speak out against him. The following passages are taken from her address to the Senate on June 1, 1950.

Mr. President [of the Senate], I would like to speak briefly and simply about a serious national condition. It is a national feeling of fear and frustration that could result in national suicide and the end of everything that we Americans hold dear. It is a condition that comes from the lack of effective leadership either in the legislative branch or the executive branch of the government. . . .

Mr. President, I speak as a Republican. I speak as a woman. I speak as a United States senator. I speak as an American.

The United States Senate has long enjoyed worldwide respect as the greatest deliberative body in the world. But recently that deliberative character has too often been debased to the level of a forum of hate and character assassination sheltered by the shield of congressional immunity. . . .

I think that it is high time for the United States Senate and its members to do some real soul-searching and to weigh our consciences as to the manner in which we are performing our duty to the people of America and the manner in which we are using or abusing our individual powers and privileges.

I think it is high time that we remembered that we have sworn to uphold and defend the Constitution. I think it is high time that we remembered that the Constitution, as amended, speaks not only of the freedom of speech but also of trial by jury instead of trial by accusation. . . .

Those of us who shout the loudest about Americanism in making character assassinations are all too frequently those who, by our own words and acts, ignore some of the basic principles of Americanism—

The right to criticize.
The right to hold unpopular beliefs.
The right to protest.
The right of independent thought.

The exercise of these rights should not cost one single American citizen his reputation or his right to a livelihood nor should he be in danger of losing his reputation or livelihood merely because he happens to know someone who holds unpopular beliefs. . . .

The American people are sick and tired of being afraid to speak their minds lest they be politically smeared as Communists or Fascists by their opponents. Freedom of speech is not what it used to be in Amer-

ica. It has been so abused by some that it is not exercised by others. . . .

As a United States senator, I am not proud of the way in which the Senate has been made a publicity platform for irresponsible sensationalism. . . .

As an American, I condemn a Republican Fascist just as much as I condemn a Democrat Communist. I condemn a Democrat Fascist just as much as I condemn a Republican Communist. They are equally dangerous to you and me and to our country. As an American, I want to see our nation recapture the strength and unity it once had when we fought the enemy instead of ourselves.

From speech by Margaret Chase Smith, *Congressional Record*, 81st Congress, 2nd Session (June 1, 1950).

1. What basic principles of Americanism did Senator Smith say were being ignored?
2. What did she say was happening to freedom of speech?

Senator Margaret Chase Smith spoke out against Senator McCarthy's activities.

3 Brown v. Board of Education

Sanctioned by the Supreme Court decision in Plessy v. Ferguson, *many areas of the nation had long maintained "separate-but-equal" educational systems for whites and blacks. In 1954, however, the Supreme Court set aside the 1896 decision when it unanimously ruled against school segregation in* Brown v. Board of Education. *Passages from the* Brown *decision follow.*

Today, education is perhaps the most important function of state and local governments. Compulsory school attendance laws and the great expenditures for education both demonstrate our recognition of the importance of education to our democratic society. It is required in the performance of our most basic public responsibilities, even service in the armed forces. It is the very foundation of good citizenship. Today it is a principal instrument in awakening the child to cultural values, in preparing him for later professional training, and in helping him to adjust normally to his environment. In these days, it is doubtful that any child may reasonably be expected to succeed in life if he is denied the opportunity of an education. Such an opportunity, where the state has undertaken to provide it, is a right which must be made available to all on equal terms.

We come then to the question presented: Does segregation of children in public schools solely on the basis of race, even though the physical facilities and other "tangible" factors may be equal, deprive the children of the minority group of equal educational opportunities? We believe that it does. . . .

We conclude that in the field of public education the doctrine of "separate but equal" has no place. Separate educational facilities are inherently unequal. Therefore, we hold that the plaintiffs and others similarly situated for whom the actions have been brought are, by reason of the segregation complained of, deprived of the equal protection of the laws guaranteed by the Fourteenth Amendment.

From *Brown v. Board of Education of Topeka, United States Report*, Vol. 347 (Washington, D.C., 1954).

---

1. For what reasons did the Court say that education was an important government function?
2. Why did the Court rule against separate school systems?

4 President Eisenhower on the Little Rock Crisis

Following the Brown *decision, some states resisted the Court's order to desegregate their schools. Serious trouble broke out in Little Rock, Arkansas, in 1957, when the local school board agreed to admit nine black students to Central High School. To ensure the safety of the black students, President Eisenhower sent federal troops to Little Rock to maintain order. On September 24, 1957, he explained his actions in an address to the nation.*

For a few minutes this evening I want to talk to you about the serious situation that has arisen in Little Rock. . . .

In that city, under the leadership of demagogic extremists, disorderly mobs have deliberately prevented the carrying out of proper orders from a federal court. Local authorities have not eliminated that violent opposition and, under the law, I yesterday issued a proclamation calling upon the mob to disperse.

This morning the mob again gathered in front of the Central High School of Little Rock, obviously for the purpose of again preventing the carrying out of the Court's order relating to the admission of Negro children to that school. . . .

In accordance with [my] responsibility, I have today issued an executive order directing the use of troops under federal authority to aid in the execution of federal law at Little Rock, Arkansas. This became necessary when my proclamation of yesterday was not observed, and the obstruction of justice still continues. . . .

Our personal opinions about the decision have no bearing on the matter of enforcement; the responsibility and authority of the Supreme Court to interpret the Constitution are very clear. . . .

Mob rule cannot be allowed to override the decisions of the courts.

Now, let me make it very clear that federal troops are not being used to relieve local and state authorities of their primary duty to preserve the peace and order of the community. Nor are the troops there for the purpose of taking over the responsibility of the school board and the other responsible local officials in running Central High School. . . . In the present case the troops are there, pursuant to law, solely for the purpose of preventing interference with the orders of the Court. . . .

Our enemies are gloating over this incident and using it everywhere to misrepresent our whole nation. We are portrayed as a violator of those standards of conduct which the people of the world united to proclaim in the Charter of the United Nations. There they affirmed "faith in fundamental human rights" and "in the dignity

In 1957, federal troops were sent to Little Rock Central High School in Arkansas to assure the safety of black students.

and worth of the human person," and they did so "without distinction as to race, sex, language, or religion."

And so, with deep confidence, I call upon citizens of the state of Arkansas to assist in bringing to an immediate end all interference with the law and its processes. If resistance to the federal court order ceases at once, the further presence of federal troops will be unnecessary and the city of Little Rock will return to its normal habits of peace and order—and a blot upon the fair name and high honor of our nation will be removed.

From address by President Dwight Eisenhower, September 24, 1957, in *Vital Speeches*, Vol. 24 (October 15, 1957).

1. What reasons did the President give for sending federal troops to Little Rock?
2. According to the President, how were America's enemies taking advantage of the Little Rock crisis?

5 President Eisenhower's "Farewell Address"

On January 18, 1961, Dwight Eisenhower spoke for the last time as President. In what was widely considered to be his "Farewell Address," he warned Americans of the dangers to their liberties posed by two new developments —the rise of the "military-industrial complex" and of government-supported scientific research.

Our military organization today bears little relation to that known by any of my predecessors, or indeed by the fighting men in World War II or Korea.

Until the latest of our world conflicts, the United States had no armaments industry. American makers of plowshares could, with time and as required, make swords as well. But now we can no longer risk emergency improvisation of national defense; we have been compelled to create a permanent armaments industry of vast proportions. Added to this, three and a half million men and women are directly engaged in the defense establishment. We annually spend on military security more than the net income of all United States corporations.

This conjunction of an immense military establishment and a large arms industry is new in American experience. The total influence—economic, political, even spiritual—is felt in every city, in every state house, every office of the federal government. We recognize the imperative need for this development. Yet we must not fail to comprehend its grave implications. Our toil, resources, and livelihood are all involved; so is the very structure of our society.

In the councils of government, we must guard against the acquisition of unwarranted influence, whether sought or unsought, by the military-industrial complex. The potential for the disastrous rise of misplaced power exists and will persist.

We must never let the weight of this combination endanger our liberties or democratic processes. We should take nothing for granted. Only an alert and knowledgeable citizenry can compel the proper meshing of the huge industrial and military machinery of defense with our peaceful methods and goals, so that security and liberty may prosper together.

Akin to, and largely responsible for the sweeping changes in our industrial-military posture, has been the technological revolution during recent decades.

In this revolution, research has become central; it also becomes more formalized, complex, and costly. A steadily increasing share is conducted for, by, or at the direction of, the federal government.

Today, the solitary inventor, tinkering in his shop, has been overshadowed by task forces of scientists in laboratories and testing fields. In the same fashion, the free university, historically the fountainhead of free ideas and scientific discovery, has experienced a revolution in the conduct of research. Partly because of the huge costs involved, a government contract becomes virtually a substitute for intellectual curiosity. For every old blackboard there are now hundreds of new electronic computers.

The prospect of domination of the nation's scholars by federal employment, project allocations, and the power of

President Dwight Eisenhower is shown with his wife, Mamie, at their home in Pennsylvania.

money is ever present and is gravely to be regarded.

Yet, in holding scientific research and discovery in respect, as we should, we must also be alert to the equal and opposite danger that public policy could itself become the captive of a scientific-technological elite.

It is the task of statesmanship to mold, to balance, and to integrate these and other forces, new and old, within the principles of our democratic system—ever aiming toward the supreme goals of our free society.

From address by President Dwight Eisenhower, *Congressional Record*, 86th Congress (February 16, 1961).

1. What specific dangers did Eisenhower see in the "military-industrial complex"?
2. What dangers did he think might arise from government involvement in scientific scholarship and research?

6 John F. Kennedy's Inaugural Address

On January 20, 1961, John F. Kennedy was sworn in as President. In his inaugural address, he stirred the nation with his eloquent words.

We observe today not a victory of party but a celebration of freedom—symbolizing an end as well as a beginning—signifying renewal as well as change. For I have sworn before you and Almighty God the same solemn oath our forebears prescribed nearly a century and three quarters ago.

The world is very different now. For man holds in his mortal hands the power to abolish all form of human poverty and to abolish all form of human life. And, yet, the same revolutionary beliefs for which our forebears fought are still at issue around the globe—the belief that the rights of man come not from the generosity of the state but from the hand of God.

John F. Kennedy took the oath of office in Washington, D.C., on January 20, 1961.

We dare not forget today that we are the heirs of that first revolution. Let the word go forth from this time and place, to friend and foe alike, that the torch has been passed to a new generation of Americans —born in this century, tempered by war, disciplined by a cold and bitter peace, proud of our ancient heritage—and unwilling to witness or permit the slow undoing of those human rights to which this nation has always been committed, and to which we are committed today.

Let every nation know, whether it wish us well or ill, that we shall pay any price, bear any burden, meet any hardship, support any friend or oppose any foe in order to assure the survival and success of liberty.

This much we pledge—and more. . . .

In your hands, my fellow citizens, more than in mine, will rest the final success or failure of our course. Since this country was founded, each generation has been summoned to give testimony to its national loyalty. The graves of young Americans who answered the call encircle the globe.

Now the trumpet summons us again— not as a call to bear arms, though arms we need—not as a call to battle, though embattled we are—but a call to bear the burden of a long twilight struggle, year in and year out, "rejoicing in hope, patient in tribulation"—a struggle against the common enemies of man: tyranny, poverty, disease, and war itself. . . .

And so, my fellow Americans: Ask not what your country can do for you—ask what you can do for your country.

My fellow citizens of the world: Ask not what America will do for you, but what together we can do for the freedom of man.

From John F. Kennedy, Inaugural Address, *Department of State Bulletin* (February 6, 1961).

1. What similarities did Kennedy see between the United States in 1961 and events 175 years earlier? What differences did he see?
2. Against what "common enemies of man" did Kennedy urge the American people to struggle?

Analysis

1. Both Senators Joseph McCarthy and Margaret Chase Smith declared in 1950 that the liberties of the American people were in jeopardy. Compare the threats that each described.

2. The Supreme Court's decision in *Brown v. Board of Education* reversed the earlier decision reached in the *Plessy v. Ferguson* case. What changes in American life since 1896 may have contributed to the 1954 decision?

3. Why would President Eisenhower's comments on the "military-industrial complex" have carried a great deal of weight?

4. In his inaugural address, what goals did John F. Kennedy set for the American people?

The Turbulent Johnson Years
1963–1968

CHAPTER

14

When Lyndon Johnson was sworn in as President in 1965, he called for a program of social legislation called the Great Society. In his State of the Union address delivered shortly thereafter, Johnson spoke of the purpose of this program:

> The Great Society asks not how much, but how good; not only how to create wealth, but how to use it; not only how fast we are going, but where we are headed. It proposes as the first test for a nation: the quality of its people.
>
> This kind of society will not flower spontaneously from swelling riches and surging power. It will not be the gift of government or the creation of Presidents. It will require of every American, for many generations, both faith in the destination and fortitude to make the journey.

In the tradition of the social reform programs of his Democratic predecessors, Lyndon Johnson's Great Society sought to alleviate economic hardships and correct injustices in American society. During the final years of Johnson's presidency, the escalation of American military involvement in the Vietnam conflict diverted the attention of his administration from domestic programs.

Passed by Congress in 1965, the Voting Rights Act abolished literacy tests and other voting restrictions. President Johnson signed the bill at a Capitol ceremony as invited guests looked on.

1 Poverty in America

Even before President Johnson launched his "war on poverty," public attention had been drawn to the plight of impoverished Americans by Michael Harrington in The Other America *(1962). Harrington, a youthful reformer and former editor of the* Catholic Worker, *gained a national reputation from his book and in 1964 served on a White House task force that developed some of the basic concepts of the antipoverty effort. In the following passages from* The Other America, *Harrington explains why so few Americans were aware of the existence of poverty in the United States.*

There is a familiar America. It is celebrated in speeches and advertised on television and in the magazines. It has the highest mass standard of living the world has ever known.

In the 1950's, this America worried about itself, yet even its anxieties were products of abundance. . . . There was introspection about Madison Avenue [advertising] and tail fins [on cars]; there was discussion of the emotional suffering that takes place in the suburbs. In all this, there was an implicit assumption that the basic grinding economic problems had been solved in the United States. In this theory the nation's problems were no longer a matter of basic human needs, of food, shelter, and clothing. Now they were seen as . . . a question of learning to live decently amid luxury.

While this discussion was carried on, there existed another America. In it dwelt somewhere between 40,000,000 and 50,000,000 citizens of this land. They were poor. They still are.

To be sure, the other America is not impoverished in the same sense as those poor nations where millions cling to hunger as a defense against starvation. This country has escaped such extremes. That does not change the fact that tens of millions of Americans are, at this very moment, maimed in body and spirit, existing at levels beneath those necessary for human decency. If these people are not starving, they are hungry, and sometimes fat with hunger, for that is what cheap foods do. They are without adequate housing and education and medical care.

The government has documented what this means to the bodies of the poor. . . . But even more basic, this poverty twists and deforms the spirit. The American poor are pessimistic and defeated, and they are victimized by mental suffering to a degree unknown in suburbia. . . .

The other America, the America of poverty, is hidden today in a way that it never was before. Its millions are socially invisible to the rest of us. . . .

There are perennial reasons that make the other America an invisible land.

Poverty is often off the beaten track. It always has been. The ordinary tourist never left the main highway, and today he rides interstate turnpikes. He does not go into the valleys of Pennsylvania where the towns look like movie sets of Wales in the [1930's]. . . .

Then, too, beauty and myths are perennial masks of poverty. The traveler comes to the Appalachians in the lovely season. He sees the hills, the streams, the foliage —but not the poor. Or perhaps he looks at a run-down mountain house and . . . decides that "those people" are truly fortunate to be living the way they are and that they are lucky to be exempt from the strains and tensions of the middle class. The only problem is that "those people," the quaint inhabitants of those hills, are uneducated, underprivileged, lack medical care, and are in the process of being forced from the land into a life in the cities, where they are misfits.

These are normal and obvious causes of the invisibility of the poor. . . . It is more important to understand that the very development of American society is creating a new kind of blindness about poverty. . . .

Now the American city has been transformed. The poor still inhabit the miserable housing in the central area, but they are increasingly isolated from contact with, or sight of, anybody else. Middle-class women coming in from suburbia on a rare trip might catch the merest glimpse of the other America on the way to an evening at the theater, but their children are segregated in suburban schools. The business or professional man may drive along the fringes of the slums in a car or bus, but it is not an important experience to him. . . .

In short, the very development of the American city has removed poverty from the living, emotional experience of millions upon millions of middle-class Americans. Living out in the suburbs, it is easy to assume that ours is, indeed, an affluent society. . . .

Then, many of the poor are the wrong age to be seen. A good number of them (over 8,000,000) are 65 years of age or better; an even larger number are under 18. The aged members of the other America are often sick, and they cannot move. An-

other group of them live out their lives in loneliness and frustration . . . in rented rooms, or . . . a house in a neighborhood that has completely changed from the old days. . . .

The young are somewhat more visible, yet they too stay close to their neighborhoods. . . .

And finally, the poor are politically invisible. . . . The people of the other America do not, by far and large, belong to unions, to fraternal organizations, or to political parties. They are without lobbies of their own; they put forward no legislative program. As a group, they . . . have no face; they have no voice.

---

1. What did Harrington mean by the term "the other America"?
2. According to Harrington, why had the poor become increasingly invisible in America?
3. Why did Harrington call the poor "politically invisible"?

2 Rachel Carson—Silent Spring

During the 1960's, Americans grew increasingly concerned about the environment. Rachel Carson, a marine biologist and author, drew the attention of millions of readers with her book Silent Spring *(1962). In* Silent Spring *she strongly criticized the wasteful and destructive use of pesticides. The book's influence was such that it led to restrictions on the use of pesticides in many parts of the world. The following passages are from the introduction to* Silent Spring.

There was once a town in the heart of America where all life seemed to live in harmony with its surroundings. The town lay in the midst of a checkerboard of prosperous farms, with fields of grain and hillsides of orchards where, in spring, white clouds of bloom drifted above the green fields. In autumn, oak and maple and birch set up a blaze of color that flamed and flickered across a backdrop of pines. Then foxes barked in the hills and deer silently crossed the fields, half hidden in the mists of the fall mornings.

Along the roads, laurel, viburnum and alder, great ferns and wildflowers delighted the traveler's eye through much of the year. Even in winter the roadsides were places of beauty, where countless birds came to feed on the berries and on the seed heads of the dried weeds rising above the snow. The countryside was, in fact, famous for the abundance and variety of its bird life, and when the flood of migrants was pouring through in spring and fall people traveled from great distances to observe them. Others came to fish the streams, which flowed clear and cold out of the hills and contained shady pools where trout lay. So it had been from the days many years ago when the first settlers raised their houses, sank their wells, and built their barns.

Then a strange blight crept over the area and everything began to change. Some evil spell had settled on the community: mysterious maladies swept the flocks of chickens; the cattle and sheep sickened and died. Everywhere was a shadow of death. The farmers spoke of much illness among their families. In the town the doctors had become more and more puzzled by new kinds of sickness appearing among their patients. There had been several sudden and unexplained deaths, not only among adults but even among children, who would be stricken suddenly while at play and die within a few hours.

There was a strange stillness. The birds, for example—where had they gone? Many people spoke of them, puzzled and disturbed. The feeding stations in the backyards were deserted. The few birds seen anywhere were moribund [near death]; they trembled violently and could not fly. It was a spring without voices. On the mornings that had once throbbed with the dawn chorus of robins, catbirds, doves, jays, wrens, and scores of other bird voices there was now no sound: only silence lay over the fields and woods and marsh.

On the farms the hens brooded, but no chicks hatched. The farmers complained that they were unable to raise any pigs—the litters were small and the young survived only a few days. The apple trees were coming into bloom but no bees droned among the blossoms, so there was no pollination and there would be no fruit.

The roadsides, once so attractive, were now lined with browned and withered vegetation as though swept by fire. These, too, were silent, deserted by all living things. Even the streams were now lifeless. An-

Rachel Carson's articles and books drew the attention of Americans to the dangers of polluting the environment.

glers no longer visited them, for all the fish had died.

In the gutters under the eaves and between the shingles of the roofs, a white granular powder still showed a few patches; some weeks before it had fallen like snow upon the roofs and the lawns, the fields and streams.

No witchcraft, no enemy action had silenced the rebirth of life in this stricken world. The people had done it themselves.

This town does not actually exist, but it might easily have a thousand counterparts in America or elsewhere in the world. I know of no community that has experienced all the misfortunes I describe. Yet every one of these disasters has actually happened somewhere, and many real communities have already suffered a substantial number of them. A grim specter has crept upon us almost unnoticed, and this imagined tragedy may easily become a stark reality we all shall know.

1. What changes came to the environment in the mythical town described by Rachel Carson?
2. On whom did Rachel Carson place responsibility for the careless use of pesticides?

3 Barry Goldwater Accepts the Republican Nomination for President

On July 16, 1964, Senator Barry Goldwater of Arizona won the Republican nomination for President. His acceptance speech, passages of which follow, was noted for its statement of Goldwater's philosophy of government.

I seek an America proud of its past, proud of its ways, proud of its dreams and determined to actively proclaim them. But our examples to the world must, like charity, begin at home.

In our vision of a good and decent future, free and peaceful, there must be room, room for the liberation of the energy and the talent of the individual. . . .

We must assure a society here which while never abandoning the needy, or forsaking the helpless, nurtures incentives and opportunity for the creative and the productive.

We must know the whole good is the product of many single contributions. And I cherish the day when our children once again will restore as heroes the sort of men and women who, unafraid and undaunted, pursue the truth, strive to cure disease, subdue and make fruitful our natural environment, and produce the inventive engines of production, science, and technology.

This nation, whose creative people have enhanced this entire span of history, should again thrive upon the greatness of all those things which we—we as individual citizens—can and should do.

During Republican years, this again will be a nation of men and women, of families proud of their role, jealous of their responsibilities, unlimited in their aspirations—a nation where all who can will be self-reliant.

We Republicans see in our constitutional form of government the great framework which assures the orderly but dynamic fulfillment of the whole man, and we see the whole man as the great reason for instituting orderly government in the first place.

We can see in private property and in economy based upon and fostering private property the one way to make government a durable ally of the whole man rather than his determined enemy.

We see in the sanctity of private property the only durable foundation for constitutional government in a free society.

And beyond that we see and cherish diversity of ways, diversity of thoughts, of motives, and accomplishments. We don't seek to live anyone's life for him. We only seek to secure his rights, guarantee him opportunity, guarantee him opportunity to strive with government performing only those needed and constitutionally sanctioned tasks which cannot otherwise be performed.

We Republicans seek a government that attends to its inherent responsibilities of maintaining a stable monetary and fiscal climate, encouraging a free and a competitive economy, and enforcing law and order.

Thus do we seek inventiveness, diversity, and creative difference within a stable order, for we Republicans define government's role where needed at many, many levels, preferably though the one closest to the people involved: our towns and our cities, then our counties, then our states, then our regional contacts and only then the national government.

That, let me remind you, is the land of liberty built by decentralized power. On it also we must have balance between the branches of government at every level. . . .

Anyone who joins us in all sincerity we welcome. Those, those who do not care for our cause, we don't expect to enter our ranks in any case. And let our Republicanism so focused and so dedicated not be made fuzzy and futile by unthinking and stupid labels.

I would remind you that extremism in defense of liberty is no vice.

And let me remind you also that moderation in pursuit of justice is no virtue.

From Barry Goldwater, Acceptance Speech, *Vital Speeches*, Vol. 30 (August 15, 1964).

---

1. What role did Goldwater want the federal government to play in the lives of Americans?
2. What did Goldwater mean when he said that "extremism in defense of liberty is no vice"?

4 Lyndon Johnson Explains the American Presence in Vietnam

Early in 1965, the first United States combat troops were sent to Vietnam. In an address to the American people, President Johnson explained his administration's policy.

The rulers in Hanoi are urged on by Peking. This is a regime which has destroyed freedom in Tibet, attacked India, and been condemned by the United Nations for aggression in Korea. It is a nation which is helping the forces of violence in almost every continent. The contest in Vietnam is part of a wider pattern of aggressive purpose.

Why are these realities our concern? Why are we in South Vietnam? We are there because we have a promise to keep. Since 1954 every American President has offered support to the people of South Vietnam. We have helped to build, and we have helped to defend. Thus, over many years, we have made a national pledge to help South Vietnam defend its independence. And I intend to keep our promise.

To dishonor that pledge, to abandon this small and brave nation to its enemy, and to the terror that must follow, would be an unforgivable wrong.

We are also there to strengthen world order. Around the globe, from Berlin to Thailand, are people whose well-being rests, in part, on the belief that they can count on us if they are attacked. To leave Vietnam to its fate would shake the confidence of all these people in the value of American commitment, the value of America's word. The result would be increased unrest and instability, and even wider war.

We are also there because there are great

Helicopters played an important part in the Vietnam War. American pilots used them to transport troops, carry the wounded to hospitals, and bring supplies to forces in the field.

stakes in the balance. Let no one think for a moment that retreat from Vietnam would bring an end to conflict. The battle would be renewed in one country and then another. The central lesson of our time is that the appetite of aggression is never satisfied. To withdraw from one battlefield means only to prepare for the next. . . .

There are those who say that all our effort there will be futile, that China's power is such it is bound to dominate all Southeast Asia. But there is no end to that argument until all the nations of Asia are swallowed up.

There are those who wonder why we have a responsibility there. We have it for the same reason we have a responsibility for the defense of freedom in Europe. World War II was fought in both Europe and Asia, and when it ended we found ourselves with continued responsibility for the defense of freedom.

Our objective is the independence of South Vietnam, and its freedom from attack. We want nothing for ourselves, only that the people of South Vietnam be allowed to guide their own country in their own way.

We will do everything necessary to reach that objective. And we will do only what is absolutely necessary.

From *Department of State Bulletin*, April 26, 1965.

1. According to President Johnson, what was the role of China in Southeast Asia?
2. What did Johnson say would happen if the United States withdrew from Vietnam?

5 Lyndon Johnson's March 31, 1968, Address on Vietnam

By 1968, many Americans were speaking out against Lyndon Johnson's handling of the conflict in Vietnam. On March 31, the President went on national television to discuss the situation in Southeast Asia. He ended his speech with a surprise announcement.

During the past four and a half years, it has been my fate and my responsibility to be commander-in-chief. I have lived—daily and nightly—with the cost of this war. I know the pain that it has inflicted. I know, perhaps better than anyone, the misgivings that it has aroused.

Throughout this entire, long period, I have been sustained by a single principle: that what we are doing now, in Vietnam, is vital not only to the security of Southeast Asia, but it is vital to the security of every American.

Surely we have treaties which we must respect. Surely we have commitments that we are going to keep. Resolutions of the Congress testify to the need to resist aggression in the world and in Southeast Asia.

But the heart of our involvement in South Vietnam—under three different Presidents, three separate administrations—has always been America's own security.

And the larger purpose of our involvement has always been to help the nations of Southeast Asia become independent and stand alone, self-sustaining, as members of a great world community—at peace with themselves, and at peace with all others.

With such an Asia, our country—and the world—will be far more secure than it is tonight.

I believe that a peaceful Asia is far nearer to reality because of what America

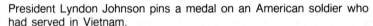

President Lyndon Johnson pins a medal on an American soldier who had served in Vietnam.

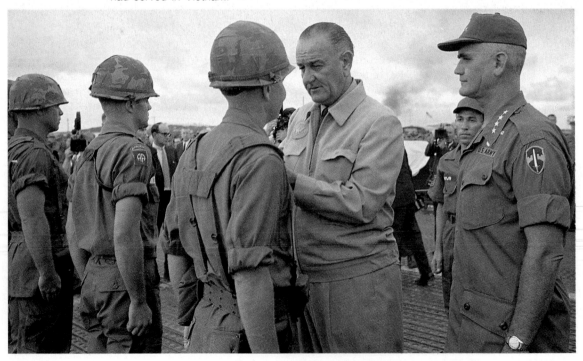

has done in Vietnam. I believe that the men who endure the dangers of battle—fighting there for us tonight—are helping the entire world avoid far greater conflicts, far wider wars, far more destruction, than this one. . . .

We are prepared to move immediately toward peace through negotiations. So tonight, in the hope that this action will lead to early talks, I am taking the first step to de-escalate the conflict. We are reducing—substantially reducing—the present level of hostilities, and we are doing so unilaterally and at once.

Tonight I have ordered our aircraft and our naval vessels to make no attacks on North Vietnam except in the area north of the demilitarized zone where the continuing enemy build-up directly threatens Allied forward positions and where the movement of their troops and supplies are clearly related to that threat.

The area in which we are stopping our attacks includes almost 90 percent of North Vietnam's population and most of its territory. Thus there will be no attacks around the principal populated areas or in the food-producing areas of North Vietnam. . . .

With America's sons in the fields far away, with America's future under challenge right here at home, with our hopes and the world's hopes for peace in the balance every day, I do not believe that I should devote an hour or a day of my time to any personal partisan causes or to any duties other than the awesome duties of this office—the presidency of your country.

Accordingly, I shall not seek, and I will not accept, the nomination of my party for another term as President.

From *Public Papers of the Presidents of the United States: Lyndon B. Johnson, 1968-1969, Book I* (Washington, D.C.: United States Government Printing Office, 1970).

1. What measure did President Johnson take to try to reduce hostilities?
2. What was President Johnson's surprise announcement?

Analysis

1. What contrast did Michael Harrington draw between suburbanites and people who lived in "the other America"?

2. Michael Harrington and Rachel Carson argued that action by the federal government was needed to deal with the problems of poverty and the environment. What response might Barry Goldwater have made to those arguments? Use statements from Goldwater's 1964 acceptance speech to support your answer.

3. Compare the views of President Johnson on resistance to communism with those of his three predecessors in the White House.

4. Compare President Johnson's address of April 26, 1965, with that of March 31, 1968. What changes in policy did he offer in the second address?

Crisis in the Presidency
1969–1976

CHAPTER

15

The primary goal of Richard Nixon's foreign policy was to reduce tensions in the world. In 1972, this policy of détente prompted President Nixon to accept an invitation to visit China and confer with the Chinese leadership. In his memoirs, Nixon described his meeting with Chairman Mao Tse-tung:

> We all sat in overstuffed armchairs set in a semicircle at the end of a long room. . . . "Mr. Chairman," I said, "I am aware of the fact that over a period of years my position with regard to the People's Republic was one that the chairman . . . totally disagreed with. What brings us together is a recognition of a new situation in the world and a recognition on our part that what is important is not a nation's internal political philosophy. What is important is its policy toward the rest of the world and toward us."

This historic trip to China was followed by one to the Soviet Union for a summit conference with the Russian leadership. Richard Nixon's foreign policy initiatives, however, were soon overshadowed by the Watergate affair, which led to his resignation in the summer of 1974.

As part of his détente policy, President Nixon visited China in 1972. Following his meetings with China's leaders, the President joined First Lady Pat Nixon for a tour of a portion of the Great Wall.

1 Vietnamization

Shortly after taking office in 1969, President Nixon announced a plan by which American troops would gradually be withdrawn from frontline positions in Vietnam and replaced with South Vietnamese forces. The following document, issued by the State Department in 1971, described the progress of the Vietnamization program.

It is clear that a majority of Americans now favor the withdrawal of United States combat forces from Vietnam and an end to the Vietnam war.

Since June, 1969, when President Nixon made his first announcement of United States troop withdrawals, the key issues have been the manner of the withdrawal and the way the war is ended.

In this photograph, three American soldiers are shown at an artillery emplacement in Vietnam.

A sudden departure of United States forces, however, could lead to a North Vietnamese take-over of the South and imposition of a dictatorship; possibly the liquidation of thousands of those associated with the long anti-Communist struggle; and a dangerous weakening of the non-Communist effort in Asia to remain neutral and independent. In that belief, this administration has followed a two-fold program for limiting and ending United States participation in the Vietnam conflict.

The program is designed to:

(1) seek a negotiated solution in Paris consistent with the legitimate interests of all parties; or,

(2) in the event that a negotiated settlement is not achieved, provide a viable alternative course of action by preparing South Vietnam to carry the full burden of its defense after United States forces are withdrawn. This is the program known as "Vietnamization"—a military-economic program of South Vietnamese development which will permit rapid but phased withdrawals of United States forces without radically upsetting the power balance in Southeast Asia. . . .

While we continue to press for a reasonable settlement through negotiations, the United States government is pursuing the alternative policy of Vietnamization. . . . The rate of withdrawal of United States troops is determined on the basis of three criteria announced by the President at the beginning of the program: (1) the level of enemy military activity; (2) progress in the Paris talks; and (3) the ability of the South Vietnamese to assume an increasing share of the burden of their own defense. Two years ago:

—The authorized American troop strength in Vietnam in 1969 was 549,000. More than 316,000 [troops] have now been withdrawn. By December 1, 1971, the authorized troop strength will be 184,000. The current pace of United States withdrawal is ahead of schedule.

—Approximately three hundred Americans

were being lost every week. This year that figure runs less than fifty.

—The ratio of South Vietnamese forces to United States forces in Vietnam changed from 2 to 1 in 1969 to 4 to 1 in early 1971.

Thus the President could announce on April 7, 1971, "The American involvement in Vietnam is coming to an end. The day the South Vietnamese can take over their own defense is in sight. Our goal is a total American withdrawal from Vietnam. We can and we will reach that goal. . . . "

The Vietnamization program, which the Communists have consistently denounced,

is in general succeeding. In some areas it is, inevitably, a mixed picture; in others, the picture is one of uniform progress.

From "A Program for Peace in Vietnam," *Current Foreign Policy*, Department of State, Bureau of Public Affairs (Washington, D.C., 1971).

1. According to this report, why had United States forces not been withdrawn from Vietnam immediately?
2. What evidence was cited to support the argument that the Vietnamization policy was succeeding?

2 The Shanghai Communiqué

Richard Nixon was the first American President to visit the People's Republic of China. The Shanghai Communiqué, released late in February, 1972, at the conclusion of the trip, summarized the discussions that had been held by President Nixon and Premier Chou En-lai. Portions of that announcement follow.

There are essential differences between China and the United States in their social systems and foreign policies. However, the two sides agreed that countries, regardless of their social systems, should conduct their relations on the principles of respect for the sovereignty and territorial integrity of all states, nonaggression against other states, equality and mutual benefit, and peaceful coexistence. International disputes should be settled on this basis, without resorting to the use or threat of force. The United States and the People's Republic of China are prepared to apply these principles to their mutual relations.

With these principles of international relations in mind the two sides stated that:
—progress toward the normalization of relations between China and the United States is in the interests of all countries;

—both wish to reduce the danger of international military conflict;

—neither should seek [domination] in the Asia-Pacific region and each is opposed to efforts by any other country or group of countries to establish such [domination];

—and neither is prepared to negotiate on behalf of any third party or to enter into agreements or understandings with the other directed at other states.

Both sides are of the view that it would be against the interests of the peoples of the world for any major country to [conspire] with another against other nations, or for major countries to divide up the world into spheres of interest.

The two sides reviewed the long-standing serious disputes between China and the United States. The Chinese side reaffirmed its position: The Taiwan question is the crucial question obstructing the normalization of relations between China and the United States; the government of the People's Republic of China is the sole legal government of China; Taiwan is a province of China which has long been returned to the motherland; the liberation of Taiwan is China's internal affair in which no other country has the right to interfere; and all United States forces and military installations must be withdrawn from Taiwan. . . .

The United States side declared: The

United States acknowledges that all Chinese on either side of the Taiwan Strait maintain there is but one China and that Taiwan is a part of China. The United States government does not challenge that position. It reaffirms its interest in a peaceful settlement of the Taiwan question by the Chinese themselves. With this prospect in mind, it affirms the ultimate objective of the withdrawal of all United States forces and military installations from Taiwan. In the meantime, it will progressively reduce its forces and military installations on Taiwan as the tension in the area diminishes.

The two sides agreed that it is desirable to broaden the understanding between the two peoples. To this end, they discussed specific areas in such fields as science, technology, culture, sports, and journalism, in which people-to-people contacts and exchanges would be mutually beneficial. Each side undertakes to facilitate the further development of such contacts and exchanges.

Both sides view bilateral trade as another area from which mutual benefit can be derived, and agreed that economic relations based on equality and mutual benefit are in the interest of the peoples of the two countries. They agree to facilitate the progressive development of trade between their two countries.

The two sides agreed that they will stay in contact through various channels, including the sending of senior United States representatives to Peking from time to time for concrete consultations to further the normalization of relations between the two countries and continue to exchange views on issues of common interest.

The two sides expressed the hope that the gains achieved during this visit would open up new prospects for the relations between the two countries. They believe that the normalization of relations between the two countries is not only in the interest of the Chinese and American peoples but also contributes to the relaxation of tension in Asia and the world.

From *Public Papers of the Presidents of the United States, Richard M. Nixon, 1972* (Washington, D.C.: United States Government Printing Office, 1973).

1. What did the communiqué say were the advantages of improved Chinese-American relations?
2. What was the main area of disagreement between the two countries?

3 Leon Jaworski on Watergate

On July 24, 1974, the Supreme Court ordered President Nixon to turn over tapes of conversations relating to the Watergate affair to Special Prosecutor Leon Jaworski and to the House Judiciary Committee. Immediately thereafter, Jaworski spoke with Theodore White, the noted political writer, about what he saw as the lessons to be learned from the situation. White described their conversation in this way.

I had lunch within an hour of the decision with Leon Jaworski, whose authority as Special Prosecutor Chief Justice Burger had just affirmed as sovereign. But as Jaworski sat at table . . . there was little of sovereign manner about him. He was an old man, today weary, tufts of white hair above the face of a friendly goblin, the voice firm, now precise, then again grandfatherly. And no elation in his voice about the victory.

Jaworski recalled that over a year ago he had first been approached to become Special Prosecutor. He had insisted on complete independence and been told he would have to operate within guidelines set by the Department of Justice, and the matter was dropped. Later his name had been suggested to Nixon as chief counsel *for* the President's defense. But nothing came of that. Six months after the first approach he had finally accepted the role of Special Prosecutor only because the President's Chief of Staff, General Alexander Haig, had specifically promised, "If necessary, you can take the President to court." He was, Jaworski insisted, "not after the President; I just want all the facts out . . . we're in search of the truth. Wherever the truth leads, we're going to prosecute them." Unless he was [pretending], it seemed to this reporter that Jaworski had no inkling, no fore-echo of what it was that Richard Nixon had been concealing, what the subpoenaed tapes would soon reveal.

Mostly, Jaworski was in a reminiscent mood, reminiscences going back to Texas, his boyhood in Waco, trials in local courts, the upward life of a successful lawyer. But through the recollections ran his underlying cause, in phrases which on any other day and occasion would have sounded trite, but now carried meaning.

"What happened this morning," said the tired man, "proved what we teach in schools, it proved what we teach in colleges, it proved everything we've been trying to get across—that no man is above the law. . . ." This case, said Jaworski, would shape what the young of America would think or say or do in this system for all of the next generation. Unless the young people believed, really believed in our institutions, the system simply would not work. He quoted Disraeli; according to his recall, Disraeli had said, "The youth of the nation are the trustees of posterity." His clients were the youth of the nation, his prosecution a defense of the system.

From Theodore H. White, *Breach of Faith: The Fall of Richard M. Nixon.* Copyright © 1975 Theodore H. White. Reprinted with the permission of Atheneum Publishers, Inc.

1. What did Jaworski identify as his goal as Special Prosecutor?
2. What did Jaworski believe was the significance of the Supreme Court's decision?

4 Betty Friedan—The Feminine Mystique

A book thought by many to have inspired the women's movement of the 1960's and 1970's was Betty Friedan's The Feminine Mystique, *published in 1963. This work challenged the belief that a woman could find fulfillment only in the home. In the following passages from* The Feminine Mystique, *Betty Friedan identifies what she calls "the problem that has no name."*

The suburban housewife—she was the dream image of the young American woman and the envy, it was said, of women all over the world. The American housewife—freed by science and labor-saving appliances from the drudgery, the dangers of childbirth, and the illnesses of her grandmother. She was healthy, beautiful, educated, concerned only about her husband, her children, her home. She had found true feminine fulfillment. As a housewife and mother, she was respected as a full and equal partner to man in his world. She was free to choose automobiles, clothes, appliances, supermarkets; she had everything that women had ever dreamed of. . . .

But on an April morning in 1959, I heard a mother of four . . . say in a tone of quiet desperation, "the problem. . . ."

Gradually, I came to realize that the problem that has no name was shared by countless women in America. As a magazine writer I often interviewed women about problems with their children, or their marriages, or their houses, or their communities. But after a while I began to recognize the telltale signs of this other problem. . . .

Just what was this problem that has no name? What were the words women used when they tried to express it? Sometimes a woman would say, "I feel empty somehow ... incomplete." Or she would say, "I feel as if I don't exist. ..."

It is no longer possible to ignore that voice, to dismiss the desperation of so many American women. ... I do not accept the answer that there is no problem because American women have luxuries that women in other times and lands never dreamed of; part of the strange newness of the problem is that it cannot be understood in terms of the age-old material problems of man: poverty, sickness, hunger, cold. It persists in women whose husbands are struggling interns and law clerks, or prosperous doctors and lawyers; in wives of workers and executives who make $5,000 a year to $50,000. It is not caused by lack of material advantages. ...

It is no longer possible today to blame the problem on loss of femininity: to say that education and independence and equality with men have made American women unfeminine. ... Women who suffer this problem, in whom this voice is stirring, have lived their whole lives in the pursuit of feminine fulfillment. ... They are women whose greatest ambition has been marriage and children. ... These women are very "feminine" in the usual sense, and yet they still suffer the problem. ...

If I am right, the problem that has no name stirring in the minds of so many American women today is not a matter of loss of femininity or too much education, or the demands of domesticity. It is far more important than anyone recognizes. It is the key to these other new and old problems which have been torturing women and their husbands and children, and puzzling their doctors and educators for years. It may well be the key to our future as a nation and a culture. We can no longer ignore that voice within women that says: "I want something more than my husband and my children and my home."

From Betty Friedan, *The Feminine Mystique.* By permission of W. W. Norton & Company, Inc., and Victor Gollancz Ltd. Copyright © 1963, 1974 by Betty Friedan.

1. Why were suburban housewives said to be the envy of people all over the world?
2. What was the problem, however, that Betty Friedan claimed American women faced?

5 The Energy Crisis

In response to United States support for Israel during the Yom Kippur War of 1973, Arab countries in OPEC declared that they would no longer sell oil to the United States. Time magazine described what the resulting shortages of gasoline meant for many Americans.

Otherwise sane citizens are in the cold grip of the nation's newest obsession: gasoline fever.

As supplies tighten in many parts of the country, people are wondering where their next gallon is coming from. ...

The full-tank syndrome is bringing out the worst in both buyers and sellers of that volatile fluid. When a motorist in Pittsburgh topped off his tank with only 11 cents worth and then tried to pay for it with a credit card, the pump attendant spat in his face. A driver in Bethel, Connecticut, and another in Neptune, New Jersey, last week escaped serious injury when their cars were demolished by passenger trains as they sat stubbornly in lines that stretched across railroad tracks. "These people are like animals foraging for food," says Don Jacobson, who runs an Amoco station in Miami. "If you can't sell them gas, they'll threaten to beat you up, wreck your station, run over you with a car." Laments Bob Graves, a Lexington, Massachusetts,

Texaco dealer: "They've broken my pump handles and smashed the glass on the pumps, and tried to start fights when we close. We're all so busy at the pumps that somebody walked in and stole my adding machine and the leukemia-fund can."

To help minimize such madness, officials in Massachusetts, Maryland, New Jersey, Washington, D.C., Dade County, Florida, and other areas last week adopted . . . rationing schemes that will allow motorists with even-numbered license plates to buy gas on even-numbered dates, and those with odd-numbered plates to buy on odd-numbered dates. Some states have begun requiring a $3 minimum purchase. . . .

The Federal Energy Office may increase gasoline allocations within the next month or two for areas that are particularly dry. Energy officials say that if service-station lines get too long, national gasoline rationing will finally be imposed. FEO Chief William Simon is still publicly opposed to rationing, but aides say that he is willing to accept it if the gasoline shortage gets much further out of hand. The administration will not have legislative authority to order rationing until Congress passes the stalled emergency energy bill.

Simon has not yet ordered oil companies to speed up their yearly refinery switch-overs from production of residual, heating, and diesel fuels to production of gasoline, which usually occurs about this time. . . . Simon fears a sudden cold snap, and he is reluctant to risk running low on residual fuel for electric utilities, or anger truckers by cutting production of diesel fuel. The energy chief still feels, as one aide put it last week, that "people would rather wait in line for gasoline than be short on heat next month."

Yet the recent rash of tank topping and other pump misbehavior indicates that many people may be more worried about mobility than warmth. Every day that refinery switch-overs are delayed brings the specter of the ration book closer.

1. How were people reacting to the gasoline shortage?
2. What steps were federal, state, and local governments taking to deal with the problems caused by the oil embargo?

Analysis

1. Compare and contrast the goals of United States involvement in Vietnam as outlined in Chapter 14 by Lyndon Johnson with those stated by the State Department in its review of the Vietnamization program in 1971.

2. President Nixon's trip to the People's Republic of China and the statements contained in the Shanghai Communiqué about that visit represented a major shift in the policies of both countries. What steps have been taken by more recent American Presidents to improve relations with China?

3. Compare and contrast Betty Friedan's views of the problems confronting American women with the views of Carrie Chapman Catt in Chapter 6.

Challenging Years
1977–1980's

CHAPTER

16

The Statue of Liberty has always signified hope for the American people and for immigrants coming to the United States to start a new life. Renovation of the statue began in 1984 and focused the attention of the country on this national monument. In an address delivered soon after work got under way, President Ronald Reagan touched on the meaning and importance of the Statue of Liberty:

> Just this past Fourth of July, the torch atop the Statue of Liberty was hoisted down for replacement. We can be forgiven for thinking maybe it was just worn out from lighting the way for 17 million new Americans. So we'll put up a new one.
>
> The poet called Miss Liberty's torch the "lamp beside the golden door." The golden door—that was the entrance to America and still is. . . .
>
> The glistening hope of that lamp is still ours. Every promise, every opportunity is still golden in this land. And through that golden door our children can walk into tomorrow with the knowledge that no one can be denied the promise that is America. . . .

The future about which President Reagan spoke is filled with opportunity for the United States. It also presents great challenges if the American nation is to be assured a prosperous and secure future.

To countless immigrants arriving in the United States, the sight of the Statue of Liberty has inspired hope. This photograph records the renovation of the statue that was carried out in the mid-1980's.

1 Jimmy Carter on the "Crisis of Confidence"

Early in 1979, when Iranian oil shipments were halted after the fall of the shah, the energy problem again became critical. On July 15, President Jimmy Carter spoke to the nation about this latest round in the energy crisis. He also discussed what he called a national "crisis of confidence." Excerpts from his speech follow.

So I want to speak to you tonight about a subject even more serious than energy or inflation. I want to talk to you right now about a fundamental threat to American democracy.

I do not mean our political and civil liberties. They will endure. And I do not refer to the outward strength of America—the nation that is at peace tonight everywhere in the world with unmatched economic power and military might. The threat is nearly invisible in ordinary ways. It is a crisis of confidence. It is a crisis that strikes at the very heart and soul and spirit of our national will.

We can see this crisis in the growing doubt about the meaning of our own lives and in the loss of a unity of purpose for our nation. . . .

We've always believed in something called progress. We've always had a faith that the days of our children would be better than our own.

Our people are losing that faith. Not only in government itself, but in their ability as citizens to serve as the ultimate rulers and shapers of our democracy. . . .

In a nation that was proud of hard work, strong families, close-knit communities and our faith in God, too many of us now tend to worship self-indulgence and consumption. Human identity is no longer defined by what one does but by what one owns.

But we've discovered that owning things and consuming things does not satisfy our longing for meaning.

We have learned that piling up material goods cannot fill the emptiness of lives which have no confidence or purpose. The symptoms of this crisis of the American spirit are all around us. For the first time in the history of our country a majority of our people believe that the next five years will be worse than that past five years. Two-thirds of our people do not even vote. The productivity of American workers is actually dropping and the willingness of Americans to save for the future has fallen below that of all other people in the Western world.

As you know there is a growing disrespect for government and for churches and for schools, the news media and other institutions. This is not a message of happiness or reassurance but it is the truth. And it is a warning. These changes did not happen overnight. They've come upon us gradually over the last generation. Years that were filled with shocks and tragedy.

We were sure that ours was a nation of the ballot, not of the bullet, until the murders of John Kennedy and Robert Kennedy and Martin Luther King, Jr. We were taught that our armies were always invincible and our causes were always just only to suffer the agony of Vietnam. We respected the presidency as a place of honor until the shock of Watergate. We remember when the phrase "sound as a dollar" was an expression of absolute dependability until ten years of inflation began to shrink our dollar and our savings. We believed that our nation's resources were limitless until 1973, when we had to face a growing dependence on foreign oil.

These wounds are still very deep. They have never been healed.

Looking for a way out of this crisis, our people have turned to the federal government and found it isolated from the mainstream of our nation's life. Washington, D.C., has become an island. The gap between our citizens and our government has never been so wide. . . .

Often you see paralysis and stagnation and drift. You don't like it.

And neither do I.

What can we do? First of all, we must face the truth and then we can change our course. We simply must have faith in each other. Faith in our ability to govern ourselves and faith in the future of this nation. Restoring that faith and that confidence to America is now the most important task we face.

Our fathers and mothers were strong men and women who shaped the new society during the Great Depression, who fought world wars and who carved out a new charter of peace for the world. We ourselves are the same Americans who just ten years ago put a man on the moon. We are the generation that dedicated our society to the pursuit of human rights and equality.

And we are the generation that will win the war on the energy problem, and in that process rebuild the unity and confidence of America. We are at a turning point in our history. There are two paths to choose. One is the path I've warned about tonight —the path that leads to fragmentation and self-interest. Down that road lies a mistaken idea of freedom.

All the traditions of our past, all the lessons of our heritage, all the promises of our future point to another path: the path of common purpose and the restoration of American values. That path leads to true freedom for our nation and ourselves. We can take the first steps down that path as we begin to solve our energy problem. Energy will be the immediate test of our ability to unite this nation.

You know we can do it. We have the natural resources. We have more oil in our shale alone than several Saudi Arabias. We have more coal than any nation on earth. We have the world's highest level of technology. We have the most skilled work force, with innovative genius.

And I firmly believe we have the national will to win this war.

From *Public Papers of the Presidents of the United States: Jimmy Carter, 1979, Book 2* (Washington, D.C.: United States Government Printing Office, 1980).

1. What examples of the "crisis of confidence" did President Carter mention?
2. What path did he say the American people should follow?
3. What reasons might President Carter have had for calling the energy crisis the "immediate test of our ability to unite this nation"?

---

2 The Hostages Return Home

After being held in captivity for more than fourteen months, the American hostages were released by Iran on the day that Jimmy Carter left office. A few days after their return to freedom, the former hostages were welcomed at the White House. Bruce Laingen, who had been Deputy Chief of Mission at the embassy in Tehran, made the following remarks.

I'm not sure I'm capable of this after that emotionally draining, but beautiful experience that all of us have just had on the streets of this magnificent city, Mr. President. I hope you were watching TV, because I don't think any of us Americans have ever seen anything quite like it, quite so spontaneous, quite so beautiful in terms of the best qualities of our people. And we are deeply grateful for it.

Mr. President, our flight to freedom is now complete: thanks to the prayers and good will of countless millions of people, not just in this country but all around the world; the assistance of those many countries and governments who understood the values and principles that were at stake in

Enthusiastic crowds turned out to cheer the return of the Americans who had been held hostage in Iran.

this crisis; and the love and affection of our countrymen from all those tens of thousands out there on the streets today, to that lady that we saw standing on a hillside as we came in from Andrews [Air Force Base], all alone, with no sign, no one around her, holding her hand to her heart —the enveloping love and affection of smalltown America of the kind we witnessed in that wonderful two-day stop in New York State . . . and last, but not least, on this flight to freedom, the United States Air Force on Freedom I.

Mr. President, I give you now 52 Americans, supplemented by a 53d, today, Richard Queen, sitting over here, overjoyed in reunion with our families, the real heroes

in this crisis; 53 Americans, proud to rejoin their professional colleagues who had made their flight to freedom earlier—our six colleagues who came here with the great cooperation and friendship of our Canadian friends, and our thirteen who came earlier. I give you now 53 Americans, proud, as I said earlier today, to record their undying respect and affection for the families of those brave eight men who gave their lives so that we might be free. . . . Fifty-three Americans who will always have a love affair with this country and who join with you in a prayer of thanksgiving for the way in which this crisis has strengthened the spirit and resilience and strength that is the mark of a truly free society.

Mr. President, we've seen a lot of signs along the road. . . . They are marvelous signs, as is the spirit and enthusiasm that accompanies this what we've been calling "a celebration of freedom." They are signs that have not been ordered. They are spontaneous, sincere signs that reflect the true feelings of the hearts of those who hold them, even those, I suppose, like "IRS [Internal Revenue Service] welcomes you"—[laughter] which we saw today as we came into town, and another one that said, "Government workers welcome you back to work." Well, we're ready.

There was another sign that said, and I think that says it as well as any as far as we're concerned: "The best things in life are free." But even better than that was a sign that we saw as we left West Point today along a superhighway . . . : "And the world will be better for this." We pray, Mr. President, that this will be so.

Mr. President, in very simple words that come from the hearts of all of us, it is good to be back. Thank you, America, and God bless all of you.

Thank you very much.

From *Historic Documents of 1981* (Washington: Congressional Quarterly, 1982).

1. According to Laingen, how had the hostages' release affected the spirit of the American people?
2. Why might the sign that read, "The best things in life are free" have had special meaning for the hostages?

3 Ronald Reagan—America "Standing Tall"

In his State of the Union message of 1984, President Ronald Reagan declared that under his leadership the mood of the nation had become one of self-assurance and pride. Passages from Reagan's address follow.

There is a renewed energy and optimism throughout the land. America is back—standing tall, looking to the '80's with courage, confidence, and hope. . . .

As we came to the decade of the '80's, we faced the worst crisis in our postwar history. In the '70's were years of rising problems and falling confidence. There was a feeling government had grown beyond the consent of the governed. Families felt helpless in the face of mounting inflation and the indignity of taxes that reduced reward for hard work, thrift, and risk-taking. All this was overlaid by an ever-growing web of rules and regulations.

On the international scene, we had an uncomfortable feeling that we had lost the respect of friend and foe. Some questioned whether we had the will to defend peace and freedom.

But America is too great for small dreams. There was a hunger in the land for a spiritual revival; if you will, a crusade for renewal. The American people said: Let us look to the future with confidence, both at home and abroad. Let us give freedom a chance.

But we know many of our fellow countrymen are still out of work, wondering what will come of their hopes and dreams. Can we love America and not reach out to tell them: You are not forgotten; we will not rest until each of you can reach as high as your God-given talents will take you.

The heart of America is strong, it's good, and true. The cynics were wrong—America never was a sick society. We're seeing rededication to bedrock values of faith, family, work, neighborhood, peace, and freedom—values that help bring us together as one people, from the youngest child to the most senior citizen. . . .

People everywhere hunger for peace and a better life. The tide of the future is a freedom tide, and our struggle for democracy cannot and will not be denied. This nation champions peace that enshrines lib-

During his years as President, Ronald Reagan expressed his confidence in America's future.

After all our struggles to restore America, to revive confidence in our country, hope for our future; after all our hard-won victories earned through the patience and courage of every citizen—we cannot, must not and will not turn back, we will finish our job. How could we do less? We are Americans. . . .

I've never felt more strongly that America's best days, and democracy's best days, lie ahead. We are a powerful force for good. With faith and courage, we can perform great deeds and take freedom's next step. And we will. We will carry on the traditions of a good and worthy people who have brought light where there was darkness, warmth where there was cold, medicine where there was disease, food where there was hunger, and peace where there was bloodshed.

Let us be sure that those who come after will say . . . that in our time we did everything that could be done: We finished the race, we kept them free, we kept the faith.

From President Ronald Reagan, State of the Union Address, *Vital Speeches*, Vol. 50 (February 15, 1984).

1. According to President Reagan, what problems had Americans faced during the 1970's?
2. What traditions did he say Americans would carry on in the years to come?

erty, democratic rights, and dignity for every individual. America's new strength, confidence, and purpose are carrying hope and opportunity far from our shores. A world economic recovery is under way. It began here. . . .

★   ★   ★

Analysis

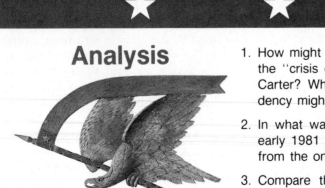

1. How might the energy crisis have played a part in the "crisis of confidence" described by President Carter? What other events during Carter's presidency might have contributed to that feeling?

2. In what ways did the release of the hostages in early 1981 contribute to a different national mood from the one described by Carter?

3. Compare the tone of Carter's speech with the tone of Ronald Reagan's 1984 State of the Union message.

HISTORICAL ATLAS AND REFERENCE SECTION

HISTORICAL ATLAS

The maps on pages 588–593 contain information about the origins, growth, and development of the United States. The map below shows some of the routes taken by the first European explorers who came to North America. It also shows the territories claimed by Spain, France, and England in 1682. In time, as shown in the maps on the next page, France lost most of its land. Spain and England, meanwhile, increased their American holdings.

The English colonies along the Atlantic coast prospered, and by 1783 they had won their independence from Great Britain. Through treaties and the purchase of land, the new nation expanded beyond its original boundaries and by

1853 had reached the Pacific. The map on pages 590–591 shows the territorial growth of the United States.

As the nation grew, explorers blazed trails through little-known regions, opening the way for miners, farmers, and other settlers. Roads, canals, and railroads were built, helping to tie the nation together. The map on pages 592–593 shows how much of the United States had been settled by 1890.

The maps, graphs, and charts on pages 594–605 contain information about the United States today. They will add to your understanding and appreciation of the American people and the nation's economy.

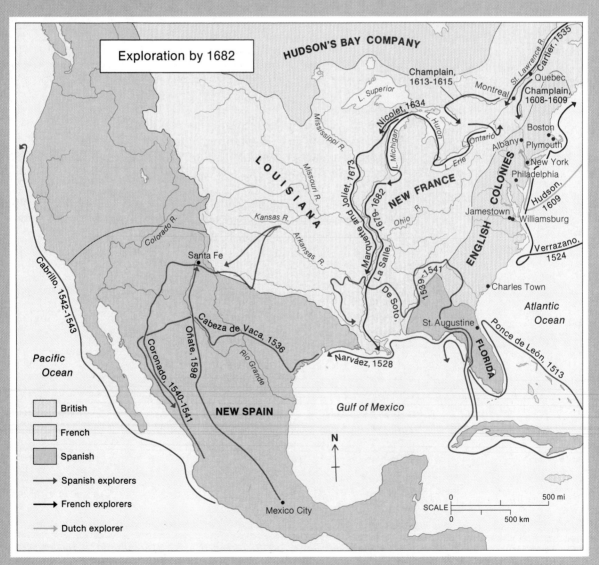

Exploration by 1682

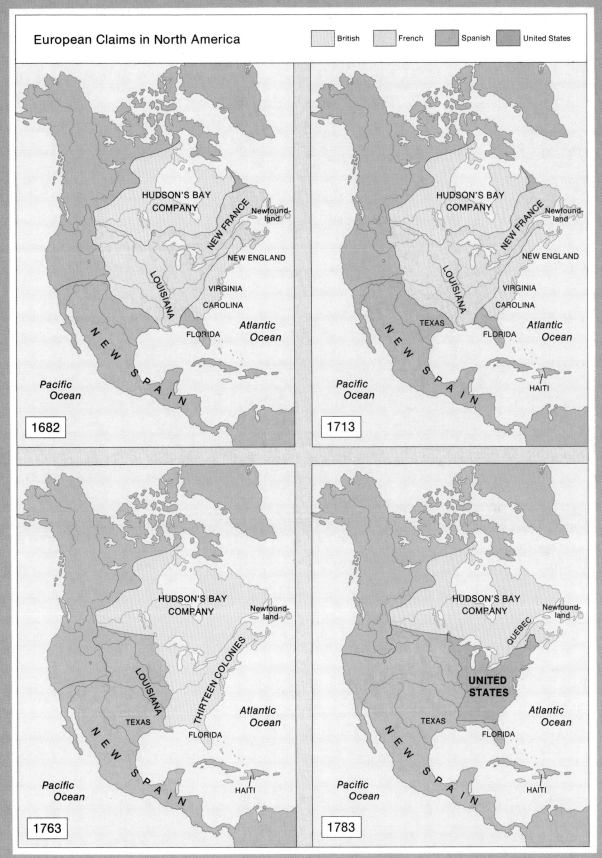

European Claims in North America

British French Spanish United States

1682

HUDSON'S BAY COMPANY

NEW FRANCE

Newfound-land

NEW ENGLAND

LOUISIANA

VIRGINIA

CAROLINA

FLORIDA

Atlantic Ocean

Pacific Ocean

NEW SPAIN

1713

HUDSON'S BAY COMPANY

NEW FRANCE

Newfound-land

NEW ENGLAND

LOUISIANA

VIRGINIA

CAROLINA

TEXAS

FLORIDA

Atlantic Ocean

Pacific Ocean

NEW SPAIN

HAITI

1763

HUDSON'S BAY COMPANY

Newfound-land

LOUISIANA

THIRTEEN COLONIES

TEXAS

FLORIDA

Atlantic Ocean

Pacific Ocean

NEW SPAIN

HAITI

1783

HUDSON'S BAY COMPANY

Newfound-land

QUEBEC

UNITED STATES

TEXAS

FLORIDA

Atlantic Ocean

Pacific Ocean

NEW SPAIN

HAITI

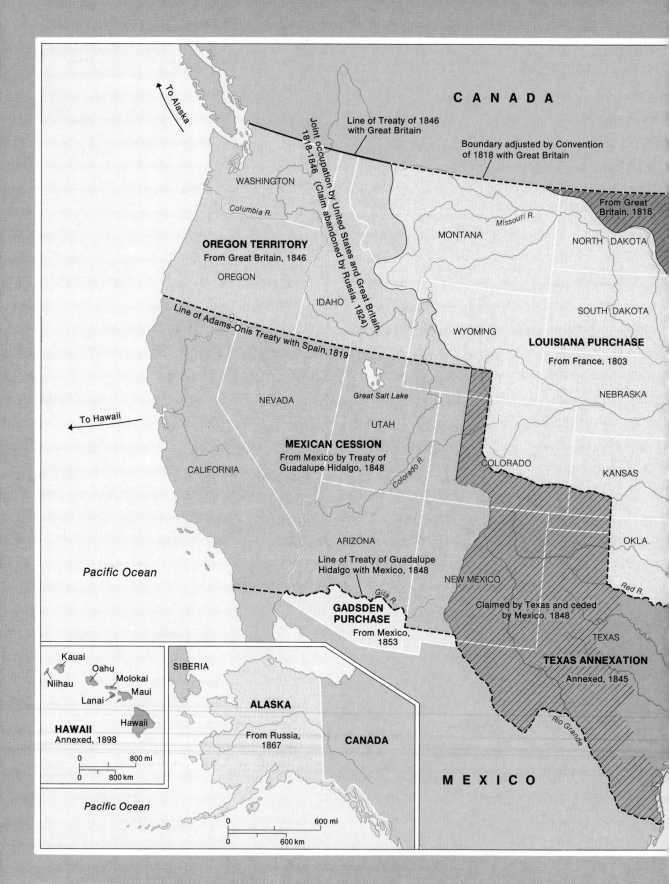

CANADA

Line of Treaty of 1846
with Great Britain

Boundary adjusted by Convention
of 1818 with Great Britain

Joint occupation by United States and Great Britain.
1818-1846 (Claim abandoned by Russia, 1824)

To Alaska

WASHINGTON

Columbia R.

Missouri R.

MONTANA

From Great
Britain, 1818

NORTH DAKOTA

OREGON TERRITORY
From Great Britain, 1846

OREGON

IDAHO

WYOMING

SOUTH DAKOTA

LOUISIANA PURCHASE
From France, 1803

Line of Adams-Onis Treaty with Spain, 1819

NEVADA

Great Salt Lake

UTAH

NEBRASKA

To Hawaii

MEXICAN CESSION
From Mexico by Treaty of
Guadalupe Hidalgo, 1848

CALIFORNIA

Colorado R.

COLORADO

KANSAS

Pacific Ocean

ARIZONA

Line of Treaty of Guadalupe
Hidalgo with Mexico, 1848

Gila R.

GADSDEN
PURCHASE

From Mexico,
1853

NEW MEXICO

OKLA.

Red R.

Claimed by Texas and ceded
by Mexico, 1848

TEXAS

TEXAS ANNEXATION
Annexed, 1845

Kauai

Oahu

Niihau

Molokai

Lanai

Maui

HAWAII
Annexed, 1898

Hawaii

0   800 mi

0   800 km

SIBERIA

ALASKA

From Russia,
1867

CANADA

MEXICO

Rio Grande

Pacific Ocean

0   600 mi

0   600 km

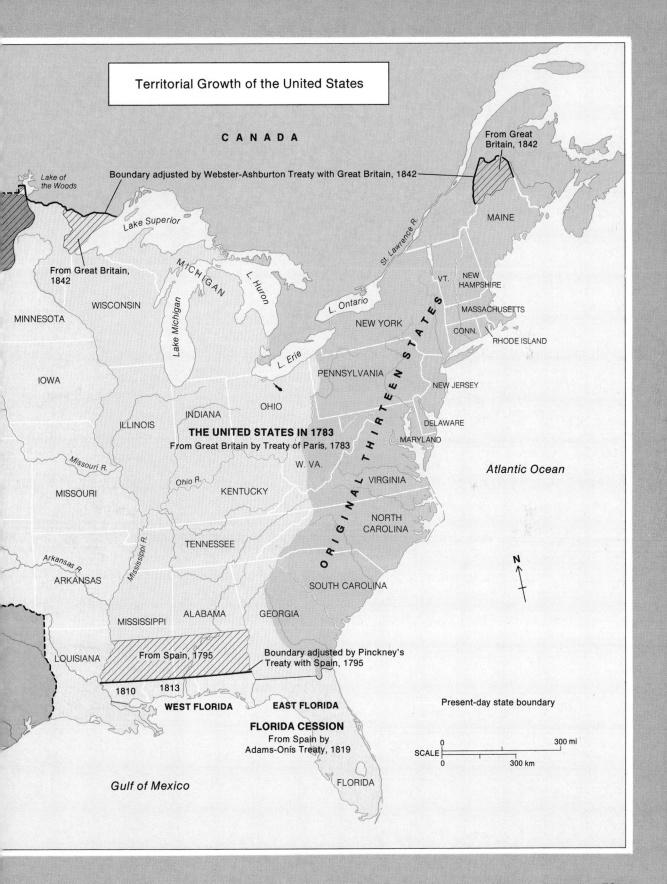

Territorial Growth of the United States

CANADA

From Great Britain, 1842

Boundary adjusted by Webster-Ashburton Treaty with Great Britain, 1842

Lake of the Woods

Lake Superior

From Great Britain, 1842

MICHIGAN

L. Huron

Lake Michigan

MAINE

St. Lawrence R.

MINNESOTA

WISCONSIN

L. Ontario

VT.

NEW HAMPSHIRE

MASSACHUSETTS

CONN.

RHODE ISLAND

IOWA

L. Erie

NEW YORK

PENNSYLVANIA

NEW JERSEY

ILLINOIS

INDIANA

OHIO

DELAWARE

MARYLAND

THE UNITED STATES IN 1783

From Great Britain by Treaty of Paris, 1783

W. VA.

Atlantic Ocean

MISSOURI

Missouri R.

Ohio R.

KENTUCKY

VIRGINIA

O R I G I N A L   T H I R T E E N   S T A T E S

NORTH CAROLINA

Arkansas R.

Mississippi R.

TENNESSEE

N

ARKANSAS

SOUTH CAROLINA

LOUISIANA

MISSISSIPPI

ALABAMA

GEORGIA

From Spain, 1795

Boundary adjusted by Pinckney's Treaty with Spain, 1795

1810   1813

WEST FLORIDA   **EAST FLORIDA**

FLORIDA CESSION

From Spain by Adams-Onís Treaty, 1819

Present-day state boundary

SCALE

0   300 mi

0   300 km

Gulf of Mexico

FLORIDA

591

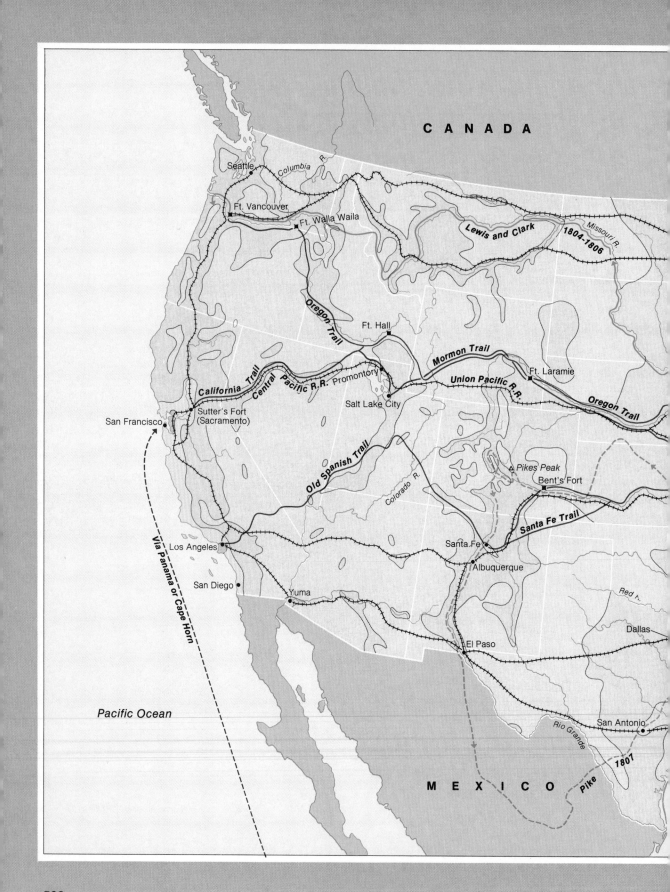

CANADA

Seattle

Columbia R.

Ft. Vancouver

Ft. Walla Walla

Lewis and Clark

1804-1806

Missouri R.

Oregon Trail

Ft. Hall

Mormon Trail

Ft. Laramie

California Trail

Central Pacific R.R.

Promontory

Union Pacific R.R.

Oregon Trail

Salt Lake City

San Francisco

Sutter's Fort
(Sacramento)

Old Spanish Trail

Pikes Peak

Bent's Fort

Colorado R.

Santa Fe Trail

Santa Fe

Los Angeles

Albuquerque

Red R.

San Diego

Yuma

Via Panama or Cape Horn

Dallas

El Paso

Pacific Ocean

San Antonio

Rio Grande

1807

M E X I C O

Pike

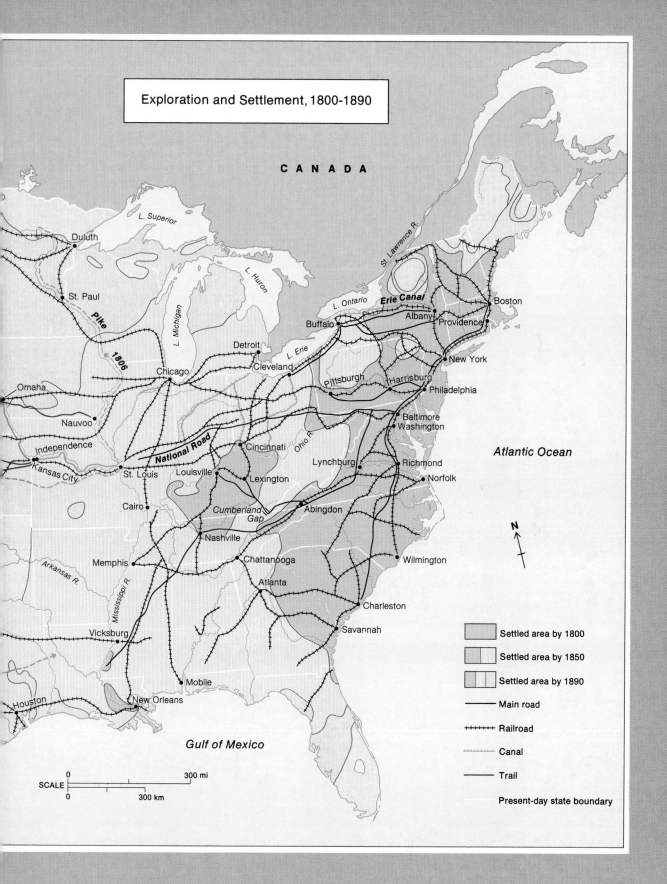

Exploration and Settlement, 1800-1890

CANADA

L. Superior

Duluth

St. Paul

Pike

1806

L. Huron

L. Michigan

Omaha

Nauvoo

Chicago

Detroit

Cleveland

L. Erie

L. Ontario

Buffalo

Erie Canal

Albany

Providence

Boston

New York

Pittsburgh

Harrisburg

Philadelphia

Independence

National Road

Cincinnati

Ohio R.

Baltimore

Washington

Kansas City

St. Louis

Louisville

Lexington

Lynchburg

Richmond

Norfolk

Cairo

Cumberland Gap

Abingdon

Atlantic Ocean

Arkansas R.

Nashville

Memphis

Mississippi R.

Chattanooga

Atlanta

Wilmington

N

Charleston

Vicksburg

Savannah

Houston

Mobile

New Orleans

Gulf of Mexico

St. Lawrence R.

Settled area by 1800

Settled area by 1850

Settled area by 1890

—— Main road

+++++ Railroad

········ Canal

—— Trail

Present-day state boundary

SCALE

0   300 mi

0   300 km

THE AMERICAN PEOPLE

It is now nearly 500 years since Columbus first reached the Americas. In those five centuries — as colonies were established and as the United States emerged as a mighty nation — millions of people immigrated to these shores. Every American today, in fact, is an immigrant or a descendant of an immigrant. As President Franklin D. Roosevelt once said, "Remember, remember always, that all of us . . . are descended from immigrants. . . ."

The following maps and graphs will tell you various things about the American people. They will also reinforce many of the themes you have read about in your study of American history. The map below, for example, shows the population density of the fifty states at the time of the 1980 census. The map also shows the nation's largest cities.

The bar graph at the top of the next page provides information about the national backgrounds of immigrants who have come to this country since 1820. It helps demonstrate the fact that in spite of recent changes in sources of immigration, the largest numbers of immigrants in the period since 1820 have come from Europe. Another graph on the next page shows the American population by age group. In recent years the group aged eighteen years and younger has been declining as a percentage of the population, while the two older age groups have been growing larger. One reason for the aging of the population is the rise in average life expectancy, the subject of the third graph on the next page. On average, an American baby born in 1980 can expect to live almost thirty years longer than could a baby born in 1900.

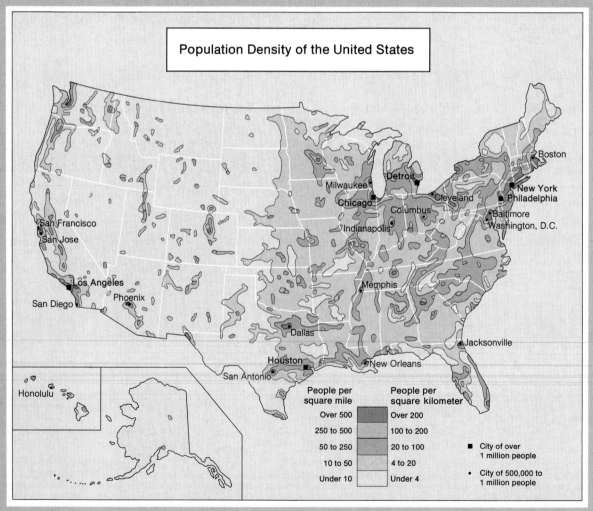

Population Density of the United States

People per square mile	People per square kilometer
Over 500	Over 200
250 to 500	100 to 200
50 to 250	20 to 100
10 to 50	4 to 20
Under 10	Under 4

■ City of over 1 million people

• City of 500,000 to 1 million people

Immigration by Country of Origin, 1820–1979

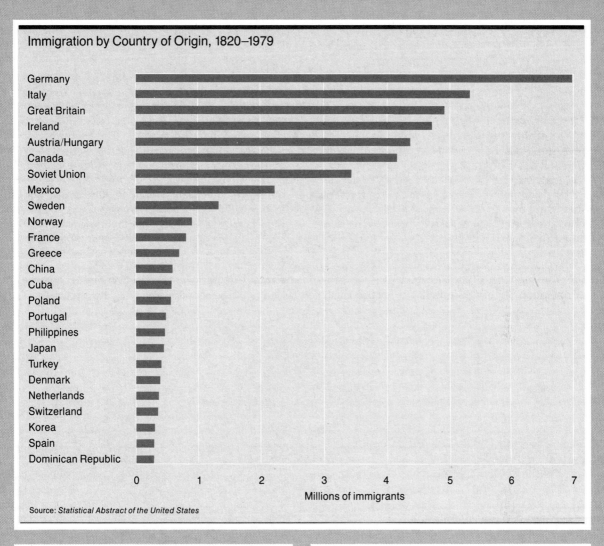

Country	Millions of immigrants

Germany, Italy, Great Britain, Ireland, Austria/Hungary, Canada, Soviet Union, Mexico, Sweden, Norway, France, Greece, China, Cuba, Poland, Portugal, Philippines, Japan, Turkey, Denmark, Netherlands, Switzerland, Korea, Spain, Dominican Republic

Millions of immigrants (0–7)

Source: *Statistical Abstract of the United States*

Population by Age Distribution, 1960–1980

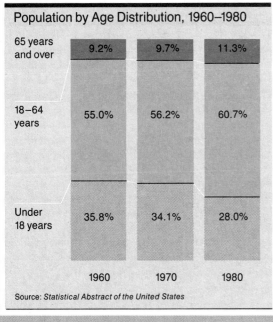

	1960	1970	1980
65 years and over	9.2%	9.7%	11.3%
18–64 years	55.0%	56.2%	60.7%
Under 18 years	35.8%	34.1%	28.0%

Source: *Statistical Abstract of the United States*

Life Expectancy at Birth, 1900–1980

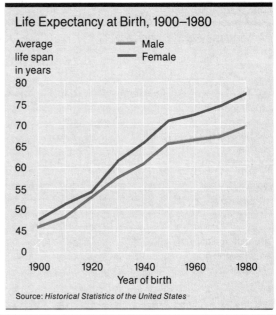

Average life span in years

— Male
— Female

Year of birth (1900–1980)

Source: *Historical Statistics of the United States*

595

POPULATION TRENDS

The Constitution of the United States provides that a census be taken every ten years, primarily to establish a basis for the apportionment of members in the House of Representatives. The Bureau of the Census is responsible for counting the American people and also for compiling statistics on other subjects.

Among the trends revealed by the 1980 census was the continued decline in the percentage of Americans living in central cities. At the same time, the percentage of elderly Americans was on the rise. As shown in the table at the bottom of this page, in 1980 there were more than 25 million Americans aged 65 and over. Another trend had to do with the movement of Americans to the sunbelt. This shift in population, which started in the 1950's, has continued to gather force. Of the states that showed either a decline in population or low population growth in the 1970's, almost all were in the Northeast or Middle West. Many states in the South and West, on the other hand, enjoyed rapid population growth. As a consequence, adjustments have been made in congressional representation.

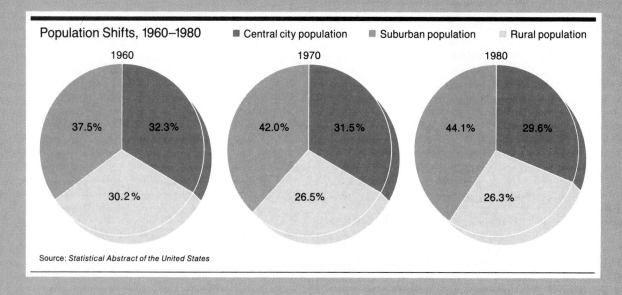

Population Shifts, 1960–1980 ■ Central city population ■ Suburban population ▨ Rural population

1960: 37.5% · 32.3% · 30.2%
1970: 42.0% · 31.5% · 26.5%
1980: 44.1% · 29.6% · 26.3%

Source: *Statistical Abstract of the United States*

Americans Aged 65 and Over

	1900	1920	1940	1960	1980	2000*
Millions of persons	3.1	4.9	9.0	16.7	25.5	31.8
As percentage of total population	4.1	4.6	6.8	9.2	11.3	12.2
As percentage of population 21 and older	7.6	8.0	10.7	15.3	17.2	17.7
Percentage of elderly who are 75 or older	29.0	29.8	29.3	33.6	39.0	45.2

Source: U.S. Bureau of the Census

*Projected

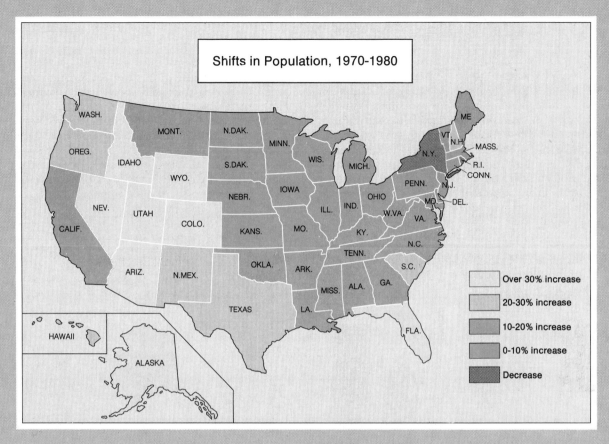

Shifts in Population, 1970-1980

Legend:
- Over 30% increase
- 20-30% increase
- 10-20% increase
- 0-10% increase
- Decrease

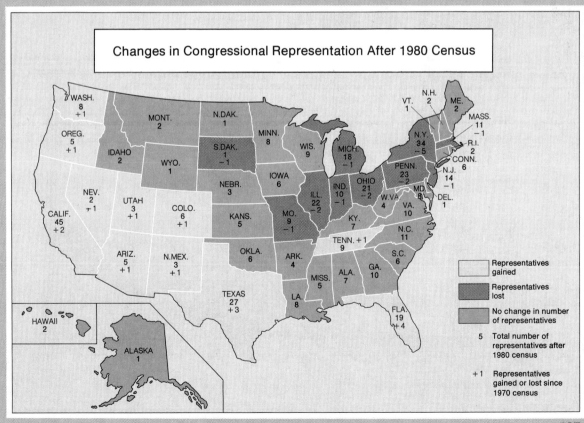

Changes in Congressional Representation After 1980 Census

WASH. 8 +1
OREG. 5 +1
MONT. 2
IDAHO 2
WYO. 1
N.DAK. 1
S.DAK. 1 -1
MINN. 8
WIS. 9
MICH. 18 -1
VT. 1
N.H. 2
ME. 2
MASS. 11 -1
N.Y. 34 -5
R.I. 2
CONN. 6
N.J. 14 -1
PENN. 23 -2
OHIO 21 -2
IND. 10 -1
ILL. 22 -2
IOWA 6
NEBR. 3
NEV. 2 +1
UTAH 3 +1
COLO. 6 +1
KANS. 5
MO. 9 -1
KY. 7
W.VA 4
MD. 8
DEL. 1
VA. 10
N.C. 11
CALIF. 45 +2
ARIZ. 5 +1
N.MEX. 3 +1
OKLA. 6
ARK. 4
TENN. +1 9
S.C. 6
GA. 10
ALA. 7
MISS. 5
TEXAS 27 +3
LA. 8
FLA. 19 +4
HAWAII 2
ALASKA 1

Legend:
- Representatives gained
- Representatives lost
- No change in number of representatives
- 5   Total number of representatives after 1980 census
- +1   Representatives gained or lost since 1970 census

THE AMERICAN ECONOMY

America's rich natural resources, its hardworking population, and the ingenuity of its inventors and scientists have all contributed to the growth of the United States economy. These pages provide information about that growth.

The chief measure of economic activity is the gross national product (GNP). Throughout the nation's history the GNP has shown remarkable growth, indicating that millions of people have found employment and that capital and natural resources have been put to good use. Another measure of economic activity is productivity. The average American farmer, for example, now produces enough food for 66 people, compared to 26 people in 1960 and only 11 people in 1940. Meanwhile, as the economy has grown, so too has the number of government workers. Federal, state, and local governments have all hired more employees to help them meet responsibilities in such vital areas as defense and education.

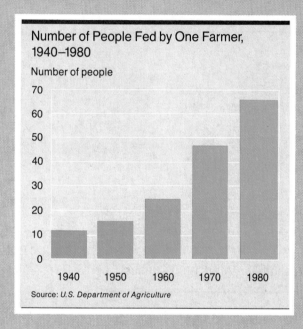

Number of People Fed by One Farmer, 1940–1980

Number of people

Source: U.S. Department of Agriculture

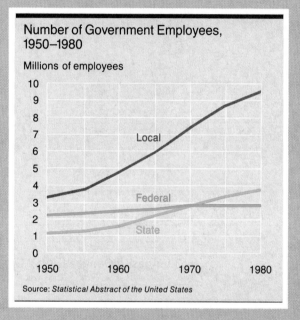

Number of Government Employees, 1950–1980

Millions of employees

Source: Statistical Abstract of the United States

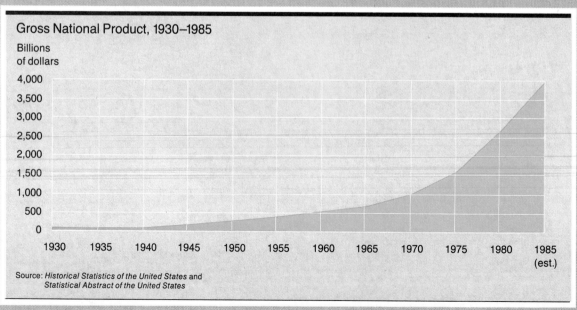

Gross National Product, 1930–1985

Billions of dollars

Source: Historical Statistics of the United States and Statistical Abstract of the United States

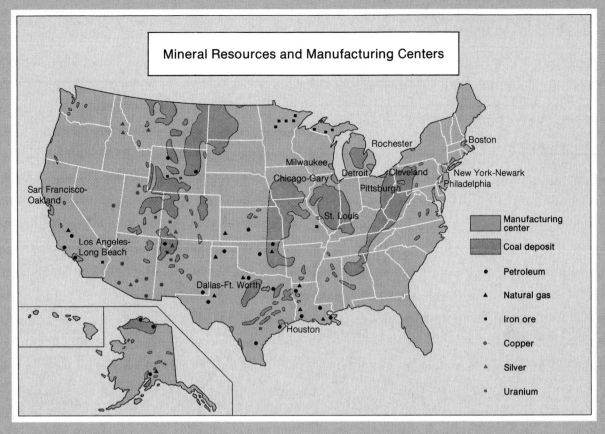

Mineral Resources and Manufacturing Centers

Rochester
Boston
Milwaukee
Chicago-Gary
Detroit
Cleveland
Pittsburgh
New York-Newark
Philadelphia
San Francisco-Oakland
St. Louis
Los Angeles-Long Beach
Dallas-Ft. Worth
Houston

- Manufacturing center
- Coal deposit
- ● Petroleum
- ▲ Natural gas
- ■ Iron ore
- ● Copper
- ▲ Silver
- ■ Uranium

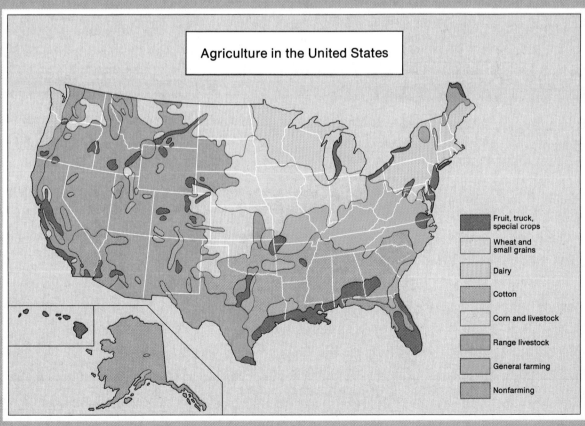

Agriculture in the United States

- Fruit, truck, special crops
- Wheat and small grains
- Dairy
- Cotton
- Corn and livestock
- Range livestock
- General farming
- Nonfarming

THE UNITED STATES
Cities and States

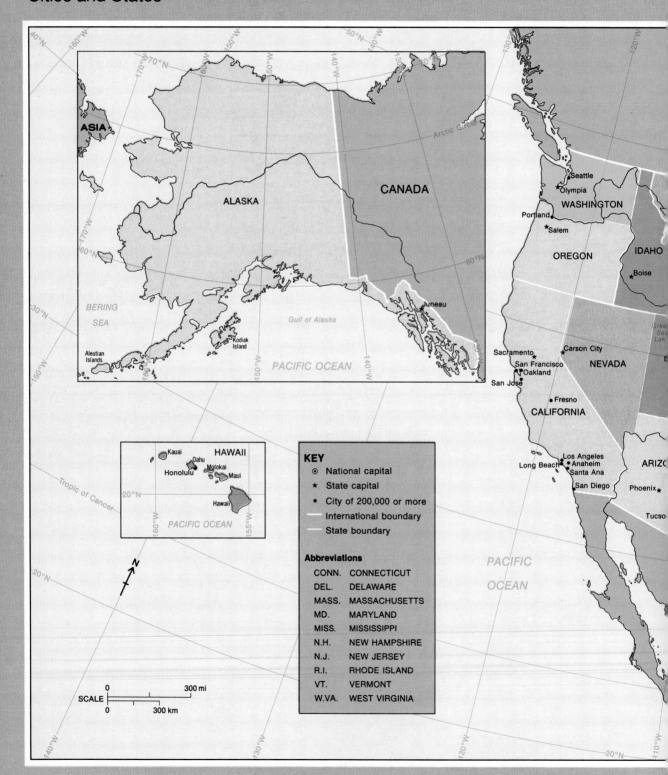

ASIA

ALASKA

CANADA

BERING
SEA

Gulf of Alaska

Juneau

Aleutian
Islands

Kodiak
Island

PACIFIC OCEAN

Arctic Circle

Seattle
Olympia
WASHINGTON
Portland
Salem
OREGON

IDAHO
Boise

Sacramento
San Francisco
Oakland
San Jose

Carson City
NEVADA

Fresno

CALIFORNIA

Los Angeles
Long Beach
Anaheim
Santa Ana
San Diego

ARIZO

Phoenix

Tucso

HAWAII

Kauai
Oahu
Honolulu
Molokai
Maui

Hawaii

PACIFIC OCEAN

Tropic of Cancer

KEY

⊙ National capital

★ State capital

• City of 200,000 or more

— International boundary

— State boundary

Abbreviations

CONN.	CONNECTICUT
DEL.	DELAWARE
MASS.	MASSACHUSETTS
MD.	MARYLAND
MISS.	MISSISSIPPI
N.H.	NEW HAMPSHIRE
N.J.	NEW JERSEY
R.I.	RHODE ISLAND
VT.	VERMONT
W.VA.	WEST VIRGINIA

PACIFIC

OCEAN

N

SCALE

0   300 mi

0   300 km

CANADA

Hudson Bay

MONTANA

Helena

NORTH DAKOTA
• Bismarck

MINNESOTA

MICHIGAN

MAINE

★ Augusta

Lake Superior

WYOMING

SOUTH DAKOTA
★ Pierre

Minneapolis St. Paul

WISCONSIN

Montpelier•
NEW
YORK
N.H.
VT.
★ Concord

Lake Huron

Lake Michigan

Lansing

Boston

NEBRASKA

Cheyenne•

IOWA

Madison•
Milwaukee•
Chicago•

Detroit•

Lake Ontario
Rochester•
Buffalo•

Albany•

MASS.
Hartford•

Providence
R.I.

• Des Moines

Cleveland•
Toledo•

Akron•

Jersey City•
Newark•
Trenton•

CONN.
New York

UTAH

Denver•

COLORADO

Colorado
Springs•

Omaha•

Lincoln•

ILLINOIS INDIANA OHIO

Columbus•

Cincinnati•

PENNSYLVANIA
Harrisburg★

Pittsburgh•

Baltimore•

Philadelphia•
N.J.
Dover★
DEL.

Indianapolis•

Dayton•

Washington, D.C.◎
MD.
Annapolis★

KANSAS

Topeka★

Kansas
City•

Springfield•

Frankfort★
Lexington•

W.VA.
Charleston★

Richmond•

Norfolk•
Virginia
Beach•

Albuquerque•

Santa Fe★

Jefferson
City★

St.
Louis•

Wichita•

Louisville•

VIRGINIA

MISSOURI

KENTUCKY

Raleigh•

ATLANTIC

OCEAN

NEW MEXICO

El Paso•

Tulsa•

Oklahoma
City★

ARKANSAS

Little
Rock★

Nashville•

TENNESSEE

Memphis•

Charlotte•

NORTH CAROLINA

SOUTH
CAROLINA
Columbia•

OKLAHOMA

Birmingham•

Atlanta•

Fort Worth• •Dallas

MISS. ALABAMA

GEORGIA

Shreveport•

Jackson★

Montgomery★

TEXAS

Austin•

Baton
Rouge•

Mobile•

Tallahassee★

Jacksonville•

San Antonio•

LOUISIANA

New Orleans•

Houston•

FLORIDA

Tampa•

St. Petersburg•

Corpus Christi•

MEXICO

Gulf of Mexico

Miami•

BAHAMAS

Tropic of Cancer

CUBA

THE UNITED STATES
Physical Features

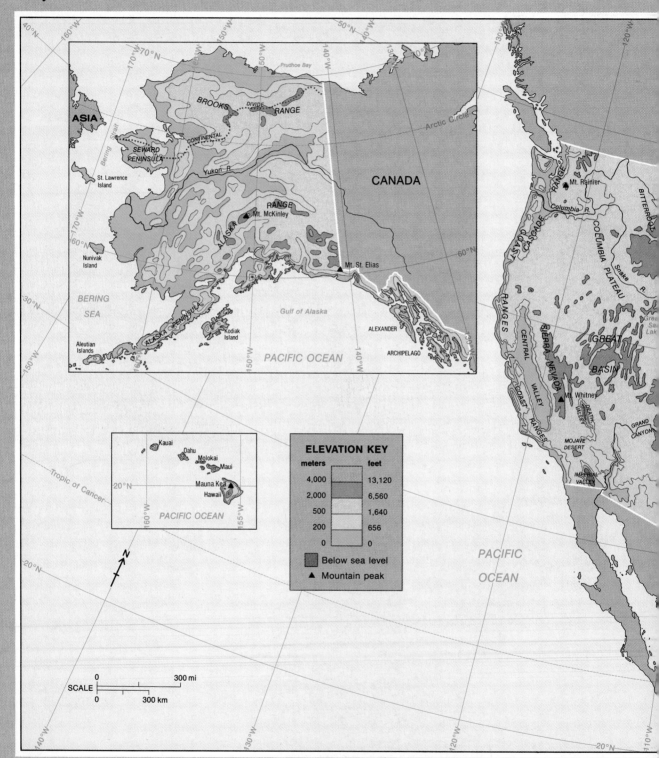

ASIA

BROOKS DIVIDE RANGE

CONTINENTAL

SEWARD PENINSULA

St. Lawrence Island

Yukon R.

CANADA

Prudhoe Bay

Arctic Circle

Mt. Rainier

Columbia R.

BITTERROOT

CASCADE RANGE

COLUMBIA PLATEAU

Snake R.

Great Salt Lake

RANGE

ALASKA RANGE

Mt. McKinley

Mt. St. Elias

Nunivak Island

BERING SEA

ALASKA PENINSULA

Kodiak Island

Gulf of Alaska

ALEXANDER

ARCHIPELAGO

COAST RANGES

CENTRAL VALLEY

SIERRA NEVADA

GREAT BASIN

Mt. Whitney

DEATH VALLEY

Aleutian Islands

PACIFIC OCEAN

MOJAVE DESERT

GRAND CANYON

COAST RANGES

IMPERIAL VALLEY

PACIFIC OCEAN

Kauai

Oahu

Molokai

Maui

Mauna Kea

Hawaii

PACIFIC OCEAN

Tropic of Cancer

ELEVATION KEY

meters		feet
4,000		13,120
2,000		6,560
500		1,640
200		656
0		0

Below sea level

▲ Mountain peak

N

SCALE	0	300 mi
	0	300 km

CANADA

Hudson Bay

50°N

100°W

R O C K Y

CONTINENTAL

DIVIDE

Missouri R.

GREAT

BLACK HILLS

Platte

MESABI RANGE

Lake Superior

Mississippi R.

Lake Michigan

Lake Huron

Lake Ontario

Lake Erie

St. Lawrence R.

ADIRONDACK MTS.

GREEN MTS.

WHITE MTS.

CATSKILL MTS.

CAPE COD

40°N

Long Island

M O U N T A I N S

Mt. Elbert ▲

Pikes Peak ▲

COLORADO PLATEAU

M O U N T A I N S

Colorado

INTERIOR

Missouri R.

PLAINS

OZARK PLATEAU

Ohio R.

CUMBERLAND PLATEAU

APPALACHIAN

BLUE RIDGE MTS.

Delaware Bay

CAPE HATTERAS

ATLANTIC

OCEAN

70°W

P L A I N S

PLATEAU

Arkansas R.

OUACHITA MTS.

Mississippi R.

ATLANTIC COASTAL PLAIN

LLANO ESTACADO

Red R.

COASTAL

PLAIN

GULF

30°N

Rio Grande

EDWARDS PLATEAU

MISSISSIPPI DELTA

CAPE CANAVERAL

EVERGLADES

BAHAMAS

MEXICO

Gulf of Mexico

FLORIDA KEYS

Tropic of Cancer

CUBA

90°W

100°W

80°W

20°N

NATIONS OF THE WORLD

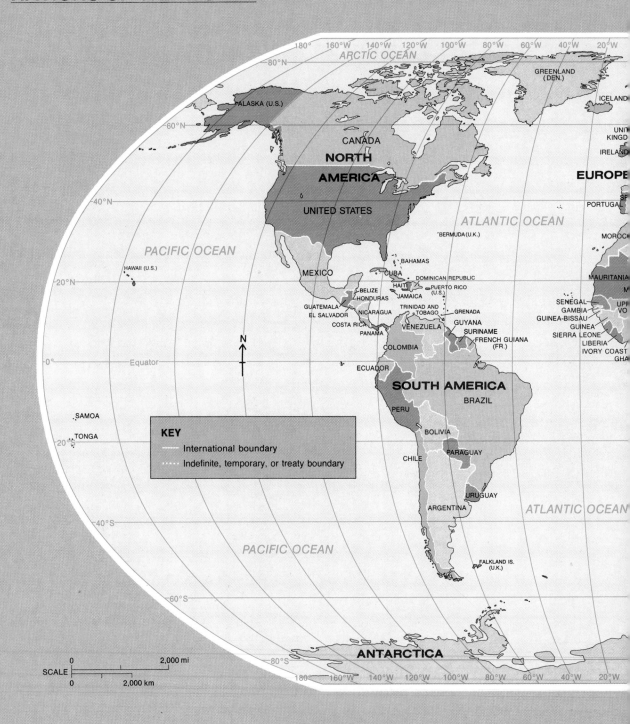

KEY

—— International boundary

······ Indefinite, temporary, or treaty boundary

SCALE
0 — 2,000 mi
0 — 2,000 km

ABBREVIATIONS

ALB. Albania
AUST. Austria
BEL. Belgium
C.AF.REP. Central African Republic

CZECH. Czechoslovakia
DEN. Denmark
E.GER. East Germany
EQ.GUINEA Equatorial Guinea

ARCTIC OCEAN

80°N

WAY. SWEDEN FINLAND

60°N

UNION OF SOVIET SOCIALIST REPUBLICS

DEN.
GER.
POLAND
W. GER.
CZECH
AUST. HUNG.
SWITZ.
YUGO.
NCE
ITALY
BULGARIA
RUMANIA
ALB.
GREECE
CYPRUS
MALTA
LEBANON
TUNISIA
ISRAEL
JORDAN

ASIA

MONGOLIA

40°N

TURKEY
SYRIA
IRAQ
IRAN
AFGHANISTAN

N. KOREA
S. KOREA
JAPAN

KUWAIT
QATAR
PAKISTAN
NEPAL BHUTAN

PEOPLE'S REPUBLIC
OF CHINA

GERIA LIBYA

EGYPT
SAUDI
ARABIA
U. ARAB EMIR.
OMAN
INDIA
BANGLADESH BURMA
LAOS

TAIWAN

20°N

NIGER

CHAD
SUDAN
YEMEN YEMEN (P.D.R.)
DJIBOUTI

THAILAND
VIETNAM

ENIN
GERIA
AFRICA

C.AF.REP.
ETHIOPIA
SRI LANKA
KAMPUCHEA
PHILIPPINES

PACIFIC OCEAN

CAMEROON
NEA
GABON
CONGO
TOMÉ
UGANDA
KENYA
SOMALIA
MALDIVES
MALAYSIA

SINGAPORE

Equator
0°

CIPE
RWANDA-
BURUNDI
ZAÏRE
TANZANIA

SEYCHELLES

INDONESIA

PAPUA
NEW GUINEA

NAURU

SOLOMON
ISLANDS

ANGOLA
MALAWI
ZAMBIA
MOZAMBIQUE
COMOROS

INDIAN OCEAN

FIJI

ZIMBABWE
MADAGASCAR

20°S

NAMIBIA

BOTSWANA
MAURITIUS

AUSTRALIA

SOUTH
AFRICA
SWAZILAND
LESOTHO

NEW
ZEALAND

40°S

60°S

ANTARCTICA

80°S

20°E 40°E 60°E 80°E 100°E 120°E 140°E 160°E 180°

The Presidents

	President	Dates	Years in Office	Party	Elected From
1	George Washington	1732–1799	1789–1797	None	Virginia
2	John Adams	1735–1826	1797–1801	Federalist	Massachusetts
3	Thomas Jefferson	1743–1826	1801–1809	Democratic–Republican	Virginia
4	James Madison	1751–1836	1809–1817	Democratic–Republican	Virginia
5	James Monroe	1758–1831	1817–1825	Democratic–Republican	Virginia
6	John Quincy Adams	1767–1848	1825–1829	National–Republican	Massachusetts
7	Andrew Jackson	1767–1845	1829–1837	Democratic	Tennessee
8	Martin Van Buren	1782–1862	1837–1841	Democratic	New York
9	William H. Harrison	1773–1841	1841	Whig	Ohio
10	John Tyler	1790–1862	1841–1845	Whig	Virginia
11	James K. Polk	1795–1849	1845–1849	Democratic	Tennessee
12	Zachary Taylor	1784–1850	1849–1850	Whig	Louisiana
13	Millard Fillmore	1800–1874	1850–1853	Whig	New York
14	Franklin Pierce	1804–1869	1853–1857	Democratic	New Hampshire
15	James Buchanan	1791–1868	1857–1861	Democratic	Pennsylvania
16	Abraham Lincoln	1809–1865	1861–1865	Republican	Illinois
17	Andrew Johnson	1808–1875	1865–1869	Republican	Tennessee
18	Ulysses S. Grant	1822–1885	1869–1877	Republican	Illinois
19	Rutherford B. Hayes	1822–1893	1877–1881	Republican	Ohio
20	James A. Garfield	1831–1881	1881	Republican	Ohio
21	Chester A. Arthur	1830–1886	1881–1885	Republican	New York
22	Grover Cleveland	1837–1908	1885–1889	Democratic	New York
23	Benjamin Harrison	1833–1901	1889–1893	Republican	Indiana
24	Grover Cleveland	1837–1908	1893–1897	Democratic	New York
25	William McKinley	1843–1901	1897–1901	Republican	Ohio
26	Theodore Roosevelt	1858–1919	1901–1909	Republican	New York
27	William H. Taft	1857–1930	1909–1913	Republican	Ohio
28	Woodrow Wilson	1856–1924	1913–1921	Democratic	New Jersey
29	Warren G. Harding	1865–1923	1921–1923	Republican	Ohio
30	Calvin Coolidge	1872–1933	1923–1929	Republican	Massachusetts
31	Herbert Hoover	1874–1964	1929–1933	Republican	California
32	Franklin D. Roosevelt	1882–1945	1933–1945	Democratic	New York
33	Harry S. Truman	1884–1972	1945–1953	Democratic	Missouri
34	Dwight D. Eisenhower	1890–1969	1953–1961	Republican	New York
35	John F. Kennedy	1917–1963	1961–1963	Democratic	Massachusetts
36	Lyndon B. Johnson	1908–1973	1963–1969	Democratic	Texas
37	Richard M. Nixon	1913–	1969–1974	Republican	New York
38	Gerald R. Ford	1913–	1974–1977	Republican	Michigan
39	Jimmy Carter	1924–	1977–1981	Democratic	Georgia
40	Ronald Reagan	1911–	1981–	Republican	California

The States

	State Name	Date of Admission	Population (1983 est.)	Number of Representatives	Capital
1	Delaware	1787	606,000	1	Dover
2	Pennsylvania	1787	11,895,000	23	Harrisburg
3	New Jersey	1787	7,468,000	14	Trenton
4	Georgia	1788	5,732,000	10	Atlanta
5	Connecticut	1788	3,138,000	6	Hartford
6	Massachusetts	1788	5,767,000	11	Boston
7	Maryland	1788	4,304,000	8	Annapolis
8	South Carolina	1788	3,264,000	6	Columbia
9	New Hampshire	1788	959,000	2	Concord
10	Virginia	1788	5,550,000	10	Richmond
11	New York	1788	17,667,000	34	Albany
12	North Carolina	1789	6,082,000	11	Raleigh
13	Rhode Island	1790	955,000	2	Providence
14	Vermont	1791	525,000	1	Montpelier
15	Kentucky	1792	3,714,000	7	Frankfort
16	Tennessee	1796	4,685,000	9	Nashville
17	Ohio	1803	10,746,000	21	Columbus
18	Louisiana	1812	4,438,000	8	Baton Rouge
19	Indiana	1816	5,479,000	10	Indianapolis
20	Mississippi	1817	2,587,000	5	Jackson
21	Illinois	1818	11,486,000	22	Springfield
22	Alabama	1819	3,959,000	7	Montgomery
23	Maine	1820	1,146,000	2	Augusta
24	Missouri	1821	4,970,000	9	Jefferson City
25	Arkansas	1836	2,328,000	4	Little Rock
26	Michigan	1837	9,069,000	18	Lansing
27	Florida	1845	10,680,000	19	Tallahassee
28	Texas	1845	15,724,000	27	Austin
29	Iowa	1846	2,905,000	6	Des Moines
30	Wisconsin	1848	4,751,000	9	Madison
31	California	1850	25,174,000	45	Sacramento
32	Minnesota	1858	4,144,000	8	St. Paul
33	Oregon	1859	2,662,000	5	Salem
34	Kansas	1861	2,425,000	5	Topeka
35	West Virginia	1863	1,965,000	4	Charleston
36	Nevada	1864	891,000	2	Carson City
37	Nebraska	1867	1,597,000	3	Lincoln
38	Colorado	1876	3,139,000	6	Denver
39	North Dakota	1889	680,000	1	Bismarck
40	South Dakota	1889	700,000	1	Pierre
41	Montana	1889	817,000	2	Helena
42	Washington	1889	4,300,000	8	Olympia
43	Idaho	1890	989,000	2	Boise
44	Wyoming	1890	514,000	1	Cheyenne
45	Utah	1896	1,619,000	3	Salt Lake City
46	Oklahoma	1907	3,298,000	6	Oklahoma City
47	New Mexico	1912	1,399,000	3	Santa Fe
48	Arizona	1912	2,963,000	5	Phoenix
49	Alaska	1959	479,000	1	Juneau
50	Hawaii	1959	1,023,000	2	Honolulu
	District of Columbia		623,000	1 (non-voting)	
			233,980,000	435	

The Declaration of Independence (1776)

When in the Course of human events, it becomes necessary for one people to dissolve the political bands which have connected them with another, and to assume among the powers of the earth, the separate and equal station to which the Laws of Nature and of Nature's God entitle them, a decent respect to the opinions of mankind requires that they should declare the causes which impel them to the separation.*

New Principles of Government

We hold these truths to be self-evident, that all men are created equal, that they are endowed by their Creator with certain unalienable Rights, that among these are Life, Liberty and the pursuit of Happiness. That to secure these rights, Governments are instituted among Men, deriving their just powers from the consent of the governed, That whenever any Form of Government becomes destructive of these ends, it is the Right of the People to alter or to abolish it, and to institute new Government, laying its foundation on such principles and organizing its powers in such form, as to them shall seem most likely to effect their Safety and Happiness. Prudence, indeed, will dictate that Governments long established should not be changed for light and transient causes; and accordingly all experience hath shown, that mankind are more disposed to suffer, while evils are sufferable, than to right themselves by abolishing the forms to which they are accustomed. But when a long train of abuses and usurpations, pursuing invariably the same Object evinces a design to reduce them under absolute Despotism, it is their right, it is their duty, to throw off such Government, and to provide new Guards for their future security. Such has been the patient sufferance of these Colonies; and such is now the necessity which constrains them to alter their former Systems of Government. The history of the present King of Great Britain is a history of repeated injuries and usurpations, all having in direct object the establishment of an absolute Tyranny over these States. To prove this, let Facts be submitted to a candid world.

Tyrannical Acts of the British King

He has refused his Assent to Laws, the most wholesome and necessary for the public good.

He has forbidden his Governors to pass Laws of immediate and pressing importance, unless suspended in their operation till his Assent should be obtained; and when so suspended, he has utterly neglected to attend to them.

He has refused to pass other Laws for the accommodation of large districts of people, unless those people would relinquish the right of Representation in the Legislature, a right inestimable to them and formidable to tyrants only.

He has called together legislative bodies at places unusual, uncomfortable, and distant from the depository of their Public Records, for the sole purpose of fatiguing them into compliance with his measures.

He has dissolved Representative Houses repeatedly, for opposing with manly firmness his invasions on the rights of the people.

He has refused for a long time, after such dissolutions, to cause others to be elected; whereby the Legislative powers, incapable of Annihilation, have returned to the People at large for their exercise; the State remaining in the mean time exposed to all the dangers of invasion from without, and convulsions within.

He has endeavoured to prevent the population of these States; for that purpose obstructing the Laws for Naturalization of Foreigners; refusing to pass others to encourage their migrations hither, and raising the conditions of new Appropriations of Lands.

---

* In punctuation and capitalization the text of the Declaration follows accepted sources.

He has obstructed the Administration of Justice, by refusing his Assent to Laws for establishing Judiciary powers.

He has made Judges dependent on his Will alone, for the tenure of their offices, and the amount and payment of their salaries.

He has erected a multitude of New Offices, and sent hither swarms of Officers to harass our People, and eat out their substance.

He has kept among us, in times of peace, Standing Armies without the Consent of our legislatures.

He has affected to render the military independent of and superior to the Civil power.

He has combined with others to subject us to a jurisdiction foreign to our constitution, and unacknowledged by our laws; giving his Assent to their Acts of pretended Legislation:

For quartering large bodies of armed troops among us:

For protecting them, by a mock Trial, from Punishment for any Murders which they should commit on the Inhabitants of these States:

For cutting off our Trade with all parts of the world:

For imposing Taxes on us without our Consent:

For depriving us in many cases, of the benefits of Trial by Jury:

For transporting us beyond Seas to be tried for pretended offenses:

For abolishing the free System of English Laws in a neighbouring Province, establishing therein an Arbitrary government, and enlarging its Boundaries so as to render it at once an example and fit instrument for introducing the same absolute rule into these Colonies:

For taking away our Charters, abolishing our most valuable Laws, and altering fundamentally the Forms of our Governments:

For suspending our own Legislatures, and declaring themselves invested with power to legislate for us in all cases whatsoever.

He has abdicated Government here, by declaring us out of his Protection and waging War against us.

He has plundered our seas, ravaged our Coasts, burnt our towns, and destroyed the lives of our people.

He is at this time transporting large Armies of foreign Mercenaries to compleat the works of death, desolation and tyranny, already begun with circumstances of Cruelty & perfidy scarcely paralleled in the most barbarous ages, and totally unworthy the Head of a civilized nation.

He has constrained our fellow Citizens taken Captive on the high Seas to bear Arms against their Country, to become the executioners of their friends and Brethren, or to fall themselves by their Hands.

He has excited domestic insurrections amongst us, and has endeavoured to bring on the inhabitants of our frontiers, the merciless Indian Savages, whose known rule of warfare, is an indistinguished destruction of all ages, sexes and conditions.

Efforts of the Colonies to Avoid Separation

In every stage of these Oppressions We have Petitioned for Redress in the most humble terms: Our repeated Petitions have been answered only by repeated injury. A Prince, whose character is thus marked by every act which may define a Tyrant, is unfit to be the ruler of a free people.

Nor have We been wanting in attentions to our British brethren. We have warned them from time to time of attempts by their legislature to extend an unwarrantable jurisdiction over us. We have reminded them of the circumstances of our emigration and settlement here. We have appealed to their native justice and magnanimity, and we have conjured them by the ties of our common kindred to disavow these usurpations, which, would inevitably interrupt our connections and correspondence. They too have been deaf to the voice of justice and of consanguinity. We must, therefore, acquiesce in the necessity, which denounces our Separation, and hold them, as we hold the rest of mankind, Enemies in War, in Peace Friends.

The Colonies Are Declared Independent

We, therefore, the Representatives of the united States of America, in General Congress, Assembled, appealing to the Supreme Judge of the world for the rectitude of our intentions, do, in the Name, and by Authority of the good People of these Colonies, solemnly publish and declare, That these United Colonies are, and of Right ought to be Free and Independent States; that they are Absolved from all Allegiance to the British Crown, and that all political connection between them and the State of Great Britain, is and ought to be totally dissolved; and that as Free and Independent States, they have full Power to Levy War, conclude Peace, contract Alliances, establish Commerce, and to do all other Acts and Things which Independent States may of right do. And for the support of this Declaration, with a firm reliance on the protection of divine Providence, we mutually pledge to each other our Lives, our Fortunes and our sacred Honor.

The Constitution of the United States

Starting on this page is the complete text of the Constitution of the United States. The actual text of the Constitution appears in the column that is printed on a colored background. In the other column you will find explanations of each part of the Constitution.

Headings and subheadings have been added to help you identify the various parts of the Constitution. The portions of the original document that are no longer in effect are printed in italics.

PREAMBLE

The Preamble states the purposes for which the Constitution was written: (1) to form a union of states that will benefit all, (2) to make laws and establish courts that are fair, (3) to maintain peace within the country, (4) to defend the nation against attack, (5) to help the people lead happy and useful lives, and (6) to make sure that this nation's people and their descendants remain free.

The opening words of the Constitution make clear that it is the people themselves who have the power to establish a government or change it.

We the people of the United States, in order to form a more perfect union, establish justice, insure domestic tranquillity, provide for the common defense, promote the general welfare, and secure the blessings of liberty to ourselves and our posterity, do ordain and establish this Constitution for the United States of America.

ARTICLE I / LEGISLATIVE BRANCH

SECTION 1 Congress

All national laws must be made by Congress. But Congress can make no laws except those permitted under the Constitution. Congress is made up of two houses—the Senate and the House of Representatives.

All legislative powers herein granted shall be vested in a Congress of the United States, which shall consist of a Senate and House of Representatives.

SECTION 2 The House of Representatives

a. Members of the House of Representatives are elected in each state every two years. Any person who has the right to vote for representatives to the state legislature has the right to vote for the state's representatives in the House of Representatives. This is the only qualification for voting listed in the original Constitution. It made sure that the House would be elected by the people themselves.

a. Election and term of members. The House of Representatives shall be composed of members chosen every second year by the people of the several states, and the electors in each state shall have the qualifications requisite for electors of the most numerous branch of the state legislature.

b. A representative must be at least 25 years old, a United States citizen for at least seven years, and a resident of the state from which he or she is elected. (By custom, a representative must also live in the congressional district from which he or she is elected.)

b. Qualification of members. No person shall be a representative who shall not have attained to the age of twenty-five years, and been seven years a citizen of the United States, and who shall not, when elected, be an inhabitant of that state in which he shall be chosen.

610

c. Appointment of representatives and of direct taxes. Representatives *and direct taxes* shall be apportioned among the several states which may be included within this Union, according to their respective numbers, *which shall be determined by adding to the whole number of free persons, including those bound to service for a term of years, and excluding Indians not taxed, three fifths of all other persons.* The actual enumeration shall be made within three years after the first meeting of the Congress of the United States, and within every subsequent term of ten years, in such manner as they shall by law direct. The number of representatives shall not exceed one for every thirty thousand, but each state shall have at least one representative; *and until such enumeration shall be made, the State of New Hampshire shall be entitled to choose three; Massachusetts, eight; Rhode Island and Providence Plantations, one; Connecticut, five; New York, six; New Jersey, four; Pennsylvania, eight; Delaware, one; Maryland, six; Virginia, ten; North Carolina, five; South Carolina, five; and Georgia, three.*

c. The number of representatives each state has is determined by the state's population. Direct taxes are to be collected from the states according to the number of people living in each state. (Amendment 16 made the income tax an exception to this rule.) A direct tax is one paid to the government by the person who is taxed. Since there now are no slaves or indentured servants in the United States and Indians are citizens, all the people of a state are counted in determining the number of representatives a state shall have. Congress decides how the population is to be counted, but a census must be taken every ten years. The House of Representatives cannot have more than one member for every 30,000 persons in the nation. But each state is entitled to one representative, no matter how small its population. In 1910 Congress limited the number of representatives to 435.

d. Filling vacancies. When vacancies happen in the representation from any state, the executive authority thereof shall issue writs of election to fill such vacancies.

d. When a state does not have all the representatives to which it is entitled—for example, when a representative resigns or dies—the governor of that state must call an election to fill the vacancy.

e. Officers; impeachment. The House of Representatives shall choose their Speaker and other officers; and shall have the sole power of impeachment.

e. The House of Representatives elects its presiding officer (the Speaker) and other officers such as the chaplain. Only the House has the right to impeach, that is, to bring charges of misdeeds in office against an official of the United States.

SECTION 3   The Senate

a. Number and election of members. The Senate of the United States shall be composed of two senators from each state, chosen *by the legislature thereof,* for six years; and each senator shall have one vote.

a. The Senate is made up of two senators from each state. Senators are no longer chosen by the legislatures of their states. Amendment 17 states that they are to be elected by the people. A senator serves a six-year term.

b. Choosing senators. Immediately after they shall be assembled in consequence of the first election, they shall be divided as equally as may be into three classes. *The seats of the senators of the first class shall be vacated at the expiration of the second year, of the second class at the expiration of the fourth year, and of the third class at the expiration of the sixth year,* so that one third may be chosen every second year; *and if vacancies happen by resignation, or otherwise, during the recess of the legislature of any state, the executive thereof may make temporary appointments until the next meeting of the legislature, which shall then fill such vacancies.*

b. Senators were divided into three groups so that their terms would not all end at the same time. Today all senators are elected for six-year terms, but only one third are elected in any election year. The provision for filling vacancies in the Senate was changed by Amendment 17.

c. Qualifications of members. No person shall be a senator who shall not have attained to the age of thirty years, and been nine years a citizen of the United States, and who shall not, when elected, be an inhabitant of that state for which he shall be chosen.

c. A senator must be at least thirty years old, a United States citizen for nine years, and a resident of the state from which he or she is elected.

d. The Vice President serves as the president of the Senate, but cannot vote except in case of a tie. This is the only duty assigned to the Vice President. In recent years the Vice President has been given more responsibilities by the President.

e. The Senate chooses its other officers, including a President pro tempore. *Pro tempore* means "for the time being." The President pro tempore presides in the Senate when the Vice President is absent or serving as President.

f. The Senate tries the case when a federal official is impeached by the House of Representatives. The Senators must formally declare that they will be honest and just. If the President of the United States is tried, the Chief Justice presides over the Senate. Two thirds of the senators present must agree that the charge is true for the impeached person to be found guilty.

g. If the Senate finds an impeached official guilty, it may only punish that official by keeping him or her from ever holding a government job again. Once out of office, however, the former official may be tried in a regular court and, if found guilty, punished like any other person.

a. The legislature of each state has the right to determine how, when, and where senators and representatives are elected, but Congress may pass election laws which the states must follow. For example, a federal law requires that secret ballots be used.

b. Congress must meet at least once a year. Amendment 20 made January 3 the day for beginning a regular session of Congress.

a. Each house of Congress has the right to decide whether its members are qualified and fairly elected. Either house may by a majority vote refuse to seat a newly elected member. A *quorum* is the number of members which must be present for official business to be carried on. The Constitution states that a majority—half the members plus one—is a quorum in either the Senate or the House.

b. Each house of Congress has the right to make rules to follow in its work. Over the years many rules have grown up concerning the procedures used in conducting business. Each house may punish its members for wrongdoing or even expel them by a two-thirds vote.

d. President of Senate. The Vice President of the United States shall be President of the Senate, but shall have no vote, unless they be equally divided.

e. Other officers. The Senate shall choose their other officers, and also a President pro tempore, in the absence of the Vice President, or when he shall exercise the office of President of the United States.

f. Trials of impeachment. The Senate shall have the sole power to try all impeachments. When sitting for that purpose, they shall be on oath or affirmation. When the President of the United States is tried, the Chief Justice shall preside; and no person shall be convicted without the concurrence of two thirds of the members present.

g. Punishment. Judgment in cases of impeachment shall not exceed further than to removal from office, and disqualification to hold and enjoy any office of honor, trust, or profit under the United States; but the party convicted shall nevertheless be liable and subject to indictment, trial, judgment, and punishment, according to law.

SECTION 4 Elections and Meetings of Congress

a. Method of holding elections. The times, places, and manner of holding elections for senators and representatives shall be prescribed in each state by the legislature thereof; but the Congress may at any time by law make or alter such regulations, *except as to the places of choosing senators.*

b. Meeting of Congress. The Congress shall assemble at least once in every year, *and such meeting shall be on the first Monday in December, unless they shall by law appoint a different day.*

SECTION 5 Organization and Rules of Each House

a. Organization. Each house shall be the judge of the elections, returns, and qualifications of its own members, and a majority of each shall constitute a quorum to do business; but a smaller number may adjourn from day to day, and may be authorized to compel the attendance of absent members, in such manner, and under such penalties as each house may provide.

b. Rules. Each house may determine the rules of its proceedings, punish its members for disorderly behavior, and with the concurrence of two thirds, expel a member.

c. Journal. Each house shall keep a journal of its proceedings, and from time to time publish the same, excepting such parts as may in their judgment require secrecy; and the yeas and nays of the members of either house on any question shall, at the desire of one fifth of those present, be entered on the journal.

d. Adjournment. Neither house, during the session of Congress, shall without the consent of the other adjourn for more than three days, nor to any other place than that in which the two houses shall be sitting.

SECTION 6 Privileges and Restrictions

a. Pay and privileges of members. The senators and representatives shall receive a compensation for their services, to be ascertained by law, and paid out of the Treasury of the United States. They shall in all cases, except treason, felony, and breach of the peace, be privileged from arrest during their attendance at the session of their respective houses and in going to and returning from the same; and for any speech or debate in either house, they shall not be questioned in any other place.

b. Holding other offices prohibited. No senator or representative shall, during the time for which he was elected, be appointed to any civil office under the authority of the United States which shall have been created, or the emoluments whereof shall have been increased during such time; and no person holding any office under the United States shall be a member of either house during his continuance in office.

SECTION 7 Method of Passing Laws

a. Revenue bills. All bills for raising revenue shall originate in the House of Representatives; but the Senate may propose or concur with amendments as on other bills.

b. How bills become laws. Every bill which shall have passed the House of Representatives and the Senate shall, before it become a law, be presented to the President of the United States; if he approves he shall sign it, but if not he shall return it, with his objections, to that house in which it shall have originated, who shall enter the objections at large on their journal, and proceed to reconsider it. If after such reconsideration two thirds of that house shall agree to pass the bill, it shall be sent, together with the objections, to the other house, by which it shall likewise be reconsidered, and

c. Each house of Congress must keep a record of what goes on at its meetings and must publish the record. The *Congressional Record* is issued daily during sessions of Congress. Parts of the record that the members of Congress believe should be kept secret may be withheld. How members of either house vote on a question may be entered in the record if one fifth of those present in that house wish this to be done.

d. When Congress is meeting, neither house may stop work for more than three days without the consent of the other house. Neither house is allowed to hold its sessions in another city without the consent of the other house.

a. Senators and representatives are paid out of the United States Treasury. Their salary is determined by law passed by Congress. At the present time the salary is $60,662 annually, plus allowances for travel, office staff, stationery, and other expenses. Members of Congress also enjoy the *franking privilege,* that is, the right to send free any official mail stamped with their name. Members of Congress may not be arrested at meetings of Congress or while going to or from such meetings unless they are suspected of treason, other serious crimes, or disturbing the peace. They may not be punished for anything they say in Congress, except by the house of which they are a member.

b. Until after their terms have ended, senators or representatives may not hold offices created by the Congress of which they are members. The same restriction applies to jobs for which Congress has voted increased pay. No person may be a member of Congress without first giving up any other federal office he or she may hold.

a. Bills for raising money for the federal government must start in the House of Representatives, but the Senate may make changes in such bills. Actually, the Senate has as much influence over revenue bills as does the House.

b. A bill (except one for raising revenue) may start in either the Senate or the House of Representatives. However, exactly the same bill must be passed by a majority vote in both houses of Congress. Differences are usually ironed out in a conference committee made up of members of both houses. When both the Senate and House have voted in favor of the bill, it is sent to the President. The President can then do one of three things: sign the bill; veto it; or return it to the house where it began. If the bill is returned, it may then be discussed again in Congress. If two thirds of both houses of Congress vote for the bill after reconsidering it, the bill becomes law without the President's signing it. In such cases, the vote of each member of Congress is recorded.

The President has ten days (not counting Sundays) to study any bill. If the President keeps a bill more than ten days without signing or vetoing it and Congress continues to meet, the bill becomes a law. But if Congress adjourns before the ten-day period ends and the President does not sign it, the bill is dead. This is known as a "pocket veto."

if approved by two thirds of that house, it shall become a law. But in all such cases the votes of both houses shall be determined by yeas and nays, and the names of the persons voting for and against the bill shall be entered on the journal of each house respectively. If any bill shall not be returned by the President within ten days (Sundays excepted) after it shall have been presented to him, the same shall be a law, in like manner as if he had signed it, unless the Congress by their adjournment prevent its return, in which case it shall not be a law.

c. Other acts which require approval of both houses of Congress take effect only if they are signed by the President or passed over a presidential veto by a two-thirds vote of both houses. However, a vote to adjourn Congress requires only a majority vote of both houses.

c. Approval or disapproval by the President. Every order, resolution, or vote to which the concurrence of the Senate and House of Representatives may be necessary (except on a question of adjournment) shall be presented to the President of the United States; and before the same shall take effect, shall be approved by him, or being disapproved by him, shall be repassed by two thirds of the Senate and House of Representatives, according to the rules and limitations prescribed in the case of a bill.

SECTION 8 Powers Granted to Congress

The Congress shall have power

a. Congress may pass laws for collecting various kinds of taxes. All federal taxes must be the same in all parts of the nation.

a. To lay and collect taxes, duties, imposts, and excises; to pay the debts and provide for the common defense and general welfare of the United States; but all duties, imposts, and excises shall be uniform throughout the United States;

b. Congress has the power to borrow money that the federal government may need and to promise to repay this money. Borrowing is generally done by issuing government bonds or certificates of indebtedness.

b. To borrow money on the credit of the United States;

c. Congress has the power to pass laws concerning trade between this country and foreign countries and between one state and another state.

c. To regulate commerce with foreign nations, and among the several states, and with the Indian tribes;

d. Congress has the power to make laws determining how citizens of other countries may become citizens of the United States. Congress also has the power to make laws regulating bankruptcy. Such laws must be the same throughout the country.

d. To establish a uniform rule of naturalization, and uniform laws on the subject of bankruptcies throughout the United States;

e. Congress controls the minting of money and decides how much each coin is worth. And it may determine the value of foreign coins used in the United States. Congress also sets up standards for measuring weight and distance.

e. To coin money, regulate the value thereof and of foreign coin, and fix the standard of weights and measures;

f. Congress passes laws punishing people who make counterfeit money and government bonds.

f. To provide for the punishment of counterfeiting the securities and current coin of the United States;

g. Congress provides for a postal system and may build and maintain roads over which the mail is carried.

g. To establish post offices and post roads;

h. To promote the progress of science and useful arts by securing for limited times to authors and inventors the exclusive right to their respective writings and discoveries;

i. To constitute tribunals inferior to the Supreme Court;

j. To define and punish piracies and felonies committed on the high seas and offenses against the law of nations;

k. To declare war, grant letters of marque and reprisal, and make rules concerning captures on land and water;

l. To raise and support armies, but no appropriation of money to that use shall be for a longer term than two years;

m. To provide and maintain a navy;

n. To make rules for the government and regulation of land and naval forces;

o. To provide for calling forth the militia to execute the laws of the Union, suppress insurrections, and repel invasions;

p. To provide for organizing, arming, and disciplining the militia, and for governing such part of them as may be employed in the service of the United States, reserving to the states respectively the appointment of the officers and the authority of training the militia, according to the discipline prescribed by Congress;

q. To exercise exclusive legislation in all cases whatsoever over such district (not exceeding ten miles square) as may, by cession of particular states and the acceptance of Congress, become the seat of the government of the United States, and to exercise like authority over all places purchased by the consent of the legislature of the state in which the same shall be for the erection of forts, magazines, arsenals, dock-yards, and other needful buildings; and

r. To make all laws which shall be necessary and proper for carrying into execution the foregoing powers, and all other powers vested by this Constitution in the government of the United States, or in any department or officer thereof.

h. Congress encourages art, science, and invention by passing laws which protect artists and inventors. Copyright and patent laws make it illegal for a person to use the work of an artist, musician, author, or inventor without permission.

i. Congress has the power to establish federal courts other than the Supreme Court.

j. Congress may specifiy what acts committed on American ships are crimes. The accused will stand trial in a federal court when the ship returns to port.

k. Congress alone has the power to declare war. *Letters of marque and reprisal* are government licenses authorizing the holders to fit out armed ships for use in capturing enemy merchant ships. This power to commission privateers to prey upon enemy commerce was used extensively in the War of 1812. The practice is no longer followed.

l. Congress may create an army for the United States. But Congress may not vote the money to support the armed forces for more than two years in advance.

m. Congress may create a navy for the United States and vote the money necessary to operate it.

n. Congress may make rules for our armed forces. While on active duty, members of the armed forces are under military law rather than civil law.

o. Congress may determine when and how the militia, the citizen soldiers of the various states, may be called into the service of the national government. The militia may be used to enforce law, to put an end to rebellion, and to drive back an invasion of the country.

p. Congress provides for organizing, arming, and disciplining the militia. The states appoint the officers and train the militia under the regulations set up by Congress. When called out by the national government, however, the militia is part of the national armed forces.

q. Congress has the power to make laws for the District of Columbia. Because it contains the national capital, the District of Columbia is not under the control of any state. Congress also makes laws regulating the use of all other property belonging to the national government—forts, arsenals, etc.

r. Congress also has the power to pass all laws needed to carry out the responsibilities assigned it by the Constitution. This provision is called the "elastic clause." It can be stretched to meet the changing needs of the nation. It is the basis for much legislation not authorized in any other provision of the Constitution.

a. In 1808 Congress prohibited further importation of slaves.

b. Congress may not take away a person's right to the writ of habeas corpus except in time of great national danger. (A *writ of habeas corpus* is a court order directing that a prisoner be given a hearing so that the court can decide whether that person should be released or held and charged with a crime.)

c. Congress may not pass a bill of attainder. (A *bill of attainder* is a legislative act which condemns a person without a trial in court.) Neither can Congress pass an *ex post facto* law. Such a law makes an act a crime after the act has been committed.

d. Congress may not levy a direct tax that is not the same for all persons taxed. Amendment 16 provides an exception in the case of the income tax.

e. Congress may not tax goods sent from one state to another or goods sent to other countries.

f. In laws concerning commerce, Congress may not favor one port over other ports. Congress must not tax goods being sent by water from one state to another state.

g. Money can be paid out of the Treasury only if Congress has voted the appropriation. (An *appropriation* is money granted for a given purpose.) An account of money received and money spent must be published from time to time.

h. The United States may not grant a title of nobility. Federal officials may not accept titles, gifts, or honors from any foreign ruler or government unless Congress gives its permission.

a. States may not make treaties, enter into agreements with foreign countries, or grant their citizens the right to make war. States cannot issue their own money or declare that any money other than that of the United States can be used as legal money.

The states are forbidden to punish people without giving them a trial or to pass laws that would punish people for acts that were not against the law at the time they were committed. State governments must not pass any laws that would make contracts or other legal agreements less binding on the people who agreed to them.

SECTION 9 Powers Denied to the Federal Government

a. *The migration or importation of such persons as any of the states now existing shall think proper to admit shall not be prohibited by the Congress prior to the year one thousand eight hundred and eight, but a tax or duty may be imposed on such importation, not exceeding ten dollars for each person.*

b. The privilege of the writ of habeas corpus shall not be suspended, unless when in cases of rebellion or invasion the public safety may require it.

c. No bill of attainder or ex post facto law shall be passed.

d. No capitation or other direct tax shall be laid, unless in proportion to the census or enumeration herein before directed to be taken.

e. No tax or duty shall be laid on articles exported from any state.

f. No preference shall be given by any regulation of commerce or revenue to the ports of one state over those of another; nor shall vessels bound to or from one state be obliged to enter, clear, or pay duties in another.

g. No money shall be drawn from the treasury, but in consequence of appropriations made by law; and a regular statement and account of the receipts and expenditures of all public money shall be published from time to time.

h. No title of nobility shall be granted by the United States; and no person holding any office of profit or trust under them shall, without the consent of Congress, accept of any present, emolument, office, or title, of any kind whatever, from any king, prince, or foreign state.

SECTION 10 Powers Denied to the States

a. No state shall enter into any treaty, alliance, or confederation; grant letters of marque and reprisal; coin money; emit bills of credit; make any thing but gold and silver coin a tender in payment of debts; pass any bill of attainder, ex post facto law, or law impairing the obligation of contracts; or grant any title of nobility.

b. No state shall, without the consent of the Congress, lay any imposts or duties on imports or exports, except what may be absolutely necessary for executing its inspection laws; and the net produce of all duties and imposts, laid by any state on imports or exports, shall be for the use of the treasury of the United States; and all such laws shall be subject to the revision and control of the Congress.

c. No state shall, without the consent of Congress, lay any duty of tonnage; keep troops or ships of war in time of peace; enter into any agreement or compact with another state or with a foreign power; or engage in war, unless actually invaded or in such imminent danger as will not admit of delay.

ARTICLE II / EXECUTIVE BRANCH

SECTION 1 President and Vice President

a. Term of office. The executive power shall be vested in a President of the United States of America. He shall hold his office during the term of four years, and, together with the Vice President chosen for the same term, be elected as follows:

b. Electors. Each state shall appoint, in such manner as the legislature thereof may direct, a number of electors, equal to the whole number of senators and representatives to which the state may be entitled in the Congress; but no senator or representative, or person holding an office of trust or profit under the United States, shall be appointed an elector.

The electors shall meet in their respective states and vote by ballot for two persons, of whom one at least shall not be an inhabitant of the same state with themselves. And they shall make a list of all the persons voted for and of the number of votes for each; which list they shall sign and certify, and transmit sealed to the seat of government of the United States, directed to the President of the Senate. The President of the Senate shall, in the presence of the Senate and House of Representatives, open all the certificates, and the votes shall then be counted. The person having the greatest number of votes shall be the President, if such number be a majority of the whole number of electors appointed; and if there be more than one who have such majority, and have an equal number of votes, then the House of Representatives shall immediately choose by ballot one of them for President; and if no person have a majority, then from the five highest on the list the said house shall in like manner choose the President. But in choosing the President the votes shall be taken by states, the representation from each state having one vote; a quorum for this purpose shall consist of a member or members from two thirds of the states, and a majority of all the

b. States may not tax goods leaving or entering their territory. However, they may charge fees to cover the costs of inspection. Any profit from such inspection fees must be turned over to the United States Treasury. Congress has the power to change the inspection laws of a state.

c. Unless Congress gives permission, a state may not tax ships entering its ports, keep an army or navy—except the militia—in time of peace, make treaties with other states or foreign countries, or make war except when it is invaded.

a. The President of the United States enforces or executes the nation's laws and is elected, as is the Vice President, for a four-year term.

b. The President and Vice President are elected by electors chosen by the states according to rules established by the legislatures. Each state has as many electors as it has senators and representatives in Congress. No senator or representative or other person holding a federal job may be an elector. Today electors usually are important party members whose votes are pledged to a given candidate.
   This clause did not work well in practice and was changed by Amendment 12.

c. Congress determines when electors are chosen and when they vote. The day is the same throughout the United States. The popular vote for electors takes place on the Tuesday after the first Monday of November in each "leap year." In mid-December the electors meet in their state capitals and cast their electoral votes.

d. To be President, a person must be a citizen of the United States by birth, at least 35 years old, and a resident of the United States for at least 14 years.

e. If the presidency becomes vacant, the Vice President becomes the President of the United States. If neither the President nor the Vice President is able to serve, Congress has the right to decide which government official shall act as President. Amendment 25 practically assures that there always will be a Vice President to succeed to the presidency.

f. The President is paid a salary fixed by Congress. That salary may not be increased or decreased during the term of office. The President may not receive any other salary from the United States or from one of the states. The salary of the President is now $200,000 a year, plus additional amounts for expenses.

g. In taking the oath of office, the President promises to preserve, protect, and defend the Constitution of the United States.

a. The President is commander-in-chief of the armed forces and of the militia when it is called out by the national government. As commander-in-chief, the President has great power, especially in time of war. The President may ask the heads of the executive departments for advice and for reports on the work of the various departments. No provision is made in the Constitution for the Cabinet or for Cabinet meetings, but the existence of executive departments is implied here.

states shall be necessary to a choice. In every case, after the choice of the President, the person having the greatest number of votes of the electors shall be the Vice President. But if there should remain two or more who have equal votes, the Senate shall choose from them by ballot the Vice President.

c. Time of elections. The Congress may determine the time of choosing the electors, and the day on which they shall give their votes; which day shall be the same throughout the United States.

d. Qualifications for President. No person except a natural-born citizen, *or a citizen of the United States, at the time of the adoption of this Constitution,* shall be eligible to the office of President; neither shall any person be eligible to that office who shall not have attained the age of thirty-five years, and been fourteen years a resident within the United States.

e. Vacancy. In case of the removal of the President from office or of his death, resignation, or inability to discharge the powers and duties of the said office, the same shall devolve on the Vice President; and the Congress may by law provide for the case of removal, death, resignation, or inability, both of the President and Vice President, declaring what officer shall then act as President; and such officer shall act accordingly, until the disability be removed or a President shall be elected.

f. The President's salary. The President shall, at stated times, receive for his services a compensation, which shall neither be increased nor diminished during the period for which he shall have been elected, and he shall not receive within that period any other emolument from the United States, or any of them.

g. Oath of office. Before he enter on the execution of his office, he shall take the following oath or affirmation: "I do solemnly swear (or affirm) that I will faithfully execute the office of President of the United States, and will to the best of my ability, preserve, protect, and defend the Constitution of the United States."

SECTION 2 Powers of the President

a. Military powers; reprieves and pardons. The President shall be Commander-in-Chief of the Army and Navy of the United States, and of the militia of the several states, when called into the actual service of the United States. He may require the opinion, in writing, of the principal officer in each of the executive departments, upon any subject relating to the duties of their respective offices, and he shall have power to grant reprieves and pardons for offenses against the United States, except in cases of impeachment.

b. Treaties and appointments. He shall have power, by and with the advice and consent of the Senate, to make treaties, provided two thirds of the senators present concur; and he shall nominate and, by and with the advice and consent of the Senate, shall appoint ambassadors, other public ministers and consuls, judges of the Supreme Court, and all other officers of the United States, whose appointments are not herein otherwise provided for, and which shall be established by law; but the Congress may by law vest the appointment of such inferior officers as they think proper in the President alone, in the courts of law, or in the heads of departments.

c. Filling vacancies. The President shall have power to fill up all vacancies that may happen during the recess of the Senate, by granting commissions which shall expire at the end of their next session.

SECTION 3   Duties of the President

He shall from time to time give to the Congress information of the state of the Union, and recommend to their consideration such measures as he shall judge necessary and expedient; he may, on extraordinary occasions, convene both houses, or either of them, and in case of disagreement between them with respect to the time of adjournment he may adjourn them to such time as he shall think proper; he shall receive ambassadors and other public ministers; he shall take care that the laws be faithfully executed, and shall commission all the officers of the United States.

SECTION 4   Impeachment

The President, Vice President and all civil officers of the United States shall be removed from office on impeachment for, and conviction of, treason, bribery, or other high crimes and misdemeanors.

ARTICLE III / JUDICIAL BRANCH

SECTION 1   The Federal Courts

The judicial power of the United States shall be vested in one Supreme Court and in such inferior courts as the Congress may from time to time ordain and establish. The judges, both of the Supreme and inferior courts, shall hold their offices during good behavior and shall, at stated times, receive for their services a compensation which shall not be diminished during their continuance in office.

b. The President may make treaties, but all treaties must be approved in the Senate by a two-thirds vote of the senators present. The President may also appoint important government officials. Such appointments must be approved in the Senate by a majority of the senators present. Congress may, however, pass laws giving the President, the courts, or the heads of departments power to appoint less important officials without the consent of the Senate.

c. If the Senate is not meeting, the President may make temporary appointments to fill vacancies. These appointments end at the close of the next session of Congress unless the Senate approves them. Congress, with the approval of the President, has given the Civil Service Commission responsibility for determining the fitness of job applicants and for ranking them on civil service lists from which appointments to many federal positions are made.

The President must report to Congress from time to time on conditions within the United States. The President may also suggest that Congress act to pass certain laws or to solve problems facing the nation. The President may call a special session of Congress if a situation arises which requires action by Congress when that body is not in regular session. In case the Senate and House cannot agree when to end a session, the President may adjourn Congress. The President receives representatives of foreign nations, sees that the laws of the nation are enforced, and commissions officers in the armed services.

The President, Vice President, and other important government officials may be removed from office if impeached and found guilty of treason, bribery, or other serious crimes.

The power to interpret the laws of the United States belongs to the Supreme Court and the other federal courts established by Congress. District courts and courts of appeal are now part of the regular court system. Federal judges are appointed by the President with the approval of the Senate. They hold office as long as they live, unless they retire, resign, or are impeached and found guilty.

a. Federal courts may try cases concerning (1) the Constitution and federal laws and treaties, (2) representatives of foreign nations, (3) laws governing ships and sailors, (4) disputes between the United States and a person or another government, (5) disputes between states, (6) disputes between citizens of different states, (7) disputes in which citizens of the same state claim lands granted by different states, and (8) disputes between a state or its citizens and a foreign state or its citizens.

b. Any case involving a representative of a foreign country or one of the states is first tried in the Supreme Court. Any other case is first tried in a lower court, but the Supreme Court may hear a case from a lower court on appeal. Since the Supreme Court is the highest court in the land, its decision cannot be appealed.

c. Except in cases of impeachment, the accused has a right to a trial by jury in the state in which the crime was committed. If the crime did not take place within a state, a law passed by Congress determines where the trial is to be held.

a. A citizen who makes war on the United States or aids this country's enemies is guilty of treason. To be judged guilty of treason, one must confess in court or be convicted by the testimony of two or more persons.

b. Congress decides what the punishment for treason will be. But the family or descendants of a guilty person may not be punished.

The records and court decisions of one state must be accepted in all states. Congress has the power to see that this is done.

SECTION 2 Jurisdiction of the Federal Courts

a. Federal courts in general. The judicial power shall extend to all cases, in law and equity, arising under this Constitution, the laws of the United States, and treaties made, or which shall be made, under their authority; to all cases affecting ambassadors, other public ministers, and consuls; to all cases of admiralty and maritime jurisdiction; to controversies to which the United States shall be a party; to controversies between two or more states; *between a state and citizens of another state;* between citizens of different states; between citizens of the same state claiming lands under grants of different states, and between a state, or the citizens thereof, and foreign states, citizens, or subjects.

b. Supreme Court. In all cases affecting ambassadors, other public ministers, and consuls, and those in which a state shall be a party, the Supreme Court shall have original jurisdiction. In all the other cases before mentioned, the Supreme Court shall have appellate jurisdiction, both as to law and fact, with such exceptions and under such regulations as the Congress shall make.

c. Rules respecting trials. The trial of all crimes, except in cases of impeachment, shall be by jury; and such trial shall be held in the state where the said crimes shall have been committed; but when not committed within any state, the trial shall be at such place or places as the Congress may by law have directed.

SECTION 3 Treason

a. Definition of treason. Treason against the United States shall consist only in levying war against them or in adhering to their enemies, giving them aid and comfort. No person shall be convicted of treason unless on the testimony of two witnesses to the same overt act, or on confession in open court.

b. Punishment for treason. The Congress shall have power to declare the punishment of treason, but no attainder of treason shall work corruption of blood, or forfeiture except during the life of the person attainted.

ARTICLE IV / THE STATES AND THE FEDERAL GOVERNMENT

SECTION 1 State Records

Full faith and credit shall be given in each state to the public acts, records, and judicial proceedings of every other state. And the Congress may by general laws prescribe the manner in which such acts, records, and proceedings shall be proved, and the effect thereof.

SECTION 2 Privileges and Immunities of Citizens

a. Privileges. The citizens of each state shall be entitled to all privileges and immunities of citizens in the several states.

a. The citizens of all states have in a given state the rights and privileges granted to the citizens of that state. For example, a citizen of Oregon going into California would be entitled to all the privileges of citizens of California.

b. Extradition. A person charged in any state with treason, felony, or other crime who shall flee from justice and be found in another state shall, on demand of the executive authority of the state from which he fled, be delivered up, to be removed to the state having jurisdiction of the crime.

b. If the governor makes the request, a person charged with a crime in one state may be returned from another state to stand trial. Such action is called *extradition.* A request for extradition may be denied, however.

c. Fugitive workers. *No person held to service or labor in one state, under the laws thereof, escaping into another shall, in consequence of any law or regulation therein, be discharged from such service or labor, but shall be delivered upon claim of the party to whom such service or labor may be due.*

c. This clause referred to slaves. Amendment 13 abolished slavery.

SECTION 3 New States and Territories

a. Admission of new states. New states may be admitted by the Congress into this Union; but no new state shall be formed or erected within the jurisdiction of any other state; nor any state be formed by the junction of two or more states, or parts of states, without the consent of the legislatures of the states concerned, as well as of the Congress.

a. Congress has the power to add new states to the Union. However, no state can have some of its territory taken away without its consent as well as the consent of Congress.

b. National territory. The Congress shall have power to dispose of and make all needful rules and regulations respecting the territory or other property belonging to the United States; and nothing in this Constitution shall be so construed as to prejudice any claims of the United States, or of any particular state.

b. Congress has the power to make rules and regulations concerning the property and the territory of the United States.

SECTION 4 Guarantees to the States

The United States shall guarantee to every state in this Union a republican form of government, and shall protect each of them against invasion; and on application of the legislature, or of the executive (when the legislature cannot be convened), against domestic violence.

It is the duty of the federal government to see that each state (1) has a republican form of government, (2) is protected from invasion, and (3) receives help to put down riots and other disorders when such help is requested by the legislature or the governor of the state.

The Constitution may be changed by amendment. An amendment may be proposed by a two-thirds vote of both houses of Congress or by a convention called at the request of the legislatures of two thirds of the states. Proposed amendments must be approved by the legislatures of three fourths of the states or by conventions called in three fourths of the states. When an amendment is approved, it becomes part of the Constitution. However, no amendment may take away equal state representation in the Senate.

ARTICLE V / AMENDING THE CONSTITUTION

The Congress, whenever two thirds of both houses shall deem it necessary, shall propose amendments to this Constitution, or, on the application of the legislatures of two thirds of the several states, shall call a convention for proposing amendments, which, in either case, shall be valid to all intents and purposes, as part of this Constitution, when ratified by the legislatures of three fourths of the several states or by conventions in three fourths thereof, as the one or the other mode of ratification may be proposed by the Congress; provided that *no amendments which may be made prior to the year one thousand eight hundred and eight shall in any manner affect the first and fourth clauses in the ninth section of the first article; and that* no state, without its consent, shall be deprived of its equal suffrage in the Senate.

ARTICLE VI / SUPREMACY OF FEDERAL LAWS

a. The framers of the Constitution agreed that the United States would be responsible for all debts contracted by the Confederation government.

a. Public debt. All debts contracted and engagements entered into, before the adoption of this Constitution, shall be as valid against the United States under this Constitution as under the Confederation.

b. The Constitution and the laws and treaties of the United States are the supreme law of the nation. If state law is in conflict with national law, it is the national law that must be obeyed.

b. Supremacy of the Constitution. This Constitution, and the laws of the United States which shall be made in pursuance thereof, and all treaties made, or which shall be made, under the authority of the United States, shall be the supreme law of the land; and the judges in every state shall be bound thereby, anything in the Constitution or laws of any state to the contrary notwithstanding.

c. All government officials, federal and state, must take an oath to support the Constitution. But no religious test can ever be required for an official to hold office.

c. Oath of office; no religious test. The senators and representatives before mentioned, and the members of the several state legislatures, and all executive and judicial officers, both of the United States and of the several states, shall be bound by oath or affirmation to support this Constitution; but no religious test shall ever be required as a qualification to any office or public trust under the United States.

ARTICLE VII / RATIFICATION OF THE CONSTITUTION

The Constitution went into effect when nine states voted to accept it.

The ratification of the conventions of nine states shall be sufficient for the establishment of this Constitution between the states so ratifying the same.

The Amendments

AMENDMENT 1 / FREEDOM OF RELIGION, SPEECH, PRESS, ASSEMBLY, AND PETITION (1791)

Congress shall make no law respecting an establishment of religion or prohibiting the free exercise thereof; or abridging the freedom of speech, or of the press; or the right of the people peaceably to assemble, and to petition the government for a redress of grievances.

This amendment protects the five basic rights of a citizen: (1) Congress must not pass laws that stop people from worshiping as they see fit. (2) Congress cannot stop people from voicing their views in private and public, as long as they do not slander or libel others or urge violent overthrow of the government. (3) Congress must respect the right of newspapers, books, and other media to express ideas and opinions, provided that no libelous or slanderous statements are made. (4) Congress must not take away the people's right to meet together for any lawful purpose, provided they do not interfere with the rights of others. (5) Congress must not take away the people's right to ask the government to correct grievances or abuses.

AMENDMENT 2 / RIGHT TO BEAR ARMS (1791)

A well-regulated militia being necessary to the security of a free state, the right of the people to keep and bear arms shall not be infringed.

Amendment 2 guarantees that the federal government cannot deny states the right to enlist citizens in the militia and to provide them with training in the use of weapons.

AMENDMENT 3 / QUARTERING OF SOLDIERS (1791)

No soldier shall, in time of peace, be quartered in any house without the consent of the owner, nor in time of war, but in a manner to be prescribed by law.

Amendment 3 was included because of the troubles caused when the British sought to quarter and supply their troops in colonists' homes. The amendment guarantees that in time of peace the federal government may not force people to have soldiers live in their homes. Even in time of war, people cannot be compelled to do this unless Congress passes a law requiring it.

AMENDMENT 4 / SEARCH AND SEIZURE (1791)

The right of the people to be secure in their persons, houses, papers, and effects, against unreasonable searches and seizures, shall not be violated, and no warrants shall issue but upon probable cause, supported by oath or affirmation and particularly describing the place to be searched and the persons or things to be seized.

This amendment extends the people's right to privacy and security by stating that the government may not search a home or arrest a person without good cause and then only after the official who makes the search or arrest has obtained a *warrant* —an official order from a judge. Judges may not issue warrants unless they believe such action is necessary to enforce the law.

AMENDMENT 5 / RIGHTS OF ACCUSED PERSONS (1791)

No person shall be held to answer for a capital or otherwise infamous crime, unless on a presentment or indictment of a grand jury, except in cases arising in

Amendment 5 says that no person may be tried in a federal court unless a grand jury decides that the person ought to be tried. (Members of the armed forces, however, may be tried in military court under military law.) People who have been tried for a crime and judged innocent cannot be tried again for the same crime. Neither can they be forced to give evidence against themselves. And no person may be executed, imprisoned, or fined except as punishment after a fair trial. A person's private property may not be taken for public use without a fair price being paid for it.

the land or naval forces, or in the militia, when in actual service in time of war or public danger; nor shall any person be subject for the same offense to be twice put in jeopardy of life or limb; nor shall be compelled in any criminal case to be a witness against himself, nor be deprived of life, liberty, or property, without due process of law; nor shall private property be taken for public use without just compensation.

AMENDMENT 6 / JURY TRIAL IN CRIMINAL CASES (1791)

In all criminal prosecutions, the accused shall enjoy the right to a speedy and public trial by an impartial jury of the state and district wherein the crime shall have been committed, which district shall have been previously ascertained by law, and to be informed of the nature and cause of the accusation; to be confronted with the witnesses against him; to have compulsory process for obtaining witnesses in his favor; and to have the assistance of counsel for his defense.

This amendment lists additional rights of an individual accused of a crime. A person accused of a crime is entitled to a prompt public trial before an impartial jury. The trial is held in the district where the crime took place. The accused must be told what the charge is. The accused must be present when witnesses give their testimony. The government must help the accused bring into court friendly witnesses. The accused must be provided a lawyer.

AMENDMENT 7 / RULES OF COMMON LAW (1791)

In suits at common law, where the value in controversy shall exceed twenty dollars, the right of trial by jury shall be preserved, and no fact tried by a jury shall be otherwise re-examined in any court of the United States than according to the rules of common law.

This amendment states that if a lawsuit involves property or settlement worth more than twenty dollars, the case may be tried before a jury. Today, cases involving lawsuits are not tried before federal courts unless large sums of money are involved.

AMENDMENT 8 / PROTECTION FROM EXCESSIVE PENALTIES (1791)

Excessive bail shall not be required, nor excessive fines imposed, nor cruel and unusual punishments inflicted.

Amendment 8 provides that persons accused of crimes may in most cases be released from jail if they or someone else posts bail. This is called "being out on bail." Bail, fines, and punishments must be reasonable.

AMENDMENT 9 / OTHER RIGHTS OF THE PEOPLE (1791)

The enumeration in the Constitution of certain rights shall not be construed to deny or disparage others retained by the people.

This amendment was included because of the impossibility of listing in the Constitution all the rights of the people. The mention of certain rights does not mean that people do not have other fundamental rights, which the government must respect.

AMENDMENT 10 / POWERS KEPT BY STATES AND THE PEOPLE (1791)

The powers not delegated to the United States by the Constitution, nor prohibited by it to the states, are reserved to the states respectively, or to the people.

This is called the "reserved-power" amendment. It states that the powers which the Constitution does not give to the United States and does not deny to the states belong to the states and to the people.

AMENDMENT 11 / SUITS AGAINST A STATE (1798)

The judicial power of the United States shall not be construed to extend to any suit in law or equity commenced or prosecuted against one of the United States by citizens of another state or by citizens or subjects of any foreign state.

This amendment was the first that was enacted to override a Supreme Court decision. It confirms that no federal court may try a case in which a state is being sued by a citizen of another state or of a foreign country. Amendment 11 changes a provision of Article III, Section 2, Clause "a."

AMENDMENT 12 / ELECTION OF PRESIDENT AND VICE PRESIDENT (1804)

The electors shall meet in their respective states and vote by ballot for President and Vice President, one of whom, at least, shall not be an inhabitant of the same state with themselves; they shall name in their ballots the person voted for as President, and in distinct ballots the person voted for as Vice President, and they shall make distinct lists of all persons voted for as President, and of all persons voted for as Vice President, and of the number of votes for each, which lists they shall sign and certify, and transmit sealed to the seat of the government of the United States, directed to the President of the Senate; the President of the Senate shall, in the presence of the Senate and House of Representatives, open all the certificates and the votes shall then be counted; the person having the greatest number of votes for President shall be the President, if such number be a majority of the whole number of electors appointed; and if no person have such majority, then from the persons having the highest numbers not exceeding three on the list of those voted for as President, the House of Representatives shall choose immediately, by ballot, the President. But in choosing the President, the votes shall be taken by states, the representation from each state having one vote; a quorum for this purpose shall consist of a member or members from two thirds of the states, and a majority of all the states shall be necessary to a choice. And if the House of Representatives shall not choose a President whenever the right of choice shall devolve upon them, *before the fourth day of March next following*, then the Vice President shall act as President, as in the case of the death or other constitutional disability of the President. The person having the greatest number of votes as Vice President shall be the Vice President, if such number be a majority of the whole number of electors appointed, and if no person have a majority, then from the two highest numbers on the list, the Senate shall choose the Vice President; a quorum for the purpose shall consist of two thirds of the whole number of senators, and a majority of the whole number shall be necessary to a choice. But no person constitutionally ineligible to the office of President shall be eligible to that of Vice President of the United States.

Amendment 12 describes the present-day procedure in the electoral college. The most important change made by this amendment was that the presidential electors would vote for President and Vice President on separate ballots. In 1800, when only one ballot was used, Thomas Jefferson and Aaron Burr received the same number of votes, and the election had to be decided by the House of Representatives. To guard against this possibility in the future, Amendment 12 calls for separate ballots.

The electors meet in their state capitals and cast their separate ballots for President and Vice President. They send them to the President of the Senate, showing the votes for each candidate. They are opened, and the electoral votes for President are counted in the presence of both houses. The candidate having a majority is declared elected. If no candidate for President receives a majority, the election goes to the House. The members of the House then vote by state for the three highest candidates. Each state casts one vote. A quorum consists of at least one member from two thirds of the states. The candidate who receives a majority of the votes of the states is elected President. If the House fails to elect a President, the Vice President acts as President.

The electoral votes for Vice President are also counted in the presence of both houses. The candidate having a majority is declared elected. If no candidate for Vice President receives a majority, the Senate chooses a Vice President from the two highest candidates. For this purpose, a quorum consists of two thirds of the total membership of the Senate. A majority of the whole number of the Senate is necessary to elect a Vice President. No person can be Vice President who does not meet the qualifications for President.

Amendment 13 is the first of three amendments that were a consequence of the Civil War. It states that slavery must end in the United States and its territories. The amendment was deemed necessary because the Supreme Court, in the Dred Scott decision, declared that ownership of slaves as a form of property was constitutional throughout the United States and its territories.

Congress may pass whatever laws are necessary to enforce Amendment 13. This statement is called an *enabling act*. Many amendments include an enabling act.

By the definition of citizenship in Amendment 14, black Americans were granted citizenship. The first section provides that all persons born or naturalized in the United States and subject to this country's laws are citizens of the United States and of the state in which they live. No state may take away the rights of citizens or take any person's life, liberty, or property except according to law. All state laws must apply equally to everyone in the state.

This section abolished the provision in Article 1, Section 2, Clause "c," which said that only three fifths of the slaves should be counted as population.

Section 3 dealt with persons who held appointive or elective offices or commissions in the armed forces which required an oath to support the Constitution of the United States and who had violated that oath by taking up arms against the United States. These officials were barred from holding any office which would again require them to take such an oath. This provision was designed to bar leaders of the Confederacy from holding federal office.

AMENDMENT 13 / SLAVERY ABOLISHED (1865)

SECTION 1. Abolition of slavery. Neither slavery nor involuntary servitude, except as a punishment for crime whereof the party shall have been duly convicted, shall exist within the United States or any place subject to their jurisdiction.

SECTION 2. Enforcement. Congress shall have the power to enforce this article by appropriate legislation.

AMENDMENT 14 / CIVIL RIGHTS GUARANTEED (1868)

SECTION 1. Definition of citizenship. All persons born or naturalized in the United States, and subject to the jurisdiction thereof, are citizens of the United States and of the state wherein they reside. No state shall make or enforce any law which shall abridge the privileges or immunities of citizens of the United States; nor shall any state deprive any person of life, liberty, or property, without due process of law; nor deny to any person within its jurisdiction the equal protection of the laws.

SECTION 2. Apportionment of representatives. Representatives shall be apportioned among the several states according to their respective numbers, counting the whole number of persons in each state, *excluding Indians not taxed.* But when the right to vote at any election for the choice of electors for President and Vice President of the United States, representatives in Congress, the executive and judicial officers of a state, or the members of the legislature thereof, is denied to any of the *male* inhabitants of such state, *being twenty-one years of age* and citizens of the United States, or in any way abridged, except for participation in rebellion, or other crime, the basis of representation therein shall be reduced in the proportion which the number of such *male* citizens shall bear to the whole number of *male* citizens *twenty-one years of age* in such state.

SECTION 3. Restrictions on public office. No person shall be a senator or representative in Congress, or elector of President and Vice President, or hold any office, civil or military, under the United States, or under any state, who, having previously taken an oath as a member of Congress, or as an officer of the United States, or as a member of any state legislature, or as an executive or judicial officer of any state, to support the Constitution of the United States, shall have engaged in insurrection or rebellion against the same, or given aid or comfort to the enemies thereof. But Congress may by vote of two thirds of each house remove such disability.

SECTION 4. Public debt of the United States valid; Confederate debt void. The validity of the public debt of the United States, authorized by law, including debts incurred for payment of pensions and bounties for services in suppressing insurrection or rebellion, shall not be questioned. But neither the United States nor any state shall assume or pay any debt or obligation incurred in aid of insurrection or rebellion against the United States, or any claim for the loss or emancipation of any slave; but all such debts, obligations, and claims shall be held illegal and void.

This section was included to settle the question of debts incurred during the Civil War. All debts contracted by the United States were to be paid. Neither the United States nor any state government, however, was to pay the debts of the Confederacy. Moreover, no payment was to be made to former slave owners as compensation for slaves who were set free.

SECTION 5. Enforcement. The Congress shall have power to enforce by appropriate legislation the provisions of this article.

AMENDMENT 15 / RIGHT TO VOTE (1870)

SECTION 1. The right of citizens of the United States to vote shall not be denied or abridged by the United States or by any state on account of race, color, or previous condition of servitude.

SECTION 2. The Congress shall have power to enforce this article by appropriate legislation.

Amendment 15 sought to protect the right of citizens to vote in federal and state elections. It states that citizens cannot be kept from voting because of their race or color or because they had once been slaves. After ratification of this amendment, states successfully kept black Americans from voting by the use of such impediments as literacy tests and poll taxes. Beginning in 1957, a series of federal civil rights acts sought to end such discrimination.

AMENDMENT 16 / INCOME TAX (1913)

The Congress shall have power to lay and collect taxes on incomes, from whatever source derived, without apportionment among the several states and without regard to any census or enumeration.

Amendment 16 authorizes Congress to tax incomes. An amendment was necessary because in 1895 the Supreme Court had decided that an income tax law, passed by Congress a year earlier, was unconstitutional.

AMENDMENT 17 / DIRECT ELECTION OF SENATORS (1913)

a. Election by the people. The Senate of the United States shall be composed of two senators from each state, elected by the people thereof, for six years; and each senator shall have one vote. The electors in each state shall have the qualifications requisite for electors of the most numerous branch of the state legislatures.

a. The Constitution originally provided that senators were to be elected by the state legislatures. Amendment 17 changed that provision to election by popular vote. Anyone qualified to vote for a state representative may vote for United States senators.

b. Vacancies. When vacancies happen in the representation of any state in the Senate, the executive authority of such state shall issue writs of election to fill such vacancies: provided that the legislature of any state may empower the executive thereof to make temporary appointments until the people fill the vacancies by election as the legislature may direct.

b. If a vacancy occurs in the United States Senate, the governor of the state affected may call a special election to fill the vacancy. The state legislature, however, may permit the governor to appoint someone to fill the vacancy until an election is held.

c. Senators chosen by state legislatures before Amendment 17 was added to the Constitution could complete their terms.

Amendment 18 forbade the manufacture, sale, or shipment of intoxicating beverages within the United States. The importation or exportation of such beverages was also forbidden. Amendment 18 was later repealed by Amendment 21.

Amendment 19 provides that a citizen who is a woman may not be denied the right to vote in a federal or state election.

When the Constitution first went into effect, means of transportation and communication were slow. There was a long period, therefore, between the President's election (November) and inauguration (March). One purpose of Amendment 20 was to shorten that waiting period. The amendment established that the terms of the President and Vice President end at noon on January 20 following a presidential election. The terms of one third of the senators and of all representatives, meanwhile, end at noon on January 3 in years ending in odd numbers. The new terms begin when the old terms end.

Section 2 provides that Congress must meet at least once a year, with the regular session beginning on January 3 unless Congress sets a different day.

c. Not retroactive. This amendment shall not be so construed as to affect the election or term of any senator chosen before it becomes valid as part of the Constitution.

AMENDMENT 18 / PROHIBITION (1919)

SECTION 1. *After one year from the ratification of this article the manufacture, sale, or transportation of intoxicating liquors within, the importation thereof into, or the exportation thereof from the United States and all territory subject to the jurisdiction thereof for beverage purposes is hereby prohibited.*

SECTION 2. *The Congress and the several states shall have concurrent power to enforce this article by appropriate legislation.*

SECTION 3. *This article shall be inoperative unless it shall have been ratified as an amendment to the Constitution by the legislatures of the several states, as provided in the Constitution, within seven years from the date of the submission hereof to the states by the Congress.*

AMENDMENT 19 / WOMEN'S VOTING RIGHTS (1920)

SECTION 1. The right of citizens of the United States to vote shall not be denied or abridged by the United States or by any state on account of sex.

SECTION 2. The Congress shall have power to enforce this article by appropriate legislation.

AMENDMENT 20 / TERMS OF OFFICE (1933)

SECTION 1. Terms of President, Vice President, and Congress. The terms of the President and Vice President shall end at noon on the 20th day of January, and the terms of senators and representatives at noon on the 3rd day of January, of the years in which such terms would have ended if this article had not been ratified; and the terms of their successors shall then begin.

SECTION 2. Sessions of Congress. The Congress shall assemble at least once in every year, and such meeting shall begin at noon on the 3rd day of January, unless they shall by law appoint a different day.

SECTION 3. Presidential succession. If, at the time fixed for the beginning of the term of the President, the President-elect shall have died, the Vice President-elect shall become President. If a President shall not have been chosen before the time fixed for the beginning of his term, or if the President-elect shall have failed to qualify, then the Vice President-elect shall act as President until a President shall have qualified; and the Congress may by law provide for the case wherein neither a President-elect nor a Vice President-elect shall have qualified, declaring who shall then act as President, or the manner in which one who is to act shall be selected, and such person shall act accordingly until a President or a Vice President shall have qualified.

Section 3 states that if the President-elect dies before being sworn in, the Vice President-elect becomes President. If the President-elect has not been chosen or does not qualify for office, the Vice President-elect acts as President until a President is chosen or qualifies. If neither the President-elect nor Vice President-elect qualifies to hold office, Congress decides who shall act as President until a President or Vice President is chosen or qualifies.

SECTION 4. Choice of President by the House. The Congress may by law provide for the case of the death of any of the persons from whom the House of Representatives may choose a President whenever the right of choice shall have devolved upon them, and for the case of the death of any of the persons from whom the Senate may choose a Vice President whenever the right of choice shall have devolved upon them.

Section 4 states that in cases in which the election is thrown into Congress because no candidate for either President or Vice President receives a majority of the electoral votes, Congress may make a law to decide what to do if one of the candidates dies.

SECTION 5. Date effective. Sections 1 and 2 shall take effect on the fifteenth day of October following the ratification of this article.

Section 5 set the date on which the first two sections of Amendment 20 were to take effect after the amendment had been approved by the states.

SECTION 6. Limited time for ratification. *This article shall be inoperative unless it shall have been ratified as an amendment to the Constitution by the legislatures of three fourths of the several states within seven years from the date of its submission.*

To become a part of the Constitution, Amendment 20 had to be approved within seven years.

AMENDMENT 21 / REPEAL OF PROHIBITION (1933)

SECTION 1. Repeal of Amendment 18. The eighteenth article of amendment to the Constitution of the United States is hereby repealed.

Amendment 21 repealed the Eighteenth Amendment, putting an end to the nationwide ban on the manufacture, sale, and shipment of alcoholic beverages. It was the only amendment submitted to special ratifying conventions instead of state legislatures.

SECTION 2. States protected. The transportation or importation into any state, territory, or possession of the United States for delivery or use therein of intoxicating liquors, in violation of the laws thereof, is hereby prohibited.

This section made it clear that intoxicating liquors may not be transported or imported into any state or territory of the United States if the laws of that state or territory prohibit the sale of liquor.

SECTION 3. Limited time for ratification. *This article shall be inoperative unless it shall have been ratified as an amendment to the Constitution by conventions in the several states, as provided in the Constitution, within seven years from the date of the submission hereof to the states by the Congress.*

Amendment 22 declares that no person may be elected President more than twice. A person who has served more than two years in the place of an elected President may be elected President only once. This limitation did not apply to President Truman, who was in office when Amendment 22 was proposed. Before this amendment was added, the Constitution placed no limit on the number of terms a President might serve. Presidents Washington, Jefferson, and Madison, however, limited themselves to two terms in office. Although Ulysses S. Grant and Theodore Roosevelt sought third terms, the precedent was not broken until 1940, when Franklin D. Roosevelt was elected for a third term.

This amendment gave the residents of the District of Columbia the right to vote in presidential elections. They may choose as many electors as does the state with the smallest population. Before this amendment was adopted, residents of the District of Columbia had not voted for President and Vice President because the Constitution provided that only states should choose presidential electors.

Amendment 24 prohibited the loss of voting rights in federal elections through failure to pay a poll tax or any other tax. The poll tax was a device used in some southern states to keep black voters from the polls. The poll tax was usually a cumulative tax.

AMENDMENT 22 / TWO-TERM LIMITATION ON PRESIDENCY (1951)

SECTION 1. Definition of limitation. No person shall be elected to the office of the President more than twice, and no person who has held the office of President, or acted as President, for more than two years of a term to which some other person was elected President shall be elected to the office of the President more than once. *But this article shall not apply to any person holding the office of President when this article was proposed by the Congress, and shall not prevent any person who may be holding the office of President, or acting as President, during the term within which this article becomes operative from holding the office of President, or acting as President during the remainder of such term.*

SECTION 2. Limited time for ratification. *This article shall be inoperative unless it shall have been ratified as an amendment to the Constitution by the legislatures of three fourths of the several states within seven years from the date of its submission to the states by the Congress.*

AMENDMENT 23 / VOTING IN THE DISTRICT OF COLUMBIA (1961)

SECTION 1. The District constituting the seat of government of the United States shall appoint, in such manner as the Congress may direct:

A number of electors of President and Vice President equal to the whole number of senators and representatives in Congress to which the District would be entitled if it were a state, but in no event more than the least populous state; they shall be in addition to those appointed by the states, but they shall be considered, for the purposes of the election of President and Vice President, to be electors appointed by a state; and they shall meet in the District and perform such duties as provided by the twelfth article of amendment.

SECTION 2. The Congress shall have power to enforce this article by appropriate legislation.

AMENDMENT 24 / POLL TAX PROHIBITION (1964)

SECTION 1. The right of citizens of the United States to vote in any primary or other election for President or Vice President, for electors for President or Vice President, or for senator or representative in Congress, shall not be denied or abridged by the United States or any state by reason of failure to pay any poll tax or other tax.

SECTION 2. The Congress shall have power to enforce this article by appropriate legislation.

AMENDMENT 25 / PRESIDENTIAL DISABILITY (1967)

SECTION 1. Accession of the Vice President. In case of the removal of the President from office or of his death or resignation, the Vice President shall become President.

SECTION 2. Replacing the Vice President. Whenever there is a vacancy in the office of the Vice President, the President shall nominate a Vice President who shall take office upon confirmation by a majority vote of both Houses of Congress.

SECTION 3. Vice President as Acting President. Whenever the President transmits to the President pro tempore of the Senate and the Speaker of the House of Representatives his written declaration that he is unable to discharge the powers and duties of his office, and until he transmits to them a written declaration to the contrary, such powers and duties shall be discharged by the Vice President as Acting President.

SECTION 4. Determining presidential disability. Whenever the Vice President and a majority of either the principal officers of the executive departments or of such other body as Congress may by law provide, transmit to the President pro tempore of the Senate and the Speaker of the House of Representatives their written declaration that the President is unable to discharge the powers and duties of his office, the Vice President shall immediately assume the powers and duties of the office as Acting President.

Thereafter, when the President transmits to the President pro tempore of the Senate and the Speaker of the House of Representatives his written declaration that no inability exists, he shall resume the powers and duties of his office unless the Vice President and a majority of either the principal officers of the executive department or of such other body as Congress may by law provide, transmit within four days to the President pro tempore of the Senate and the Speaker of the House of Representatives their written declaration that the President is unable to discharge the powers and duties of his office. Thereupon, Congress shall decide the issue, assembling within forty-eight hours for that purpose, if not in session. If

This meant that to register to vote a citizen had to pay all the back taxes for the years since coming of voting age. In 1966, the Supreme Court ruled that payment of poll taxes was also an unconstitutional precondition for voting in state and local elections.

Amendment 25 clarifies Article 2, Section 1, Clause "e," which deals with filling vacancies in the presidency. It also establishes procedures to follow when the President is too ill to serve. Section 1 states clearly that if the President dies or resigns, the Vice President becomes President.

Section 2 seeks to keep the office of Vice President filled so that there will always be an immediate successor to the President. It states that when there is a vacancy in the office of Vice President, the President may appoint a person to be Vice President.

Section 3 deals with the difficult problem of presidential disability. It declares that a President who is ill or unable to carry out official duties may assign those duties to the Vice President by notifying the Speaker of the House and the President pro tempore of the Senate. The Vice President then acts as President until the President is again able to serve.

Section 4 provides that when it is determined that the President is ill or unable for other reasons to carry out official duties and is unable or unwilling to assign those duties to the Vice President, the Vice President and a majority of the Cabinet must notify the Speaker of the House and the President pro tempore of the Senate. The Vice President then acts as President. The President cannot again assume official duties unless the Vice President and a majority of the Cabinet agree that he is fit to do so. If the Vice President and a majority of the Cabinet do not believe that the President is fit, Congress must meet and make a decision within 21 days. If two thirds of both houses of Congress vote that the President is unable to carry out the duties of his office, the Vice President continues to act as President. Otherwise, the President again takes over the duties of the presidency.

the Congress, within twenty-one days after receipt of the latter written declaration, or, if Congress is not in session, within twenty-one days after Congress is required to assemble, determines by two-thirds vote of both Houses that the President is unable to discharge the powers and duties of his office, the Vice President shall continue to discharge the same as Acting President; otherwise, the President shall resume the powers and duties of his office.

AMENDMENT 26 / VOTING AGE (1971)

SECTION 1. The right of citizens of the United States who are eighteen years of age or older to vote shall not be denied or abridged by the United States or by any state on account of age.

SECTION 2. The Congress shall have power to enforce this article by appropriate legislation.

Amendment 26 grants citizens 18 years of age or older the right to vote in federal and state elections. Prior to its ratification, most states limited the vote to citizens 21 years of age or older. In the Voting Rights Act of 1970, Congress lowered the minimum age to 18 in both federal and state elections. When the Supreme Court limited this law to federal elections, Congress proposed Amendment 26.

Important Dates

1000 Vikings cross Atlantic.
1487 Dias rounds Cape of Good Hope.
1492 Columbus reaches America.
1493 Line of Demarcation.
1498 Da Gama reaches India.
1513 Balboa reaches Pacific Ocean.
1519 Magellan begins voyage around world.
1521 Cortés conquers Aztecs.
1535 Cartier explores St. Lawrence River.
1541 De Soto reaches Mississippi River.
1565 Spanish settle St. Augustine.
1580 Drake circumnavigates world.
1607 Jamestown settled.
1608 Champlain founds Quebec.
1609 Santa Fe settled.
1619 Virginia House of Burgesses first meets.
1620 Pilgrims settle Plymouth.
1625 Dutch settle New Amsterdam.
1630 Puritans establish Massachusetts Bay Colony.
1634 Maryland founded.
1636 Roger Williams settles Providence.
1639 Fundamental Orders of Connecticut.
1649 Maryland Toleration Act.
1663 Carolina charter granted.
1664 English capture New Amsterdam.
1673 Marquette and Joliet explore Mississippi River.
1679 New Hampshire receives charter.
1681 Pennsylvania charter granted.
1682 La Salle reaches mouth of Mississippi River.
1733 Georgia founded.
1754 French and Indian War starts.
1759 British capture Quebec.
1765 Stamp Act.
1767 Townshend Acts.
1770 Boston Massacre.
1773 Boston Tea Party.
1774 Intolerable Acts.
     First Continental Congress meets.

1775 Battles of Lexington and Concord.
     Second Continental Congress meets.
     Battle of Bunker Hill.
1776 British evacuate Boston.
     American colonies declare independence.
1777 Burgoyne surrenders at Saratoga.
1778 Treaty of alliance signed with France.
1779 George Rogers Clark captures Vincennes.
1781 Cornwallis surrenders at Yorktown.
     Articles of Confederation go into effect.
1783 Treaty of Paris signed.
1785 Land Ordinance passed.
1786 Shays's Rebellion.
1787 Northwest Ordinance.
1788 Constitution ratified.
1789 George Washington becomes President.
1790 First American textile mill.
1791 Bill of Rights added to Constitution.
1793 Whitney invents cotton gin.
1794 Whiskey Rebellion.
1797 John Adams becomes President.
     XYZ Affair.
1798 Alien and Sedition Acts.
1801 Thomas Jefferson becomes President.
     Marbury v. Madison decision.
1803 Louisiana Purchase.
1804 Lewis and Clark expedition begins.
1807 Chesapeake Affair.
     Embargo Act.
1809 James Madison becomes President.
1811 Battle of Tippecanoe.
1812 War with Britain begins.
1814 Treaty of Ghent.
1817 James Monroe becomes President.
1819 Adams-Onís Treaty.
1820 Missouri Compromise.

1821 First public high school (Boston).
1822 Americans settle in Texas.
1823 Monroe Doctrine proclaimed.
1825 John Quincy Adams becomes President.
     Erie Canal completed.
1829 Andrew Jackson becomes President.
1830 Webster-Hayne debate.
     Indian Removal Act.
1831 Nat Turner organizes slave revolt.
1832 Jackson vetoes Bank Bill.
1833 Compromise tariff.
1834 Whig Party organized.
     National Trades Union formed.
1836 Texas declares independence from Mexico.
     Battle of the Alamo.
1837 Martin Van Buren becomes President.
     Oberlin College accepts women students.
     Panic of 1837.
1838 Cherokee forced west.
1841 William Henry Harrison becomes President.
     John Tyler becomes President on Harrison's death (April).
1842 Webster-Ashburton Treaty.
1845 James K. Polk becomes President.
     Texas and Florida become states.
1846 War with Mexico starts.
1847 Mormons settle in Utah.
1848 Treaty of Guadalupe-Hidalgo.
     Women's rights convention at Seneca Falls.
1849 Zachary Taylor becomes President.
1850 Millard Fillmore becomes President on Taylor's death (July).
     Compromise of 1850.
1852 *Uncle Tom's Cabin* published.
1853 Franklin Pierce becomes President.
     Gadsden Purchase.

1854 Kansas-Nebraska Act.
Republican Party formed.
Ostend Manifesto.
1857 James Buchanan becomes President.
Dred Scott decision.
1859 John Brown raids Harpers Ferry.
1861 Abraham Lincoln becomes President.
Civil War begins.
First Battle of Bull Run.
1862 Battle of Antietam.
Homestead Act.
1863 Emancipation Proclamation.
Battle of Gettysburg.
1864 Sherman takes Atlanta.
1865 Lee surrenders at Appomattox.
1865 Andrew Johnson becomes President on Lincoln's assassination (April).
Thirteenth Amendment abolishes slavery.
1866 National Labor Union formed.
1867 Reconstruction Act of 1867.
Alaska purchased.
Grange movement started.
1868 Congress impeaches Johnson.
Fourteenth Amendment defines American citizenship.
1869 Ulysses S. Grant becomes President.
First transcontinental railroad completed.
Knights of Labor formed.
1870 Fifteenth Amendment states voters' rights.
1873 Barbed wire developed.
1876 Battle of Little Bighorn.
Bell demonstrates telephone.
1877 Rutherford B. Hayes becomes President.
Chief Joseph surrenders.
Munn v. Illinois decision.
Last federal troops leave South.
1878 Bland-Allison Act.
1879 Edison invents electric light.
1881 James A. Garfield becomes President.
Chester A. Arthur becomes President on Garfield's assassination (September).
1882 John D. Rockefeller organizes Standard Oil Company.
1883 Civil Service Commission established.
Brooklyn Bridge completed.
1885 Grover Cleveland becomes President.
First skyscraper built in Chicago.

1886 Haymarket Riot.
American Federation of Labor formed.
1887 Interstate Commerce Act.
Dawes Act assigns land to Indians.
1889 Benjamin Harrison becomes President.
Jane Addams founds Hull House.
1890 First Pan-American Congress meets.
Sherman Antitrust Act.
Sherman Silver Purchase Act.
1892 Homestead strike.
1893 Grover Cleveland becomes President for second time.
Sherman Silver Purchase Act repealed.
1894 Pullman strike.
1896 *Plessy v. Ferguson* decision.
1897 William McKinley becomes President.
1898 Spanish-American War: U.S. acquires Philippines, Puerto Rico, Guam; frees Cuba.
Hawaii annexed.
1899 Open Door Policy proposed.
U.S. acquires American Samoa.
1900 Gold Standard Act.
Boxer Rebellion.
1901 Theodore Roosevelt becomes President on McKinley's assassination (September).
1903 U.S. leases Canal Zone in Panama.
Wright brothers make first successful airplane flight.
1904 Roosevelt Corollary.
1905 Treaty of Portsmouth ends Russo-Japanese War.
1906 Pure Food and Drug Act.
1909 William H. Taft becomes President.
1910 Mexican Revolution starts.
NAACP formed.
1911 National Urban League organized.
1913 Woodrow Wilson becomes President.
Sixteenth Amendment makes income tax legal.
Seventeenth Amendment provides for election of senators by voters.
Federal Reserve Act.
1914 World War I begins in Europe.
Federal Trade Commission created.
1915 *Lusitania* sunk by Germans.
1916 Border campaign against Villa.

1917 Virgin Islands purchased from Denmark.
U.S. enters World War I.
Communists seize power in Russia.
1918 Signing of armistice ends World War I.
1919 Eighteenth Amendment establishes prohibition.
Treaty of Versailles.
Boston police strike.
1920 Nineteenth Amendment gives women the vote.
First American radio broadcasting station.
1921 Warren G. Harding becomes President.
Washington Conference begins.
1923 Calvin Coolidge becomes President on Harding's death (August).
1924 Dawes Plan.
1927 Lindbergh flies nonstop to Paris.
1928 Kellogg-Briand Pact.
1929 Herbert Hoover becomes President.
Great Depression begins.
1931 Japan invades Manchuria.
1933 Twentieth Amendment provides that presidential and congressional terms begin earlier.
1933 Franklin D. Roosevelt becomes President.
New Deal begins.
Roosevelt pledges Good Neighbor Policy.
Hitler takes power in Germany.
Twenty-First Amendment repeals prohibition.
1934 Indian Reorganization Act.
1935 Wagner Act.
Social Security Act.
Italy attacks Ethiopia.
1936 Supreme Court declares AAA unconstitutional.
Germany occupies Rhineland.
Hoover Dam completed.
1937 Roosevelt's "court-packing" plan rejected.
Japan invades China.
1938 CIO organized.
1939 World War II begins in Europe.
1941 Lend-Lease Act.
United States enters World War II.
1942 Battle of the Coral Sea.
Allies land in North Africa.
1943 Allies invade Italy.

1944 Allies land in France.
Battle of the Bulge.
1945 Yalta Conference.
*1945 Harry S. Truman becomes
President on Roosevelt's death*
(April).
Germany surrenders (V-E
Day).
Japan surrenders (V-J Day).
United Nations organized.
1947 Marshall Plan proposed.
Taft-Hartley Act.
1948 Berlin airlift begins.
1949 NATO formed.
Communists take control of
China.
1950 Korean War begins.
1951 Twenty-Second Amendment
puts two-term limit on
presidency.
1952 Puerto Rico becomes self-
governing commonwealth.
*1953 Dwight D. Eisenhower
becomes President.*
Korean armistice signed.
1954 Supreme Court decision on
school segregation.
1955 AFL-CIO merger.
1956 Suez Canal crisis.
Hungarian uprising.
1957 Eisenhower Doctrine
proclaimed.
Soviet Union launches first
Sputnik.
1959 Castro leads Cuban revolt.
Landrum-Griffin Act.
1960 Summit meeting canceled
over U–2 incident.

*1961 John F. Kennedy becomes
President.*
Peace Corps formed.
Twenty-Third Amendment
allows D.C. residents to vote
for President.
Berlin Wall built.
1962 Cuban missile crisis.
First U.S. manned orbital
space flight.
1963 Nuclear test-ban treaty.
*1963 Lyndon Johnson becomes
President on Kennedy's
assassination* (November).
1964 Twenty-Fourth Amendment
abolishes poll tax.
Civil Rights Act.
Gulf of Tonkin Resolution.
Johnson defeats Goldwater.
1965 Voting Rights Act.
Immigration quota system
ended.
1967 Twenty-Fifth Amendment
establishes procedures in case
of presidential disability.
Six-Day War in Middle East.
1968 Martin Luther King, Jr., and
Robert Kennedy assassinated.
*1969 Richard M. Nixon becomes
President.*
American astronauts land on
moon.
1971 Twenty-Sixth Amendment
lowers voting age to eighteen
years.
1972 Nixon visits China and Soviet
Union.
Watergate break-in.

1973 Last American troops leave
Vietnam.
Yom Kippur War in Middle
East.
*1974 Gerald R. Ford becomes
President on resignation of
Richard Nixon* (August).
1975 South Vietnam falls to
Communists.
1976 U.S. celebrates two-
hundredth birthday.
*1977 Jimmy Carter becomes
President.*
1978 Camp David accords signed.
1979 Iranians seize U.S. embassy
and take hostages.
Soviet Union invades
Afghanistan.
*1981 Ronald Reagan becomes
President.*
American hostages released
by Iran.
First woman appointed to
Supreme Court.
1982 Reagan announces "New
Federalism."
1983 American forces sent to
Grenada.
1984 Kissinger Commission issues
report on Central America.
First woman nominated to
run for vice presidency.

Citizens and Their Government

"Proclaim liberty throughout the land unto all the inhabitants thereof." This inscription on the Liberty Bell in Philadelphia is an enduring reminder of the American belief in the right of free people to govern themselves. The Constitution of the United States expresses this belief in the language of government—in its powers, in its laws, and in the rights it guarantees. The following pages will help you learn more about the American system of government, and about the rights and responsibilities of citizens of our nation.

Our government, as you know, is dedicated to the proposition that people have the capacity to make wise decisions and to govern themselves. The United States is a *republic* because the people choose representatives to act for them in governing. Our country is also a *democracy* because all citizens who are eighteen years of age or older have the privilege of voting. The people, therefore, determine the kind of government we have. Not only do they vote representatives into and out of office, but they can work with others to bring their needs to the attention of public officials.

The struggle for the right to self-government began in 1215 when English barons forced King John to accept Magna Charta and thus to recognize certain limits to royal power. Since then the people of English-speaking countries—as well as other peoples throughout the world—have worked continuously to extend their rights to govern themselves.

Self-government is not the only goal for which people have struggled through the centuries. Another objective has been the attainment of what Thomas Jefferson, in writing the Declaration of Independence, called "unalienable rights"—rights that human beings have simply because they are human beings. Recognition of these rights grows out of two basic beliefs: (1) that all human beings are important; and (2) that ordinary citizens are capable of governing themselves wisely.

The American government guarantees citizens their fundamental rights. These guarantees are found in the Constitution itself, in the Bill of Rights, and in other amendments to the Constitution. The Bill of Rights, for instance, protects freedom of speech, press, and religion, and also the right to petition. It also guarantees personal security, protects the rights of persons accused of crimes, and affirms that the United States government has only the powers granted to it by the Constitution.

Along with the privilege of living in a free society come responsibilities. It is not enough, after all, simply to proclaim freedom. No republic can remain strong unless its citizens are deeply dedicated to freedom and willing to give thought and time to the business of self-government. In other words, Americans must fulfill the responsibilities of *citizenship*. Some of the ways in which good citizens meet those responsibilities are as follows:

- vote intelligently
- keep well-informed
- help create public opinion
- serve on juries
- pay taxes
- perform military service
- help in the work of political parties

When Americans carry out the responsibilities of good citizens, they help to preserve their freedom and to decide the future of the United States.

Words to Remember

Americans are proud of their great nation and of the freedom for which it stands. Throughout the years, that pride has been expressed in solemn pledges, memorable speeches, and rousing anthems, all of which celebrate freedom and express love of country.

THE PLEDGE OF ALLEGIANCE
Francis Bellamy

I pledge allegiance to the flag of the United States of America and to the republic for which it stands; one nation under God, indivisible, with liberty and justice for all.

GREAT AMERICANS ON PATRIOTISM

Where liberty dwells, there is my country.

BENJAMIN FRANKLIN,
1706–1790

God grants liberty only to those who live it, and are always ready to guard and defend it.

DANIEL WEBSTER,
1782–1852

Our country, right or wrong. When right, to be kept right; when wrong, to be put right.

CARL SCHURZ,
1829–1906

There are no days of special patriotism. There are no days when you should be more patriotic than on other days, and I ask you to wear every day in your heart our flag of the Union.

WOODROW WILSON,
1856–1924

Ask not what your country can do for you—ask what you can do for your country.

JOHN F. KENNEDY,
1917–1963

"THE STAR-SPANGLED BANNER"
Words by Francis Scott Key

O say, can you see, by the dawn's early light,
What so proudly we hailed at the twilight's last
  gleaming?
Whose broad stripes and bright stars, through the
  perilous fight,
O'er the ramparts we watched were so gallantly
  streaming!
And the rockets' red glare, the bombs bursting in air,
Gave proof through the night that our flag was still
  there:
O say, does that star-spangled banner yet wave
O'er the land of the free and the home of the brave?

———

On the shore, dimly seen through the mists of the
  deep,
Where the foe's haughty host in dread silence
  reposes,
What is that which the breeze, o'er the towering
  steep,
As it fitfully blows, now conceals, now discloses?
Now it catches the gleam of the morning's first
  beam,
In full glory reflected now shines on the stream:
'Tis the star-spangled banner! O long may it wave
O'er the land of the free and the home of the brave!

———

O thus be it ever, when freemen shall stand
Between their loved homes and the war's desolation!
Blest with victory and peace, may the heaven-
  rescued land
Praise the power that hath made and preserved
  us a nation.
Then conquer we must, when our cause it is just,
And this be our motto: "In God is our trust,"
And the star-spangled banner in triumph shall wave
O'er the land of the free and the home of the brave!

Principles of American Government

Americans are proud to say that ours is "a government of laws and not of men." This means that all actions of government are based upon the Constitution and the laws that have been passed in accordance with it. The principle of *government by law* keeps government officials from exceeding their rightful powers.

How do Americans maintain their control of government and yet make sure that it meets their needs? The answer lies in the principle of *representative government.* Under this principle, the voters elect representatives who have the authority to enact laws for the benefit of all. Representative government preserves the principle of majority rule. The Constitution, however, is not concerned only with majority rule; it is equally concerned with the protection of minority rights.

Another important feature of American government is that the Constitution established a *federal system.* Under a federal system, two governments join and act together in some ways, but each of them maintains its own well-defined powers and functions.

How does our federal system of government work? The chart below shows that (1) certain *enumerated powers* may be exercised only by the United States; (2) certain *reserved powers* may be exercised only by the states; and (3) certain *concurrent powers* may be exercised by both the national and state governments.

Constitutional government is limited government. The limits in our system are set in two ways. The framers of the Constitution were influenced, first of all, by the principle of government called *separation of powers.* Under this principle, the legisla-

The Federal System

Enumerated Powers (federal powers)	Concurrent Powers (powers common to both)	Reserved Powers (state powers)
• Coin money	• Collect taxes	• Provide for education
• Regulate foreign and interstate commerce	• Borrow money	• Conduct elections
• Pass naturalization and immigration laws	• Charter banks	• Provide for local governments
• Grant patents and copyrights	• Protect health and safety of the people	• Ratify constitutional amendments
• Declare war and make peace	• Make and enforce laws	• Regulate intrastate commerce
• Admit new states and govern territories	• Maintain courts	• Issue licenses
• Maintain armed services		• Make laws about wills, contracts, and domestic relations
• Fix standards of weights and measures		• Incorporate businesses
• Provide for common defense		
• Conduct foreign relations		

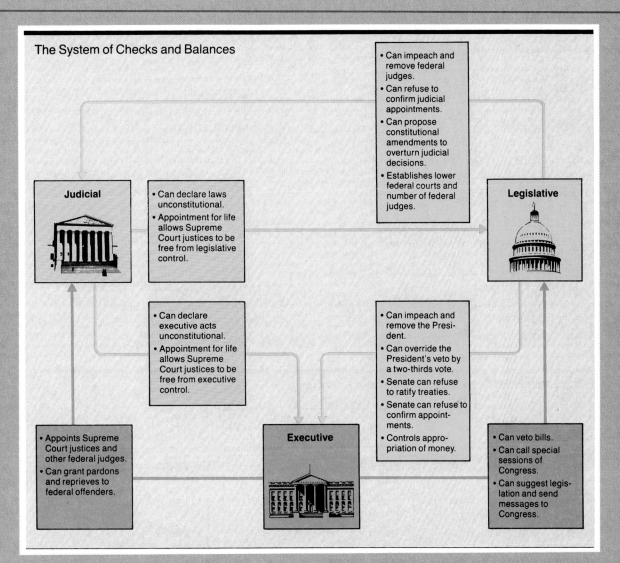

The System of Checks and Balances

Judicial

- Can declare laws unconstitutional.
- Appointment for life allows Supreme Court justices to be free from legislative control.

- Can impeach and remove federal judges.
- Can refuse to confirm judicial appointments.
- Can propose constitutional amendments to overturn judicial decisions.
- Establishes lower federal courts and number of federal judges.

Legislative

- Can declare executive acts unconstitutional.
- Appointment for life allows Supreme Court justices to be free from executive control.

- Can impeach and remove the President.
- Can override the President's veto by a two-thirds vote.
- Senate can refuse to ratify treaties.
- Senate can refuse to confirm appointments.
- Controls appropriation of money.

Executive

- Appoints Supreme Court justices and other federal judges.
- Can grant pardons and reprieves to federal offenders.

- Can veto bills.
- Can call special sessions of Congress.
- Can suggest legislation and send messages to Congress.

tive branch of government makes the laws; the executive branch administers them; and the judicial branch interprets and applies them in specific cases.

Although the three branches of government are separate, they are not entirely independent of one another. Through a system of *checks and balances*, each branch of government limits the powers of the other branches. The chart above illustrates this principle.

The American Constitution has remained the basis of the government of a great people for a longer time than any other single written document. The changes that have been made in the original work are remarkably few. Over the years, of course, the Constitution has been modified through custom and usage. Amendments also provide a way of changing the Constitution (though relatively few amendments have been made in our nation's history). It is a very great tribute to the framers of the Constitution that the system of government which they worked out, almost 200 years ago, has endured through the many startling changes that have taken place in this nation and in the world.

The Executive Branch

The framers of the Constitution of the United States feared a strong centralized government. From their colonial experience, they opposed having the same people make, enforce, and interpret laws; therefore, they created three branches of government—separate but not entirely independent of one another. The legislative powers granted by the Constitution are held by Congress, executive powers are held by the President, and judicial power rests in the Supreme Court and in the lower courts created by Congress.

The executive branch of the national government has the responsibility of administering federal laws. The President of the United States is head of the executive branch. The Executive Office of the President and the Cabinet advise the Chief Executive and help him carry out his duties.

The Executive Office includes the President's staff, advisers, and experts on national security, economics, and the federal budget. The Cabinet consists of the heads of the various executive departments, which administer particular areas of government policy. In addition, several agencies and commissions operate independently as part of the executive branch. The chart below shows the offices and departments of the executive branch, and many of the federal independent agencies.

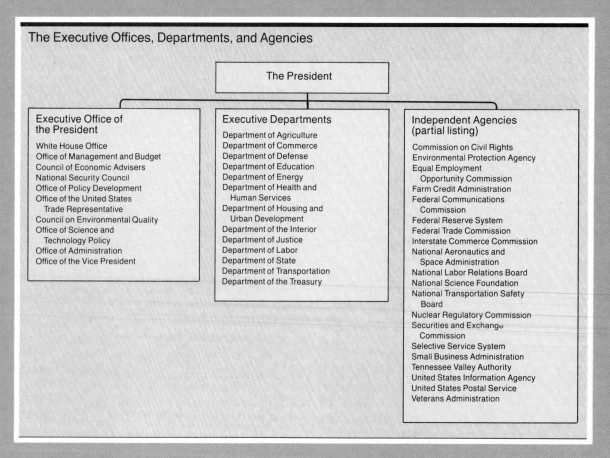

The Executive Offices, Departments, and Agencies

The President

Executive Office of the President

White House Office
Office of Management and Budget
Council of Economic Advisers
National Security Council
Office of Policy Development
Office of the United States
   Trade Representative
Council on Environmental Quality
Office of Science and
   Technology Policy
Office of Administration
Office of the Vice President

Executive Departments

Department of Agriculture
Department of Commerce
Department of Defense
Department of Education
Department of Energy
Department of Health and
   Human Services
Department of Housing and
   Urban Development
Department of the Interior
Department of Justice
Department of Labor
Department of State
Department of Transportation
Department of the Treasury

Independent Agencies (partial listing)

Commission on Civil Rights
Environmental Protection Agency
Equal Employment
   Opportunity Commission
Farm Credit Administration
Federal Communications
   Commission
Federal Reserve System
Federal Trade Commission
Interstate Commerce Commission
National Aeronautics and
   Space Administration
National Labor Relations Board
National Science Foundation
National Transportation Safety
   Board
Nuclear Regulatory Commission
Securities and Exchange
   Commission
Selective Service System
Small Business Administration
Tennessee Valley Authority
United States Information Agency
United States Postal Service
Veterans Administration

The Judicial Branch

A cornerstone of American government is the principle that all individuals are equal before the law. Federal and state courts guarantee that the law is carried out fairly.

The Supreme Court is at the head of the judicial branch and can overrule decisions made in any of the federal or state courts. The Supreme Court also exercises the power of judicial review: that is, it may decide whether an action of the President, a law passed by Congress, or a state law violates the Constitution.

Cases involving federal law are first heard in the United States District Courts and can be appealed to the United States Court of Appeals. From time to time, Con-gress designates special federal courts to handle specific matters. These courts do not have general jurisdiction, but handle only those specific matters designated by Congress. They deal with such issues as claims against the United States, customs law, patent law, and territorial matters.

Each state has its own court system to interpret state laws. Most cases involving state law are first heard in general trial courts. In some states, intermediate courts hear appeals from the trial courts. Each state has a court of last appeal, usually called the supreme court. The chart below shows how federal and state courts in the United States are organized.

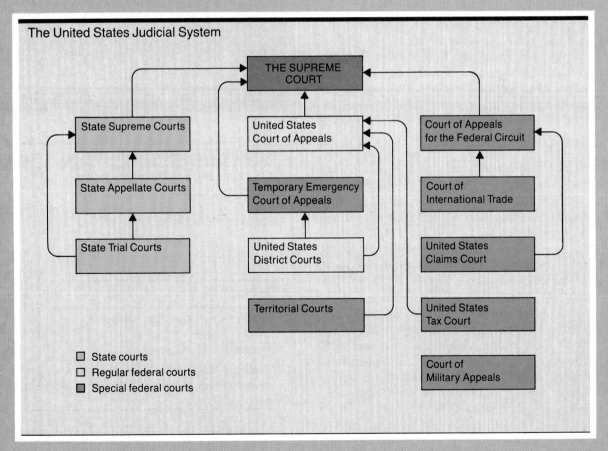

The United States Judicial System

- ☐ State courts
- ☐ Regular federal courts
- ■ Special federal courts

The Legislative Branch

Congress—the Senate and the House of Representatives—is the legislative, or law-making, branch of government. Congress is organized to give representation to the various interests and needs of the American people. The Senate has one hundred members, two from each state. The 435 members of the House are apportioned among the states on the basis of population, with each state having at least one representative.

Each house of Congress has a presiding officer. The Speaker of the House is the presiding officer of the House of Representatives. As leader of the majority party in the House, the Speaker plays an important role in determining whether a particular measure will pass or be defeated. The Vice President of the United States presides over the Senate, but cannot take part in debates and can vote only in case of a tie.

In both the House and Senate, each political party chooses a floor leader and a party whip. A floor leader is responsible for carrying out the party's legislative program. The whip serves as a link between the floor leader and party members.

To speed up and smooth out the process of lawmaking, both the House and Senate maintain standing, or permanent, committees. These committees determine which matters are brought before the House or Senate for consideration. In addition to the standing committees (chart, right), Congress from time to time establishes joint committees of the House and Senate that deal with matters of mutual concern.

The President may call Congress into special joint session if he feels it necessary, as, for example, in the case of a national emergency. In addition, Congress meets annually in joint session to hear the President's State of the Union Message (photograph, right).

HOUSE OF REPRESENTATIVES

435 members, apportioned according
  to state population

Speaker of the House

| Majority Floor Leader | Majority Whip |
| Minority Floor Leader | Minority Whip |

SENATE

100 members, two from each state

President of the Senate

| Majority Floor Leader | Majority Whip |
| Minority Floor Leader | Minority Whip |

Standing Committees

Agriculture
Appropriations
Armed Services
Banking, Finance, and
   Urban Affairs
Budget

District of Columbia
Education and Labor
Energy and Commerce
Foreign Affairs
Government Operations
House Administration
Interior and Insular
   Affairs

Judiciary
Merchant Marine and
   Fisheries
Post Office and Civil
   Service
Public Works and
   Transportation
Rules

Science and
   Technology
Small Business
Standards of Official
   Conduct
Veterans' Affairs
Ways and Means

Standing Committees

Agriculture, Nutrition,
   and Forestry
Appropriations
Armed Services

Banking, Housing, and
   Urban Affairs
Budget
Commerce, Science,
   and Transportation
Energy and Natural
   Resources

Environment and
   Public Works
Finance
Foreign Relations
Governmental Affairs
Judiciary

Labor and Human
   Resources
Rules and
   Administration
Small Business
Veterans' Affairs

Thinking About Careers

During this school year you learned that in the early days of the American republic, most people earned a living by farming. By 1920, manufacturing had replaced agriculture as the nation's major economic activity. Then, forty years later, a second major shift began to take place. Manufacturing started being replaced by high-technology and service industries. Since 1970, jobs in manufacturing have declined, while those in high-technology and service industries have expanded. Three out of every four new jobs will be created in service industries.

YOUR INTERESTS, VALUES, AND SKILLS

Before you begin to consider a career, you should think about your interests, values, and skills. You can determine your interests by examining the kinds of things you like to do. Do you prefer group activities? Or would you rather spend your time working on your own? Do you prefer working with words or with your hands, with ideas or with things? Answering questions like these will help you identify your interests.

Your values indicate what you consider important in life. Is acquiring wealth important to you? Would you want to stay in your home community, or would you prefer to live elsewhere? How many years are you willing to invest in training for a career? Is job security important to you? Or would you be willing to take risks in the hope of achieving greater returns? Your values will affect your choice of a career.

Many skills can be learned, but most people find certain skills easier to master than others. Different career fields, furthermore, have different skill requirements. For example, good eyesight and quick reflexes are more important for a police officer than for a social worker. You should choose a career that matches your skills.

LEARNING MORE ABOUT CAREERS

There are many sources of information that can help you explore a career field. Government agencies, business firms, trade associations, labor unions, fraternal and patriotic groups, and educational institutions all publish a great deal of useful material. You might start with the *Dictionary of Occupational Titles*, put out by the Department of Labor. It describes about 20,000 different kinds of jobs. Another good government source is the *Occupational Outlook Handbook*, published every two years by the Bureau of Labor Statistics. In addition to information about job requirements and earnings, it predicts which industries will grow and which will shrink over the next few years. You can probably find both titles in your school or local library.

Another good source of career information is your school counselor or adviser. Counselors can discuss with you what your interests, values, and skills are and arrange for you to take tests that will help you assess these factors. They know the curriculum and costs of various schools and training programs. They are also familiar with the job market.

In recent years, various agencies have begun providing career information for special groups. For example, women's centers run by community organizations or local colleges offer suggestions about jobs. Vocational-rehabilitation agencies provide information aimed at the handicapped. Specialized magazines such as *The Black Collegian* and *Minority Engineer* deal with problems that members of minority groups may face.

The way you choose to earn your living is important not only to you but also to our nation. To meet future challenges, the United States needs skillful and responsible citizens.

Suggested Reading

General List

American Heritage Book of Indians. American Heritage. A beautifully illustrated history of the Indians of North America.

American Heritage Pictorial Atlas of United States History. American Heritage. A basic source.

Barzman, Sol. *The First Ladies.* Cowles. Brief but reflective biographies of the Presidents' wives from Martha Washington to Pat Nixon.

A Cartoon History of United States Foreign Policy. Foreign Policy Association. A lively way of examining America's relations with other nations.

Commager, Henry Steele, ed. *Documents of American History.* Appleton-Century-Crofts. A basic collection.

Dinnerstein, Leonard, and David Reimers. *Ethnic Americans: A History of Immigration and Assimilation.* Harper and Row. A concise treatment of this stirring theme.

Dulles, Foster R. *America Learns to Play.* Peter Smith. Popular recreation traced from 1607 to the eve of World War II.

Franklin, John Hope. *From Slavery to Freedom,* 5th ed. Alfred A. Knopf. An award-winning history of black Americans.

Graff, Henry F., ed. *The Presidents: A Reference History.* Charles Scribner's Sons. Noted historians examine the Chief Executives in individual essays on their terms of office.

Hofstadter, Richard. *The American Political Tradition and the Men Who Made It.* Alfred A. Knopf. A collection of provocative and informative essays on political leaders.

Hughes, Langston; Milton Meltzer; and C. Eric Lincoln, eds. *A Pictorial History of Black-Americans.* Crown. An illustrated account of black people in American society.

Lingeman, Richard. *Small Town America.* Houghton Mifflin. A history of small-town life, from 1620 to the present.

Morris, Richard B., and Jeffrey B. Morris, eds. *Encyclopedia of American History.* Harper and Row. A standard reference work.

Ryan, William, and Desmond Guinness. *The White House.* McGraw-Hill. The first complete biography of America's most famous home. Profusely and handsomely illustrated.

Wertheimer, Barbara M. *We Were There.* Pantheon. The story of working women in the United States.

Unit One: The Nation Transformed

American Heritage History of the Confident Years. American Heritage. A survey of the period from 1865 to 1914; combines pictures, narrative, and primary sources.

Brown, Dee. *Bury My Heart at Wounded Knee.* Holt, Rinehart and Winston. The westward expansion of the United States told from the viewpoint of Native Americans.

Callow, Alexander B., Jr. *The Tweed Ring.* Oxford. A close look at the famous political machine.

Garbedian, H. Gordon. *Thomas Alva Edison.* Julian Messner. A biography of the nation's most celebrated inventor.

Glad, Paul W. *McKinley, Bryan, and the People.* J. B. Lippincott. An analysis of the individuals and issues that shaped the 1896 election.

Handlin, Oscar. *The Uprooted.* Grosset & Dunlap. The classic study of late nineteenth-century immigration.

Harlow, Alvin. *Andrew Carnegie.* Julian Messner. A biography of the prototypical "rags-to-riches" American.

Josephson, Matthew. *Politicos.* Harcourt Brace Jovanovich. An overview of national politics in the post-Civil War years, with intimate accounts of the chief participants.

Katz, William Loren. *The Black West.* Doubleday. An account of black cowboys, cavalrymen, ranchers, and farmers in the West.

McCullough, David. *The Great Bridge.* Simon and Schuster. An account of the construction of the Brooklyn Bridge.

Maddow, Ben. *A Sunday Between Wars: The Course of American Life from 1865–1917.* W. W. Norton. A presentation of nineteenth-century life from the ordinary American's point of view.

Meltzer, Milton. *Bread and Roses.* Alfred A. Knopf. A history of the American labor movement from 1865 to 1915.

O'Connor, Edwin. *The Last Hurrah.* Atlantic-Little, Brown. A novel about the final campaign of an urban political boss.

Riis, Jacob. *How the Other Half Lives.* Harvard University Press. The classic work that focused attention on slum-dwelling.

Schlissel, Lillian. *Women's Diaries of the Westward Journey.* Schocken Books. A stirring portrayal of the westward adventure from the viewpoint of women.

Stiller, Richard. *Queen of Populists: The Story of Mary Elizabeth Lease.* T. Y. Crowell. A biography of one of the most colorful Populist leaders.

Strasser, Susan. *Never Done: A History of American Housework.* Pantheon. A lively, eye-opening account of the relationship between an industrializing economy and the household.

Thorndike, Joseph J., Jr. *The Very Rich.* American Heritage. A well-illustrated portrayal of rich families and their ways of life in the late 1800's.

Unit Two: Crusading at Home and Abroad

Addams, Jane. *Twenty Years at Hull-House.* Macmillan. The autobiography of one of the leaders of the settlement-house movement.

Archer, Jules. *World Citizen: Woodrow Wilson.* Julian Messner. A biography of the twenty-eighth President, with emphasis on his fight for the League of Nations.

Beale, Howard. *Theodore Roosevelt and the Rise of America to World Power.* Johns Hopkins University Press. An analysis of Roosevelt's influence on the nation's foreign policies.

Fleming, Alice. *Ida Tarbell.* T. Y. Crowell. A biography of the journalist who exposed the pricing tactics of the Standard Oil Company.

Flexner, Eleanor. *Century of Struggle.* Belknap Press. A history of the first hundred years of the fight for women's rights.

Garraty, John A. *Theodore Roosevelt: The Strenuous Life.* American Heritage. A study that shows how Roosevelt's belief in action expressed itself in both his personal and political life.

Ginger, Ray. *Eugene V. Debs.* Macmillan. A biography of the labor leader and presidential candidate who was a leading opponent of American involvement in World War I.

Jantzen, Steven. *Hooray for Peace, Hurrah for War.* Alfred A. Knopf. A description of World War I that uses such primary sources as letters, diaries, drawings, speeches, and songs.

La Follette, Robert M. *Autobiography.* University of Wisconsin Press. The autobiography of a leading progressive.

McCullough, David C. *The Path Between the Seas.* Simon and Schuster. The best presentation of the complex story of the construction of the Panama Canal.

May, Ernest R. *The Progressive Era.* Time-Life Books. A well-illustrated account of the politics and personalities of the period.

Rouveral, Jean. *Pancho Villa: A Biography.* Doubleday. A biography of the controversial Mexican leader.

Sinclair, Upton. *The Jungle.* Airmont Publishing. The novel whose description of the meat-packing industry helped bring about passage of the Pure Food and Drugs Act.

Swanberg, W. A. *Citizen Hearst.* Charles Scribner's Sons. A biography of the newspaper publisher whose drive for higher circulation helped encourage American war fever in 1898.

Tuchman, Barbara. *The Guns of August.* Macmillan. A suspenseful account of the early days of World War I.

Unit Three: Good Times, Hard Times, and War

Allen, Frederick Lewis. *Lords of Creation.* Harper and Row. Biographies of financial leaders of the United States.

Alsop, Joseph. *FDR: A Centenary Remembrance.* Viking. A combination of biographical essay, memoir, and history.

Ambrose, Stephen E. *Ike from Abilene to Berlin.* Harper and Row. A biography of Dwight D. Eisenhower from his childhood through victory in Europe.

Anderson, Jervis. *This Was Harlem.* Farrar, Straus & Giroux. A portrait of the writers, musicians, and artists of the Harlem Renaissance.

Buchanan, A. Russell. *The United States and World War II.* Harper and Row. A full account of the military history of World War II.

Burner, David. *Herbert Hoover: The Public Life.* Alfred A. Knopf. The most authoritative biography of the thirty-first President.

Burns, James M. *Roosevelt: The Lion and the Fox.* Harcourt Brace Jovanovich. A study of Roosevelt as a political leader.

Considine, Bob, and Ted Lawson. *Thirty Seconds Over Tokyo.* Random House. The gripping story of the first American air strikes on Japan's capital.

Handlin, Oscar. *Al Smith and His America.* Little, Brown. A biography that offers considerable insight into urban politics.

Kennan, George F. *American Diplomacy, 1900-1950.* University of Chicago Press. A thoughtful survey of the principles of American foreign policy.

Lord, Walter. *Day of Infamy.* Holt, Rinehart and Winston. A highly readable account of the Japanese attack on Pearl Harbor and the American response.

Marling, Karal Ann. *Wall-to-Wall America.* University of Minnesota Press. An account of the social and political significance of the murals painted under federal patronage during the Great Depression; well-illustrated.

Meltzer, Milton. *Brother, Can You Spare a Dime?* Alfred A. Knopf. The story of the Great Depression from the stock market crash to the New Deal, with numerous primary sources.

Meltzer, Milton. *Never to Forget: The Jews of the Holocaust.* Harper and Row. A searing account of the historical background of German anti-Semitism, Hitler's rise to power, and the Nazi death camps, combined with the recorded experiences of individual Jews.

Sherwood, Robert E. *Roosevelt and Hopkins.* Harper and Row. An intimate account of the President's relationship with his chief associate.

Sward, Keith. *The Legend of Henry Ford.* Russell and Russell. A biography of the man who revolutionized both American industry and the American way of life.

Williams, T. Harry. *Huey Long.* Vintage Books. A well-balanced biography of the Louisiana political leader.

Unit Four: Confidence and Concern

Carter, Paul. *Another Part of the Fifties.* Columbia University Press. A fresh look at the 1950's.

Daniels, Jonathan. *The Man of Independence.* Kennikat. An illuminating biography of Harry S. Truman.

Ewald, William B. *Eisenhower the President: Crucial Days.* Prentice-Hall. An account of the eight years in office of the thirty-fourth President.

Goulden, Joseph C. *Korea: The Untold Story of the War.* Times Books. A well-documented portrayal of the individuals and events of the Korean War.

King, Martin Luther, Jr. *Stride Toward Freedom.* Harper and Row. A vivid account of the Montgomery bus boycott that led to the desegregation of public transportation.

Lewis, Anthony. *Gideon's Trumpet.* Random House. An account of the Supreme Court decision that poor people are entitled to legal counsel in criminal cases.

Nixon, Richard. *Six Crises.* Warner Books. Recounts the author's role in several controversial issues that arose in his career before he was President.

O'Neill, William L. *Coming Apart: An Informal History of America in the 1960's.* Quadrangle. An account of the political and social protests that marked the decade.

Robinson, Jackie. *I Never Had It Made.* G. P. Putnam's Sons. The autobiography of the first player to break the color bar in major league baseball.

Ross, Lillian. *Adlai Stevenson.* J. B. Lippincott. A biography of the able Democratic candidate for the presidency who lost to Eisenhower twice.

Schechter, Betty. *The Peaceable Revolution.* Houghton Mifflin. The development of nonviolent resistance in America from Thoreau to King.

Schwartz, Bernard. *Super Chief: Earl Warren and His Supreme Court — A Judicial Biography.* New York University Press. A biography that explains how Earl Warren guided the Court into issuing numerous landmark decisions in the area of individual rights.

Walton, Richard J. *America and the Cold War.* Seabury. A well-balanced analysis by a United Nations correspondent for the Voice of America.

White, Theodore H. *The Making of the President, 1960* and *The Making of the President, 1964.* Atheneum. Inside views of the campaigns by a leading political journalist.

Wicker, Tom. *JFK and LBJ.* Penguin. A comparison of the two Presidents, their personalities, and their administrations.

Unit Five: Toward a New Century

Amrine, Michael. *The Great Decision.* G. P. Putnam's Sons. A gripping history of the development of the atomic bomb.

Bernstein, Carl, and Bob Woodward. *All the President's Men.* Simon and Schuster. The step-by-step story of Watergate as told by the reporters most responsible for uncovering the scandal.

Cohen, Warren I. *America's Response to China.* John Wiley. A significant examination of Sino-American relations.

Gaddis, John L. *Russia, the Soviet Union, and the United States.* John Wiley. An outstanding examination of the subject reduced to its essentials.

Greenstein, Fred, ed. *The Reagan Presidency: An Early Assessment.* Johns Hopkins University Press. Scholars and policy-makers attempt to judge Reagan in four major policy areas — fiscal, foreign, defense, and domestic.

Grose, Peter. *Israel in the Mind of America.* Alfred A. Knopf. An account of the role of the United States in the re-establishment of a Jewish homeland.

Handlin, Oscar, ed. *Children of the Uprooted.* George Braziller. How the descendants of turn-of-the-century immigrants from eastern and southern Europe have fared in America.

Herring, George C. *America's Longest War.* John Wiley. A balanced overview of the conflict in Vietnam.

McGinniss, Joe. *The Selling of the President, 1968.* Pocket Books. A study of the role of image-making in presidential elections.

Meier, Matt S., and Feliciano Rivera. *The Chicanos: A History of Mexican-Americans.* Hill and Wang. A valuable primer on the subject.

Pierce, Neal, and Jerry Hagstrom. *The Book of America: Inside 50 States Today.* W. W. Norton. Detailed information about each of the states.

Sale, Kirkpatrick. *Power Shift.* Random House. The movement of population, industry, and political power from the Northeast to the South and West since the end of World War II.

Sitkoff, Harvard. *The Struggle for Black Equality: 1954–1981.* Hill and Wang. A leading survey of the civil-rights movement.

Glossary

The glossary defines important words and terms used in this book. Remember that many words have more than one meaning. The definitions given here are the ones that will be most helpful in your reading of this book.

abolitionist: a person who worked in the movement to do away with slavery.

amnesty: a general pardon by a government for political offenses.

anarchist: a person who favors abolishing all forms of government.

annex: to incorporate territory into an existing country or state.

appeasement: the granting of concessions to a potential enemy in order to maintain peace.

apprentice: a youth who is bound to a skilled person in order to learn a trade.

arbitration: a process by which the parties to a dispute submit their differences to the judgment of an impartial party.

assembly line: a line of factory workers and equipment along which work being assembled passes from one operation to the next until completion.

automation: the automatic operation of manufacturing processes.

black codes: state laws that restricted the activities of southern blacks in the years after the Civil War.

blacklist: a list of workers whom employers refuse to hire because of their union activities.

blockade: to close off an area by the use of naval or other forces.

bond: a certificate issued by a corporation or a government in exchange for a loan of money.

boycott: to express protest by refusing to deal with a certain party.

brinkmanship: a strategy by which a nation displays its willingness to risk war in order to make an adversary back down.

bureaucracy: administration of a government, chiefly by unelected officials.

Cabinet: the executive department heads who advise the President.

capital: wealth, in the form of money or property, that is owned by an individual or a business organization.

capitalist: a person who invests money in business in order to make a profit.

charter: a document creating a corporation.

checks and balances: a system that allows each branch of government to limit the power of the other branches.

cloture: a parliamentary procedure by which debate may be limited and a vote taken on the matter under discussion.

collective bargaining: discussions carried on between a union and an employer to determine such things as wages, hours, and working conditions.

collective security: the increased protection gained when nations stand together against aggression.

containment: a policy aimed at checking the expansion of a hostile power by diplomatic, economic, or military means.

cooperative: a business owned and operated by its workers.

corporation: a business chartered by a state and owned by shareholding investors.

craft union: an organization of workers in which all members practice the same trade.

democracy: a philosophy of government that recognizes the people's right to take part directly or indirectly in controlling their political institutions; the practices of society as a whole that enlarge opportunities for people and place emphasis on the dignity of the individual.

depression: a period of drastic decline in business activity accompanied by rising unemployment.

détente: a relaxing of tensions between nations.

direct primary: a preliminary election in which a political party's candidates are chosen by popular vote.

disarmament: the reduction or abolition of weapons and military forces.

dividend: the portion of a corporation's profits paid to a shareholder.

dry farming: a method of farming in arid areas without irrigation.

duty: a tax on imported goods.

elector: a person chosen by a state to cast one of its votes in a presidential election.

emancipate: to set free from bondage or oppression.

excise tax: a tax on certain goods produced, sold, or used within a country.

federal system: a system of government in which states that retain their local powers are united under a strong central government.

filibuster: the use of certain tactics, such as the making of prolonged speeches, for the purpose of delaying legislative action.

finance capitalist: a banker who invests in businesses and helps them obtain capital and credit.

free enterprise system: the economic system of private ownership of farms, factories, and other businesses; capitalism.

gold standard: the valuing of currency on the basis of gold.

greenbacks: paper money that was authorized by Congress in 1862 and was not backed by a gold or silver reserve.

gross national product: the total value of all goods and services produced by a nation.

holding company: a corporation formed to gain control of another corporation by buying its stock.

homestead: free federal land claimed by settlers under the Homestead Act of 1862.

impeach: to accuse a public official before a proper tribunal of misconduct in office.

imperialism: a national policy of extending political or economic control over other countries.

inflation: a continuing increase in prices resulting from an abnormal rise in the amount of money and credit in circulation in proportion to the goods available.

initiative: a process by which citizens may propose legislation and have it submitted to the voters.

injunction: a court order forbidding a specific action.

interchangeable parts: identical parts that can be substituted for one another in the manufacturing or repair of a given product.

interlocking directorate: a means of controlling an industry by having the same people serve as directors for several companies.

irrigation: the use of ditches, channels, or pipes to bring water to dry farmland.

isolationist: a person who favors a national policy of avoiding foreign entanglements.

Jim Crow laws: laws introduced following reconstruction that imposed or enforced segregation.

judicial review: the power of the federal courts to declare unconstitutional acts of Congress or of state legislatures.

long drive: the annual herding of cattle from Texas to railroad towns farther north.

loose construction: an interpretation of the Constitution holding that the federal government has broad powers.

mandate system: an arrangement by which the victorious Allies at the close of World War I were given the responsibility of preparing the former colonies of Germany and Turkey for independence.

massive retaliation: a strategy calling for swift, all-out military action against a nation committing aggression against a neighboring country.

mercenary: a soldier who serves in a foreign army for pay.

merger: the union of two or more commercial interests or corporations.

merit system: a government employment system based on competitive examinations.

minister: a representative of a government, next in rank to an ambassador.

mission: a settlement, founded by priests, usually consisting of a church, a village, a fort, and farmland.

monopoly: exclusive control over the supply of a particular product or service.

mortgage: a pledge of property to a lender as security for a loan.

muckraker: a writer in the Progressive Era who exposed social and political evils.

nationalism: devotion to one's nation; the belief that national interests are more important than international considerations.

navigation: the science of charting the course of a ship or aircraft.

neutral: not actively favoring either side, as in a war.

nullification: the doctrine that a state may refuse to enforce a federal law it deems unconstitutional.

Pan-Americanism: a movement to promote economic and political cooperation among the nations of the Western Hemisphere.

patent: a government document that grants an inventor for a period of time the sole right to build and sell his or her invention.

piedmont: the region in the eastern United States extending eastward from the Appalachians to the fall line.

pocket veto: a President's indirect veto of a bill, exercised by retaining the bill unsigned until Congress adjourns.

pool: an arrangement among businesses in the same industry for the purpose of establishing control over prices and production.

preamble: an opening statement explaining the purpose of a document.

prohibition: a ban on the manufacture, sale, and distribution of alcoholic beverages.

ratification: official approval of a constitution or a treaty.

recall: the procedure by which a public official may be voted out of office before his or her term is ended.

recession: a moderate slump in business activity.

referendum: a process by which citizens may vote on a proposed law or other public measure.

reparations: compensation required from a defeated nation for war damages.

republic: a form of government controlled by the people through elected representatives.

repudiate: to refuse to recognize or pay.

reservation: a tract of land set aside for permanent settlement by a specific Indian tribe.

right-to-work laws: laws that allow workers to obtain and keep jobs without being required to join a union.

satellite: a nation dominated politically by another.

secede: to withdraw formally from membership in an alliance or organization.

secret ballot: a method of voting by which voters mark and cast their ballots in secrecy.

segregation: the separation of one race (or class) from another.

separation of powers: the division of government power into executive, legislative, and judicial branches.

sharecropper: a farm tenant who pays the landlord a share of the crops as rent.

Socialist: an advocate of government ownership of the means of production.

spoils system: the practice of giving government jobs to party supporters after an election victory.

states' rights: the principle that upholds the powers of the states as opposed to the powers of the federal government.

stock: a certificate representing ownership in a corporation.

strict construction: an interpretation of the Constitution holding that the powers of the federal government are strictly defined.

strike: a work stoppage by employees.

suffrage: the right to vote; also, the exercise of that right.

sunbelt: the part of the United States that stretches from the southeastern Atlantic coast to southern California.

tariff: a tax on imported goods.

temperance movement: a campaign against the consumption of alcoholic beverages.

tenement: a crowded slum dwelling.

third party: a party organized in opposition to the two major political parties.

totalitarian: designating a policy by which a government's main characteristic is its absolute control over citizens' lives.

trunk line: the main line of a transportation or communication system, to which subsidiary lines are connected.

trust: a form of business uniting several companies into one system, often creating a monopoly.

turnpike: a highway on which users pay tolls.

vigilante: a member of a citizens' group operating to enforce the law, without authority.

yellow dog contract: an employment agreement, now illegal, in which working people promised not to join a union.

Acknowledgments

Text Credits

Grateful acknowledgment is made to authors, publishers, and other copyright holders for permission to reprint (and in some selections to adapt slightly) copyright material listed below.

Page 56: From *Sketches In Crude-Oil* by John J. McLavrin, 1896. **Page 91:** From "The Story of a Sweatshop Girl" by Sadie Frowne. *The Independent*, Sept. 25, 1902. **Page 114:** From *A Son of The Middle Border* by Hamlin Garland. Copyright © 1917, Hamlin Garland, renewed 1945 by Mary I. Lord and Constance G. Williams. Reprinted by permission of Macmillan Publishing Company. **Page 139:** From the *Autobiography of George Dewey*. Charles Scribner's Sons, 1913. **Page 156:** From *Victory: How Women Won It* by The National American Women Suffrage Association. Copyright © 1940, The H. W. Wilson Company. Reprinted by permission of the H. W. Wilson Company. **Page 188:** From "Over There" by George M. Cohan. Copyright © 1917, renewed 1945 Leo Feist Inc., New York. Rights assigned to CBS CATALOG PARTNERSHIP. All rights controlled and administered by CBS FEIST CATALOG INC. All rights reserved, used by permission. **Page 193:** From *American in France* by Major Frederick Palmer. Copyright © 1918 Dodd, Mead and Company. Reprinted by permission of Dodd, Mead and Company, Inc. **Page 223:** From *Middletown, A Study in American Culture* by Robert S. and Helen M. Lynd. Copyright © 1929 Harcourt, Brace & Jovanovich, Inc., renewed 1957 by Robert S. and Helen M. Lynd. Reprinted by permission of Harcourt, Brace & Jovanovich, Inc. and Constable Publishers **Page 232:** From *Movin' On Up* by Mahalia Jackson. Copyright © 1966 Mahalia Jackson and Evan McLeod Wylie. Reprinted by permission of E. P. Dutton, Inc. **Page 279:** From *In Search of Light: The Broadcasts of Edward R. Murrow 1938–1961* by Edward R. Murrow, edited by Edward Bliss, Jr. Copyright © 1967 the Estate of Edward R. Murrow. Reprinted by permission of Alfred A. Knopf, Inc. **Page 294:** From *Americans Remember the Home Front* by Ray Hoopes. Copyright © 1977 Ray Hoopes. Reprinted by permission of the author. **Page 299:** From the song "I Double Dare You" by Terry Shand and Jimmy Eaton. Copyright © 1937, renewed by Shapiro, Bernstein & Company, Inc. Reprinted by permission of Shapiro, Bernstein & Company, Inc. **Page 323:** From *On My Own* by Eleanor Roosevelt. Copyright © 1958 the Estate of Eleanor Roosevelt. Reprinted by permission of Franklin Roosevelt, Jr. **Page 353:** From *Letters From the Peace Corps* edited by Iris Luce. Copyright © 1964 Robert B. Luce, Inc. Reprinted by permission of Robert B. Luce, Inc. **Page 358:** From "I Have A Dream" by Martin Luther King, Jr. Copyright © 1963 Martin Luther King, Jr. Reprinted by permission of Joan Daves. **Page 369:** From *The Making of the President—1964* by Theodore H. White. Copyright © 1965 Theodore H. White. Reprinted by permission of Atheneum Publishers and the Julian Bach Literary Agency, Inc. **Page 402:** From "Notes and Comment," *The New Yorker* magazine, July 19, 1976. Copyright © 1976 The New Yorker Magazine, Inc. Reprinted by permission of the New Yorker Magazine, Inc. **Page 415:** From "An End to a Long Ordeal" by Ed Magnuson, *Time* magazine, February 2, 1981. Copyright © 1981 Time Inc. Reprinted by permission of *Time*. **Page 435:** From "The Building of the Ship" by Henry Wadsworth Longfellow, 1849.

Art Credits

Cover: Concept by John Caswell and Ligature Publishing Services, Inc. Eagle watercolor rendering by Elizabeth Moutal, 1938, of wood carving by John Haley Bellamy, late 19th century. Coll: Index of American Design, National Gallery of Art, Washington, D.C.

Half-title: Eagle watercolor rendering by Alfred H. Smith, of wood carving by William Beal, 19th century. Coll: Index of American Design, National Gallery of Art, Washington, D.C.

Frontispiece: "Flags, Fourth of July, 1916," by Childe Hassam. Coll: Mr. and Mrs. Frank Sinatra. Photo: Hirschl & Adler Galleries.

Maps: All maps by Dick Sanderson, except those on pages 600–603, 604–605 by Donnelley Cartographic Services (pages 604–605, Robinson Projection).

Time lines and table on pages 642–643 by Gary Shellehamer.

Graphs and diagrams by Omnigraphics, Inc.

"Achievements in Technology" art by John D. Dawson.

The following abbreviations are used for some sources from which several illustrations were obtained:

ASKB—Ann S. K. Brown Military Collection **BA**—Bettmann Archive. **BB**—Brown Brothers. **CHS**—Chicago Historical Society. **CP**—Culver Pictures. **FDRL**—Franklin D. Roosevelt Library. **GC**—Granger Collection. **HSP**—Historical Society of Pennsylvania. **IWM**—Trustees of the Imperial War Museum. **LC**—Library of Congress. **MMA**—Metropolitan Museum of Art. **NA**—National Archives. **NGA**—National Gallery of Art, Washington, D.C. **NPG**—National Portrait Gallery, Washington, D.C. **NYHS**—New-York Historical Society. **NYPL**—New York Public Library. **RISD**—Museum of Art, Rhode Island School of Design. **SI**—Smithsonian Institution. **UPI**—United Press International. **WHHA**—White House Historical Association. **WM**—Henry duPont Francis Winterthur Museum. **WW**—Wide World. **YU**—Yale University Art Gallery.

7 "Interior of Fort Laramie," by Alfred Jacob Miller. Coll: Walters Art Gallery. **9** FDR and Churchill by Raymond P. R. Neilson, 1941. Coll: IWM. **10** Wally McNamee/Woodfin Camp and Associates. **12** "Detroit Industry," south wall (detail), by Diego Rivera, 1932-1933. Coll: Detroit Institute of Arts, Founders Society, purchase, Edsel B. Ford Fund and gift of Edsel B. Ford. **13** BA. **14** UPI. **15** Larry Dale Gordon/Image Bank. **17** "Route of Magellan," from Baptista Agnese's Atlas, HM 25, ff. 12v-13r. Coll: Huntington Library, San Marino, California. **18** Courtesy of the Boston Athenaeum. Photo: Charles Hogg.

21 "The Mayflower" (detail), by Halsall. Coll: The Pilgrim Society, Plymouth, Massachusetts. **22** "Old Bruton Parish Church," by Wordsworth Thompson. Coll: MMA. **23** "Colonel George Washington," by Charles Wilson Peale. Coll: Washington/Curtis/Lee Collection, Washington and Lee University, Virginia. **24** "Congress Voting Independence," by Pine and Savage. Coll: HSP. **25** GC. **27** "Boarding The Chesapeake," by Thomas Hemy, 1895. Coll: The Honorable Mrs. H. M. Llewellyn. **28** "Lincoln Raising the Flag at Independence Hall," by J. L. G. Ferris. Coll: Archives of 76.

31 "Hunting Buffalo," by Alfred Jacob Miller. Coll: Stark Museum of Art. **33** "Ten Bears-Comanche Chief" (detail). Coll: SI. **34** "Interior of Fort Laramie," by Alfred Jacob Miller. Coll: Walters Art Gallery. **35** LC, #747 162 19725. **39** "The Roundup" (detail), by Charles M. Russell, 1913. Coll: MacKay Collection, Montana Historical Society. **40** CHS. **47** Solomon D. Butcher Collection, Nebraska State Historical Society. **49** Kansas State Historical Society. **55** "Bessemer Converter" (detail), by S. B. Shiley, 1895. Coll: Bethlehem Steel Corporation. **56** NYPL. **59** "Night Scene at an American Railway Junction," by Currier and Ives. Coll: LC, #3652. **62** University of Washington, Henry Art Gallery, Special Collections. **65** Coll: NPG. Photo: Rolland G. White. **75** BB. **77** *(left)* Courtesy American Heritage Publishing Co., Inc. *(right)* L.C. #USZ62-36986. *(bottom)* Photo by Jacob A. Riis, from Jacob A. Riis Collection, Museum of the City of New York. **83** "Washington Street, Indianapolis at Dusk," by Theodore Groll, 1892. Coll: Indianapolis Museum of Art, gift of a couple of old Hoosiers. **85** Photo by Irving Underhill, from LC, #USZ62-24063. **86** MMA. **87** Photo by Byron, from The Byron Collection, Museum of the City of New York. **89** New York University, Tamiment Collection. **91** Photo by Lewis Hine, from International Museum of Photography, George Eastman House. **92** "Virginia-Tenth Annual Convention of the Knights of Labor at Richmond," by Joseph Becker. Photo: CP. **94** Coll: George Meany Memorial Archives. **96** "Great Battle of Homestead, Defeat and Capture of the Pinkerton Invaders July 6, 1892." Coll: LC. **97** "King Debs," by W. A. Rogers. Coll: LC #USZ62-2115. **103** "Electioneering," by Edward Lamson Henry. Coll: Kennedy Galleries. **105** Cartoon by Thomas Nast. Coll: NYPL. **111** "The Lost Bet" (detail), by Joseph Klir, 1892. Coll: CHS. **113** LC. **114** "Gift for the Grangers" (detail). Coll: LC. **116** "Harvest Time," by William Hahn. Coll: Fine Arts Museum of San Francisco, gift of Mrs. Harold McKinnon and Mrs. Harry L. Brown. **119** GC.

127 "The Naval Parade, 1899," by Fred Pansing. Coll: Museum of the City of New York. **129**

Bishop Museum. **131** From *New York Herald Tribune*. Coll: NYPL, Special Collections. **134** Theodore Roosevelt Collection, Harvard College Library. **137** "Destruction of the U.S. Battleship Maine in Havana Harbor, Feb. 15, 1898." Coll: CHS. **138** *San Francisco Examiner*, April 12, 1898. Photo: Bell and Howell Labs. **139** "Commodore George Dewey" (detail), by N. M. Miller. Coll: U. S. Naval Academy. Photo: Dermott Hickey. **141** "Charge of the Rough Riders Up San Juan Hill," by Frederic Remington. Coll: Remington Art Museum. **142** "Surrender of Puerto Rico" (detail), anonymous. Coll: CHS. **144** "The Boxer Rebellion" (detail). Coll: LC. **151** "Central Park, 1901," by Maurice Prendergast. Coll: Whitney Museum of American Art. Photo: Geoffrey Clements. **153** The Ida M. Tarbell Collection, Pelletier Library, Allegheny College. **156** CHS. **157** BB. **159** BA. **162** *(left)* Coll: Museo Civico, "L. Bailo," Commune Di Treviso. *(right)* Staten Island Historical Society. *(bottom)* "Looking Down at Yosemite Valley from Glacier Point," by William Hahn, 1874. Coll: California Historical Society. **164** NA. **167** "The Great White Fleet" (detail), by Henry Reuterdahl. Coll: U. S. Naval Academy Museum. Photo: Dermott Hickey. **169** GC. **172** "Reading the Death Warrant," by C. R. Macauley, 1913. Photo: GC. **173** WW. **177** Photo by Harlan Marshall, from Manchester Historical Association. **179** GC. **180** "Guerre 14/18: La Mobilisation sur les Boulevards," by A. Leveille. Coll: Musée de la Guerre. Photo: Edimedia/SNARK. **182** BB. **184** *(left)* Coll: Staatsgalerie Stuttgart. *(right)* Poster by A. Leete. Coll: IWM. **185** Princeton University Library. **188** "Over There" by George M. Cohan, © 1917 (Renewed 1945) LEO FEIST, INC. All Rights of LEO FEIST, INC. Assigned to CBS CATALOGUE PARTNERSHIP. All Rights Controlled by CBS FEIST CATALOG. International Copyright Secured. All Rights Reserved. Used by Permission. Song sheet illustration copyright F. B. Rockwell. **189** BBC Hulton Picture Library/BA. **192** "Douglas Campbell-World War I Pilot," by John T. McCoy, Jr. Coll: Aviation Americana. **193** "Doughboy" (detail), by Captain Harvey Dunn. Coll: SI. **195** "Troops at Saint-Mihiel," anonymous. Coll: SI. **197** "Signing of the Peace" (detail), by W. Orpen. Coll: IWM.

207 "Detroit Industry," south wall (detail), by Diego Rivera, 1932–1933. Coll: Detroit Institute of Arts, Founders Society, purchase, Edsel B. Ford Fund and gift of Edsel B. Ford. **209** WW. **211** Frank Driggs Collection. **213, 215** LC. **219** CP. **222** "The Great White Way — Times Square New York City" (detail), by How-ard Thain, 1925. Coll: NYHS. **223** Photo by Lewis W. Hine, from International Museum of Photography at George Eastman House. **224** *(top left)* "Teaching Old Dogs," by John Held Jr., Photo: GC. *(bottom left)* UPI. *(middle)* CP. *(right)* Baltimore Sun Papers. **229** "Employment Agency" (detail), by Isaac Soyer, 1937. Coll: Whitney Museum. Photo: Geoffrey Clements. **231** LC. **232** Springer/BA. **233** Herbert Hoover Presidential Library/AP. **235** FDRL, AP. **237** BB. **238** NA. **239** BA. **245** Cartoon by William Gropper. Coll: VANITY FAIR copyright 1935 (renewed 1963) by The Conde Nast Publications. Photo: Boston Public Library. **246** "Construction of a Dam" (detail), by William Gropper. Coll: U.S. Dept. of the Interior. **248** LC. **249** UPI. **250** FDRL. **252** Cartoon by J. N. "Ding" Darling. Coll: J. N. "Ding" Darling Conservation Foundation, Des Moines. **253** FDRL. **261** "American Landscape," by Charles Sheeler, 1930. Coll: Museum of Modern Art, gift of Abby Aldrich Rockefeller. **265** BB. **267** BA. **269** Coll: Office of the Governor, Puerto Rico. **272, 275** BA. **278** "Battle of Dunkirk" (detail), by Charles Cundall. Coll: IWM. **279** UPI. **281** Coll: IWM. **285** FDR and Churchill by Raymond P. R. Neilson, 1941. Coll: FDRL. **286** NA. **289** NA #80-a-30517. **291** Pictorial Parade. **292** NA #242-GAP-181A-4. **294** Bureau of the Public Debt. **295** U.S. Air Force. **296** *(left)* "Calship Burner," by Edna Reindel, 1943. Coll: Life Collection of World War II Art. Photo: U.S. Army. *(right)* Poster by Norman Rockwell. Coll: National Infantry Museum. *(bottom)* BA. **298** FDRL. **300** "Tank Break-Through at St. Lo," by Ogden Pleissner. Coll: City Commission of Detroit. Photo: *The Life History of the United States: New Deal and Global War*, Time-Life Books, Inc., Publisher © 1964 Time Inc. **303** U. S. Army. **305** UPI. **307** U. S. Army.

315 BB. **318** "Pre-Fourth Fizzle," by Edward Keukes from *The Plain Dealer*. **319** WW. **321** UPI. **323** FDRL. **324** Werner Wolf/Black Star. **326** UPI. **328** Walter Sanders, LIFE Magazine © 1948 Time Inc. **331** WW. **333** UPI. **335** George Skadding, LIFE Magazine © 1952 Time Inc. **339** Herman J. Kokojan/Black Star. **340** Dwight D. Eisenhower Library. **342** Lessing/Magnum. **344** Thomas Hovland/Grant Heilman. **347** *(left)* Farrell Grehan/Photo Researchers. *(right)* J.R. Eyerman, LIFE Magazine © 1953 Time Inc. *(bottom)* BB. **348** John Launois/Black Star. **350** UPI. **351** Cornell Capa/Magnum. **353** Marc and Evelyne Bernheim/Woodfin Camp and Associates. **354** Berlin Bild/Black Star. **357** NASA, courtesy

LIFE MAGAZINE, © Time, Inc. **359** Cecil Stoughton/Lyndon B. Johnson Library. **360** *(left)* "Join or Die," by Benjamin Franklin, woodcut, from the May 9, 1754, issue of the *Pennsylvania Gazette.* Courtesy of The Library Company of Philadelphia. *(right)* cartoon by Warren King, from *New York Daily News,* October 21, 1962. **361** "National Park as the People Inherited It," cartoon by Herbert Johnson. Photo: National Park Service History Collection. **365** Fred Ward/Black Star. **366** "Hope I Know Where We're Goin'," by Shanks, *The Buffalo Evening News.* **367** Bruce Roberts/Photo Researchers. **368** Max Scheber-Stern/Black Star. **369** Popperfoto. **371** Leonard Freed/Magnum. **375** WW. **377** Lyndon B. Johnson Library. **378** H. Kubota/Magnum. **380** Ted Rozumalski/Black Star. **381** UPI. **382** SI.

389 WW. **391** Sven Simon. **392** Wally McNamee/Woodfin Camp and Associates. **394** Doug Wilson/Black Star. **395** Pictorial Parade. **397** Fred Ward/Black Star. **399** Alex Webb/Magnum. **400** UPI. **401** Dennis Brack/Black Star. **402** Peter B. Kaplan/Photo Researchers. **403** Dennis Brack/Black Star. **409** Robert Llewellyn. **411, 412** Wally McNamee/Woodfin Camp and Associates. **413** Ledru/Sygma. **415** Laffont/Sygma. **417** Michael Evans/Sygma. **419** *(left)* Jim Pickerell. *(right)* Billy E. Barnes/Uniphoto. *(center)* U. S. Bureau of Census. *(bottom)* Owen Franken/Stock, Boston. **425** Uniphoto. **427** Larry Dale Gordon/Image Bank. **428** UPI. **429** M. Philippot/Sygma. **431** A. Keler/Sygma. **433** Alex Webb/Mag-

num. **434** P. F. Bentley/Photo Reporters. **435** Dennis Brack/Black Star.

441, 443 GC. **445** Idaho Historical Society. **446** Nebraska State Historical Society. **451, 453** GC. **459** NYHS. **461** Byron Collection, Museum of the City of New York. **463, 467** GC. **469, 471** BA. **474** Minnesota Historical Society. **477** Scala/Art Resource. **479** BA. **480** Untitled painting by F.C. Yohn. Coll: Society of Illustrators, Museum of American Illustration, New York. **482** GC. **485** "Winter in Union Square" (detail), by Childe Hassam. Coll: MMA, gift of Miss Ethelyn McKinney, 1943, in memory of her brother, Glenn Ford McKinney. **488** GC. **489** BB. **491** GC. **492** BB. **495** GC. **496** BA. **499** GC. **502** BA. **505** GC. **509, 511, 512** *(both)* BA. **515** LC. **517, 518, 520** BA. **525** Time-Life Picture Agency. Photo: Hugo Jaeger/Time Inc. **526** *(left)* BA. *(right)* IWM. **528** Historical Picture Service. **533** GC. **534** LC. **537** BA. **539** WW. **540** CP. **543** UPI/BA. **544** © Karsh, Ottawa/Woodfin Camp and Associates. **546** Black Star. **549** BA. **550** WW. **553** Magnum. **554** Robert Phillips/Black Star. **556** WW. **558, 559** Burt Glinn/Magnum. **560** Black Star. **563** Time-Life Picture Agency. Photo: Stan Wayman/Time Inc. **566** Erich Hartmann/Magnum. **569** Phillip Jones Griffith/Magnum. **570** Black Star. **573** Magnum. **574** Phillip Jones Griffith/Magnum. **581** Andy Levin/Black Star. **584** John Troha/Black Star. **586** Sebastiano Salgado/Magnum.

642-643 Dennis Brack/Black Star.

Index

This index includes references not only to the text but to pictures (p), charts (c), graphs (g), maps (m), and readings (r) as well. Page numbers that are marked n. refer to footnotes.

Atomic bomb, 305–306; dropped on Japan, 307; Soviet, 321
Australian ballot, 154
Austria, 197, m 199, 208, 275, m 276, m 301, m 329
Austria-Hungary, 179, 181, m 194; immigrants from, 75
Automation, 345, 426
Automobiles, 173, 219–220, 248, 293, 348; sales, in 1920's, g 221
Axis powers, 274, m 276, 285, 288, 290–291, 292, m 301
"Axis Sally," 299

Baker, Ray Stannard, 152, 158
Baltimore, Md., 57, 66, 88; population growth, c 82; riots in, 90, 372
Baltimore and Ohio Railroad, 60, m 60; strike on, 90, 105
Banks, and finance capitalists, 70; Federal Reserve, 172, 229, 252, 425; failures of, 233, 235; bank holiday, 237; reform of system, 240–241; loans to Europe by, 262
Barbed wire, 46–47; in World War I, 195
Baruch, Bernard M., 189, 237; quoted, 240
Baseball, 224, 319
Bastogne, France, 300
Bataan Peninsula, 288, m 306
Batista, Fulgencio, 352
Bay of Pigs, 354
Beck, Dave, 346
Beecher, Henry Ward, quoted, 90
Begin, Menachem, 411, p 411, 412
Beirut, Lebanon, m 414, 430–431, 432
Belgium, m 276; in World War I, 181–182, m 194; in World War II, 278, 300, m 301; in NATO, 329, m 329
Bell, Alexander Graham, 68–69
Bell, Mabel Hubbard, 69
Bellamy, Edward, 152
Belleau Wood, 193, m 194
Bell Telephone Company, 68–69
Benson, Ezra Taft, 344
Berle, Adolf A., 237
Berlin, Communists in, 208; division of, 300, 328, 343; taken by Russians, 303; Soviet blockade of, 328, 329; airlift to, p 328, 328–329; Berlin Wall, 354, p 354
Berryman, Clifford K., 159 n.
Bessemer, Henry; Bessemer process, 64
Bethune, Mary McLeod, p 253, 254
Beveridge, Albert J., quoted, 133, 142
Bicentennial, 402

Big business, mining as, 43; and political corruption, 103; monitoring of, 160; bootlegging as, 212; advertising as, 221; government as, 255
Birmingham, Ala., 358
Bismarck, N.D., m 42, 48
Bissell, George H., 57
Bitter Cry of the Children, The (Spargo), 153
Bituminous Coal Conservation Act, 249, 250
Black Hills, m 42, 43, 48
Black Kettle, 34, 35
Blacklist, 95
Blackmun, Harry A., 394
Black Muslims, 372
Black nationalism, 211
Black-power movement, 372
Blacks, as cowboys, 38; in unions, 88, 92, 248; excluded from AFL, 94; vote Republican, 104; discrimination against, 108, 157–158, 254, 295, 296, 319, 349; in Farmers' Alliance, 115; segregation of, 116, 157, 158, 349; in Spanish-American War, 140, 141; laws restricting, 157, 158; denied civil rights, 157, 158, 370; denied right to vote, 157, 319 n.; education for, 158; in World War I, 188, 189, 210; move to cities and to North, 190; violence against, 210, 212; achievements of, 210–211, 254, 319, 324 n., 356–357, 370, 371–372; in Great Depression, 253; and WPA, 253–254; shift to Democratic Party, 254; in World War II, 295–296; and civil rights movement, 319, 349–350; and Montgomery bus boycott, 349–350; steps to secure rights of, 356, 357–358; and voter-registration drives, 370, 371; leaders of, 370, 372; at political conventions, 396; population in 1970's, 420
Black Star Steamship Line, 211
Blaine, James G., 106, 108, 109, 111, 130
Blaine, Mrs. James G., 108
Bland-Allison Act, 118
Blockade, in World War I, 181; Berlin, 328, 329; Cuban, 355
Boeing, William, 225
Bogardus, James, 84
Bogota, Colombia, 164, m 165
Bolsheviks, 192, 208, 272, 325
Bonds, 61, 65, 189, 293
Bonneville Dam, 241
Bonus Army march, 233–234
Books, new ideas in, 133; public opinion and, 151–153
Bootlegging, 212, 213
Borah, William E., 198, 263, 264; quoted, 274, 277

Bork, Robert, 398
Bosnia, 179, m 194
Boss system, 107, 108
Boston, Mass., 68, 76, 82, 84; and police strike, 207–208; growth of, c 294, 295
Boulder, Colo., 41, m 42
Boulder Dam, 241
Bow, Clara, 221
Boxer Rebellion, 145
Boycott, secondary, 318; bus, in Montgomery, Ala., 349–350; of Olympic Games, 416
Boy Scouts, 157
Bradley, Omar, 299; quoted, 333
"Brain trust," 236–237
Brazil, 178
Brest-Litovsk, Treaty of, 192
Brezhnev, Leonid, 393
Briand, Aristide, 264
Bricker, John W., 297
Brinkmanship, 340
Britain, Battle of, 279, 280
British Expeditionary Force, 182
British Guiana, 131, 132
Brooke, Edward, 372
Brooklyn Bridge, 84–85
Brown, Jerry, 416
Brown v. Board of Education of Topeka, 349; r 556–557
Bryan, William Jennings, 120, 121, 168, 171, 176; quoted, 120, 144
Bryce, James, 154; r 468
Budapest uprising, 342
Budget, national, 252, 344, 424–425, 428, 434
Buenos Aires peace conference, 277
Buffalo, p 31, 32–33
Buffalo, N.Y., growth, c 82
Bulgaria, m 194, m 199, m 276, 300, m 301, 325, m 329
Bulge, Battle of the, 300, m 301, p 539
Bull Moose Party, 170, 185
Bunau-Varilla, Philippe, 163–164
Bunche, Ralph, 324, p 324
Bunyan, John, 152
Bureaucracy, 189, 255
Burger, Warren E., 394, 398, 399, p 428
Burgess, John W., quoted, 133
Burns, Lucy, 155
Buses, 83, 220; Montgomery boycott, 349–350; discrimination prohibited on, 356
Bush, George, 416, 434
Business, in Civil War, 58; corporations, 58, 69; leaders of, 64–69, 70–71, 104; cooperatives, 92; opposition of, to unions, 95; unfair practices, 172; black, 211; in 1920's, 218; and recession, 252, 344. See also Big business
Butler, Benjamin, 115

Cabinet, of Hayes, 104–105; of Harrison, 111; of Harding, 214; of F. D. Roosevelt, 236
Calamity Jane, 43
California, 79, 347, m 600
Calles, Plutarco, 266
Cambodia, 341, m 376, 390, 392
Cambridge, Mass., 68
Camp David accords, 343, 410, 411–412, 430
Camp Fire Girls, 157
Canada, railroads in, 73; gold in, 121; self-government achieved, 123; food imported from, 217; in NATO, 329
Canal Zone, 164, m 165, 267, 268
Cannon, Joseph, 169
Canon City, Colo., 41, m 42
Cantigny, France, 192, m 194
Capital, capitalists, 57–58, 70, 71
Capone, Al, 213
Caporetto, Battle of, 192, m 194
Caribbean Sea, U.S. interests in, 127, 128, m 165, 165–166, 177; Spanish-American War in, 140–142; invasion of Grenada, 434
Carnegie, Andrew, 64–65, 70, 144, p 491; quoted, 71; portrait, p 65
Carnegie Steel Company, 95
Caroline Islands, 304
Carranza, Venustiano, 178, 179
Carson, Rachel, p 566; r 565–567
Carter, Jimmy, 403, p 403; as President, 408, 409–412, p 411, p 412, 413–414, 415; in 1980 election, 416, 417; r 582–583
Casablanca Conference, 297–298
Cash-and-carry program, 274, 275, 278
Castle, Irene, 223
Castro, Fidel, 352–353
Catholics, prejudice against, 79, 109, 157, 209, 212; in Philippines, 142 n.; and Kennedy's nomination, 351–352
Catt, Carrie Chapman, 155; r 489–490
Cattle, 37–41, p 39, m 42, 63
Centennial Exposition, 68
Central America, Panama Canal across, 163–165, m 165; recent fighting in, 432–433
Central Pacific Railroad, m 42, m 60, 61, 62
Central Powers, World War I, 179, 181, 186, m 194, 197
Century of Dishonor (Jackson), 37
Cervera, Admiral, 140, 141
Chamberlain, Neville, 275
Chambers, Whittaker, 321
Chaplin, Charlie, 221
Chapultepec, Act of, 277
Charles River, 85
Charter, United Nations, 322
Chateau-Thierry, Battle of, 193, m 194
Checks and balances, 639, c 639
Cherokee Indians, 31, 32

Chevrolet cars, 220
Cheyenne, Wyo., 40, m 42, m 60
Cheyenne Indians, 32, 34, 35
Chiang Kai-shek, 275, 285, 286, 302, 330, 331
Chiang Kai-shek, Madame, 330
Chicago, m 42, 49, 84, 86, 152, 153; livestock trade in, 39, p 40; as railroad center, 60, 61, immigration to, 76, 77; growth of, 82, m 82; Haymarket Riot in, 93; nominating conventions in, 106, 234, 235, 280, 334, 382; ghetto in, 190; race riots in, 210; organized crime in, 213; airmail to, 225
Chickasaw Indians, 31
Chile, 178
China, immigrants from, 61, 79; spheres of influence in, 144, m 145; Boxer Rebellion in, 145; Open Door in, 145, 264; territorial integrity of, 166–167, 264; republic established in, 175; Japanese aggression in, 273, 275, 285; in World War II, 288; in UN, 323; communism in, 330–331; in Korean War, 333; and Vietnam, 341; and France, 374; and Soviet Union, 374, 392; under Mao, 385; Nixon visits, p 392, 392–393; recognized by U.S., 412
Chinese Exclusion Act, 79
Chisholm Trail, 39, m 42
Chivington, J. M., 34
Choctaw Indians, 31
Chou En-lai, 392, 393
Chrysler cars, 220
Churchill, Winston, 279, 281, p 285, 291; at Casablanca, 297–298; at Yalta, 300–302; "iron curtain" speech, 326, p 326; quoted, 284, 292, 302, 326, 524; portrait, p 544; r 544–545
Cicero, Ill., 213
Cincinnati, c 82, 86, 106, 247
Cisneros, Evangelina, 136
Cities, immigration to, 55, 75–76, 77, 86; skyscrapers in, 64, 84–85; manufacturing in, 82; largest, in 1860, 1880, 1890, c 82; problems of, 82, 152, 153, 154; growth of, 82–87; transportation in, 83–84; housing in, 85–86; advantages of life in, 86–87; riots in, 93, 210, 371, 372; political machines in, 107, 108; new ways of governing, 154; blacks move to, 190; in depression, 232; and urban renewal, 356, 370; youth movement in, 374; loss of population, 420
City-manager government, 154
Civilian Conservation Corps, 238
Civil rights, violations of, 208; publicizing issue of, 319
Civil Rights Acts, 349, 366, 370, 372 n.

Civil Rights Commission, 319, 349
Civil rights movement, 349–350, 356–357, 358–359
Civil Service Commission, 108, 159
Civil service reform, 105, 107–108
Civil War, 31–32, 58
Civil Works Administration (CWA), 238, 245
Clark, "Champ," 188
Clark, J. Reuben; Clark Memorandum, 266
Clark, Mark W., 299
Clarke, John H., 262
Clawson, Augusta, r 540–541
Clayton, Antitrust Act, 172
Clayton-Bulwer Treaty, 163
Clemenceau, Georges, 196
Cleveland, Frances Folsom, 109
Cleveland, Grover, 97, 108, 109–110, 111–112, 120; and Venezuelan dispute, 131, 132; quoted, 110, 130
Cleveland, Ohio, 65, 66, 154, 190, 250, 420; immigration to, 75; riots in, 372
Clothing industry, 76, 77–78
Cloture, 366
Coal, 55–56, 63; strikes, 89–90, 159, 208, 317; regulation, 249; and Carter program, 410
Coal Conservation Act, 249, 250
Cody, William F., 33
Cohan, George M., 188
Cold war, 322, 326, 335, 340, 341, 353
Collective bargaining, 239
Collective security, 262
Collier, John, 254
Collins, Michael, 394
Colombia, 163, 164, 165, m 165
Colon, Panama, 164, m 165
Colorado, 33, 34, m 36, 41, 155
Colorado River, 241, 242–243, m 243
Colorado Territory, 32, 34
Colored Farmers' Alliance, 115
Colt, Samuel, 32
Columbia (space shuttle), p 427, 427–428
Columbia River, 241
Comanche Indians, 35
Commission form of city government, 154
Committee for Industrial Organization (CIO), 247
Committee on Public Information, 190
Communism, in Russia, 192, 273, 276, 325; fear of, 208, 318, 340, 375; in U.S., 318, 320–321; and internal security, 321–322, 334, 345, 346; in East Germany, 324; in China, 330–331; in Korea, 332; in Vietnam, 341, 355, 376, 377, 379, 391, 392; in Cuba, 352–353; in Central America, 432–433

Macy, R. R., and Company, 86
Madama Butterfly, 319
Madero, Francisco, 178
Magnuson, Ed, quoted, 415
Mahan, Alfred Thayer, 134; r 478
Mail-order houses, 86
Maine, 212, *m* 601
Maine, sinking of, 136–137
Malay Peninsula, 288, *m* 306
Malcolm X, 372
Manchuria, *m* 145, 273, 302, *m* 306, 307, 331, *m* 332
Mandate system, 198
Manhattan Project, 305–306
Manila, 138–139, *m* 143, *m* 145, 288, 305
Manufacturing, *m* 599; growth of, 54, 58; in cities, 82; of automobiles, 219–220; automation in, 345, 426. *See also* Factories; Industry
Mao Tse-tung, 330, 331, 385
Mariana Islands, 304, *m* 306
Marne River, Battles of, 182, 193, *m* 194, 195
Marshall, George C., in World War I, 195; in World War II, 292; as Secretary of State, 327; awarded Nobel Prize, 327 n.; quoted, 327
Marshall, Thurgood, 356–357, *p* 381
Marshall Islands, 304, *m* 306
Marshall Plan, 327
Martinique, 163, *m* 165
Maryland, *m* 601
Masaryk, Tomás, 227
Massachusetts, *m* 601
Massive retaliation, 340
Mass media, mass marketing, 221
Maximilian of Mexico, 130
Meany, George, 345
Meat Inspection Act, 160–161
Medicaid, 427
Medicare, 370
Mein Kampf (Hitler), 272
Mellon, Andrew W., 214, 229
Memphis, *m* 60, 82, 381
Mennonites, 53
Meredith, James, 357
Mergers, corporate, 69
Merit system, 105, 108, 154
Merritt, Leonidas, 57
Merritt, Lesley, 140
Mesabi Range, 56–57, *m* 60
Mesa Verde, 161, 422
Metropolitan Museum of Art, New York, 86, *p* 86
Meuse River, *m* 194, 195
Mexican Americans, 254, 297
Mexico, French puppet ruler in, 130; Revolution in, 177–178, 254; Wilson and, 178, 179; and resettlement program, 254; constitution of, 265; relations with, 265; today, *m* 604
Mexico City, 266, 277
Miami, Fla., 383, 396
Michigan, 56, 212, *m* 601

Middle class, 151, 231, 348
Middle East, Arab-Israeli conflict in, 324, 341–342, 375, 393, *p* 411, 411–412, *m* 414; and oil embargo, 393–394; and Lebanon crisis, 430–431, 432
Midway, *m* 306; annexation of, 129, *m* 143; Battle of, 289
Migrant laborers, 254
Miles, Nelson A., 141, 268
Miller, William, 367
Millionaires, 43, 64, 70, 71
Milwaukee, 247, *m* 601
Mineral resources, *m* 599
Minimum wage laws, 250, 251, 253, 320
Mining, 41–43, *m* 42, 55–56, 208, 248
Minneapolis, *m* 42, 49
Minnesota, 57, 114, 120, 435, *m* 601
Minnesota Territory, 33–34
Mississippi, *m* 240, 241, 357, 390
Mississippi River, *m* 42, 61, 85, *m* 240
Missouri, 38, *m* 240
Missouri (ship), 307
Mitchell, Billy, 195, 283
Mitchell, John (Attorney General), 397
Mitchell, John (UMW leader), 159
Mobile, Ala., *m* 60, 61
Moley, Raymond, 237
"Molly Maguires," 96
Molotov, Vyacheslav, 314
Moltke, Helmuth von, 182
Mondale, Walter, 403, 416, 434, 435
Money, capital investments, 57–58; finance capitalists, 70, 71; silver-backed paper, 111, 112; greenbacks, 115; borrowing of, 117, 229, 233, 293, 317; gold and silver, ratio of, 117–118, 120; increased supply of, 121; for World War I, 181, 189; protection of, 241; and Keynes theory, 252. *See also* Debt
Monopoly, oil, 66, 69–70; efforts to control, 111, 152, 153, 160, 172
Monroe Doctrine, 277; strengthened, 130–132; Roosevelt corollary to, 166, 265, 266
Montana, 35–36, *m* 42, 43, 48, 212
Montana Territory, 32, 43
Montgomery, Ala., 83; bus boycott in, 349–350; march from Selma to, 370
Montgomery, Bernard Law, 291, 292
Montgomery Ward, 86
Moon landing, 394, *p* 395
Morgan, J. Pierpont, 61, 65, 70, 112, 160, 162
Morgan, J. P., and Company, 230
Morocco, 168, 291, *m* 301
Morrow, Dwight W., 266

Morse, Samuel F. B., 66
Mortgages, farm, 116–117
Morton, Oliver P., r 469–470
Moscow, 290, *m* 301, 355
Mount Pelée, 163
Movies, 221–222
Muckrakers, 152–153, 158
Mugwumps, 108, 109, 151–152
Muir, John, 422
Muir Woods, 161
Munich agreement, 275
Munn v. Illinois, 115
Muñoz Marin, Luis, 269
Muñoz Rivera, Luis, 268
Murrow, Edward, *p* 279; quoted, 279
Museums, 86
Muskie, Edmund, 382, 396
Muslims, Black, 372, 432; in Iran and Afghanistan, 413, 415; in Middle East, 433
Mussolini, Benito, *p* 272, 272–273, 274, 276, 291, 298, 299

Nagasaki, *m* 306, 307
Naples, Italy, 299, *m* 301
Nashville (warship), 164
Nasser, Gamal Abdel, 341
National Association for the Advancement of Colored People (NAACP), 158
National Equal Rights Party, 109
National Farmers' Holiday Association, 236
National Grange. *See* Grange
National Guard, 185, 370, 371, 390
National Industrial Recovery Act, 239
Nationalism, 180; black, 211
Nationalist government, Chinese, 330, 331, 393
National Labor Reform Party, 88
National Labor Relations Act, 247, 251; National Labor Relations Board (NLRB), 248, 317
National Labor Union, 88
National Organization of Women (NOW), 421
National Origins Act, 210
National parks, 161, 422–423, *m* 423
National Recovery Administration (NRA), 239–240, 248, 249
National (Cumberland) Road, 60
National Urban League, 190
National Woman Suffrage Association, 155
National Youth Administration (NYA), 246, 254
Native Americans. *See* Indians
Natural resources, 55–57, 599; conservation of, 161, 293
Navy, 185, 225; modernization of, 108, 129, 134; decline of, 127; in Spanish-American War, 138–140, 141; in World War I, 188; blacks in, 188; naval disarma-

Paul, Alice, 155

Peace, efforts to achieve, 168, 322–324, 430, 431, 432, 433

Peace Corps, 352, 353, 367

Pearl Harbor, 129, *m* 143, 271, *m* 271, *p* 286; in World War II, 287, 288, *m* 306

Pecos Trail, 40, *m* 42

Pedro, Emperor of Brazil, 68

Peking, 145, *m* 145

Pendleton, George H.; Pendleton Act, 108

Pennsylvania, 57, 75, 89–90, 95, *m* 601

Pennsylvania Railroad, 60, *m* 60, 70, 90

Pension bills, 109, 110

People's Party. *See* Populist Party

People's Republic of Korea. *See* North Korea

Perkins, Frances, 236, *p* 520; *r* 520–521

Permanent Court of International Arbitration, 168

Perry, Matthew C., 128–129, 307

Pershing, John J., 178, *p* 179, 192, *p* 502; quoted, 141

Peru, 352

Pétain, Henri Philippe, 278

Petrified Forest, 161

Philadelphia, manufacturing in, 58; and rail service, 60, *m* 60, 61; Centennial Exposition in, 68; immigration to, 76, 77; growth of, 82, *c* 82, 83; nominating conventions in, 250, 320

Philadelphia Coal and Iron Company, 90

Philippine Islands, *m* 145, 267, *m* 267; and Spanish-American War, 137, 138–40, *m* 143; annexation of, 142; resist American rule, 143; independence for, 269, 337; in World War II, 288–289; liberated, 304–305, *m* 306

Phillips, David Graham, 152

Phonograph, 66

Pickett, Bill, 38

Pickford, Mary, 221

Pierre, S.D., *m* 42, 48

Pikes Peak, 41, *m* 42

Pilgrim's Progress (Bunyan), 152

Pinchot, Gifford, 169

Pine Ridge reservation, *p* 35

Pinkerton, Allan; Pinkerton detectives, 95

Pioneers, 46, 47. *See also* Frontier

Pit, The (Norris), 153

Pittsburgh, 64, 85, 90, *m* 601

Plains Indians, *p* 31, 32; resettlement of, 31–37

Plantations, *p* 129

Platt, Thomas, 106–107

Platt Amendment, 268, 277

Playgrounds, 154, 157

"Pledge of Allegiance," text of, 637

Plessy v. Ferguson, 157, 349

Plow, steel, 47

Poland, *m* 194; immigrants from 75, 76; new boundaries for, 197, *m* 199; threatened by Hitler, 276; invaded, *m* 276, 277, 278; in World War II, 300, *m* 301; controlled by Russia, 302, 322; Communist government in, 325; and Solidarity, 429, *p* 429

Political parties, and corruption, 103–105, 106; nominating conventions of, 106, 119, 170, 215, 218, 234, 235, 250–251, 280, 320, 334, 351, 368, 382, 383, 396, 403; third parties, 112, 383

Poll tax, 319 n.; outlawed, 357

Pollution, 220, 395

Pools, 69

Pope, John, 33, 34

Population, *m* 594, *c* 595; Indian, 37; increasing, 48, 55, 82, 83, 116, *g* 210, 346–347; in West, 48, 116; 1860–1900, 55; foreign-born, in 1900, *m* 78; urban, 82, 83, 419–420; 1870–1920, *g* 210; shifts in, 347–348, 418–421, *c* 596, *m* 597; 1930–1980, *g* 420

Populist Party, 111, 112, 119, 120, 121, 151, 155

"Pork-barrel" proposals, 111

Portland, Ore., *m* 42, *m* 60, 62, 63

Portsmouth, Treaty of, 166

Portugal, 329, 407

Potsdam Conference, 306, 324, 325

Poverty, 152, 255; war on, 367, 370

Powderly, Terence V., 92; quoted, 93

Powell, John Wesley, *r* 447–448

Powell, Lewis F., Jr., 394

"Prairie schooners," 41, 117

Pratt and Whitney Aircraft, 225

Precipitation, yearly, 44–45, *m* 45

Prejudice, against foreign-born, Catholics, Jews, 79, 109, 157, 190, 209, 212, 351–352; in unions, 94

President, expanded powers of, 188, 281; tradition of only two terms for, broken, 280; limited to two terms, 318; presidential succession, 318

Price controls, 294, 396

Price-support payments, 345

Progress and Poverty (George), 152

Progressive Movement, 151–153, 154, 155, 156, 158; peace efforts, 168; and Taft, 169; and Wilson, 171; American life changed by, 173

Progressive Party, 170, 217, 320

Prohibition, 212–213; repealed, 235

Promise of American Life (Croly), 169

Promontory, Utah, *m* 60, 62

Prospectors, 41, 42

Public opinion, molding of, 135, 136, 151–153; and trust-busting, 160; and World War I, 190; expression of, 248, 320, 365, 383; and civil rights movement, 358

Public Works Administration (PWA), 239

Public works programs, 252, 356

Puerto Rico, 267; acquired by U.S., 141–142, *m* 143, *m* 165; self-government in, 268; commonwealth status for, 269

Puget Sound, *m* 60, 63

Pulitzer, Joseph, 135, *p* 479; *r* 479

Pullman, George; Pullman strike, 96–97

Pure Food and Drug Act, 160

Pusan, 332, *m* 332

Pyle, Ernie, *r* 537–538

"Quarantine speech," 275

Quay, Matt, 110

Quotas, immigration, 210

Radio, 221, 255

Railroad Administration, 189

Railroads, to West, 32, 35, 48, 63; cattle shipped by, 39; transcontinental, 41, *m* 60, 61–63; mileage, by 1900, 59; southern, 59, 61; trunk lines, 60–61; influence of, on American life, 63; and time zones, 63–64; capital for, 73; strikes on, 90, 92, 96–97; regulation of, 110, 160; and Granger laws, 114–115; government operation of, 189, 317; discrimination forbidden on, 356

Ranching, 37–41, 48

Randolph, A. Philip, 295, 319

Rankin, Jeanette, 288

Ratification of constitutional amendments, 155, 212, 222, 357, 370, 398

Rationing, in World War II, 293

Reagan, Ronald, 408; governor of California, 383; in 1976 election, 402, 403; in 1980 election, 416–417, *p* 417, 418; as President, 424–425, *p* 425, 427, 428, 429–430, 431, 433, 434, *p* 586; in 1984 election, 434–435, *p* 435; quoted, 387, 408, 580; *r* 585–586

Rearmament, 329, 340, 354

Rebates, railroad, 160

Recall, 154

Recession, 252, 344, 401, 424

Reconcentration camps, Spanish, 135

Reconstruction Finance Corporation (RFC), 233

Recovery legislation, 238, 239–241

Red Army, 290, 300, 322, 325
Red River, m 42, 48
Red River War, 35
"Red scare," 208
Reed, Thomas B., 111
Referendum, 154
Reform movement, 111, 112, 115; Indian rights, 37; housing, 86; political corruption, 104, 105, 107–108, 171, civil service, 105, 107–108; progressivism, 151–153, 154–157; municipal and state, 154; peace movement, 168; New Deal and, 238, 240–241, 242, 247, 253. See also Progressive movement
Rehnquist, William H., 395
Relief legislation, 218, 238, 244–246, 252, 356
Remington, Frederic, 135
Rentschler, Frederick B., 225
Reparations, war, 197, 261, 262, 302
Republican Party, dominance of, 104; Liberal Republicans, 105; Mugwumps, 108, 109; and farm vote, 116; and peace delegation, 196; and tax cut, 318; South returns to, 334; in 1980's, 416–418, 425–427, 435
Republic of Korea, 332
Republic Steel Company, 248
Reservations, Indian, 34–35, p 35, m 36
Resettlement Administration, 247
Resumption Act, 115
Reuther, Walter, 345
Revenue Act, 366
Reza Pahlevi, Mohammed, 413, 414
Rheims, France, m 301, 303
Rhineland, 274, m 276
Rhode Island, m 601
Richardson, Elliot, 398
Richmond, Va., m 60, 61, 84
Rickenbacker, Eddie, 195, 225
Ridgway, Matthew B., 334
Right-to-work laws, 318
Rihbany, Abraham, r 460–461
Riis, Jacob, 152; r 462–464
Rio Grande, m 243
Riots, race, 79, 210, 297, 357, 371, 372, 381; labor, 90, 93; political, 382
River projects, 161, 241
Roads, expanded system of, 348; beautification and safety of, 370
"Roaring Twenties," 206
Robinson, Jackie, 319
Robots, 426
Rockefeller, John D., 65–66, 69, 160; quoted, 66, 71; r 454–455
Rockets, Saturn V, p 373
Rocky Mountains, 30, m 42, m 45; mining in, 41–43
Roebling, John A., 85
Rogers, Will, 255
Roman Catholics. See Catholics
Rome, Italy, 299, m 301

Rommel, Erwin, 290, 291, 292, p 292
Roosevelt, Alice, p 157, 159
Roosevelt, Eleanor, 234, 237, p 253, 255, 297 n., 302, p 323
Roosevelt, Franklin D., 192, 213, 214, 218, 228, 235, p 235, 245, 252, 255, 281, 318; as governor of New York, 232, 234; as Assistant Secretary of Navy, 234; First Inaugural Address, 236, p 518; "brain trust" of, 236–237; and banks, 237; recovery program, 239; and gold standard, 240; and conservation, 241; public assistance programs, 244, 254; and income tax, 247; and labor, 248; and NRA, 248–249; broadcasting, p 249; and Supreme Court, 250, 251; re-elected, 250, 251, 254, 280, 297; and minorities, 253, 254, 295; recognizes Soviet Union, 273; imposes arms embargo, 274; "quarantine speech," 275; and Good Neighbor Policy, 277; lifts arms embargo, 277–278; and aid to Britain, 279–280; and Atlantic Charter, 284; war message to Congress, 287; in World War II, 287–288, 291, 293, 294, 295, p 298; at Casablanca, 297–298; at Yalta, 300–302; death of, 302; and atomic bomb, 305; quoted, 251, 274, 275, 277–278, 280, 281, 288, 532; r 526–527, r 529–530
Roosevelt, James, 234
Roosevelt, Quentin, 159
Roosevelt, Sara Delano, 234
Roosevelt, Theodore, 134, 150, 158–159, p 159, 185; as Assistant Secretary of Navy, p 134, 137, 159; in Spanish-American War, 140, 141; as Vice President, 144, 159; as President, 157, 160–163, 164–165, 166, 167, 168, 173, 234; and coal strike, 159; and trusts, 159–160; and conservation, 161; and railroad regulation, 161; and foreign affairs, 163–168; awarded Nobel Prize, 167; re-enters politics, 169, 170, 171; quoted, 125, 137, 138, 152, 160, 168–169, 171, 184; r 482–483
Roosevelt Corollary to Monroe Doctrine, 166, 265, 266
Rosenberg, Julius and Ethel, 322
Rough Riders, 140, 141
Rowan, Carl, 357
Ruby, Jack, 359, 365
Ruckelshaus, William, 398
Rumania, 186, m 194, 300, m 301, 322, 325, m 329
Rum-running, 212
Rural Electrification Administration (REA), 247
Rusk, Dean, 376; quoted, 355

Russia, immigrants from, 53, 75, 77, m 81; railroads in, 73; Alaska bought from, 128; war with Japan, 166; 1905 Revolution in, 175; in World War I, 179, 182, 183, 186, m 194; 1907 agreement with England, 180; 1917 Revolution in, 187, 208; and Treaty of Brest-Litovsk, 192; Communist regime in, 192. See also Soviet Union
Russo-Japanese War, 166
Ruth, Babe, 199, 224

Sacco, Nicola, 208–209
Sacramento, Calif., m 42, m 60, 61
Sadat, Anwar, 411, p 411, 412, 430
Saigon, m 376, 379, 390, 392
St. John, Vincent, 95
St. Louis, Mo., 60, m 60, 61, c 82, 85, 119, 120
St. Mihiel, France, m 194, 195, 200, m 200
St. Nazaire, France, 290, m 301
St. Paul, Minn., m 42, 48, m 60, 63
Saipan, 304, m 306
Sakhalin, 273, m 306
Sakharov, Andrei, 437
Samaná Bay, 127
Samoa Islands, 129, m 143
Sampson, William T., 140; quoted, 141
San Antonio, Tex., 38, m 42, m 60
Sand Creek Massacre, 34, m 36
San Francisco, m 42, m 60, 167, 225, 322, 374
San Juan Hill, Battle of, 141, p 141
Santa Fe, m 60, 63
Santa Fe Railroad, m 42, 48, m 60, 63
Santa Fe Trail, 63
Santiago, Battle of, 140, 141, m 143
Sarajevo, 179, m 194
Saratoga, N.Y., 79
Satellites, nations, 325–326; space, 356
"Saturday Night Massacre," 398
Saudi Arabia, 324, 393, m 414
Savannah, Ga., m 60, 61
Scandinavian immigrants, 48, p 49, 75, m 81
Schechter v. United States, 248
Schley, Winfield Scott, 140
Schlieffen, Alfred von, 182
Schurz, Carl, 104–105, 144; quoted, 637; r 470–472
Schwab, Charles M., 236
Scorched-earth policy, 290
Scott, Thomas A., 64
Scouting (Boy, Girl Scouts), 157
Seaboard Air Line Railroad, m 60, 61
Seattle, Wash., m 42, 48
Securities and Exchange Commission (SEC), 239

Sedition Acts, 190
Segregation, of blacks, 116, 157, 158, 349, 350; of Japanese American children, 167; Wilson and, 173; in armed forces, 296; steps to end, 319; demonstrations against, 358
Selective Service Act, 188, 280, 293. *See also* Draft, military
Self-determination, 191
Self-government, 123, 198, 268–269
Seligman, Joseph, 79
Selma, Ala., 370
Seminole Indians, 31
Senate, 642; election to, 107, 155; and noninterference policy, 168; opposes Versailles Treaty, 198; and disarmament treaties, 264; McCarthy in, 345, *p* 554; investigates union corruption, 346; and civil rights, 366; blacks in, 372; and Vietnam War, 379; and Supreme Court nominations, 394; confirms Ford as Vice President, 398; organization of, *c* 642–643
Seoul, 332, *m* 332, 333
Separate-but-equal concept, 157, 349
Separation of powers, 638
Serbia, 179, *m* 194
Servicemen's Readjustment Act, 315–317
Settlement houses, 153
Sewall, Arthur, 120
Seward, William H., 127, 128, 132
Shafter, William R., 140
Shawnee Trail, 38, *m* 42
Sheeler, Charles, painting by, *p* 261
Shepard, Alan, 356
Sheridan, Philip H., 35
Sherman, John, 111
Sherman, William T., 35
Sherman Antitrust Act, 69, 70, 111, 160
Sherman Silver Purchase Act, 111, 112, 118
Shipbuilding, 189
Shipping, of cattle, 38, 39; special freight rates, 66; protected by convoys, 188, 290
Shipping Board, 189
Ships, ocean liners, 259; and naval disarmament, 263–264
Shotwell, James T., 264
Shriver, R. Sargent, 396
Sicily, *m* 194, 298, *m* 301
Silver, mining of, 42–43, 117; and gold, ratio of, in coinage, 117–118, 120
Simpson, "Sockless Jerry," 118
Sims, William S., 188
Sinclair, Harry F., 215
Sinclair, Upton, 152
Singapore, 288, *m* 306
Sioux Falls, S.D., *m* 42, 48
Sioux Indians, 33–34, 35, 37

Sirhan, Sirhan, 382
Sit-in, 350. *See also* Demonstrations
Six-Day War, 375
Skyscrapers, 64, 84
Slavs, 75
Slums, 86, 152
Smith, Alfred E., 215, 218, 234, 244, 351; quoted, 235
Smith, Jess, 215
Smith, Margaret Chase, *p* 556; *r* 555–556
Smuggling, 212
Socialists, 153, 160, 208
Social problems, 151–153, 154, 220, 318, 367, 369–370
Social Security, 244, 251, 252, 320, 370
Soil Conservation and Domestic Allotment Act, 249
Solidarity (Poland), 429, *p* 429
Solomon Islands, 289, *m* 306
Solzhenitsyn, Alexander, 437
Somme, Battle of the, 183, *m* 194
Somoza, Anastasio, 265
Soo Canal, 56
Souls of Black Folk (Du Bois), 158
South, railroads in, 59, *m* 60, 61; Democrats strong in, 104; Jim Crow laws in, 157, 158; blacks leave, 190; depression in, for blacks, 253; returns to Republican Party, 334; voter-registration drives in, 370, 371
South Carolina, *m* 240
South Dakota, *m* 42, 43, 48, 154, 212; Battle of Wounded Knee, *m* 36, 37; population, 1880–1890, 116
Southeast Asia, French withdraw from, 355; American involvement in, 355, 356. *See also* Vietnam; Vietnam War
Southern Alliance (Farmers'), 115, 116
Southern Christian Leadership Conference (SCLC), 350
Southern Pacific Railroad, *m* 60, 63
Southern Railway, *m* 60, 61
South Korea, 332, *m* 332, *p* 333, 340
South Vietnam, 355, 356, 376, *m* 376, 377, 378, 379, 382, 383, 390, 391–392
Soviet Union, 192 n., 321, *m* 329; under Stalin, 272; recognized by U.S., 273; in Baltic countries, 276; German invasion of, *m* 276, 281; invades Poland, 278; in World War II, 288, 290, 291, 300, *m* 301, 302, 303, 307, 326; tests atomic bomb, 321, cold war with, 322, 326, 340, 341, 353; in UN, 323; Eastern Europe controlled by, 325–326, 327, 342; rejects Marshall Plan, 327; and division of Germany, 328; Berlin blockade by, 328,

329; and China, 331, 374, 392; walks out of UN, 332; and Egypt, 341; and Vietnam, 341; and U-2 flight, 343; Nixon visits, 343, 393; and Cuba, 353, 355; and Berlin Wall, 354; launches *Sputnik*, 356; invades Afghanistan, 415–416; recent relations with Poland, 428–429; and missiles in Europe, 430; downs Korean plane, 430; dissidents in, 437. *See also* Russia
Space program, 356, *p* 373; moon landing, 394, *p* 395; shuttle flights, *p* 427, 427–428
Spain, 168; heritage of, 38; Cuban uprising against, 134–135; in Spanish-American War, 136, 137, 138–142; civil war in, 274; in recent years, 407
Spanish-American War, 138–142, *m* 143, 145, 163
Spargo, John, 153; *r* 487–488
"Speakeasies," 212
Spheres of influence, 144, *m* 145
Spindletop oil field, 221
Spirit of St. Louis, 225
Spoils system, 105, 107, 108, 109, 111
Sports, professional, 224, 319
Sprague, Frank, 84
Sputnik, 356
Square Deal, 158, 235
Stagecoaches, 83
Stalin, Joseph, 272, 297, 306, 321, 326 n.; in World War II, 292, 300, 303; at Yalta and Potsdam, 300–302, 325; purges by, 325; death of, 339
Stalingrad, 290, *p* 291, *m* 301
Stalwarts (Republican wing), 106, 108
Standard Oil Company, 66, 69, 152, 160
Stanton, Elizabeth Cady, 155
"Star-Spangled Banner, The," text of, 637
States, corruption in, 103; reform in, 154; aid in depression, 232–233; court systems, 641, *c* 641
States' rights, 383
States' Rights Democratic Party, 320
Statue of Liberty, *p* 75, 97, *p* 297
Steamboat, 65
Steel industry, 64–65; 1860–1900, *g* 65; strikes in, 95, 208, 248; and unions, 248
Steel plow, 47
Steffens, Lincoln, 152; *r* 486–487
Steinbeck, John, 246
Stephens, Uriah S., 91–92
Stevenson, Adlai E., 334, 345
Stevenson, John, 83
Steward, Ira, 89
Stimson, Henry L., 265, 266, 273; quoted, 286
Stimson Doctrine, 273
Stock market, 218; crash of, 230